CLYMER®

KAWASAKI

VN800 VULCAN & VULCAN CLASSIC
1995-1998

The world's finest publisher of mechanical how-to manuals

INTERTEC PUBLISHING
P.O. Box 12901, Overland Park, Kansas 66282-2901

FIRST EDITION
First Printing June, 1999

Printed in U.S.A.

CLYMER and colophon are registered trademarks of Intertec Publishing.

ISBN: 0-89287-718-9

Library of Congress: 98-75603

Technical photography by Ed Scott.

Technical and photographic assistance by Curt Jordan, Jordan Engineering, Oceanside, California.

Technical illustrations by Mitzi McCarthy and Robert Caldwell.

COVER: Photographed by Mark Clifford, Mark Clifford Photography, Los Angeles, California.

Intertec Book Division

President Raymond E. Maloney
Vice President, Book Division Ted Marcus

The following books and guides are published by Intertec Publishing.

CLYMER SHOP MANUALS
Boat Motors and Drives
Motorcycles and ATVs
Snowmobiles
Personal Watercraft

ABOS/INTERTEC/CLYMER BLUE BOOKS AND TRADE-IN GUIDES
Recreational Vehicles
Outdoor Power Equipment
Agricultural Tractors
Lawn and Garden Tractors
Motorcycles and ATVs
Snowmobiles and Personal Watercraft
Boats and Motors

AIRCRAFT BLUEBOOK-PRICE DIGEST
Airplanes
Helicopters

AC-U-KWIK DIRECTORIES
The Corporate Pilot's Airport/FBO Directory
International Manager's Edition
Jet Book

I&T SHOP SERVICE MANUALS
Tractors

INTERTEC SERVICE MANUALS
Snowmobiles
Outdoor Power Equipment
Personal Watercraft
Gasoline and Diesel Engines
Recreational Vehicles
Boat Motors and Drives
Motorcycles
Lawn and Garden Tractors

CONTENTS

QUICK REFERENCE DATA

TIRE SIZE AND INFLATION PRESSURE (COLD)*

	Tire size
Front	
VN800	80/90-21 48H tube
VN800 Classic	130/90-16 67H tube
Rear	140/90-16 71H tube

Tire Pressure

	Front		Rear	
Load	psi	kPa	psi	kPa
Up to 215 lbs (97.5 kg)				
VN800	28	200	32	200
VN800 Classic	28	200	28	200
215 to 397 lbs (97 to 180 kg)	28	200	32	225

*Tire inflation pressure for factory equipped tires. Aftermarket tires may require different inflation pressure; refer to manufacturer's specifications.

RECOMMENDED LUBRICANTS AND FLUIDS

Fuel	Regular unleaded
Octane	87 [(R + M)/2 method] or 91 or higher
Capacity	15.0 L (3.96 U.S. gal [3.3 Imp. gal])
Engine oil	
Grade	API SE, SF or SG
Viscosity	SAE 10W/40, 10W/50, 20W/40 or 20W/50
Capacity	
Oil change only	2.7 L (2.9 U.S. qt. [2.4 Imp. qt.])
Change and filter	2.9 L (3.1 qt. [2.6 Imp. qt.])
When engine completely dry	3.2 L (3.4 U.S. qt. [2.8 Imp. qt.])
Coolant	Ethylene glycol
Capacity at large	2.4 L (2.5 qt. [2.1 Imp. qt.])
Brake fluid	DOT 4
Battery	Maintenance free
Fork oil	
Viscosity	SAE 10W fork oil
Capacity per leg	
Oil change only	
VN800	290 ml (9.80 U.S. oz. [10.21 Imp. oz.])
VN800 Classic	265 ml (8.96 oz. [9.33 Imp. oz.])
After disassembly	
VN800	336-344 ml (11.36-11.63 U.S. oz. [11.83-12.11 Imp. oz.])
VN800 Classic	306-314 ml (10.35-10.62 U.S. oz. [10.77-11.05 Imp. oz.])
Oil level each leg (fully compressed, without spring)	
VN800	290-294 mm (11.42-11.65 in.)
VN800 Classic	284-288 mm (11.18-11.34 in.)
Cables	SAE 10W/30 motor oil
Pivot points	SAE 30

MAINTENANCE AND TUNE UP TIGHTENING TORQUES

Item	N•m	in.-lb.	ft.-lb.
Oil drain plug	20	—	15
Oil filter	18	—	13
Front brake caliper mounting bolts	34	—	25
Engine coolant drain plugs	11	97	—

TUNE-UP SPECIFICATIONS

Spark plug type	NGK CR7E or ND U22ESR-N
Spark plug gap	0.7-0.8 mm (0.028-0.031 in.)
Idlespeed	
U.S. and Swiss models	1300 50 rpm
All other models	1000 50 rpm
Cylinder compression	855-1315 kPa (124-191 psi)

REPLACEMENT BULBS

U.S. and Canadian Models	
Item	**Voltage/wattage**
Headlight (high/low beam)	12V 60/55W
Tail/brake light	12V 8/27W
Turn signals	
Front/running position light	12V 23/8W
Rear	12V 23W
Turn signal indicator light	12V 3.4W
Coolant temperature warning light	12V 1.7W
Oil pressure warning light	12V 1.7W
Speedometer lights	12V 1.7W
Neutral indicator light	12V 3W
High beam indicator light	12V 3W
Other than U.S. and Canadian Models	
Item	**Voltage/wattage**
Headlight (high/low beam)	12V 60/55W
City light	12V 4W
Tail/brake light	12V 5/21W
Turn signals	
Front	12V 21W
Rear	12V 21W
Turn signal indicator light	12V 3.4W
Coolant temperature warning light	12V 1.7W
Oil pressure warning light	12V 1.7W
Speedometer lights	12V 1.7W
Neutral indicator light	12V 3W
High beam indicator light	12V 3W
License plate light	
VN800 Classic	12V 5W

CLYMER®

KAWASAKI

VN800 VULCAN & VULCAN CLASSIC
1995-1998

CHAPTER ONE

GENERAL INFORMATION

This detailed, comprehensive manual covers the Kawasaki VN800 and VN800 Classic from 1995-on. The expert text gives complete information on maintenance, tune-up, repair and overhaul. Hundreds of photos and drawings guide you through every step. The book includes all you need to know to keep your Kawasaki running right.

A shop manual is a reference. You want to be able to find information fast. As in all Clymer books, this one is designed with you in mind. All chapters are thumb tabbed. Important items are extensively indexed at the rear of the book. All procedures, tables and photos in this manual are for the reader who may be working on the bike for the first time or using this manual for the first time. Frequently used specifications and capacities are summarized in the *Quick Reference Data* pages at the front of the book.

Keep the book handy in your tool box. It will help you better understand how your bike runs, lower repair costs and generally improve your satisfaction with the bike.

Kawasaki uses a letter and numeral designation in the model number to identify the model year of their bikes. For example the 1996 Vulcan 800 is a VN800-A2, while and 1996 Vulcan 800 Classic is a VN800-B1. Refer to **Table 1** at the end of this chapter for the letter-to-year designation information and the VIN numbers.

Table 1 lists model coverage with VIN and engine serial numbers.

Table 2 lists general vehicle dimensions.

Table 3 lists vehicle weight.

Table 4 lists decimal and metric equivalents.

Table 5 lists general torque specifications.

Table 6 lists conversion tables.

Table 7 lists technical abbreviations.

Table 8 lists metric tap sizes.

Tables 1-8 are at the end of this chapter.

MANUAL ORGANIZATION

All specifications in this manual are expressed in ISO (International Organization for Standardization) metric units. An equivalent, expressed in U.S. standard units is also provided.

This chapter provides general information and discusses equipment and tools useful both for preventive maintenance and troubleshooting.

Chapter Two provides methods and suggestions for quick and accurate diagnosis and repair of problems. Troubleshooting procedures discuss typical symptoms and logical methods to pinpoint the trouble.

Chapter Three explains all periodic lubrication and routine maintenance necessary to keep your Kawasaki running well. Chapter Three also includes recommended tune-up procedures, eliminating the need to constantly consult chapters on the various assemblies.

Subsequent chapters describe specific systems such as the engine, lower end, clutch, transmission, fuel, exhaust, cooling, suspension and brakes. Each chapter provides disassembly, inspection, repair and assembly procedures in simple step-by-step form. Specifications concerning a particular system are included at the end of the appropriate chapter.

If a repair is impractical for a home mechanic, it is so indicated. It is usually faster and less expensive to take such repairs to a dealership or competent repair shop.

Some of the procedures in this manual require special tools. In most cases, the tool is illustrated either in actual use or alone. Well equipped mechanics may find they can substitute similar tools already on hand or fabricate a suitable tool.

NOTES, CAUTIONS AND WARNINGS

The terms NOTE, CAUTION and WARNING have specific meanings in this manual. A NOTE provides additional information to make a step or procedure easier or more clear. Disregarding a NOTE could cause inconvenience, but would not cause equipment damage or personal injury.

A CAUTION emphasizes areas where equipment damage could result. Disregarding a CAUTION could cause mechanical damage; however, personal injury is unlikely.

A WARNING emphasizes areas where personal injury or even death could result from negligence. Mechanical damage may also occur. WARNINGS *are to be taken seriously.* Serious injury or death can result from disregarding a warning.

SAFETY FIRST

Professional mechanics can work for years and never sustain a serious injury. If you observe a few rules of common sense and safety, you can enjoy many safe hours servicing your machine. If you ignore these rules you can hurt yourself or damage the equipment.

1. Never use gasoline as a cleaning solvent.
2. Never smoke or use a torch in the vicinity of flammable liquids, such as cleaning solvent in an open container.
3. If welding or brazing is required on the bike, remove the fuel tank to a safe distance, at least 50 feet (15 m) away.
4. Use the proper sized wrenches to avoid damage to fasteners and injury to yourself.
5. When loosening a tight or stuck nut, be guided by what would happen if the wrench should slip. Be careful and protect yourself accordingly.
6. When replacing a fastener, make sure to use one with the same measurements and strength as the old one. Incorrect or mismatched fasteners can result in damage to the bike and possible personal injury. Beware of fastener kits filled with cheap and poorly made nuts, bolts, washers and cotter pins. Refer to *Fasteners* in this chapter for additional information.
7. Keep all hand tools and power tools in good condition. Wipe greasy and oily tools after using them. They are difficult to hold and can cause injury. Replace or repair worn or damaged tools.
8. Keep your work area clean and uncluttered.
9. Wear safety goggles (**Figure 1**) during all operations involving drilling, grinding, the use of a cold chisel or anytime you feel unsure about the safety of your eyes. Safety goggles should also be worn when using solvent and compressed air to clean parts.
10. Keep an approved fire extinguisher nearby. It must be rated for gasoline (Class B) and electrical (Class C) fires.
11. When drying bearings or other rotating parts with compressed air, never allow the air jet to rotate the bearing or part. The air jet is capable of rotating

them at speeds more than those for which they were designed. The bearing or rotating part is very likely to disintegrate and cause serious injury and damage. To prevent bearing damage when using compressed air, hold the inner bearing race by hand (**Figure 2**).

SERVICE HINTS

Most of the service procedures covered are straightforward and can be performed by anyone reasonably handy with tools. However, consider your capabilities carefully before attempting any operation involving major disassembly of the engine assembly.

Take your time and do the job right. Do not forget that a newly rebuilt engine must be broken-in the same way as a new one; refer to Chapter Four.

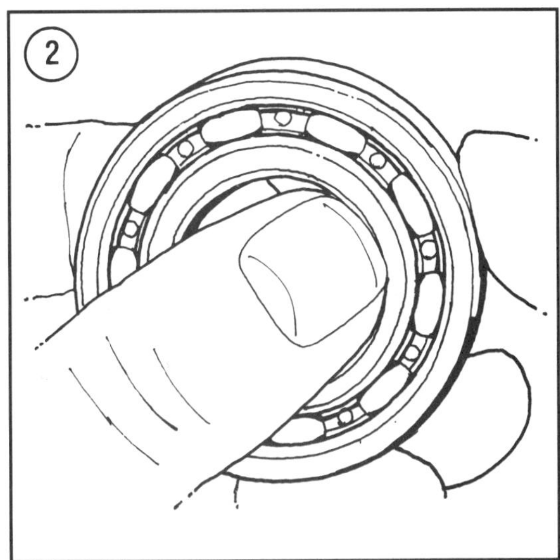

1. Front, as used in this manual, refers to the front of the bike; the front of any component is the end closest to the front of the bike. The left- and right-hand sides refer to the position of the parts as viewed by a rider sitting on the seat facing forward. For example, the throttle control is on the right-hand side. These rules are simple, but confusion can cause a major inconvenience during service.
2. Whenever servicing the engine or clutch or when removing a suspension component, the bike should be secured in a safe manner.
3. Disconnect the negative battery cable (**Figure 3**) before disconnecting any electrical wires or when working on or near the electrical, clutch or starter systems. On most batteries, the negative terminal is marked with a minus (–) sign and the positive terminal is marked with a plus (+) sign.
4. Tag all similar internal parts for location and mark all mating parts for position. Record shim number, thickness and alignment when removed. Identify and store small parts in plastic sandwich bags. Seal and label them with masking tape.
5. Place parts from a specific area of the engine like the cylinder head, cylinder, clutch and shift mechanism into plastic boxes to keep them separated.
6. When disassembling transmission shaft assemblies, use an egg flat (the type that restaurants get their eggs in). Set the parts from a shaft in one of the depressions in the same order in which it was removed.
7. Label all electrical wiring and connectors before disconnecting them. Again, do not rely on memory alone.
8. Protect finished surfaces from physical damage or corrosion. Keep gasoline, brake fluid and clutch fluid off painted surfaces.
9. Use penetrating oil on frozen or tight bolts, then strike the bolt head a few times with a hammer and punch (use a screwdriver on screws). Avoid the use of heat where possible, as it can warp, melt or affect the temper of parts. Heat also ruins finishes, especially paints and plastics.
10. Unless specified in the procedure, parts should not require unusual force during disassembly or assembly. If a part is difficult to remove or install, find out why before continuing.
11. To prevent small objects and abrasive dust from falling into the engine, cover all openings after exposing them.

12. Read each procedure *completely* while looking at the actual parts before starting a job. Make sure you thoroughly understand each step, then follow the procedure, step by step.

13. The recommendation is occasionally made to refer service or maintenance to a Kawasaki dealership or a specialist in a particular field. In these cases, the work will be done more quickly and economically than if you performed the job yourself.

14. In procedural steps, the term *replace* means to discard a worn or defective part and replace it with a new or exchange unit. *Overhaul* means to remove and disassemble a major system or assembly, inspect all its parts, then replace worn or defective parts as required during reassembly and reinstallation.

15. Some operations require the use of a hydraulic press. It is wiser to have these operations performed at a shop equipped for such work, rather than to try to do the job yourself with makeshift equipment that may damage your machine.

16. Repairs go much faster and easier if your machine is clean before you begin work. There are many special cleaners on the market, like Bel-Ray Degreaser, for washing the engine and related parts. Follow the manufacturer's directions on the container for the best results. Clean all oily or greasy parts with cleaning solvent as you remove them.

WARNING

***Never** use gasoline as a cleaning agent. It presents an extreme fire hazard. Be sure to work in a well-ventilated area when using cleaning solvent. Keep a fire extinguisher, rated for gasoline fires, nearby in any case.*

CAUTION

*If you use a car wash to clean your bike, do **not** direct the high pressure water at steering bearings, carburetor hoses, suspension components, wheel bearings or electrical components. High-pressure water will flush grease out of the bearings or damage the seals.*

17. Many of the dealership labor charges are for the time involved during the removal, disassembly, assembly and reinstallation of other parts to reach the defective part. It is frequently possible to perform the preliminary operations yourself, then take the defective unit to the dealership for repair at considerable savings.

18. When special tools are required, arrange to get them before you start. It is frustrating and time-consuming to start a job and then be unable to complete it.

19. Make diagrams (or take a Polaroid picture) wherever similar-appearing parts are found.You may think you can remember where everything came from, but mistakes are costly. There is also the possibility that you may be sidetracked and not return to work for days or even weeks in which time carefully laid out parts may become disturbed.

20. When assembling parts, be sure all shims and washers are replaced exactly as they came out.

21. Whenever a rotating part butts against a stationary part, look for a shim or washer. Use new gaskets if there is any doubt about the condition of the old ones. A thin coat of oil on non-pressure type gaskets may help them seal more effectively.

22. Use heavy grease to hold small parts in place if they tend to fall out during assembly. However, keep grease and oil away from electrical and brake components.

WASHING THE BIKE

Regular cleaning of the bike is an important part of its overall maintenance. After riding your bike, clean it thoroughly. Doing this will make maintenance and service procedures quick and easy. More important, proper cleaning will prevent dirt from falling into critical areas undetected. Failing to clean the bike or cleaning it incorrectly will add to your maintenance costs and shop time because dirty parts wear out prematurely. It is unlikely that your bike will break because of improper cleaning, but it can happen. When cleaning your Kawasaki, you need a few tools, shop rags, scrub brush, bucket, liquid

cleaner and access to water. Many riders use a coin-operated car wash. Coin-operated car washes are convenient and quick, but with improper use the high water pressure can do more damage than good to your bike.

NOTE
Simple Green is a biodegradable, non-toxic and nonflammable liquid cleaner that works well for washing your bike and for removing grease and oil from engine and suspension parts. Simple Green can be bought through some supermarkets, hardware and garden stores, and discount supply houses. Follow the directions on the container for recommended mixing ratios.

When cleaning your bike and especially when using a spray type degreaser, remember that what goes on the bike will rinse off and drip onto your driveway or into your yard. If you can, use a degreaser at a coin-operated car wash. If you are cleaning your bike at home, place thick cardboard or newspapers underneath the bike to catch the oil and grease deposits as they are rinsed off.

CAUTION
Some of the steps in this procedure relate to a bike that has been subjected to extremely dirty conditions, like mud or severe road dirt. To avoid surface damage, carefully scrub the plastic side covers with a soft sponge or towel—do not use a brush on these covers as you will scratch the surfaces.

1. Place the bike on level ground on a sidestand.
2. Check the following before washing the bike:

a. Make sure the fuel cap (**Figure 4**) is closed and locked.
b. Make sure the engine oil fill cap (**Figure 5**) is on tight.
c. Plug the muffler openings.
d. Cover the air box air inlet opening(s) with plastic or duct tape.

3. First, wash the bike from top to bottom with soapy water. Use the scrub brush to get excess dirt out of the wheel rims and engine crannies. Concentrate on the upper controls, engine, side panels, front fairing and gas tank. Do not forget to wash dirt and mud from underneath the fenders, suspension and engine crankcase.
4. Next, concentrate on the frame tube members and suspension.
5. Direct the hose underneath the engine and swing arm. Wash this area thoroughly.
6. Finally, use cold water without soap, and spray the entire bike again. Use as much time and care when rinsing the bike as when washing it. Soap deposits will quickly corrode electrical connections and remove the natural oils from tires, causing premature cracks and wear. Make sure you thoroughly rinse off the bike.
7. Tip the bike from side to side to allow any water that has collected on horizontal surfaces to drain off.
8. Remove the plastic cover or duct tape from air box air inlet(s).
9. Unplug the muffler openings.
10. Start the engine and let it idle so the engine will burn off the internal moisture.
11. Before taking the bike into the garage, wipe it dry with a soft terry cloth or chamois. Inspect the machine as you dry it for additional dirt and grime. Make a quick visual inspection of the clear coat and other painted pieces on the frame, swing arm and front forks. Spray any worn-down spots with WD-40 or Bel-Ray 6-in-1 to prevent rust from building on the bare metal. When the bike is back at your work area you can repaint the bare areas with touch-up paint (clear or color) after cleaning off the WD-40.

SPECIAL TIPS

Because of the extreme demands placed on a bike, several points should be kept in mind when performing service and repair. The following items are general suggestions that may improve the overall life of the machine and help avoid costly failures.

1. Use a threadlocking compound such as ThreeBond TB1342 (blue) or Loctite 242 (blue) on all bolts and nuts, even if they are secured with lockwashers. This type of locking compound allows easy removal of the bolt or nut. A screw or bolt lost from an engine cover or bearing retainer could easily cause serious and expensive damage before its loss is noticed. Make sure the threads are clean and free of grease and oil. Clean with contact cleaner before applying the locking compound. When applying the locking compound, use a small amount. If too much is used, it can work its way down the threads and enter bearings or seals. Keep a tube of the various locking compounds in your tool box.
2. Use a hammer-driven impact tool to remove tight fasteners, particularly engine cover screws. These tools help prevent rounding off fastener heads.
3. When replacing missing or broken fasteners, especially on the engine or frame components, always use Kawasaki replacement parts. They are specially hardened for each application. The wrong fastener could easily cause serious and expensive damage, not to mention rider injury.
4. When installing gaskets in the engine, always use genuine Kawasaki replacement gaskets. Kawasaki gaskets are manufactured using material of the precise thickness required. Also, install gaskets without sealant, unless instructed otherwise.

TORQUE SPECIFICATIONS

Improper bolt tightening can cause components to leak, warp or fail. An undertightened fastener will work loose and fall out. An overtightened fastener may break or could warp or crack a component. Overtightening a bolt or cap screw deforms its threads and stretches it beyond its elastic limit. To ensure that fasteners are properly tightened, use an accurate torque wrench and the correct tightening specification.

Torque specifications in this manual are given in Newton-meters (N•m) and foot-pounds (ft.-lb.). Performing a simple conversion—move the decimal point one place to the right (3.5 m-kg equals 35 N•m) allows the use of older torque wrenches calibrated in meter kilograms. This conversion is accurate enough for mechanical work even though the exact mathematical conversion is 3.5 m-kg equals 34.3 N•m.

To convert foot-pounds to Newton meters multiply the foot pounds specification by 1.3558 to achieve a N•m equivalent. (150 ft.-lb. × 1.3558 equals 203 N•m).

Refer to **Table 2** for standard torque specifications for various size screws, bolts and nuts not listed in the respective chapter tables. To use the table, first determine the size of the bolt or nut. Use a vernier caliper and measure the inside of the threads of a nut (**Figure 6**) and across the threads of a bolt (**Figure 7**).

FASTENERS

The materials and designs of the various fasteners used on your Kawasaki are not arrived at by chance

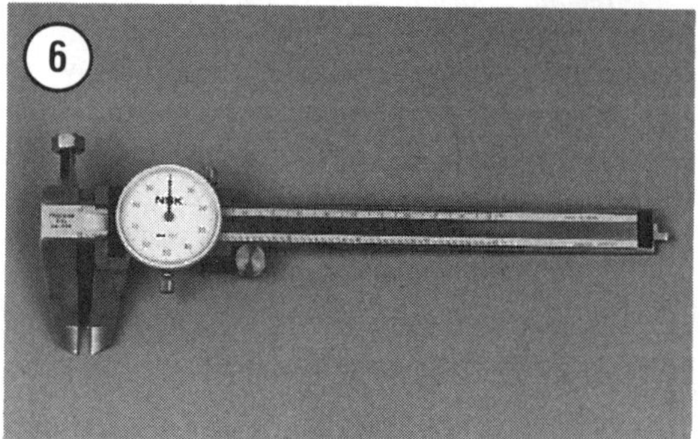

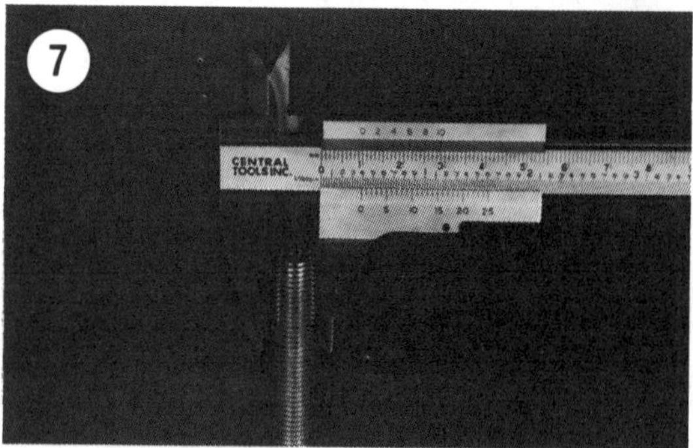

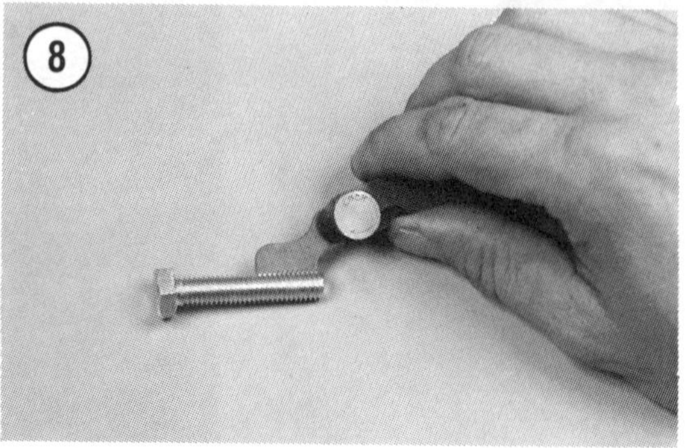

or accident. Fastener design determines the type of tool required to work the fastener. Fastener material is carefully selected to decrease the possibility of physical failure.

Nuts, bolts and screws are manufactured in a wide range of thread patterns. To join a nut and bolt, the diameter of the bolt and the diameter of the hole in the nut must be the same. It is just as important that the threads on both be properly matched.

The best way to tell if two fastener threads match is to turn the nut onto the bolt (or the bolt into the threaded hole in a piece of equipment) with fingers only. Be sure both pieces are clean. If excessive force is required, check the thread condition on each fastener. If the thread condition is good but the fasteners jam, the threads are not compatible. A thread pitch gauge (**Figure 8**) can be used to determine pitch. Kawasaki motorcycles are manufactured with ISO (International Organization for Standardization) metric fasteners. The threads are cut differently than those of U.S. standard fasteners (**Figure 9**).

Most threads are cut so that the fastener must be turned clockwise to tighten it. These are called right-hand threads. Some fasteners have left-hand threads; they must be turned counterclockwise to be tightened. Left-hand threads are used in locations where normal rotation of the equipment would tend to loosen a right-hand threaded fastener.

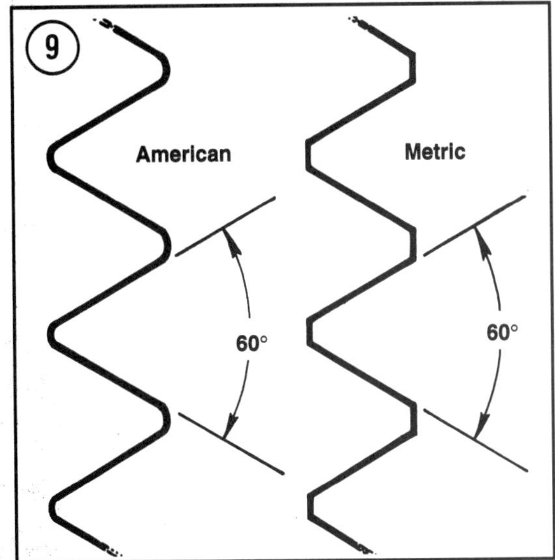

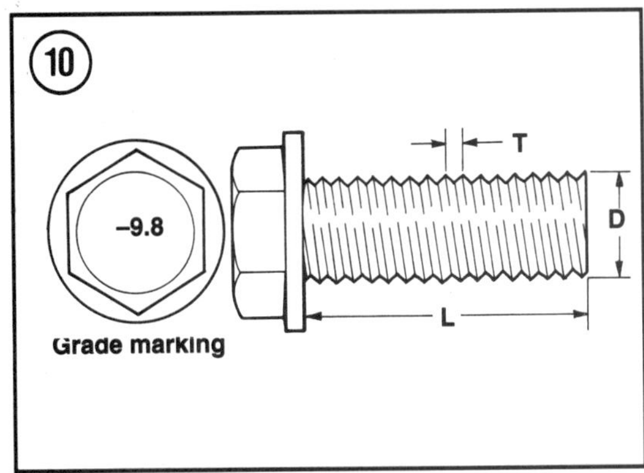

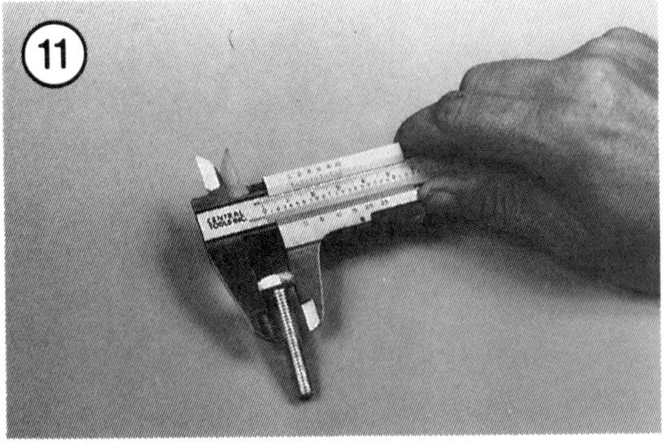

ISO Metric Screw Threads

ISO (International Organization for Standardization) metric threads are available in three standard thread sizes: coarse, fine and constant pitch. The ISO coarse pitch is used for almost all common fastener applications. The fine pitch thread is used on certain precision tools and instruments. The constant pitch thread is used mainly on machine parts and not for fasteners. The constant pitch thread, however, is used on all metric thread spark plugs.

Metric screws and bolts are classified by length (L, **Figure 10**), diameter (D) and distance between thread crests (T). A typical bolt might be identified by the numbers 8–1.25 × 130, which indicates that the bolt has a diameter of 8 mm, the distance between thread crests is 1.25 mm and bolt length is 130 mm.

CAUTION

*Do **not** install screws or bolts with a lower strength grade than installed originally by the manufacturer. Doing so may cause engine or equipment failure and possible injury.*

The measurement across two flats on the head of the bolt (**Figure 11**) indicates the proper wrench size to use. **Figure 12** shows how to determine bolt diameter. When buying a bolt, it is important to know how to specify bolt length. The correct way to measure bolt length is by measuring the length starting from underneath the bolt head to the end of the bolt (**Figure 13**). Always measure bolt length in this manner to avoid buying bolts that are too long.

Machine Screws

There are many different types of machine screws. **Figure 14** shows a number of screw heads requiring different types of turning tools. Heads are also designed to protrude above the metal (round) or slightly recessed in the metal (flat).

Nuts

Nuts are manufactured in a variety of types and sizes. Most are hexagonal (6-sided) and fit on bolts, screws and studs with the same diameter and pitch. **Figure 15** shows several types of nuts. The common nut is generally used with a lockwasher. Self-locking nuts have a nylon insert that prevents the nut from loosening. No lockwasher is required. Wing nuts are

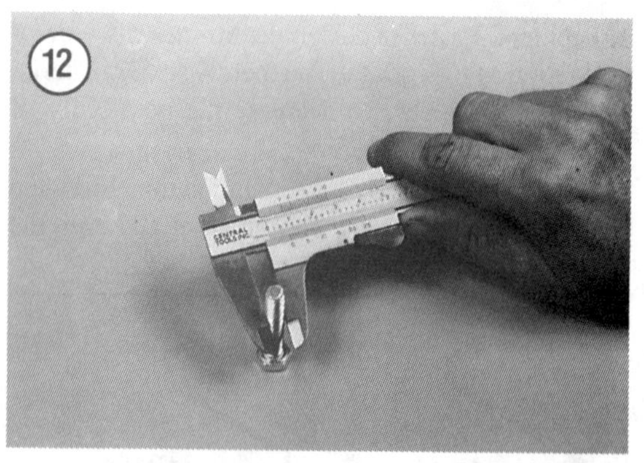
12

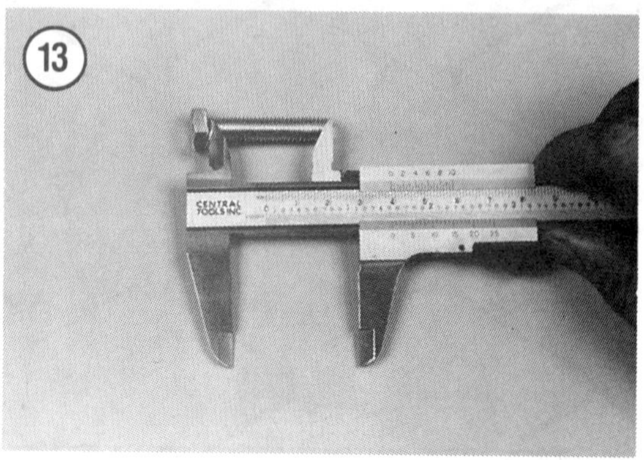
13

14

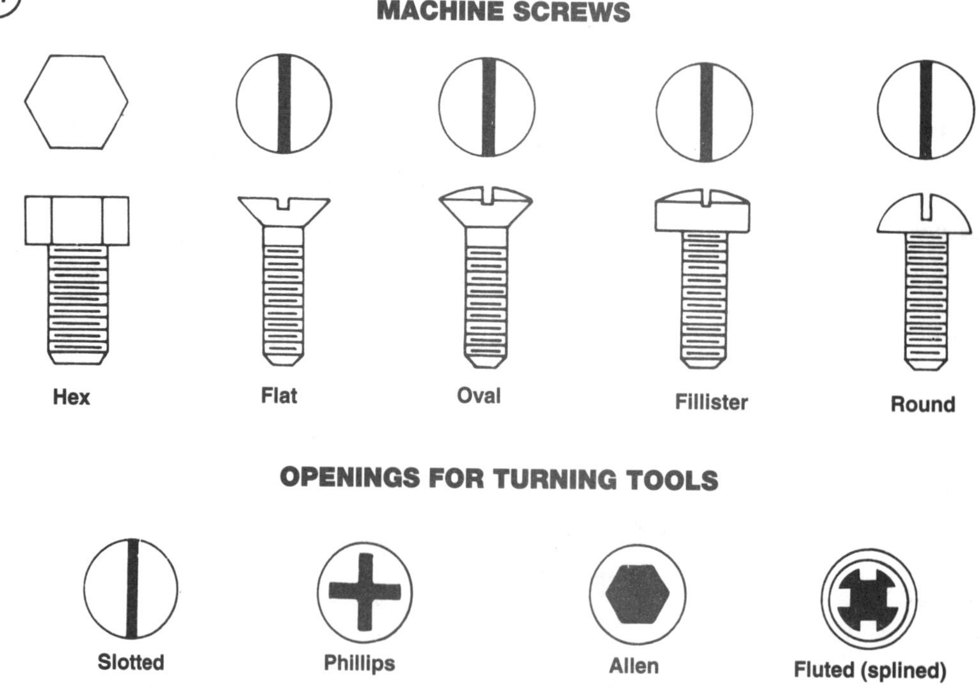

MACHINE SCREWS

Hex · Flat · Oval · Fillister · Round

OPENINGS FOR TURNING TOOLS

Slotted · Phillips · Allen · Fluted (splined)

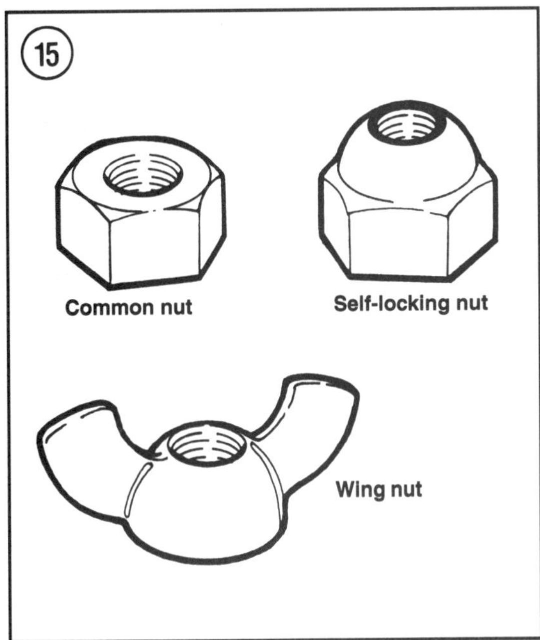

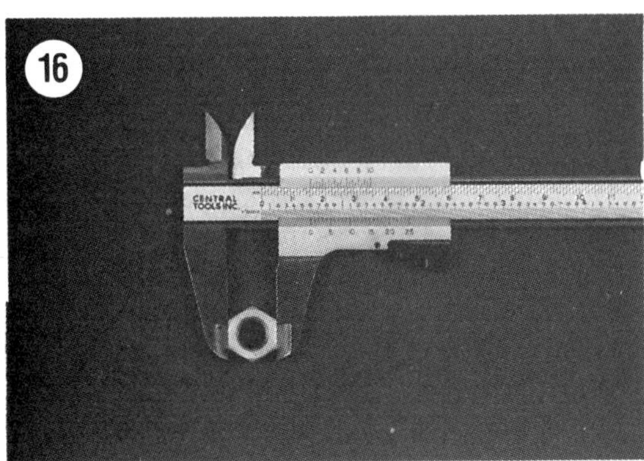

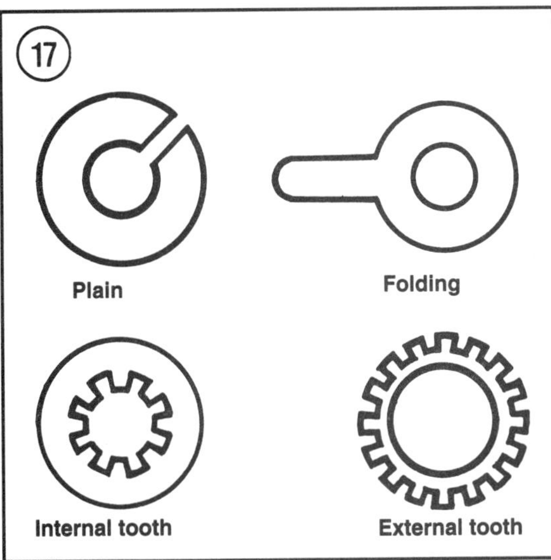

designed for fast removal by hand. Wing nuts are used for convenience in non-critical locations.

To indicate the size of a metric nut, manufacturers specify the diameter of the opening and the thread pitch. This is similar to bolt specifications, but without the length dimension. The measurement across two flats on the nut indicates the proper wrench size to be used (**Figure 16**).

Self-Locking Fasteners

Several types of bolts, screws and nuts incorporate a system that develops an interference between the bolt, screw, nut or threaded hole. Interference is achieved in various ways: by distorting threads, coating threads with dry adhesive or nylon, distorting the top of an all-metal nut or using a nylon insert in the center or at the top of a nut.

Self-locking fasteners offer greater holding strength and better vibration resistance than standard fasteners. Some self-locking fasteners can be reused if in good condition. Others, like the nylon insert nut, form an initial locking condition when the nut is first installed; the nylon forms closely to the bolt thread pattern, thus reducing any tendency for the nut to loosen. For greatest safety, *always discard* previously used self-locking fasteners and install new ones during reassembly.

Washers

There are two basic types of washers: flat washers and lockwashers. Flat washers are simple discs with a hole to fit a screw or bolt. Lockwashers are designed to prevent a fastener from working loose due to vibration, expansion and contraction. **Figure 17** shows several types of washers. Washers can be used in the following functions:

a. As spacers.

b. To prevent galling or damage of the equipment by the fastener.

c. To help distribute fastener load during torquing.

d. As seals.

Note that flat washers are often used between a lockwasher and a fastener to provide a smooth bearing surface.

NOTE
Give as much care to the selection of washers as that given to bolts, nuts and other fasteners. Beware of washers that are made of thin and weak materials. These will deform and crush the first time they are used in a high torque application.

Cotter Pins

In certain applications, a fastener must be secured so it cannot possibly loosen. The rear axle nut on the VN800 is one such application. For this purpose, a cotter pin (**Figure 18**) and slotted or castle nut is often used. To use a cotter pin, first make sure the pin fits snugly, but not too tight. Then, align a slot in the fastener with the hole in the bolt or axle. Insert the cotter pin through the nut and bolt or axle and bend the ends over to secure the cotter pin tightly. If the holes do not align, tighten the nut just enough to obtain the proper alignment. Unless specifically instructed to do so, never loosen the fastener to align the slot and hole. Because the cotter pin is weakened after installation and removal, never reuse a cotter pin. Cotter pins are available in several styles, lengths and diameters. Measure cotter pin length from the bottom of its head to the tip of its shortest prong.

Circlips (Snap Rings)

Circlips (snap rings) can be internal or external design. They are used to retain items on shafts (external type) or within tubes (internal type). In some applications, circlips of varying thickness are used to control the end play of assemblies. These are often called selective circlips. Circlips should be replaced during installation, as removal weakens and deforms them.

Two basic styles of circlips are available: machined and stamped circlips. Machined circlips (**Figure 19**) can be installed in either direction (shaft or housing) because both faces are machined, thus creating two sharp edges. Stamped circlips (**Figure 20**) are manufactured with one sharp edge and one rounded edge. When installing stamped circlips in a thrust situation (such as transmission shafts and fork tubes), the sharp edge must face away from the part producing the thrust. When installing circlips, observe the following:

a. Compress or expand circlips only enough to install them.

b. After the circlip is installed, make sure it is completely seated in its groove.

c. Transmission circlips become worn with use. For this reason, always use new circlips whenever a transmission is reassembled.

LUBRICANTS

Periodic lubrication helps ensure long life for any type of equipment. The type of lubricant used is just as important as the lubrication service itself, although in an emergency the wrong type of lubricant is better than none at all. The following paragraphs describe the types of lubricants most often used on motorcycle equipment. Be sure to follow the manufacturer's recommendations for lubricant types.

Generally all liquid lubricants are called oil. They may be mineral-based (including petroleum bases), natural-based (vegetable and animal bases), synthetic-based or emulsions (mixtures). Grease is an oil to which a thickening base has been added so the end product is semi-solid. Grease is often classified by the type of thickener added; lithium soap is commonly used.

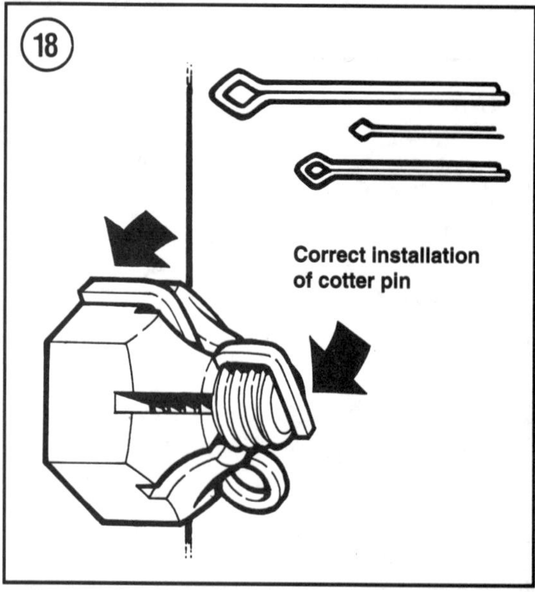

Engine Oil

Four-stroke oil for motorcycles is graded by the American Petroleum Institute (API) and the Society of Automotive Engineers (SAE). Oil containers display these ratings on the label. API oil grade is indicated by letters; oils for gasoline engines are identified by an S. Kawasaki models described in this manual require SE, SF or SG grade oil.

Viscosity is an indication of the oil's thickness. The SAE uses numbers to indicate viscosity. Thin oils have low numbers while thick oils have high numbers. A W after the number indicates that the viscosity testing was done at low temperature to simulate cold-weather operation. Engine oils fall into the 5 to 50 range.

Multigrade oils (for example 10W-40) are less viscous (thinner) at low temperatures and more viscous (thicker) at high temperatures. This allows the oil to perform efficiently across a wide range of engine operating conditions. The lower the number, the better the engine will start in cold climates.

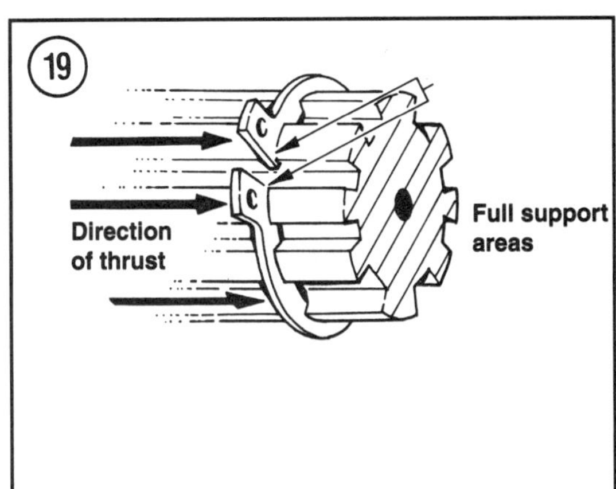

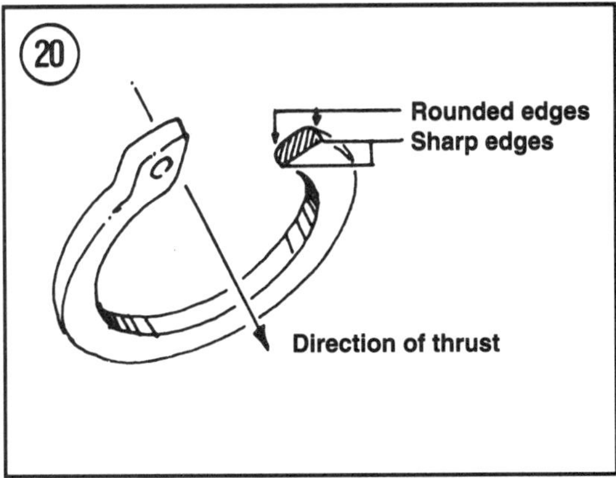

Higher numbers are usually recommended when operating an engine in hot weather.

Grease

Greases are graded by the National Lubricating Grease Institute (NLGI). Greases are graded by number according to the consistency of the grease; these range from No. 000 to No. 6, with No. 6 being the most solid. A typical multipurpose grease is NLGI No. 2. For specific applications, equipment manufacturers may require grease with an additive such as molybdenum disulfide.

RTV GASTET SEALANT

Room temperature vulcanizing (RTV) sealant is used on some gaskets and to seal some components. RTV is a silicone gel supplied in tubes and can be purchased in a number of different colors.

Moisture in the air causes RTV to cure. RTV has a shelf life of one year and will not cure properly after the shelf life has expired. Check the expiration date on an RTV tube before using it. Always replace the cap on the tube as soon as possible and keep partially used tubes tightly sealed.

Applying RTV Sealant

Before applying RTV sealant, the mating surfaces must be absolutely free of gasket material, sealant, dirt, oil, grease or other contamination. Lacquer thinner, electrical contact cleaner, acetone and isopropyl alcohol work well for cleaning mating surfaces. Avoid using solvent with an oil, wax or petroleum base; RTV sealant will not adhere to a surface with a petroleum, oil or wax film. Remove all RTV gasket material from blind attaching holes. If left in place, it can cause a hydraulic effect and influence bolt torque.

Apply RTV sealant in a continuous bead. Circle all mounting holes unless otherwise specified. Torque mating parts within ten minutes after application.

GASKET REMOVER

Stubborn gaskets can present a problem during engine service. They can take a long time to remove and incorrect use of a gasket scraping tool can damage the gasket mating surfaces. To quickly and safely remove stubborn gaskets, use a spray gasket remover. Spray gasket remover can be purchased through automotive parts houses. Follow the manufacturer's directions for use.

THREADLOCKING COMPOUND

Use a threadlocking compound to help secure many of the fasteners used on your bike. Threadlocking compound locks fasteners against loosening by vibration loosening and protects the seal against leaks. The following thread locking compounds are recommended for many threadlock requirements described in this manual.

a. ThreeBond 1342 (blue): low strength, frequent repair.
b. Loctite 242 (blue): low strength, frequent repair.
c. ThreeBond 1360 (green): medium strength, high temperature.
d. ThreeBond 1333B (red): medium strength, bearing and stud lock.
e. ThreeBond 1303 (orange): high strength, frequent repair.
f. Loctite 271 (red): high strength, frequent repair.

There are other quality threadlock brands on the market.

EXPENDABLE SUPPLIES

Certain expendable supplies are required during maintenance and repair work. These include grease, oil, gasket cement, wiping rags and cleaning solvent. Ask your dealer for the special locking compounds, lubricants and other products that make bike maintenance simpler and easier. Cleaning solvent or kerosene is available at some service stations, paint or hardware stores.

Be sure to follow the manufacturer's instructions and warnings listed on the label of the product you are using. Some cleaning supplies are very caustic and are dangerous if not used properly.

WARNING
Having a stack of clean shop rags on hand is important when performing engine and suspension service. However, to prevent spontaneous combustion from a pile of solvent soaked rags, store them in a sealed metal container until they can be washed or properly discarded.

NOTE
To prevent solvent and other chemicals from being absorbed into your skin, wear a pair of petroleum-resistance gloves when cleaning parts. These can be bought through industrial supply houses or well-equipped hardware stores.

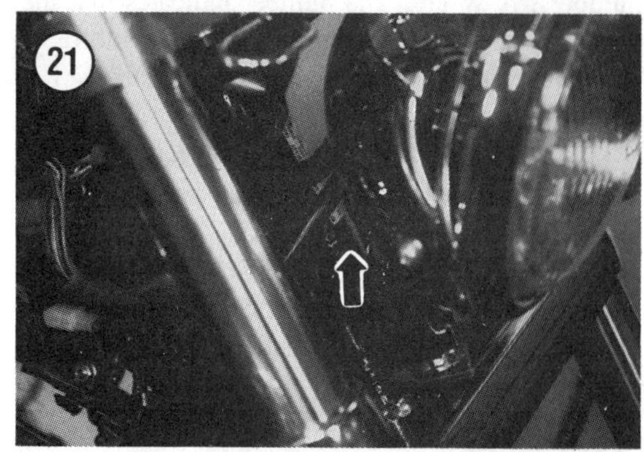

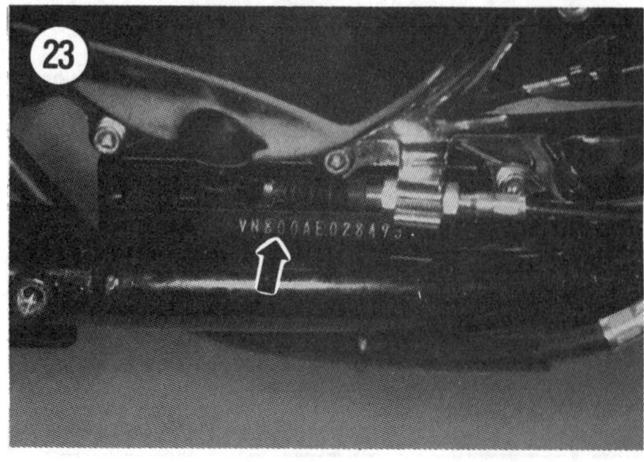

SERIAL NUMBERS

Kawasaki makes frequent changes during a model year, some minor, some relatively major. When you order parts, always order by VIN and engine/frame serial numbers. The frame serial number is stamped on the right-hand side of the steering head (**Figure 21**). The VIN plate (vehicle identification number) is attached to the left-hand side of the steering head (**Figure 22**). The engine number is stamped on the right-hand side of the crankcase (**Figure 23**). The carburetor serial number is on the side of the carburetor body (**Figure 24**).

Table 1 lists VIN and engine serial numbers for the models covered in this manual.

WARNING AND INFORMATION LABELS

A number of warning labels are attached to your Kawasaki. These labels contain information that is important to your safety when operating, transporting and storing your bike. Refer to information labels behind the side covers (**Figure 25**) and underneath the seat. Refer to your owner's manual for a description and location of each label. If a label is missing, order a replacement label from a Kawasaki dealership.

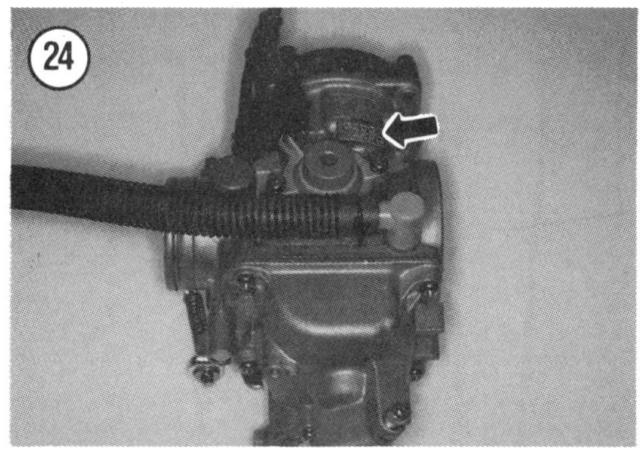

24

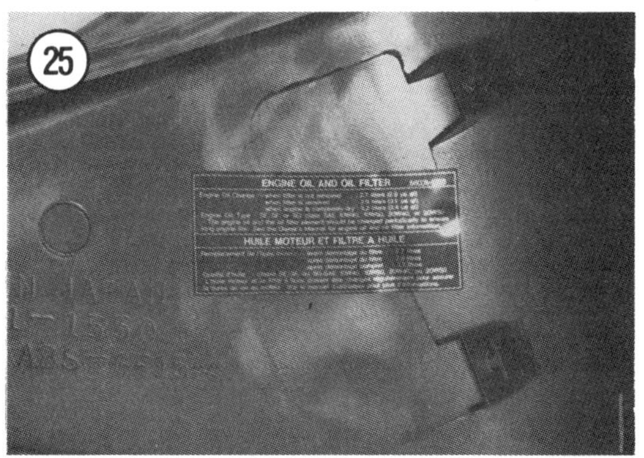

25

BASIC HAND TOOLS

Many of the procedures in this manual can be carried out with simple hand tools and test equipment familiar to the average home mechanic. Keep your tools clean and in a tool box. Keep them organized with related tools stored together. After using a tool, wipe off dirt and grease with a clean cloth and return the tool to its correct place.

Top quality tools are essential; they are also more economical in the long run. If you are now starting to build your tool collection, avoid the advertised specials featured at some parts houses, discount stores and chain drug stores. These are usually poor grade tools that can be sold cheaply, and that is exactly what they are—cheap. They are usually made of inferior materials and are thick, heavy and clumsy. Their rough finish makes them difficult to clean and they usually do not last very long. If it is ever your misfortune to use such tools, you will probably find out that the wrenches do not fit the heads of bolts and nuts correctly and damage the fastener.

Quality tools are made of alloy steel and are heat treated for greater strength. They are lighter and better balanced than cheap ones. Their surface is smooth, making them a pleasure to work with and easy to clean. The initial cost of good quality tools may be more, but they are less expensive in the long run. Do not try to buy everything in all sizes in the beginning. Buy a few at a time until you have the necessary tools.

Screwdrivers

The screwdriver is a very basic tool, but if used improperly it will do more damage than good. The slot on a screw has a particular dimension and shape. A screwdriver must be selected to conform to that shape. Use a small screwdriver for small screws and a large one for large screws or the screw head will be damaged.

Two basic types of screwdrivers are required: slotted (flat-blade) screwdrivers (**Figure 26**) and Phillips screwdrivers (**Figure 27**).

Screwdrivers are available in sets, which often include an assortment of common and Phillips blades. If you buy them individually, buy at least the following:

a. Slotted screwdriver—5/16 × 6 in. blade.

b. Slotted screwdriver—3/8 × 12 in. blade.

c. Phillips screwdriver—size 2 tip, 6 in. blade.

d. Phillips screwdriver—size 3 tip, 6 and 10 in. blade.

Use screwdrivers only for driving screws. Never use a screwdriver for prying or chiseling metal. Do not try to remove a Phillips or Allen head screw with a common screwdriver (unless the screw has a combination head that will accept either type); you can damage the head so that even the proper tool will be unable to remove it. Keep screwdrivers in the proper condition and they will last longer and perform better. Always keep the tip of a common screwdriver in good condition. **Figure 28** shows how to grind the tip to the proper shape if it becomes damaged. Note the symmetrical sides of the tip.

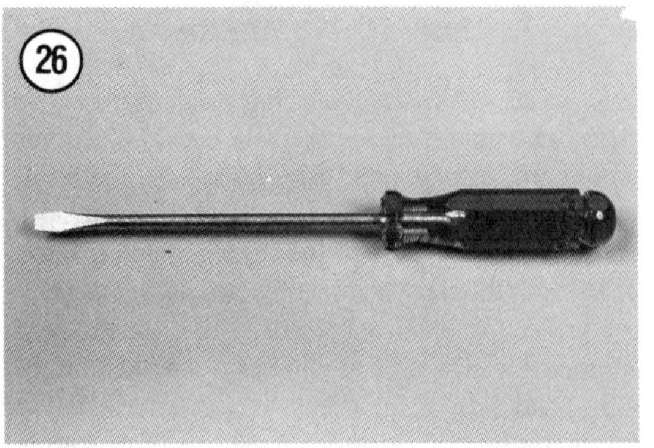

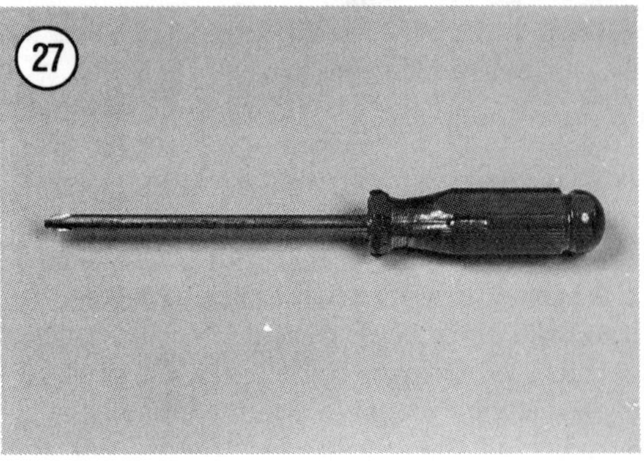

28

FRONT

SIDE

CORRECT WAY TO GRIND BLADE

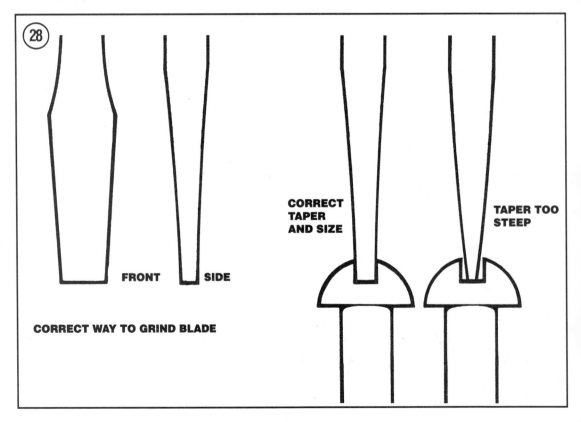

CORRECT TAPER AND SIZE

TAPER TOO STEEP

Pliers

Pliers come in a wide range of types and sizes. Pliers are useful for cutting, bending and crimping. Do not use them to cut hardened objects or to turn bolts or nuts. **Figure 29** shows several pliers useful in motorcycle repair. Each type of plier has a specialized function. Slip-joint pliers are general purpose pliers. These are used mainly for holding things and for bending.

Needlenose pliers are used to hold or bend small objects. Adjustable pliers can be adjusted to hold various sizes of objects; the jaws remain parallel to grip around objects such as pipe or tubing. There are many more types of pliers. The ones described here are most suitable for bike repairs.

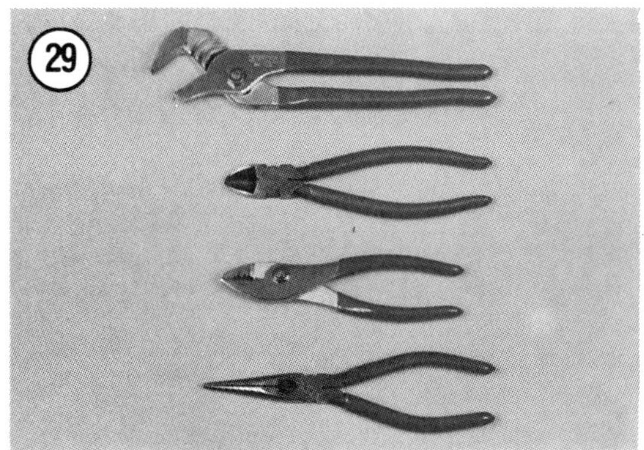

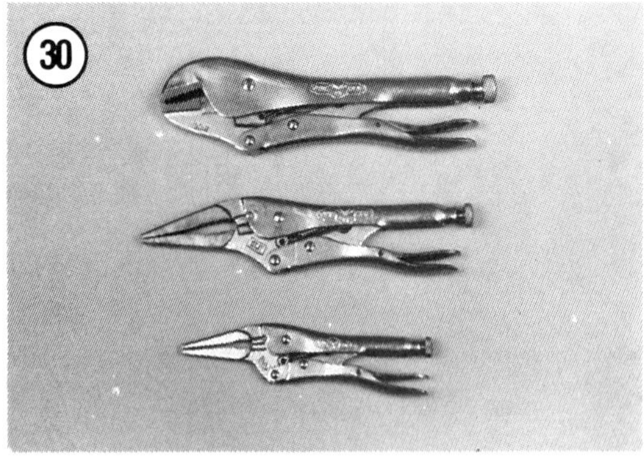

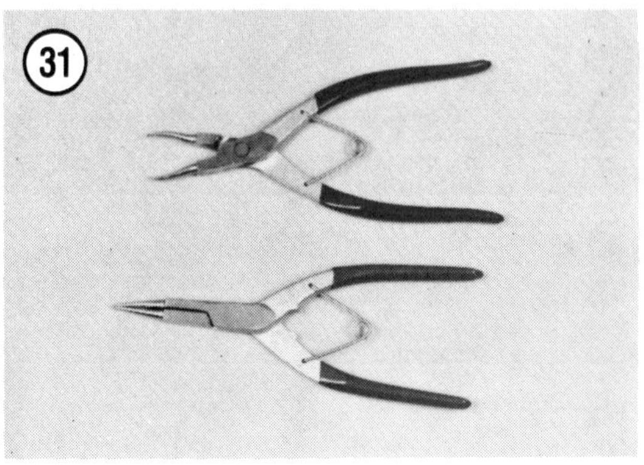

Locking Pliers

Locking pliers (**Figure 30**) are used to hold objects very tightly like a vise. Avoid using them unless necessary since their sharp jaws will permanently scar any objects they hold. Locking pliers are available in many types for more specific tasks.

Circlip (Snap Ring) Pliers

Circlip (snap ring) pliers (**Figure 31**) are made for removing and installing circlips. External pliers (spreading) are used to remove circlips that fit on the outside of a shaft. Internal pliers (squeezing) are used to remove circlips which fit inside a gear or housing.

WARNING

Because circlips can sometimes slip and fly off, always wear safety glasses when removing and installing them.

Box, Open-end and Combination Wrenches

Box-end, open-end and combination wrenches are available in sets or separately in a variety of sizes. On open- and box-end wrenches, the number stamped near the end refers to the distance between two parallel flats on the hex head bolt or nut. On combination wrenches, the number is stamped near the center.

Box-end wrenches require clear overhead access to the fastener but can work well in situations where the fastener head is close to another part. They grip on all six edges of a fastener for a very secure grip. They are available in either 6-point or 12-point. The 6-point gives superior holding power and durability, but it requires a greater swinging radius. The 12-point works better in situations where the swinging radius is limited.

Open-end wrenches are speedy and work best in areas with limited overhead access. Their wide flat jaws make them unsuitable for situations where the bolt or nut is sunken in a well or close to the edge of a casting. These wrenches grip only two flats of a fastener so if either the fastener head or the wrench jaws are worn, the wrench may slip off.

Combination wrenches (**Figure 32**) have an open-end on one side and box-end on the other with both ends being the same size. Professional mechanics favor these wrenches because of their versatility.

Adjustable (Crescent) Wrenches

An adjustable wrench (sometimes called a crescent wrench) can be adjusted to fit nearly any nut or bolt head that has clear access around its entire perimeter. An adjustable wrench (**Figure 33**) is best used as a backup wrench to keep a large nut or bolt from turning while the other end is being loosened or tightened with a proper wrench.

Adjustable wrenches have only two gripping surfaces which make them more subject to slipping off the fastener and damaging the part and possibly injuring your hand. The fact that one jaw is adjustable only aggravates this shortcoming.

These wrenches are directional; the solid jaw must be the one transmitting the force. If you use the adjustable jaw to transmit the force, it will loosen and possibly slip off.

Adjustable wrenches come in many sizes; one in the 6 to 8 in. and 12 to 14 in. range is recommended.

Socket Wrenches

This type is undoubtedly the fastest, safest and most convenient wrench to use. Sockets, which attach to a ratchet handle, are available with 6-point or 12-point openings and with 1/4, 3/8, 1/2 and 3/4 in. drives. The drive size indicates the size of the square hole which mates with the ratchet handle (**Figure 34**).

Allen Wrenches

Allen wrenches are available in sets or separately in a variety of sizes. These sets come in U.S. customary and metric size, so be sure to buy a metric set. Allen bolts are sometimes called socket bolts. Sometimes the bolts are difficult to reach and it is suggested that a variety of Allen wrenches to purchase like the socket driven, T-handle and extension type that are shown in **Figure 35**.

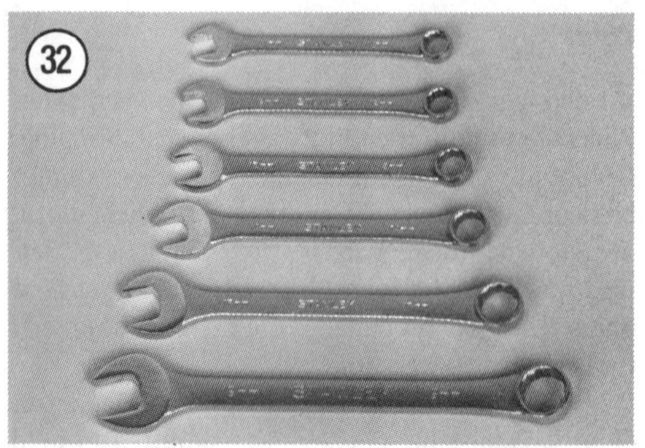
32

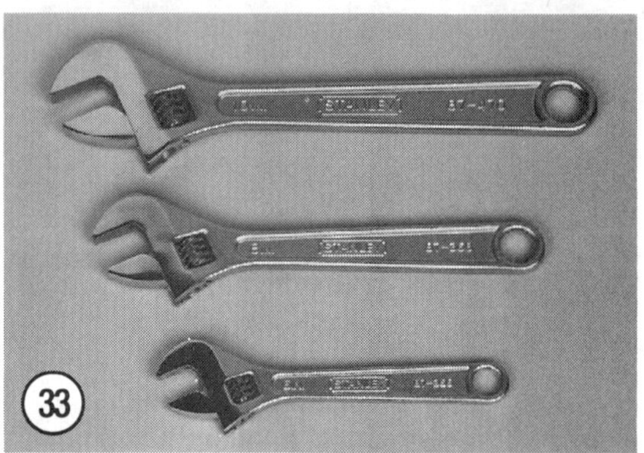
33

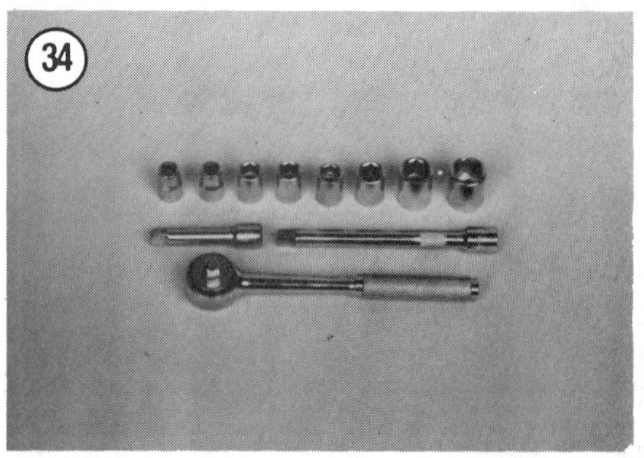
34

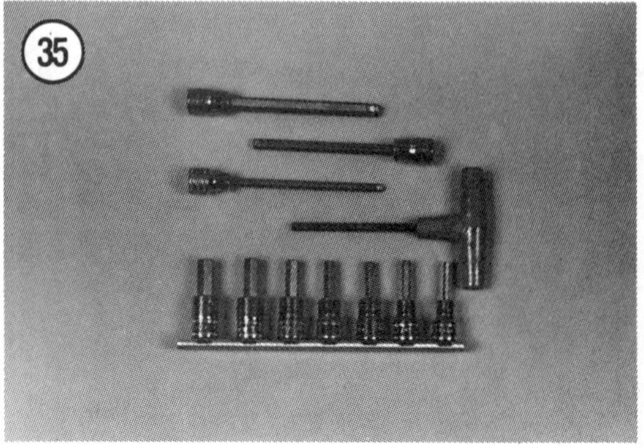
35

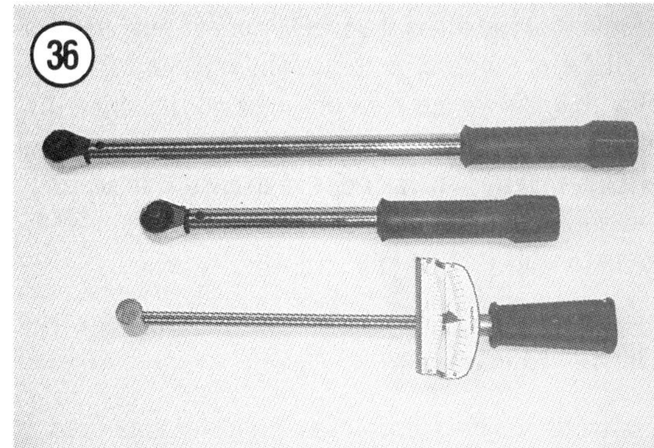

36

Torque Wrench

A torque wrench is used with a socket to measure how tightly a nut or bolt is installed. They come in a wide price range and with either 1/4, 3/8 or 1/2 in. square drive (**Figure 36**). The drive size indicates the size of the square drive that mates with the socket.

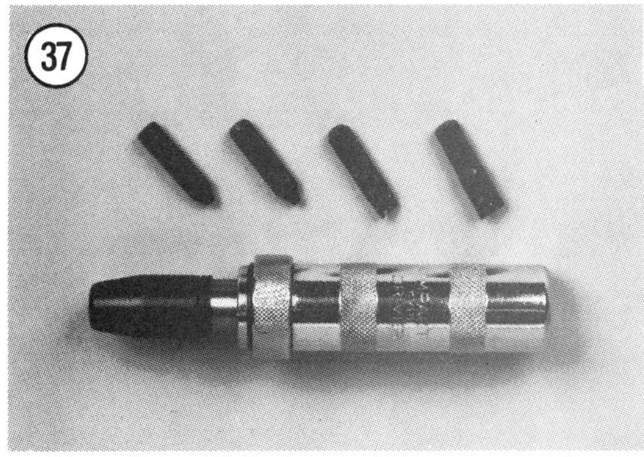

37

Impact Driver

This tool might have been designed with the motorcycle rider in mind. An impact driver makes removal of fasteners easy and eliminates damage to bolts and screw slots. Impact drivers (**Figure 37**) and interchangeable bits are available at most large hardware, motorcycle or auto parts stores. Sockets can also be used with a hand impact driver; however, make sure that the socket is designed for use with an impact driver or air tool. Do not use regular hand sockets. They may shatter during use.

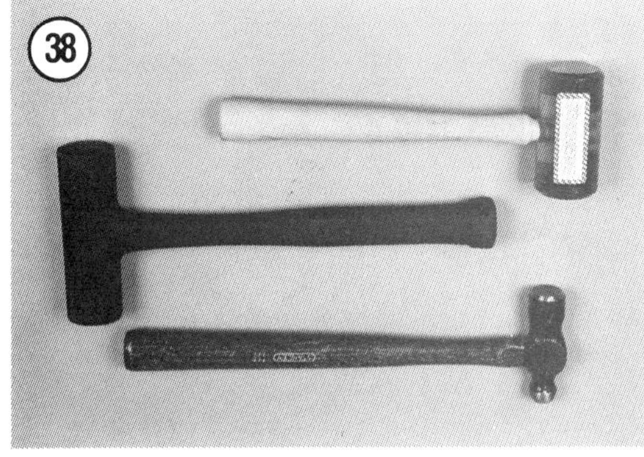

38

Hammers

The correct hammer (**Figure 38**) is necessary for certain repairs. A soft-faced hammer (rubber or plastic) or a soft-faced hammer filled with lead or steel shot is sometimes necessary during engine disassembly. Never use a metal-faced hammer on engine or suspension parts. Severe damage will result in most cases. You can produce the same amount of force with a soft-faced hammer. The shock of a metal-faced hammer, however, is required for using a hand impact driver or cold chisel.

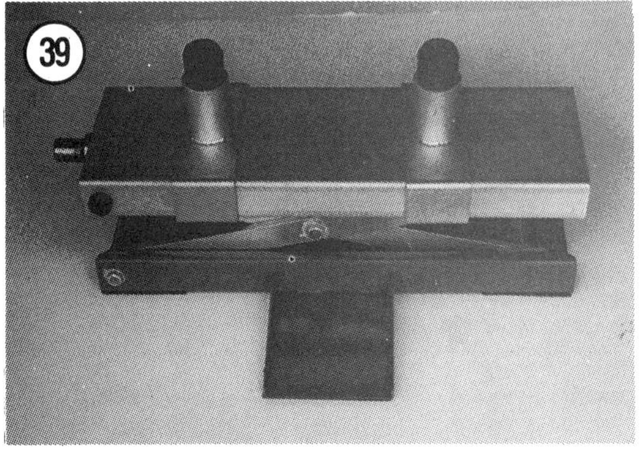

39

Support Jacks

The correct type of support jack is necessary for many routine service or major component replacement procedures on the bike. The centerstand scissor jack available through Kawasaki dealerships from K&L Supply, Santa Clara, CA (**Figure 39**) is suitable for most service procedures on this series of bikes. It is adjustable and is very stable for use with the frame configuration of this vehicle.

PRECISION MEASURING TOOLS

Measurement is an important part of engine and suspension service. When performing many of the service procedures in this manual, you will be required to make a number of measurements. These include basic checks such as engine compression and spark plug gap. When performing engine disassembly and service, measurements will be required to determine the size and condition of the piston and cylinder bore, crankshaft runout and so on. When making these measurements, the degree of accuracy will dictate which tool is required. Precision measuring tools are expensive. If this is your first experience at engine or suspension service, it may be worthwhile to have the checks and measurements made at a Kawasaki dealership, a competent independent motorcycle repair shop or a machine shop. However, as your skills and enthusiasm for service work increase, you may want to buy some of these specialized tools. The following is a description of the measuring tools required to perform the various service procedures described in this manual.

Feeler Gauge

Feeler gauges come in assorted sets and types (**Figure 40**). The feeler gauge is made of either a piece of a flat or round hardened steel of a specified thickness. Round gauges are used to measure spark plug gap. Flat gauges are used for other measurements. Feeler gauges are also designed for specialized uses. For example, the end of a gauge is can be small and angled to facilitate checking valve clearances.

Vernier Caliper, Dial Caliper and Digital Electronic Caliper

These are valuable tools for reading inside, outside and depth measurements. The vernier caliper is shown in **Figure 41**. Although this type of tool is not as precise as a micrometer, they allow reasonably accurate measurements, typically to within 0.025 mm (0.001 in.). Common uses of a vernier caliper are measuring the length of the clutch springs, the thickness of clutch plates, shims and thrust washers, brake pad or lining thickness or the depth of a bearing bore. The jaws of the caliper must be clean and free of burrs at all times to obtain an accurate measurement. There are several types of vernier calipers available. The standard vernier caliper has a highly accurate graduated scale on the handle (**Figure 42**) in which the measurements must be calculated. A dial caliper is equipped with a small dial and needle that indicates the measurement reading. The digital electronic type, however, uses an LCD display that shows the measurement on the small display screen. Some vernier calipers must be zeroed prior to making a measurement to ensure an accurate measurement. Refer to the manufacturer's instructions for this procedure.

Outside Micrometers

An outside micrometer is a precision tool used to accurately measure parts using the decimal divisions

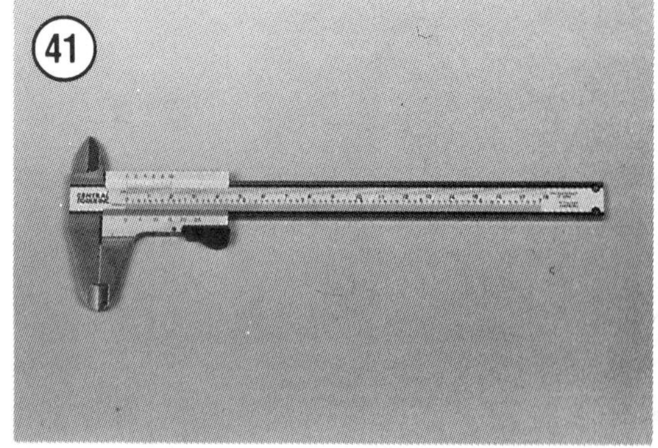

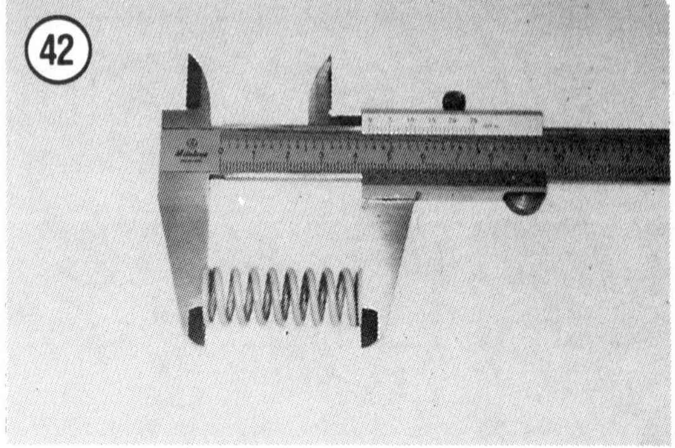

of the inch or meter (**Figure 43**). While there are many types and styles of micrometers, this section describes steps on how to use the outside micrometer. The outside micrometer is the most common type of micrometer used when servicing a motorcycle. It accurately measures the outside diameter, length and thickness of parts used on these vehicles. These parts include pistons, piston pins, crankshaft, piston rings, transmission shafts and various shims. The outside micrometer is also used to measure the dimension taken by a small hole gauge or a telescoping gauge described later in this section. After the small hole gauge or telescoping gauge has been carefully expanded within the bore of the component, carefully remove the gauge and measure the outer dimension of the gauge with the outside micrometer.

Other types of micrometers include the depth micrometer and screw thread micrometer. **Figure 44** identifies the various parts of the outside micrometer.

DECIMAL PLACE VALUES*

0.1	Indicates 1/10 (one tenth of an inch or millimeter)
0.01	Indicates 1/100 (one one-hundredth of an inch or millimeter)
0.001	Indicates 1/1,000 (one one-thousandth of an inch or millimeter)

* This chart represents the values of figures placed to the right of the decimal point. Use it when reading decimals from one-tenth to one one-thousandth of an inch or millimeter. It is not a conversion chart (for example: 0.001 in. is not equal to 0.001 mm.).

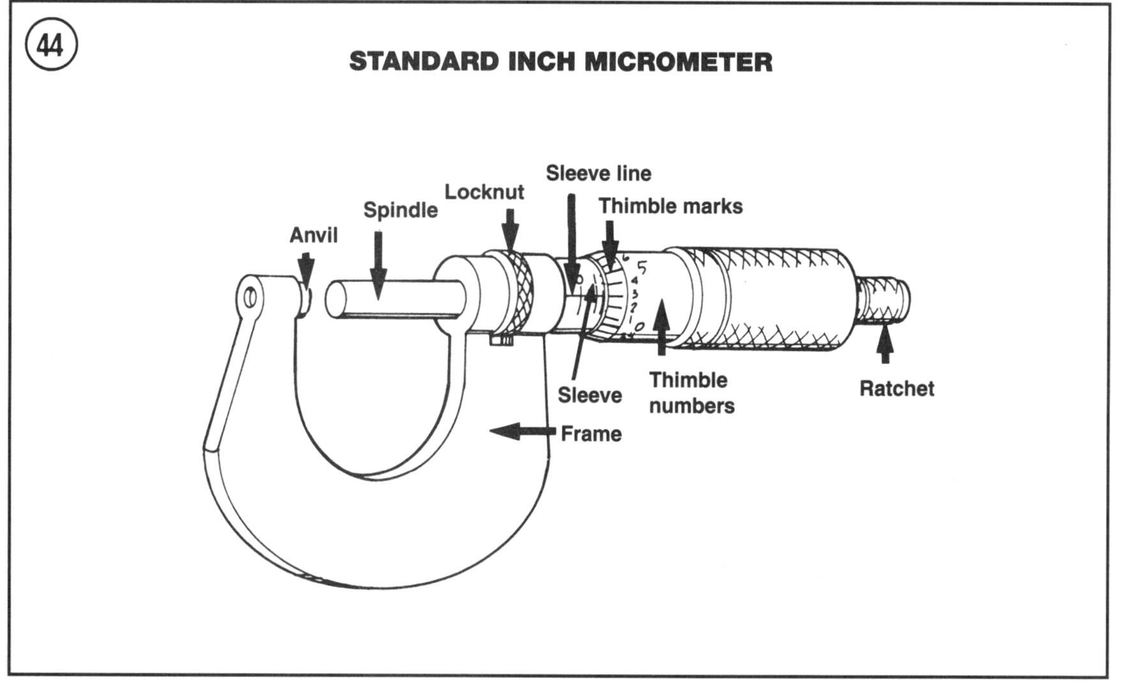

Micrometer Range

A micrometer's size indicates the minimum and maximum size of a part that it can measure. The usual sizes are: 0-1 in.(0-25 mm), 1-2 in.(25-50 mm), 2-3 in. (50-75 mm) and 3-4 (75-100 mm). These micrometers use fixed anvils.

Some micrometers use the same frame with interchangeable anvils of different lengths. This allows the installation of the correct length anvil for a particular job. For example, a 0-4 in. interchangeable micrometer is equipped with four different length anvils. While purchasing one or two micrometers to cover a range from 0-4 in, or 0-6 inches is less expensive, its overall frame size makes it less convenient to use.

How To Read a Micrometer

When reading a micrometer, numbers are taken from different scales, then added together. The following sections describe how to read the standard inch micrometer, the vernier inch micrometer, the standard metric micrometer and the metric vernier micrometer.

Standard inch micrometer

The standard inch micrometer is accurate to one-thousand of an inch (0.001 in.). The heart of the micrometer is its spindle screw with 40 threads per inch. Every turn of the thimble moves the spindle 1/40 of an inch or 0.025 inch.

Before you learn how to read a micrometer, study the markings and part names in **Figure 44**. Turn the micrometer's thimble until its zero mark aligns with the zero mark on the sleeve line. Now turn the thimble counterclockwise and align the next thimble mark with the sleeve line. The micrometer now reads 0.001 in. (one one-thousandths) of an inch. Thus, each thimble mark is equal to 0.001 in. Every fifth thimble mark is numbered to help with reading: 0, 5, 15 and 20.

Reset the micrometer so the thimble and sleeve-line zero marks align. Then turn the thimble counterclockwise one complete revolution and align the thimble zero mark with the first line in the sleeve line. The micrometer now reads 0.025 in. (twenty-five thousandths) of an inch. Thus each sleeve line represents 0.025 inch.

Now turn the thimble counterclockwise while counting the sleeve line marks. Every fourth mark on the sleeve line is marked with a number ranging from 1 through 9. Manufacturers usually mark the last mark on the sleeve with a 0. This indicates that you have reached the end of the micrometer's measuring range. Each sleeve number represents 0.100 in. For example, the number 1 represents 0.100 in. and the number 9 represents 0.900 inch.

When reading a standard micrometer, take the following three measurements described and add them together. The sum of the three readings will give you the measurement in thousandths of an inch.

To read a micrometer, perform the following steps and refer to the example in **Figure 45**.

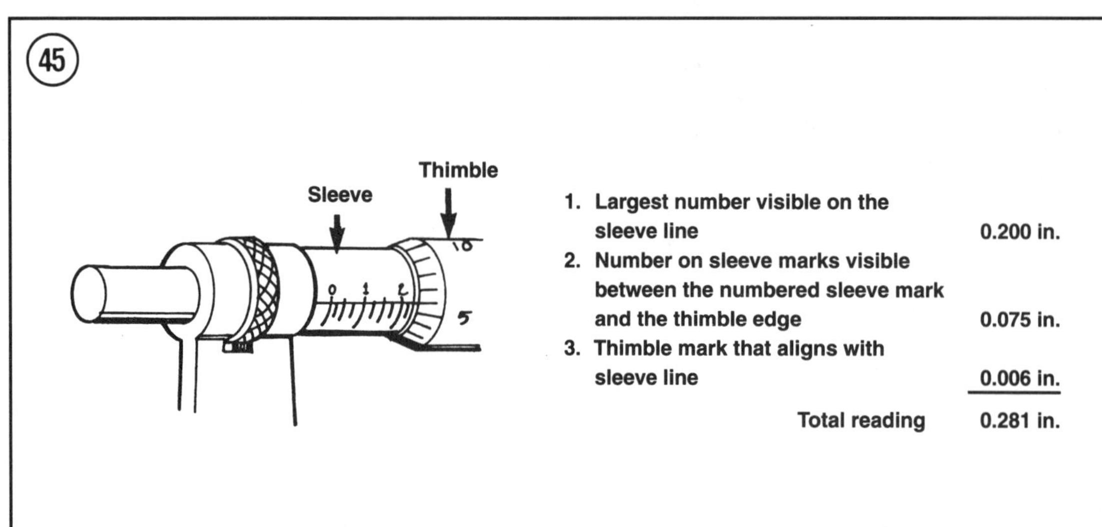

45
Thimble
Sleeve
1. Largest number visible on the sleeve line 0.200 in.
2. Number on sleeve marks visible between the numbered sleeve mark and the thimble edge 0.075 in.
3. Thimble mark that aligns with sleeve line 0.006 in.
Total reading 0.281 in.

1. Read the sleeve line to find the largest number visible—each sleeve number mark equals 0.100 inch.
2. Count the number of sleeve marks visible between the numbered sleeve mark and the thimble edge—each sleeve mark equals 0.025 inch. If there is no visible sleeve mark, continue to Step 3.
3. Read the thimble mark that lines up with the sleeve line—each thimble mark equals 0.001 inch.

NOTE
If a thimble mark does not align exactly with the sleeve line but falls between two lines, estimate the fraction of decimal amount between the lines.

4. Add the micrometer readings in Steps 1, 2 and 3 to obtain the actual measurement.

Vernier inch micrometer

A vernier micrometer can accurately measure in ten-thousandths of an inch (0.0001 in.) increments. While it has the same markings as the standard inch micrometer, a vernier scale scribed on the sleeve (**Figure 46**) makes it unique . The vernier scale consists of eleven equally spaced lines marked 0-9 with a 0 on each end. These lines run parallel on the top of the sleeve where each line is equal to 0.0001 inch. Thus, the vernier scale divides a thousandth of an inch (0.001 in.) into ten-thousandths of an inch (0.0001 in.).

To read the vernier micrometer, perform the following steps and refer to the example in **Figure 47**:

1. Read the micrometer in the same way as the standard inch micrometer. This is the initial reading.
2. If a thimble mark aligns exactly with the sleeve line, reading the vernier scale is not necessary. If a thimble mark does not align exactly with the sleeve line, read the vernier scale in Step 3.
3. Read the vernier scale to find which vernier mark aligns with the one thimble mark. The number of that vernier mark is the number of ten-thousandths of an inch to add to the initial reading taken in Step 1.

Metric micrometer

The metric micrometer is very similar to the standard inch micrometer. The differences are the graduations on the thimble and sleeve as shown in **Figure 48**.

The standard metric micrometer accurately measures to one one-hundredths of a millimeter (0.01 mm). On the metric micrometer, the spindle screw is ground with a thread pitch of one-half millimeter (0.5 mm). Thus, every turn of the thimble will move the spindle 0.5 mm.

The sleeve line is graduated in millimeters and half millimeters. The marks on the upper side of the

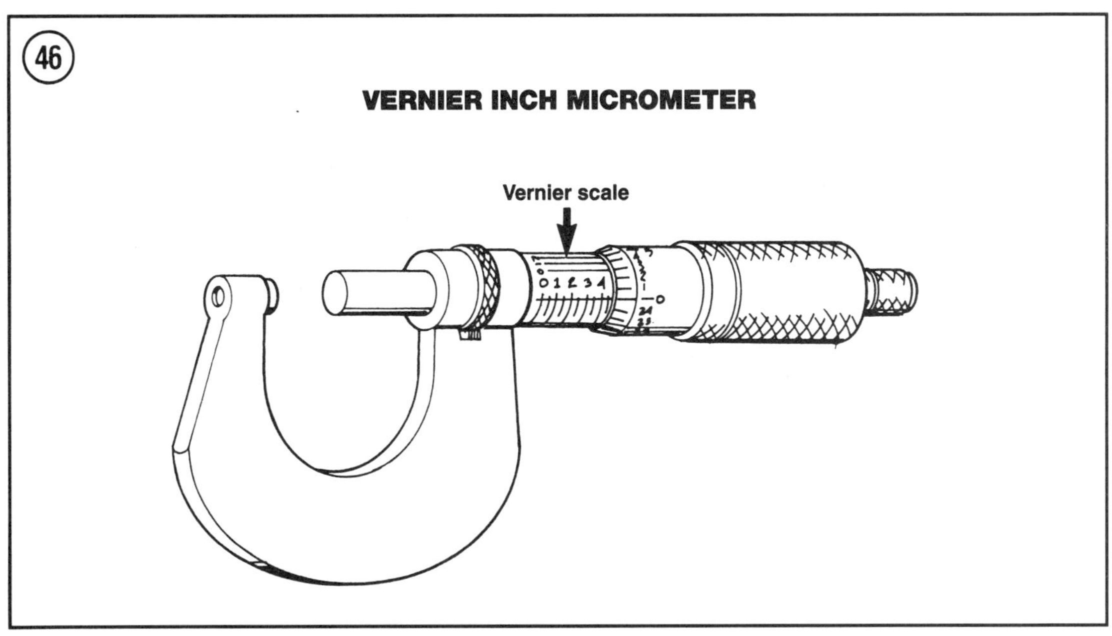

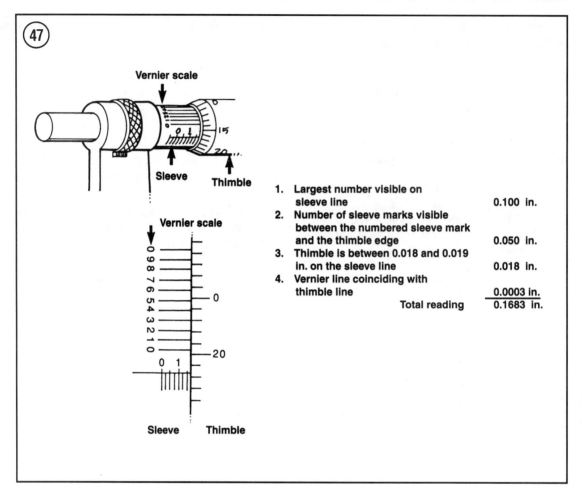

(47)

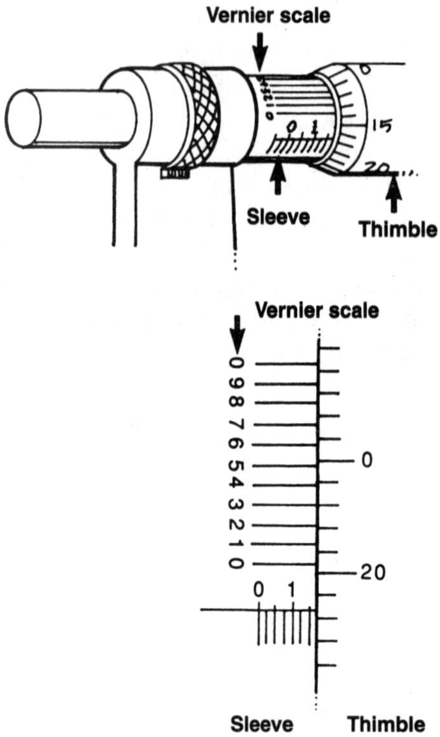

Vernier scale

Sleeve

Thimble

1.	Largest number visible on sleeve line	0.100 in.
2.	Number of sleeve marks visible between the numbered sleeve mark and the thimble edge	0.050 in.
3.	Thimble is between 0.018 and 0.019 in. on the sleeve line	0.018 in.
4.	Vernier line coinciding with thimble line	0.0003 in.
	Total reading	0.1683 in.

(48)

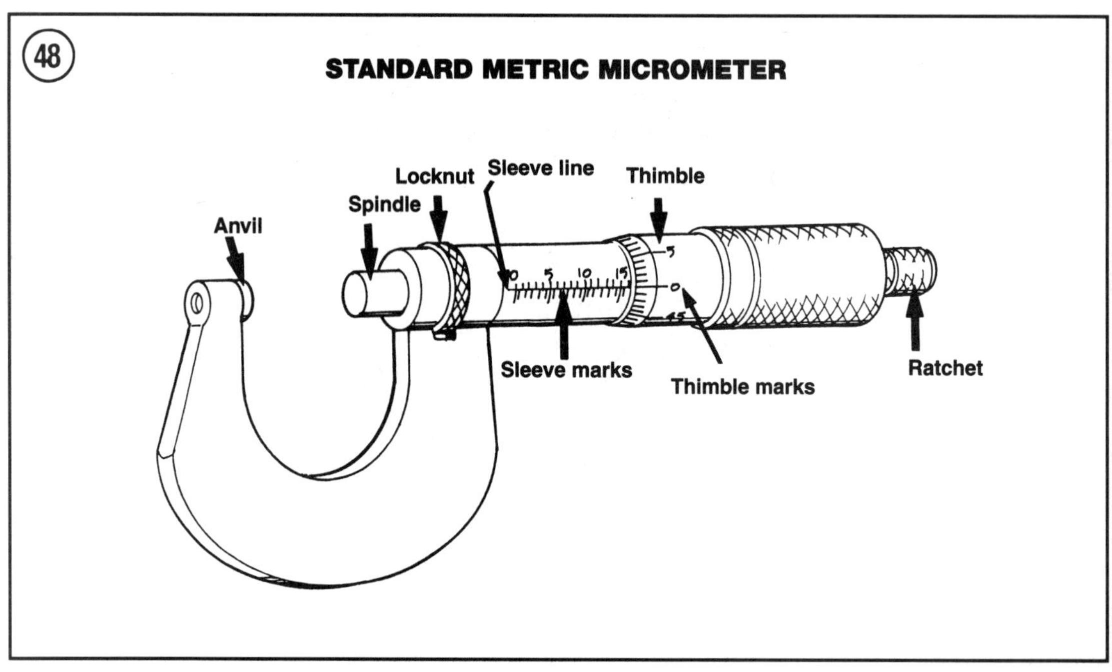

sleeve line are equal to 1.00 mm . Every fifth mark above the sleeve line is marked with a number. The actual numbers depend on the size of the micrometer. For example, on a 0-25 mm micrometer, the sleeve marks are numbered 0, 5, 10, 15, 20 and 25. On a 25-50 mm micrometer, the sleeve marks are numbered 25, 30, 35, 40, 45 and 50. This numbering sequence continues with larger micrometers (50-75 and 75-100). Each mark on the lower side of the sleeve line is equal to 0.5 mm.

The thimble scale is divided into fifty graduations where one graduation is equal to 0.01 mm. Every fifth graduation is numbered to help with reading from 0-45. The thimble edge is used to indicate which sleeve markings to read.

To read the metric micrometer add the number of millimeters and half-millimeters on the sleeve line to the number of one one-hundredth millimeters on the thimble. To do so, perform the following steps and refer to the example in **Figure 49**:

1. Take the first reading by counting the number of marks visible on the upper sleeve line. Record the reading.

2. Look below the sleeve line to see if a lower mark is visible directly past the upper line mark. If so, add 0.50 to the first reading.

3. Now read the thimble mark that aligns with the sleeve line. Record this reading.

NOTE

If a thimble mark does not align exactly with the sleeve line but falls between the two lines, estimate the decimal amount between the lines. For an accurate reading, you must use a metric vernier micrometer.

4. Add the micrometer readings in Steps 1, 2 and to obtain the actual measurement.

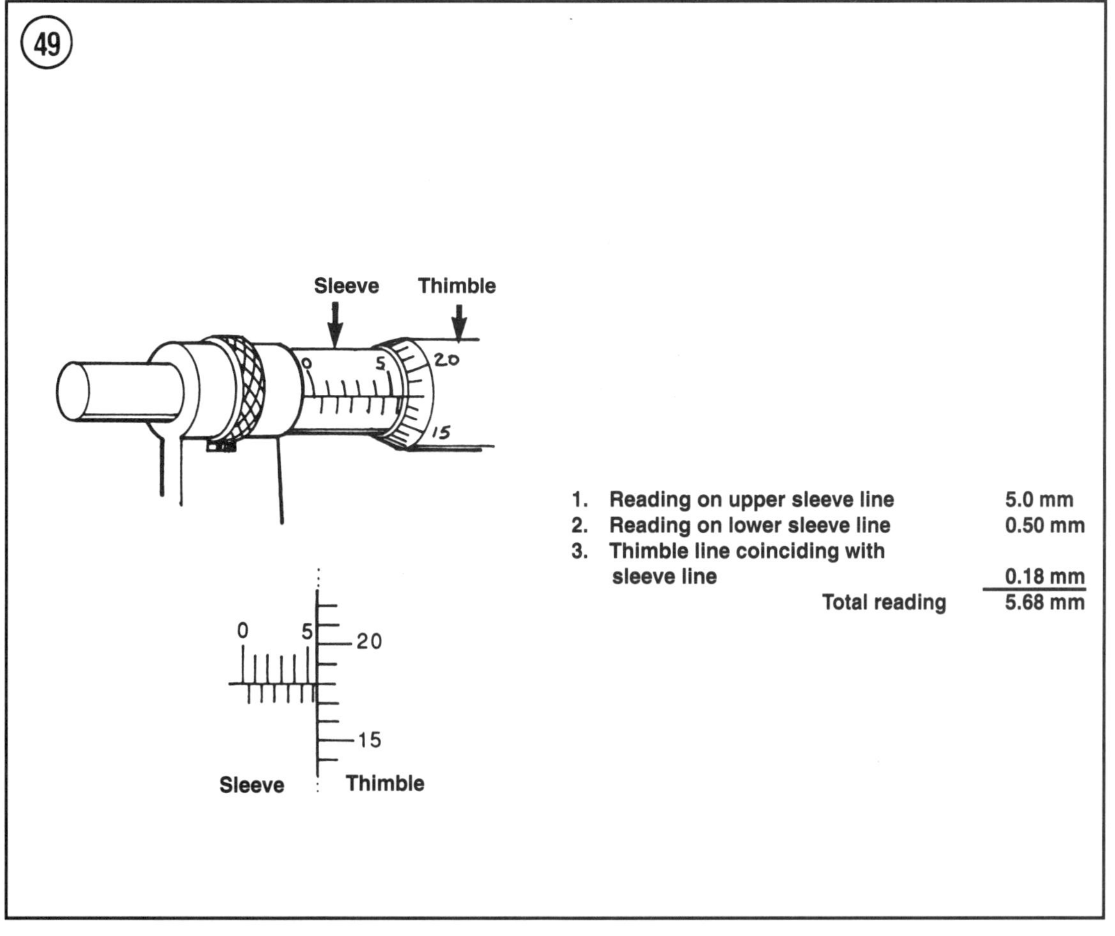

Metric vernier micrometer

A metric micrometer can accurately measure to two thousandths of a millimeter (0.002 mm). While it has the same markings as the standard metric micrometer, a vernier scale scribed on the sleeve (**Figure 50**) makes it unique. The vernier scale consists of five equally spaced lines 0, 2, 4, 6 and 8. These lines run parallel on the top of the sleeve where each line is equal to 0.002 mm.

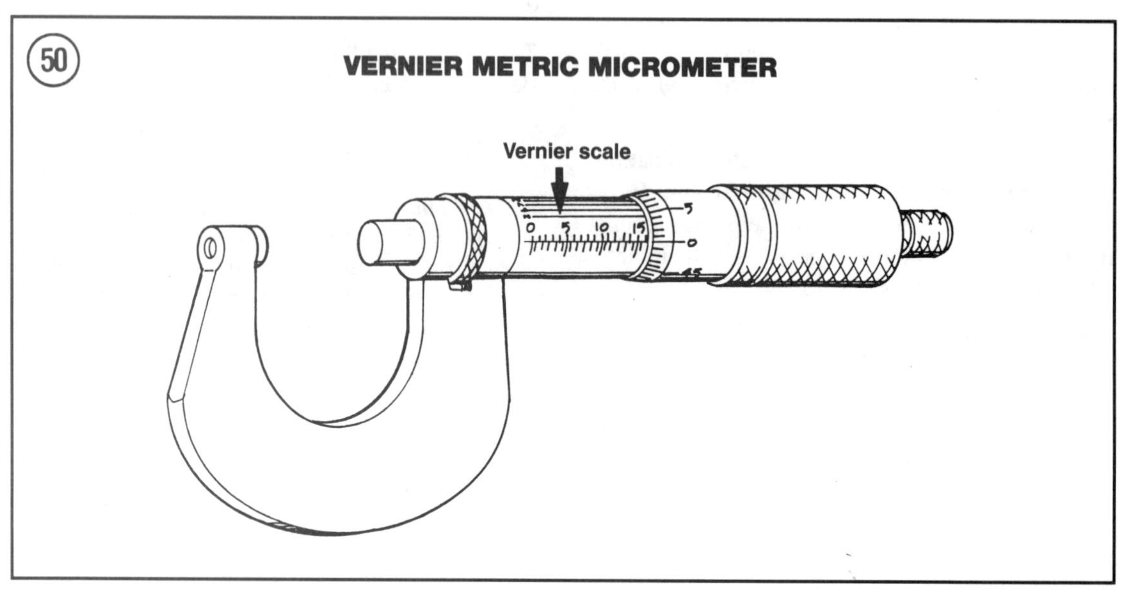

(50) **VERNIER METRIC MICROMETER**

(51)

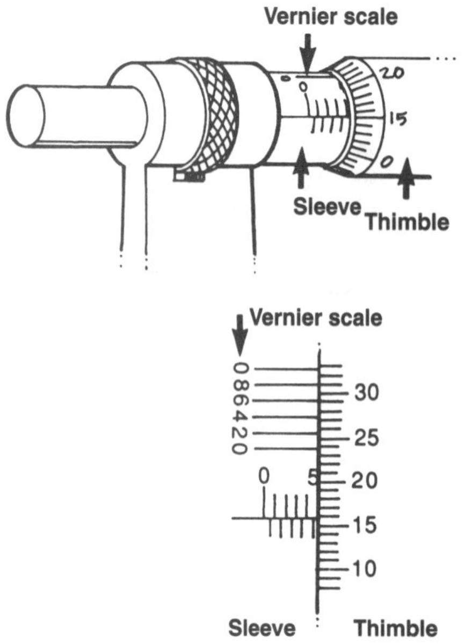

Vernier scale

Sleeve

Thimble

Vernier scale

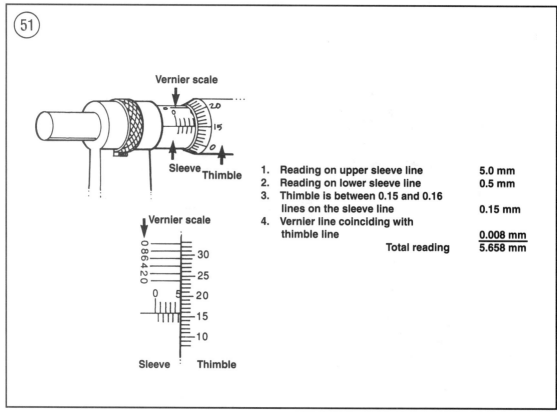

Sleeve

Thimble

1. Reading on upper sleeve line — 5.0 mm
2. Reading on lower sleeve line — 0.5 mm
3. Thimble is between 0.15 and 0.16 lines on the sleeve line — 0.15 mm
4. Vernier line coinciding with thimble line — 0.008 mm

Total reading — 5.658 mm

To read the metric vernier micrometer, perform the following steps and refer to the example in **Figure 51**:

1. Read the metric vernier micrometer the same way as with the metric standard micrometer. This is the initial reading.
2. If a thimble mark aligns exactly with the sleeve line, reading the vernier scale is not necessary. If a thimble line does not align exactly with the sleeve line, read the vernier scale in Step 3.
3. Read the vernier scale to find which mark aligns with one thimble mark. The number of the vernier mark is the number of thousands of a millimeter to add to the initial reading taken in Step 1.

Micrometer Accuracy Check

The micrometer must be checked frequently to ensure accuracy as follows:

1. Make sure the anvil and spindle faces (**Figure 44**) are clean and dry.
2. To check a 0-1 in. (0-25 mm) micrometer, perform the following:
   a. Turn the spindle until the spindle contacts the anvil. If the micrometer has a ratchet stop, use it to ensure that the proper amount of pressure is applied against the contact surfaces.
   b. Read the micrometer. If the adjustment is correct, the 0 mark on the thimble will be aligned exactly with the 0 mark on the sleeve line. If the 0 marks do not align, the micrometer is out of adjustment.
   c. To adjust the micrometer, follow its manufacturer's instructions provided with the micrometer.
3. To check the accuracy of a micrometer above the 1 inch (25 mm) size, perform the following:
   a. Manufacturers usually supply a standard gauge with their micrometers. A standard is a steel block, disc or rod that is ground to an exact size to check the accuracy of the micrometer. For example, a 1-2 inch micrometer is equipped with a 1 inch standard gauge. A 25-50 mm micrometer is equipped with a 25 mm standard gauge.
   b. Place the standard gauge between the micrometer's spindle and anvil and measure its outside diameter or length. Read the micrometer. If the adjustment is correct, the 0 mark on the thimble will be aligned exactly with the sleeve line. If the 0 marks do not align, the micrometer is out of alignment.
   c. To adjust the micrometer, follow its manufacturer's instructions provided with the micrometer.

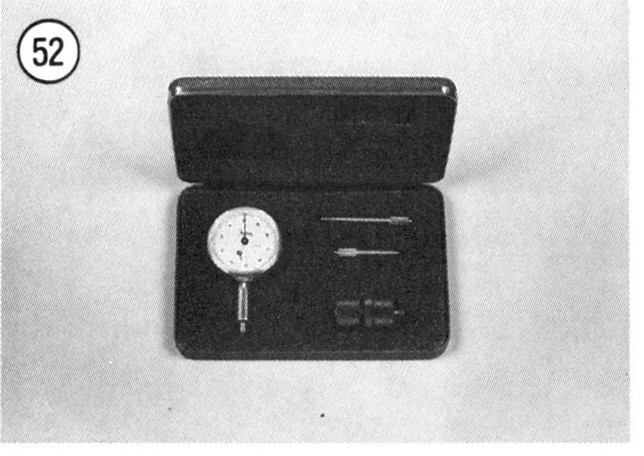

Proper Care of a Micrometer

Because the micrometer is a precision instrument, it must be used correctly and with great care. When using and storing a micrometer, refer to the following:

1. Store a micrometer in its box or in a protected place where dust, oil and other debris cannot come in contact with it. Do not store micrometers in a drawer with other tools nor hang them on a tool board.
2. When storing a 0-1 in. (0-25 mm) micrometer, the spindle and anvil must not contact each other. If they do, this may cause rust to form on the contact ends or spindle and will be damaged from temperature changes.
3. Do not clean a micrometer with compressed air. Dirt forced under pressure into the tool can cause premature damage.
4. Occasionally lubricate the micrometer with light oil to prevent rust and corrosion.
5. Before using a micrometer, check its accuracy as previously described in this section.

Dial Indicator

A dial indicator (**Figure 52**) is a precision tool used to check dimensional variations, both radial and axial runout, of machined parts such as transmission shafts and to check crankshaft runout and end play. A dial indicator may also be used to locate the piston at a specific position when checking ignition timing. For motorcycle service procedures, select a dial indicator with a continuous dial (**Figure 53**). Several different mounting types are available, including magnetic stands that attaches to iron or steel surfaces, a clamp that can be attached to various components and a spark plug adapter that locates the probe of the dial indicator through the spark plug hole. See *Magnetic Stand* in this chapter. The measurement taken determines the type of mount you will need. The text in each chapter indicates the type of mount necessary for each specific measuring procedure.

Cylinder Bore Gauge

The cylinder bore gauge is a very specialized precision tool. The gauge set shown in **Figure 54** consists of a dial indicator, handle and a number of different length adapters for different bore sizes. The bore gauge is used to make cylinder bore measurements such as bore size, taper and out-of-round. Depending on the bore gauge, it can sometimes be used to measure brake caliper and master cylinder bore sizes. In some cases, an outside micrometer must be used to calibrate the bore gauge to a specific bore size.

Select the correct length adapter (A, **Figure 55**) for the size of the bore to be measured. Zero the bore gauge according to its manufacturer's instructions and insert the bore gauge into the cylinder. Carefully move the gauge around in the bore to make sure it is centered and that the gauge foot (B, **Figure 55**) is sitting correctly on the bore surface. This is necessary to obtain a correct reading.

Small Hole Gauges

A set of small hole gauges (**Figure 56**) allows you to measure a hole, groove or slot. A small hole gauge is required to measure rocker arm bore and brake master cylinder bore diameters. The small hole gauge does not have a scale for direct readings. An outside micrometer must be used together with the small hole gauge to determine the bore dimension.

Carefully insert the small hole gauge into the bore of the component to be measured. Tighten the knurled end of the gauge to carefully expand the gauge fingers inside the bore (**Figure 57**)—*do not overtighten* the gauge as there is no built-in release feature. If tightened too much, the gauge fingers can damage the bore surface. Carefully remove the gauge, and measure the outside dimension of the

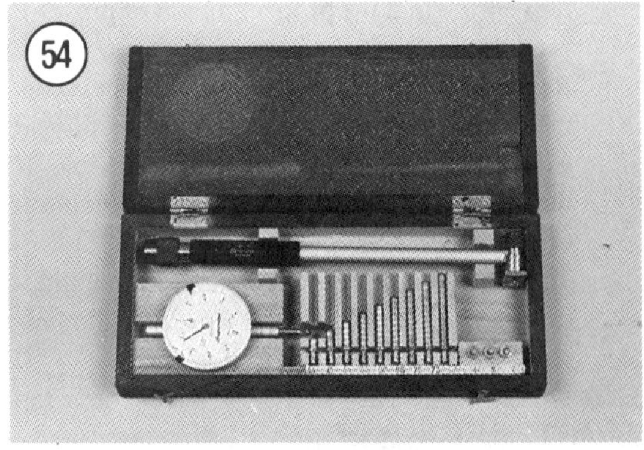

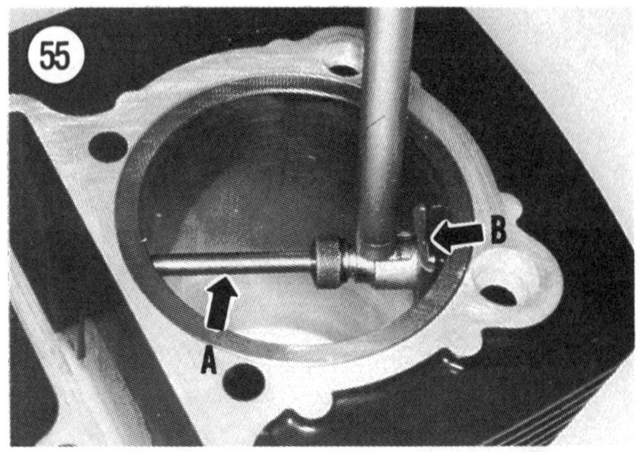

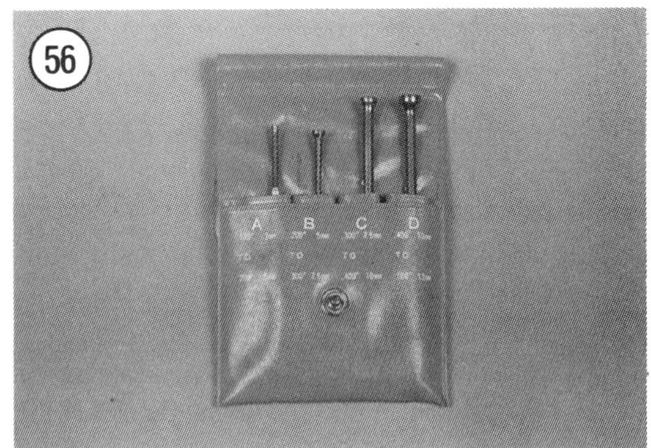

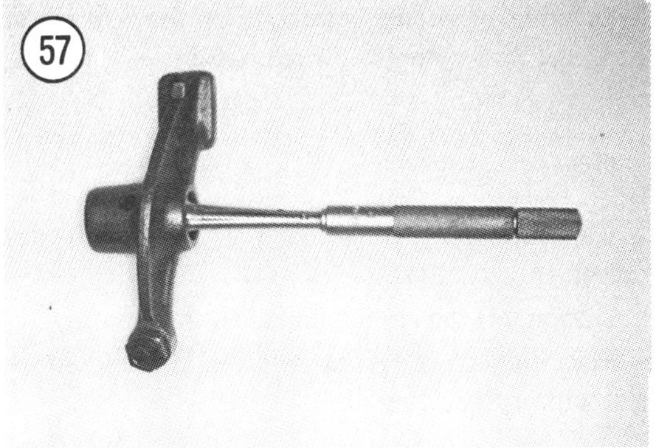

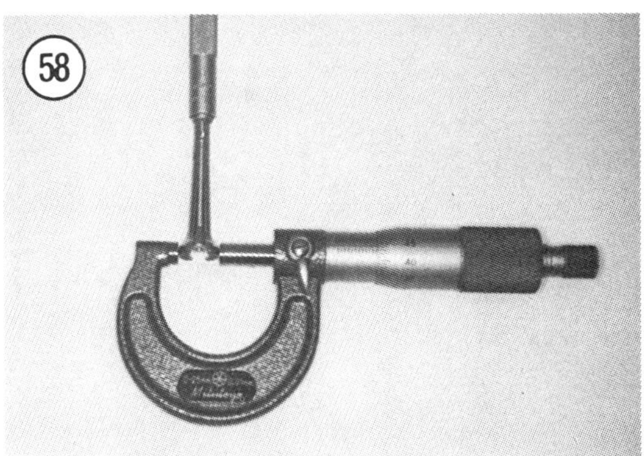

gauge with a micrometer (**Figure 58**), as described in this chapter.

Telescoping Gauges

A telescoping gauge (**Figure 59**) is used to measure hole diameters from approximately 8 mm (5/16 in.) to 150 mm (6 in.). For example, it could be used to measure brake caliper bore and cylinder bore diameters. Like the small hole gauge, the telescoping gauge does not have a scale for direct reading. An outside micrometer must be used together with the telescoping gauge to determine the bore dimension.

Select the correct-size telescoping gauge for the bore to be measured. Compress the moveable side of the gauge post and carefully install the gauge into the bore, and then release the movable post against the bore. Carefully center the gauge in the bore. Tighten the knurled end of the gauge to hold the movable gauge post in this position. Carefully remove the gauge and measure the outside dimension of the gauge posts using a micrometer as described in this chapter.

Compression Gauge

An engine with low compression cannot be properly tuned and will not develop full power. A compression gauge (**Figure 60**) measures engine compression. The one shown has a flexible stem with an extension that can allow you to hold it while cranking the engine. Open the throttle all the way when checking engine compression as described in Chapter Three.

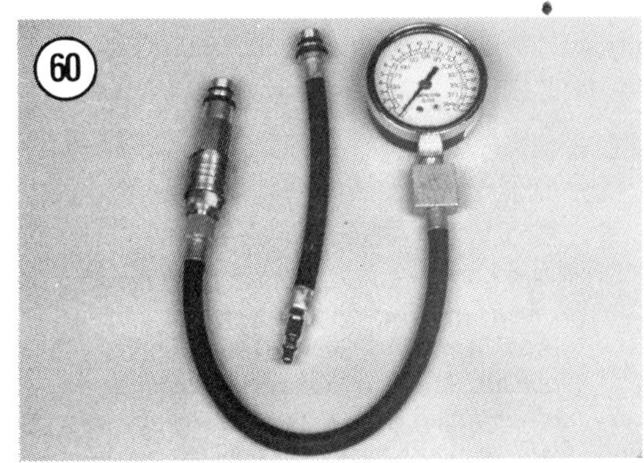

Multimeter or VOM

A VOM (Volt and Ohm Meter) (**Figure 61**) is a valuable tool for all electrical system troubleshooting . The voltage application is used to indicate the voltage applied or available to various electrical components. The ohmmeter portion of the meter is used to check for continuity and to measure the resistance of a component. Some tests are easily accomplished using meter with a sweeping needle (analog), but other tests require a digital VOM (DVOM).

In some electrical tests, the internal design of a meter affects the test readings. In these instances, the vehicle's manufacturer instructs you to use their specific meter because another meter may produce inaccurate results. The text in this book notes when you must use a particular meter to perform a test.

To measure voltage

NOTE

Make sure the negative (–) or ground surface that you will be using is clean and free of paint and/or grease. If possible, use a unpainted bolt that is attached directly to the frame.

1. Make sure the meter battery power source is at full power. If its condition is questionable, install a new battery(s).
2. Select the meter voltage range to *one scale higher* than the indicated voltage value of the circuit to be tested.
3. Touch the red test probe to the *positive* (+) end and the black test probe to the *negative* (–), or ground, end of the circuit.
4. Read the position of the needle on the VOLTS or VOLTAGE scale of the meter face, or the digital readout. Refer to the manufacturer's instruction for any special conditions relating to the meter that you are using.

To calibrate an analog ohmmeter

NOTE

Every time an analog ohmmeter is used to measure resistance it must be calibrated in order to obtain a correct measurement. Most digital ohmmeters are not equipped with a zero ohms adjust feature—when turned on they are automatically set at zero (providing the meter battery is at full power).

1. Make sure the meter's battery power source is at full power. If its condition is questionable, install a new battery(s).
2. Make sure the test probes are clean and free of corrosion.
3. Touch the two test probes together and observe the meter needle location on the OHMS scale on the meter face. The needle must be on the 0 mark at the end of the scale.
4. If necessary, rotate the ohms adjust knob on the meter until the needle is directly on the 0 mark on the scale. The meter is now ready for use.

To measure resistance

1. Calibrate the analog meter as previously described.
2. Disconnect the component from the circuit.
3. Place the test probes at each end of the component and read the meter.

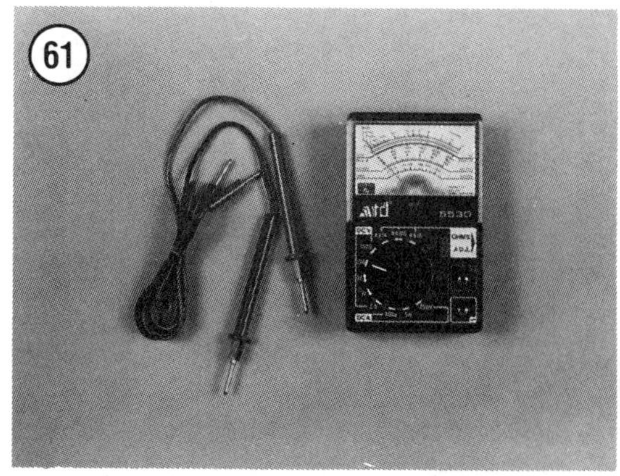

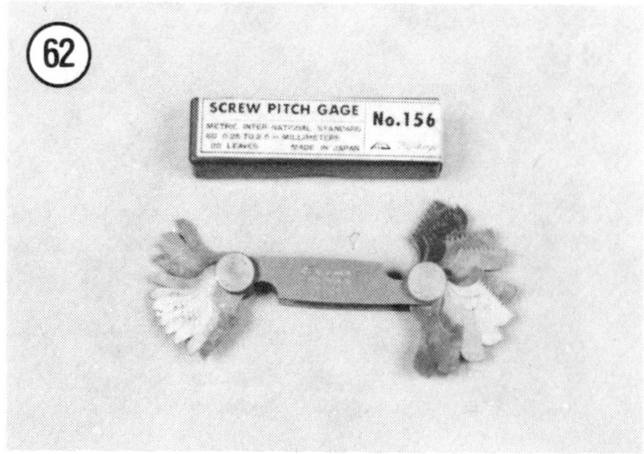

4. Replace the component if it is not within specification.
5. If the component is within specification, reinstall it in the circuit.

Continuity test

A continuity test is used to determine the integrity of a circuit, wire or component.

Continuity is indicated by a low resistance reading, usually zero ohms, on the meter. No continuity is indicated by an infinity reading. A broken or open circuit has no continuity, while a complete circuit has continuity. A continuity test is also useful to check components for a short to ground. A shorted component has a complete circuit (continuity) between the component and ground.

1. Calibrate the analog meter as previously described.
2. Place the test probes at each end of the component, or circuit and read the meter.
3. If no continuity is present, the meter will indicate an infinity reading. A zero or a low ohm reading generally indicates that continuity is present in the circuit or component.

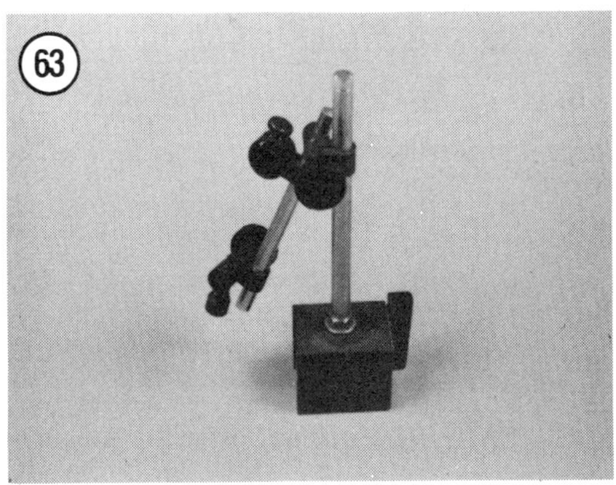
63

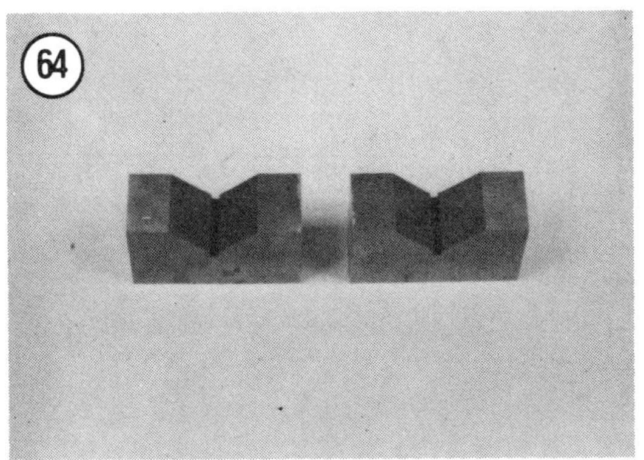
64

Screw Pitch Gauge

A screw pitch gauge (**Figure 62**) determines the thread pitch of threaded fasteners. The gauge is made up of a number of thin plates. Each plate has a thread shape cut on one edge to match one thread pitch. When using a screw pitch gauge to determine a thread pitch size, try to fit different blade sizes onto the fastener threads until both threads match exactly.

Magnetic Stand

A magnetic stand (**Figure 63**) is used to hold a dial indicator securely when checking the runout of a round object or when checking the end play of a shaft.

V-Blocks

V-blocks (**Figure 64**) are precision ground blocks used to hold a round object when checking its runout or condition. In motorcycle repair, V-blocks can be used when checking the runout of such items as transmission shafts, crankshaft, wheel axles and other shafts and collars.

Surface Plate

A surface plate (**Figure 65**) is used to check the flatness of parts. While industrial quality surface plates are quite expensive, the home mechanic can improvise. A piece of thick, flat metal or plate glass can sometimes be used as a surface plate. The quality of the surface plate will affect the accuracy of the measurement being taken. The surface plate can have a piece of fine grit paper mounted on its surface to assist in cleaning and smoothing a flat surface of a part. The machined surfaces of the cylinder head, cylinder, crankcase and other close fitting parts may require a very good-quality surface plate to smooth nicked or damaged surfaces.

SPECIAL TOOLS

A few special tools may be required for major service. These are described in the appropriate chapters and are available either from a Kawasaki dealership or other manufacturer as indicated.

This section describes special tools unique to this type of bike's service and repair.

65

Clutch Holding Tool

The clutch holding tool (**Figure 66**) (Kawasaki part No. 57001-1243) is a special tool used to hold various parts, like the clutch hub, sprockets and gears, when loosening and tightening fasteners.

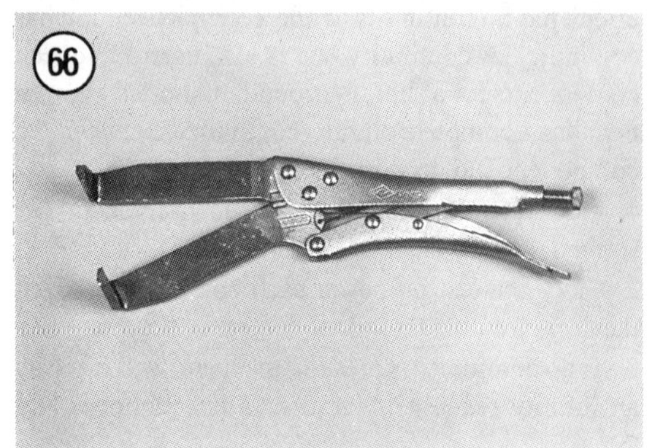
66

Piston Ring Compressor

The piston ring compressor (**Figure 67**) or (**Figure 68**) is used to compress the piston rings during cylinder installation to prevent piston ring damage.

Pressure Cable Lube Tool

A cable lube tool is used to force cable lubricant throughout a control cable.

This tool (**Figure 69**) (Kawasaki part No. K56019-021) is clamped to one end of a control cable. It has a tube fitting that allows pressurized cable lubricant to be forced throughout the entire length of the cable.

67

Tire Levers

When changing tires, use a good set of tire lever (**Figure 70**). Never use a screwdriver in place of a tire lever; refer to Chapter Eleven for its use. Before using a tire lever, check the working end of the tool and remove any burrs with a file. Do not use a tire lever for prying anything but tires.

FABRICATING TOOLS

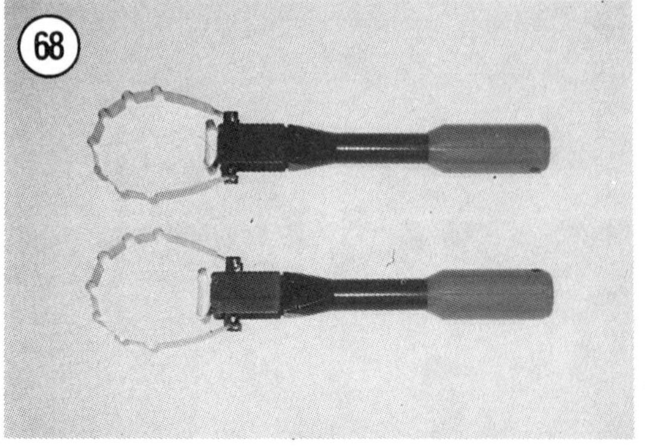
68

Some of the procedures in this manual require the use of special tools. The resourceful mechanic can, in many cases, think of acceptable substitutes for special tools. This can be as simple as using a few pieces of threaded rod, washer and nuts to remove or install a bearing. If you find that a special tool can be designed and safely made, but it will require some type of machine work, contact a local community college or high school that has a machine shop curriculum. Some shop teachers welcome outside

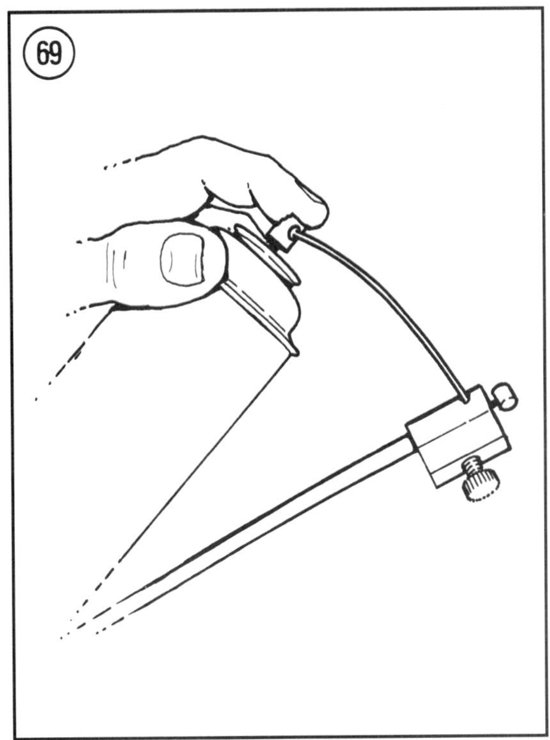

69

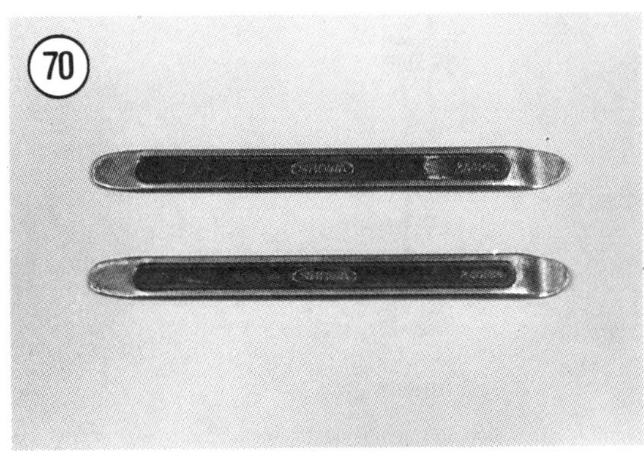

70

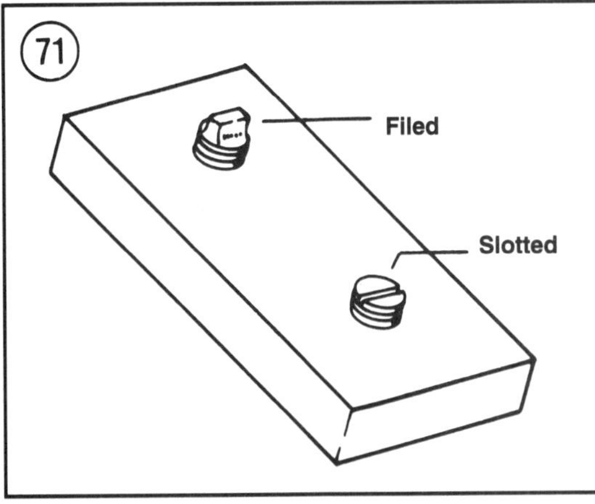

71

work that can be used as practical shop applications for advanced students.

MECHANIC'S TIPS

Removing Frozen Nuts and Screws

If a fastener rusts and cannot be removed, several methods may be used to loosen it. First, apply penetrating oil such as Liquid Wrench or WD-40 (available at hardware or auto supply stores). Apply it liberally and let it penetrate for 10-15 minutes. Rap the fastener several times with a small hammer; do not hit it hard enough to cause damage. Reapply the penetrating oil if necessary.

For frozen screws, apply penetrating oil as described, then insert a screwdriver in the slot and rap the top of the screwdriver with a hammer. This loosens the rust so the screw can be removed. If the screw head is too damaged to use this method, grip the head with locking pliers and twist the screw out.

Avoid applying heat unless specifically instructed. The heat may melt, warp or remove the temper from parts.

Removing Broken Screws or Bolts

If the head breaks off a screw or bolt, several methods are available for removing the remaining portion. If a large portion of the remainder projects out, try gripping it with locking pliers. If the projecting portion is too small, file it to fit a wrench or cut a slot in it to fit a screwdriver. See **Figure 71**.

If the head breaks off flush, use a screw extractor. To do this, centerpunch the exact center of the remaining portion of the screw or bolt. Drill a small hole in the screw and tap the extractor into the hole. Back the screw out with a wrench on the extractor. See **Figure 72**.

Remedying Stripped Threads

Occasionally, threads are stripped through carelessness or impact damage. Often the threads can be repaired by running a tap (for internal threads on nuts) or die (for external threads on bolts) through the threads. See **Figure 73**. To clean or repair spark plug threads, a spark plug tap can be used (**Figure 74**).

NOTE
*Tap and dies can be bought individually or in a set as shown in **Figure 75**.*

If an internal thread is damaged, it may be necessary to install a Helicoil (**Figure 76**) or other type of thread insert. Follow the manufacturer's instructions when installing their insert.

If it is necessary to drill and tap a hole, refer to **Table 8** for metric tap drill sizes.

BALL BEARING REPLACEMENT

Ball bearings (**Figure 77**) are used throughout the engine and drive assembly to reduce power loss, heat and noise resulting from friction. Because ball bearings are precision-made parts, they must be properly lubricated and maintained. If a bearing is damaged, it must be replaced immediately. However, use caution when installing a new bearing to prevent damage to the new bearing. While bearing replacement is described in the individual chapters where applicable, use the following as a guideline.

NOTE
Unless otherwise specified, install bearings with their manufacturer's mark or number facing outward.

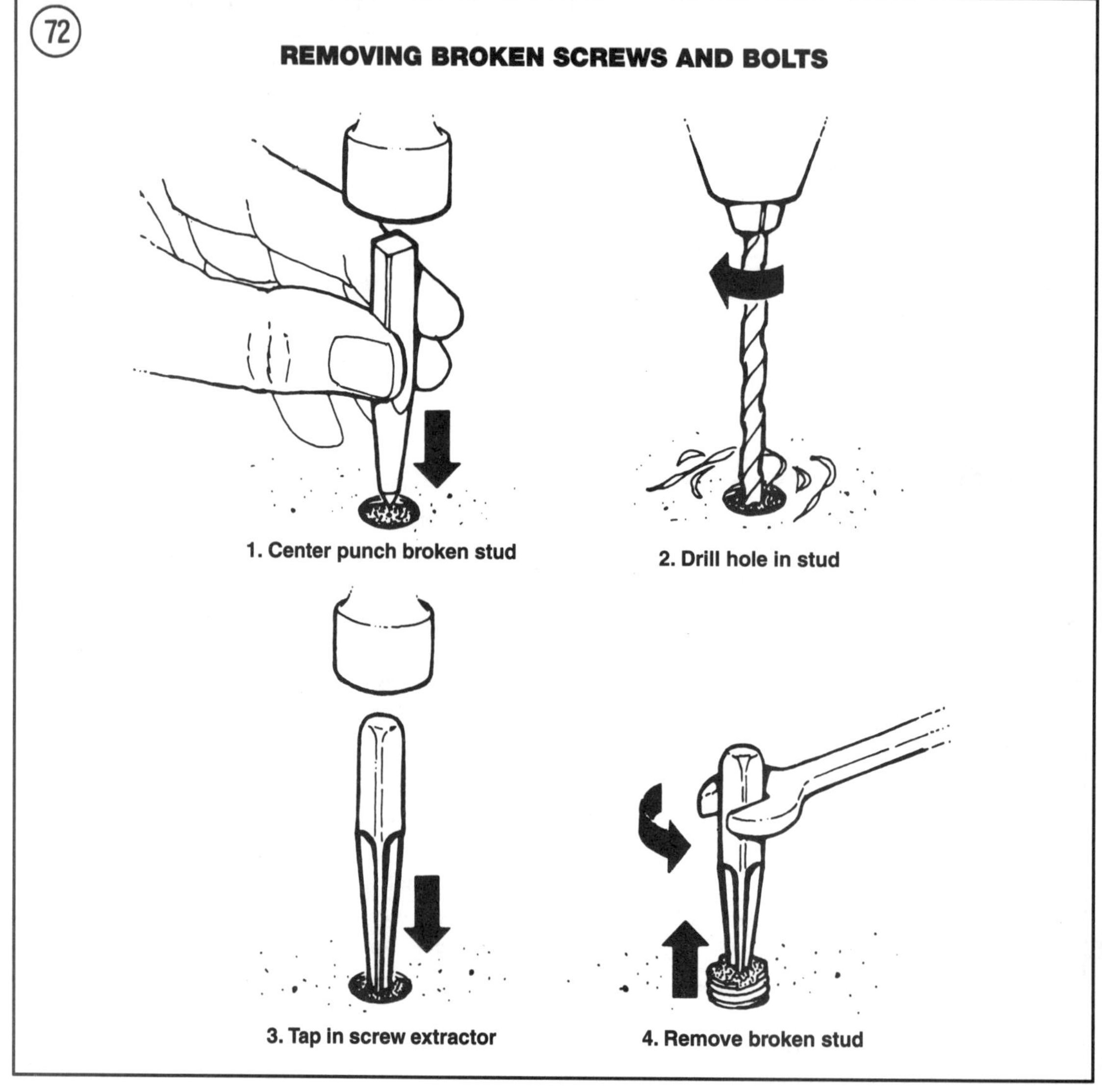
72
REMOVING BROKEN SCREWS AND BOLTS
1. Center punch broken stud
2. Drill hole in stud
3. Tap in screw extractor
4. Remove broken stud

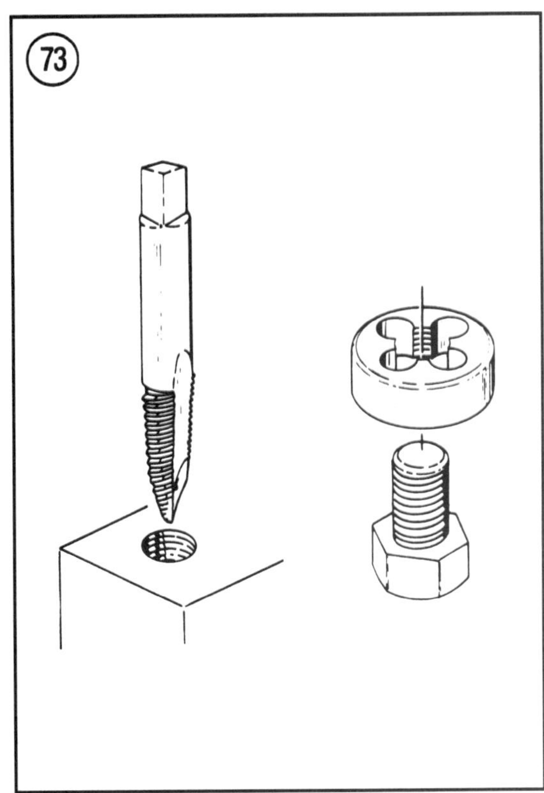

Bearing Removal

While bearings are normally removed only if damaged or worn, there may be times when it is necessary to remove a bearing that is in good condition. However, improper bearing removal will damage the bearing and maybe the shaft or housing. Note the following when removing bearings.

1. When using a puller to remove a bearing from a shaft, make sure the shaft is not damaged. Always place a piece of metal between the end of the shaft and the puller screw. In addition, place the puller arms next to the inner bearing race. See **Figure 78**.
2. When using a hammer to remove a bearing from a shaft, do not strike the hammer directly against the shaft. Instead, use a brass or aluminum driver between the hammer and shaft (**Figure 79**). Make sure to support both bearing races as shown.
3. A hydraulic press is the ideal tool for bearing removal. However, certain procedures must be followed or damage may occur to the bearing, shaft or bearing housing. Note the following when using a press:
   a. Always support the inner and outer bearing (**Figure 80**). If you only support the outer race,

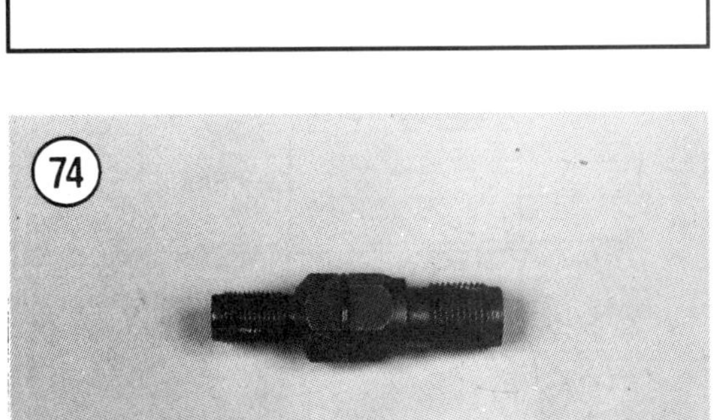

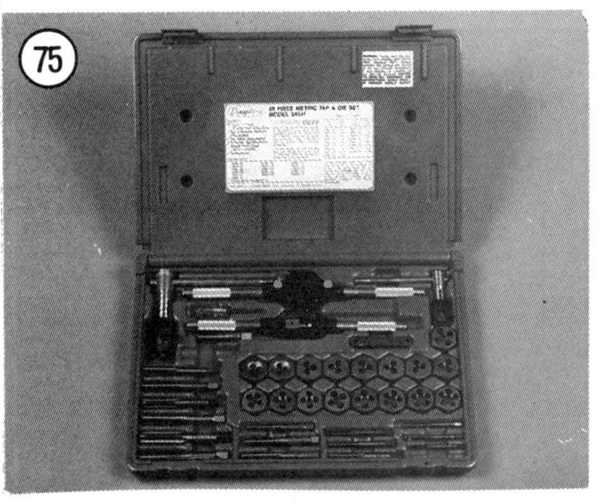

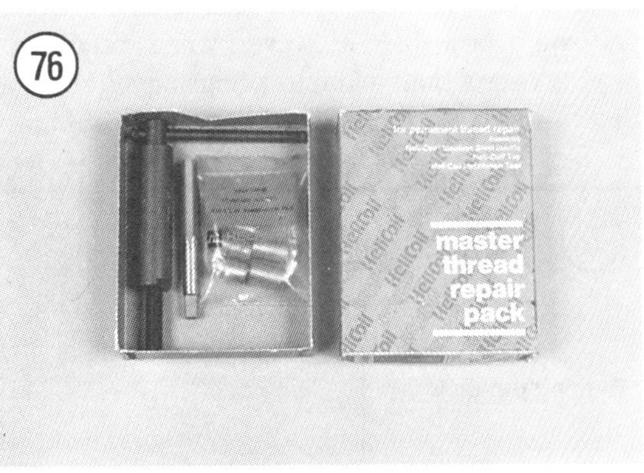

pressure applied against the balls and/or the inner race will damage them.

b. Always make sure the press ram (**Figure 80**) aligns with the center of the shaft. If the ram is not centered, it may damage the bearing and/or shaft.

c. The moment the shaft is free of the bearing, it will drop to the floor. Secure or hold the shaft to prevent it from falling.

Bearing Installation

1. When installing a bearing in a housing, pressure must be applied to the *outer* bearing race (**Figure 81**). When installing a bearing on a shaft, pressure must be applied to the *inner* bearing race (**Figure 82**).
2. When installing a bearing as described in Step 1, some type of driver is required. Never strike the bearing directly with a hammer or the bearing will be damaged. When installing a bearing, a piece of pipe or driver with a diameter that matches the bearing race is required. **Figure 83** shows the correct way to use a driver and hammer when installing a bearing.
3. Step 1 describes how to install a bearing in a case half and over a shaft. However, when installing a bearing over a shaft and into a housing at the same time, a snug fit is required for both outer and inner

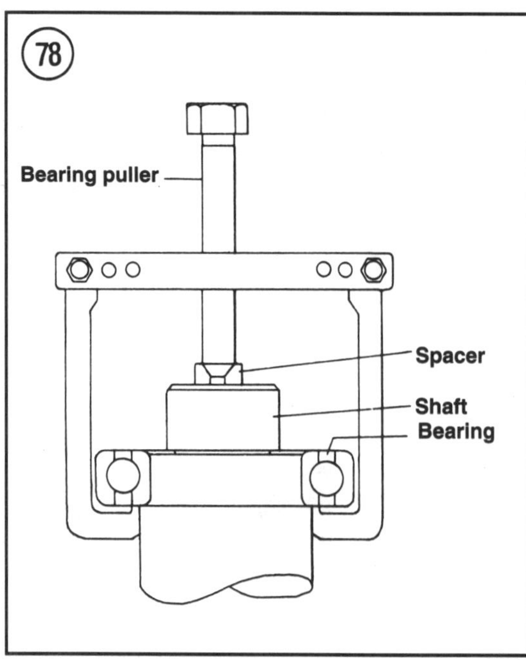

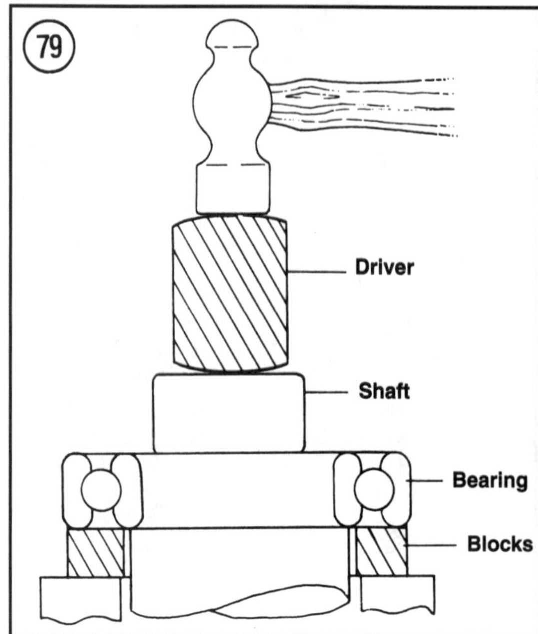

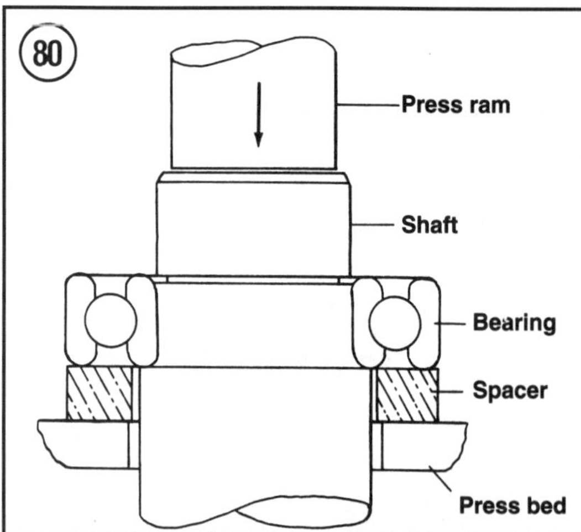

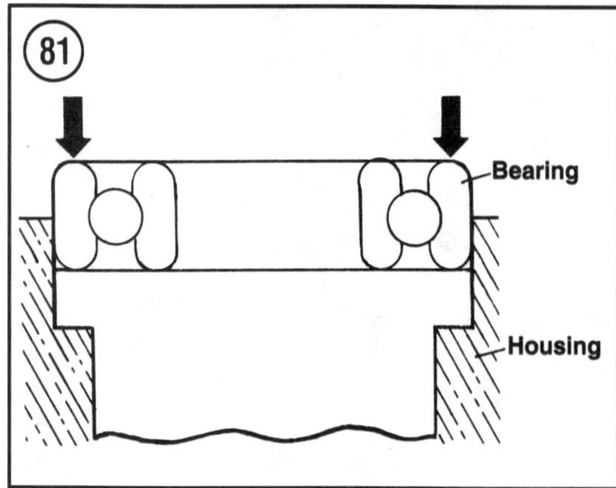

bearing races. In this situation, a spacer must be installed underneath the driver tool so pressure is applied evenly across both races. See **Figure 84**. If the outer race is not supported as shown in **Figure 84**, the balls will push against the outer bearing track and damage it.

Shrink Fit

1. Installing a bearing over a shaft: When a tight fit is required, the bearing inside diameter will be smaller than the shaft. In this case, driving the bearing on the shaft may cause bearing damage. Instead, heat the bearing before installation. Note the following:

a. Secure the shaft so that it is ready for bearing installation.

b. Clean all residue from the bearing surface of the shaft. Remove burrs with a file or sandpaper.

c. Fill a suitable pot or beaker with clean mineral oil. Place a thermometer (rated higher than 120° C [248° F]) in the oil. Support the thermometer so it does not rest on the bottom or side of the pot.

d. Secure the bearing with a piece of heavy wire bent to hold it in the pot. Hang the bearing in the pot so it does not touch the bottom or sides of the pot.

e. Turn the heat on and monitor the thermometer. When the oil temperature rises to approximately 120°C (248° F), remove the bearing from the pot and quickly install it. If necessary, place a driver on the inner bearing race and tap the bearing into place. As the bearing chills, it will tighten on the shaft so you must work quickly when installing it. Make sure the bearing is installed all the way.

2. Installing a bearing in a housing: Bearings are generally installed in a housing with a slight interference fit. Driving the bearing into the housing may damage the housing or cause bearing damage. In-

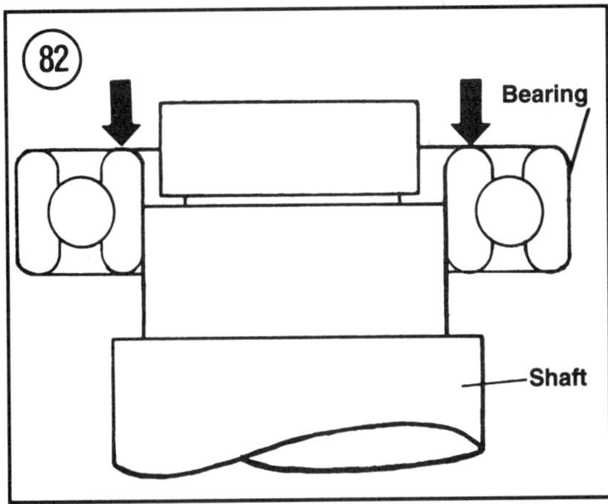

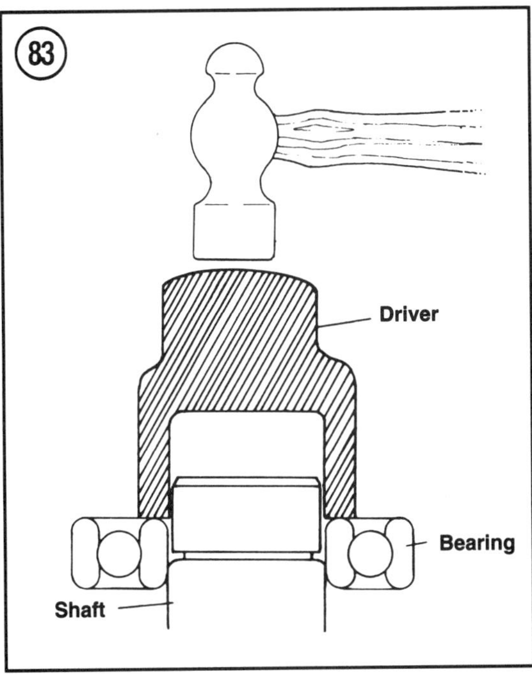

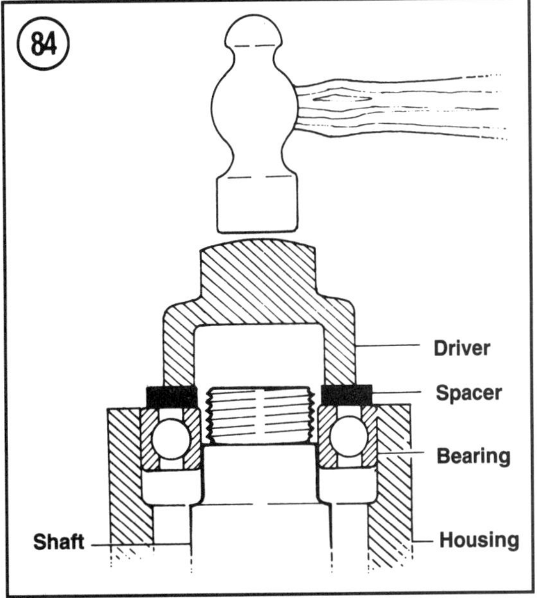

stead, heat the housing before the bearing is installed. Note the following:

CAUTION
Before heating the crankcases in this procedure, wash the cases thoroughly with detergent and water. Rinse and rewash the cases as required to remove all traces of oil and other chemical deposits.

a. The housing must be heated to a temperature of about 212° F (100°C) in an oven or on a hot plate. An easy way to check that it is at the proper temperature is to place tiny drops of water on the case; if they sizzle and evaporate immediately, the temperature is correct. Heat only one housing at a time.

CAUTION
Do not heat the housing with a torch (propane or acetylene)—never bring a flame into contact with the bearing or housing. The direct heat will destroy the case hardening of the bearing and will likely warp the housing.

b. Remove the housing from the oven or hot plate. Hold onto the housing with a kitchen pot holder, heavy gloves, or heavy shop cloth—it is hot.

NOTE
A suitable size socket and extension works well for removing and installing bearings.

c. Hold the housing with the bearing side down and tap the bearing out. Repeat for all bearings in the housing.
d. Prior to heating the bearing housing, place the new bearing in a freezer, if possible. Chilling a bearing will slightly reduce its outside diameter while the heated bearing housing assembly is slightly larger due to heat expansion. This will make bearing installation much easier.

NOTE
Always install bearings with their manufacturer's mark or number facing outward.

e. While the housing is still hot, install the new bearing(s) into the housing. Install the bearings by hand, if possible. If necessary, lightly tap the bearing(s) into the housing with a socket placed on the outer bearing race. Do not install new bearings by driving on the inner bearing race. Install the bearing(s) until it seats completely.

SEALS

Seals (**Figure 85**) are used to contain oil, water, grease or combustion gasses in a housing or shaft. Improper removal of a seal can damage the housing or shaft. Improper installation of the seal can damage the seal. Note the following:

a. Prying is generally the easiest and most effective method of removing a seal from a housing. However, always place a rag underneath the pry tool to prevent damage to the housing.
b. Pack waterproof grease in the seal lips before the seal is installed.
c. Install seals with their manufacturer's numbers or marks facing out, unless specified otherwise..
d. Install seals with a driver placed on the outside of the seal as shown in **Figure 86**. Make sure the seal is driven squarely into the housing. Never install a seal by hitting against the top of the seal with a hammer.

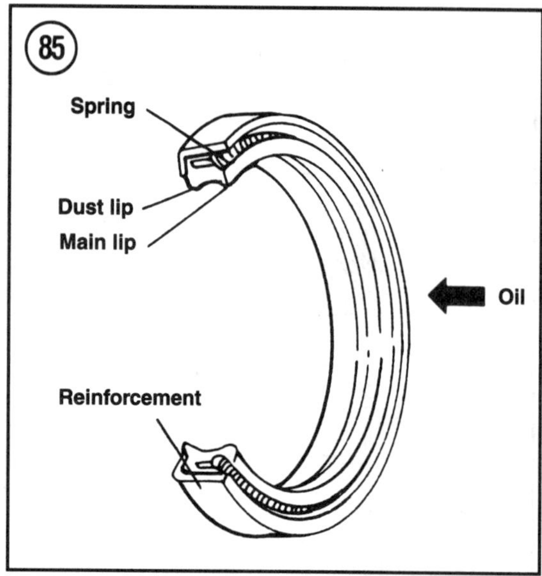

RIDING SAFETY

General Tips

1. Read your owner's manual and know your machine. Refer to the Daily Safety Check decal (**Figure 87**) located behind the right-hand side cover and follow these instructions.
2. Check the throttle and brake controls before starting the engine.
3. Know how to make an emergency stop.
4. Never add fuel while anyone is smoking in the area or when the engine is running.
5. Never wear loose scarves, belts or boot laces that could catch on moving parts.
6. Always wear eye protection, head protection and protective clothing to protect your entire body.
7. Riding in the winter months requires a good set of clothes to keep your body dry and warm, otherwise your entire trip may be miserable. Even mild temperatures can be very uncomfortable and dangerous when combined with a strong wind or traveling at high speed. Always dress for the wind-chilled temperature, not the ambient temperature.
8. Never allow anyone to operate the bike without proper instruction. This is for their protection and to keep your machine from damage or destruction.
9. Use the buddy system for long trips, just in case you have a problem or run out of fuel.
10. Never attempt to repair your machine with the engine running except when necessary for certain tune-up procedures.
11. Check all of the machine components and hardware frequently, especially the wheels and the steering.

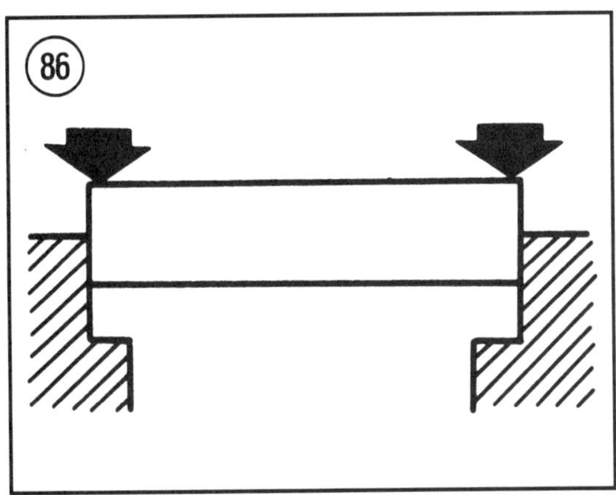
86

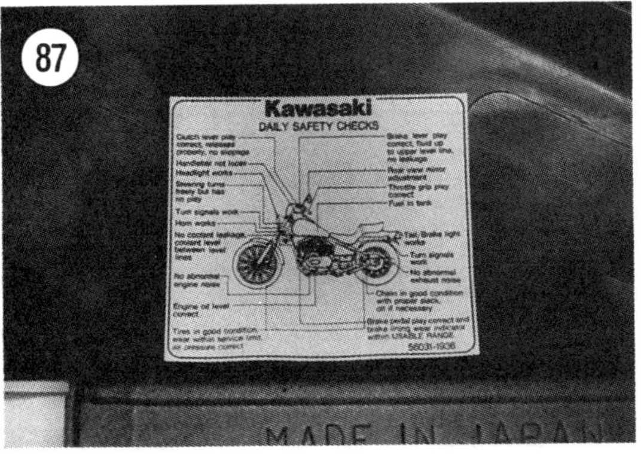

87

STORAGE

Several months of inactivity can cause serious problems and general deterioration of your bike. This is especially important in areas with cold winters.

Selecting a Storage Area

Most cyclists store their motorcycles in their home garage. If you do not have a garage, there are other facilities for rent or lease in most areas. When selecting an area, consider the following points.

1. The storage area must be dry. A heated area is not necessary, but it should be insulated to minimize extreme temperature variation.
2. Avoid buildings with large window areas. If this is not possible, mask the window to keep direct sunlight off the bike.
3. Avoid buildings in industrial areas where factories emit corrosive fumes. Also avoid buildings near large bodies of saltwater.
4. Select an area where there is minimum risk of fire, theft or vandalism. Check with your insurance agent to make sure that your insurance covers the motorcycle where it is stored.

Preparing Motorcycle for Storage

Careful preparation will minimize deterioration and make it easier to restore the bike to service later. Use the following procedure.

1. Wash the bike thoroughly. Make certain you remove all the dirt and mud which may have accumulated during the riding season. Thoroughly clean all plastic and metal components. Apply a plastic pre-

servative such as Armor-All to all plastic parts including the tires. Make sure you follow the manufacturer's instructions when applying the plastic preservative.
2. Run the engine until it reaches operating temperature. Drain the engine oil regardless of the riding time since the last change. Fill the engine with the recommended type and quantity of fresh oil.
3. Make sure the coolant is topped off, and that the mixture is 50% water and 50% antifreeze as specified in Chapter Ten.
4. Drain all the gasoline from the fuel tank, fuel line and carburetor. Run the engine at idle speed until the fuel in the carburetor is used up.
5. Remove the fuel tank as described in Chapter Eight. Pour about 250 ml (1/2 pint) of engine oil into the fuel tank. Move the tank around to distribute the oil all over the interior surfaces of the tank, then pour out the excess oil. Reinstall the tank and close the filler cap.
6. Remove the spark plugs and add a small quantity of engine oil into each cylinder. Place a rag over the cylinder head and slowly roll the engine over a few times to distribute the oil, then reinstall the spark plugs.
7. Check the tire pressures, reduce the normal inflation pressure by 20% and move the machine to the storage area.
8. Place the bike securely on a stand, or wooden blocks so both wheels are off the ground. If not possible, place a piece of wood (plywood) under the tires to keep moisture from the tire rubber.

After Storage

1. Before returning the motorcycle to service, thoroughly check all fasteners, suspension components and brake components. Move the front suspension through several complete strokes to make sure the fork seals are not leaking.
2. Pour out any remaining engine oil from the fuel tank, then fill the fuel tank with a fresh tank of gasoline.
3. Check all controls and cables. Replace any cables that are frayed or kinked.
4. Make sure both brakes, the clutch and the throttle operate smoothly. Adjust the controls if necessary.
5. Ensure that all the wiring is correctly routed and all connections are tight and corrosion-free. Make sure the STOP button will stop the engine. Check horn operation. Make sure none of the wires are positioned against the exhaust pipe.
6. Before starting the engine, remove the spark plugs and crank the engine over a few times to blow out the excess storage oil. Place a rag over the cylinder head to keep the oil off the engine. Install new spark plugs and connect the spark plug leads.

Table 1 SERIAL NUMBERS

U.S. and Canadian Models Year/model	VIN number	Engine number
1995		
VN800-A1	JKBVNCA1 SA000001-030000	VN800AE000001-on
1996		
VN800-A2	JKBVNCA1 TA030001-050000	VN800AE000001-on
VN800-B1	JKBVNCB1 TA030001-050000	VN800AE000001-on
1997		
VN800-A3	JKBVNCA1 VA050001-on	VN800AE000001-on
VN800-B2	JKBVNCB1 VA050001-on	VN800AE000001-on

(continued)

Table 1 SERIAL NUMBERS (continued)

U.S. and Canadian Models (continued) Year/model	VIN number	Engine number
1998		
VN800-A4		
U.S. mfgr*	JKBVNCA1 WB500001-on	VN800AE000001-on
Japan mfgr**	JKBVNCA1 WA063001-on	VN800AE000001-on
VN800-B3		
U.S. mfgr*	JKAVNCB1 WB500005-on	VN800AE000001-on
Japan mfgr**	JKBVNCB1 WA063001-on	VN800AE000001-on
European Models **Year/model**	**Frame number**	**Engine number**
1995		
VN800-A1	VN800A-000001~030000	VN800AE000001-on
1996		
VN800-A2	VN800A-030001-050000	VN800AE000001-on
VN800-B1	VN800A-030001-050000	VN800AE000001-on
	VN800B-000001-005000 (Germany only)	
1997		
VN800-A3	VN800A-050001-on	VN800AE000001-on
VN800-B2	VN800A-050001-on	VN800AE000001-on
	VN800B-005001-on (Germany only)	

* Models manufactured in Lincoln, Nebraska U.S.A.
** Models manufactured in Japan

Table 2 GENERAL VEHICLE DIMENSIONS

Overall length	
VN800	
U.S. and Canadian models	2360 mm (92.9 in.)
Other than U.S. and Canadian models	2370 mm (93.3 in.)
VN800 Classic	
U.S. and Canadian models	2375 mm (93.5 in.)
Except U.S. and Canadian models	2390 mm (94.1 in.)
Overall Width	
VN800	825 mm (32.5 in.)
VN800 Classic	
U.S. and Canadian models	930 mm (36.6 in.)
Except U.S. and Canadian models	940 mm (37.0 in.)
Overall height	
VN800	1170 mm (46.1 in.)
VN800 Classic	
U.S. and Canadian models	1125 mm (44.3 in.)
Except U.S. and Canadian models	1130 mm (44.5 in.)
Wheelbase	
VN800	1625 mm (64.0 in.)
VN800 Classic	1600 mm (63.0 in.)
Road clearance	
VN800	160 mm (6.3 in.)
VN800 Classic	135 mm (5.3 in.)
Seat height	
VN800	710 mm (27.0 in.)
VN800 Classic	705 mm (27.8 in.)

Table 3 VEHICLE WEIGHT

Dry mass	
VN800	
California models	225.5 kg (497.1 lb.)
Except California models	225 kg (496.0 lb.)
VN800 Classic	
California models	234.5 kg (517.0 lb.)
U.S. and Canadian models	234 kg (515.9 lb.)
Except U.S., California, and Canadian models	235 kg (518.1 lb.)
Curb mass	
Front	
VN800	107 kg (235.9 lb.)
VN800 Classic	
U.S. and Canadian models	115 kg (253.5 lb.)
Except U.S. and Canadian models	116 kg (255.7 lb.)
Rear	
VN800	
California models	137.5 kg (303.1 lb)
Except California models	137 kg (302.0 lb.)
VN800 Classic	
California models	138.5 kg (305.3 lb.)
Other than California models	138 kg (304.2 lb.)

Table 4 DECIMAL AND METRIC EQUIVALENTS

Fractions	Decimal in.	Metric mm	Fractions	Decimal in.	Metric mm
1/64	0.015625	0.39688	33/64	0.515625	13.09687
1/32	0.03125	0.79375	17/32	0.53125	13.49375
3/64	0.046875	1.19062	35/64	0.546875	13.89062
1/16	0.0625	1.58750	9/16	0.5625	14.28750
5/64	0.078125	1.98437	37/64	0.578125	14.68437
3/32	0.09375	2.38125	19/32	0.59375	15.08125
7/64	0.109375	2.77812	39/64	0.609375	15.47812
1/8	0.125	3.1750	5/8	0.625	15.87500
9/64	0.140625	3.57187	41/64	0.640625	16.27187
5/32	0.15625	3.96875	21/32	0.65625	16.66875
11/64	0.171875	4.36562	43/64	0.671875	17.06562
3/16	0.1875	4.76250	11/16	0.6875	17.46250
13/64	0.203125	5.15937	45/64	0.703125	17.85937
7/32	0.21875	5.55625	23/32	0.71875	18.25625
15/64	0.234375	5.95312	47/64	0.734375	18.65312
1/4	0.250	6.35000	3/4	0.750	19.05000
17/64	0.265625	6.74687	49/64	0.765625	19.44687
9/32	0.28125	7.14375	25/32	0.78125	19.84375
19/64	0.296875	7.54062	51/64	0.796875	20.24062
5/16	0.3125	7.93750	13/16	0.8125	20.63750
21/64	0.328125	8.33437	53/64	0.828125	21.03437
11/32	0.34375	8.73125	27/32	0.84375	21.43125
23/64	0.359375	9.12812	55/64	0.859375	22.82812
3/8	0.375	9.52500	7/8	0.875	22.22500
25/64	0.390625	9.92187	57/64	0.890625	22.62187
13/32	0.40625	10.31875	29/32	0.90625	23.01875
27/64	0.421875	10.71562	59/64	0.921875	23.41562
7/16	0.4375	11.11250	15/16	0.9375	23.81250
29/64	0.453125	11.50937	61/64	0.953125	24.20937
15/32	0.46875	11.90625	31/32	0.96875	24.60625
31/64	0.484375	12.30312	63/64	0.984375	25.00312
1/2	0.500	12.70000	1	1.00	25.40000

Table 5 STANDARD TIGHTENING TORQUES

Fastener size or type	N•m	in.-lb.	ft.-lb.
5 mm screw	4	35	—
5 mm bolt and nut	5	44	—
6 mm screw	9	80	—
6 mm bolt and nut	10	88	—
6 mm flange bolt (8 mm head, small flange)	9	80	—
6 mm flange bolt (10 mm head) and nut	12	106	—
8 mm bolt and nut	22	—	16
8 mm flange bolt and nut	27	—	20
10 mm bolt and nut	35	—	25
10 mm flange bolt and nut	40	—	29
12 mm bolt and nut	55	—	40

Table 6 CONVERSION TABLES

Multiply	By	To get equivalent of
Length		
Inches	25.4	Millimeter
Inches	2.54	Centimeter
Miles	1.609	Kilometer
Feet	0.3048	Meter
Millimeter	0.03937	Inches
Centimeter	0.3937	Inches
Kilometer	0.6214	Mile
Meter	3.281	Mile
Fluid volume		
U.S. quarts	0.9463	Liters
U.S. gallons	3.785	Liters
U.S. ounces	29.573529	Milliliters
Imperial gallons	4.54609	Liters
Imperial quarts	1.1365	Liters
Liters	0.2641721	U.S. gallons
Liters	1.0566882	U.S. quarts
Liters	33.814023	U.S. ounces
Liters	0.22	Imperial gallons
Liters	0.8799	Imperial quarts
Milliliters	0.033814	U.S. ounces
Milliliters	1.0	Cubic centimeters
Milliliters	0.001	Liters
Torque		
Foot-pounds	1.3558	Newton-meters
Foot-pounds	0.138255	Meters-kilograms
Inch-pounds	0.11299	Newton-meters
Newton-meters	0.7375622	Foot-pounds
Newton-meters	8.8507	Inch-pounds
Meters-kilograms	7.2330139	Foot-pounds
Volume		
Cubic inches	16.387064	Cubic centimeters
Cubic centimeters	0.0610237	Cubic inches
Temperature		
Fahrenheit	(F − 32) 0.556	Centigrade
Centigrade	(C × 1.8)	Fahrenheit

Table 7 TECHNICAL ABBREVIATIONS

ABDC	After bottom dead center
ATDC	After top dead center
BBDC	Before bottom dead center
BDC	Bottom dead center
BTDC	Before top dead center
C	Celsius (Centigrade)
cc	Cubic centimeters
CDI	Capacitor discharge ignition
cu. in.	Cubic inches
F	Fahrenheit
ft.-lb.	Foot-pounds
gal.	Gallons
H/A	High altitude
hp	Horsepower
in.	Inches
kg	Kilogram
kg/cm2	Kilograms per square centimeter
kgm	Kilogram meters
km	Kilometer
L	Liter
m	Meter
MAG	Magneto
ml	Milliliter
mm	Millimeter
N•m	Newton-meters
oz.	Ounce
psi	Pounds per square inch
PTO	Power take off
pt.	Pint
qt.	Quart
rpm	Revolutions per minute

Table 8 METRIC TAP DRILL SIZES

Metric (mm)	Drill size	Decimal equivalent	Nearest fraction
3 × 0.50	No. 39	0.0995	3/32
3 × 0.60	3/32	0.0937	3/32
4 × 0.70	No. 30	0.1285	1/8
4 × 0.75	1/8	0.125	1/8
5 × 0.80	No. 19	0.166	11/64
5 × 0.90	No. 20	0.161	5/32
6 × 1.00	No. 9	0.196	13/64
7 × 1.00	16/64	0.234	15/64
8 × 1.00	J	0.277	9/32
8 × 1.25	17/64	0.265	17/64
9 × 1.00	5/16	0.3125	5/16
9 × 1.25	5/16	0.3125	5/16
10 × 1.25	11/32	0.3437	11/32
10 × 1.50	R	0.339	11/32
11 × 1.50	3/8	0.375	3/8
12 × 1.50	13/32	0.406	13/32
12 × 1.75	13/32	0.406	13/32

CHAPTER TWO

TROUBLESHOOTING

Every motorcycle engine requires an uninterrupted supply of fuel and air, proper ignition and adequate compression. If any of these is lacking, the engine will not run.

Diagnosing mechanical and electrical problems is relatively simple if you use an orderly procedure and keep a few basic principles in mind.

The troubleshooting procedures in this chapter analyze typical symptoms and show logical methods for isolating causes. These are not the only adequate troubleshooting methods. There may be several ways to solve a problem, but only a systematic approach can guarantee success.

Never assume anything. Do not overlook the obvious. If you are riding along and the bike suddenly quits, check the easiest, most accessible problem spots first.

If nothing obvious turns up during a quick check, look a little further. Learning to recognize and describe symptoms will make repairs easier for you or a mechanic at the shop. Describe problems accurately and fully.

Gather as much information as possible to aid in diagnosis. Note whether the engine lost power gradually or all at once. Remember that the more complicated a machine is, the easier it is to troubleshoot because symptoms point to specific problems.

After defining the symptoms, test and analyze the areas that could cause those symptoms. Guessing at the cause of a problem may provide the solution, but it can easily lead to frustration, wasted time and a series of expensive, unnecessary parts replacements.

You do not need expensive equipment or complicated test gear to determine whether repairs can be attempted at home. A few simple checks could save a large repair bill and lost time while the bike sits in a dealer's service department. On the other hand, be realistic and do not attempt repairs beyond your abilities. Service departments tend to charge heavily for putting together a disassembled engine that may have been abused. Some will not even take on such a job, so use common sense and do not get in over your head.

OPERATING REQUIREMENTS

An engine needs three basic elements to run properly: correct fuel/air mixture, compression and a spark at the correct time (**Figure 1**). If one or more are missing, the engine will not run. Four-stroke engine operating principles are described in Chapter Four.

If the machine has been sitting for any length of time and refuses to start, check and clean the spark plugs, then look to the gasoline delivery system. This includes the fuel tank, fuel shutoff valve and fuel line to the carburetor. Gasoline deposits may have formed and gummed up the carburetor jets and air passages. Gasoline tends to lose its potency after standing for long periods. Condensation may contaminate the fuel with water. Drain the old fuel (fuel tank, fuel lines and carburetor) and try starting with a tank of fresh fuel.

TROUBLESHOOTING INSTRUMENTS

Refer to **Chapter One** for a list of the instruments needed.

STARTING THE ENGINE

If experiencing engine starting troubles, it is easy to forget the basic engine starting procedure. The following sections will guide you through the basic starting procedure. In all cases, make sure that there is an adequate supply of fuel in the tank.

Starting Notes

1. A sidestand ignition cutoff system is used on all models. The position of the sidestand will affect engine starting as follows:
   a. The engine cannot start when the sidestand is down and the transmission is in gear.
   b. The engine can start when the sidestand is down and the transmission is in NEUTRAL. The engine will stop, however, if the transmission is put in gear with the sidestand down.
   c. The engine can be started when the sidestand is up and the transmission is in NEUTRAL. If the sidestand is up, the engine will also start if the transmission is in gear and the clutch lever is pulled in.
2. Before starting the engine, shift the transmission into NEUTRAL and confirm that the engine stop switch is set to RUN.
3. Turn the ignition switch to ON and confirm the following:
   a. The neutral indicator light is ON (when transmission is in NEUTRAL).
   b. The engine oil pressure warning light is ON.
4. The engine is now ready to start. Refer to the starting procedure in this section that best meets the air temperature and engine condition.
5. If the engine idles at a fast speed for more than 5 minutes or if the throttle is repeatedly snapped on and off at normal air temperature, the exhaust pipes may discolor.
6. Excessive choke use can cause an excessively rich fuel mixture. This condition can wash oil off of the piston and cylinder walls, causing piston and cylinder scuffing.

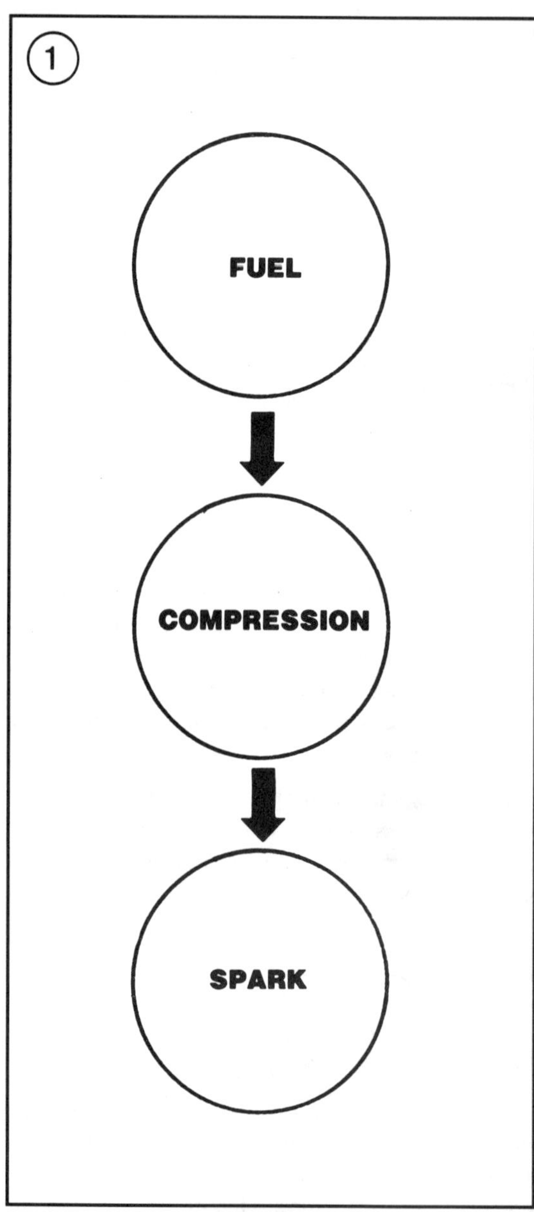

CAUTION

The red oil pressure warning light should turn off a few seconds after the engine starts. If the light stays on longer than a few seconds, stop the engine immediately. Check the engine oil level as described in Chapter Three. If the oil level is good, the oil pressure may be too low or the oil pressure switch may be shorted. Check the oiling system and correct the problem before starting the engine. If the oil pressure switch is in good condition, the system is warning you that oil is not being delivered to the engine. Severe engine damage will occur if the engine is run with low oil pressure. Refer to ***Engine Lubrication*** *in this chapter.*

CAUTION

Do not operate the starter motor for more than 5 seconds at a time. Wait approximately 10 seconds between starting attempts.

2

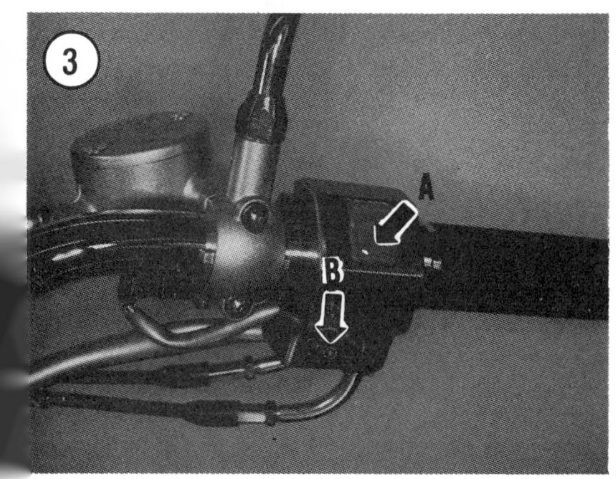

3

2

Starting a Cold Engine

1. Shift the transmission into NEUTRAL.
2. Turn the fuel shutoff valve to the ON position.
3. Insert the ignition key and turn the ignition switch to ON.
4. Pull the choke knob (**Figure 2**) to the fully ON position.
5. Make sure the engine stop switch (A, **Figure 3**) is in the RUN position.
6. Depress the starter button (B, **Figure 3**) and start the engine. Do not open the throttle when pressing the starter button.

NOTE

Do not open the throttle when attempting to start a cold engine. The throttle must be closed for the choke to operate properly. Opening the throttle with the choke in the ON position will result in a lean mixture and cause hard starting.

7. Once the engine is running, open the throttle slightly to help warm the engine. Continue warming the engine until the choke can be turned to the fully OFF position and the engine accelerates cleanly without hesitation.

Starting a Warm or Hot Engine

1. Shift the transmission into NEUTRAL.
2. Turn the fuel shutoff valve (**Figure 4**) to the ON position.
3. Install the ignition key and turn the ignition switch to ON.
4. Make sure the engine stop switch (A, **Figure 3**) is in the RUN position.
5. Make sure the choke knob (**Figure 2**) is in the fully OFF position.
6. Open the throttle slightly and depress the starter button (B, **Figure 3**). Do not use the choke.

Starting a Flooded Engine

If the engine will not start and you smell gasoline, the engine is probably flooded. To start a flooded engine, open the throttle all the way and operate the starter. Do not open the choke. Holding the throttle completely open allows more air to reach the cylinders.

EMERGENCY TROUBLESHOOTING

If the bike is difficult to start, or will not start at all, it does not help to wear down the battery using the electric starter. Check for obvious problems even before getting out your tools. Go down the following list step by step. Do each one. You may be embarrassed to find the engine stop switch off, but that is better than wearing down the battery. If the bike still will not start, refer to the appropriate troubleshooting procedure in this chapter.

1. Is there fuel in the tank? Open the fuel cap and rock the bike. Listen for fuel sloshing around.

WARNING
Do not use an open flame to check in the tank. A serious explosion is certain to result.

2. Is the fuel valve in the ON position? Turn the valve to the ON position (**Figure 4**) or the RES position (**Figure 5**). The reserve position ensures you get the last remaining gas in the tank.
3. Is the engine stop switch in the correct position? The engine should start and operate when the switch is in the RUN position (A, **Figure 3**). This switch is used primarily as an emergency or safety switch. Place the switch in the RUN position when starting the engine. Test the switch as described in Chapter Nine.
4. Are both spark plug caps on tight? Push the spark plug cap (**Figure 6**) firmly onto each spark plug. Slightly rotate each cap to clean the electrical connection between the plug and the connector.
5. Is the choke knob (**Figure 2**) in the right position? The choke knob should be OFF for a warm engine and ON for a cold engine.

ENGINE STARTING TROUBLESHOOTING

An engine that refuses to start or is difficult to start is very frustrating. More often than not, the problem is minor and can be found with a simple and logical troubleshooting approach.

First, review the engine starting procedure in this chapter. If the engine will not start by following the engine starting steps, continue with this section.

The following are beginning points from which to isolate engine starting problems.

NOTE
Do not operate the starter motor for more than 5 seconds at a time. Wait approximately 10 seconds between starting attempts.

Engine Fails to Start (Spark Test)

Perform the following spark test to determine if the ignition system is operating properly.

1. Remove the spark plug from each cylinder head as described in Chapter Three.

NOTE
If the spark plugs are wet after attempting to start the engine or if they appear fouled, refer to ***Carburetor Troubleshooting*** *in this chapter.*

2. Insert a new spark plug, or spark tester, into the spark plug cap, and touch the spark plug base to a good ground like the engine cylinder head. Position the spark plug so you can see the electrode.

WARNING
Be sure the spark plug or the spark plug tester is away from the spark plug holes in the cylinder so the spark cannot ignite the mixture in the cylinder. If the engine is flooded, do not perform this test. The firing of the spark plug can ignite fuel ejected from the opened spark plug hole.

WARNING
During the next step, do not hold the spark plugs or connectors with your fingers or a serious electrical shock may result. If necessary, use a pair of insulated pliers to hold the spark plugs or wires. The high voltage generated by the ignition system could produce serious or fatal shocks.

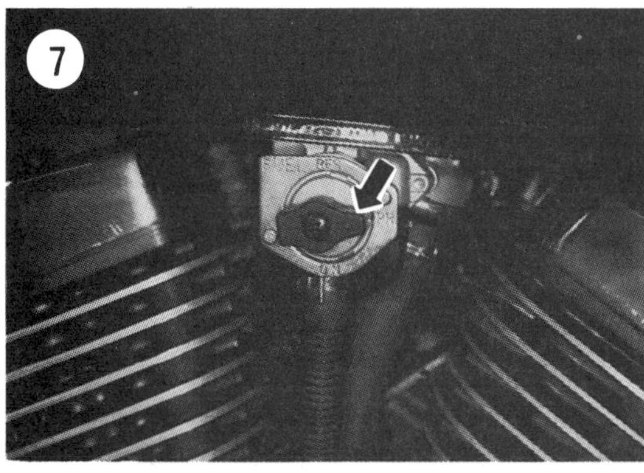
7

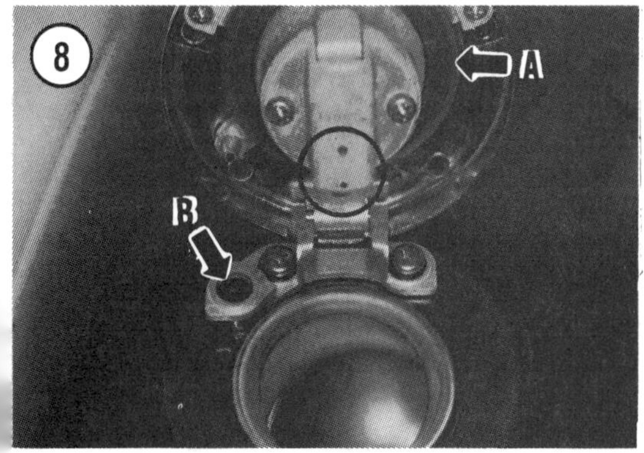

8

3. Crank the engine with the starter. A fat blue spark should be evident across the spark plug electrode or spark tester terminals. Repeat for the other cylinder. If the spark is good, continue with Step 4. If the spark is weak or if there is no spark, perform Step 6.

NOTE
If the starter does not operate or if the starter motor rotates but the engine does not turn, refer to Engine Will Not Crank in this section.

4. Check engine compression as described in Chapter Three. If the compression is good, perform Steps 5-7. If the compression is low, check for one or more of the following:
   a. Leaking cylinder head gasket(s).
   b. Cracked or warped cylinder head(s).
   c. Worn piston rings, pistons and cylinders.
   d. Valve stuck open.
   e. Seized valve(s).
   f. Worn or damaged valve seat(s).
   g. Incorrect valve timing.
5. Turn the fuel valve to the ON (**Figure 4**) or RES (reserve) position (**Figure 5**). Disconnect the fuel line from the shutoff valve and connect a spare line to the fuel valve.
6. Insert the open end of the spare fuel line into a clear container.
7. Turn the fuel shutoff valve to PRI (prime) as shown in **Figure 7**. A steady flow of fuel should be noticed with the shutoff valve in the PRI position. The fuel flow should stop when the valve is turned to the ON or RES positions. If the fuel flow is good, check for one or more of the following:
   a. Clogged fuel line.
   b. Stuck or clogged carburetor float valve.

If there is no fuel flow or if the flow is slow or intermittent, check for one or more of the following conditions:
   a. Empty fuel tank.
   b. Plugged fuel tank cap vent hole (**Figure 8**).
   c. Plugged vacuum line.
   d. Plugged shutoff valve.
8. If the spark is weak or if there is no spark at one or both plugs, note the following:

a. If there is no spark at both plugs, there may be a problem in the input side of the ignition system IC ignitor, pickup coil, sidestand switch or neutral switch. Test these parts as described in Chapter Nine.
b. If there is no spark at one of the spark plugs, the spark plug is probably faulty or there is a problem with the spark plug wire or plug cap. Replace the spark plug and retest. If there is still no spark at that one plug, test the spark plug wire and plug cap as described in Chapter Nine. If these test good, the problem may be in the primary side of the ignition system (ignition coil or IC ignitor). Test these parts as described in Chapter Nine.

Engine Will Not Crank

Check for one or more of the following possible malfunctions:

1. Blown fuse.
2. Discharged battery.
3. Defective starter motor, starter relay or start switch.
4. Seized piston(s).
5. Seized crankshaft bearings.
6. Broken connecting rod(s).
7. Locked-up transmission or clutch assembly.
8. Defective starter clutch.

ENGINE PERFORMANCE

This checklist will serve as a starting point from which to isolate a performance malfunction. Where ignition timing is mentioned as a problem, remember that there is no method of adjusting the ignition timing. If you check the ignition timing with a timing light and it is incorrect, there is a faulty part within the ignition system. The individual parts must be checked and the faulty part(s) replaced.

Engine Will Not Start or Is Hard to Start

1. Fuel tank empty.
2. Obstructed fuel line, fuel shutoff valve or fuel filter.
3. Sticking float valve in carburetor.
4. Carburetor incorrectly adjusted.
5. Improper choke operation.
6. Improper throttle operation.
7. Fouled or improperly gapped spark plug(s).
8. Ignition timing incorrect.
9. Broken or shorted ignition coil(s).
10. Weak or faulty IC ignitor or pickup coils.
11. Improper valve timing.
12. Plugged air filter element.
13. Contaminated fuel.
14. Engine flooded with fuel.

Engine Starts but Then Stops

1. Incorrect choke adjustment.
2. Incorrect pilot air screw setting (closed).
3. Incorrect ignition timing.
4. Contaminated fuel.
5. Intake manifold air leak.

Engine Will Not Idle

1. Carburetor incorrectly adjusted (too lean or too rich).
2. Fouled or improperly gapped spark plug(s).
3. Leaking head gasket(s) or vacuum leak.
4. Ignition timing incorrect.
5. Improper valve timing.
6. Obstructed fuel line or fuel shutoff valve.
7. Low engine compression.
8. Choke stuck in the on position.
9. Incorrect pilot screw adjustment.
10. Plugged pilot jet in the carburetor.
11. Plugged air filter element.
12. Valve(s) and valve seat(s) require service.

Poor High Speed Performance

1. Check the ignition timing as described in Chapter Three. If ignition timing is correct, perform Step 2. If the timing is incorrect, test the following ignition system components as described in Chapter Nine:
   a. IC ignitor.
   b. Pickup coil(s).
   c. Ignition coils.
2. Turn the fuel valve to the ON (**Figure 4**) or RES position (**Figure 5**). Connect a spare hose to the fuel valve.
3. Insert the open end of the spare fuel line into a clear glass container.
4. Turn the fuel valve to prime (**Figure 7**). A steady flow of fuel should be noticed with the fuel valve in the PRI position. The fuel flow should stop when the

valve is turned to the ON or RES positions. If the fuel flow is good, check for one or more of the following:

a. Plugged fuel line.
b. Stuck or clogged carburetor float valve.

If there is no fuel flow or if the flow is slow or intermittent, check for one or more of the following conditions:

a. Empty fuel tank.
b. Plugged fuel tank cap vent hole (**Figure 8**).
c. Plugged vacuum line.
d. Plugged shutoff valve.

5. Remove the carburetor as described in Chapter Eight. Then remove the float bowl and check for contamination and plugged jets. If any contamination is found, disassemble and clean the carburetor. You should also pour out and discard the remaining fuel in the fuel tank and flush the fuel tank thoroughly. If no contamination is found and the jets are not plugged, perform Step 6.
6. Incorrect valve timing and worn or damaged valve springs can cause poor high-speed performance. If the valve timing was set just prior to the onset of this type of problem, the valve timing may be incorrect. If the valve timing was not set or changed, and you performed all of the other inspection procedures in this section without locating the problem area, the cylinder head covers should be removed and the valve train assembly inspected.

Low or Poor Engine Power

1. Support the bike with the rear wheel off the ground, and then spin the rear wheel by hand. If the wheel spins freely, perform Step 2. If the wheel does not spin freely, check for the following conditions:
   a. Dragging rear brake.
   b. Excessive rear axle tightening torque.
   c. Worn or damaged rear wheel bearings.
2. Check the clutch adjustment and operation. If the clutch slips, refer to *Clutch* in this chapter.
3. Test ride the bike and accelerate lightly. If the engine speed increases according to throttle position, perform Step 4. If the engine speed does not increase, check for one or more of the following problems:
   a. Plugged or damaged air filter.
   b. Restricted fuel flow.
   c. Plugged fuel tank cap vent.
   d. Incorrect choke adjustment or operation.
   e. Plugged or damaged muffler.
4. Check for one or more of the following problems:
   a. Low engine compression.
   b. Fouled spark plug(s).
   c. Clogged carburetor jet(s).
   d. Incorrect ignition timing.
   e. Incorrect oil level (too high or too low).
   f. Contaminated oil.
   g. Worn or damaged valve train assembly.
   h. Engine overheating.

2

Engine Overheating

1. Incorrect coolant level.
2. Incorrect carburetor adjustment or jet selection.
3. Improper spark plug heat range.
4. Cooling system malfunction.
5. Plugged radiator and/or cooling fins.
6. Oil level low.
7. Oil not circulating properly.
8. Valves leaking.
9. Heavy engine carbon deposits.
10. Dragging brake(s).
11. Clutch slipping.

Engine Overheating (Cooling System Malfunction)

Note the above, then proceed with the following items:

1. Plugged radiator.
2. Thermostat stuck closed.
3. Worn or damaged radiator cap.
4. Water pump worn or damaged.
5. Fan relay malfunction.
6. Thermostatic fan switch malfunction.
7. Damaged fan blade(s).
8. Plugged or blocked coolant passages in radiator, hoses or engine.

Excessive Exhaust Smoke and Engine Runs Roughly

1. Plugged air filter element.
2. Carburetor adjustment incorrect; mixture too rich.
3. Choke not operating correctly.
4. Water or other contaminants in fuel.
5. Plugged fuel line.
6. Spark plugs fouled.

7. Ignition coil defective.
8. Loose or defective ignition circuit.
9. Short circuit from damaged wire insulation.
10. Loose battery cable connection(s).
11. Valve timing incorrect.

Engine Lacks Acceleration

1. Carburetor mixture too lean.
2. Restricted fuel line.
3. Improper ignition timing.
4. Dragging brake(s).
5. Slipping clutch.

Engine Backfires

1. Improper ignition timing.
2. Carburetor improperly adjusted.
3. Lean fuel mixture.

Engine Misfires During Acceleration

1. Improper ignition timing.
2. Lean fuel mixture.

ENGINE NOISES

Often the first evidence of an internal engine problem is a strange noise. A knocking, clicking or tapping sound may be warning you of impending trouble.

While engine noises can indicate problems, they are difficult to interpret correctly; they can seriously mislead inexperienced mechanics.

Professional mechanics often use a special stethoscope for isolating engine noises. You can do nearly as well with an ordinary piece of doweling or a section of small hose. By placing one end in contact with the area you wish to listen to and the other end to the front of your ear (not directly on your ear), you can hear sounds emanating from that area. The first time you do this, you may be confused by the strange sounds coming from even a normal engine. If you can, have an experienced friend or mechanic help you sort out the noises.

Consider the following when troubleshooting engine noises:

1. *Knocking or pinging during acceleration*—Caused by using a lower octane fuel than recommended. May also be caused by poor fuel. Pinging can also be caused by a spark plug of the wrong heat range or carbon buildup in the combustion chamber. Check the spark plugs and engine compression as described Chapter Three.
2. *Slapping or rattling noises at low speed or during acceleration*— May be caused by piston slap (excessive piston-to-cylinder wall clearance).

NOTE
Piston slap is easier to detect when the engine is cold and before the pistons have expanded. Once the engine is warm, piston expansion reduces piston-to-cylinder clearance.

3. *Knocking or rapping while decelerating*—Usually caused by excessive rod bearing clearance.
4. *Persistent knocking and vibration on every crankshaft rotation*—Usually caused by worn rod or main bearing(s). Can also be caused by broken piston rings or damaged piston pins.
5. *Rapid on-off squeal*—Compression leak around cylinder head gasket(s) or spark plug(s).
6. *Valve train noise—Check for the following:*
   a. Valve sticking in guide.
   b. Low oil pressure.
   c. Damaged camshaft cap or loose mounting bolts.

ENGINE LUBRICATION

An improperly operating engine lubrication system will quickly lead to engine seizure. Check the engine oil level each week as described in Chapter Three. Oil pump service is described in Chapter Five.

Oil Consumption High or Engine Smokes Excessively

1. Worn valve guides.
2. Worn or damaged piston rings.

Excessive Engine Oil Leaks

1. Plugged air filter breather hose.
2. Loose engine parts.
3. Damaged gasket sealing surfaces.

Black Smoke

1. Plugged air filter.
2. Incorrect carburetor fuel level (too high).
3. Choke stuck open.
4. Incorrect main jet (too large).

White Smoke

1. Worn valve guide.
2. Worn valve stem seal.
3. Worn piston ring oil ring.
4. Excessive cylinder and/or piston wear.
5. Coolant leaking into cylinders.

Oil Pressure Too High

1. Plugged oil filter.
2. Plugged oil gallery or metering orifices.
3. Pressure relief valve stuck closed.

Low Oil Pressure

1. Low oil level.
2. Damaged oil pump.
3. Plugged oil screen.
4. Plugged oil filter.
5. Internal oil leakage.
6. Pressure relief valve stuck open.

No Oil Pressure

1. Damaged oil pump.
2. Excessively low oil level.
3. No oil in crankcase.
4. Internal oil leakage.
5. Damaged oil pump drive chain.
6. Damaged oil pump drive shaft.

Oil Pressure Warning Light Stays On

1. Low oil pressure.
2. No oil pressure.
3. Damaged oil pressure switch.
4. Short circuit in warning light circuit.

Oil Level Too Low

1. Oil level not maintained at correct level.
2. Worn piston rings.
3. Worn cylinder(s).
4. Worn valve guides.
5. Worn valve stem seals.
6. Piston rings incorrectly installed.
7. External oil leakage.
8. Oil leaking into the cooling system.

Oil Contamination

1. Blown cylinder head gasket(s).
2. Water contamination.
3. Oil and filter not changed at specified intervals.

CLUTCH

The most common clutch problems and causes are listed in this section.

Excessive Clutch Lever Operation

If the clutch lever is too hard to pull in, check the following:

1. Clutch cable not properly adjusted.
2. Clutch cable requires lubrication.
3. Clutch cable improperly routed or bent.
4. Damaged clutch lifter bearing.
5. Push rod bent.

Rough Clutch Operation

This condition can be caused by excessively worn, grooved or damaged clutch housing slots.

Clutch Slippage

If the engine accelerates, but the bike does not, the clutch is probably slipping. Some of the main causes of clutch slipping are:

1. Worn clutch or friction plates.
2. Weak clutch springs.
3. No clutch lever free play.
4. Clutch inner cable sticking.
5. Clutch release mechanism.
6. Engine oil /clutch plates contaminated.

Clutch Drag

If the clutch will not disengage or if the bike creeps with the transmission in gear and the clutch disengaged, the clutch is dragging. Some of the main causes of clutch drag are:

1. Excessive clutch lever free play.
2. Warped clutch or friction plates.
3. Damaged clutch release mechanism.
4. Loose clutch housing locknut.
5. Clutch hub splines damaged.
6. Friction plates incorrectly installed.
7. Uneven clutch spring compression.
8. Engine oil level too high.
9. Incorrect oil viscosity.
10. Engine oil additive being used.

GEARSHIFT LINKAGE

The gearshift linkage assembly connects the gearshift pedal to the shift drum (internal shift mechanism).

The external shift mechanism can be examined after removing the external shift mechanism cover on the left-hand side of the crankcase. The internal shift mechanism can only be examined once the engine is removed from the frame and the crankcase disassembled. Common gearshift linkage problems are listed below.

Transmission Jumps Out of Gear

1. Bent or worn shift fork.
2. Bent shift fork shaft.
3. Gear groove worn.
4. Damaged stopper arm.
5. Weak or damaged stopper arm spring.
6. Loose or damaged shifter cam.
7. Worn gear dogs or slots.
8. Damaged shift drum grooves.

Difficult Shifting

1. Damaged clutch system.
2. Incorrect oil viscosity.
3. Bent shift fork shaft(s).
4. Bent or damaged shift fork(s).
5. Worn gear dogs or slots.
6. Damaged shift drum grooves.

TRANSMISSION

Transmission symptoms are sometimes hard to distinguish from clutch symptoms. Common transmission problems and the likely causes are listed below. Refer to Chapter Seven for transmission service procedures. Prior to working on the transmission, make sure the clutch or gearshift linkage are not causing the problem.

Difficult Shifting

1. Damaged clutch system.
2. Incorrect oil viscosity.
3. Bent shift fork shaft.
4. Bent or damaged shift fork.
5. Worn gear dogs or slots.
6. Damaged shift drum grooves.

Jumps out of Gear

1. Loose or damaged shift drum stopper arm.
2. Bent or damaged shift fork(s).
3. Bent shift fork shaft(s).
4. Damaged shift drum grooves.
5. Worn gear dogs or slots.
6. Broken shift linkage return spring.

Incorrect Shift Lever Operation

1. Bent shift lever.
2. Stripped shift lever splines.
3. Damaged shift lever linkage.

Excessive Gear Noise

1. Worn bearings.
2. Worn or damaged gears.
3. Excessive gear backlash.

ELECTRICAL TROUBLESHOOTING

This section describes the basics of electrical troubleshooting, how to use test equipment and the basic test procedures with the various pieces of test equipment.

Electrical troubleshooting can be very time-consuming and frustrating without proper knowledge and a suitable plan. Refer to the wiring diagrams at the end of the book and to the individual system diagrams included with the charging system, ignition system and starting system sections in this chapter. Wiring diagrams will help you determine how the circuit should work by tracing the current paths from the power source through the circuit components to ground. Also check any circuits that share the same fuse, ground or switch. If the other circuits work properly, the shared wiring is good and the cause must be in the wiring used only by the suspect circuit. If all related circuits are faulty at the same time the probable cause is a poor ground connection or a blown fuse(s).

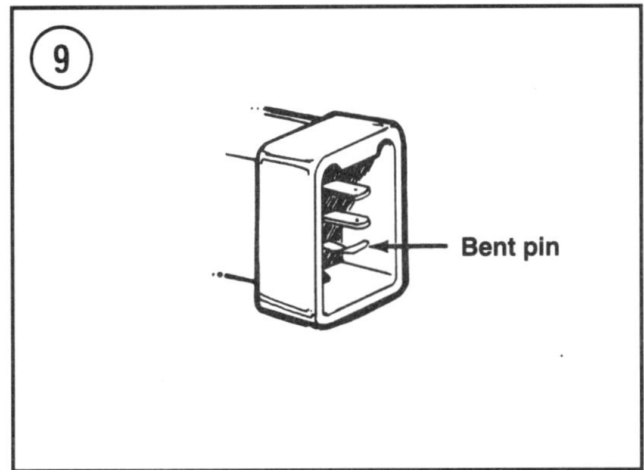

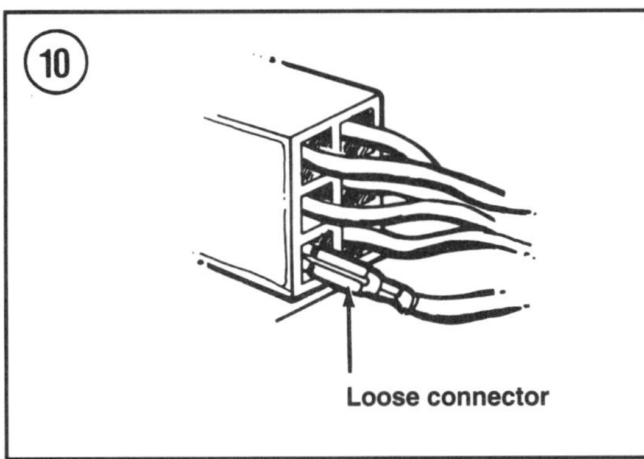

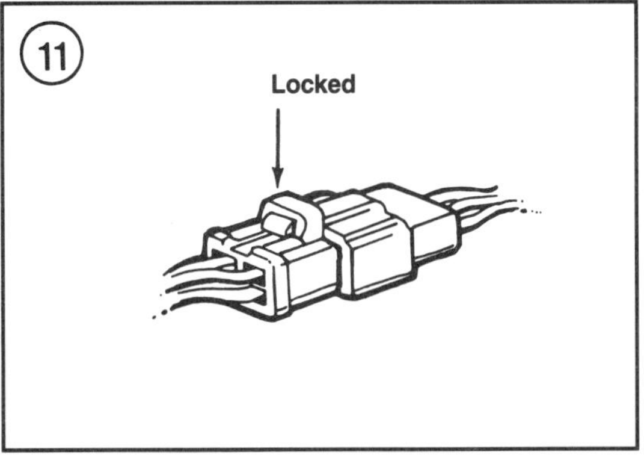

As with all troubleshooting procedures, analyze typical symptoms in a systematic procedure. Never assume anything and do not overlook the obvious like a blown fuse or an electrical connector that has separated. Test the simplest and most obvious cause first and try to make tests at easily accessible points on the bike.

2

Preliminary Checks and Precautions

Prior to starting any electrical troubleshooting procedure perform the following:

1. Check the main fuse; make sure it is not blown. Replace if necessary.
2. Check the individual fuse(s) for each circuit; make sure it is not blown. Replace if necessary.
3. Inspect the battery. Make sure it is fully charged and that the battery leads are clean and securely attached to the battery terminals as described in Chapter Nine.
4. Disconnect each electrical connector in the suspect circuit and make sure there are no bent metal pins on the male side of the electrical connector (**Figure 9**). A bent pin will not connect to its mate in the female end of the connector, causing an open circuit.
5. Check each female end of the connector. Make sure that the metal connector on the end of each wire (**Figure 10**) is pushed all the way into the plastic connector. If not, carefully push them in with a small screwdriver.
6. Check all wires where they enter the individual metal terminal in both the male and female plastic connector.
7. Make sure all electrical connectors within the plastic connector are clean and free of corrosion. Clean, if necessary, and pack the connectors with dielectric grease.
8. Push the connectors together and make sure they are fully engaged and locked together (**Figure 11**).
9. Never pull on the wires when disconnecting an electrical connector—pull only on the connector plastic housing.
10. Never use a self-powered test light on circuits that contain solid-state devices. The solid-state devices may be damaged.

TEST EQUIPMENT

Test Lamp or Voltmeter

A test lamp can be constructed of a 12-volt bulb with a pair of test leads carefully soldered to the bulb. To check for battery voltage (12 volts) in a circuit, attach one lead to ground and the other lead to various points along the circuit. Where battery voltage is present the lamp bulb will light.

A voltmeter is used in the same manner as the test lamp to find out if battery voltage is present in any given circuit. The voltmeter, unlike the test lamp, will also indicate how much voltage is present at each test point. When using a voltmeter, attach the red lead (+) to the component or wire to be checked and the negative (–) lead to a good ground.

Self-powered Test Lamp and Ohmmeter

A self-powered test lamp can be constructed of a 12-volt bulb, a pair of test leads and a 12-volt battery. When the test leads are touched together the bulb will go on.

Use a self-powered test light as follows:

1. Touch the test leads together to make sure the bulb goes on. If not, correct the problem prior to using it in a test procedure.
2. Disconnect the bike's battery or remove the fuse(s) that protects the circuit to be tested.
3. Select two points within the circuit where there should be continuity.
4. Attach one lead of the self-powered test lamp to each point.
5. If there is continuity, the self-powered test lamp will come on.
6. If there is no continuity, the self-powered test lamp will not come on.

An ohmmeter can be used in place of the self-powered test light. The ohmmeter, unlike the test lamp, will also indicate how much resistance is present between each test point. Low resistance means good continuity in a complete circuit. Before using an analog ohmmeter, it must first be calibrated. This is done by touching the leads together and turning the ohms calibration knob until the meter reads zero.

CAUTION

An ohmmeter must never be connected to any circuit which has power applied to it. Always disconnect the battery negative lead before using the ohmmeter.

Jumper Wire

When using a jumper wire always install an inline fuse/fuse holder (available at most auto supply stores or electronic supply stores) to the jumper wire. Never use a jumper wire across any load (a component that is connected and turned on). This would result in a direct short and will blow the fuse(s) and/or damage components and wiring in that circuit.

BASIC TEST PROCEDURES

Voltage Testing

Unless otherwise specified, perform all voltage tests with the electrical connector still connected. Insert the test leads into the backside of the connector and make sure the test lead touches the wire or metal terminal within the plastic connector. If the test lead only touches the wire insulation you will get a false reading.

Always check both sides of the connector as one side may be loose or corroded thus preventing electrical flow through the connector. This type of test can be performed with a test lamp or a voltmeter. A voltmeter will give the best results.

1. Attach the negative test lead (if using a voltmeter) to a good ground (bare metal). If necessary, scrape away paint from the frame or engine (retouch later with paint). Make sure the part used for ground is not insulated with a rubber gasket or rubber grommet.
2. Attach the positive test lead (if using a voltmeter) to the point you want to check.
3. Turn the ignition switch on. If using a test lamp, the test lamp will come on if voltage is present. If using a voltmeter, note the voltage reading. The reading should be within 1 volt of battery voltage. If the voltage is 11 volts or less there is a problem in the circuit.

Voltage Drop Test

Since resistance causes voltage to drop, resistance can be measured on an active circuit using a voltmeter. This is the voltage drop test. A voltage drop test determines the difference between the voltage at the beginning of a circuit from the voltage at the end of the circuit, while the circuit is active. If the circuit has no resistance, there will be no voltage drop (the meter will indicate zero volts). The more resistance present in the circuit, the higher the voltage reading will be. Generally, a voltage drop of 1 or more volts is considered excessive. The chief advantage to a voltage drop test over a resistance test is that the circuit is tested while under operation.

The voltage drop test is an excellent way to test solenoids and relays, battery cables and high-current leads. To perform a voltage drop test, connect the red voltmeter lead to the electric source (where electricity is coming from) and the black lead to the load (where electricity is going).

Continuity Test

A continuity test is used to determine the integrity of a circuit or component. A complete circuit has continuity; a broken wire or open circuit has no continuity. Continuity is indicated by a zero ohms reading if using an ohmmeter. If using a self-powered test lamp, continuity is indicated by a glowing light. No continuity is indicated by an infinity reading on an ohmmeter or lack of a light on a self-powered test lamp.

1. Disconnect the negative battery cable from the battery.
2. Isolate (disconnect) the circuit or component being tested. Attach one test lead to one end of the circuit being tested.
3. Attach the other test lead to the other end of the circuit.
4. If continuity is present, the test lamp will glow or the ohmmeter will indicate zero ohms. If no continuity is present, the test lamp will not glow or the ohmmeter will indicate infinity.

Testing for a Short Circuit Using Self-powered Test Lamp or Ohmmeter

This test can be performed with either a self-powered test lamp or an ohmmeter.

1. Disconnect the battery negative lead as described in Chapter Three.
2. Remove the blown fuse from the fuse panel.
3. Connect one test lead of the test lamp or ohmmeter to the load side (battery side) of the fuse terminal in the fuse panel.
4. Connect the other test lead to a good ground (bare metal). If necessary, scrape away paint from the frame or engine (retouch later with paint). Make sure the part used for a ground is not insulated with a rubber gasket or rubber grommet.
5. With the self-powered test lamp or ohmmeter attached to the fuse terminal and ground, wiggle the wiring harness relating to the suspect circuit at 6 in. (15.2 cm) intervals. Start next to the fuse panel and work your way away from the fuse panel. Watch the self-powered test light or ohmmeter as you progress along the harness.
6. If the test lamp blinks or the needle on the ohmmeter moves, there is a short-to-ground at that point in the harness.

Testing For a Short with a Test Lamp or Voltmeter

This test can be performed with either a test lamp or voltmeter.

1. Remove the blown fuse from the fuse panel.
2. Connect the test lamp or voltmeter across the fuse terminals in the fuse panel. Turn the ignition switch on and check for battery voltage.
3. With the test lamp or voltmeter attached to the fuse terminals, wiggle the wiring harness relating to the suspect circuit at 6 in. (15.2 cm) intervals. Start next to the fuse panel and work your way away from the fuse panel. Watch the test lamp or voltmeter as you progress along the harness.
4. If the test lamp blinks or the needle on the voltmeter moves, there is a short-to-ground at that point in the harness.

ELECTRICAL PROBLEMS

If light bulbs burn out frequently, the cause may be excessive vibration, a loose connection that permits sudden current surges or the installation of the wrong type of bulb.

Most light and ignition problems are caused by loose or corroded ground connections. Check these prior to replacing a light bulb or electrical component.

CHARGING SYSTEM TROUBLESHOOTING

The charging system (**Figure 12**) consists of the battery, alternator and a voltage regulator/rectifier. A 30-amp main fuse protects the circuit.

Alternating current generated by the alternator is rectified to direct current. The voltage regulator maintains the voltage to the battery and additional electrical loads at a constant voltage regardless of variations in engine speed and load.

The most common charging system complaints are:

1. Battery discharging.
2. Battery overcharging.

Battery Discharging

1. Visually check the connections at the battery. If the polarity is reversed, check for a damaged regulator/rectifier.
2. Check for loose or corroded battery cable connectors.
3. Inspect all wiring between the battery and alternator stator for worn or cracked insulation or looses connections. Replace the wiring or clean and tighten the connectors as required.

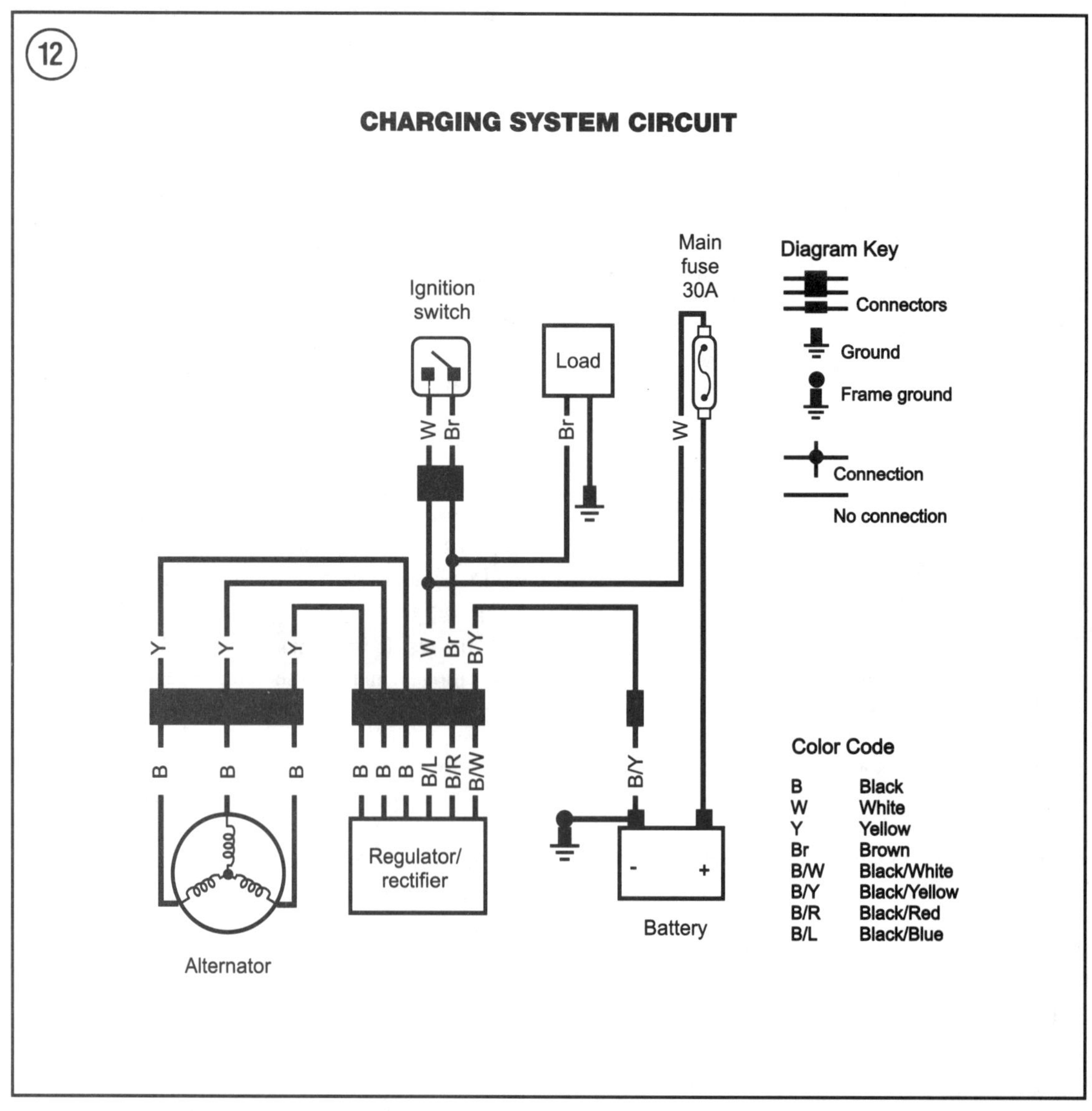

NOTE

If you do not have access to a battery tester, remove the battery from the bike and take it to a Kawasaki dealership for testing.

4. Check the condition of the battery. Clean and recharge the battery as described in Chapter Three.

5. Perform the *Battery Drain Test* as described in Chapter Nine. Then, check the charging system output and test the voltage regulator/rectifier as described in Chapter Nine.

Battery Overcharging

If the battery is overcharging, the voltage regulator/rectifier unit is faulty. Replace the regulator/rectifier unit as described in Chapter Nine.

IGNITION SYSTEM TROUBLESHOOTING

The ignition system (**Figure 13**) consists of an IC ignitor, two ignition coils, a pickup coil assembly and two spark plugs. The most common ignition system complaints are:

a. No spark at both spark plugs.

b. No spark at one spark plug.

c. Engine starts and runs but sidestand switch does not operate.

Prior to troubleshooting the ignition system, perform the following:

1. Check the battery to make sure it is fully charged and in good condition. A weak battery will result in a slower engine cranking speed.

2. Perform the spark test as described under *Engine Fails to Start (Spark Test)* in this chapter. Then refer to the appropriate ignition system complaint.

3. Because a loose or dirty electrical connector can prevent the ignition system from operating properly, check for dirty or loose-fitting connector terminals. The ignition system electrical diagram and the wiring diagrams at the end of this book can be used to locate the appropriate electrical connectors. Also, refer to *Preliminary Checks and Precautions* in this chapter for additional information.

No Spark at Both Spark Plugs

1. Check for dirty or loose-fitting connector terminals as described in this chapter. Clean and repair as required.

2

NOTE

If the ignition system does not operate properly after inspecting and cleaning the connector terminals, proceed with Step 2.

2. Measure the IC ignitor resistance as described as described in Chapter Nine. Note the following:

a. If the resistance reading is incorrect, the IC ignitor is faulty and should be replaced.

b. If the resistance reading is correct, check for an open circuit between the IC ignitor and the pickup coil assembly.

NOTE

The IC ignitor is located the electrical box under the seat.

NOTE

When switching between ohmmeter scales, always calibrate an analog meter to ensure a correct reading.

3. Measure the pickup coil resistance as described in Chapter Nine. Note the following:

a. If the resistance reading is incorrect, the pulse generator is faulty and should be replaced.

b. If the resistance reading is correct, check for an open circuit between the ignition control module and the pulse generator.

NOTE

The pickup coil connector is behind the left-hand frame cover.

4. Test the neutral switch as described in Chapter Nine. Note the following:

a. If the neutral switch is faulty, replace it and retest.

b. If the neutral switch is good, check for an open circuit between the neutral switch and the ignition control module.

5. Test the sidestand switch as described in Chapter Nine. Note the following:

a. If the sidestand switch is faulty, replace it and retest.

b. If the sidestand switch is good, check for an open circuit between the sidestand switch and the ignition control module.

6. When finished, install all previously removed parts.

No Spark at One Spark Plug

If there is no spark at one spark plug, replace the plug and repeat the spark test. If the new plug will not fire, perform the following.

1. Measure the ignition coil's secondary resistance as described in Chapter Nine. Note the following:

a. If the test results are incorrect, perform Step 2.

b. If the test results are correct, repeat the spark test by switching the ignition coils. If you now have a spark, the original coil is faulty and should be replaced.

2. Remove the spark plug wire from the ignition coil and repeat the test made in Step 1. Note the following:

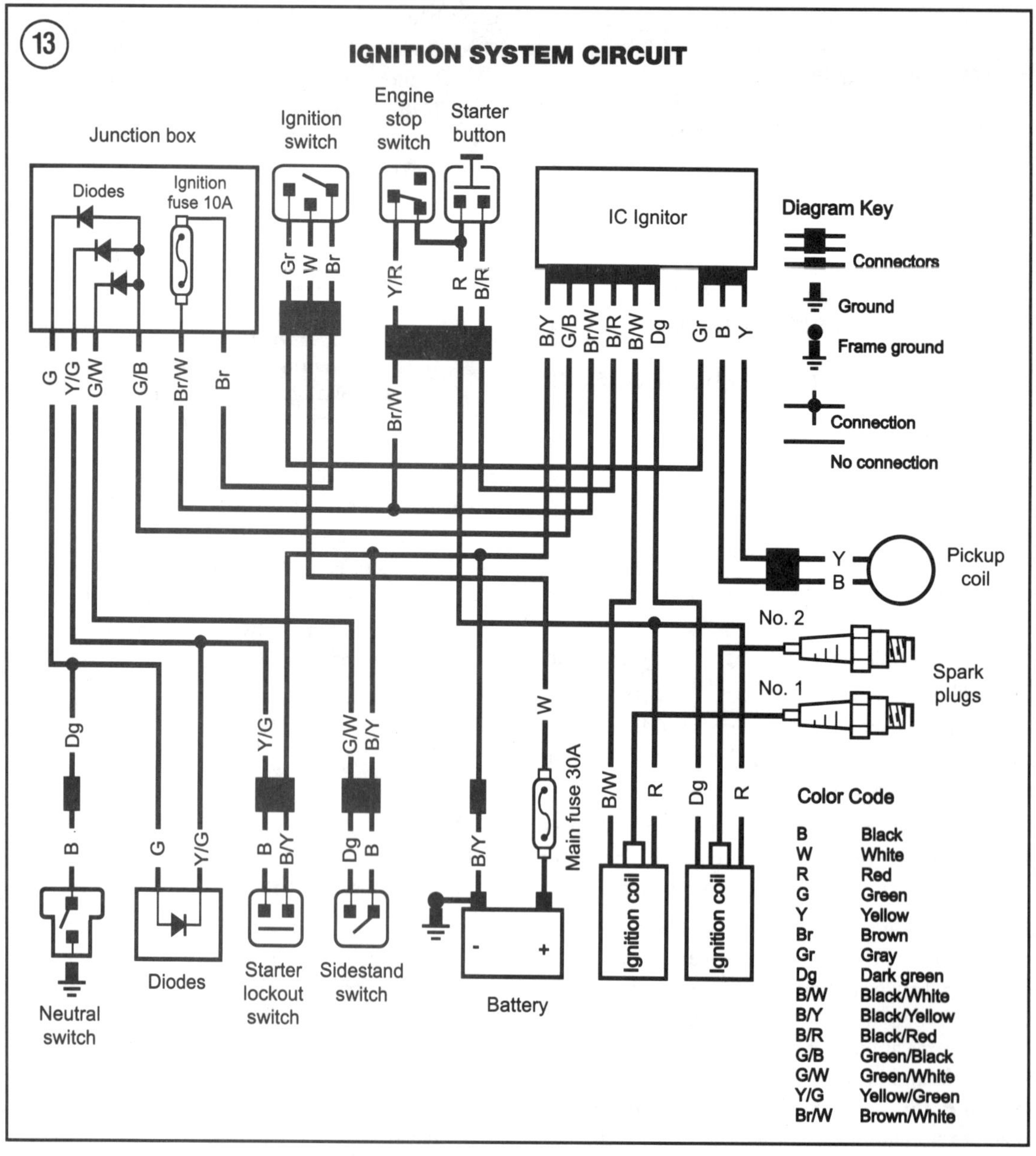

a. If the test results are still incorrect, the ignition coil is faulty and should be replaced.
b. If the test results are now correct, check for poor contact between the spark plug wire and coil. If the connection is in good condition, the spark plug wire is faulty and should be replaced.

Sidestand Switch Inoperative

When the engine is running and the transmission is in NEUTRAL, it should continue to run when the sidestand is moved down.

When the engine is running and the transmission is in gear, the engine should stop when the sidestand is moved down.

Check the sidestand switch continuity as described in Chapter Nine. Note the following:

1. If there is no continuity, the sidestand switch is faulty; replace the switch and retest.
2. If there is continuity, check for an open circuit in the ungrounded wire (brown wire on U.S. and Canadian models or black/yellow wire, on all other models) or for dirty or loose-fitting sidestand switch connector terminals.

STARTER SYSTEM TROUBLESHOOTING

The starting system (**Figure 14**) consists of the starter motor, starter gears, starter relay, starter button, ignition switch, starter lockout switch (clutch switch), neutral switch, main and auxiliary fuses and the battery.

When the starter button is pressed, it allows current flow through the solenoid coil. The coil contacts close, allowing electricity to flow from the battery to the starter motor.

CAUTION

Do not operate the starter for more than 5 seconds at a time. Let it rest approximately 10 seconds, then use it again.

The starter should turn when the starter button is depressed if the transmission is in neutral and the clutch disengaged. If the starter does not operate properly, perform the following test procedure. Starter troubleshooting is grouped under the following:

1. Starter motor does not turn.
2. Starter motor turns slowly.
3. Starter motor turns but the engine does not.
4. Starter motor and engine turn but the engine does not start.
5. Check the battery to make sure it is fully charged and in good condition. Refer to Chapter Three for battery service.
6. Check the starter electrical cables for loose or damaged connections.
7. Check the battery electrical cables for loose or damaged connections.
8. If the starter does not operate correctly after making these checks, perform the test procedure that best describes the starting problem.

2

Starter Motor Does Not Turn

1. Remove the seat as described in Chapter Fourteen to expose the starter relay. (**Figure 15**).
2. Check the starter relay connector for dirty or loose-fitting terminals. Clean and repair as required.
3. Check the starter relay. Turn the ignition switch on and depress the starter switch button. When the starter button is depressed, the starter relay should click once. Note the following:
   a. If the relay clicks, perform Step 4.
   b. If the relay does not click, perform Step 5.

CAUTION

Because of the large amount of current that will flow from the battery to the starter in Step 4, use a large cable to make the connection.

4. Remove the starter from the motorcycle as described in Chapter Nine. Using an auxiliary battery, apply battery voltage directly to the starter. The starter should turn when battery voltage is directly applied. Note the following:
   a. If the starter motor does not run, disassemble and inspect the starter motor as described in Chapter Nine. Test the starter components and replace worn or damaged parts as required.
   b. If the starter motor now runs, check for loose or damaged starter cables. If the cables are in good condition, check the starter relay as described in Chapter Nine. Replace the starter relay if necessary.
5. Remove the starter relay (**Figure 15**). Note the following:
   a. Connect the positive (+) lead of a fully charged 12-volt battery to the starter relay yellow/red

wire terminal and the battery negative wire to the black/yellow wire terminal.

b. Connect an ohmmeter between the battery lead terminal and the starter motor lead terminal of the starter relay.

c. There should be continuity when the battery leads are connected to the starter relay and no continuity when they are disconnected.

6. If continuity is present during each test, perform Step 7. If there is no continuity in one or more tests, check for dirty or loose-fitting terminals; clean and repair as required and retest. Then check for a short circuit in the wiring. If the connectors and wiring are good, test the following components as described in Chapter Nine:

a. Starter lockout switch.

b. Starter lockout switch diode.

c. Neutral switch.

d. Sidestand switch.

7. Pull the rubber cover away from the starter relay electrical connector to expose the wire terminals in the connector (**Figure 15**). Then connect a voltmeter

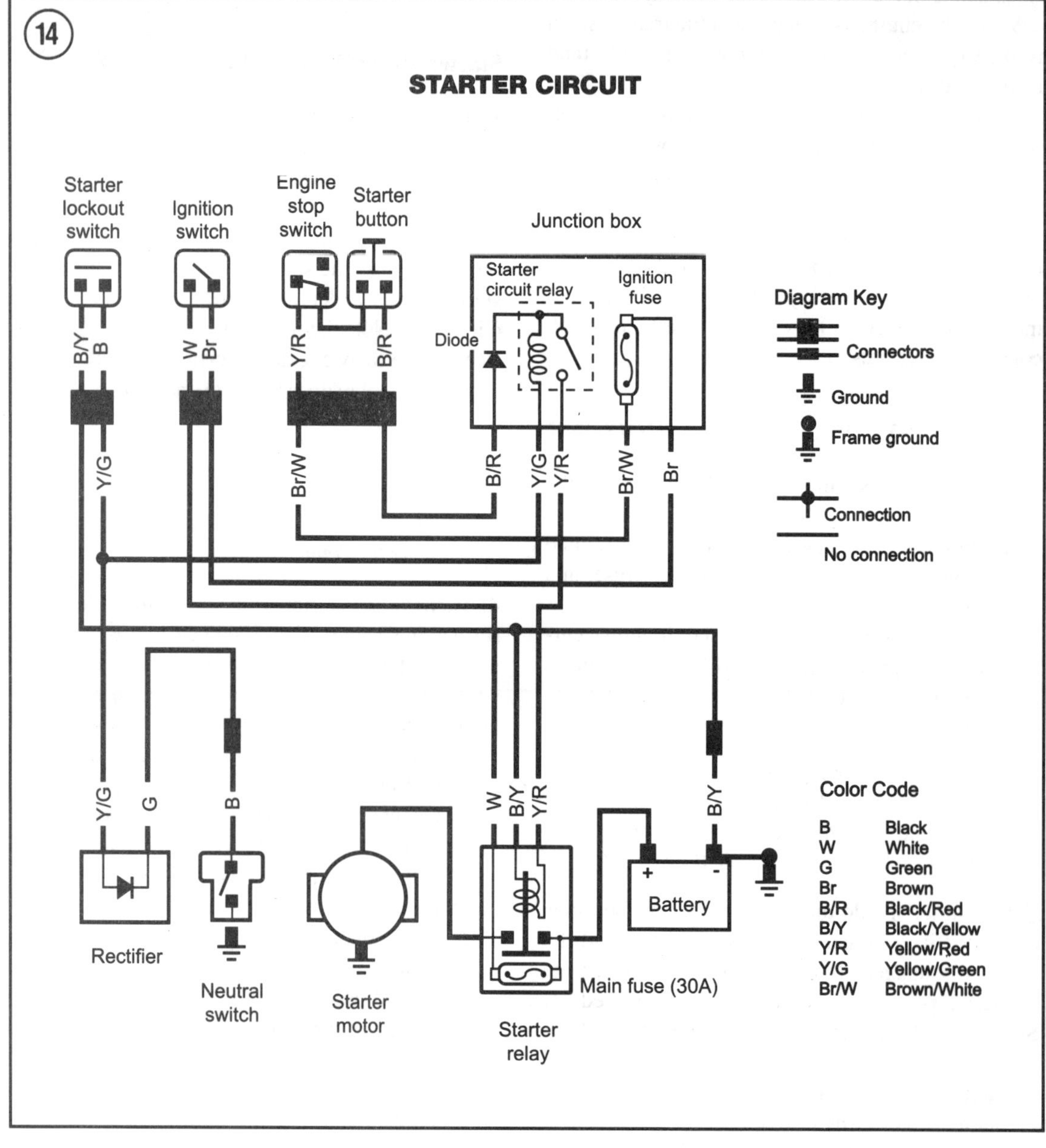

between the starter relay connector yellow/red terminal (+) and ground (–). Turn the ignition switch to ON and the engine stop switch to RUN. Press the starter button and read the voltage indicated on the voltmeter. It should be battery voltage. Turn the ignition switch off and note the following:

a. If battery voltage is shown, perform Step 8.
b. If no voltage is shown, check for a blown main or subfuse as described in Chapter Nine. If the fuses are good, check for an open circuit in the wiring harness or for dirty or loose-fitting terminals. If the wiring and connectors are in good condition, check for a faulty ignition and/or starter switch as described in Chapter Nine.

8. Test the starter relay as described in Chapter Nine. Note the following:

a. If the starter relay is in good condition, check for dirty or loose-fitting terminals in its connector block.
b. If the starter relay is faulty, replace it and retest.

Starter Motor Turns Slowly

If the starter motor turns slowly and all engine components and systems are normal, perform the following:

1. Test the battery as described in Chapter Three.
2. Check for the following:
   a. Loose or corroded battery terminals.
   b. Loose or corroded battery ground cable.
   c. Loose starter motor cable.
3. Remove, disassemble and bench test the starter as described in Chapter Nine.
4. Check the starter for binding during operation. Disassemble the starter and check the armature shaft for bending or damage. Also check the starter clutch as described in Chapter Five.

Starter Motor Turns but the Engine Does Not

If the starter motor turns but the engine does not, perform the following:

1. If the starter motor is running backward and the starter was just reassembled or if the starter motor cables were disconnected and then reconnected to the starter:
   a. The starter motor is reassembled incorrectly.
   b. The starter motor cables are incorrectly installed.
2. Check for a damaged starter clutch (Chapter Five).
3. Check for a damaged or faulty starter pinion gear (Chapter Five).
4. Check for damaged starter clutch and reduction gears (Chapter Five).

Starter Relay Clicks but Engine Does Not Turn

1. Excessive reduction gear friction.
2. Crankshaft cannot turn because of mechanical failure.

Starter Motor Inoperative with Transmission in Gear, Clutch Lever Pulled In and Sidestand Up

1. Test the starter lockout switch (clutch switch) as described in Chapter Nine. Note the following:
   a. Starter lockout switch functions correctly, perform Step 2.
   b. Starter lockout switch faulty, replace the switch and retest.
2. Test the sidestand switch as described in Chapter Nine. Note the following:
   a. Sidestand switch functions correctly, perform Step 3.
   b. Sidestand switch faulty, replace the switch and retest.
3. Check for an open circuit in the wiring harness. Check for loose or damaged electrical connector.

CARBURETOR TROUBLESHOOTING

The following lists isolate basic carburetor problems under specific complaints.

Engine Will Not Start

If the engine will not start and the electrical and mechanical systems are working correctly, check the following:

1. If there is no fuel going to the carburetors, note the following:
   a. Plugged fuel tank breather cap hole.
   b. Plugged fuel tank-to-carburetor tube.
   c. Plugged fuel shutoff valve screen.
   d. Incorrect float adjustment.
   e. Stuck or clogged float valve in carburetor.
2. If the engine is flooded (too much fuel), note the following:
   a. Flooded carburetor. Float valve in carburetor stuck open.
   b. Plugged air filter element.
3. A faulty emission control system (if equipped) can cause fuel problems. Note the following:
   a. Faulty purge control valve (PCV).
   b. Faulty air injection control valve (AICV).
   c. Loose, disconnected or plugged emission control system hoses.
4. If you have not located the problem in Steps 1-3, check for the following:
   a. Contaminated or deteriorated fuel.
   b. Intake manifold air leak.
   c. Plugged pilot or choke circuit.

Engine Starts but Idles and Runs Poorly or Stalls Frequently

An engine that idles roughly or stalls may have one or more of the following problems:

1. Plugged air cleaner.
2. Contaminated fuel.
3. Incorrect pilot screw adjustment.
4. Incorrect idle speed.
5. Bystarter or slow circuit clogged.
6. Loose, disconnected or damaged fuel and emission control vacuum hoses.
7. Intake air leak.
8. Lean fuel mixture.
9. Rich fuel mixture.

Incorrect Fast Idle Speed

An excessive fast idle speed can be due to one of the following problems:

1. Idle adjust screw incorrectly set.
2. Incorrect choke cable free play.

Poor Fuel Economy and Engine Performance

Poor fuel economy and engine performance can be caused by infrequent engine tune-ups. Check your records against the recommended tune-up intervals in Chapter Three. If your last tune-up was within the specified service interval, check for one or more of the following problems:

1. Plugged air filter.
2. Plugged fuel system.
3. Loose, disconnected or damaged fuel and emission control vacuum hoses.

Rich Fuel Mixture

A rich carburetor fuel mixture can be caused by one or more of the following conditions:

1. Plugged or dirty air filter.
2. Worn or damaged fuel valve and seat.
3. Plugged air jets.
4. Incorrect float level (too high).
5. Flooded carburetor.

Lean Fuel Mixture

A lean carburetor fuel mixture can be caused by one or more of the following conditions:

1. Plugged carburetor air vent hole.
2. Plugged fuel filter.
3. Restricted fuel line.
4. Intake air leak.
5. Incorrect float level (too low).
6. Worn or damaged float valve.
7. Faulty throttle valve.
8. Faulty vacuum piston.

Engine Backfires

1. Lean fuel mixture.
2. Incorrect carburetor adjustment.

Engine Misfires During Acceleration

If there is a pause before the engine responds to the throttle, the engine may be misfiring. An engine misfire can occur when starting from a stop or at any speed. An engine misfire may be due to one of the following:

1. Lean fuel mixture.
2. Faulty ignition coil secondary wires. Check for cracking, hardening or bad connections.
3. Faulty vacuum hoses. Check for kinks, splits or bad connections.
4. Vacuum leak at the carburetor and/or intake manifold(s).
5. Fouled spark plug(s).
6. Low engine compression, especially at one cylinder only. Check engine compression as described in Chapter Three. Low compression can be caused by worn engine components.

EXCESSIVE VIBRATION

Usually this is caused by loose engine mounting hardware. If the mounting hardware is in good condition, vibration can be difficult to find without disassembling the engine.

FRONT SUSPENSION AND STEERING

Poor handling may be caused by improper tire pressure, a damaged frame or front steering components, a worn front fork assembly, worn wheel bearings or dragging brakes.

Bike Steers to One Side

1. Bent axle.
2. Bent frame.
3. Worn or damaged front wheel bearings.
4. Worn or damaged swing arm pivot bearings.
5. Damaged steering head bearings.
6. Uneven front fork adjustment.
7. Incorrectly installed wheels.

Suspension Noise

1. Loose mounting fasteners.
2. Damaged fork(s) or rear shock absorber.
3. Incorrect front fork oil.

Wobble/Vibration

1. Loose front or rear axle.
2. Loose or damaged wheel bearing(s).
3. Damaged wheel rim(s).
4. Damaged tire(s).
5. Loose swing arm pivot bolt.
6. Unbalanced tire and wheel.

Hard Suspension (Front Forks)

1. Insufficient tire pressure.
2. Damaged steering head bearings.
3. Incorrect steering head bearing adjustment.
4. Bent fork tubes.
5. Binding slider.
6. Incorrect fork oil or excessive fork oil level.
7. Plugged fork oil hydraulic passage.

Hard Suspension (Rear Shock Absorbers)

1. Excessive tire pressure.
2. Bent damper rod.
3. Incorrect shock adjustment.
4. Damaged shock absorber bushing(s).
5. Damaged shock absorber bearing.
6. Damaged swing arm pivot bearing.

Soft Suspension (Front Forks)

1. Insufficient tire pressure.
2. Insufficient fork oil level or fluid capacity.
3. Incorrect oil viscosity.
4. Weak or damaged fork springs.

Soft Suspension (Rear Shock Absorbers)

1. Insufficient tire pressure.
2. Weak or damaged shock absorber spring.
3. Damaged shock absorber.
4. Incorrect shock absorber adjustment.
5. Leaking damper unit.

BRAKE PROBLEMS

Sticking disc brakes may be caused by a stuck piston(s) in a caliper assembly or a warped pad shim(s) or improper rear brake adjustment.

Brake Drag

1. Plugged or restricted brake hydraulic system.
2. Sticking caliper pistons.
3. Sticking master cylinder piston.
4. Incorrectly installed brake caliper.
5. Warped brake disc.
6. Sticking caliper side slide pin.
7. Incorrect wheel alignment.
8. Worn or weak drum return springs.
9. Sticking pivot and cam bushings.

Brakes Grab

1. Contaminated brake pads or linings.
2. Incorrect wheel alignment.
3. Warped brake disc or out-of-round brake drum.
4. Glazed pads or linings.

Brake Squeal or Chatter

1. Contaminated brake pads or linings.
2. Incorrectly installed brake caliper.
3. Warped brake disc.
4. Incorrect wheel alignment.
5. Antirattle spring missing in caliper.

Soft or Spongy Front Brake Lever

1. Low brake fluid level.
2. Air in brake hydraulic system.
3. Leaking brake hydraulic system.

Hard Front Brake Lever Operation

1. Plugged brake hydraulic system.
2. Sticking caliper pistons.
3. Sticking master cylinder piston.
4. Glazed or worn brake pads.

CHAPTER THREE

3

LUBRICATION, MAINTENANCE AND TUNE-UP

A motorcycle, even in normal use, is subjected to tremendous heat, stress and vibration. When neglected, any bike becomes unreliable and actually dangerous to ride.

To gain the utmost in safety, performance and useful life from your Kawasaki Vulcan, it is necessary to make periodic inspections and adjustments. Frequently, minor problems are found during these inspections that are simple and inexpensive to correct. If they are not found and corrected at this time, they could lead to major and more expensive problems later on.

Start out by doing simple tune-up, lubrication and maintenance, then perform more involved jobs as you become more acquainted with the bike.

Table 1 is a suggested factory maintenance schedule. **Tables 1-6** are located at the end of this chapter.

NOTE
Where differences occur relating to the United Kingdom (U.K.) models, they are identified. If there is no (U.K.) designation relating to a procedure, photo or illustration, it is identical to the United States (U.S.) models.

ROUTINE INSPECTION

Engine Oil Level

Refer to *Engine Oil Level Check* in this chapter.

Fuel

All Vulcan engines are designed to use gasoline that has an antiknock index number (RON+MON)/2 of 87 or higher or gasoline with a research octane number (RON) of 91 or higher. The pump octane number is normally displayed at service station fuel pumps. Using a gasoline with a lower octane number can cause detonation and engine damage.

When filling the fuel tank, note the following:

NOTE
On California models, never overfill the fuel tank. If the fuel tank is overfilled, heat may cause the fuel to expand and the fuel will overflow into the evaporative emission control system resulting in hard starting and engine hesitation.

1. When filling the tank, do not overfill it. Fuel expands in the tank due to engine heat or heating by the sun. Stop adding fuel when the fuel level reaches the bottom of the filler tube inside the fuel tank.

2. To help meet clean air standards in some areas of the United States and Canada, oxygenated fuels are being used. Oxygenated fuels are conventional gasolines that are blended with an alcohol or ether compound. If using an oxygenated fuel, make sure that it meets the minimum octane rating as previously specified.

3. Because oxygenated fuel can damage plastic and paint, avoid spilling fuel onto the fuel tank during fuel stops.

4. An ethanol (ethyl or grain alcohol) gasoline that contains more than 10% ethanol by volume may cause engine starting and performance related problems.

5. Gasoline that contains more than 5% methanol by volume may cause engine starting and performance related problems. Gasoline that contains methanol must have corrosion inhibitors to protect the metal, plastic and rubber parts in the fuel system from damage.

Coolant Level

Check the coolant level in the reservoir only when the engine is COOL, preferably prior to the first ride of the day.

WARNING

Do not remove the radiator cap when the engine is HOT. The coolant is under pressure and scalding and severe burns could result.

1. Securely support the bike in an upright position on a level surface.

2. Check the coolant level gauge on the side of the reservoir. The coolant level should be between the LOW level line and the FULL level line (A, **Figure 1**) on the side of the reservoir. If necessary, add coolant to the reservoir.

NOTE

If the coolant level is very low, there may be a leak in the cooling system. If this condition exists, check the system as described in this chapter.

NOTE

Never add pure water to the system as this will dilute the coolant-to-water mixture to an unsafe level.

3. Unscrew the cap (B, **Figure 1**) from the reservoir and insert a long funnel into the radiator filler neck. Add a 50:50 mixture of distilled water and antifreeze to bring the level to the FULL level line (A, **Figure 1**) on the tank.

4. Remove the funnel, and install the cap. Tighten the cap securely.

General Inspection

1. Quickly inspect the engine for oil, fuel or coolant leakage.

2. Check the tires for embedded stones. Pry them out with a suitable tool.

3. Make sure all lights work.

Tire Pressure

Check tire pressure with the tires cold. Correct tire pressure varies with the load you are carrying or if you have a passenger. See **Table 2**.

Brake Operation

Make sure the brakes operate with full hydraulic (front) or mechanical (rear) advantage. Check the front brake fluid level as described under *Disc Brake Fluid Level Inspection* in this chapter. Makes sure there is no brake fluid leakage from the front master cylinder, front calipers or brake lines.

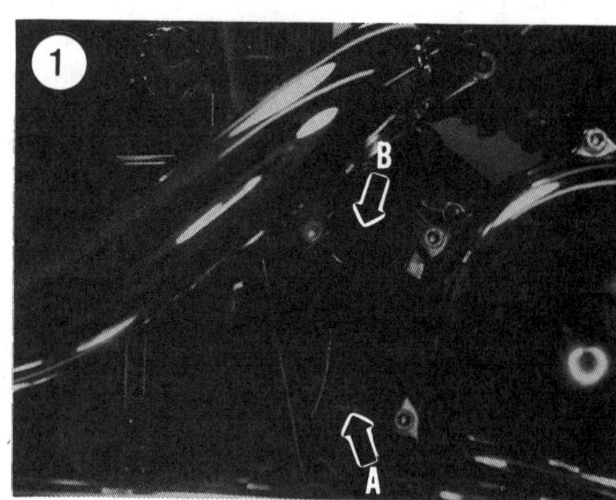

Throttle

With the brake ON, the transmission in NEUTRAL and the engine idling, sit on the bike and move the handlebars from side to side. The engine idle speed should not change (increase nor decrease) as the handlebars are moved. Make sure the throttle moves smoothly in all steering positions. Shut off the engine.

Engine Stop Switch

The engine stop switch (**Figure 2**) is designed primarily as an emergency switch. It is part of the right-hand switch assembly next to the throttle housing. The engine stop switch has two operating positions: OFF and RUN. When the switch is in the OFF position, the engine will not start or run. In the RUN position, the engine should start and run with the ignition switch on. If you move the switch to OFF with the engine idling, the engine should turn off.

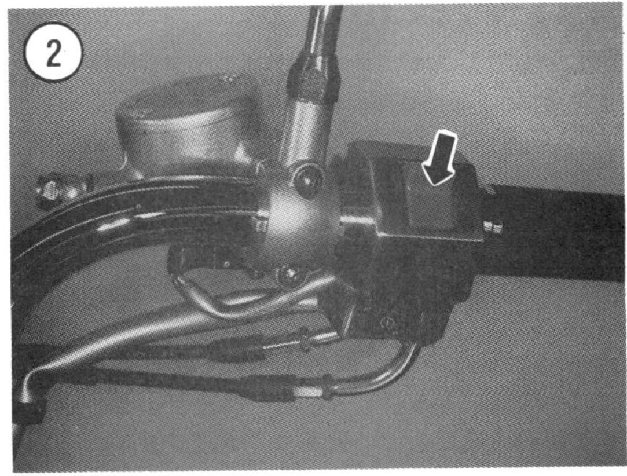

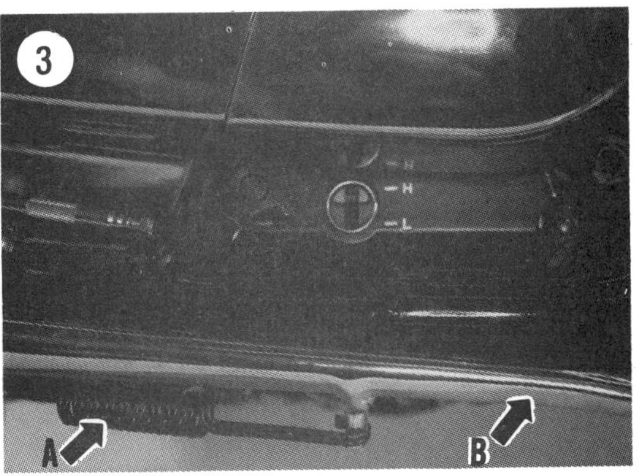

Sidestand and Switch Inspection

1. Place the bike on level ground. Use wooden blocks or a scissors jack to securely support it so the rear wheel is off the ground.
2. Check the sidestand spring (A, **Figure 3**). Make sure the spring is in good condition and has not lost tension.
3. Swing the sidestand (B, **Figure 3**) down and up a few times. The sidestand should swing smoothly and the spring should provide proper tension in the raised position.
4. While sitting on the motorcycle, shift the transmission into NEUTRAL and move the sidestand up.
5. Start the engine and allow it to warm up. Then pull in the clutch lever and shift the transmission into gear.
6. Lower the sidestand with your foot. The engine should stop as the sidestand is lowered.
7. If the engine does not stop when you lower the sidestand, inspect the sidestand switch as described in Chapter Nine.

Crankcase Breather Hose

Inspect the hose for cracks and deterioration and make sure that the hose clamps are tight.

Evaporative Emission Control System (California Models)

Inspect the hoses to make sure they are not kinked or cracked and that they are securely connected to their respective parts.

Lights and Horn

With the engine running, check the following.

1. Pull the front brake lever on and check that the brake light comes on.
2. Push the rear brake pedal down and check that the brake light comes on soon after you begin depressing the pedal. If necessary, adjust the brake light switch as described in Chapter Nine.

3A. On U.S., Canadian and Australian models, make sure the headlight and taillight are on when the engine is running.

3B. On units other than U.S., Canadian or Australian models, move the headlight switch between ON and

OFF and make sure the headlight and taillights operate.

4. Move the dimmer switch between the HI and LO positions and make sure that both headlight elements are working in the headlight.

5. Push the turn signal switch to the left and right positions and check that all four turn signals are working.

6. Push the horn button and make sure that the horn blows loudly.

7. If the horn or any of the lights fail to operate properly, refer to Chapter Nine.

PRE-RIDE INSPECTION

Perform the following inspection prior to the first ride of the day.

1. Inspect all fuel lines and fittings for leaks.
2. Make sure the fuel tank is full of fresh gasoline.
3. Make sure the engine oil level is correct.
4. Make sure the drive chain is properly lubricated
5. Check the operation of the front brake. Add hydraulic fluid to the front brake master cylinder if necessary.
6. Check the operation of the rear brake. Adjust the rear brake pedal free play as described in this chapter if necessary.
7. Check the operation of the clutch. Adjust the clutch free play as described in this chapter if necessary.
8. Check the throttle operation. Make sure it operates properly with no binding.
9. Inspect the front and rear suspension. Make sure they have a good solid feel with no looseness.
10. Check tire pressure. Refer to **Table 2**.
11. Check the exhaust system for damage.
12. Check the tightness of all fasteners, especially engine mounting hardware.

SERVICE INTERVALS

The factory-recommended maintenance schedule is shown in **Table 1**. Strict adherence to these recommendations will help ensure long service from your Kawasaki. If the bike is run in an area of high humidity, the lubrication services must be done more frequently to prevent possible rust damage.

For convenience, most of the services shown in these tables are described in this chapter. However, those procedures that require more than minor disassembly or adjustment are covered in the appropriate chapter. The *Table of Contents* and *Index* can help you locate a particular service procedure.

TIRES AND WHEELS

Tire Pressure

Tire pressure should be checked and adjusted to maintain the tire profile, good traction and handling and to get the maximum life out of the tire. A simple, accurate gauge (**Figure 4**) can be purchased for a few dollars and should be carried in your motorcycle tool kit. Tire pressure should be checked when the tires are cold. The appropriate tire pressures are shown in **Table 2**.

NOTE

*After checking and adjusting the air pressure, make sure to install the valve stem cap (**Figure 5**). The cap prevents small pebbles and dirt from collecting in the valve stem; this could allow air leakage or result in incorrect tire pressure readings.*

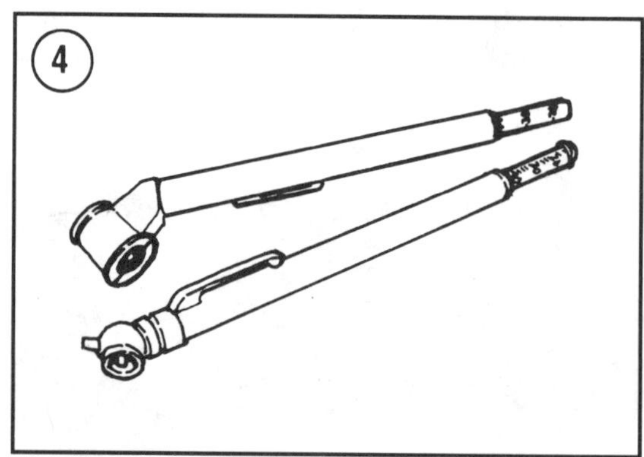

NOTE

A loss of air pressure may be due to a loose or damaged valve core. Put a few drops of water on the top of the valve core. If the water bubbles, tighten the valve core and recheck. If air still leaks from the valve after tightening it, replace the valve core.

Tire Inspection

The tires take a lot of punishment so inspect them periodically for excessive wear. Inspect the tires for the following:

1. Deep cuts and imbedded objects. If you find a nail or other object in a tire, mark its location with a light crayon prior to removing it. This will help you locate the hole for repair. Refer to Chapter Eleven for tire changing and repair information.
2. Flat spots.
3. Cracks.
4. Separating plies.
5. Sidewall damage.

Tire Wear Analysis

Analyze any abnormal tire wear to determine its cause. The most common cause of abnormal tire wear is incorrect tire pressure (**Figure 6**). Under-inflation will cause excessive tire temperature, hard or imprecise steering and excessive wear on both edges of the tire contact patch. Over-inflation will cause a harsh ride and excessive wear in the center of the tire contact patch. Other causes of abnormal tire wear are:

1. Overloading.

2. Incorrect balance—be sure to balance the tire/wheel assembly when a new tire or tube is installed or if the tire is removed/installed on the wheel.

Tread Depth

Check local traffic regulations concerning minimum tread depth. Measure the tread depth at the center of tire and to the center of the tire tread (**Figure 7**) using a tread depth gauge (**Figure 8**) or a small ruler. Kawasaki recommends replacing original equipment tires when the tread depth reaches the wear limit. Refer to the specifications in **Table 2**.

WARNING

If you operate the bike at speeds over 130 km/h (80 mph), replace the original equipment rear tire when the tread depth is 3.0 mm (4/32 in.) or less.

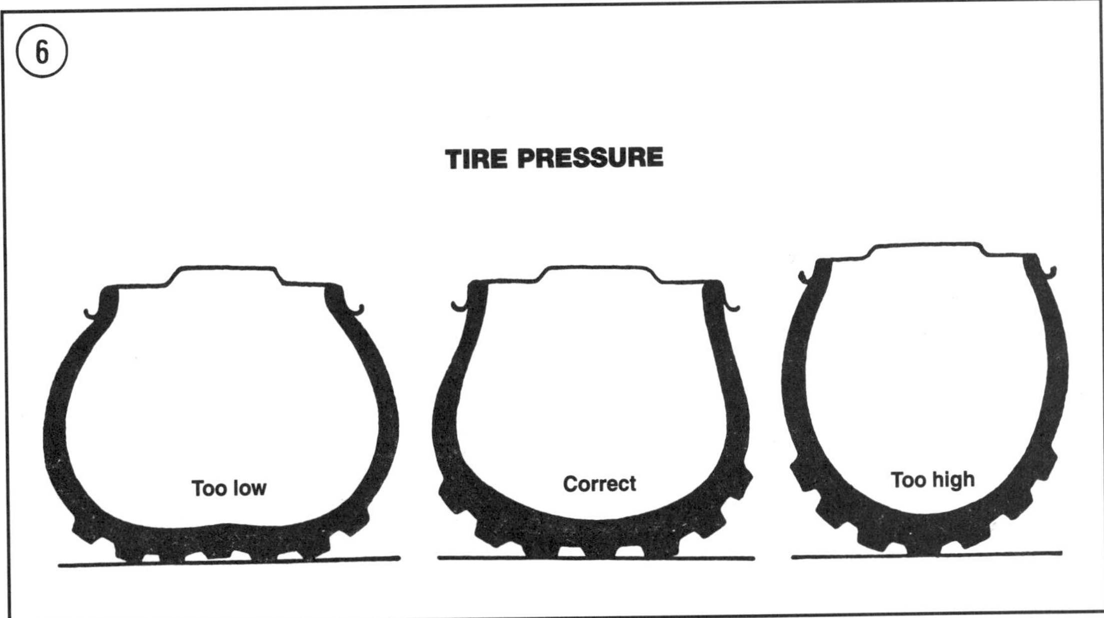

Wheel Spoke Tension

CAUTION

During the break-in period for a new or respoked wheel, check the spoke tension at 15 minute intervals during the first hour of riding. Most spoke seating takes place during the initial use.

Tap each spoke with a wrench and listen to the sound it makes. The higher the pitch, the tighter the spoke; the lower the pitch, the looser the spoke. A *ping* is good. A *klunk* says the spoke is too loose.

If one or more spokes are loose, tighten them as described in Chapter Eleven.

NOTE

Most spokes loosen as a group rather than individually. Excessively loose spokes should be tightened carefully. Burying just a few spokes tightly into the rim will put improper pressure across the wheel. Never tighten a spoke so much that the spoke wrench rounds off the nipple flats.

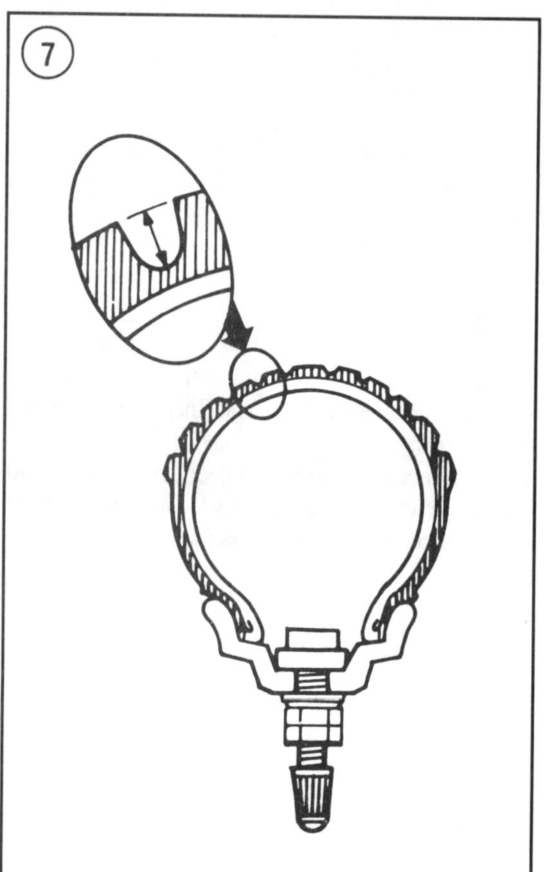

Rim Inspection

Frequently inspect the wheel rims. If a rim is damaged, the wheel assembly might also be misaligned. Improper wheel alignment can cause severe vibration and result in an unsafe riding condition. If the rim portion of an alloy wheel is damaged, the wheel must be replaced as it cannot be serviced or repaired.

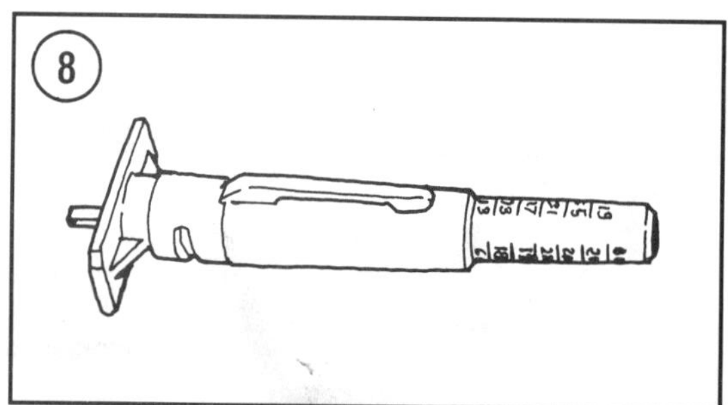

BATTERY

The battery is an important component in the electrical system. It is also the one most frequently neglected. Clean and inspect the battery at periodic intervals listed in **Table 1**. During hot weather, frequent checks are recommended.

Removal and Installation

1. Securely support the bike on level ground.
2. Remove the seat as described in Chapter Fourteen.
3. Remove the bolts securing the battery bracket (A, **Figure 9**). Remove the bracket and protective pad.

4. Disconnect the battery negative (–) cable (B, **Figure 9**), then disconnect the battery positive (+) cable (C, **Figure 9**).
5. Remove the battery by carefully pulling it straight up and out of the battery box.
6. Set the battery on some newspapers or shop cloths to protect the workbench surface.

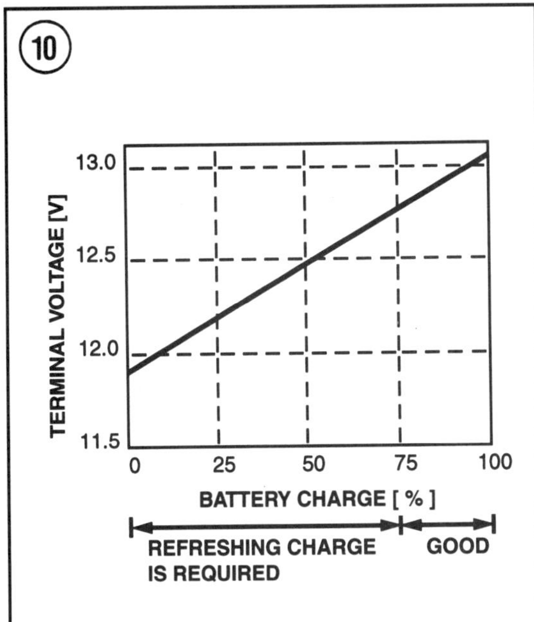

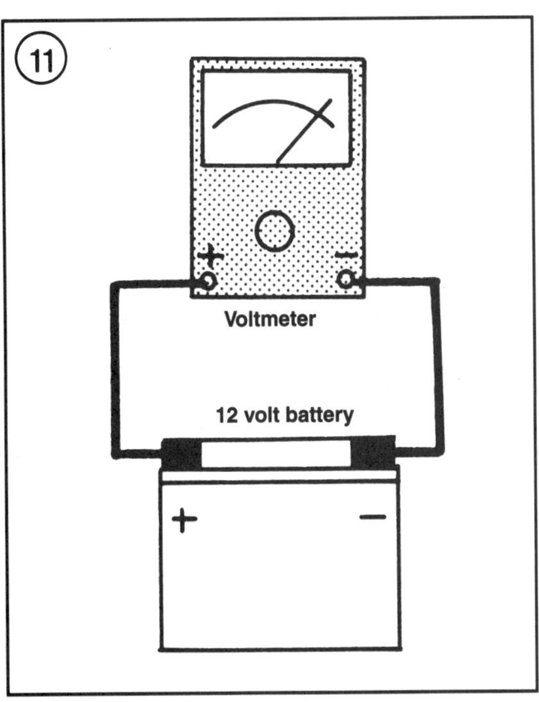

7. Install the battery by reversing these removal steps.

Inspection and Testing

The battery used in the Vulcan is a maintenance free battery. Check the battery state of charge by measuring terminal voltage and comparing the reading to the chart in **Figure 10**.

The battery does not require periodic electrolyte inspection or refilling. In fact, the electrolyte level cannot be serviced. Never attempt to remove the sealing bar from the top of the battery.

WARNING
Always wear safety glasses whenever you service the battery. Even though this is a sealed battery, electrolyte could leak from a cracked battery case. Protect your eyes, skin and clothing. Electrolyte is corrosive and can cause severe burns as well as permanent injury. If electrolyte gets into your eyes, flush your eyes thoroughly with clean, running water, and get immediate medical attention.

1. Remove the battery from the motorcycle as described in this chapter. Do not clean the battery while it is mounted in the bike.
2. Clean the battery case with warm water and household dish washing detergent. Rinse it thoroughly with clean water.
3. Inspect the physical condition of the battery. Look for bulges, corrosion buildup, cracks in the case or leaking electrolyte.
4. Clean the battery terminals, bolts and cable ends with sandpaper and then rinse with water.
5. Check the cables for chafing, deterioration or other damage.
6. Check the state of charge by connecting a voltmeter between the battery negative and positive leads (**Figure 11**).
   a. If the battery voltage is greater than 12.8 volts (at 20° C [68° F]) the battery is fully charged.
   b. If the battery voltage is less than 12.6 volts (at 20° C [68° F]) the battery is undercharged.

Charging

WARNING
During the charging process, a small amount of highly explosive hydrogen

gas is released from the battery. The battery should be charged only in a well-ventilated area away from any open flames (including pilot lights on home gas appliances). Do not allow any smoking in the area. Never check the charge by arcing (connecting pliers or other metal objects) across the terminals; the resulting spark can ignite the hydrogen gas.

CAUTION
*Do **NOT** use an automotive-type battery charger; you will run the risk of overheating the battery and causing internal plate damage. Use only a small trickle charger designed specifically for use on motorcycle batteries.*

CAUTION
Always disconnect the battery cables from the battery before charging. The charger could destroy the voltage regulator/rectifier if the cables are left connected.

1. Remove the battery from the bike as described in this chapter.
2. Connect the positive (+) charger lead to the positive (+) battery terminal and the negative (–) charger lead to the negative (–) battery terminal.
3. Set the charger to 12 volts. If the output of the charger is variable, it is best to select a low setting. See **Table 3** for the recommended charge rate and charge time.
4. Turn the charger ON.
5. After the battery has charged for the specified amount of time, turn the charger off and disconnect the leads.
6. Check the charge by connecting a voltmeter between the battery negative and positive terminals. A fully charged battery will read 13.0-13.2 volts. If the voltage is 12.6 or less, the battery is undercharged.
7. If the battery remains stable at the specified voltage for one hour, the battery is charged.
8. Clean the battery terminals and the surrounding case. Coat the terminals with a thin layer of dielectric grease to retard corrosion and decomposition of the battery terminals.
9. To ensure good electrical contact, the cables must be clean and tight on the battery's terminals. Refer to *Battery Electrical Cable Connectors* in this chapter.
10. Reinstall the battery as described in this chapter.

NEW BATTERY INSTALLATION

When replacing a maintenance free battery, be sure to install another maintenance free battery. Also be sure the battery is charged completely before installing it. Failure to do so will reduce the life of the battery.

NOTE
***Recycle your old battery**. When you replace the old battery, be sure to turn in the old battery at that time. The lead plates and the plastic case can be recycled. Most motorcycle dealerships will accept your old battery in trade when you purchase a new one. If they will not, many automotive supply stores certainly will. Never place an old battery in your household trash. It is illegal in most states to place any acid or lead (heavy metal) contents in landfills.*

BATTERY ELECTRICAL CABLE CONNECTORS

To ensure good electrical contact between the battery and the electrical cables, the cables must be clean and free of corrosion.

1. If the electrical cable terminals are badly corroded, disconnect them from the bike's electrical system.
2. Thoroughly clean each connector with a wire brush and then with a water and baking soda solution. Rinse thoroughly with clean water and wipe dry with a clean cloth.

3. After cleaning, apply a thin layer of dielectric grease to the battery terminals before reattaching the cables.
4. After connecting the electrical cables, apply a light coating of dielectric grease to the electrical terminals of the battery to retard corrosion and decomposition of the terminals.

PERIODIC LUBRICATION

Oil

Oil is graded according to its viscosity, which is an indication of how thick it is. The Society of Automotive Engineers (SAE) distinguishes oil viscosity by numbers. Thick oils have higher viscosity numbers than thin oils. For example, an SAE 5 oil is a thin oil while an SAE 90 oil is thick. If the oil is tested in cold weather it is denoted with a W after the number as SAE 10W.

Grease

A good-quality grease (preferably waterproof) should be used whenever grease is recommended. In a pinch, though, the wrong lubricant is better than none at all.

Engine Oil Level Check and Adding Oil

Check the engine oil level at the oil level inspection window (**Figure 12**), located below the engine sprocket cover on the left-hand side of the engine.

1. Securely support the bike on level ground.
2. Start the engine and let it idle for 1-2 minutes.

3. Shut off the engine and let the oil settle for 1-2 minutes.
4. Support the motorcycle so it is in the true vertical position. A false reading will be given if the bike is tipped to either side.
5. Look at the oil level inspection window. The oil level should be between the two lines (**Figure 12**). If the level is below the low (L) line, add the recommended engine oil to correct the oil level.
6. Remove the oil filler cap (**Figure 13**).
7. Insert a funnel into the oil filler hole and fill the engine with the correct viscosity and quantity of oil. Refer to **Table 4**.
8. Remove the funnel, install the oil filler cap and tighten it securely.
9. Repeat Steps 2-5 and recheck the oil level.

Engine Oil and Oil Filter Change

Change the engine oil and oil filter at the interval indicated in **Table 1**. This assumes that the motorcycle is operated in moderate climates. In extreme climates, change the oil and filter every 30 days. The time interval is more important than the mileage interval because acids formed by combustion blowby will contaminate the oil even if the motorcycle is not run for several months. If the motorcycle is operated under dusty conditions, the oil will get dirty more quickly and should be changed more frequently.

CAUTION

***Do not use SH rated motor oil** in this motorcycle. This type of motor oil was developed to optimize the fuel economy in automobile engines. An SH oil contains friction modifiers (not always listed on the container) that reduce internal frictional losses thus achieving a higher fuel economy rating. This type of oil will create slippage with the wet multiplate clutch assembly as well as the one-way starter clutch assembly. It may cause transmission wear and pitting due to the decreased shear stability of the oil.*

Use only a high-quality detergent motor oil with an API rating of SE, SF or SG. The API rating is printed on the label on the plastic bottle. Try to use the same brand of oil at each change. Use of oil additives is not recommended. Kawasaki recommends the use of SAE 10W-40, 10W-50, 20W-40 or 20W-50 oil viscosity under normal conditions.

To change the engine oil and filter you need the following:

a. Drain pan.
b. Funnel.
c. Box- or open-end wrench (drain plug).
d. Kawasaki oil filter wrench or equivalent.
e. Oil (refer to **Table 4** for quantity).
f. New oil filter element.

There are a number of ways to discard the old oil safely. Some service stations and oil retailers will accept your used oil for recycling. Some may even pay you for it. Never drain the oil onto the ground nor place it in your household trash.

NOTE
If you are going to recycle the oil, do not add any other type of chemical (fork oil or brake fluid) to the oil as the oil recycler will probably not accept the oil.

1. Start the engine and let it reach operating temperature; 15-20 minutes of stop-and-go riding is usually sufficient.
2. Turn the engine off. Use wooden blocks or a scissors jack to securely support the bike so it is perpendicular to the ground.
3. Place a drain pan under the engine drain plug (**Figure 14**) and remove the drain plug along with its gasket. Removing the oil filler cap will quicken the flow of oil.
4. While the oil is draining, inspect the gasket. Replace it if it is worn or damaged.
5. When the oil has completely drained from the crankcase, reinstall the engine drain plug and gasket. Torque the drain plug to the specification given in **Table 5**.
6. Move the drain pan under the left-hand rear portion of the crankcase below the oil screen drain plug.

NOTE
A spring, washer and oil screen are behind the drain plug. When the drain plug is removed, the spring and washer may come off with it. If they fall off or come out while the draining, be sure to remove them from the oil pan after the draining is complete.

WARNING
Do not try to catch the spring and washer. The HOT oil draining from the

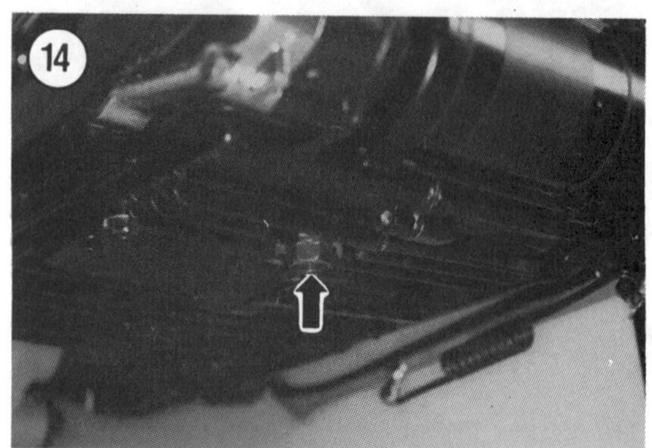
14

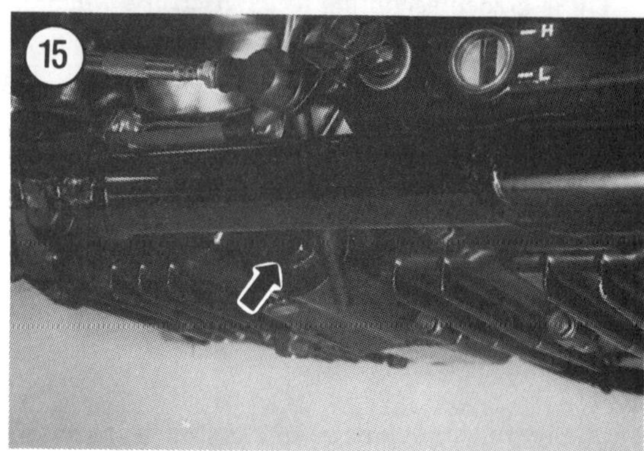

15

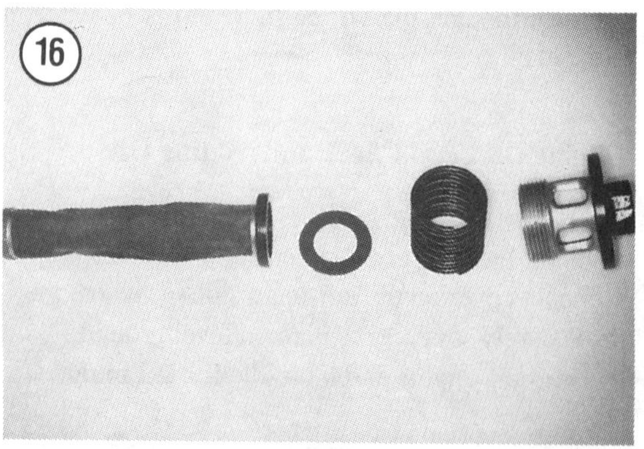
16

17

crankcase could burn your fingers. Wait until later and remove them from the drain pan.

NOTE

Steps 8-12 are shown with the engine removed from the frame for clarity. It is not necessary to remove the engine for this procedure.

7. Unscrew and remove the oil screen drain plug (**Figure 15**).

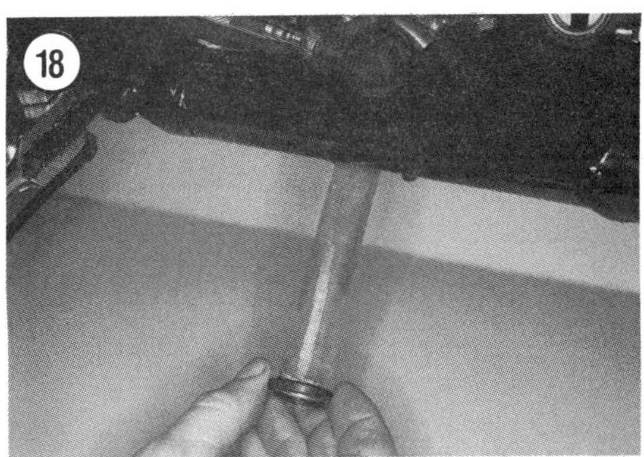

18

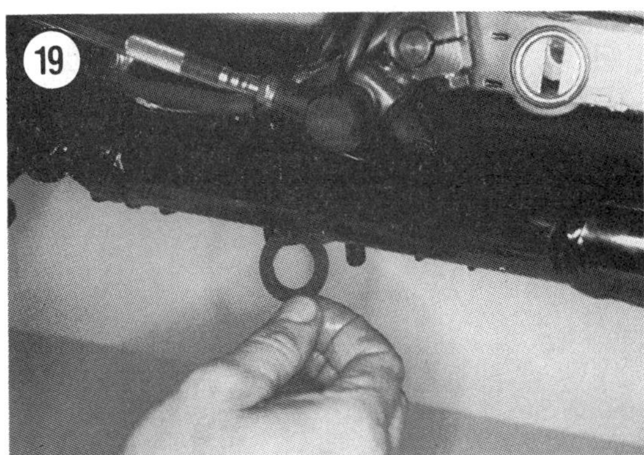

19

20

8. Remove the spring, washer and oil screen from the crankcase.

9. Thoroughly clean the oil screen in a cleaning solvent. During the cleaning process, check for any small metal particles that may indicate internal engine damage. Dry with compressed air and inspect the oil screen (**Figure 16**) for any damage, broken areas or holes. Replace the oil screen as necessary.

10. Inspect the O-ring seal (**Figure 17**) on the crankcase drain plug. Replace if its condition is in doubt.

11. Install the oil screen (**Figure 18**), washer (**Figure 19**) and spring (**Figure 20**).

12. Install the drain plug with the O-ring in place. Tighten the plug to the torque specification listed in **Table 5**.

NOTE

Before removing the oil filter, clean all road dirt and any oil residue from around it.

13. Move the drain pan under the oil filter at the front of the engine.

NOTE

*The easiest way to remove the oil filter is to use a Kawasaki cap-type oil filter wrench, part No. 57001-1249 (**Figure 21**).*

14. Use the special tool and socket wrench and unscrew the oil filter (**Figure 22**) from the engine. Place the old filter in a reclosable plastic bag and close it to prevent residual oil from draining out. Discard the used oil filter properly.

15. Clean the oil filter mating surface on the crankcase with a shop rag and cleaning solvent. Remove any sludge or road dirt. Wipe it dry with a clean, lint-free cloth.

16. Apply a light coat of clean engine oil to the O-ring seal on the new oil filter.

17. Screw on the new oil filter by hand until the O-ring seal contacts the crankcase-mating surface, then tighten to the torque specification listed in **Table 5**.

18. Insert a funnel into the oil fill hole and fill the engine with the correct quantity of oil. Refer to **Table 4**.

19. Install the oil filler cap (**Figure 13**) and tighten securely.

20. Start the engine, let it run at idle speed and check for leaks.
21. Turn the engine off and check for correct oil level as described in this chapter; adjust as necessary.

Engine Oil Pressure Test

Perform this procedure after reassembling the engine or when troubleshooting the lubrication system. You will need the following special tools, or equivalent, to perform this test:

a. Oil pressure gauge – Kawasaki part No. 57001-164
b. Oil pressure gauge adapter – Kawasaki part No. 57001-1033

1. Securely support the bike on level ground.
2. Check the engine oil as described in this chapter. It must be at the proper level.
3. Start the engine and let it reach normal operating temperature.
4. Turn off the engine, and attach a portable tachometer following its manufacturer's instructions.
5. Place an oil pan under the oil pressure switch at the front of the engine.

NOTE
The engine has been removed for clarity. Do not remove the engine to perform this procedure.

6. Pull the cover (**Figure 23**) from the oil pressure switch.
7. Unscrew the electrical terminal from the end of the oil pressure switch and remove the wire from the switch.

CAUTION
Some oil will flow from the oil pressure switch fitting when you remove the switch in the next step. Take care so this oil does not burn you.

8. Carefully unscrew the oil pressure switch (**Figure 24**) from the fitting in the crankcase.
9. Install the oil pressure gauge and adapter into the oil pressure switch fitting.
10. Start the engine and let it idle. Increase engine speed to 4000 rpm and read the oil pressure on the gauge. It should be within the range specified in **Table 6**.
11. Shut off the engine.
12. If the oil pressure is lower than specified, check the following

a. Plugged oil filter.
b. Oil leak from the oil passageway.
c. Damaged seal(s).
d. Oil pump.
e. Relief valve.
f. Combination of the above.

13. If the oil pressure is higher than specified, check the following:

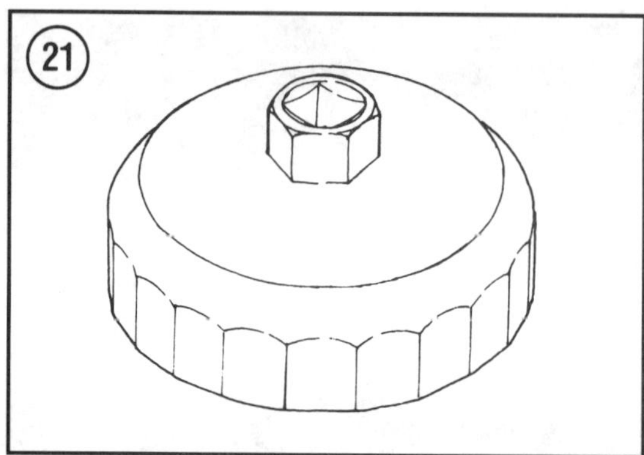
21

22

23

a. The oil viscosity is too heavy (drain the oil and install lighter oil).

b. Plugged oil passageway

c. Combination of the above.

14. Apply a light coat of RTV sealant to the threads of the oil pressure switch.

CAUTION
Some oil will flow from the oil pressure switch fitting when you remove the test equipment in the next step. Take care so this oil does not burn you.

15. Remove the test equipment and install the oil pressure switch (**Figure 24**) into the fitting in the crankcase. Tighten the switch to the torque specification listed in **Table 5**.

16. Connect the oil pressure switch wire to the switch and tighten the screw securely.

17. Fit the cover (**Figure 23**) in place over the oil pressure switch.

18. Check the oil level. Adjust it as necessary.

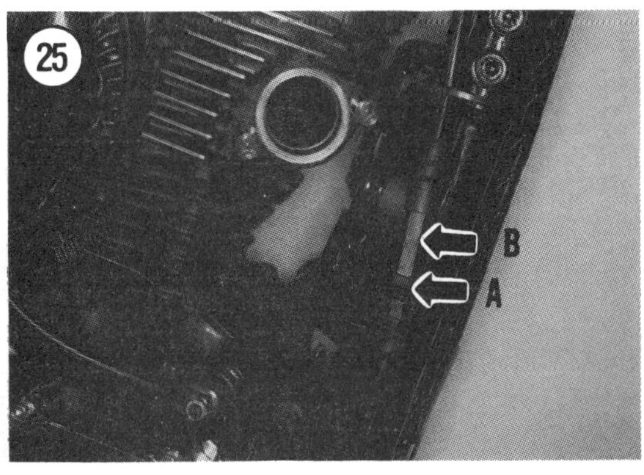

Front Fork Oil Change

Changing the fork oil requires more than minor disassembly. The front forks must be removed from the motorcycle and the oil poured from each fork. Refer to Chapter Eleven for this procedure.

Control Cables

Lubricate the control cables at the cable inspection intervals specified in **Table 1** or if they become stiff or sluggish. Whenever you lubricate a cable, also take the time to inspect the cable for fraying and check the sheath for chafing. The cables are relatively inexpensive and should be replaced if damaged or excessively worn.

Lubricate the cables using cable lubricant and a cable lubricator.

CAUTION
If the stock cable has been replaced with a nylon-lined cable, do not lubricate it as described in the following procedure. Oil and most cable lubricants will cause the liner to expand, pinching the liner against the cable. Nylon-lined cables are normally used dry. When servicing nylon-lined cables, follow the cable manufacturer's instructions.

NOTE
The main cause of cable breakage or cable stiffness is improper lubrication. Maintaining the cables as described in this section will ensure long service life.

1. Disconnect the clutch cable as follows:

a. At the mid-cable adjuster, loosen the cable adjuster locknut (A, **Figure 25**) and turn the adjuster (B, **Figure 25**) all the way in to allow maximum slack in the cable.

b. At the clutch lever on the handlebar, loosen the cable adjuster locknut (A, **Figure 26**), and turn the adjuster (B, **Figure 26**) all the way in to allow maximum slack in the cable.

c. Align the slot in the cable adjuster locknut with the slot in the lever assembly and release the cable from the adjuster and the hand lever.

2. Disconnect the throttle cables as follows:

a. At the throttle control on the handlebar, loosen both cable adjuster locknuts (A, **Figure 27**) and turn both adjusters (B, **Figure 27**) all the way in to allow maximum slack in both cables.

b. Remove the screws securing the right-hand switch assembly (C, **Figure 27**) together to gain access to the throttle cable ends. Separate the switch assembly.

c. Disconnect the throttle cables from the grip assembly and the upper portion of the switch assembly.

d. Remove the fuel tank as described in Chapter Eight.

3. Disconnecting the choke cable requires removing the carburetor. Refer to Chapter Eight for this procedure.

4. Disconnecting the rear brake cable/rod assembly requires removing the storage box. Refer to Chapter Thirteen for this procedure.

5. Attach a lubricator following its manufacturer's instructions (**Figure 28**).

6. Place a clean shop cloth at the other end of the cable to catch the excess lubricant as it exits the cable end.

7. Insert the nozzle of the lubricant can in the lubricator. Inject lubricant into the cable until the lubricant begins to flow out of the other end of the cable.

8. Remove the lubricator, reconnect the cable(s) and adjust the cable(s) as described in this chapter:

a. Throttle free play adjustment.

b. Clutch lever free play adjustment.

c. Rear brake free play adjustment.

d. Choke cable adjustment

Brake System

Lubricate the following brake components with silicone grease (specified for brake use) whenever the components are removed for service:

1. Brake lever pivot bolt.

2. Brake caliper bracket

Brake Pedal Pivot Shaft Lubrication

Remove the brake pedal periodically, as described in Chapter Thirteen, and lubricate the pivot shaft with water-resistant grease.

Speedometer Cable Lubrication

Lubricate the inner speedometer cable periodically or if needle operation is erratic. At the same time, check the outer cable for damage.

1. Remove the bolt securing the meter assembly to the fuel tank, then lift the meter assembly from the tank.

2. Unscrew the knurled ring on the speedometer cable (**Figure 29**) from the speedometer case.

3. Remove the muffler as described in Chapter Eight.

4. At the rear brake panel, remove the speedometer cable set screw (A, **Figure 30**) and remove the cable from speedometer gear housing in the brake panel (B, **Figure 30**).

5. Pull the cable from the sheath.

6. Clean the cable with a clotch soaked in solvent. Thoroughly dry the cable with a lint-free cloth.

7. Examine the cable ends for damage. Check the cable for bending or broken strands. Replace the cable if necessary.

8. Thoroughly coat the cable with a good grade of multipurpose grease and insert the cable back into the sheath. Push the cable back and forth through the

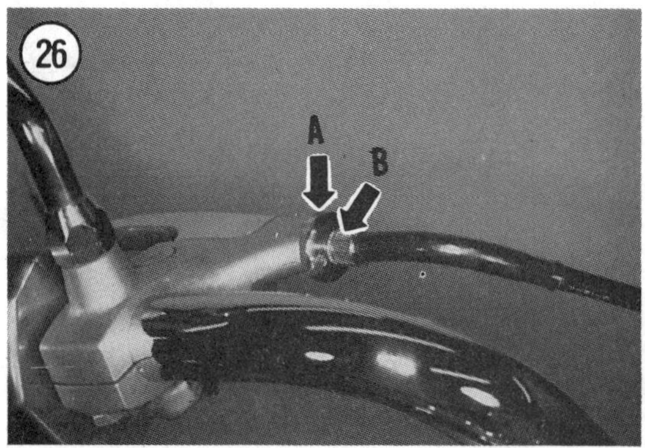

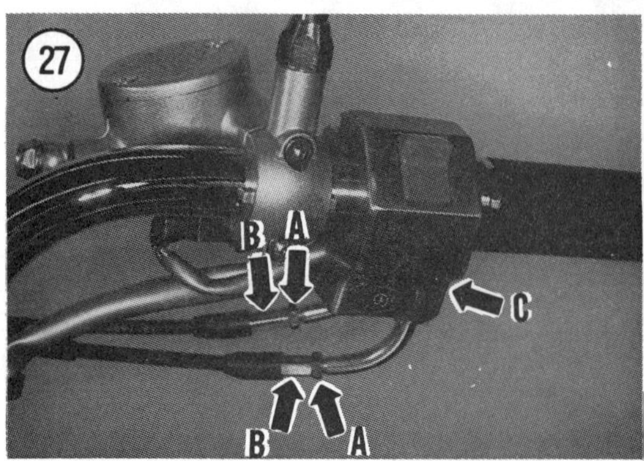

sheath making sure there is no binding or roughness. The cable must move smoothly.

9. Reconnect the speedometer cable by reversing the above procedure.

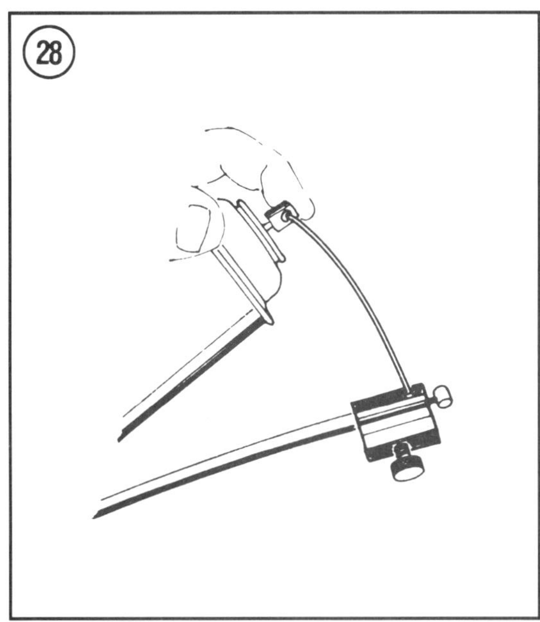

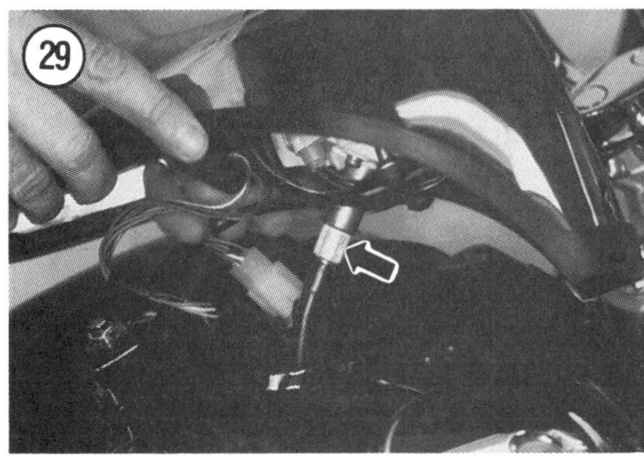

Steering Stem Lubrication

Remove, clean and lubricate the retainer-type ball bearings used in the steering system as described in Chapter Eleven.

Drive Chain Lubrication

Kawasaki recommends using heavy oil, such as SAE 90, for chain lubrication. It is less likely to be thrown off the chain than lighter oil. Many of the commercial drive chain lubricants also do an excellent job.

NOTE
If the drive chain is very dirty, remove and clean it as described under Drive Chain Cleaning in this chapter.

CAUTION
*The factory drive chain is equipped with O-rings between the side plates (**Figure 31**) that seal grease between the pins and bushings. To prevent O-ring damage, only clean the chain with kerosene or diesel fuel. Do not use gasoline or other solvents. These will cause the O-rings to swell or deteriorate. Refer to the cleaning procedure later in this chapter.*

1. Ride the bike a few miles to warm the drive chain. A warm chain increases lubricant penetration.
2. Support the bike with wooden blocks or a scissors jack so the rear wheel clears the ground.
3. Lubricate the bottom chain run with SAE 90 oil or with commercial chain lubricant *recommended* for use on O-ring drive chains. Concentrate on getting the oil down between the side plates of the chain links (**Figure 31**). Apply oil to the sides of the rollers so oil will find its way to the rollers and bushings. Also be sure the O-rings are thoroughly coated with oil.

CAUTION
Not all commercial chain lubricants are recommended for use on O-ring drive chains. Read the label carefully before purchasing chain lube. Be sure it is formulated for O-ring chains.

4. Rotate the chain and continue applying oil until the entire chain is lubricated.

5. Wipe off any oil or chain lubricant from the swing arm or rear wheel.

Miscellaneous Lubrication Points

Lubricate the clutch lever, front brake lever, sidestand pivot point and the footpeg pivot points. Use SAE 10W-40 engine oil.

PERIODIC MAINTENANCE

Periodic maintenance intervals are listed in **Table 1**.

Drive Chain/Sprocket Inspection (Chain Installed)

Inspect the drive chain frequently and replace it if excessively worn or damaged. A quick check will give you an indication of when to actually measure chain wear. At the rear sprocket, pull one of the links away from the sprocket (**Figure 32**). If the link pulls away more than ½ the height of a sprocket tooth, the chain is excessively worn. Measure drive chain wear by performing the following:

1. Remove the cotter pins, and loosen the axle nut (A, **Figure 33**) and the torque link nut (B, **Figure 33**).
2. Loosen the chain adjuster locknut on each side of the wheel (C, **Figure 33**).
3. Tighten each chain adjuster nut (D, **Figure 33**) to move the wheel rearward until the chain is tight (no slack).
4. Measure the distance between 21 pins (20 links) in the chain (**Figure 34**). If the drive chain is worn to the service limit listed in **Table 6**, replace the drive chain, engine sprocket and rear sprocket.
5. Check the inner faces of the inner plates. They should be lightly polished on both sides. If they show considerable wear on both sides, the sprockets are not aligned. Adjust chain alignment as described in this chapter.
6. Check the engine sprocket and the rear sprocket for wear (**Figure 35**) or missing teeth. If any wear is noticed on the teeth, replace both sprockets and the drive chain. Never install a new drive chain over worn sprockets or a worn drive chain over new sprockets.
7. Adjust the drive chain tension as described in this chapter.

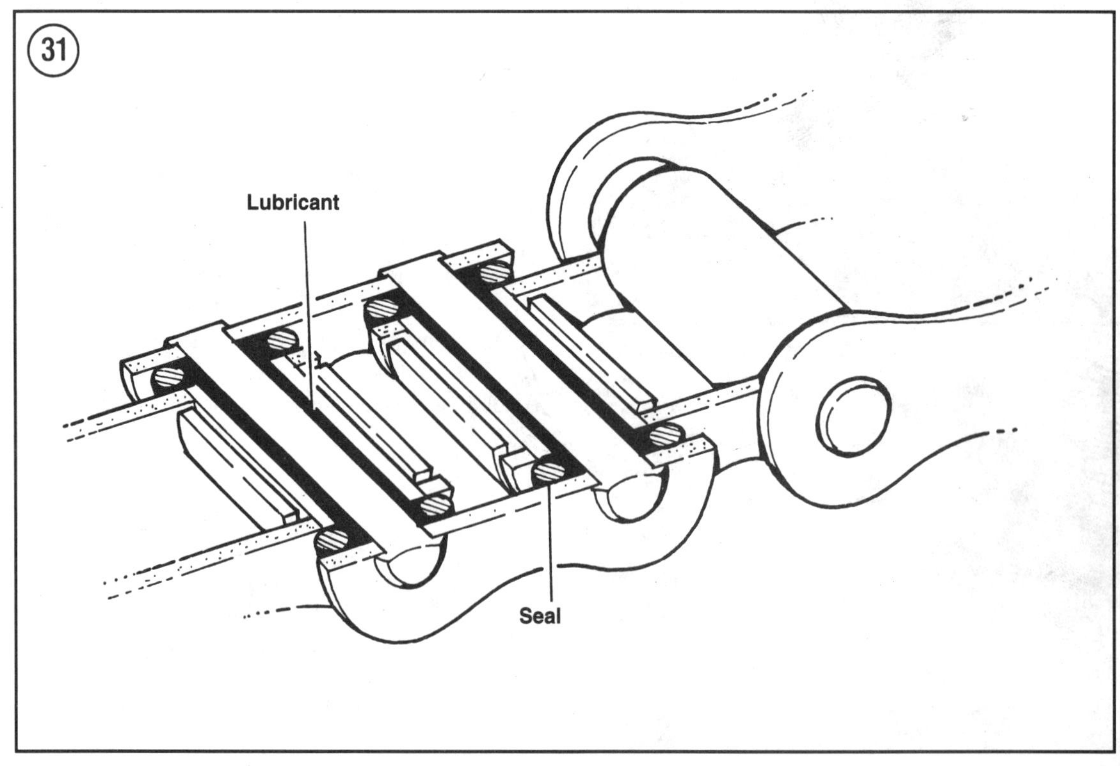

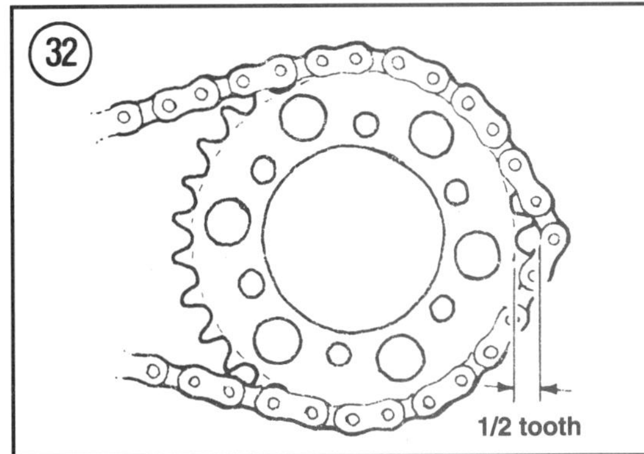

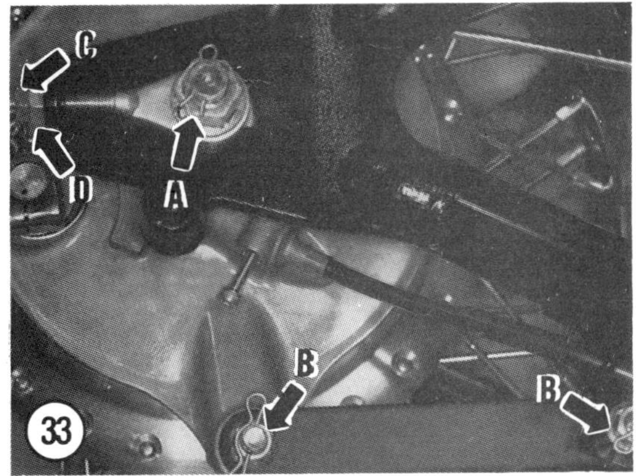

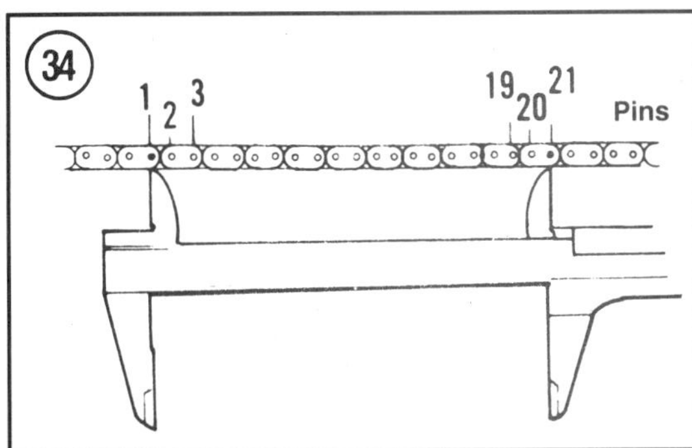

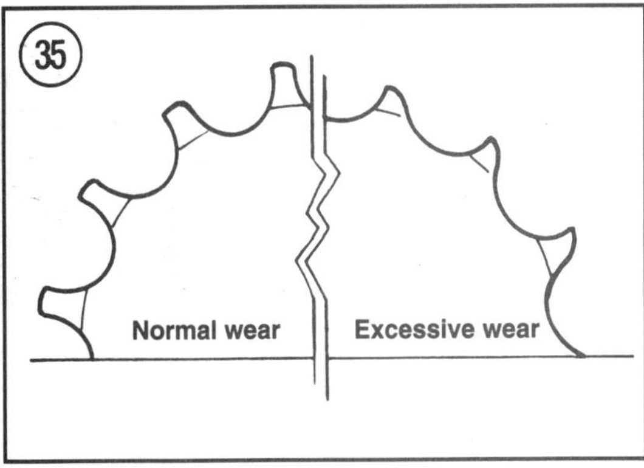

Drive Chain Cleaning and Inspection

Clean and lubricate the drive chain at the interval listed in **Table 1** or more frequently if the bike is often ridden in wet, dusty or muddy conditions. A properly maintained chain will provide maximum service life and reliability.

1. Remove the drive chain as described in Chapter Twelve.

CAUTION

*The factory drive chain is equipped with O-rings between the side plates (**Figure 31**) that seal grease between the pins and bushings. To prevent O-ring damage, only clean the chain with kerosene or diesel fuel. Do not use gasoline or other solvents. These will cause the O-rings to swell or deteriorate.*

2. Immerse the chain in a pan of kerosene or diesel. Let is soak for about 5 minutes. Move the chain around and flex it during this period so the dirt between the pins and rollers works its way out.
3. Scrub the rollers and side plates with a soft brush and rinse away loosened grit. Rinse the chain in fresh kerosene or diesel a couple times to make sure all dirt is washed out.
4. Immediately dry the chain with compressed air.
5. Stretch out the chain on the workbench, and measure the distance between 21 pins (20 links) in the chain (**Figure 34**). If the drive chain is worn to the service limit listed in **Table 6**, replace the drive chain, engine sprocket and rear sprocket.

NOTE

*Always check the engine sprocket and the rear sprocket every time the drive chain is removed (**Figure 35**). If any wear is noticed on the teeth, replace both sprockets and the drive chain. Never install a new drive chain over worn sprockets or a worn drive chain over new sprockets.*

6. Check the inner faces of the inner plates. They should be lightly polished on both sides. If they show considerable wear on both sides, the sprockets are not aligned. Adjust chain alignment as described in this chapter.
7. Lubricate the drive chain with SAE 90 oil or a good-grade drive chain lubricant formulated for O-ring chains. Carefully follow the manufacturer's in-

structions. Make sure all portions of the drive chain are thoroughly lubricated.

8. Install the chain as described in Chapter Twelve.

9. Adjust the drive chain tension as described in this chapter.

Drive Chain Tension Inspection

Adjust the chain at the intervals specified in **Table 1**. If the bike is operated at sustained high speeds or if it is repeatedly accelerated very hard, check the drive chain adjustment more often. Excessive drive chain slack may damage the frame or swing arm.

1. Turn the engine off and shift the transmission into NEUTRAL.

2. Using wooden blocks or a scissors jack, support the bike so the rear wheel clears the ground.

NOTE
As the drive chain wears, it becomes tighter at one point. The chain tension must be checked and adjusted at this point.

3. Turn the rear wheel slowly, stop it, and check the chain tension. Continue until you locate the tightest point. Mark this spot with chalk and turn the wheel so the mark is located midway between both drive sprockets on the chain's lower run.

NOTE
If the drive chain is kinked or feels tight, it may require cleaning and lubrication. Refer to ***Drive Chain Lubrication*** *in this chapterA. If the chain is still tight, it may be damaged due to swollen O-*

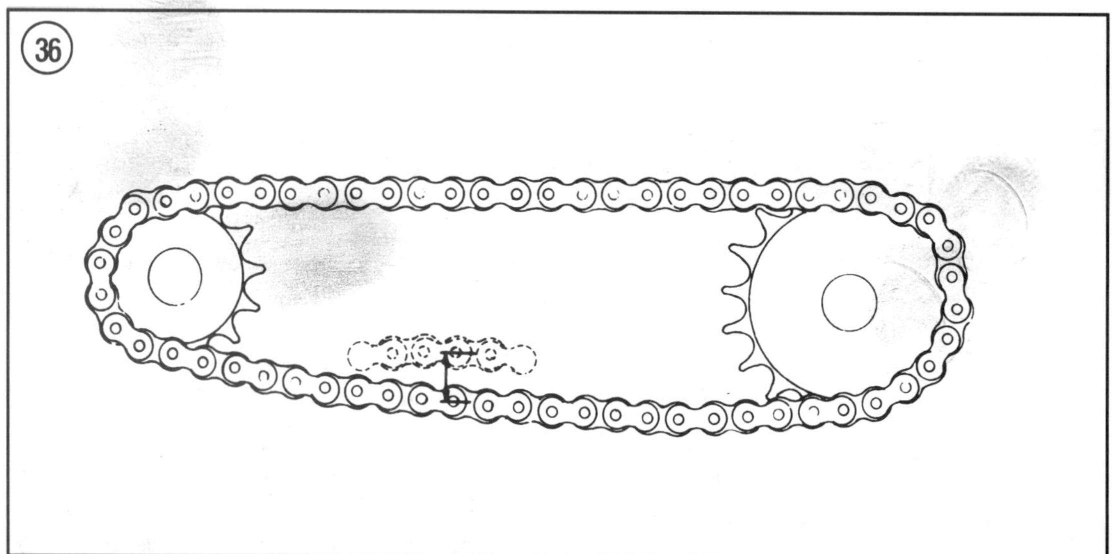
36

37

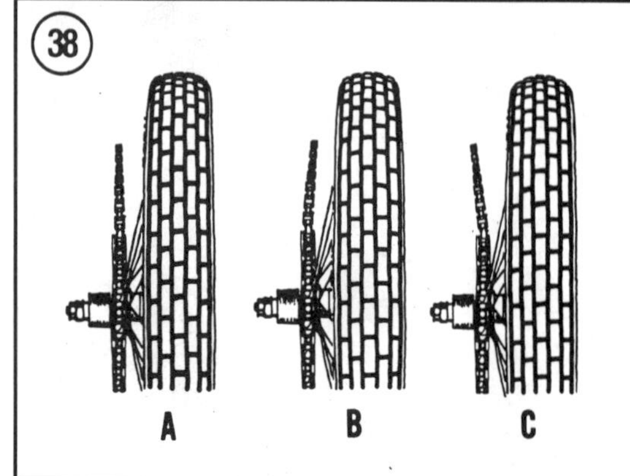

38

rings, damaged rollers, loose pins or binding links. Refer to Chapter Twelve.

4. Take the bike off its support and set it on its sidestand.
5. With your thumb and forefinger, lift the chain up and down at the center of the bottom chain run. Measure the distance the chain moves vertically (**Figure 36**).
6. The amount of vertical travel should be within the drive chain slack specification in **Table 6**. If necessary, adjust the chain as described in the following procedure.

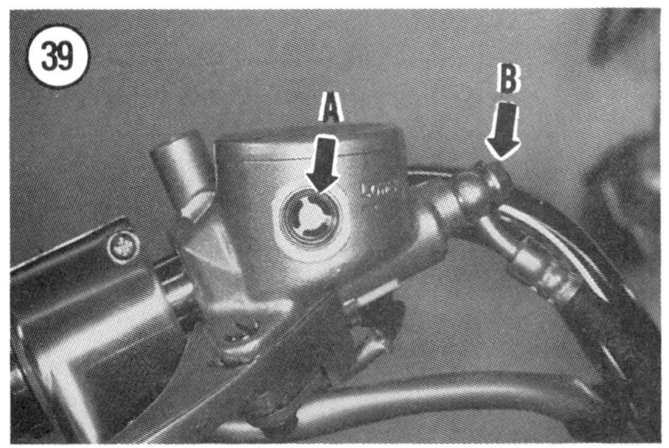

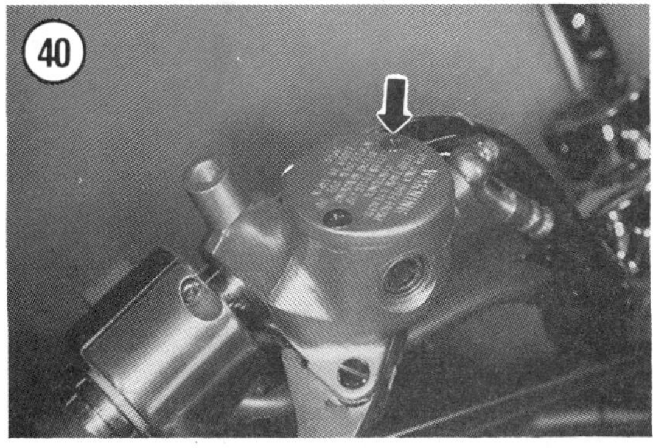

Drive Chain Tension Adjustment.

1. Remove the exhaust pipes as described in Chapter Eight.
2. Remove the cotter pins, loosen the axle nut (A, **Figure 33**) and the torque link nut (B, **Figure 33**).
3. Loosen the chain adjuster locknut on each side of the wheel (C, **Figure 33**).
4. Turn each chain adjuster nut (D, **Figure 33**) an equal number of turns to obtain the correct drive chain slack listed in **Table 6**. Be sure the indexing mark on each chain adjuster aligns with the same alignment mark on each side of the swing arm (**Figure 37**).
5. To verify the wheel alignment, remove the drive chain guard and sight along the drive chain as it runs over the rear sprocket. It should not appear to move sideways (B or C, **Figure 38**).
6. Tighten both chain adjuster locknuts securely.
7. Torque the axle nut to the specification in **Table 5**.
8. Recheck the drive chain slack.
9. Tighten the torque link nut to the specification in **Table 5**.
10. Install a new cotter pin in the axle nut and in the torque link nut.

Disc Brake Fluid Level

1. Support the bike on level ground.
2. Position the handlebars so the front master cylinder reservoir is horizontal.
3. The fluid level in the reservoir window (**A, Figure 39**) should be above the lower level line on the side of the master cylinder reservoir. If the brake fluid level is at or below the lower level line, add fresh brake fluid by performing the following:
   a. Clean the top of the master cylinder of all dirt and foreign matter.
   b. Remove the screws securing the cover (**Figure 40**). Remove the cover and diaphragm (**Figure 41**) from the reservoir .
   c. Add DOT 4 brake fluid until the level is even with the upper level line. Use fresh brake fluid from a sealed brake fluid container.

WARNING

Use brake fluid from a sealed container clearly marked DOT 4 only (specified for disc brakes). Others may cause brake failure. Do not intermix different

3

brands or types of brake fluid as they may not be compatible. Do not intermix a silicone based (DOT 5) brake fluid as it can cause brake system failure.

CAUTION
Be careful when handling brake fluid. Do not spill it on painted or plated surfaces or plastic parts as it will destroy the surface. Wash the area immediately with soapy water and thoroughly rinse it off.

d. Reinstall the diaphragm and the cover (**Figure 40**). Tighten the screws securely.

Front Disc Brake Line

Check hydraulic brake line (B, **Figure 39**) between the front master cylinder and the front brake caliper (A, **Figure 42**). If there is any leakage, tighten the connections and bleed the brakes as described in Chapter Thirteen. If this does not stop the leak or if a brake line is obviously damaged, cracked or chafed, replace the brake line and bleed the system as described in Chapter Thirteen.

Disc Brake Pad Wear

Inspect the brake pads for excessive or uneven wear and scoring. Also check for oil or grease on the friction surface.

1. Place the bike on level ground and securely support it with wooden blocks or a scissors jack.
2. Remove the bolts (B, **Figure 42**) securing the caliper assembly to the fork slider.
3. Carefully pull the caliper off the disc and check the wear lines on the brake pads.
4. If either pad is worn to the wear line (**Figure 43**), replace both brake pads as described in Chapter Thirteen.
5. Reinstall the caliper assembly onto the brake disc being careful not to damage the leading edge of the pads during installation.
6. Tighten the mounting bolts to the torque specification listed in **Table 5**.

Disc Brake Fluid Change

Every time the reservoir cap is removed, a small amount of dirt and moisture can enter the brake fluid. The same thing happens if a leak occurs or if any part of the hydraulic system is loosened or disconnected. Dirt can plug the system and cause unnecessary wear. Water will contaminate the brake fluid and impair the hydraulic action, reducing the brake's stopping ability.

To maintain peak performance, change the brake fluid at the interval indicated in **Table 1**. To change brake fluid, follow the procedure in Chapter Thirteen. Continue adding new fluid to the master cylinder and bleeding it from the caliper until the fluid leaving the caliper is clean and free of contaminants.

WARNING
Use brake fluid from a sealed container clearly marked DOT 4 only (specified for disc brakes). Do not intermix different brands or types of brake fluid as they may not be compatible. Do not intermix a silicone based (DOT 5) brake fluid as it can cause brake system failure.

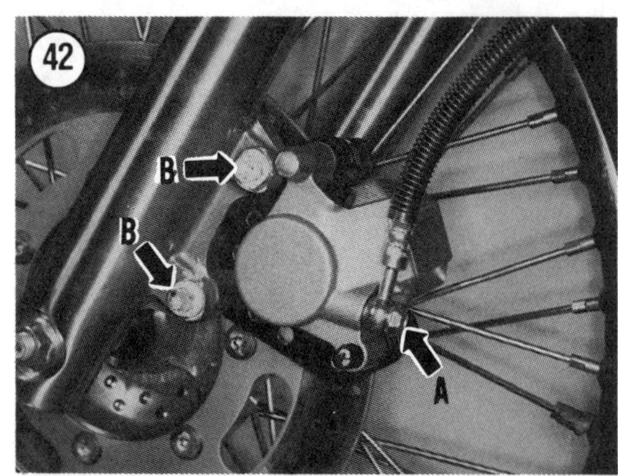

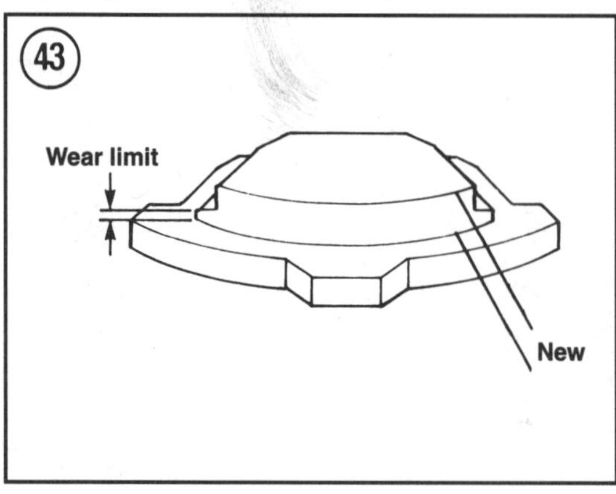

Rear Drum Brake Lining Wear Indicator

The rear drum brake is equipped with a brake lining wear indicator. This enables you to check the brake lining condition without removing the rear wheel and brake assembly.

1. Apply the rear brake fully.

2. Observe the wear indicator (A, **Figure 44**) on the brake panel.

3. If the indicator falls within the usable range (B, **Figure 44**) embossed on the brake panel, the brake lining thickness is within specification and does not require service.
4. If the wear indicator lines fall outside of this usable range, the brake linings are worn and should be replaced.
5. If necessary, replace the rear brake linings as described in Chapter Thirteen.

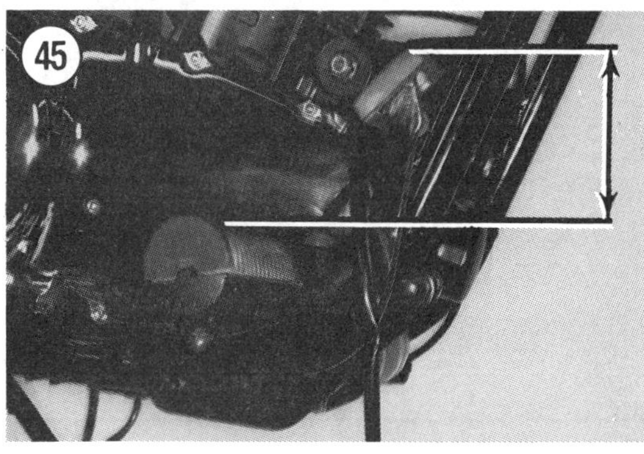

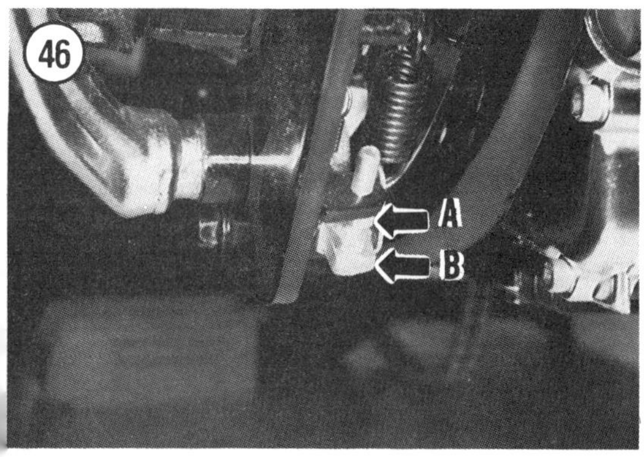

3

Rear Brake Pedal Height Adjustment

Adjust the rear brake pedal height at the interval listed in **Table 1**. The brake pedal height is, the distance from the top of the brake pedal to the top surface of the footpeg as shown in **Figure 45**. Brake pedal height changes as the brake linings wear.
1. Make sure the brake pedal is in the at-rest position.
2. To change height position, loosen the locknut (A, **Figure 46**) and turn the adjusting bolt (B, **Figure 46**) until the correct height is achieved (**Table 6**). Tighten the locknut securely.

Rear Brake Pedal Free Play Adjustment

Set the pedal free play to the specification listed in **Table 6**.
1. Make sure the brake pedal is in the at-rest position.
2. Depress the brake pedal lightly by hand until the brake shoes make contact with the drum. This is the free play.
3. To change the free play adjustment, turn the adjust nut (A, **Figure 47**) at the end of the brake rod (B, **Figure 47**). Turn the adjust nut until the correct amount of free play is achieved.
4. After adjusting the free play, securely support the bike on a level surface with the rear wheel off the ground and check for brake drag. Make any necessary adjustments.

Rear Brake Cam Lever Angle Adjustment

When the rear brake is fully applied, the rear brake cam lever should be within the range specified in **Table 6**. Rear braking effectiveness is greatly reduced if this angle exceeds specification.
1. Have an assistant apply the rear brake and observe the rear brake cam lever. Note the angle of the lever (C, **Figure 47**) in relation to the brake rod (B, **Figure 47**). If this angle (D, **Figure 47**) is not within

the range specified in **Table 6**, the cam lever must be repositioned on the camshaft to maintain full braking ability.

2. Remove the rear exhaust pipe as described in Chapter Eight.
3. At the rear brake panel, completely unscrew the adjust nut (A, **Figure 47**).
4. Depress the brake pedal and disconnect the brake rod (B, **Figure 47**) from the pivot joint in the brake panel cam lever. Remove the pivot joint and reinstall the joint and the adjust nut onto the rod to avoid misplacing them.
5. Use a fine-line permanent marking pen and mark the existing location of the cam lever split in relation to the end of the camshaft (A, **Figure 48**).
6. Loosen the pinch bolt (B, **Figure 48**) securing the brake cam lever and remove the brake cam lever from the camshaft.
7. Reposition the cam lever on the camshaft to achieve the recommended angle. Reinstall the cam lever so it moves only one spline from its original position.
8. Install the pinch bolt and tighten it securely.
9. Reinstall the brake rod, pivot joint and adjust nut.
10. Adjust the rear brake free play as described in this chapter.
11. Repeat Step 1; readjust if necessary.

Clutch Lever Free Play Adjustment

NOTE
After adjusting the clutch lever free play, always start the engine and check clutch operation. Improper free play adjustment could lead to clutch slippage and damage.

1. Loosen the locknut (A, **Figure 49**) at the clutch lever and turn the adjuster (B, **Figure 49**) until the gap between the clutch lever and the lever housing is within the specification in **Table 6**.
2. Tighten the clutch lever locknut.
3. If you cannot set the free play at the clutch lever, adjust clutch free play at the mid-cable adjuster by performing the following:
   a. Loosen the locknut (A, **Figure 50**) at the mid-cable adjuster .
   b. Turn the mid-cable adjuster (B, **Figure 50**) until the clutch lever free play is within specification. Tighten the mid-adjuster locknut.
4. If you cannot set free play at the mid-cable adjuster, use the adjuster at the clutch release lever by performing the following:
   a. Loosen the locknut at the clutch lever and turn the adjuster until 5-6 mm (0.20-0.24 in.) of threads are exposed (C, **Figure 49**).
   b. Loosen both locknuts (A, **Figure 51**) at the clutch cable bracket on the right-side crankcase cover.

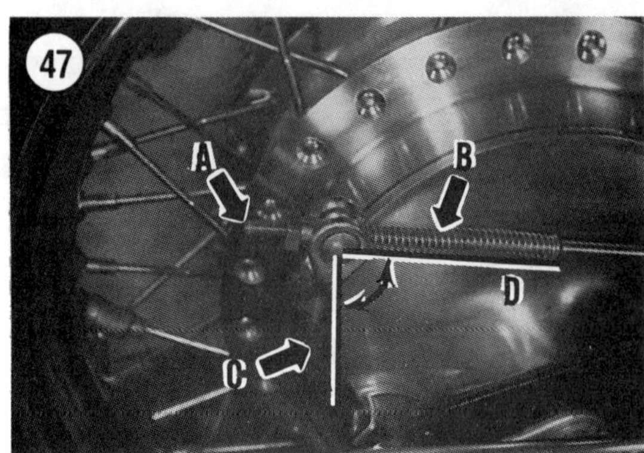

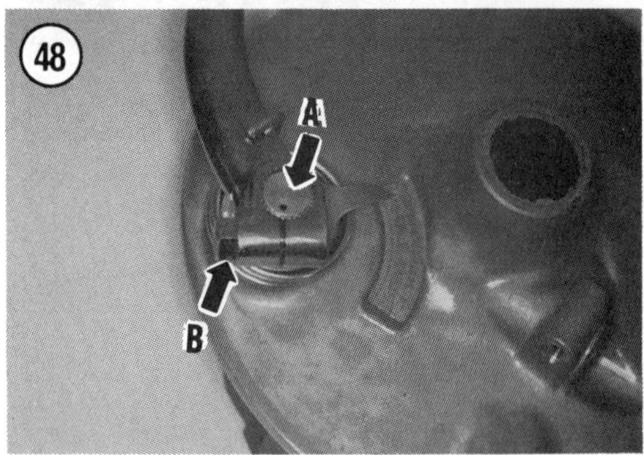

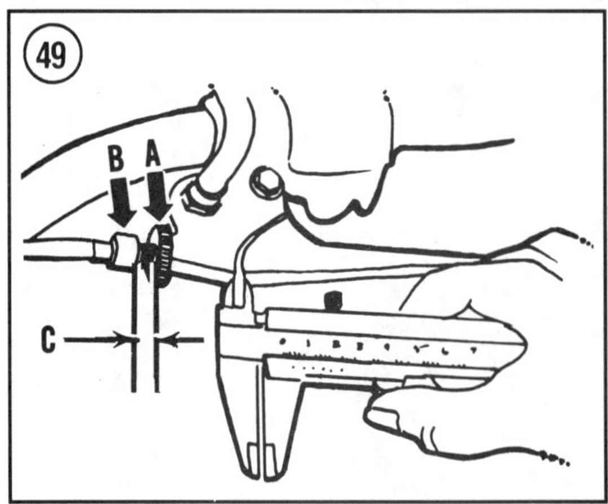

c. Pull the clutch cable outer cover (B, **Figure 51**) toward the clutch release lever until the cable is taut. Hold the cable in this position while you tighten both locknuts (A, **Figure 51**).

d. Use the adjuster at the clutch lever and set the clutch lever free play to the specification listed in **Table 6**. Tighten the locknut.

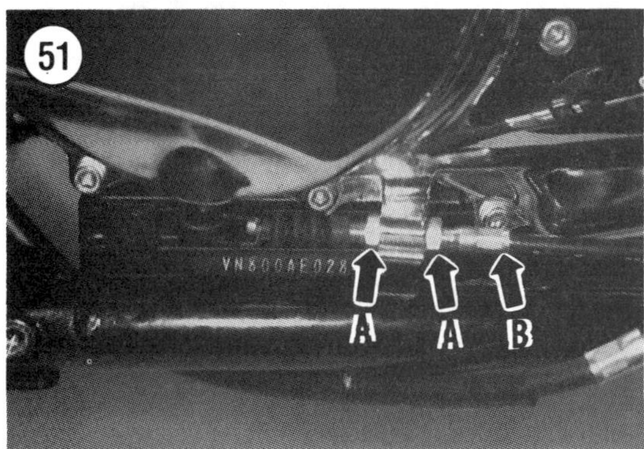

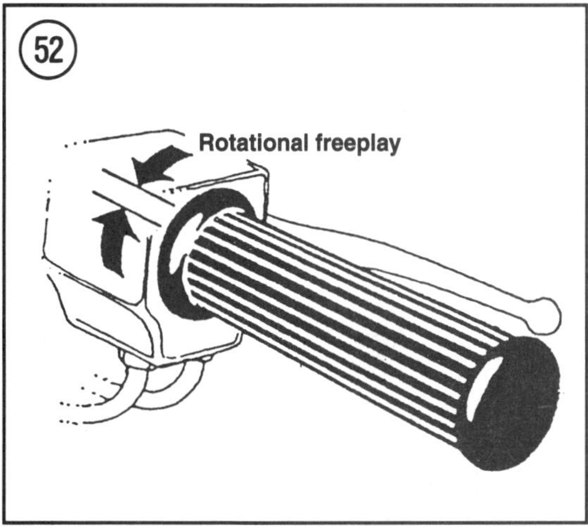

5. Start the engine and check the operation of the clutch.

Throttle Free Play Adjustment

Always check the throttle cables before you make any carburetor adjustments. Too much free play causes delayed throttle response; too little free play causes unstable idling.

Check the throttle cables from grip to carburetor. Make sure they are not kinked or chafed. Replace the cables as necessary.

Make sure that the throttle grip rotates smoothly from fully closed to fully open. Be sure that the throttle grip returns and closes properly in all steering positions. If not, lubricate the throttle cables as described in this chapter. If necessary, remove the throttle grip and apply lithium base grease to the rotating surfaces. At the same time, clean and lubricate the throttle grip housing with a light oil. If the throttle still does not return properly, the cables are probably kinked or routed incorrectly.

Check the free play at the throttle grip (**Figure 52**). It should be within the range specified in **Table 6**.

WARNING

If idle speed increases when the handlebars are turned to the right or left, check throttle cable routing or look for a damaged throttle cable(s). Correct this problem immediately. Do not ride the bike in this unsafe condition.

1. To adjust the free play at the throttle grip:
   a. Loosen the locknuts (A, **Figure 53**) on both the pull and push throttle cables.
   b. Turn the adjusters in (B and C, **Figure 53**) to attain plenty of free play.
   c. Rotate the throttle grip until it is completely closed.
   d. Turn out the adjuster on the push cable (C, **Figure 53**) until the cable becomes tight. Tighten the push cable locknut.
   e. Turn the adjuster on the pull cable (B, **Figure 53**) until proper throttle grip free play is attained. Tighten the push cable locknut.
2. If proper free play cannot be attained by turning the adjusters at the throttle grip, use the mid-cable adjusters.

a. At the throttle end, turn in the adjusters on the push and pull cables to provide the maximum amount of free play. Tighten both locknuts.
b. Remove the fuel tank as described in Chapter Eight.
c. Loosen the locknuts (A, **Figure 54**) at the mid-cable adjusters on the push and pull cables.
d. Turn each mid-cable adjuster (B and C, **Figure 54**) to provide the maximum amount of slack in each cable.
e. Rotate the throttle grip until it is completely closed.
f. Turn the push cable adjuster (B, **Figure 54**) until the inner cable is just barely taut. Tighten the push cable locknut.
g. Turn the pull cable adjuster (C, **Figure 54**) until the proper throttle grip free play is attained. Tighten the push cable locknut.
h. At the throttle grip end, tighten the adjuster locknuts on both cables.

3. If the proper amount of free play cannot be achieved using this procedure, the cables have stretched and must be replaced. Refer to Chapter Eight for this procedure.
4. Check the throttle grip operation. It should be adjusted properly. If not, the throttle cables may be stretched and should be replaced.
5. Reinstall all previously removed parts.
6. Sit on the bike and start the engine with the transmission in NEUTRAL. Turn the handlebars from right to left and listen for abnormal idle speed variation.

WARNING

If idle speed increases during this movement, the throttle cable may need adjusting or may be incorrectly routed through the frame. Correct this problem immediately. Do not ride the bike in this unsafe condition.

Choke Cable Tension Adjustment

1. Pull out the choke knob.
2. Adjust the friction on the cable by turning the cable friction nut (**Figure 55**).
3. Apply the minimal amount of friction necessary to hold the choke open while also permitting smooth operation of the cable.

Camshaft Chain Tensioner Adjustment

There is no provision for manual adjustment of the camshaft chain tension on this engine. Camshaft chain tension is maintained automatically.

Exhaust System

Check for leakage at all fittings. Tighten all bolts and nuts; replace any gaskets as necessary. Refer to Chapter Eight.

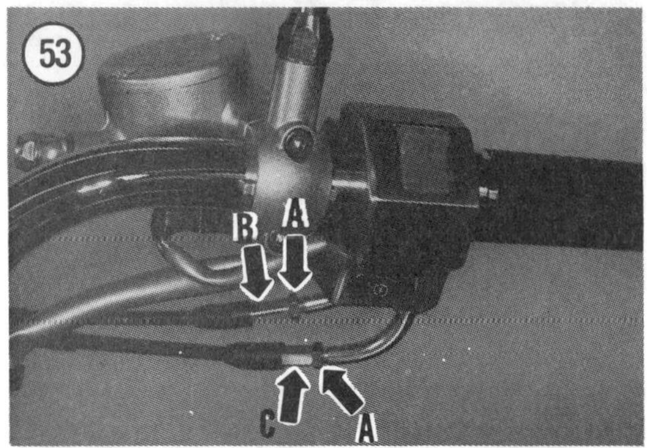

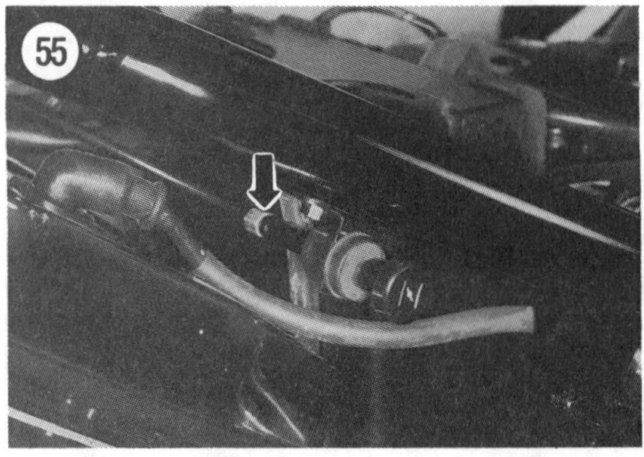

Air Filter Elements

Remove and clean the air filter element at the interval listed in **Table 1**. The air filter removes dust and abrasive particles from the air before they enter the carburetor and the engine. Without an air filter, very fine particles will enter the engine and cause rapid wear of the piston rings, cylinders and bearings and will plug small passages in the carburetor. Never run the bike without the air filter element installed.

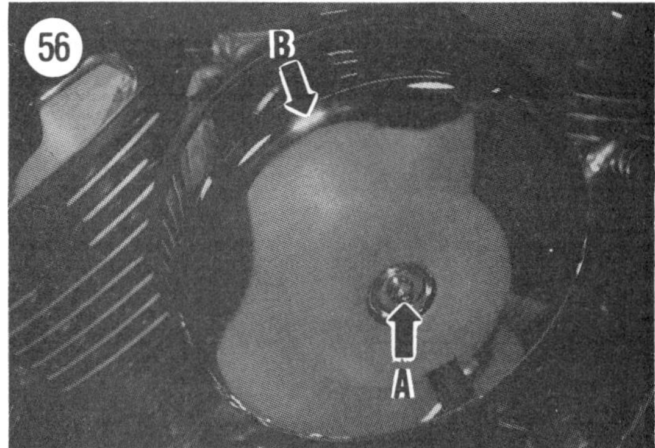

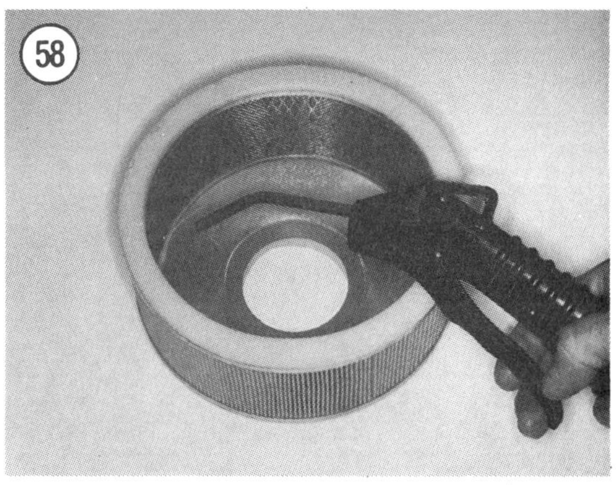

Proper air filter servicing can do more to ensure long service from your engine than almost any other single item.

Air Filter Removal/Installation

1. Remove the screw (A, **Figure 56**) securing the air filter cover and remove the cover (B, **Figure 56**).
2. Remove the air filter (**Figure 57**) from the housing.
3. Clean and inspect the elements as described in this chapter.
4. Install the air filter element by reversing the removal procedure.

Element Cleaning and Inspection

1. Carefully remove the air filter element from its housing.
2. Lightly tap the element to loosen dust.
3. Clean the element with compressed air. Blow the element from the inside to the outside (**Figure 58**).
4. Visually inspect the air filter element for tears.
5. Inspect the element's gasket for tears.
6. Replace the element if it cannot be cleaned with compressed air or if you find any tears in the element or in its gasket.

Fuel Line Inspection

Inspect the fuel line (**Figure 59**) from the fuel shutoff valve to the carburetor. Replace the fuel line if it is cracked or starting to deteriorate. Make sure the hose clamps are in place and holding securely.

WARNING
A damaged or deteriorated fuel line presents a very dangerous fire hazard to both the rider and the vehicle if fuel should spill onto a hot engine or exhaust pipe.

Vacuum Line Inspection

Inspect the condition of all vacuum lines for cracks or deterioration and replace if necessary. Make sure the hose clamps are in place and holding securely.

3

Cooling System Inspection

Inspect the following items at the interval indicated in **Table 1**. If you do not have the test equipment, a Kawasaki dealership, automobile dealership, radiator shop or service station can do the tests.

WARNING
*Do not remove the radiator cap (**Figure 60**) if the engine is HOT. Severe scalding could result if the escaping coolant comes in contact with your skin. Allow the cooling system to cool prior to loosening the cap. Loosen the cap slowly to the first detent to allow any pressure to escape safely.*

1. Remove the meter assembly from the tank, and remove the radiator cap (**Figure 60**).
2. Test the radiator cap pressure (**Figure 61**). The cap must be able to sustain the pressure specified in **Table 6** for a minimum of 10 seconds. Replace the radiator cap if it does not hold pressure or if the relief pressure is too high or too low.

CAUTION
Do not exceed the indicated test pressure. If test pressure is excessive, the radiator may be damaged.

3. Install the tester onto the radiator filler neck (**Figure 62**).
4. Pressure test the entire cooling system. Pressurize the cooling to, but do not exceed, the test pressure specified in **Table 6**. The system must sustain this pressure for a minimum of 6 seconds. If the pressure does not hold steady, check the system for leaks. Replace or repair any component that fails this test.
5. Test the specific gravity of the coolant with an antifreeze tester to ensure adequate temperature and corrosion protection. The system must have at least a 50:50 mixture of antifreeze and distilled water. Never let the mixture become less than 40% antifreeze or corrosion protection will be impaired.
6. Remove the fuel tank and check all cooling system hoses for damage or deterioration. Refer to **Figure 63**, **Figure 64** and **Figure 65**. Replace any hose that is questionable. Make sure all hose clamps are tight.
7. Remove the radiator cover (**Figure 66**).
8. Carefully clean the front surface of the radiator core (**Figure 67**). Use a whisk broom, compressed

59

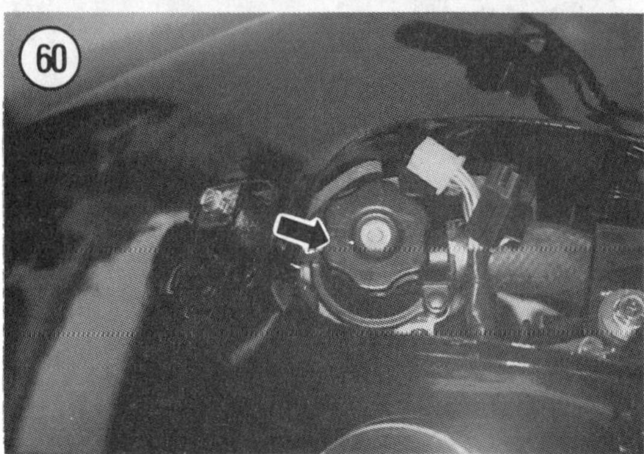
60

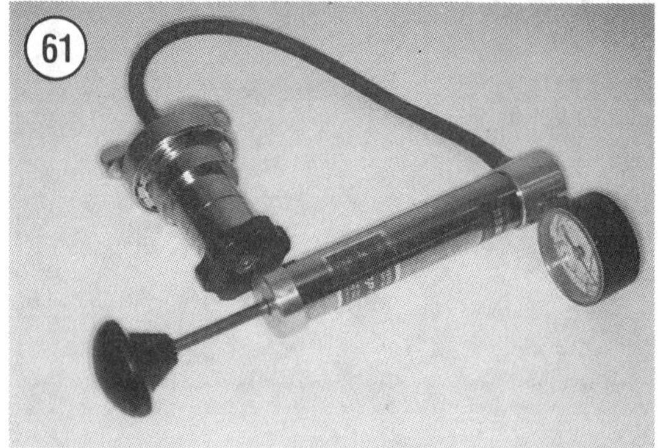
61

62

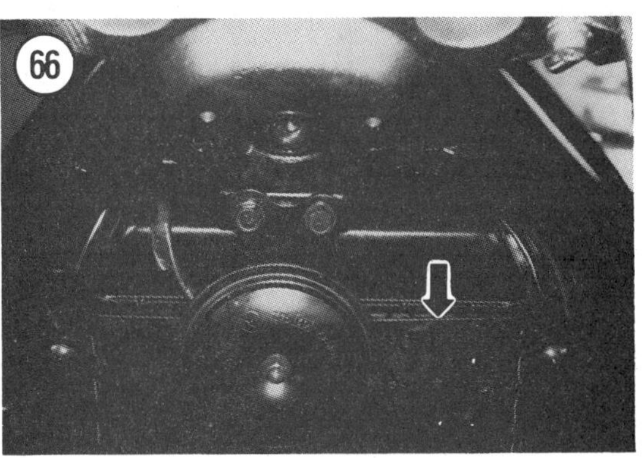

air or low-pressure water. If the radiator has been hit by a small rock or other item, carefully straighten out the fins with a screwdriver.

NOTE
If the radiator has been damaged across approximately 20% or more of the frontal area, the radiator should be recored or replaced as described in Chapter Nine.

9. Install all removed parts.

Coolant Change

Drain and refill the cooling system at the interval indicated in **Table 1**.

It is sometimes necessary to remove the radiator or drain the coolant from the system in order to perform a service procedure on some parts of the bike. If the coolant is still in good condition, the coolant can be reused if it is kept clean. Drain the coolant into a clean drain pan and pour it into a clean sealable container like a plastic milk or bleach bottle. This coolant can then be reused if it is still clean.

CAUTION
Antifreeze is poisonous and has a sweet taste that is attractive to animals. Do not leave the drained coolant where it is accessible to children or animals.

CAUTION
Use only a high-quality ethylene glycol antifreeze specifically labeled for use with aluminum engines. Do not use an alcohol-based antifreeze.

The following procedure must be performed when the engine is cool.

WARNING
*Do **not** change the coolant while the engine is still hot or even warm. Do **not** remove the radiator cap (**Figure 60**) when the engine is HOT. The coolant is very hot and is under pressure. Severe scalding could result if the escaping coolant comes in contact with your skin. Allow the cooling system to cool prior to loosening the cap and then loosen the cap slowly to the first detent to allow pressure to escape safely.*

CAUTION
Be careful not to spill antifreeze on painted surfaces. Antifreeze will destroy painted surfaces. Wash a spill immediately with soapy water and rinse thoroughly with clean water. Coolant is also slippery. Be sure to clean spilled coolant from the ground or tire threads.

1. Support the bike on the wooden blocks or with a scissors jack.
2. Remove the meter assembly from the fuel tank.

NOTE
Use a clean drain pan to collect the spent coolant so the coolant can be inspected for possible internal engine problems.

3. Place a clean drain pan under coolant drain bolt under the right-hand crankcase.

NOTE
Remove the coolant drain bolt first as this will relieve the internal pressure prior to removing the radiator cap.

4. Remove the coolant drain bolt (**Figure 68**) and drain the coolant from the engine and radiator.
5. Remove the radiator cap (**Figure 60**) to quicken the draining process.
6. Remove the reservoir cap (A, **Figure 69**). Use a siphon, pump, syringe or other suitable tool to remove the coolant from the reservoir.
7. Take the bike off the blocks and lean the bike from side to side to drain any residual coolant from the cooling system. Support the bike on wooden blocks.
8. Visually inspect the condition of the coolant as follows:
   a. White cotton-like sediment in the coolant indicate that aluminum parts in the cooling system are corroded.
   b. Brownish color indicates that iron parts in the cooling system are rusting.
   c. An abnormal smell of the coolant may be indicate an exhaust or combustion leak into the cooling system.
9. If the drained coolant is contaminated or very dirty, flush the cooling system with freshwater. Securely support the bike on wooden blocks or a scissors jack. Allow the water to run through the cooling system for approximately 5 minutes. Shut off the water and allow the water to drain.
10. Take the bike off the blocks and tip the bike from side to side to drain all residual water from the cooling system. Support the bike on wooden blocks.
11. Inspect the gasket on the drain plug; replace if necessary. Install the drain plug and gaskets. Refer to **Figure 68**. Tighten the plug to the torque specification listed in **Table 5**.
12. Refill the cooling system as follows:
   a. Insert a small funnel into the radiator filler neck.

CAUTION
Do not use a higher percentage of coolant-to-water than 50:50. A higher concentration of antifreeze (60% or greater) will actually decrease the performance of the cooling system.

   b. Slowly add a 50:50 mixture of distilled water and antifreeze to the radiator until the fluid level is even with the cap inlet fitting on the filler neck. Add the coolant slowly to help purge the system of trapped air.

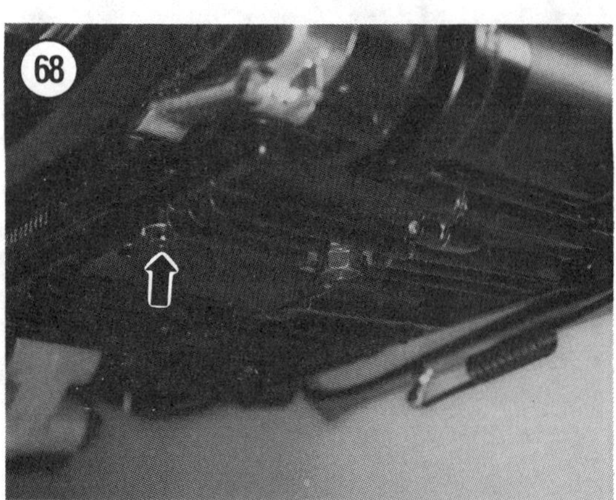
68

c. Use a long-neck funnel and add coolant to the reservoir until the fluid level is even with the full FULL line on the side of the tank (B, **Figure 69**). Install the cap.

d. Lean the bike from side to side to bleed out as much air from the system as possible.

e. Install the radiator cap (**Figure 60**) and turn it clockwise until it stops turning.

f. Install the fuel tank as described in Chapter Eight.

13. Reinstall the removed parts and start the engine. Let it run at idle speed until the engine reaches normal operating temperature. Shut off the engine.

14. Allow the engine to cool. Then, with the engine cool, check the coolant level in the reservoir. If the coolant level is below the LOW mark, add coolant until it is even with the FULL mark (B, **Figure 69**).

15. Check for coolant leaks at all drain plugs. Tighten if necessary.

16. Test ride the bike and readjust the coolant level if necessary after the cooling system has cooled.

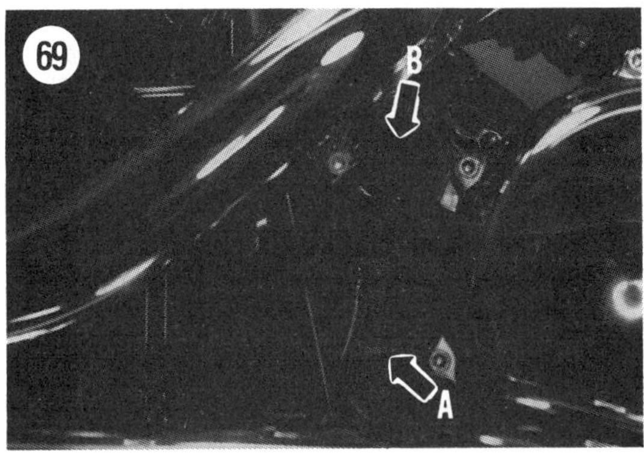

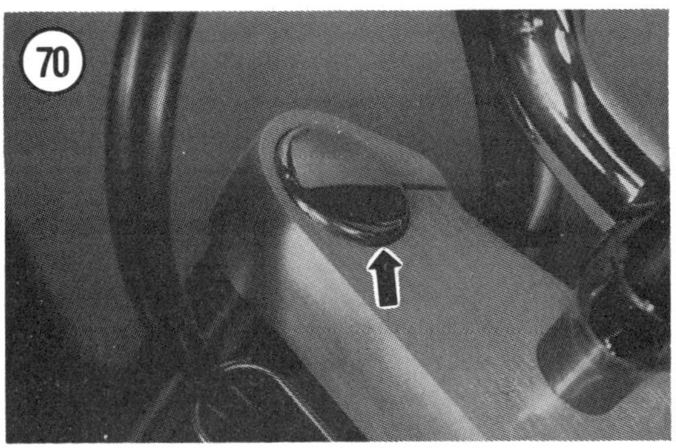

Evaporative Emission Control System (California Models Only)

Fuel vapor from the fuel tank is routed into a charcoal canister when the engine is stopped. When the engine is started this vapor is drawn through the separator and into the carburetor and burned in the engine. Make sure all vacuum hoses are correctly routed and attached. Inspect the hoses and replace any if necessary.

Refer to Chapter Eight for detailed information on the evaporative emission control system and for vacuum hose routing.

Wheel Bearings

There is no factory-recommended mileage interval for cleaning and repacking the wheel bearings. They should be inspected and serviced, if necessary, every time the wheel is removed or whenever there is a likelihood of water contamination. The correct service procedures are covered in Chapter Eleven and Chapter Twelve.

Front Suspension Check

1. Apply the front brake and pump the forks up and down as vigorously as possible. Check for smooth operation and check for any fork oil leaks around the seal area on each fork leg.
2. Remove the cap (**Figure 70**) from the top of each fork tube.
3. Make sure the retaining ring is seated correctly in the fork tube groove (**Figure 71**).
4. Make sure the upper and lower fork bridge clamp bolts (**Figure 72**) are tight on both fork legs.

NOTE

Figures 73-75 *show the handlebar clamps for 1997 and 1998 VN800 models and for VN800 Classics models. A different-type of handlebar clamp is used on 1995 and 1996 VN800 models.*

5. Make sure the handlebar clamp bolts (**Figure 73**) are tight and that the handlebar clamps are secured to the upper fork bridge.
6. Make sure the front axle pinch bolt (**Figure 74**) and front axle nut (**Figure 75**) are tight.

Rear Suspension Check

1. Place the bike on level ground. Use wooden blocks or a scissors jack to securely support the bike with the rear wheel off the ground.
2. Push hard on the rear wheel (sideways) to check for side play in the rear swing arm bearings. Remove the wooden blocks.

NOTE
Partial disassembly is required to check the shock absorber and other suspension mounts. Refer to Chapter Twelve for details.

3. Check the shock absorber's upper and lower mounts. Be sure they are tight.
4. Check the shock absorber for leakage.
5. Check the Uni-Trak linkage. Be sure all nuts and bolts are tight.
6. Make sure the rear axle nut (A, **Figure 76**) is tight and that the cotter pin is in place.
7. Be sure the rear brake torque arm nuts (B, **Figure 76**) are tight and their pins are in place.

Nuts, Bolts and Other Fasteners

Constant vibration can loosen many of the fasteners on the motorcycle. Check the tightness of all fasteners, especially the following:

a. Engine mounting hardware.
b. Engine crankcase covers.
c. Handlebar and front fork.
d. Gearshift lever.
e. Brake pedal and lever.
f. Exhaust system.
g. Lighting equipment.

Steering Head Adjustment Check

Check the steering head bearings for looseness at the interval listed in **Table 1**.

1. Place a wooden block(s) or scissors jack under the engine to support the bike securely with the front wheel off the ground.
2. Hold the front fork tubes and gently rock the fork assembly back and forth. If you feel looseness, refer to Chapter Eleven.

71

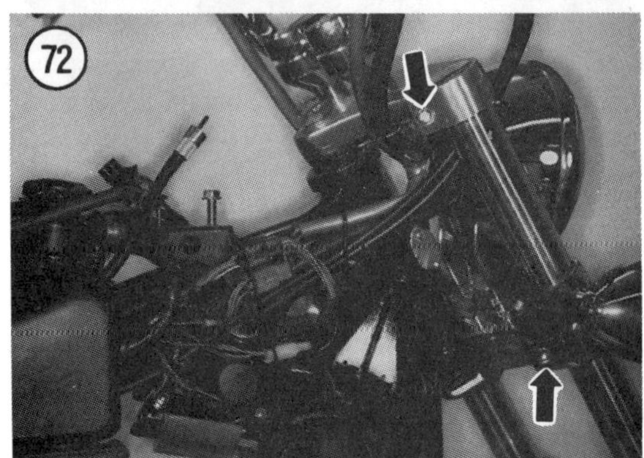
72

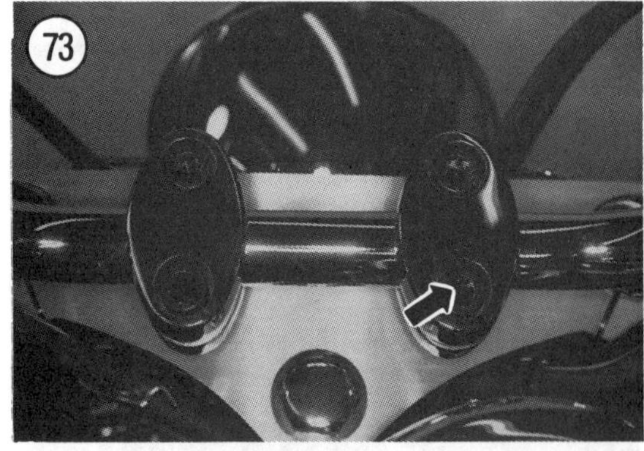
73

74

TUNE-UP

For normal riding, perform a complete tune-up at the interval listed in **Table 1**. More frequent tune-ups may be required if the bike is ridden in stop-and-go traffic. The purpose of the tune-up is to restore the performance lost due to normal wear and deterioration of parts.

If engine performance is reduced or if the spark plug electrodes are worn, replace both spark plugs as a set. In addition, this is a good time to clean the air filter element.

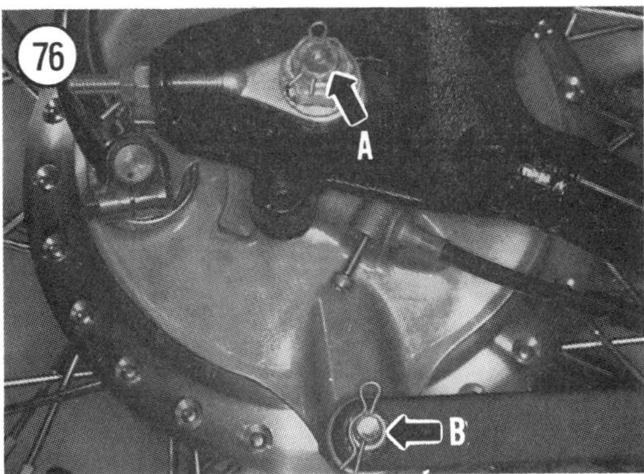

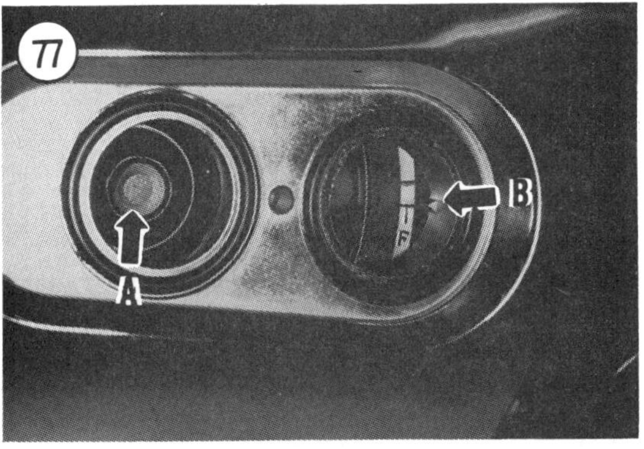

Perform the tune-up procedure in the following order:

1. Adjust valve clearance.
2. Run a compression test.
3. Change spark plugs.
4. Check ignition timing.
5. Set the idle speed.

Table 6 includes tune-up specifications.

6. To perform a tune-up on your Kawasaki, you need the following tools and equipment:
   a. 18 mm (5/8 in.) spark plug wrench.
   b. Socket wrench and assorted sockets.
   c. Compression gauge.
   d. Spark plug feeler gauge and gap adjusting tool.
   e. Portable tachometer.

Valve Clearance Measurement and Adjustment

NOTE
Be sure the engine is cold before measuring valve clearance.

1. Remove the cylinder head covers as described in Chapter Four.
2. Remove the timing cover from the alternator cover.
3. Rotate the engine counterclockwise until the front piston is at top dead center (TDC) on the compression stroke.
   a. Use a 17 mm socket to turn the alternator rotor (A, **Figure 77**) counterclockwise until the front cylinder timing mark (TF) on the rotor aligns with the pointer (B, **Figure 77**).
   b. Check the index line on the front cylinder camshaft sprocket. It should be aligned with the top surface of the cylinder head (**Figure 78**). If it is not, rotate the engine 360° counterclockwise until the camshaft sprocket index line is correctly aligned with the cylinder head and the TF mark on the alternator rotor is aligned with the pointer (B, **Figure 77**).
4. Place a clean shop rag over the cam sprocket and cam chain cavity so nothing will be dropped into the crankcase.
5. Use a feeler gauge to check the clearance between the rocker arm and the shim on each valve in the front cylinder (**Figure 79**). Record the valve clearance for each valve.

6. Now set the rear piston to top dead center on the compression stroke. Use the 17 mm socket to turn the alternator 305° counterclockwise. The rear cylinder timing mark on the rotor (TR) should align with the pointer (**Figure 80**)

7. Measure the clearance of the valves in the rear cylinder. Record the valve clearance for each valve in the rear cylinder.

8. Compare the valve clearances to the specifications listed in **Table 6**. To adjust the clearance of any valve that is not within specification, remove the old shim from the top of the valve stem and replace it with a new shim that brings the clearance within specification.

 a. Slide the rocker arm sideways in the camshaft cap. Insert the head of a 6 mm bolt (**Figure 81**) between the rocker arm and the cam cap. This will hold the rocker arm away from the shim for easy removal and installation.
 b. Use a magnet or tweezers to remove the shim from between the valve keepers (**Figure 82**).
 c. Mark the shim and record its location.
 d. Measure the shim thickness with a micrometer (**Figure 83**). Record the thickness.
 e. Determine the new shim thickness by using the following equation:

$a = (b - c) + d$

Where: a is the thickness of the new shim, b is the measured valve clearance, c is the specified valve clearance and d is the thickness of the old shim.

NOTE
*The following numbers are for **example only.** Use the numbers you wrote down when you measured the valve clearance and old shim thickness.*

For example, if the measured valve clearance is 0.25 mm, the old shim thickness is 2.60 mm and the specified valve clearance is 0.15 mm, then:

a = (0.25 - 0.15) + 2.60

a (new shim thickness) = 2.70

 f. Apply clean engine oil to both sides of the new shim and install the shim between the valve keepers.

9. Repeat the procedure for each valve that needs to be adjusted.

10. Recheck the valve clearance. Readjust as needed.

Compression Test

Check the cylinder compression at the interval indicated in **Table 1**. Record the results and compare them to the results at the next interval. A running record will show trends in deterioration so that corrective action can be taken before complete failure.

The results when properly interpreted, can indicate general cylinder, piston ring and valve condition.

78

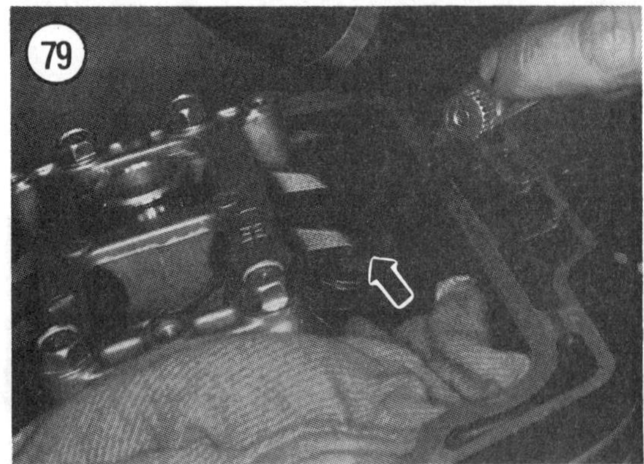
79

80

Warm the engine to normal operating temperature, then shut it off.

Remove the spark plug from each cylinder as described in this chapter.

3. Connect the compression tester to one cylinder following its manufacturer's instructions.

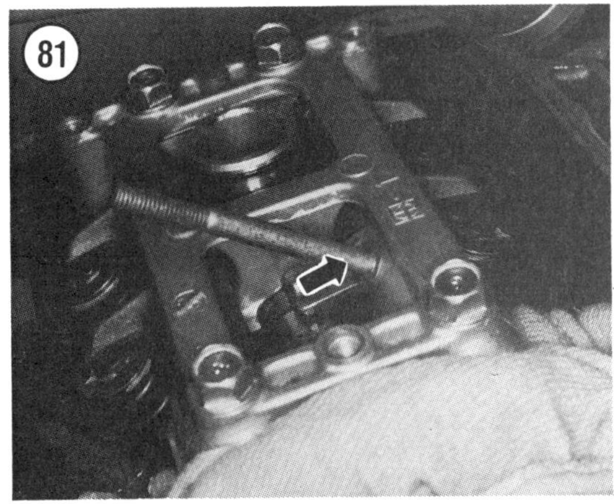

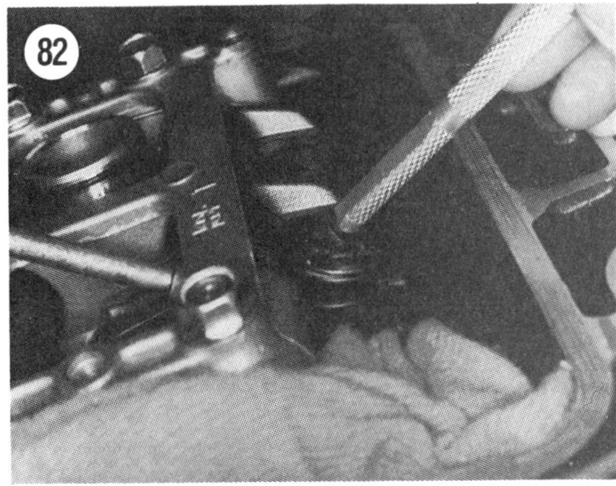

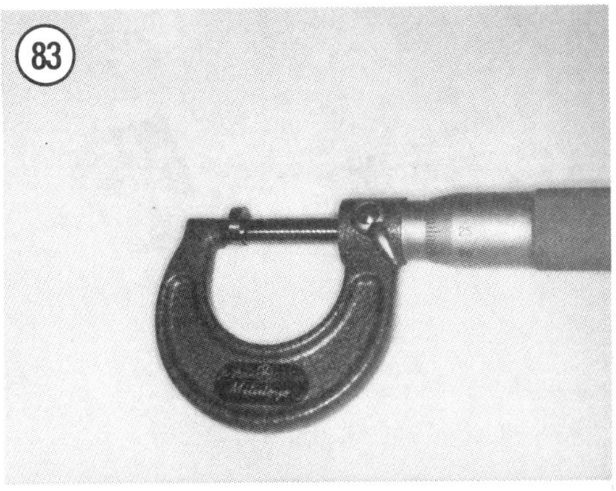

4. Hold the throttle in the wide-open position. Crank the engine until there is no further rise in pressure.

5. Remove the tester and record the reading. Repeat for the other cylinder.

6. When interpreting the results, actual compression is not as important as the difference in pressure between cylinders. For optimum performance, compression pressure must be within 10% between cylinders.

7. A low compression reading generally indicates a problem with the piston, piston rings and cylinder, or a leaking valve(s). If a low reading is obtained, pour a teaspoon of clean engine oil into the cylinder through the spark plug hole. Crank the engine to clear excess oil, then repeat the compression test. If compression increases significantly, the piston rings and possibly the cylinder are excessively worn. If the compression does not increase, a leaking valve(s) is indicated.

Spark Plug Selection

Select plugs in a heat range designed for the loads and temperature conditions under which the engine will operate. Using an incorrect heat range can cause piston seizure, scored cylinder walls or damaged piston crowns.

In general, use a hotter plug for low speeds, low loads and low temperatures. Use a colder plug for high speeds, high engine loads and high temperatures.

NOTE

In areas where seasonal temperature variations are great, the factory recommends a two-plug system: a cold plug for hard summer riding and a hot plug for slower winter operation. This may prevent spark plug and engine problems. The plug should operate hot enough to burn off unwanted deposits, but not so hot that it is damaged or causes pre-ignition.

A spark plug of the correct heat range will show a light tan color on the insulator.

The reach (length) of a plug is also important (**Figure 84**). A longer than normal plug could interfere with the valves and pistons, causing severe damage. The recommended spark plugs are listed in **Table 6**.

3

Spark Plug Removal/Cleaning

1. Remove the seat.
2. Grasp each spark plug lead and carefully pull it off the plug. If the boot is stuck to the plug, twist it slightly to break it loose.

CAUTION

If any dirt falls into the cylinder when the plugs are removed, it could cause serious engine damage.

3. Use compressed air and blow away any dirt that may have accumulated in the spark plug well.
4. Remove both spark plugs using a 16 mm spark plug wrench. Keep the front and rear plugs separate. If anything turns up during the inspection step, you will then know which cylinder it came from.

NOTE

If a plug is difficult to remove, apply penetrating oil around base of the plug and let it soak about 10-20 minutes.

5. Inspect the spark plug carefully. Look for a broken center porcelain, excessively eroded electrodes and excessive carbon or oil fouling. Replace such a plug. If deposits are light, the plug may be cleaned in solvent with a wire brush. Regap the plug as explained in this chapter.

NOTE

Spark plug cleaning with the use of a sand-blast type device is not recommended. While this type of cleaning is thorough, the plug must be perfectly free of all abrasive cleaning material when done. If not, it is possible for the cleaning material to fall into the engine during operation and cause damage.

84

Reach

Too short Correct Too long

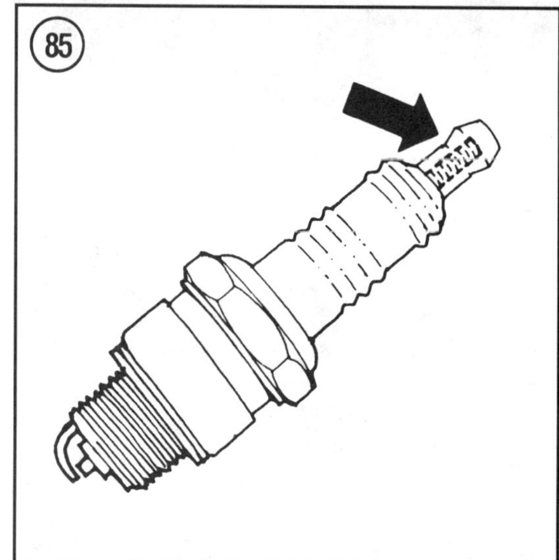

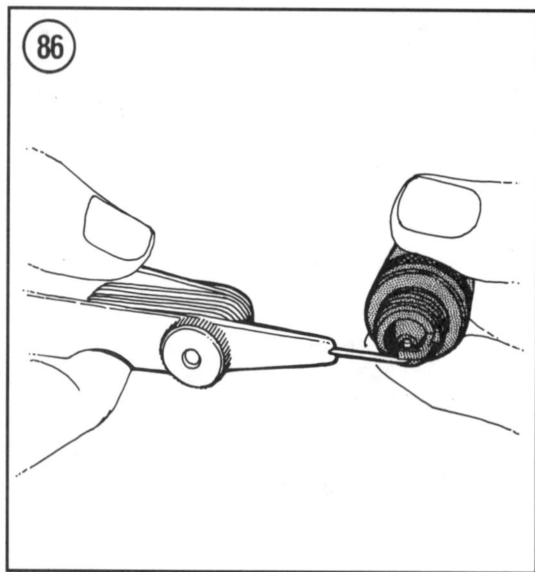

Spark Plug Gapping and Installation

Carefully adjust the electrode gap on a new plug to ensure a reliable, consistent spark. You must use a special spark plug gapping tool with a wire feeler gauge.

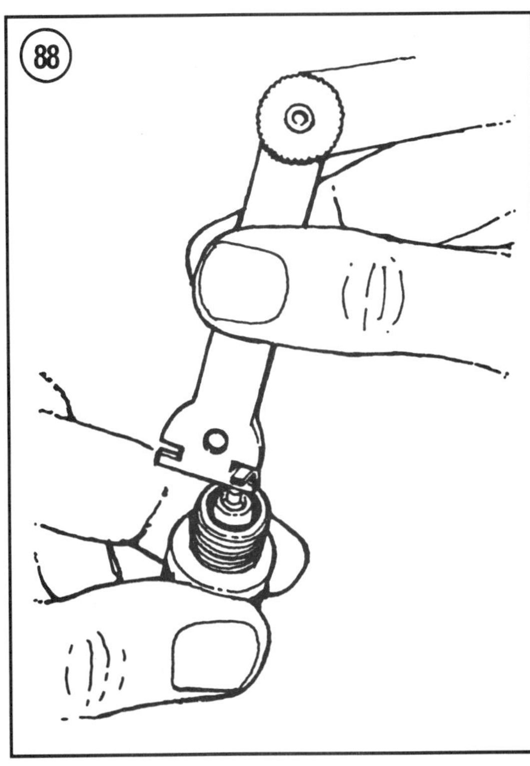

1. If installed, unscrew the small terminal from the end of the spark plug (**Figure 85**). This terminal is not used.
2. Insert a round feeler gauge between the center and side electrode of each plug (**Figure 86**). The correct gap (**Figure 87**) is listed in **Table 6**. If the gap is correct, you will feel a slight drag as you pull the feeler gauge through. If there is no drag or the gauge will not pass through, bend the side electrode with the gapping tool (**Figure 88**) to set the proper gap.
3. Put a small drop of oil or aluminum antiseize compound on the threads of the spark plug.
4. Screw each spark plug in by hand until it seats. Very little effort is required. If force is necessary, you may have the plug cross-threaded; unscrew it and try again.

NOTE

If a spark plug is difficult to install, the cylinder head threads may be dirty or slightly damaged. To clean the threads, apply grease to the threads of a spark plug tap and screw it carefully into the cylinder head. Turn the tap slowly until it is completely installed. If the tap cannot be installed, the threads are severely damaged and must be repaired.

5. Tighten the spark plugs an additional 1/2 turn after the gasket contacts the head. If you are reinstalling the old plug, only tighten an additional 1/4 turn.

CAUTION

Do not over tighten. Besides making the plug difficult to remove, the excessive torque will crush the gasket and destroy its sealing ability.

6. Install the spark plug leads; make sure the leads are on tight.

Reading Spark Plugs

Much information about engine and spark plug performance can be determined by careful examination of the spark plugs. This information is only valid after performing the following steps.

1. Ride the bike a short distance at full throttle in any gear.
2. While riding at wide-open throttle, move the stop switch (**Figure 89**) to the OFF position (without closing the throttle) and simultaneously pull in the clutch or shift into neutral. Coast and brake to a stop.
3. Remove one spark plug at a time and examine it. Compare it to **Figure 90**. If the insulator is white or burned, the plug is too hot and should be replaced with a colder one.

NOTE
A plug that is too cold will have sooty or oily deposits ranging in color from dark brown to black. Replace with a hotter plug and check for excessively rich carburetion or evidence of oil blowby at the piston rings. If the plug has a light tan or gray colored deposit and no abnormal gap wear or electrode erosion is evident, the plug and plug and carburetion are correct. If the plug exhibits a black insulator tip, a damp and oily film over the firing end and a carbon layer over the entire nose, it is oil fouled. An oil fouled plug can be cleaned, but it is better to replace it.

4. Repeat for the other spark plug. If either spark plug is in unserviceable condition, replace them both.

Ignition Timing

All models are equipped with a solid state ignition system consisting of a pickup coil and timing rotor assembly, an IC igniter unit, two ignition coils and two spark plugs. This system uses no breaker points and requires no maintenance.

Since there are no components to wear, adjusting the ignition timing is not necessary nor possible. If you suspect an ignition-related problem, inspect the ignition coils, pickup coil and IC igniter unit as described in Chapter Nine.

Incorrect ignition timing can cause a drastic loss of engine performance and efficiency. It may also cause overheating.

Carburetor Idle Speed Adjustment

Prior to making this adjustment, the air filter element must be clean and the engine must have adequate compression. See *Compression Test* in this chapter. Otherwise this procedure cannot be done properly.

1. Start and run the engine until it reaches normal operating temperature. Make sure the choke is pushed in all the way (**Figure 91**).
2. Connect a portable tachometer following its manufacturer's instructions.
3. On the right-hand side of the bike, turn the idle adjust screw (**Figure 92**) in or out to adjust idle speed.
4. The correct idle speed is listed in **Table 6**.

NOTE
The throttle linkage must stop against the idle adjust screw with the throttle in the completely closed position.

5. Open and close the throttle a couple of times and check for variations in idle speed. Readjust if necessary.

WARNING
With the engine running at idle speed, move the handlebar from side to side. If the idle speed increases during this movement, the throttle cable may need adjusting or it may be incorrectly routed through the frame. Correct this problem immediately. Do not ride the bike in this unsafe condition.

Carburetor Idle Mixture

The idle mixture (pilot air screw) is preset at the factory and is not to be reset. Do not adjust the pilot air screw unless the carburetor is overhauled. If so, refer to Chapter Eight.

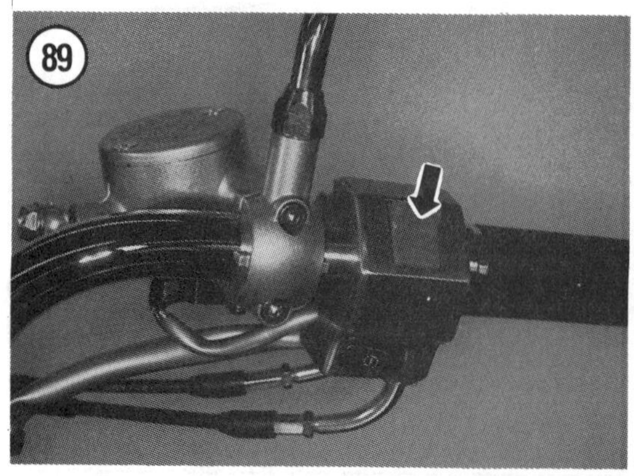
89

SPARK PLUG CONDITION

NORMAL

- Identified by light tan or gray deposits on the firing tip.
- Can be cleaned.

GAP BRIDGED

- Identified by deposit buildup closing gap between electrodes.
- Caused by oil or carbon fouling. If deposits are not excessive, the plug can be cleaned.

OIL FOULED

- Identified by wet black deposits on the insulator shell bore and electrodes.
- Caused by excessive oil entering combustion chamber through worn rings and pistons, excessive clearance between valve guides and stems or worn or loose bearings. Can be cleaned. If engine is not repaired, use a hotter plug.

CARBON FOULED

- Identified by black, dry fluffy carbon deposits on insulator tips, exposed shell surfaces and electrodes.
- Caused by too cold a plug, weak ignition, dirty air cleaner, too rich a fuel mixture or excessive idling. Can be cleaned.

LEAD FOULED

- Identified by dark gray, black, yellow or tan deposits or a fused glazed coating on the insulator tip.
- Caused by highly leaded gasoline. Can be cleaned.

WORN

- Identified by severely eroded or worn electrodes.
- Caused by normal wear. Should be replaced.

FUSED SPOT DEPOSIT

- Identified by melted or spotty deposits resembling bubbles or blisters.
- Caused by sudden acceleration. Can be cleaned.

OVERHEATING

- Identified by a white or light gray insulator with small black or gray brown spots and with bluish-burnt appearance of electrodes.
- Caused by engine overheating, wrong type of fuel, loose spark plugs, too hot a plug or incorrect ignition timing. Replace the plug.

PREIGNITION

- Identified by melted electrodes and possibly blistered insulator. Metallic deposits on insulator indicate engine damage.
- Caused by wrong type of fuel, incorrect ignition timing or advance, too hot a plug, burned valves or engine overheating. Replace the plug.

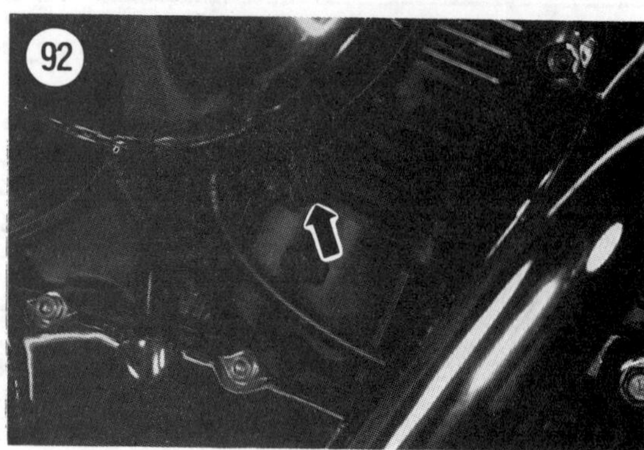

Table 1 MAINTENANCE SCHEDULE*

Prior to each ride	Inspect the tires and rims, and check inflation pressure Check brake operation, and check for fluid leaks Check fuel supply. Make sure there is enough fuel for the intended ride Check for fuel leaks Check for coolant leaks Check all lights for proper operation Check engine oil level Check for smooth throttle operation Check gearshift pedal operation Check clutch operation, and check for fluid leaks
Every 185 miles (300 km)	Lubricate the drive chain
Initial 500 miles (800 km)	Replace engine oil and filter
Initial 600 miles (1,000 km)	Clean oil screen Clean air filter element Check engine idle speed Check valve clearance Check evaporative emission control system** Check throttle grip free play Check clutch lever free play Check rear brake pedal free play Check fluid level in front brake master cylinder; add fluid if necessary Check brake light switch operation Inspect entire brake system Check spoke tightness and rim runout Check all hoses--fuel, vacuum, emission, brake and coolant Check tightness of all fasteners Inspect steering for smooth operation
Every 3,100 miles (5,000 km)	Replace engine oil and filter Clean oil screen Clean and inspect spark plugs Check engine idle speed; adjust if necessary Check air suction valve Check evaporative emission control system**

(continued)

Table 1 MAINTENANCE SCHEDULE* (continued)

	Check clutch lever free play
	Check the drive chain for wear
	Inspect the brake pads and shoes for wear
	Check fluid level in front brake master cylinder
	Check rear brake pedal free play
	Check brake light switch operation
	Inspect steering for smooth operation
	Check tire wear
	Check spoke tightness and rim runout
	Lubricate all pivot points
	Lubricate control cables (throttle, choke, clutch, rear brake)
Every 6,200 miles (10,000 km)	Check valve clearance
	Clean air filter elements
	Check throttle grip free play
	Check the fuel system
	Lubricate the swing arm and uni-trak linkage
	Lubricate all pivot points
	Check the rear shock and front forks for leakage
	Check tightness of all fasteners
Every 12,400 miles (20,000 km) or every 2 years	Replace air filter elements (or after five cleanings)
	Drain and replace hydraulic brake fluid
	Drain and replace coolant
	Lubricate rear brake camshaft
	Lubricate steering stem bearings
	Replace rear brake cable
	Replace the front brake master cylinder and dust seal
	Replace the front caliper piston seal and dust seal
Every 18,600 miles (30,000 km) or every 2 years	Change the front fork oil
Every 4 years	Replace the brake hose
	Replace all coolant hoses
	Replace the fuel lines

* Consider this schedule a guide to general maintenance and lubrication intervals. Harder than normal use and exposure to mud, water, sand and high humidity naturally dictates more frequent attention to most maintenance items.
** California models only.

Table 2 TIRE SPECIFICATIONS

Tire Size	
VN800	
Front	80/90-21 48H tube
Rear	140/90-16 71H tube
VN800 Classic	
Front	130/90-16 67H tube
Rear	140/90-16 71H tube
Minimum tread depth	
Front	1 mm (0.04 in.)
Rear	
To 130 km/h (90 mph)	2 mm (0.8 in.)
Over 130 km/h (90mph)	3 mm (0.12 in.)

(continued)

Table 2 TIRE SPECIFICATIONS (continued)

Tire inflation (cold)*	
Up to 215 lb. (97.5 kg)	
Front	28 psi (193 kPa)
Rear	38 psi (193 kPa)
215-397 lb. (97-180kg)	
Front	32 psi (220 kPa)
Rear	32 psi (220 kPa)

*Tire pressure is for origninal equipement tires. Aftermarket tires may require different pressures; refer to the aftermarket tire manufacture's specifications.

Table 3 BATTERY CHARGE RATE

Terminal voltage	Charge rate	Charge period
11.5- 12.5 volts	1.4 amps	5-10 hours
Less than 11.5 volts	1.4 amps	20 hours

Table 4 RECOMMENDED LUBRICANTS AND FLUIDS

Fuel	Regular unleaded
Octane	
U.S. models	87 [(R + M)/2 method] or 91 or higher
Capacity	15.0 L (3.96 U.S. gal [3.3 Imp. gal])
Engine oil	
Grade	API SE, SF or SG
Viscosity	SAE 10W-40, 10W-50, 20W-40 or 20W-50
Capacity	
Oil change only	2.7 L (2.9 U.S. qt. [2.4 Imp. qt.])
Change and filter	2.9 L (3.1 qt. [2.6 Imp. qt.])
When engine completely dry	3.2 L (3.4 U.S. qt. [2.8 Imp. qt.])
Coolant	Ethylene glycol
Capacity	2.4 L (2.5 qt. [2.1 Imp. qt.])
Brake fluid	DOT 4
Battery	Maintenance free
Fork oil	
Viscosity	SAE 10W
Capacity per leg	
Oil change only	
VN800	290 ml (9.80 U.S. oz. [10.21 Imp. oz.])
VN800 Classic	265 ml (8.96 oz. [9.33 Imp. oz.])
After disassembly	
VN800	336-344 ml (11.36-11.63 U.S. oz. [11.83-12.11 Imp. oz.])
VN800 Classic	306-314 ml (10.35-10.62 U.S. oz. [10.77-11.05 Imp. oz.])
Cables	SAE 10W-30 motor oil
Pivot points	SAE 30
Drive chain	SAE 90

Table 5 MAINTENANCE AND TUNE UP TIGHTENING TORQUES

Item	N•m	in.-lb.	ft.-lb.
Oil drain plug	20	—	15
Oil filter	18	—	13.0
Oil screen drain plug	20	—	15

(continued)

Table 5 MAINTENANCE AND TUNE UP TIGHTENING TORQUES (continued)

Item	N•m	in.-lb.	ft.-lb.
Oil pressure switch	20	—	15
Front brake caliper mounting bolts	34	—	25
Engine coolant drain plug	11	97	—
Radiator drain plug	11	97	—
Rear axle nut	98	—	72
Torque link nut	34	—	25
Spark plugs	18	—	13.0

Table 6 MAINTENANCE AND TUNE-UP SPECIFICATIONS

Spark plug type	NGK CR7E or ND U22ESR-N
Spark plug gap	0.7-0.8 mm (0.028-0.031 in.)
Idle Speed	
U.S. and Swiss models	1250-1350 rpm
All other models	950-1050 rpm
Valve clearance	
Intake	0.10-0.15 mm (0.004-0.006 in.)
Exhaust	0.25-0.30 mm (0.010-0.012 in.)
Cylinder compression (useable range)	855-1315 kPa (124-191 psi)
Engine oil pressure @ 4000 rpm	355-410 kPa (51-60 psi) with oil at 100° C (212° F)
Radiator cap relief pressure	93-123 kPa (14-18 psi)
Coolant system test pressure	123 kPa (18 psi)
Brake pad wear limit	1 mm (0.039 in.)
Brake shoe	
Lining thickness	4.9-5.5 mm (0.19-0.25 in.)
Wear limit	2.6 mm (0.10 in.)
Rear brake cam lever angle	80-90 degrees
Rear brake pedal free play	20-30 mm (0.79-1.18 in.)
Brake pedal height	65 mm (2.6 in.)
Throttle grip free play	2-3 mm (0.079-0.118 in.)
Clutch lever free play	2-3 mm (0.079-0.118 in.)
Drive chain slack	25-30 mm (0.98-1.18 in.)
Wear limit	35 mm (1.38 in.)
Drive chain 20-link length	317.5-318.2 mm (12.50-12.53 in.)
Wear limit	323 mm (12.72 in.)

CHAPTER FOUR

ENGINE UPPER END

The engine is a liquid-cooled, four-stroke V-twin design. The cylinders are offset and configured in a 45-degree angle. They fire on alternate crankshaft rotations. Each cylinder is equipped with a single camshaft and four valves. The crankshaft is supported by two main bearings in a vertically split crankcase.

Both engine and transmission share a common case and the same wet sump oil supply. The clutch is a wet-type located on the right-hand side of the engine. Refer to Chapter Six for clutch service and Chapter Seven for transmission service procedures.

This chapter provides complete procedures and information for removal, inspection, service and reassembly of the engine upper end. Refer to Chapter Five for engine removal and lower end service procedures.

NOTE
Many of the upper end components on this engine are similar, but slight variations do exist. These variations mean the component must be installed in the correct location either on the front cylinder assembly or on the rear cylinder assembly. Where these similarities exist, they are noted in the text. Where it is necessary, mark parts with an F (front cylinder) or R (rear cylinder) to avoid confusion during assembly.

Table 1 provides specifications for the engine upper end and **Table 2** lists upper end torque specifications. **Tables 1-3** are located at the end of this chapter.

Before beginning work, read Chapter One of this book. You will do a better job with this information fresh in your mind.

ENGINE PRINCIPLES

Figure 1 explains how the engine works. This will be helpful when troubleshooting or repairing the engine.

SERVICING ENGINE IN FRAME

The following components can be serviced while the engine is mounted in the frame (the bike's frame is a great holding fixture for breaking loose stubborn bolts and nuts):

a. Clutch (except for clutch outer housing).
b. Carburetor.
c. Starter motor.
d. Alternator and electrical systems.

CYLINDER HEAD COVER

Removal

The following procedure shows the removal and installation of the front cylinder head cover. The procedure is similar for both cylinders except for minor differences, which are noted.

1. Securely support the bike on wooden blocks or on a scissors jack.
2. Remove the seat as described in Chapter Fourteen.

(1)

4-STROKE ENGINE PRINCIPLES

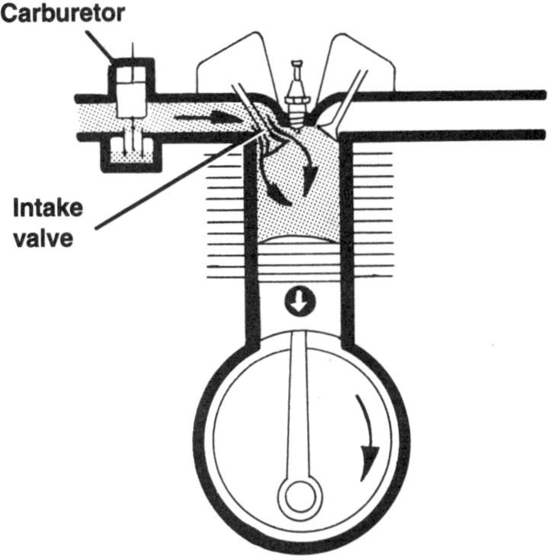

As the piston travels downward, the exhaust valve is closed and the intake valve opens, allowing the new air-fuel mixture from the carburetor to be drawn into the cylinder. When the piston reaches the bottom of its travel (BDC), the intake valve closes and remains closed for the next 1 1/2 revolutions of the crankshaft.

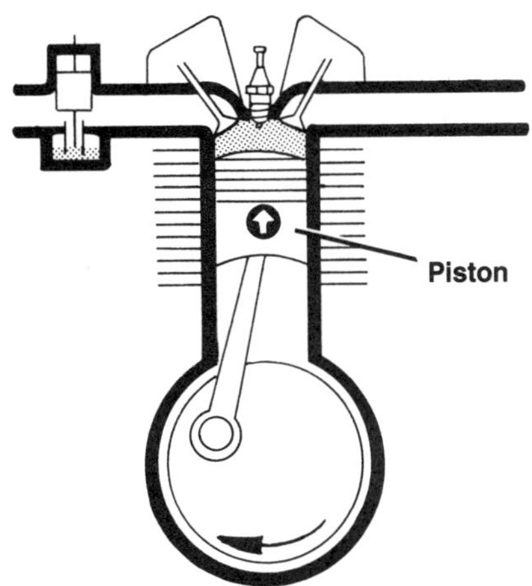

While the crankshaft continues to rotate, the piston moves upward, compressing the air-fuel mixture.

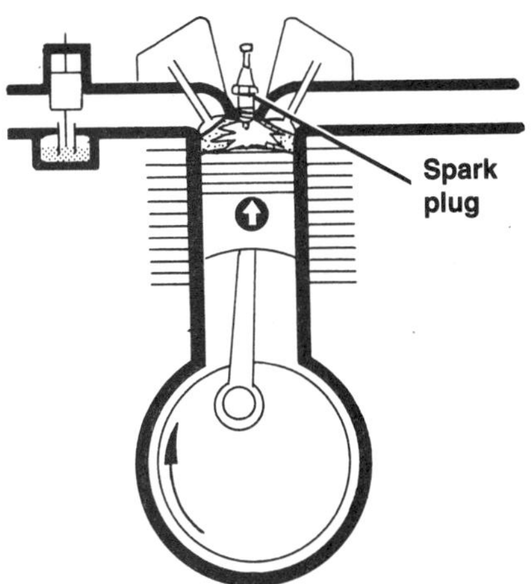

As the piston almost reaches the top of its travel, the spark plug fires, igniting the compressed air-fuel mixture. The piston continues to top dead center (TDC) and is pushed downward by the expanding gases.

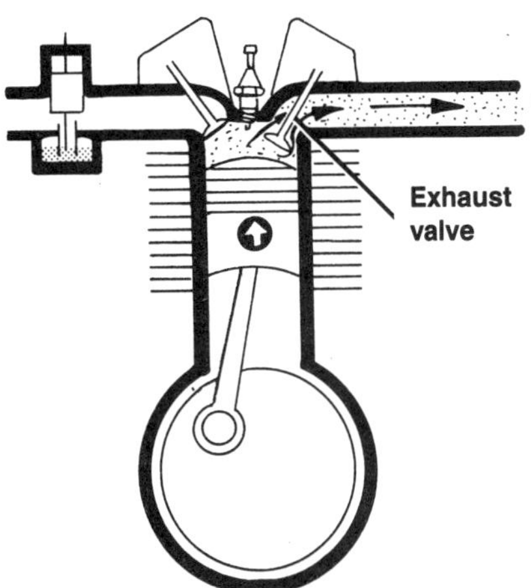

When the piston almost reaches BDC, the exhaust valve opens and remains open until the piston is near TDC. The upward travel of the piston forces the exhaust gases out of the cylinder. After the piston has reached TDC, the exhaust valve closes and the cycle starts all over again.

3. Remove the fuel tank as described in Chapter Eight.
4. Remove the air filter assembly, carburetor and the vacuum switch valve as described in Chapter Eight. Move the throttle and choke cables out of the way.
5. When servicing the rear cylinder, remove the exhaust pipe as described in Chapter Eight.
6. Remove the spark plug cap.
7. Remove the cylinder head cover bolts and remove the cover (**Figure 2**). Be sure you do not lose the washer under each bolt or the locating pin (A, **Figure 3**) from the cylinder.
8. Installation is the reverse of the removal procedure. Pay attention to the following:
   a. If the spark plug pipe (B, **Figure 3**) was removed, apply grease to the O-rings at each end of the pipe, and reinstall the pipe with the chamfered end facing upward.
   b. Be sure the locating pin (A, **Figure 3**) and the air suction valve (C, **Figure 3**) are in place in the cylinder head.
   c. Install a new cylinder head cover gasket.
   d. When installing the cylinder head cover bolts, be sure the metal side of the washers face upward (**Figure 2**). Torque the bolts to the specification listed in **Table 2**.

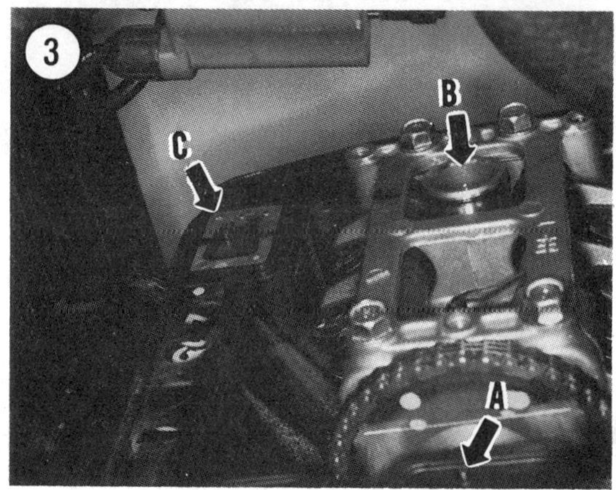

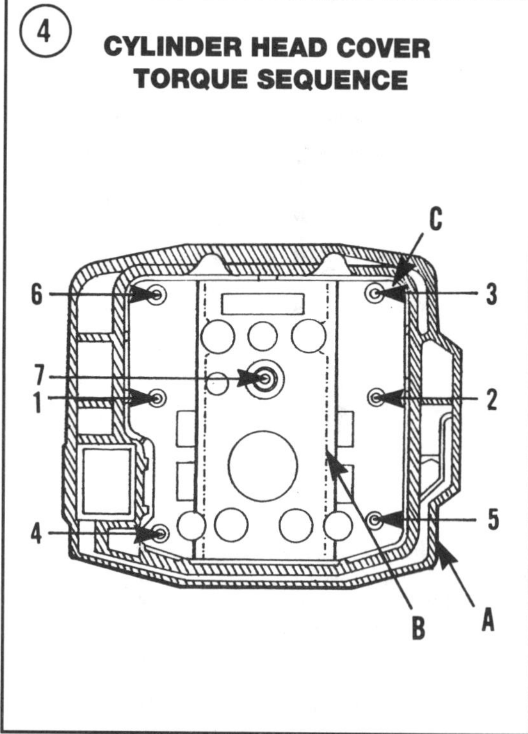

Disassembly

1. Remove the seven damper plate bolts from inside the cylinder head cover (A, **Figure 4**).
2. Remove the damper plate (C, **Figure 4**) and the damper (B, **Figure 4**).
3. Assembly is the reverse of the disassembly procedure. Note the following:
   a. Apply Loctite 242 to the damper plate bolts and tighten the bolts in the sequence shown in **Figure 4**.
   b. Tighten the cylinder head bolts to the specification given in **Table 2**.

CAMSHAFT

The following procedure shows the removal and installation of the front cylinder camshaft. The procedure is similar for both cylinders except for minor differences, which are noted.

Refer to **Figure 5** for this procedure.

Removal

1. Remove the engine as described in Chapter Five.
2. Remove the cylinder head cover as described in this chapter.
3. Remove the timing cover (**Figure 6**) from the alternator cover.
4. Rotate the engine counterclockwise until the front piston is at top dead center (TDC) on the compression stroke.

CAMSHAFT/CAM CHAIN ASSEMBLY

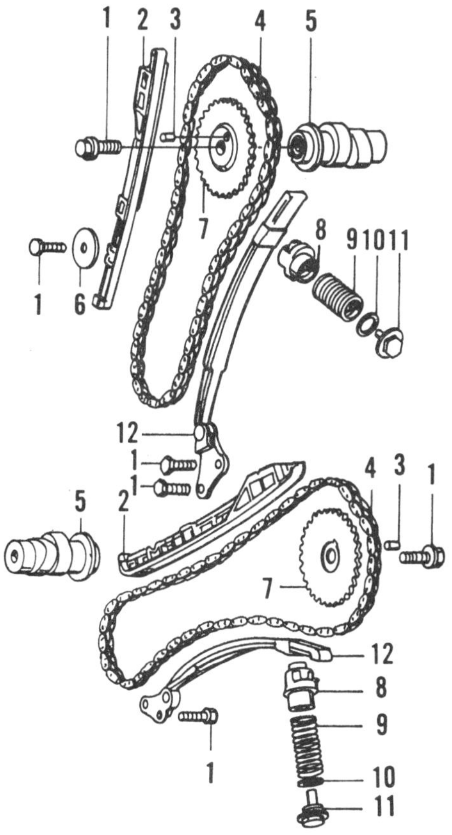

1. Bolt
2. Chain guide (white)
3. Pin
4. Cam chain
5. Camshaft
6. Washer (front cylinder only)
7. Sprocket
8. Tensioner body
9. Spring
10. Gasket
11. Tensioner bolt
12. Chain guide/tensioner (black)

5

a. Use a 17 mm socket to turn the alternator rotor (A, **Figure 7**) counterclockwise until the front cylinder timing mark TF on the rotor aligns with the pointer on the left-side crankcase cover (B, **Figure 7**).

NOTE

*TF is the timing mark for the front cylinder. The timing mark for the rear cylinder is TR. When setting the rear cylinder to TDC, turn the engine counterclockwise until the TR mark on the rotor aligns with the pointer (**Figure 8**).*

If the front cylinder is already at top dead center on the compression stroke, rotating the engine 305° counterclockwise sets the rear cylinder to TDC on the compression stroke.

b. Confirm that the index line on the front cylinder camshaft sprocket is aligned with the top surface of the cylinder head (**Figure 9**). If it is not, rotate the engine 360° counterclockwise until the camshaft sprocket index line is correctly aligned with the cylinder head and the TF mark on the alternator rotor is aligned with the pointer on the left-side crankcase cover.

6

7

4

NOTE
In the following photographs, the rear cylinder is removed for clarity.

5. Remove the cam chain tensioner cap bolt (**Figure 10**), the gasket and the tensioner spring from the cylinder.

CAUTION
The tensioner body is loose in the cylinder when the tensioner cap bolt is removed. ***Do not*** *rotate the crankshaft while the tensioner cap bolt is out. You could damage the tensioner body or the cylinder.*

6. Release the tensioner push rod by performing the following:
   a. Insert a screwdriver down the cam chain cavity and release the stopper (A, **Figure 11**).
   b. Insert a second screwdriver and depress the push rod (B, **Figure 11**) into the tensioner body (C, **Figure 11**).
   c. Temporarily reinstall the tensioner cap bolt so the tensioner body will not fall into the crankcase.

NOTE
The camshaft caps in this engine are not interchangeable. Each camshaft cap is machined to fit a particular cylinder head and must be used only in that head. If you are servicing both cylinders, mark the front and rear camshaft caps so they can be easily identified and reinstalled in their respective cylinder heads.

7. Remove the four camshaft cap bolts (A, **Figure 12**), and remove the camshaft cap from the cylinder head (B, **Figure 12**). Do not lose the two locating dowels under the camshaft cap (**Figure 13**).
8. Disengage the cam chain from the sprocket and remove the camshaft from the cylinder head. Tie a wire to the cam chain and secure the wire to the outside of the engine **(Figure 14)** so the chain will not fall into the crankcase.
9. Inspect all parts as described in this chapter.

CAUTION
The crankshaft may be turned while the camshaft is removed. However, the cam chain ***must*** *be pulled taut whenever the crankshaft is rotated. If it is not, the cam chain could kink on the crankshaft*

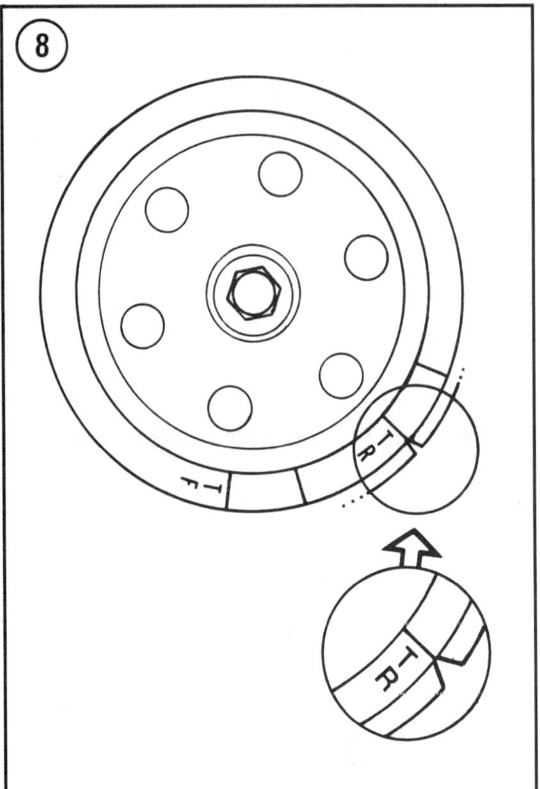

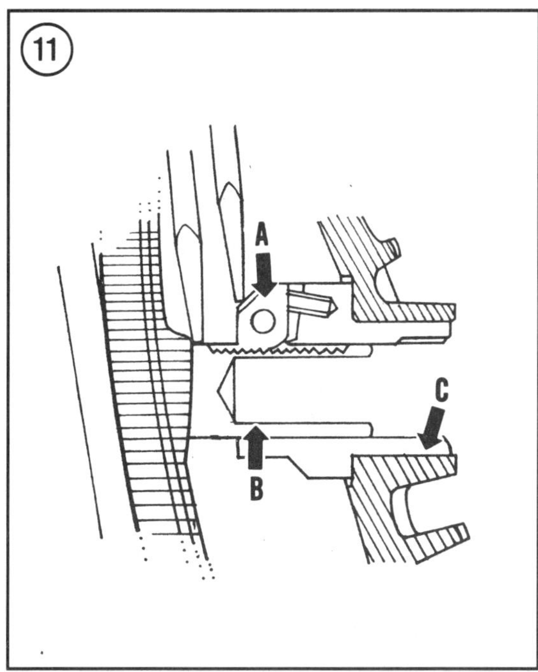

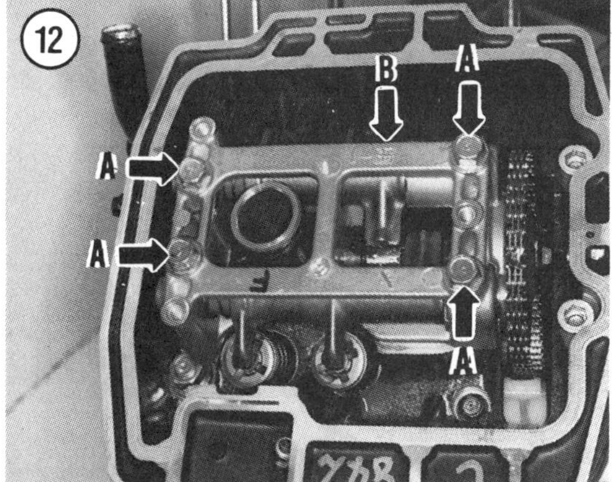

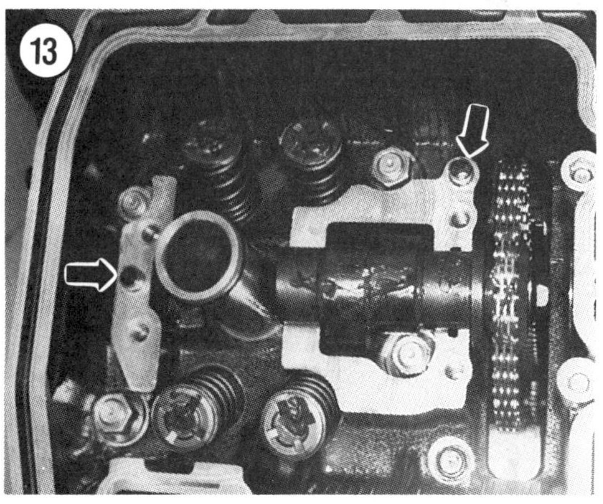

sprocket, which could damage both the chain and sprocket.

Installation

NOTE

The front and rear camshafts are not identical. The rear camshaft has a radial groove in its locating boss ***(Figure 15)*** *that is not found on the front camshaft. Be sure you are installing the correct camshaft into each cylinder.*

1. Set the cylinder to top dead center on the compression stroke. Refer to *Camshaft Removal* in this chapter.
2. Apply oil to the camshaft journals and to the bearing surfaces in the cylinder head.
3. Untie the wire from the cam chain. Fit the camshaft under the chain and into place in the cylinder head.
4. Rotate the camshaft sprocket until the index line on the sprocket aligns with the top surface of the cylinder head. Lower the cam chain so it properly engages the teeth on the sprocket (**Figure 9**).

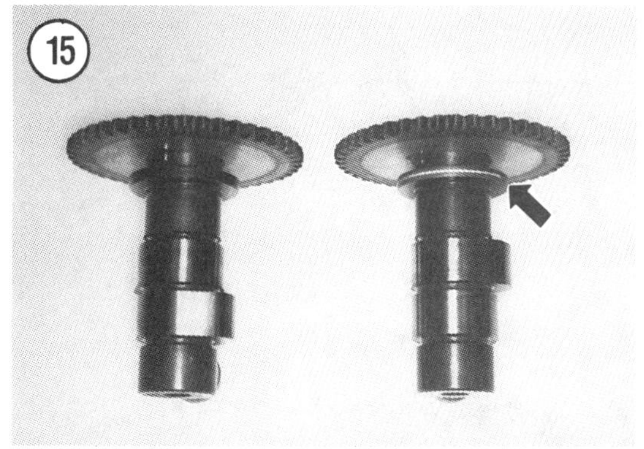

4

5. Check that the camshaft cap locating dowels are in place in the cylinder head (**Figure 13**).

6. Be sure the cutouts in the rocker shafts face inward (**Figure 16**). Also be sure that the cutouts and the holes in the rocker shafts align with the mounting holes in the camshaft cap (**Figure 17**).

7. Lower the camshaft cap (B, **Figure 12**) in place over the camshaft so that the cap engages the locating dowels.

8. Install the four camshaft cap bolts (A, **Figure 12**). Gradually tighten them in a crisscross pattern. Torque the camshaft cap bolts to the specification listed in **Table 2**.

9. Remove the cap bolt from the chain tensioner.

10. Hold the tensioner body while you gently push the push rod until it *lightly* touches the chain guide (**Figure 18**).

11. Install the chain tensioner spring, washer and the cap bolt (**Figure 19**). Torque the cap bolt to the specification listed in **Table 2**.

12. Reinstall the cylinder head cover as described in this chapter.

Camshaft Inspection

1. Inspect the camshaft bearing journals (A, **Figure 20**) for wear.

2. Measure both camshaft bearing journals (**Figure 21**) with a micrometer. Compare the measurements to the specifications given in **Table 1**. Replace the camshaft if either journal is worn to the service limit.

3. Check the camshaft lobes (B, **Figure 20**) for wear. The lobes must not be scored and the edges must be square. Slight damage may be removed with a silicone carbide oilstone. Use No. 100-120 grit stone initially, then polish with a No. 280-320 grit stone.

16

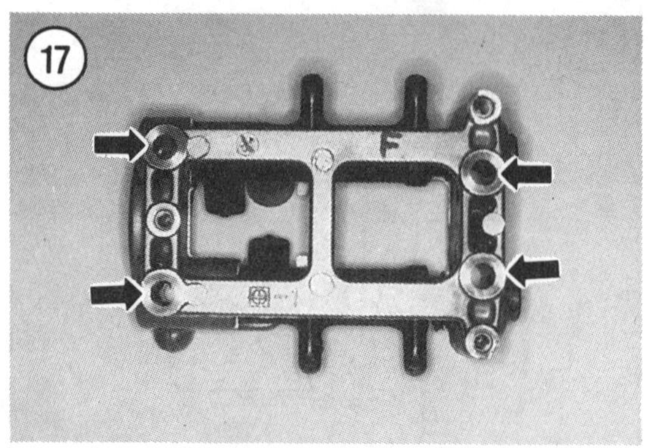
17

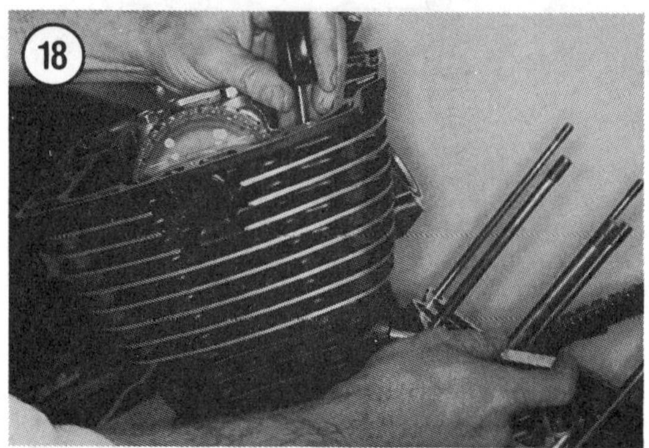
18

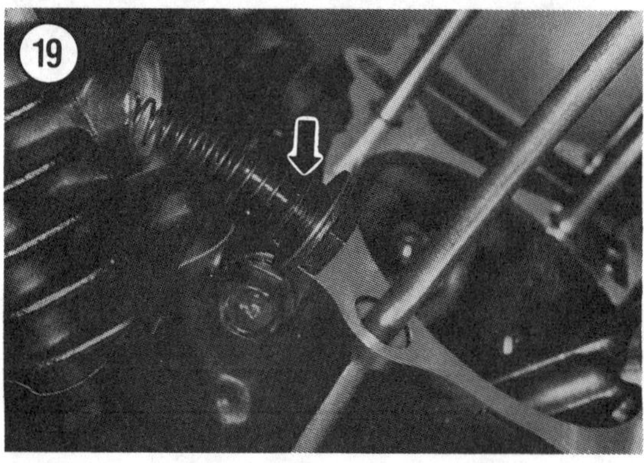
19

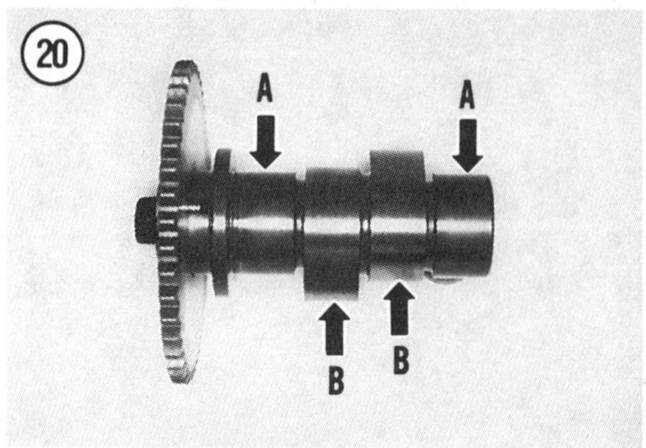

20

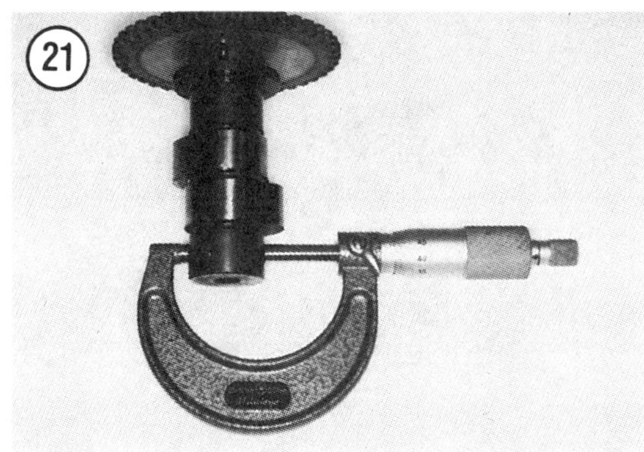

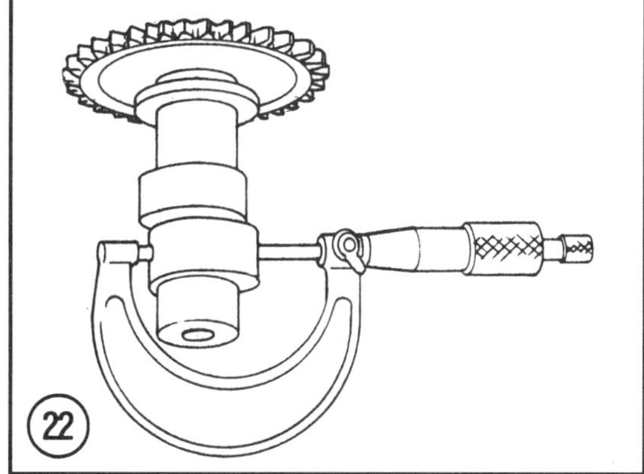

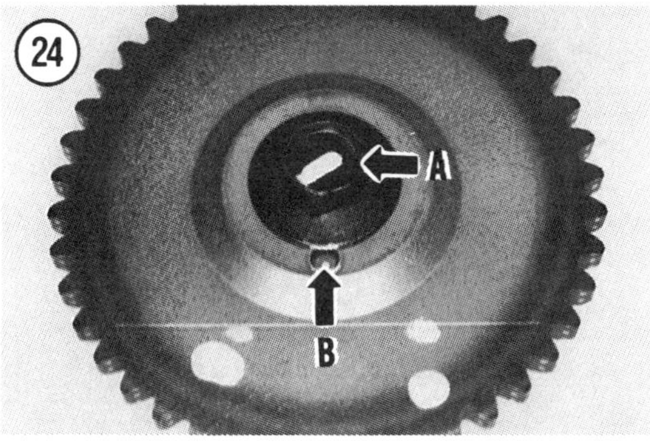

4. Even if the camshaft lobe surface appears to be satisfactory, with no visible wear, measure the camshaft lobe height with a micrometer (**Figure 22**). Compare the measurements to the dimensions given in **Table 1**. Replace the camshaft if worn to the service limit.

5. Inspect the camshaft locating boss (A, **Figure 23**) for wear or damage. If worn or damaged, replace the camshaft.

6. Inspect the camshaft sprocket teeth (B, **Figure 23**) for wear; replace if necessary.

   a. Remove the camshaft sprocket bolt (A, **Figure 24**) and remove the sprocket from the camshaft. Do not lose the locating pin (B, **Figure 24**) when removing the sprocket .
   b. Clean the threads of the sprocket bolt.
   c. Install the new sprocket onto the camshaft. Be sure the locating pin engages both the camshaft and the sprocket (C, **Figure 23**).
   d. Apply Loctite 242 to the threads of the camshaft sprocket bolt. Install the bolt, and torque it to the specification given in **Table 2**.

7. Inspect the camshaft bearing surfaces in the cylinder head (A, **Figure 25**) and in the camshaft cap (**Figure 26**) for damage, wear or burrs. Clean the surfaces if damage is minimal. They should not be scored or excessively worn. Replace the cylinder head and camshaft cap as a set if the bearing surfaces are worn or scored.

Camshaft Bearing Clearance Measurement

The most efficient method to measure camshaft bearing clearance is by using Plastigage. Plastigage consists of a crushable plastic material and a graduated scale printed on the Plastigage envelope. Plas-

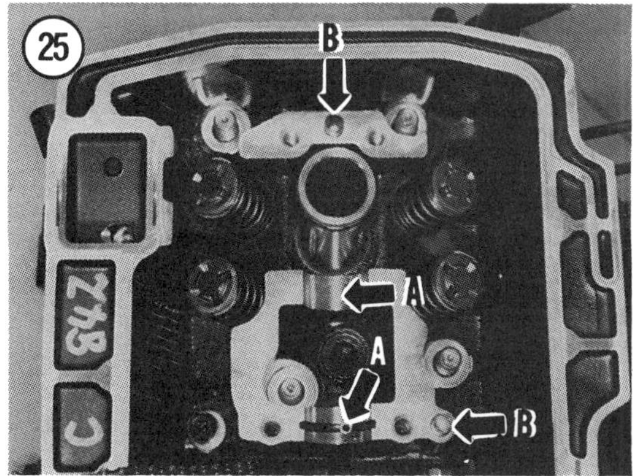

tigage is available in four sizes, with each size covering a particular clearance range.

The camshaft, camshaft bearing cap and bearing surfaces in the cylinder head must be absolutely clean and free of oil residue when using the Plastigage.

1. Make sure both locating dowels (B, **Figure 25**) are in place in the cylinder head.
2. Install the camshaft (**Figure 27**) into the cylinder head.
3. Place a strip of Plastigage material on top of both camshaft-bearing journals parallel to the camshaft.
4. Install the camshaft cap.
   a. Be sure the cutouts in the rocker shafts face inward (**Figure 16**), and that the holes in the rocker shaft are aligned with the mounting holes in the camshaft cap (**Figure 17**).
   b. Lower the camshaft cap (B, **Figure 12**) into place over the camshaft so that the cap engages the locating dowels.
   c. Install the four camshaft cap bolts (A, **Figure 12**). Gradually tighten them in a crisscross pattern. Torque the camshaft cap bolts to the specification listed in **Table 2**.

CAUTION
Do not rotate the camshafts with the Plastigage material in place.

5. Loosen the camshaft-bearing cap in 2-3 stages in a crisscross pattern, then remove the bolts.
6. Carefully remove the camshaft-bearing cap.
7. Measure the width of the flattened Plastigage material at its widest point, according to its manufacturer's instructions.

CAUTION
Although the Plastigage is oil soluble, be sure to remove all traces of Plastigage material from the bearing journals in the cylinder head and camshaft cap.

8. Remove *all* Plastigage material from the camshafts.
9. If the camshaft journal oil clearance is greater than specified in **Table 1**, and if the camshaft journal outside diameter is within specification, perform the following:
   a. Remove the camshaft from the cylinder head.
   b. Install the camshaft cap as described in Step 4.

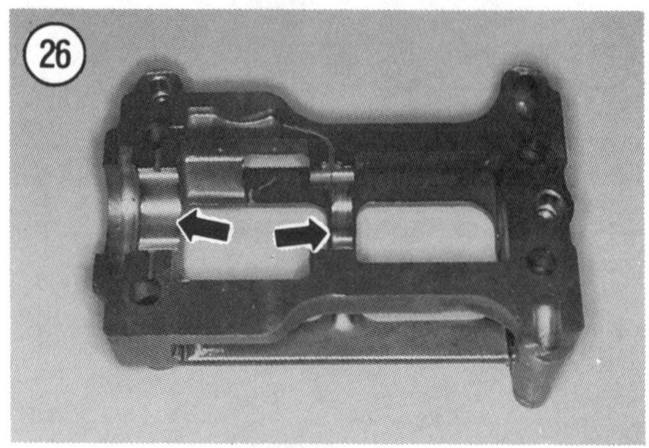
26

27

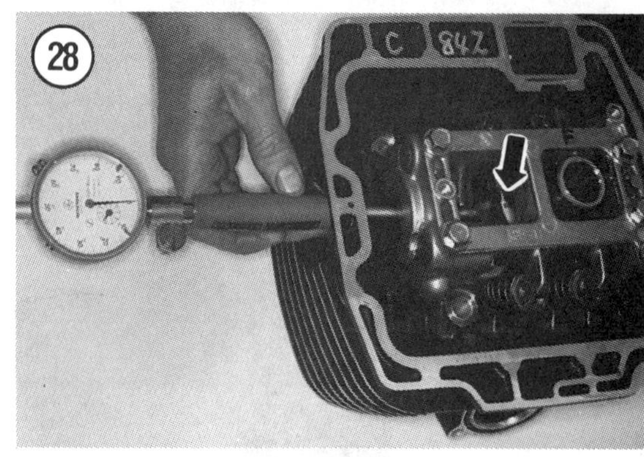
28

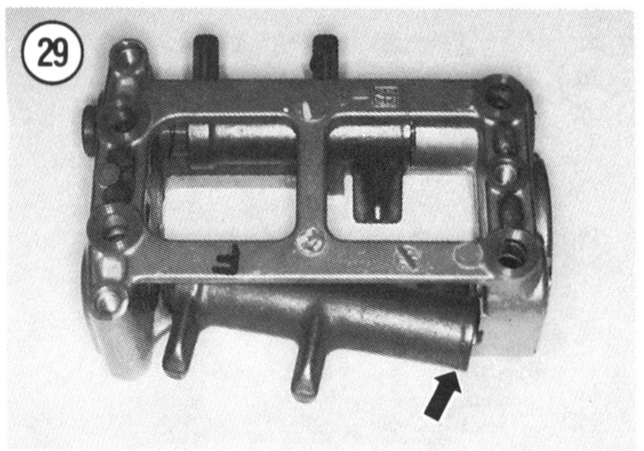
29

c. Measure the camshaft bearing inside diameter with a bore gauge (**Figure 28**) at both bearing surface locations. Compare the measurements to the specifications given in **Table 1**. If wear exceeds the service limit, replace the cylinder head and camshaft cap as a set.

ROCKER ARMS/ROCKER SHAFT

Rocker arm/rocker shaft assemblies should be disassembled, inspected and then reassembled one at a time to avoid intermixing parts. This is especially true for a high-mileage engine. Once a wear pattern develops on these parts, they must only be installed as they were removed or excessive wear may occur.

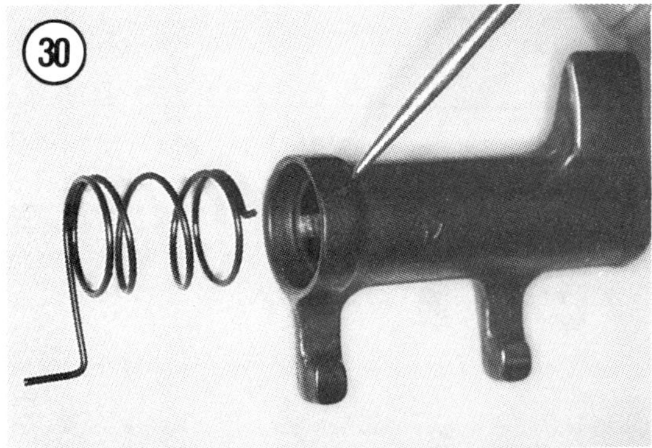

Disassembly

1. Remove the engine as described in Chapter Five.
2. Remove the cylinder head cover as described in this chapter.
3. Remove the camshaft cap as described in this chapter.
4. Disassemble the exhaust side of the camshaft cap by performing the following:
   a. Slide the intake rocker shaft from the camshaft cap (**Figure 16**).
   b. Slide the rocker arm against the rocker spring and remove the rocker arm along with its rocker arm spring (**Figure 29**).
   c. Mark the parts and keep them together so they can be identified and reinstalled as an assembly.
5. Disassemble the intake side of the camshaft cap. Mark the parts and keep them together so they can be identified and reinstalled in the intake side of the camshaft cap.
6. Inspect the parts as described below.

Assembly

1. Apply molybdenum disulfide grease to the intake rocker shaft.

NOTE
The intake rocker arm spring is painted red.

2. Fit the rock arm spring into the intake rocker arm. Be sure the short tang on the spring engages the hole in the rocker arm (**Figure 30**).
3. Install the rocker arm/spring assembly into the intake side of the camshaft cap by performing the following:
   a. Fit the long tang on the rocker arm spring into the hole in the camshaft cap (**Figure 31**).
   b. Press the rocker arm against the spring, and pivot the rocker arm into position in the camshaft cap (**Figure 32**).
4. Slide the intake rocker shaft (**Figure 33**) into the cap so it passes through the spring, through the

rocker arm and then out the other side of the camshaft cap. Be sure the notched end (A, **Figure 34**)of the rocker shaft is at the spring end of the camshaft cap (B, **Figure 34**).

5. Repeat this procedure for the exhaust side of the camshaft cap.

Rocker Arm Inspection

1. Wash all parts in solvent and thoroughly dry them with compressed air.
2. Inspect the rocker arm bore where it rides on the rocker shaft. If the bore is scratched or unevenly worn, also inspect the rocker shaft for scoring or damage. Replace any part that is worn or damaged.
3. Measure the inside diameter of each rocker arm (**Figure 35**) and the outside diameter of each rocker shaft (**Figure 36**). Compare the measurements with the specifications in **Table 1**. Replace any part with wear that exceeds the service limit.
4. Inspect the rocker arm pad where it rides on the cam lobe (A, **Figure 37**) and where the rocker arm rides on the valve stem (B, **Figure 37**). If the pad is scratched or unevenly worn, inspect the camshaft lobe for scoring, chipping or flat spots. Replace the rocker arm if it is worn or damaged.
5. Check the overall condition of the rocker arm and rocker shaft for fractures, wear or damage, replace if necessary.

CAM CHAIN AND CHAIN GUIDES

Removal
Front Cylinder Cam Chain

1. Remove the engine as described in Chapter Five.

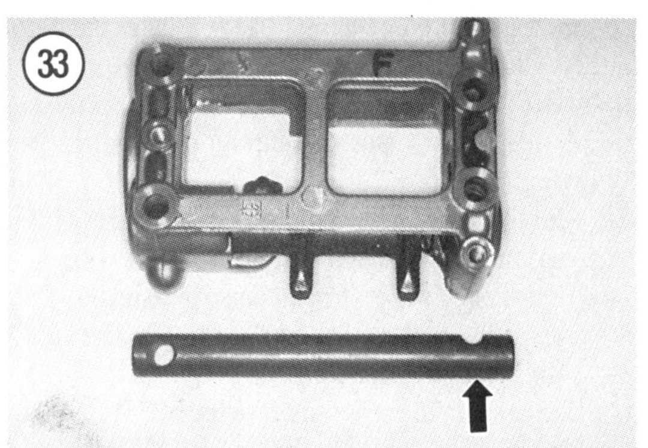

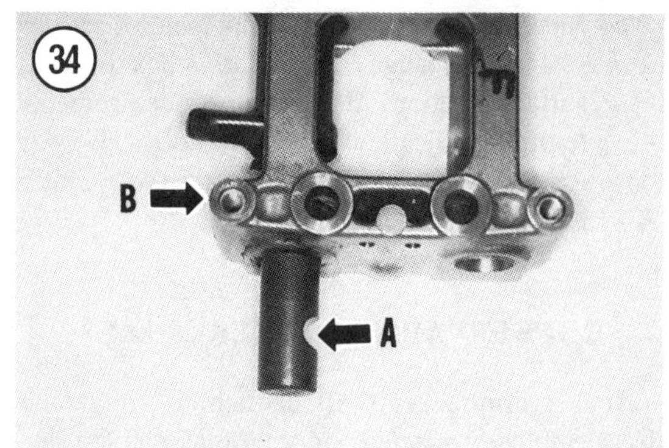

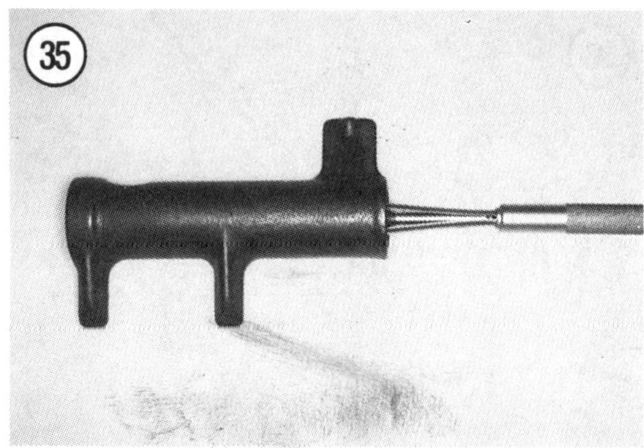

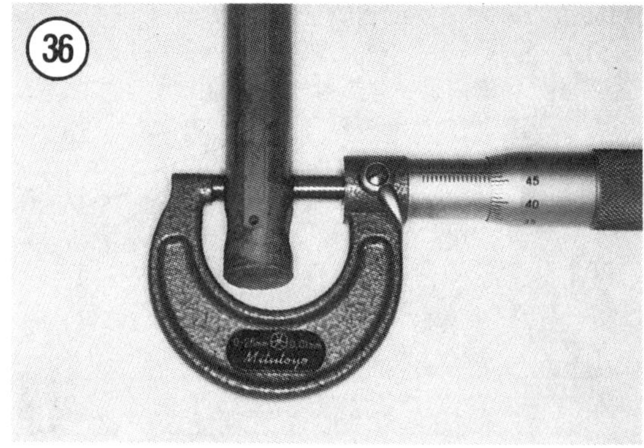

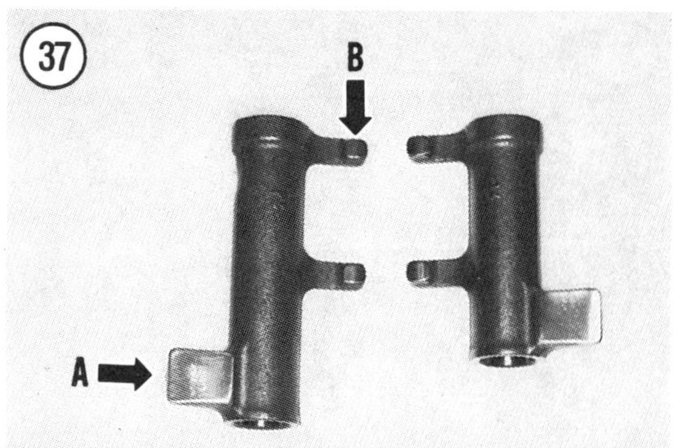

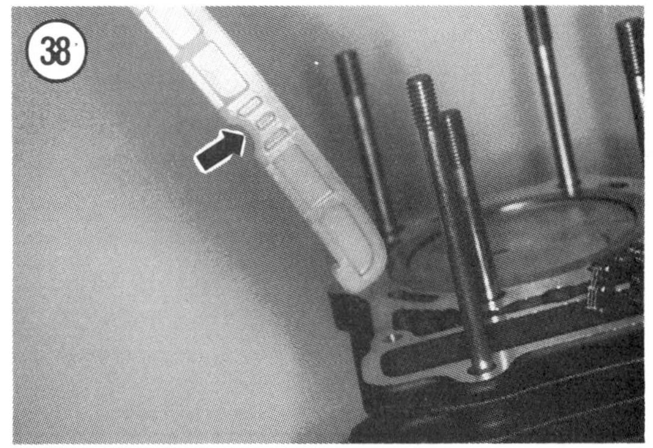

38

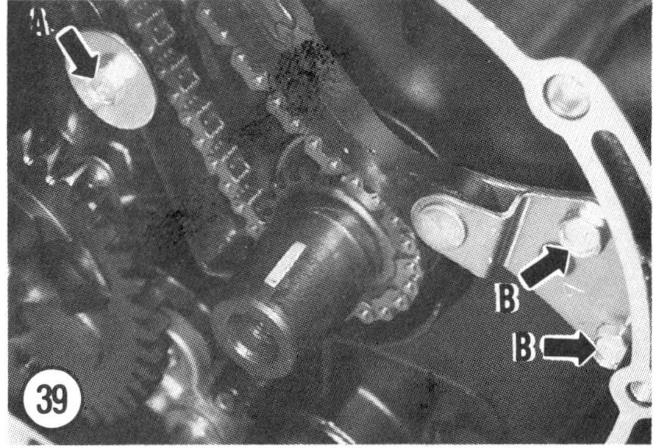

39

40

41

2. Remove the camshaft as described in chapter Five.

3. Remove the alternator rotor as described in Chapter Nine.

NOTE
The chain guides can be removed with the cylinder head installed. In the following photographs, the cylinder head has been removed for clarity.

4. Pull the white chain guide from its seat and lift the guide from the cam chain cavity. When the white chain guide is properly installed, the notch in the chain guide (**Figure 38**) rests against the securing bolt (A, **Figure 39**) on the chain guide seat. You should be able to pull the chain guide past this bolt. If necessary, remove the securing bolt and washer, and then remove the white chain guide.

5. Remove the bolts (B, **Figure 39**) securing the black chain guide/tensioner to the crankcase and remove the black chain guide/tensioner.

6. Disengage the cam chain from the crankshaft sprocket and remove the cam chain from the engine.

7. Inspect all parts as described in this chapter.

Removal
Rear cylinder cam chain

1. Remove the engine as described in Chapter Five.

2. Remove the camshaft as described in this chapter.

3. Wipe the outer circumference of the alternator rotor to remove any oil, then hold the rotor using a flywheel holder.

4. Remove the primary gear bolt (A, **Figure 40**) and washer (B, **Figure 40**), then remove the primary gear (C, **Figure 40**) from the crankshaft. Do not lose the crankshaft woodruff key (A, **Figure 41**)

5. Remove the clutch as described in Chapter Six.

6. Remove the bolts (B, **Figure 41**) securing the black chain guide to the crankcase and remove the black chain guide.

7. Lift the white chain guide (C, **Figure 41**) from its seat on the crankcase and remove the guide from the cam chain cavity.

8. Disengage the cam chain from the crankshaft sprocket and remove the cam chain from the engine.

9. Inspect all parts as described in this chapter.

Cam Chain and Chain Guide Inspection

1. Lay the cam chain on a workbench and stretch a 20-pin segment as shown in **Figure 42**. Measure the 20-pin length at several places around the chain. Replace the chain if any measurement exceeds the service limit in **Table 1**.
2. Visually inspect the chain for damage or wear. If the chain is worn, also inspect the sprockets for wear or damage. They may also require replacement.
3. Visually inspect the sliding surfaces (**Figure 43**) on each cam chain guide (white) and guide/tensioner (black) for wear or damage. Replace any worn part.
4. Visually inspect the mounting and/or pivot areas (**Figure 44**) of the chain guides and guide/tensioners for wear or damage. Replace any worn part.

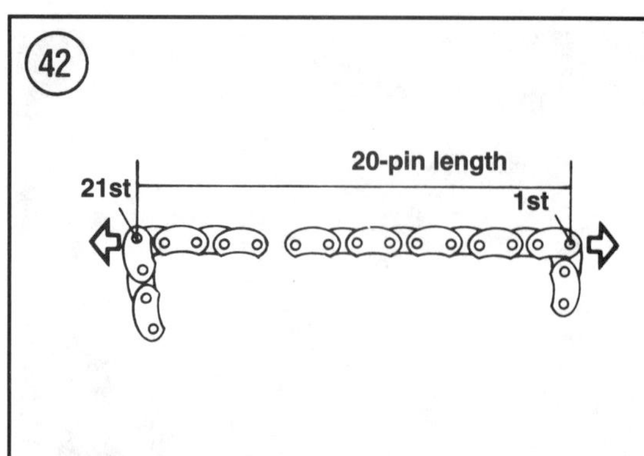

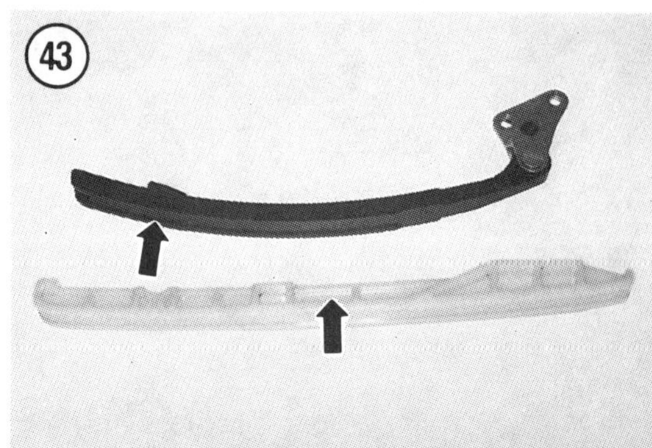

Cam Chain and Chain Guides Installation

1. Be sure the cam chain tensioner cap bolt is in place.
2. Lower the cam chain down the cam chain cavity and fit the chain onto the crankshaft sprocket.
3. Attach a wire to the chain and secure wire to the outside of the engine so the chain will not fall into the crankcase.
4. Lower the black chain guide/tensioner down the cam chain cavity, and secure it to the crankcase with the two mounting bolts (B, **Figure 39** [front cylinder]; B, **Figure 41** [rear cylinder]). Apply Loctite 242 to the threads of the chain guide/tensioner bolts and torque the bolts to the specification in **Table 2**.

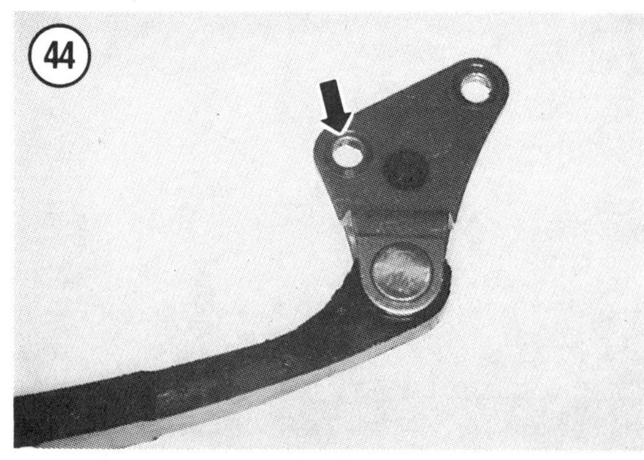

NOTE:
The cam chain guides can be removed and installed with the cylinder head in place. The cylinder head has been removed in the following for clarity.

5. Lower the white chain guide down the cam chain cavity and into its seat in the crankcase.
   a. On the front cylinder, press the chain guide down into the cam chain cavity until the guide bottoms in its seat in the crankcase. Be sure the cutout in the chain guide (**Figure 38**) snaps into place against the securing bolt (A **Figure 39**). If this bolt was removed, apply Loctite 242 to the threads of the chain guide bolt and install the securing bolt along with its washer. Torque the bolt to the specification in **Table 2**.

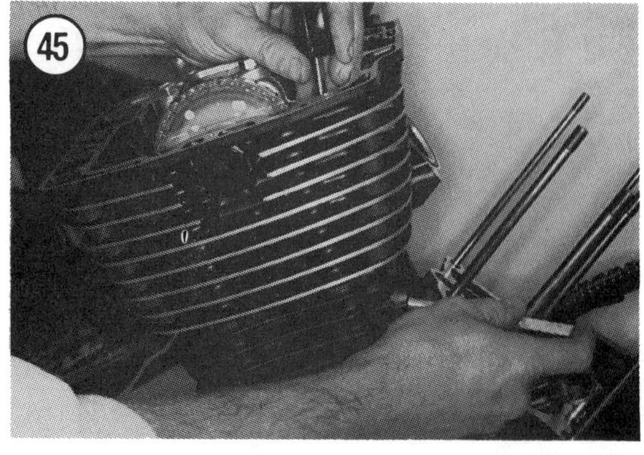

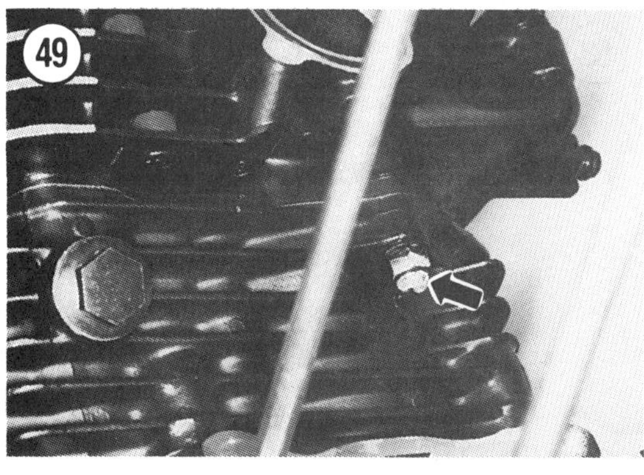

   b. On the rear cylinder, lower the white chain guide into the cam chain cavity until the guide bottoms against its seat on the crankcase (C, **Figure 41**). There is no securing bolt for the white chain guide on the rear cylinder.

6. Remove the cap bolt from the chain tensioner.
7. Hold the tensioner body while you gently push the tensioner rod until it *lightly* touches the black chain guide/tensioner (**Figure 45**).
8. Install the chain tensioner spring and washer, then the chain tensioner cap bolt (**Figure 46**). Torque the cap bolt to the specification listed in **Table 2**.
9. When working on the front cylinder, perform the following,
   a. Reinstall the alternator rotor as described in Chapter Nine.
   b. Reinstall the left-side crankcase cover.
10. When working on the rear cylinder, perform the following:
   a. Be sure the woodruff key (A, **Figure 41**) is in place on the crankshaft, and reinstall the primary gear (C, **Figure 40**).
   b. Apply Loctite 242 to the threads of the primary gear bolt (A, **Figure 40**) and install the bolt along with its washer (B, **Figure 40**).
   c. Hold the alternator rotor. Use a flywheel holder and torque the primary gear bolt to the specification given in **Table 2**.
   d. Reinstall the clutch as described in Chapter Six.
11. Reinstall the camshaft and the cylinder head cover as described in this chapter.

CYLINDER HEAD

Removal

1. Remove the engine as described in this Chapter Five.
2. Remove the cylinder head cover as described in this chapter.
3. Remove the camshaft as described in this chapter.
4. Remove the four intake manifold bolts (A, **Figure 47**) and remove the manifold (B, **Figure 47**)
5. Loosen the cylinder head mounting nuts and bolts in the following order:
   a. The two external cylinder head cap nuts. (**Figure 48** and **Figure 49**).
   b. The internal cylinder head bolt (A, **Figure 50**).

c. The two internal 8 mm Allen nuts (B, **Figure 50**) at the top of the cam chain cavity.

d. And finally the four internal 10 mm cylinder head nuts (C, **Figure 50**).

6. Remove all the hardware loosened in the step 5.

7. If you are removing the rear cylinder head, remove the breather hose from its fitting (**Figure 51**).

8. Loosen the cylinder head by lightly tapping around its perimeter with a soft-faced mallet. If necessary, *gently* pry the cylinder head loose with a broad-tipped screwdriver. Separate the cylinder head from the cylinder.

9. Pull the cylinder head (**Figure 52**) straight up and off the crankcase studs. Do not lose the two locating dowels.

10. Place the cylinder head right side up on a clean surface on the work bench.

CAUTION

If the crankshaft must be rotated with the camshaft removed, pull up on the cam chain. Be sure to keep the chain taut so it remains properly engaged with the crankshaft sprocket as the crankshaft is rotated. If this step is not followed, the chain may become kinked and the chain, sprocket and crankcase may be damaged.

11. Inspect the cylinder head as described in this chapter.

12. If you need to inspect the cam chain tensioner body, remove the tensioner cap bolt (**Figure 53**) along with the gasket and spring, then remove the tensioner body (**Figure 54**) from the cylinder.

Cylinder Head Installation

NOTE

The following procedure describes the installation of the front cylinder head. The procedure is similar for both cylinders except for minor differences, which are noted.

The front and rear cylinder heads are similar but *not* interchangeable. The rear cylinder head has a breather pipe fitting that is not found on the front cylinder head. Be sure you do not confuse the front and rear cylinder heads during reassembly.

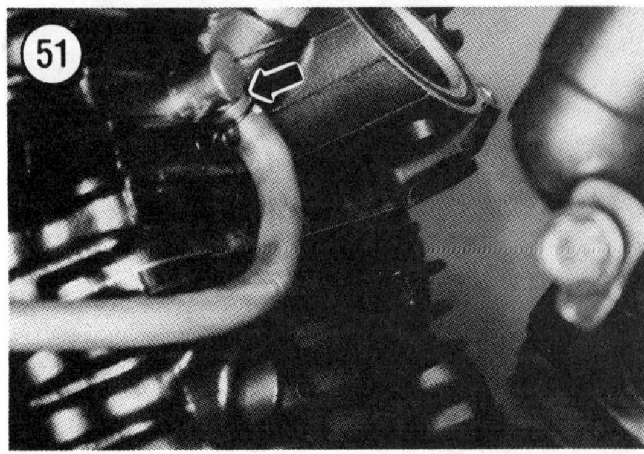

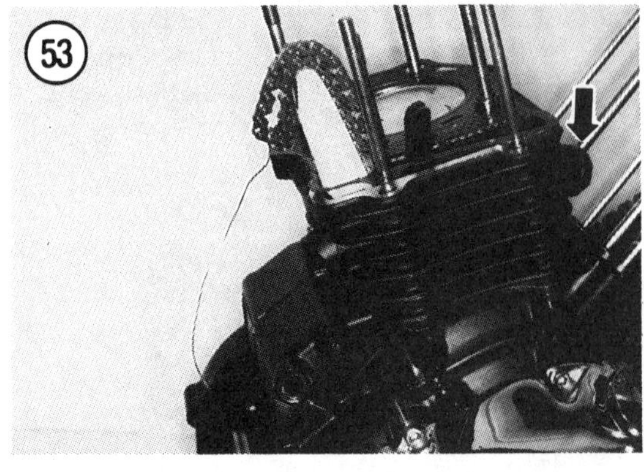

NOTE
Step 1 is only necessary if the crankshaft has been rotated after the front cylinder head was removed (the front cylinder is no longer at TDC on the compression stroke). If the engine has **not** *been disturbed, the front cylinder should still be positioned at TDC on the compression stroke and Step 1 is not necessary. Proceed to Step 2.*

1. If it is necessary to place the front cylinder at TDC on the compression stroke, refer to *Camshaft Removal* in this chapter for the correct timing procedure.

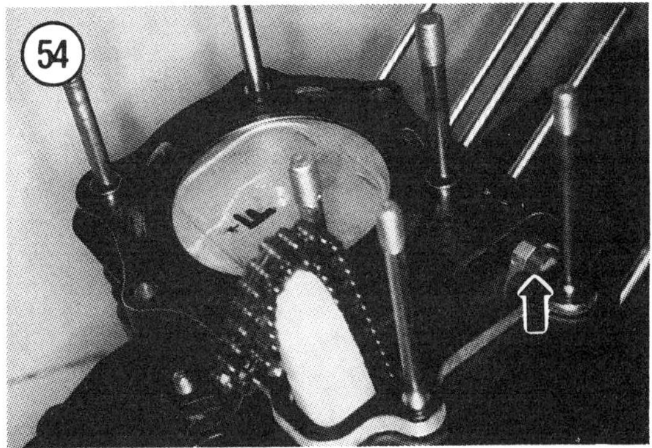
54

55

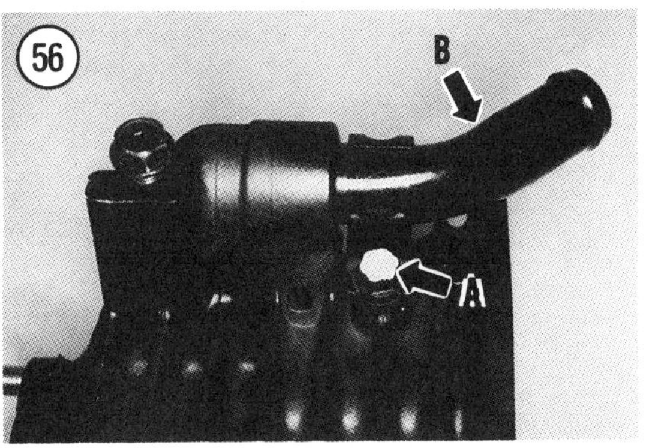

56

2. If removed, install the cam chain tensioner body into its housing in the cylinder, and install the spring and cap bolt along with the gasket (**Figure 53**).

3. If removed, install the spark plug pipe into the cylinder head (**Figure 55**). Apply grease to both O-rings on the pipe and install the pipe so its chamfered end faces up.

4. If removed, install the coolant pipe (B, **Figure 56**) into the coolant fitting on the cylinder head. Insert the pipe into the fitting and secure the pipe to the cylinder head with its mounting screw (A, **Figure 56**). Torque the bolt to the specification in **Table 2**.

5. Remove the cap bolt from the cam chain tensioner. Release the stopper (A, **Figure 57**) and push

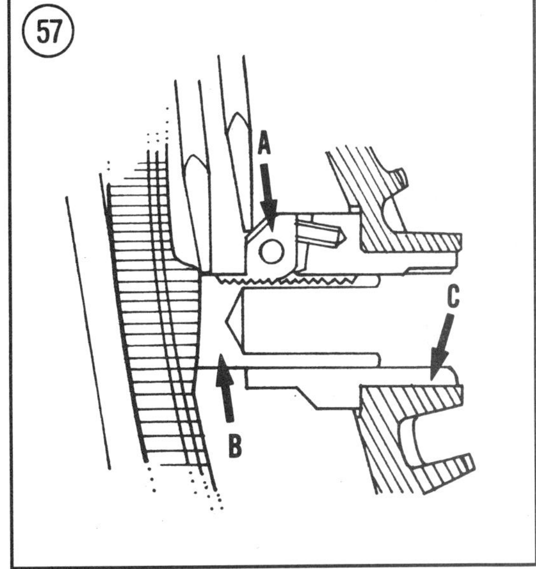

57

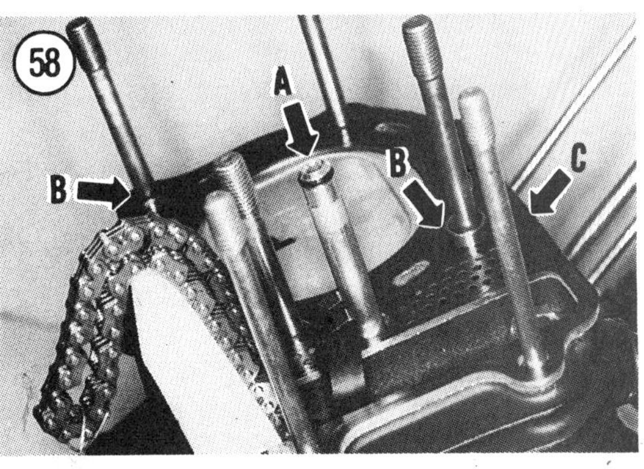

58

the rod (B) into the tensioner body (C). Reinstall and fingertighten the cap bolt.

6. If removed, install the oil pipe (A, **Figure 58**) into the cylinder.

7. If removed, install the two locating dowels (B, **Figure 58**) around the studs in the cylinder block.

8. Apply RTV sealant to the mating surface of the cylinder block, and install a new cylinder head gasket (C, **Figure 58**). Make sure all holes are aligned correctly.

9. If removed, install the white cam chain guide.
   a. When installing the front cylinder head, lower the white chain guide through the cam chain cavity in the cylinder and press the white chain guide into its seat on the left side of the crankcase. Be sure the notch on the chain guide (**Figure 38**) snaps into place against its securing bolt (A, **Figure 39**).
   b. When installing the rear cylinder head, lower the white chain guide through the cam chain cavity in the cylinder and fit the white chain guide into its seat on the right side of the crankcase (C, **Figure 41**).

10. Carefully slide the cylinder head down the crankcase studs while guiding the cam chain and the chain guides up through the cam chain cavity in the cylinder head. Tie a piece of wire to the cam chain and attach the wire to the exterior of the engine.

11. Push the cylinder head down until it bottoms against the cylinder block.

12. Install all bolts and nuts securing the cylinder head to the cylinder block and tighten only fingertight.

13. Tighten the cylinder head mounting bolts and nuts to the torque specification listed in **Table 2**. Tighten the bolts in the following order:
   a. The four internal 10 mm nuts (1-4, **Figure 59**) on the crankcase studs—use a crisscross pattern and tighten them in 2-3 steps.
   b. The two internal 8 mm Allen nuts (5 and 6, **Figure 59**) at the cam chain side of the cylinder.
   c. The single internal cylinder head bolt (7, **Figure 59**).
   d. The two external 8 mm cap nuts (**Figure 48 and Figure 49**) securing the cylinder head to the cylinder.

14. When installing the rear cylinder head, fit the breather hose onto its fitting (**Figure 51**) on the head and secure the hose in place with the hose clamp.

15. Apply grease to the O-rings on both intake ports and install the intake manifold. Torque the intake manifold bolts to the specification in **Table 2**

16. Reinstall the camshaft as described in this chapter.

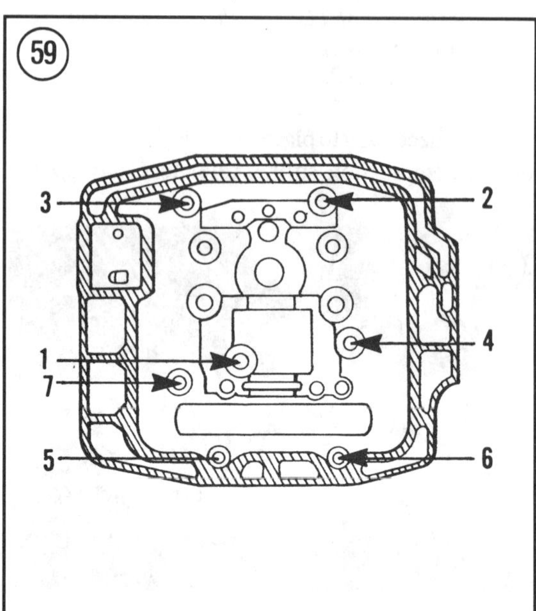

17. If removed, install the air suction valve into its housing in the cylinder head. Position the valve so the valve stopper faces down into the cylinder head (**Figure 60**).

18. Reinstall the cylinder head cover as described in this chapter.

CYLINDER HEAD INSPECTION

1. Remove the spark plug pipe (**Figure 55**) from the cylinder head. Inspect the O-ring seal at each end (**Figure 61**). Replace the O-rings if they are starting to deteriorate or harden.

2. Remove the bolt (A, **Figure 56**) securing the coolant pipe to the cylinder head and remove the pipe (B, **Figure 56**) from the fitting.

3. Inspect the O-ring (**Figure 62**) on the coolant pipe . Replace the O-ring if it is hard or deteriorated. Do not apply grease to the O-ring.

4. Remove the air suction valve (**Figure 60**) from its housing in the cylinder head. Inspect the valve as described in Chapter Eight.

5. Remove all traces of gasket material from the cylinder head-to-cylinder block (A, **Figure 63**) mating surfaces. Do not scratch the gasket surface.

6. Clean any RTV residue from the cylinder head and cylinder block.

7. *Without removing the valves,* remove all carbon deposits from the combustion chamber (B, **Figure 63**) and valve ports with a wire brush. A blunt screwdriver or chisel may be used if care is taken not to damage the head, valves and spark plug threads.

8. Examine the spark plug threads (C, **Figure 63**) in the cylinder head for damage. If damage is minor or if the threads are dirty or plugged with carbon, use a spark plug thread tap to clean the threads following its manufacturer's instructions. If thread damage is severe, refer further service to a dealership or competent machine shop.

9. Clean the entire head in solvent after removing carbon from the combustion chamber and the valve port and after repairing the spark plug threaded holes (if required). Dry with compressed air.

10. Clean all carbon from the piston crown. Do **not**, however, remove the carbon ridge from the top of the cylinder bore.

11. Check for cracks in the combustion chamber and exhaust port (A, **Figure 64**). A cracked head must be replaced.

12A. On VN800 Classic models and 1997 and 1998 VN800 models, inspect the threads on the exhaust port studs (B, **Figure 64**) for damage. Repair damaged threads with an appropriate size metric die if necessary.

12B. On 1995 and 1996 VN800 models, inspect the threads on the exhaust pipe mounting hole in the exhaust port.

NOTE
The cylinder head and the camshaft cap are mated. They must be replaced as a set. If the following step reveals that the

(62)

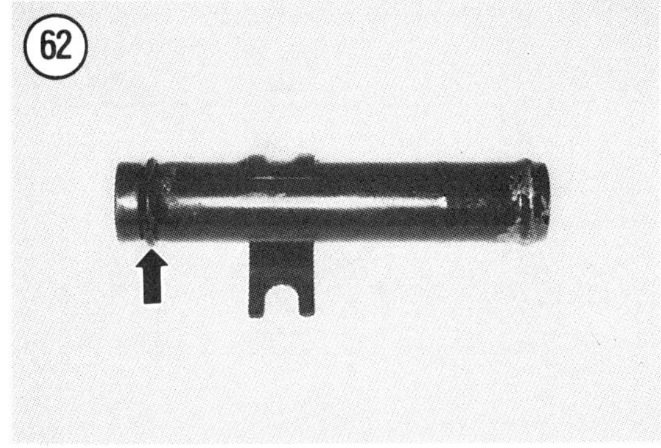

(63)

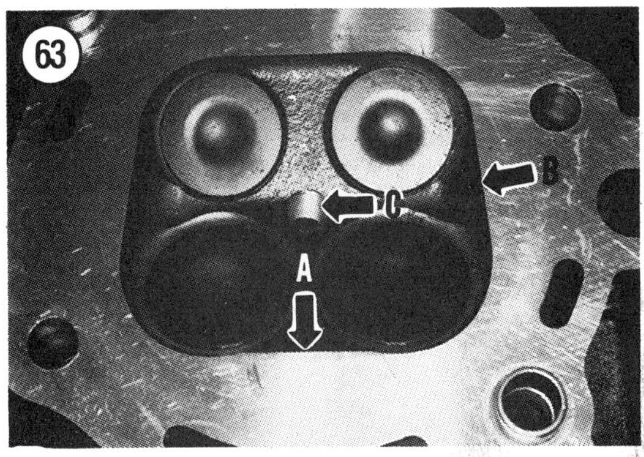

(64)

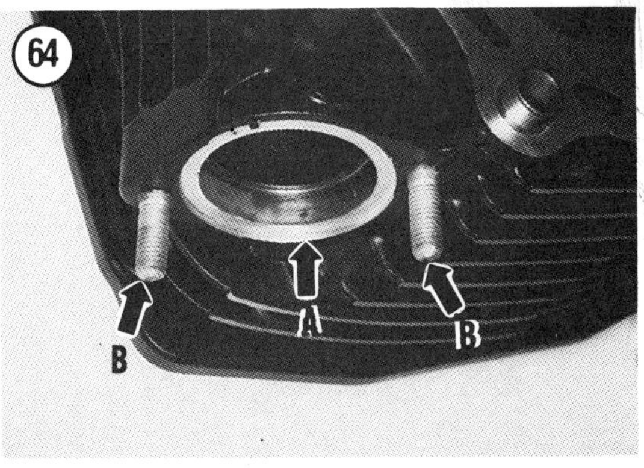

cylinder head must be replaced, you must also replace the camshaft cap.

13. Inspect the camshaft bearing surfaces (**Figure 65**) in the cylinder head for damage, wear or burrs. Clean the bearing surfaces if damage is minimal. They should not be scored or excessively worn. Replace the cylinder head and camshaft cap as a set if the bearing surfaces are worn or scored.
14. Inspect the camshaft bearing surfaces (**Figure 66**) in the camshaft cap for damage, wear or burrs. Clean the bearing surfaces if damage is minimal. They should not be scored or excessively worn. Replace the cylinder head and camshaft cap as a set if the bearing surfaces are worn or scored.
15. Inspect the decorative cooling fins (A, **Figure 67**) for cracks or damage. The fins provide minimal cooling, but they can still be damaged.
16. Inspect the threads on the short studs (B, **Figure 67**) for damage. Clean the threads with an appropriate size metric die if necessary. Make sure the studs are tightly secured in the cylinder head.
17. After the head is thoroughly cleaned, place a straightedge across the cylinder head/cylinder block gasket surface at several points. Measure the cylinder head warp by inserting a flat feeler gauge between the straightedge and the cylinder head at several locations (**Figure 68**). If cylinder head warp exceeds the service limit given in **Table 1**, the cylinder head must be replaced.
18. Inspect the valves and valve guides as described in this chapter.
19. Inspect the cylinder head cover (**Figure 69**) for damage, wear or burrs. Clean up damage if it is minimal; replace the cylinder head cover as necessary.
20. Repeat for the other cylinder head.

CAM CHAIN TENSIONER BODY INSPECTION

1. Inspect the cam chain tensioner body (**Figure 70**) if you removed it. Visually check for wear or damage and be sure the ratchet operates correctly.
2. Inspect the gasket on the tensioner cap bolt (**Figure 71**) for hardness or deterioration. Replace if necessary.
3. If any part of the tensioner assembly is worn or damaged, replace the entire assembly. Replacement parts are not available.

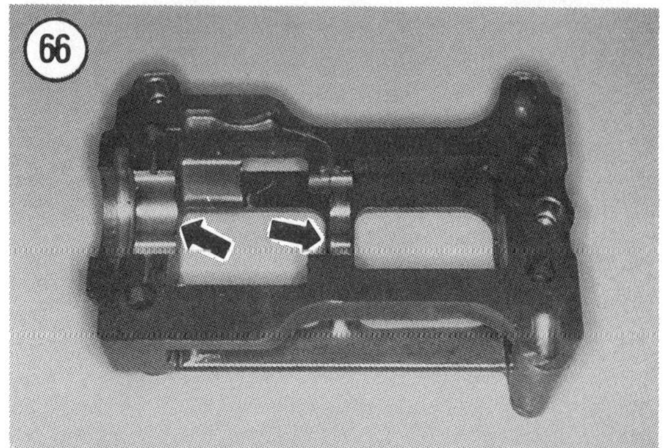

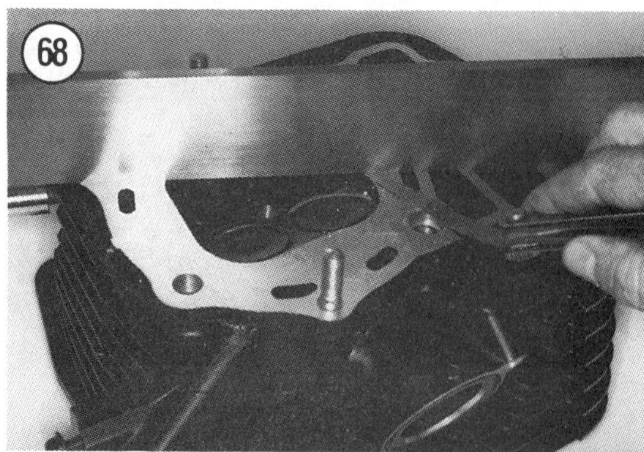

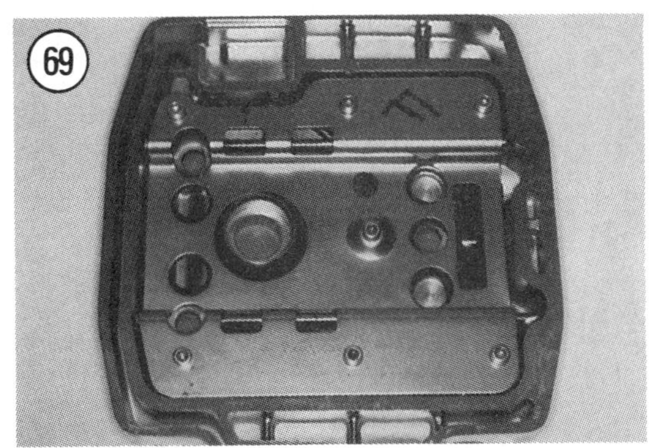

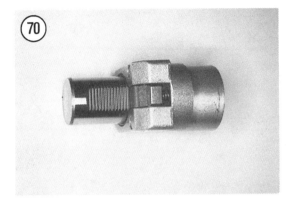

70

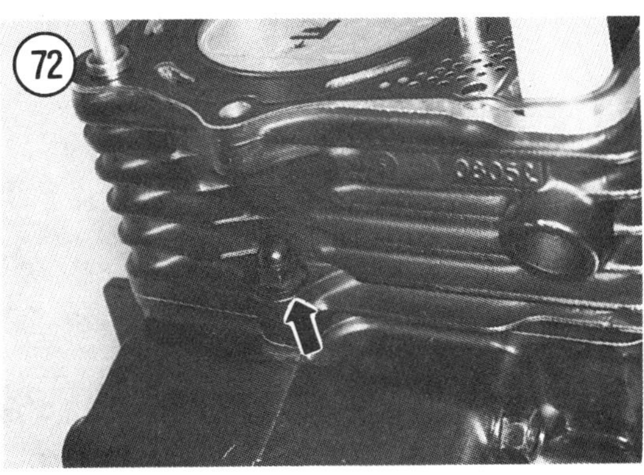

CYLINDER BLOCK

Removal

NOTE
The following procedure describes the removal of the front cylinder block. The procedures are similar for both cylinders except for minor differences, which are noted.

1. Remove the engine as described in Chapter Five.
2. Remove the cylinder head as described in this chapter.
3. Remove the cam chain, white chain guide and black chain guide/tensioner as described in this chapter.

4A. Remove the cap nut (**Figure 72**) from the front cylinder block.

4B. Remove the cap nut (**Figure 73**) from the rear cylinder block.

CAUTION
The small cooling fins are fragile and may be damaged if tapped or pried too hard. Never use a metal hammer on the cylinder block.

5. Loosen the cylinder block by tapping around its base using a rubber or soft-faced mallet. If necessary, *gently* pry the cylinder block loose from the crankcase with a broad-tipped screwdriver.
6. Remove the cylinder base gasket and discard it. Do not lose the locating dowels.
7. Place a clean shop cloth into the openings in the crankcase to prevent the entry of foreign matter.
8. Repeat for the other cylinder block.

9. Inspect the cylinder block as described in this chapter.

Cylinder Block Installation

1. If used, remove the clean shop cloth from the openings in the crankcase opening.
2. Apply a liberal coat of clean engine oil to the cylinder wall especially at the lower end where the piston will be entering.
3. Also apply clean engine oil to the piston and piston rings. This will make it easier to guide the piston into the cylinder bore.
4. Check that the top surface of the crankcase and the bottom surface of the cylinder are clean prior to installing a new base gasket.
5. If removed, install the two locating dowels (A, **Figure 74** and A, **Figure 75**).
6. Install a new cylinder base gasket (B, **Figure 74**).
7. Make sure the end gaps of the piston rings are *not* aligned with each other— they must be staggered.

> *NOTE*
> *The cylinder blocks are almost identical and can accidentally be installed in the wrong location on the crankcase. The cam chain tensioner mounting hole in the cylinder block* ***must face rearward*** *as shown in B,* ***Figure 75****.*

8. If removed, install the tensioner body into the cylinder (**Figure 76**) and install the tensioner cap bolt along with its gasket and spring (**Figure 77**).
9. Position the cylinder block with the camshaft chain tensioner mounting hole facing toward the rear of the crankcase. Move the cylinder block into position on the crankcase studs.
10. Start the cylinder block down over the piston while you compress each piston ring (C, **Figure 74**) with your fingers as it enters the cylinder.
11. Slide the cylinder block down until it bottoms on the crankcase.

12A. Install the cap nut (**Figure 72**) at the front cylinder block. Torque the cylinder cap nut to the specification listed in **Table 2**.

12B. Install the cap nut (**Figure 73**) at the rear cylinder. Torque the cylinder cap nut to the specification listed in **Table 2**.

13. Install the cam chain and chain guides as described in this chapter.

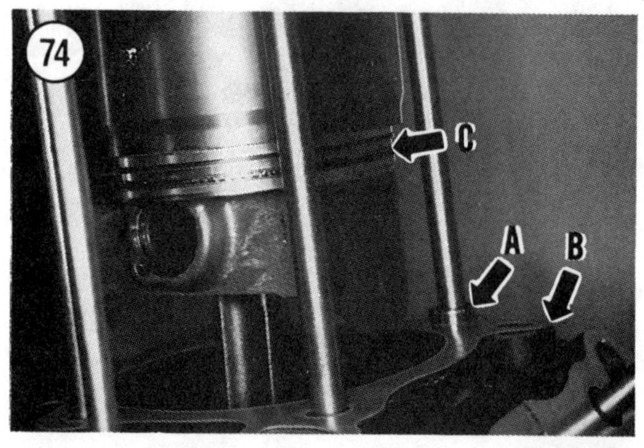

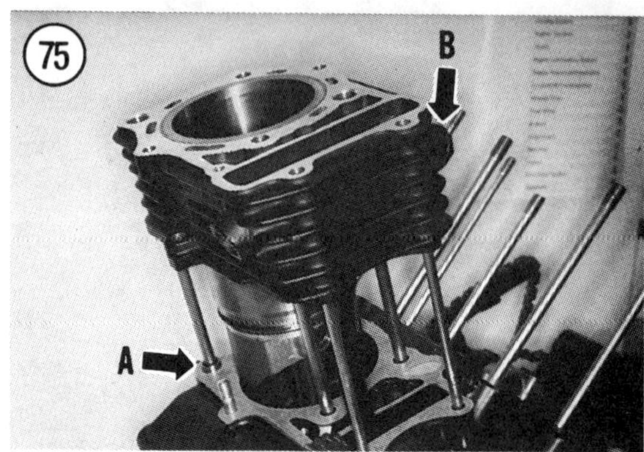

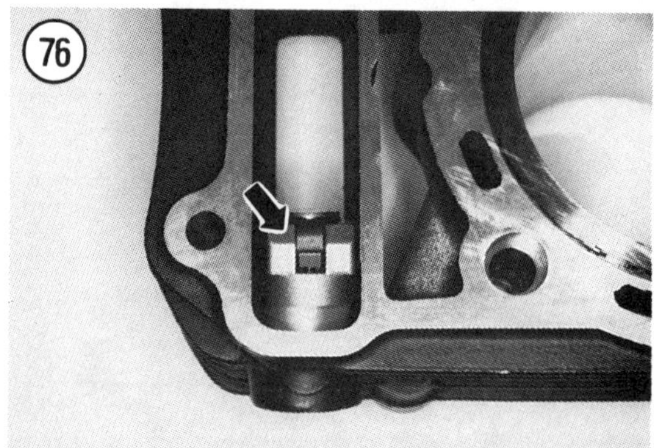

14. Install the cylinder head and camshaft as described in this chapter.

15. Repeat the procedure for the other cylinder if necessary.

Cylinder Block Inspection

1. Soak old gasket material on the cylinder with solvent. Refer to A, **Figure 78** and **Figure 79**. Use a *dull*, gasket scraper and gently remove all gasket residue. Do not gouge the sealing surface or oil, coolant and air leaks will result.

2. Measure the cylinder bore (**Figure 80**) using a bore gauge or inside micrometer at the three points shown in **Figure 81**. Take two measurements at each point—aligned with the piston pin and at 90° to the piston pin.

3. If any measurement exceeds the wear limit in **Table 1**, the cylinder must be bored to the next oversize and a new piston and rings installed. Bore both cylinders even if only one is worn.

4

NOTE

*Purchase the new pistons before the cylinders are bored so the pistons can be measured. Slight manufacturing tolerances must be taken into account to determine the actual size and working clearance. The recommended piston-to-cylinder clearance is listed in **Table 1**.*

NOTE

*The maximum cylinder bore diameter is listed in **Table 1**. If the cylinder diameter exceeds this limit, it must be replaced. Never bore a cylinder if the finished*

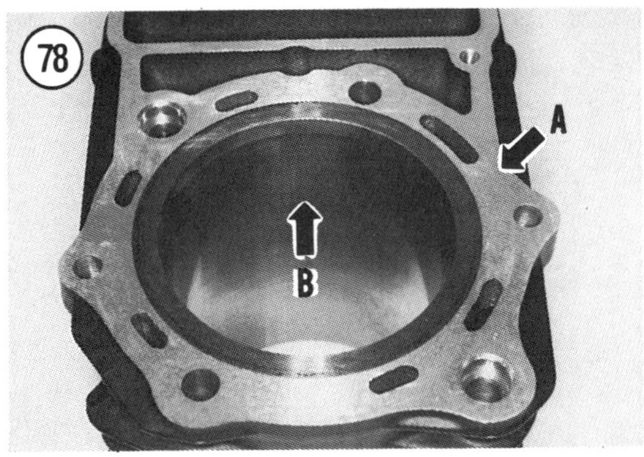

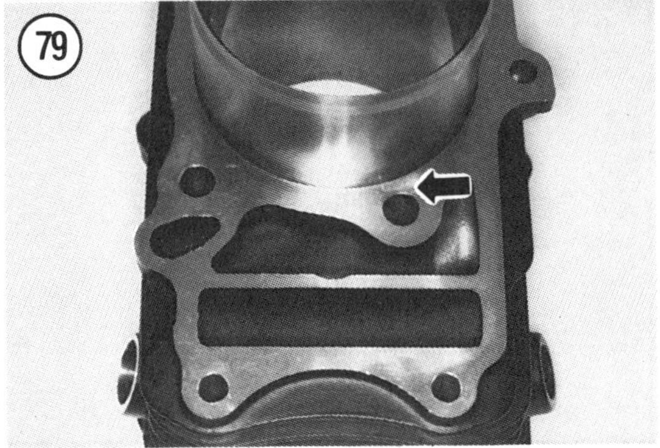

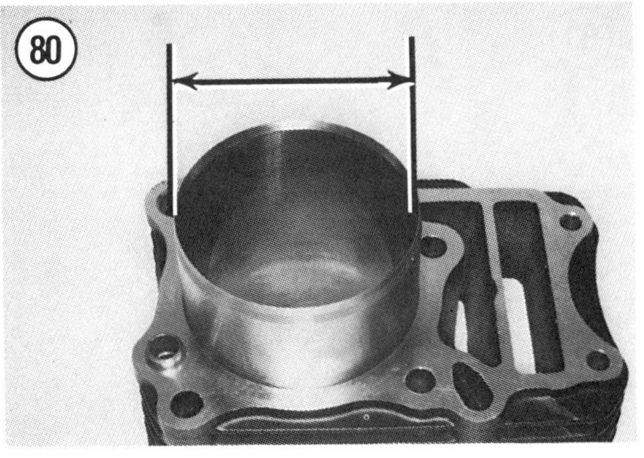

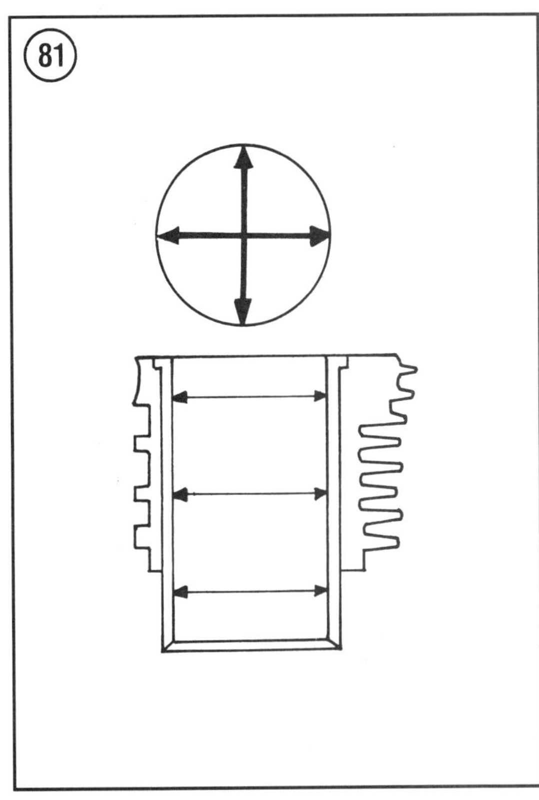

diameter will equal or exceed this wear limit.

4. If the cylinder is within specification, thoroughly check the bore surface (B, **Figure 78**) for scratches or gouges. If damaged in any way, the cylinder requires boring and reconditioning.
5. If the cylinders require boring, remove all dowel pins from the cylinders and take them to a dealership or machine shop for service.
6. After the cylinders are serviced, perform the following:

CAUTION
A combination of soap and hot water is the only solution that will completely clean the cylinder walls. Solvent and kerosene cannot wash fine grit out of cylinder crevices. Any grit left in the cylinders will cause premature wear to the new rings.

a. Wash each cylinder bore with hot soapy water. This is the only way to clean the cylinders of the fine grit material left from the bore and honing procedure.
b. Also wash out any fine grit material from the cooling passages surrounding each cylinder.
c. After washing the cylinder walls, run a clean white cloth through each cylinder wall. It should *not* show any traces of grit or debris. If the cloth is the slightest bit dirty, the wall is not thoroughly cleaned and must be rewashed.
d. After the cylinder is cleaned, lubricate the cylinder walls with clean engine oil to prevent the cylinders from rusting.

7. Inspect the small cooling fins for cracks or damage.
8. Remove the tensioner cap bolt (**Figure 77**) along with its gasket and spring, and remove the tensioner body (**Figure 76**) from the cylinder.
9. Inspect the tensioner body as described in this chapter.
10. Repeat for the other cylinder block.

VALVES AND VALVE COMPONENTS

General practice among those who do their own service is to remove the cylinder heads and take them to a machine shop or dealership for inspection and service. Since the cost is relative to the required

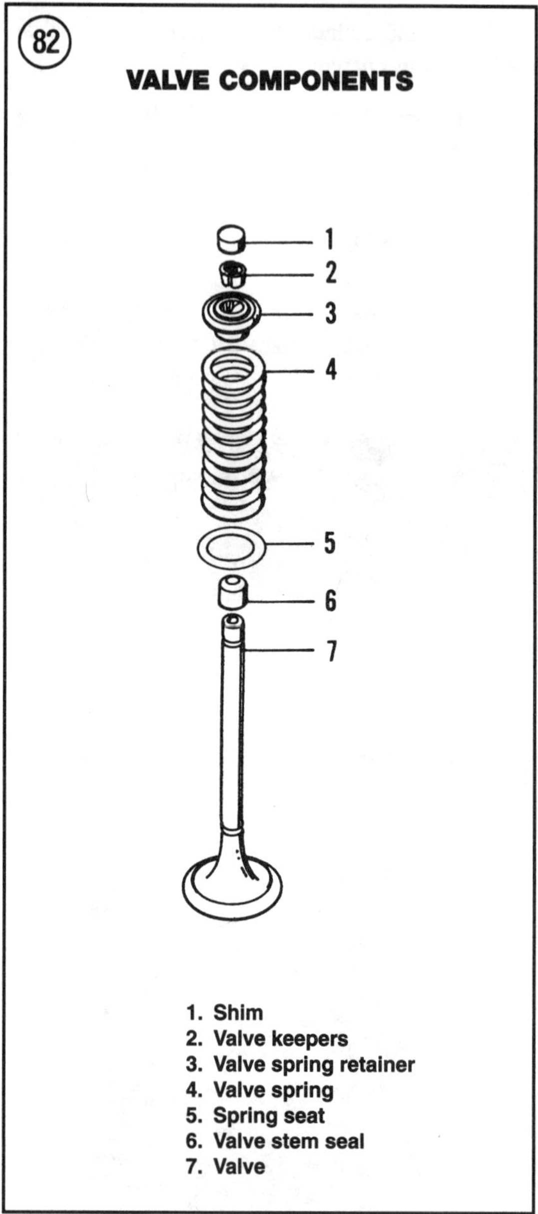

1. Shim
2. Valve keepers
3. Valve spring retainer
4. Valve spring
5. Spring seat
6. Valve stem seal
7. Valve

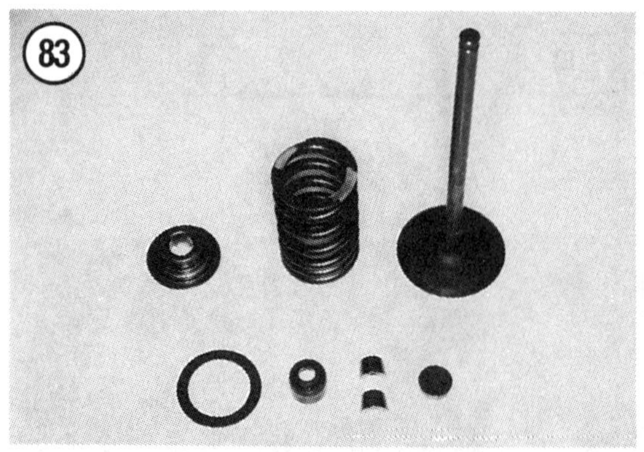

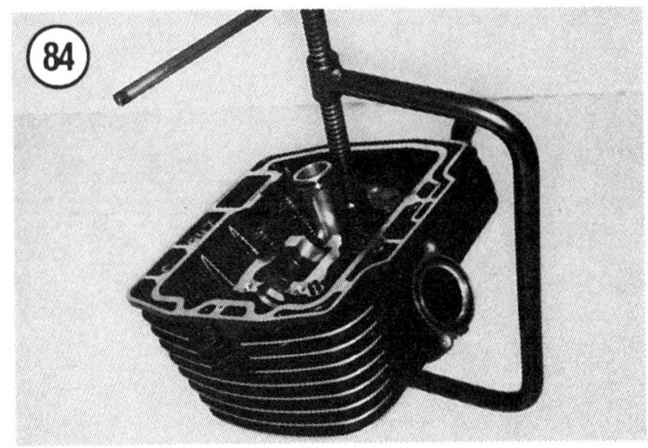
84

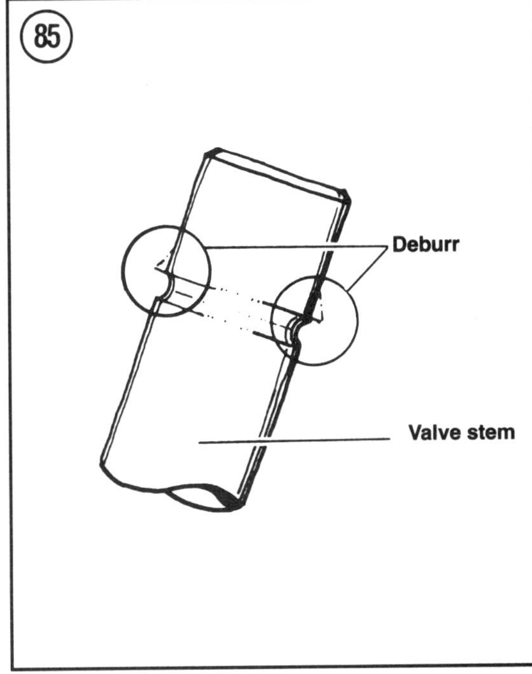

85

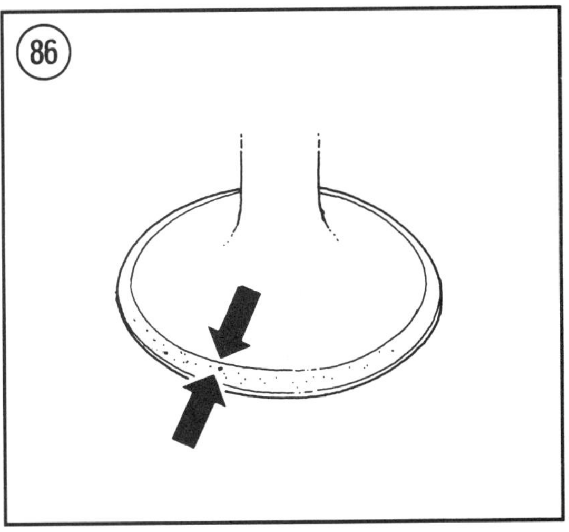
86

effort and equipment, this is the best approach even for the experienced mechanics.

This procedure is included for those who chose to do their own valve service.

Refer to **Figure 82** for this procedure.

Valve Removal

1. Remove the cylinder head(s) as described in this chapter.

NOTE
*Mark each part (**Figure 83**) as it is disassembled so it can be identified and reinstalled in its original location.*

2. Remove the shim from between the valve keepers.

CAUTION
To avoid loss of spring tension, do not compress the spring any more than necessary to remove the keepers.

3. Compress the valve spring with a valve compressor (**Figure 84**). Remove the valve keepers and release the compression. Remove the valve compressor.
4. Remove the valve spring retainer and the valve spring.
5. Prior to removing the valve, remove any burrs from the valve stem (**Figure 85**) using a fine-cut file.
6. Remove the valve.
7. Remove the valve stem seal and spring seat from the valve guide.
8. Repeat Steps 2-7 for the remaining valves. The exhaust valves are adjacent to the exhaust port and the intake valves are next to the intake port.

Valve Inspection

1. Clean the valves with a soft-wire brush and solvent.
2. Inspect the face of each valve (**Figure 86**) for burning or pitting. Uneven wear on the contact surface is an indication that the valve is not serviceable. Because the valve face cannot be resurfaced, replace the valve if the seating surface is not in acceptable condition.

3. Measure each valve stem diameter (**Figure 87**). Replace the valve if the stem diameter is less than the specification in Table 1.

4. Measure the valve head thickness as shown in (**Figure 88**). Replace the valve if the head thickness is less than the specification in Table 1.

5. Remove all carbon and varnish from each valve guide with a stiff spiral wire brush.

6. To measure valve stem-to-valve guide clearance using the wobble or tilt method, perform the following:

   a. Insert a *new* valve in a guide.

   b. Hold the valve with the head just slightly off the valve seat and rock it sideways in 2 directions perpendicular to each other as shown in **Figure 89**.

   c. If the valve-to-valve guide clearance exceeds the limit listed in **Table 1**, replace the cylinder head.

7. Measure the valve spring free length with a vernier caliper (**Figure 90**). The spring should be within the length specified in **Table 1** with no bends or distortion (**Figure 91**). Replace any defective springs.

8. Check the valve spring retainer and valve keepers. If they are in good condition, they may be reused.

9. Inspect the valve seats (**Figure 92**) in the cylinder head. If worn or burned, they must be reconditioned as described in this chapter.

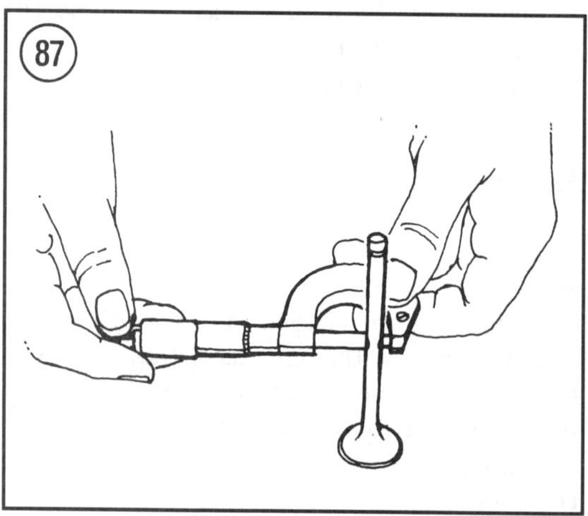

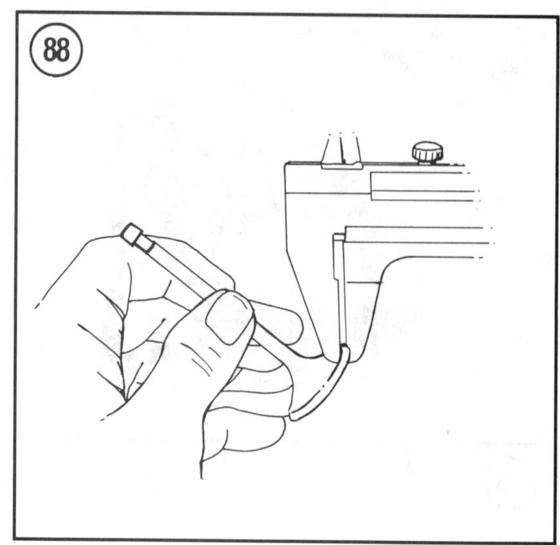

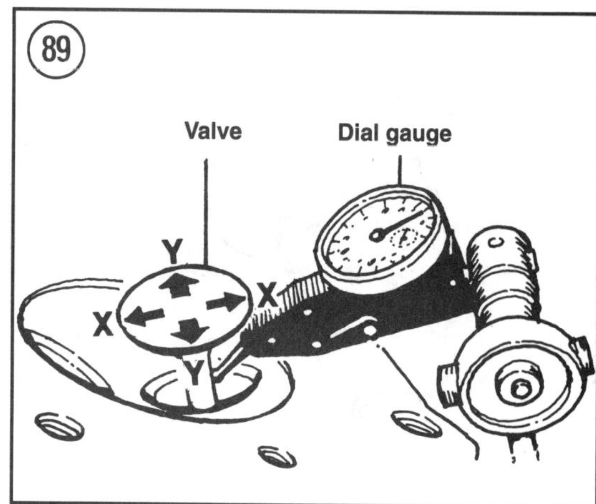

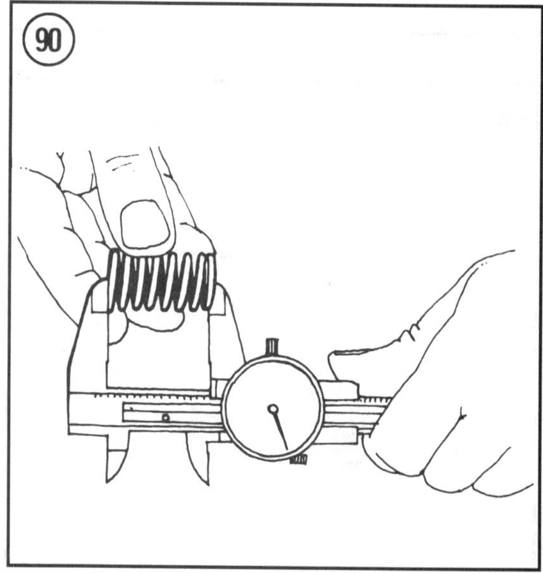

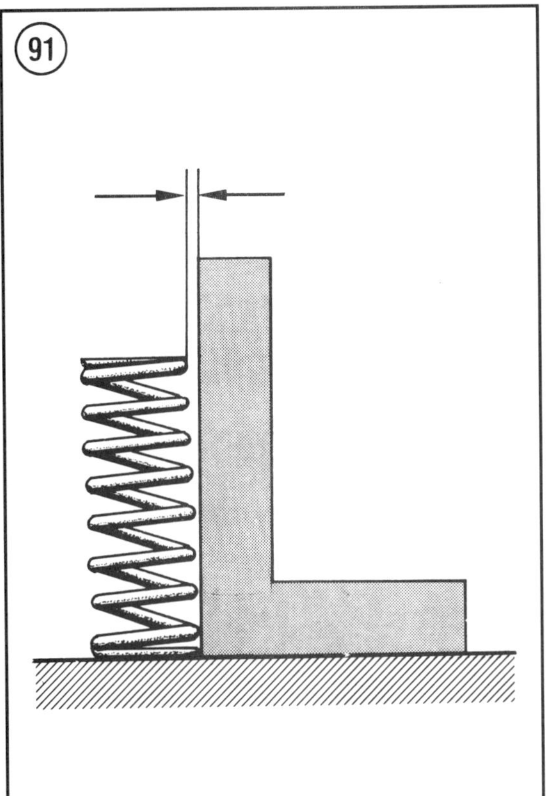

Valve Installation

1. Install the spring seat (**Figure 93**) over the valve guide and push it down until it bottoms.
2. Install a new seal (**Figure 94**) and push it down until it is seated (**Figure 95**).
3. Coat the valve stems with molybdenum disulfide grease. To avoid damage to the valve stem seal, turn the valve slowly while inserting the valve into the cylinder head. Push the valve all the way in until it closes and the stem protrudes beyond the valve guide (**Figure 96**).

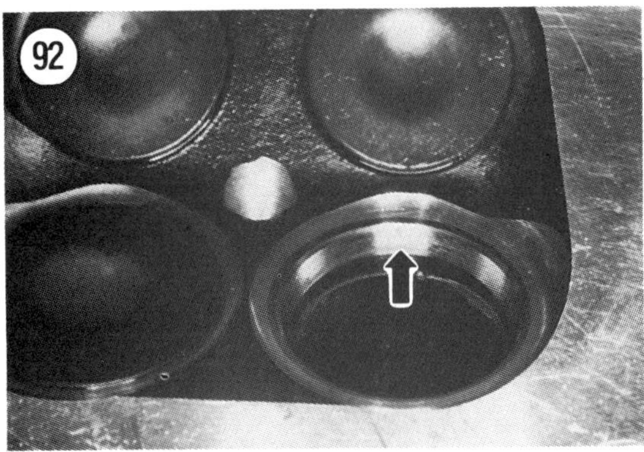

4. Install the valve spring, with its closer wound coils (**Figure 97**) facing down, on to the cylinder head (**Figure 98**).
5. Position the valve spring retainer with the small shoulder side facing the valve spring, and set the valve spring retainer (**Figure 99**) on top of the valve spring.

CAUTION
To avoid loss of spring tension, do not compress the spring any more than necessary to install the keepers.

6. Compress the valve spring with a compressor (A, **Figure 100**).
7. Apply a small amount of cold grease to each valve keeper and install both keepers (B, **Figure 100**). Make sure the keepers fit snugly into the rounded groove in the valve stem.
8. Remove the compressor tool.
9. Gently tap the end of the valve stem with a soft aluminum or brass drift and a hammer. This will ensure that the keepers are properly seated (**Figure 101**).
10. Reinstall the valve shim between the keepers (**Figure 102**). If reusing a shim, be sure it's the same shim you removed from this particular valve
11. Repeat for all valve assemblies and for the other cylinder head if necessary.
12. Install the cylinder head as described in this chapter.

Valve Guide Replacement

The valve guides cannot be replaced on these models. If valve guides are worn so there is excessive valve stem-to-guide clearance or excessive valve tipping, replace the cylinder head.

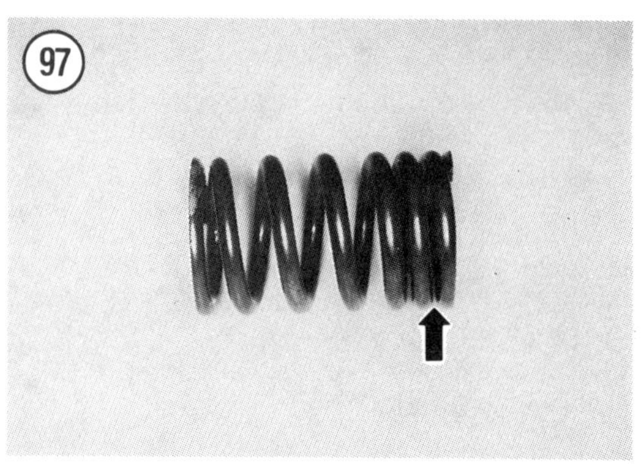

NOTE:
The camshaft cap and cylinder head are mated. You must replace the camshaft cap and cylinder head as a set.

Valve Seat Inspection

1. Remove the valves as described in this chapter.
2. Using Prussian Blue or machinist's marking compound is an accurate way to check if a valve is seating completely. Both are available at auto parts stores or machine shops. To check valve seal with Prussian Blue or machinist's marking compound, proceed as follows:
   a. Thoroughly clean all carbon deposits from the valve face with solvent or detergent and thoroughly dry the valve.

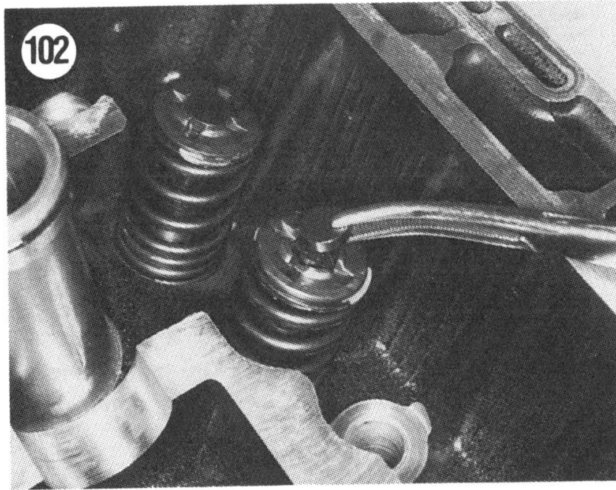

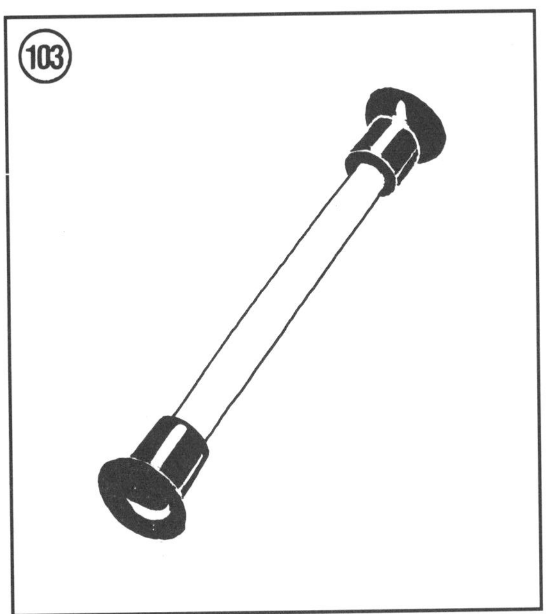

   b. Spread a thin layer of Prussian Blue or machinist's marking compound evenly on the valve face.
   c. Moisten the end of a suction cup valve tool (**Figure 103**) and attach it to the valve. Insert the valve into the guide.
   d. Using the suction cup tool, tap the valve up and down in the cylinder head. Do *not* rotate the valve. This will yield false results.
   e. Remove the valve and examine the impression left by the Prussian Blue or machinist's marking compound. If the impression left (on the valve or in the cylinder head) is not even and continuous or if the valve seat width (**Figure 104**) is not within the specified tolerance listed in **Table 1**, the cylinder head valve seat must be reconditioned.
3. Closely examine the valve seat (**Figure 92**) in the cylinder head. It should be smooth and even with a polished seating surface.
4. If the valve seat is in good condition, install the valve as described in this chapter.
5. If necessary, recondition the valve seat as described in this chapter.

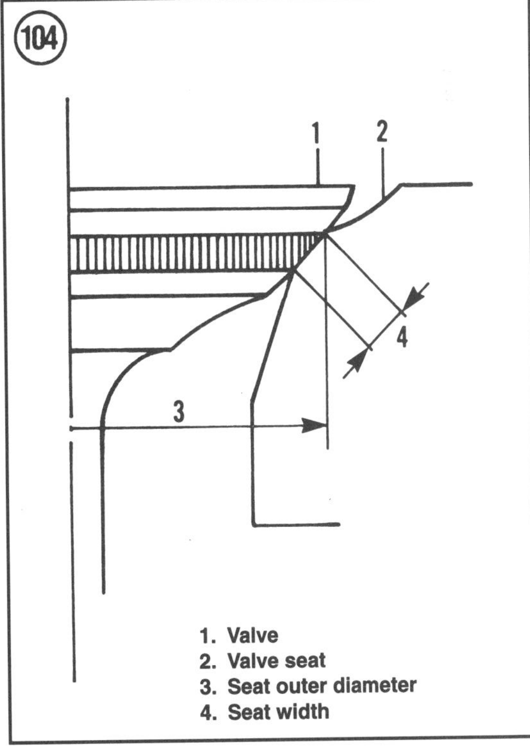

1. Valve
2. Valve seat
3. Seat outer diameter
4. Seat width

4

Valve Seat Reconditioning

Properly reconditioning the valve seats in the cylinder heads requires special valve cutter tools and considerable expertise. You can save considerable money by removing the valves and taking just the cylinder heads to a dealership or machine shop and have the valve seats reconditioned.

The following procedure is provided if you choose to perform this task yourself. The following tools are required:

a. Valve seat cutters (see a Kawasaki dealer for part numbers).
b. Vernier caliper.
c. Machinist's marking compound.
d. Valve lapping tool.

The valve seat for both the intake and exhaust valves are machined to the same angles. The valve contact surface is cut to a 45° angle and the area above the contact surface (closest to the combustion chamber) is cut to a 32° angle (**Figure 105**).

1. Install a 45° cutter onto the valve tool. Lightly cut the seat to remove roughness and clean the valve seat with one or two turns (**Figure 106**).

CAUTION

Measure the valve seat after each cut to make sure the contact area is correct and to prevent removing too much material. If too much material is removed, the cylinder head must be replaced.

2. If the seat is still pitted or burned, turn the 45° cutter additional turns until the surface is clean. Refer to the previous CAUTION. Do *not* remove too much material from the valve seat.

3. Measure the seat width with a vernier caliper. Record the measurement to refer to when performing the following.

4. Remove the 45° cutter and install the 32° cutter onto the valve tool. Lightly cut the seat to remove 1/4 of the existing valve seat.

CAUTION

The 60° cutter removes material quickly. Work carefully and check your progress often.

5. Remove the 32°cutter and install the 60° cutter onto the valve tool. Lightly cut the seat to remove the lower 1/4 of the existing valve seat.

NOTE

The 32° and 60° cutters are used to make the valve seat a consistent width around the entire surface. The 32° and 60° cutters are also used to shift the seat up and down, depending on readings taken with machinist's blue.

6. Measure the valve seat with a vernier caliper. If necessary, fit the 45° cutter onto the valve tool and cut the valve seat to the specified seat width listed in **Table 1**.

7. Check that the finish is smooth. The final seating will take place when the engine is first run.

8. Repeat Steps 1-6 for all remaining valve seats.

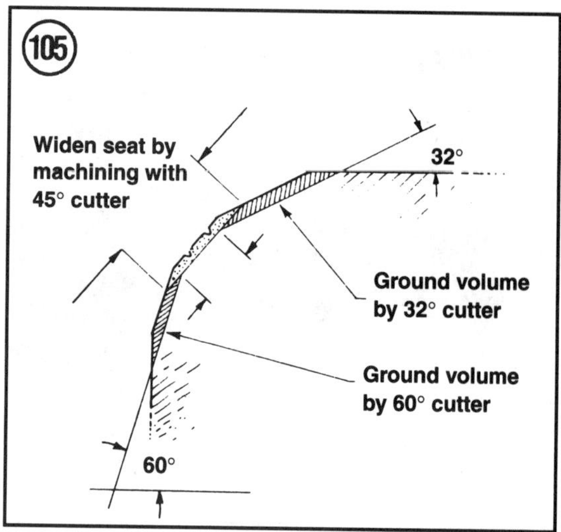

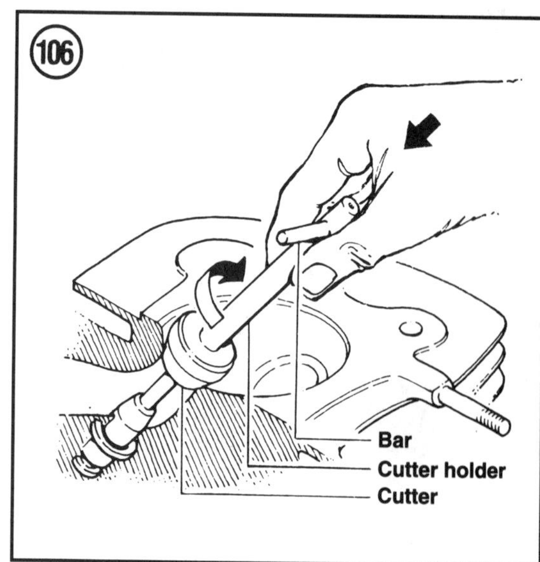

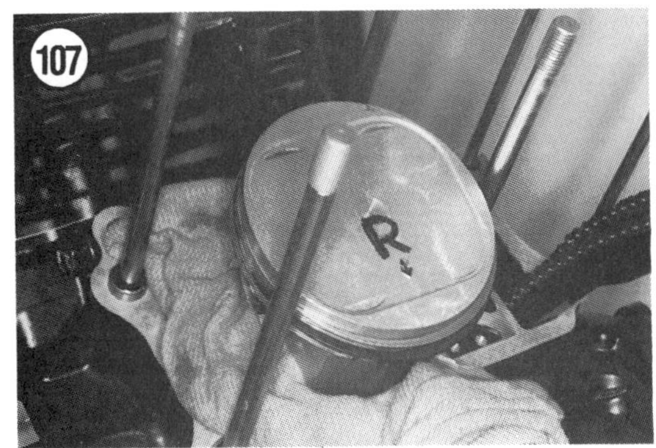

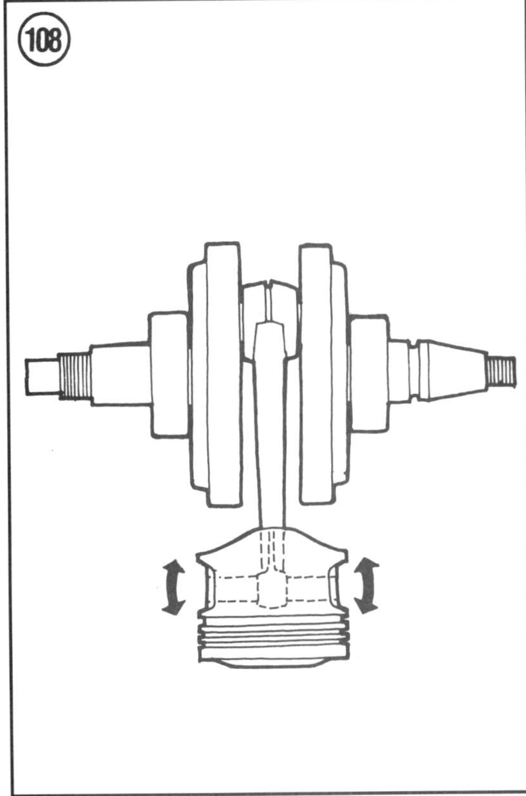

9. Thoroughly clean the cylinder head and all valve components in solvent or in detergent and hot water.
10. Install the valve assemblies as described in this chapter and fill the ports with solvent to check for leaks. If any leaks are present, the valve seats must be inspected for foreign matter or burrs that may be preventing a proper seal.
11. Apply a light coat of engine oil to all bare metal steel surfaces to prevent rust.

PISTONS AND PISTON RINGS

The pistons are made of aluminum alloy and the piston pins are made of steel. Each piston pin is a precision fit and is held in place by a clip at each end of the piston pin bore.

Piston Removal/Installation

1. Remove the cylinder head and cylinder block as described in this chapter.
2. Stuff clean shop cloths into the cylinder bore crankcase openings (**Figure 107**) to prevent objects from falling into the crankcase.
3. Lightly mark the top of the pistons with an F (front) or R (rear) so they will be installed into the correct cylinder. Also make an arrow (**Figure 107**) to indicate the exhaust side of the piston.
4. If necessary, remove the piston rings as described in this chapter.
5. Before removing the piston, hold the rod tightly and rock the piston as shown in **Figure 108**. Any rocking motion (do not confuse with the normal sliding motion) indicates wear on the piston pin, piston pin bore or connecting rod small-end bore (more likely a combination of these). Mark the piston and pin so that thcy will be reassembled as a set.
6. Remove the clips (A, **Figure 109**) from each side of the piston pin bore with a small screwdriver, scribe or needlenose pliers. Hold your thumb over one edge of the clip when removing it to prevent the clip from springing out.
7. Use a proper size wooden dowel or socket extension and push out the piston pin.

CAUTION

Be careful when removing the pin to avoid damaging the connecting rod. If it is necessary to gently tap the pin to remove it, be sure that the piston is properly supported so that lateral shock is not transmitted to the connecting rod lower bearing.

8. If the piston pin is difficult to remove, heat the piston and pin with a butane torch. The pin will probably push right out. Heat the piston to only about 140° F (60° C), until it is too warm to touch, but not excessively hot. If the pin is still difficult to push out, use a tool as shown in **Figure 110**.

9. Lift the piston off the connecting rod, and inspect it as described in this chapter.

10. If the piston is going to be left off for some time, place a piece of foam insulation tube over the end of the connecting rod to protect it.

11. Apply molybdenum disulfide grease to the inside surface of the connecting-rod piston-pin bore.

12. Oil the piston pin with assembly oil or fresh engine oil, and install it in the piston until its end extends slightly beyond the inside of the boss (**Figure 111**).

13. Correctly position the piston on the connecting rod as follows:

   a. Refer to the arrow mark (**Figure 112**) made during disassembly and install the piston with the arrow pointing to the front of the engine (front cylinder), or pointing to the rear of the engine (rear cylinder).
   b. If the pistons were not marked, or if new pistons are being installed, position the piston with the arrow mark on the crown pointing toward the *exhaust valve side* of the cylinder.

14. Place the piston over the connecting rod.

15. Align the piston pin with the hole in the connecting rod. Push the piston pin through the connecting rod and into the other side of the piston until it is even with the piston pin clip grooves.

CAUTION

If it is necessary to tap the piston pin into the connecting rod, do so gently with a block of wood or a soft-faced hammer. Make sure you support the piston to prevent the lateral shock from being transmitted to the connecting rod lower bearing.

NOTE

In the next step, install the piston pin clips so each clip's end gap is opposite the cutout in the piston ***(B, Figure 109).***

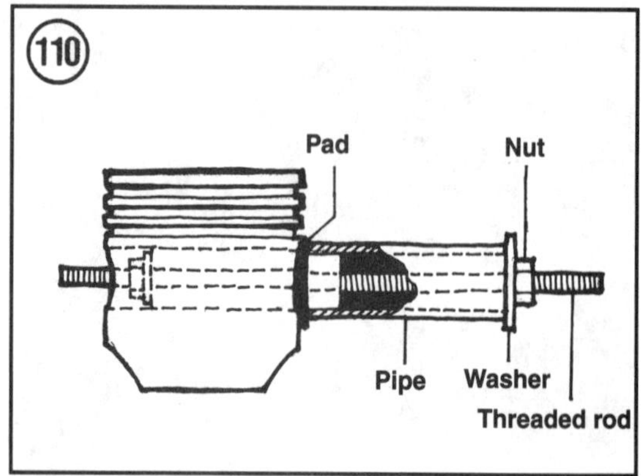

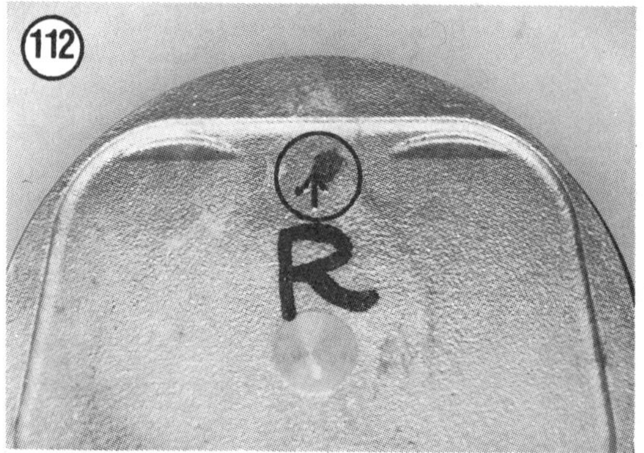

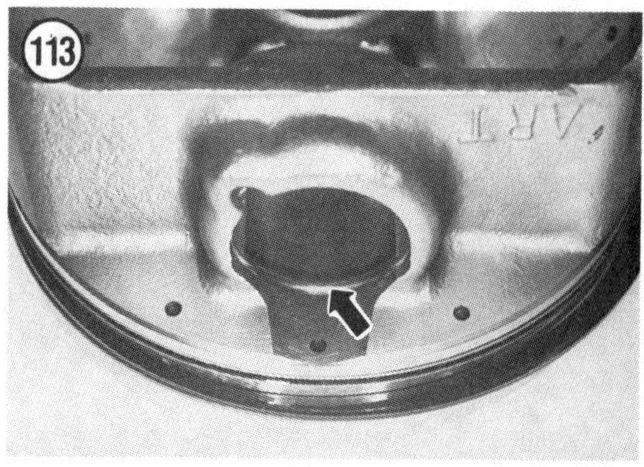

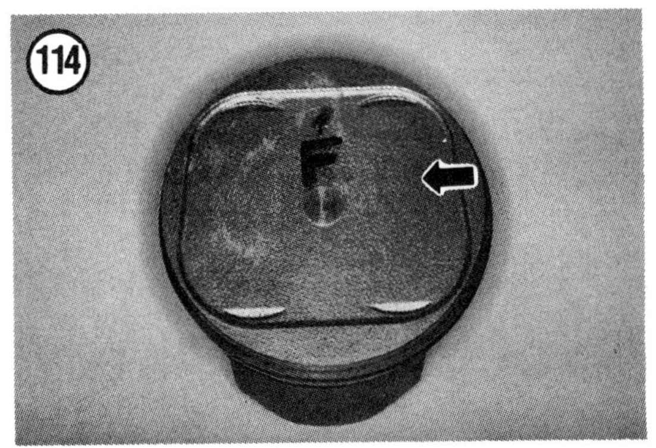

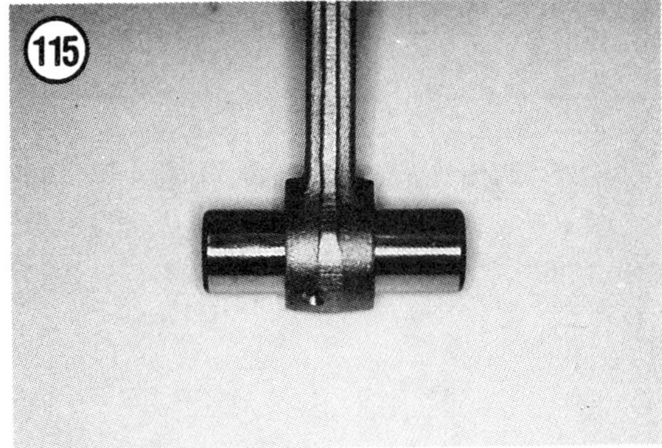

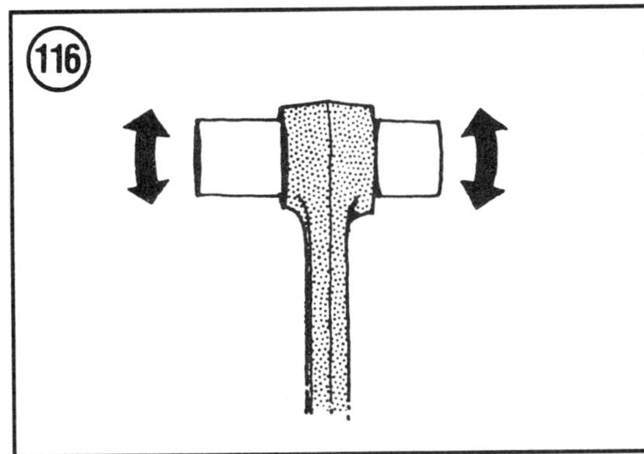

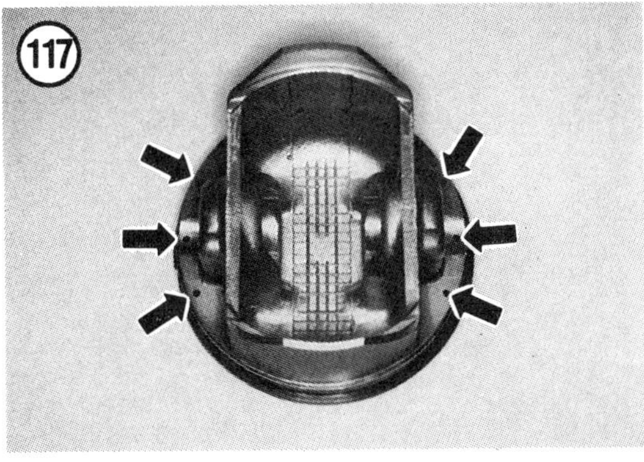

16. Install a *new* piston pin clip (A, **Figure 109**) into both ends of the pin boss. Make sure each pin is seated in the groove (**Figure 113**) in the piston.
17. Check the installation by rocking the piston back and forth around the pin axis and from side to side along the axis. It should rotate freely back and forth but not from side to side.
18. Install the piston rings as described in this chapter.
19. Repeat Steps 1-18 for the other piston.

Piston Inspection

1. Carefully clean the carbon from the piston crown (**Figure 114**) with a chemical remover or with a soft scraper. Do not remove or damage the carbon ridge around the circumference of the piston above the top ring. If the piston, rings and cylinder are dimensionally correct and can be reused, removal of the carbon ring from the top of the piston or the carbon ridge from the top of the cylinder will promote excessive oil consumption.

CAUTION
Do not wire brush the piston skirts or ring lands. A wire brush will mar and remove the Teflon coating from the piston skirts. Wiring brushing also removes aluminum, which increases piston clearance and it rounds the corners of the ring lands, which results in decreased support for the piston rings.

2. Examine each ring groove for burrs, dented edges and wear. Pay particular attention to the top compression ring groove. It usually wears more than the other grooves.
3. If damage or wear indicates that piston replacement is required, select a new piston as described in this chapter.
4. Oil the piston pin and install it in the connecting rod (**Figure 115**). Slowly rotate the piston pin and check for radial and axial play (**Figure 116**). If any play exists, the piston pin should be replaced, providing the rod bore is in good condition.
5. Check the oil control holes in the piston for carbon or oil sludge buildup. Refer to **Figure 117** and **Figure 118**. Clean the holes with a small diameter drill bit and blow out with compressed air.
6. Check the piston skirt for galling and abrasion, which may have been caused by piston seizure. If

light galling is present, smooth the affected area with No. 400 emery paper and oil or a fine oilstone. However, if galling is severe or if the piston is deeply scored, replace it.

7. Inspect the grooves in the piston pin bore on each side of the piston. If either groove is damaged, replace the piston.

8. If piston replacement is required, select a new piston as described in this chapter.

9. Inspect the piston pin (**Figure 119**) for chrome flaking or cracks. Replace if necessary.

Piston Clearance Measurement

1. Make sure the piston and cylinder walls are clean and dry.

2. Measure the inside diameter of the cylinder bore at a point 1/2 in. (13 mm) from the upper edge with a bore gauge.

3. Measure the outside diameter of the piston across the skirt (**Figure 120**) at a right angle to the piston pin. Measure at a distance 5 mm (0.20 in.) up from the bottom of the piston skirt.

4. Subtract the piston diameter from the cylinder diameter. Compare this difference to the piston/cylinder clearance listed in **Table 1**. If clearance is excessive, the piston should be replaced and the cylinder should be bored to the next oversize. Purchase the new piston first; measure its diameter and add the specified clearance to determine the proper cylinder bore diameter.

Piston Ring Removal/Installation

WARNING

*The edges of all piston rings **(Figure 121)** are very sharp. Be careful when handling them to avoid cutting your fingers.*

1. Measure the ring side clearance of each ring with a flat feeler gauge (**Figure 122**) and compare to specification given in **Table 1**. If the clearance is greater than specified, the rings must be replaced. If the clearance is still excessive with the new rings, the piston must also be replaced.

2. Remove the old rings with a ring expander tool (**Figure 123**) or by spreading the ends with your thumbs just enough to slide the ring up over the piston (**Figure 124**). Repeat for the remaining rings.

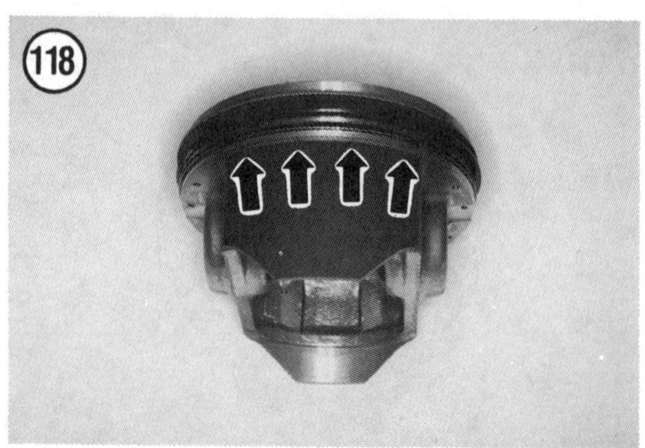

118

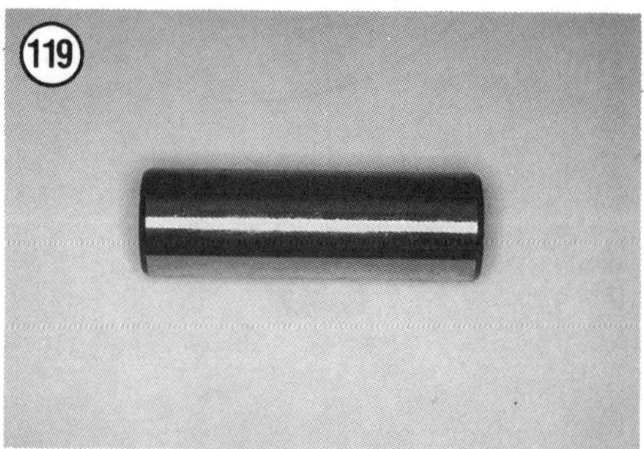

119

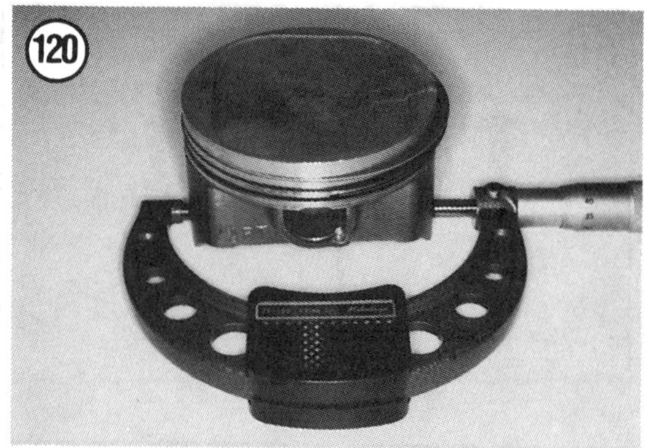

120

121

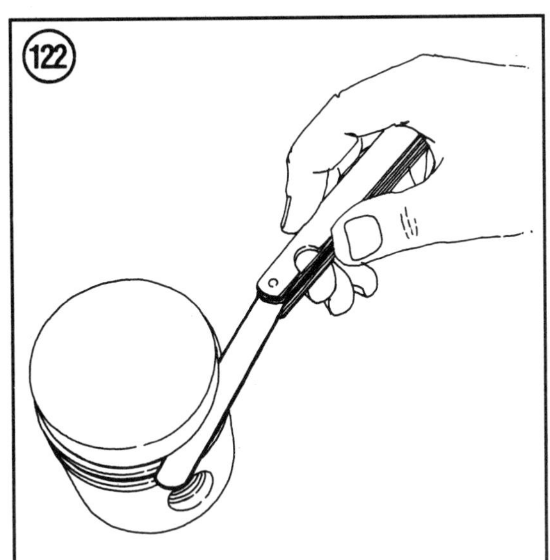

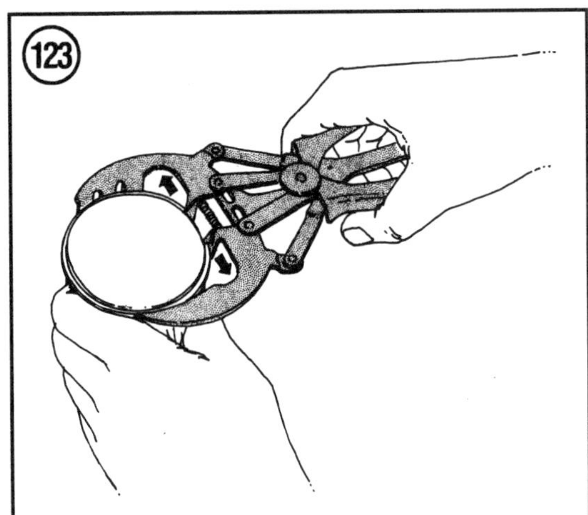

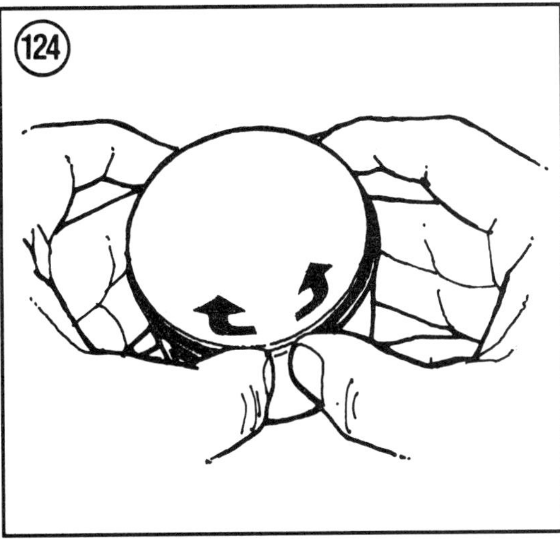

3. Carefully remove all carbon buildup from the ring grooves with a broken piston ring (**Figure 125**).

4. Inspect the grooves carefully for burrs, nicks or broken and cracked lands. Recondition or replace the piston if necessary.

5. Check the end gap of each ring. To check the ring, insert a ring into the bottom of the cylinder bore, and push it about 20 mm (5/8 in.) into the bore. Push the ring with the crown of the piston to ensure that the ring is square in the cylinder bore. Measure the gap with a flat feeler gauge (**Figure 126**) and compare the gap to the specification in **Table 1**. If the ring end

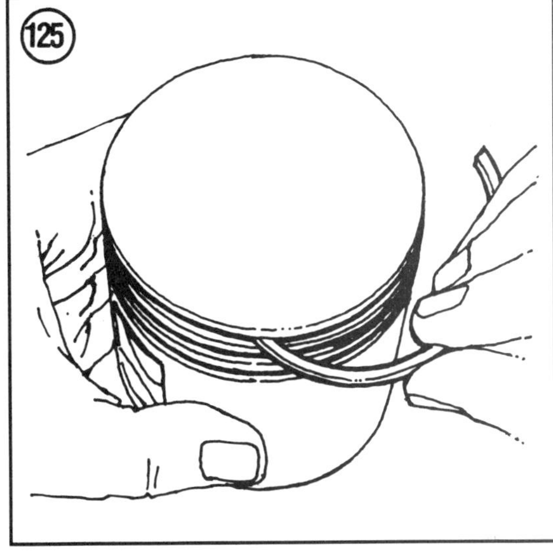

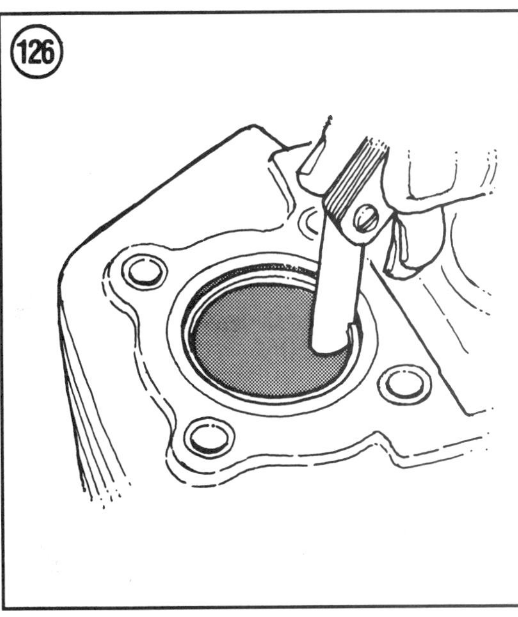

gap is greater than specified, the rings should be replaced. When installing new rings, measure their end gap in the same manner as for old ones. If the gap is less than specified, carefully file the ends with a fine-cut file until the gap is correct.

6. Roll each ring around its piston groove as shown in **Figure 127** to check for binding. If there is any binding, there may still be carbon in the groove. Reclean the ring groove with solvent. After cleaning with solvent, clean the groove with a broken piston ring (**Figure 125**).

7. Do not confuse the top and second rings. They can be identified by the manufacturer's marks shown in **Figure 128**.

8. Install the piston rings. Install the bottom oil control ring assembly first, then the second ring, then the top ring. Carefully spread the ends of each ring with your thumbs and slip the ring over the top of the piston. The piston rings must be installed with the manufacturer's mark or paint mark facing the top of the piston. Install the rings as follows:

   a. Install the oil control ring assembly. First, install the oil control expander. Be sure the ends of the expander butt together as shown in **Figure 129**. They must not overlap. Next, install the oil ring lower steel rail and finally the oil ring upper steel rail.

   b. Install the second ring. The second ring is not symmetrical and must be installed as shown in **Figure 128**.

   c. Install the top ring. The top ring is also not symmetrical and must be installed as shown in **Figure 128**.

9. Make sure the rings are seated completely in their grooves all the way around the piston and that the end gaps are distributed around the piston as shown in **Figure 130**. Be sure that the ring gaps are not aligned with each other when installed in the cylinder.

10. If new rings are installed, measure the ring/groove side clearance of each installed ring with a flat feeler gauge (**Figure 122**). Compare the measurements to the dimensions given in **Table 1**.

11. After the rings are installed, apply clean engine oil to the rings. Rotate the rings several complete revolutions in their respective grooves.

BREAK-IN

Following cylinder servicing (boring, honing, new rings or pistons) and major lower end work, the engine should be broken-in just as if it were new. The

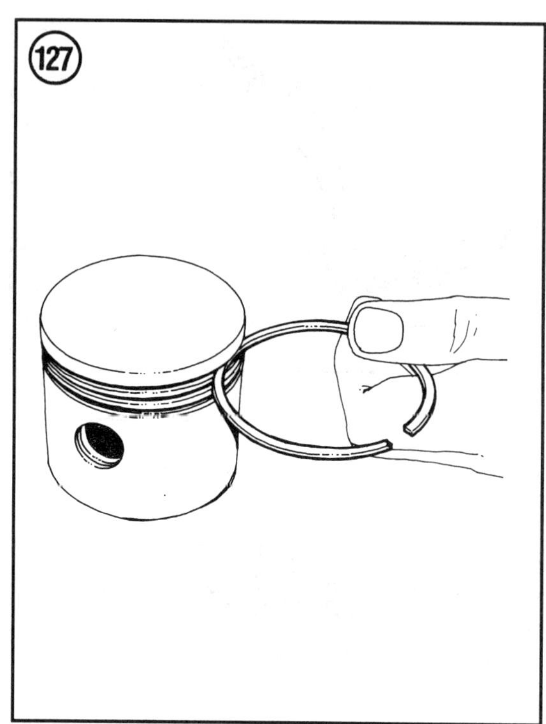

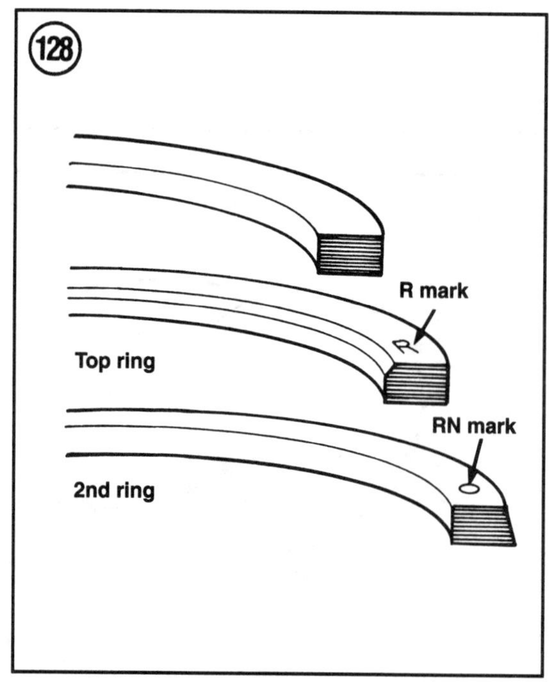

performance and service life of the engine depends greatly on a careful and sensible break-in. For the first 500 miles, use no more than one-third throttle and vary the speed as much as possible within the one-third throttle limit. Avoid prolonged, steady running at one speed, no matter how moderate. Also avoid hard acceleration.

Following the 500-mile service, increasingly more throttle can be used but avoid full throttle until the motorcycle has covered at least 1000 miles and then limit full throttle operation to short bursts until 1500 miles have been logged.

During the break-in period, oil consumption may be higher than normal. It is therefore important to frequently check and correct the oil level. At no time, during break-in or later, should the oil level be allowed to drop below the bottom line on the inspection window. If the oil level is low, the oil will overheat causing insufficient lubrication and increased wear.

500-Mile Service

It is essential that the oil and filter be changed after the first 500 miles. In addition, it is a good idea to change the oil and filter at the completion of break-in (about 1500 miles). This ensures that all of the particles produced during break-in are removed from the lubrication system. The small added expense is a smart investment that will pay off in increased engine life.

4

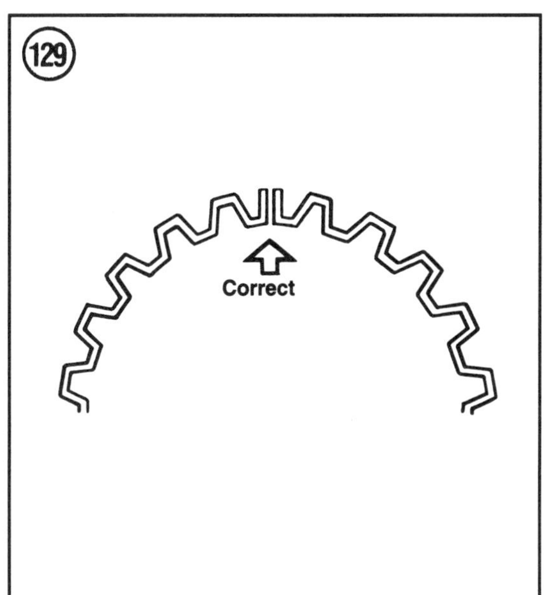

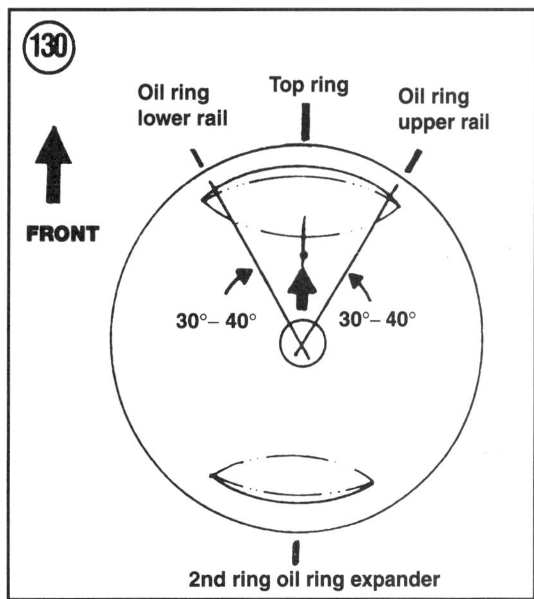

Table 1 ENGINE UPPER END SPECIFICATIONS

	Specification	Wear limit
Camshaft		
Cam lobe height		
Intake	35.305-35.413 mm (1.3800-1.3942 in.)	35.21 mm (1.3862 in.)
Exhaust	35.033-35.141 mm (1.3792-1.3835 in.)	34.93 mm (1.3752 in.)
Journal diameter	26.950-26.972 mm (1.0610-1.0619 in.)	26.92 mm (1.0598 in.)
Bearing inner diameter	27.000-27.021 mm (1.0630-1.0638 in)	27.08 mm (1.0661 in.)

(continued)

Table 1 ENGINE UPPER END SPECIFICATIONS (continued)

	Specification	Wear limit
Camshaft (continued)		
Journal to camshaft cap clearance	0.028-0.071 mm (0.0011-0.0027) in.	0.16 mm (0.00663 in.)
Camshaft runout		0.01 mm (0.0004 in.)
Rocker arm inside diameter	16.000-16.018 mm (0.6299-0.6306 in.)	16.05 mm (0.6319 in.)
Rocker shaft diameter	15.965-15.984 mm (0.6285-0.6292 in.)	15.94 mm (0.62756 in.)
Cam chain 20-link length	127.00-127.36 mm (5.000-5.014 in.)	128.9 mm (5.0745 in.)
Cylinder head warp	—	0.05 mm (0.0019 in.)
Valves and valve springs		
Valve clearance		
Intake	0.10-0.15 mm (0.004-0.006 in.)	
Exhaust	0.25-0.30 mm (0.010-0.012 in.)	
Valve stem diameter		
Intake	4.975-4.990 mm (0.1959-0.1965 in.)	4.96 mm (0.1953 in.)
Exhaust	4.955-4.970 mm (0.1951-0.1957 in.)	4.94 mm (0.1945 in.)
Valve stem runout	0.01 mm (0.0004 in.) or less	0.05mm (0.002 in.)
Valve guide inner diameter	5.000-5.012 mm (0.1969-0.1973 in.)	5.07 mm (0.1996 in.)
Valve stem-to-guide clearance (wobble method)		
Intake	0.03-0.12 mm (0.0012-0.0047 in.)	0.26 mm (0.0102 in.)
Exhaust	0.10-0.18 mm (0.0039 -0.0071 in.)	0.32 mm (0.0126 in.)
Valve head thickness		
Intake	0.5 mm	—
	(0.020 in.)	—
Exhaust	0.8 mm	—
	(0.031 in.)	—
Valve seat surface		—
Width		—
Intake and exhaust	0.5-1.0 mm (0.0196-0.039 in.)	—
Outside diameter		
Intake	30.9-31.1 mm (1.217-1.224 in.)	—
Exhaust	26.9-27.1 mm (1.059-1.067 in.)	—
Valve seat cutting angle	45, 32, 60 degrees	
Valve spring free length	40.5 mm (1.594 in.)	38.6 mm (1.520 in.)
Cylinders		
Bore diameter	88.000-88.012 mm (3.4646-3.4650 in.)	88.11 mm (3.4689 in.)
Oversize pistons and rings	+0.5 mm (0.020 in.)	
Piston diameter	87.975-87.990 mm (3.4629-3.4642 in.)	87.83 mm (3.4579 in.)
Piston/cylinder clearance	0.010-0.037 mm (0.0004-0.0015 in.)	—

(continued)

Table 1 ENGINE UPPER END SPECIFICATIONS (continued)

	Specification	Wear limit
Piston ring groove width		
Top	1.02-1.04 mm (0.0401-0.0409 in.)	1.12 mm (0.044 in.)
Second	1.01-1.03 mm (0.0397-0. 0405 in.)	1.11 mm (0.0437 in.)
Piston rings		
Ring/groove clearance		
Top	0.03-0.07 mm (0.0012-0.0027 in.)	0.17 mm (0.0067 in.)
Second	0.02-0.06 mm (0.0008-0.0024 in.)	1.16 mm (0.0457 in.)
Ring thickness		
Top and second	0.97-0.99 mm (0.0381-0.0389 in.)	0.90 mm (0.0354 in.)
Ring end gap		
Top	0.25-0.40 mm (0.0098-0.0157 in.)	0.7 mm (0.0275 in.)
Second	0.40-0.55 mm) (0.0157-0.0216 in.	0.9 mm (0.0354 in.)

4

Table 2 UPPER END TIGHTENING TORQUES

Item	N•m	in.-lb.	ft.-lb.
Intake manifold bolts	12	106	—
Cylinder head cover bolts	12	106	—
Cylinder head cover damper plate bolts	12	106	—
Cylinder head bolt	12	106	—
Cylinder head nuts			
8 mm	25	—	18
10 mm	39	—	29
Cylinder head cap nuts	25	—	18
Cylinder cap nut	25	—	18
Camshaft cap bolts	25	—	18
Camshaft sprocket bolt	49	—	36
Cam chain tensioner cap bolts	20	—	15
Cam chain guide bolt	11	97	—
Cam chain guide/tensioner bolts	11	97	—
Primary gear bolt	155	—	114
Coolant pipe mounting bolt	11	97	—

Table 3 GENERAL ENGINE SPECIFICATIONS

	Specification	Wear limit
Type and number of cylinders	V-2 cylinder, SOHC, liquid cooled	
Bore × stroke	88.0 × 66.2 mm (3.46 × 2.61 in.)	
Displacement	805 cc (49.12 cu. in.)	
Compression ratio	9.5:1	
Compression pressure	855-1315 kPa (124-191 psi)	

CHAPTER FIVE

ENGINE LOWER END

ENGINE

Removal/Installation

1. Drain the engine oil and cooling system as described in Chapter Three.
2. Remove the seat and both frame side covers as described in Chapter Fourteen.
3. Remove the fuel tank as described in Chapter Eight.
4. Remove the exhaust pipes as described in Chapter Eight.
5. Remove the air filter assembly, carburetor assembly and the vacuum switch valve as described in Chapter Eight. Move the throttle and choke cables out of the way.
6. Remove the radiator and fan assembly as described in Chapter Ten.
7. Remove the coolant hose fittings from the cylinder heads.
8. Disconnect the clutch cable from the release arm as described in Chapter Six. Move the cable out of the way.
9. Remove the engine sprocket as described in this chapter.
10. Disconnect the spark plug leads from both spark plugs. Move both leads out of the way.

NOTE

After disconnecting the following electrical wires, move the loose ends out of the way and secure them to the frame. This will reduce the chance of their being caught on the engine during removal from the frame.

11. Disconnect the following electrical wires:
    a. The starter motor lead (A, **Figure 1**).
    b. The oil pressure switch lead (B, **Figure 1**).
    c. The ignition switch lead (A, **Figure 2**).
    d. Alternator connector (B, **Figure 2**).
    e. Pickup coil connector (C, **Figure 2**).
    f. Neutral switch lead (A, **Figure 3**).
    g. Engine ground (A, **Figure 4**).
12. Remove the shift pedal/lever assembly as described in Chapter Seven.
13. Remove the rear brake pedal assembly as described in Chapter Thirteen.
14. Support the frame with a scissors jack.
15. Place wooden blocks and a small hydraulic jack under the engine to support it securely.
16. Take a final look all over the engine to make sure everything is disconnected.
17. Make sure the hydraulic jack is still in place and supporting the engine securely.

CAUTION
The following steps require the aid of a helper to safely remove the engine assembly from the frame.

18. Loosen, but do not remove, all frame downtube and engine mounting bolts.
19. Remove the hardware in the following order:
    a. Remove the lower rear bolts (B, **Figure 3**) securing the frame downtube to the frame.
    b. Remove the upper front bolts (**Figure 5**) securing the frame downtube to the frame.
    c. Remove the two bolts (A, **Figure 6**) securing the front engine bracket to the frame downtube, and then remove the frame downtube (B, **Figure 6**).
    d. Remove the nut and through-bolt from the front engine mount (C, **Figure 6**).
    e. Remove the nut and through-bolt from upper rear engine bracket (B, **Figure 4**).
    f. Loosen the bolts (C, **Figure 4**) securing the upper rear engine bracket to the frame and remove the bracket.
    g. Remove the nut and lower rear through bolt (C, **Figure 3**).

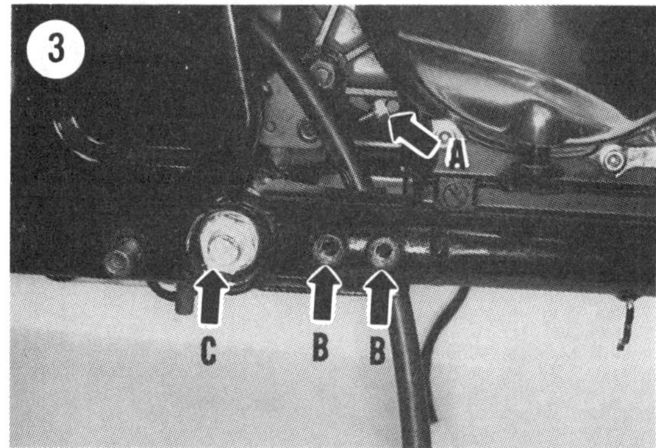

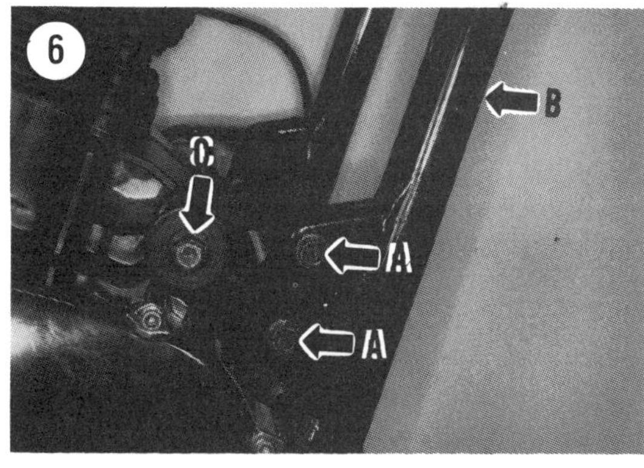

20. Once again, confirm that everything is disconnected from the engine.

21. Slowly move the engine forward and toward the right-hand side.

22. Slightly lower the engine on the jack and continue to move the engine forward and toward the right-hand side until the engine clears the frame members.

23. Take the engine to a workbench for further disassembly.

24. Install by reversing these removal steps while noting the following:

a. Install each engine mounting through-bolt from the left-hand side of the motorcycle so its mounting nut can be installed on the right-hand side.
b. Route the air filter drain tube behind the frame downtube mounting bolts and nut and secure the drain tube with a tie-wrap to keep it away from the rear exhaust pipe.
c. Torque the engine mounting bolts to the specifications in **Table 2**.
d. Fill the engine with oil as described in Chapter Three.
e. Refill the cooling system as described in Chapter Three.
f. Start the engine and check for leaks.

OIL PUMP

Removal/Installation

1. Remove the engine from the frame and split the crankcase halves as described in this chapter.

2. Remove the crankshaft assembly as described in this chapter.

3. Remove the circlip (A, **Figure 7**) securing the oil pump driven sprocket (B, **Figure 7**) to the oil pump shaft.

4. Remove the driven sprocket, oil pump drive chain and balancer shaft as an assembly. Slide the balancer shaft (A, **Figure 8**) out of its bearing in the left-hand crankcase half along with the oil pump drive chain (B, **Figure 8**) and driven sprocket (C, **Figure 8**).

5. Remove the sprocket from the drive chain, remove the drive chain from the balancer shaft and leave the balancer shaft resting in the crankcase.

NOTE
The oil pump mounting screws are secured with threadlocking compound. They may be difficult to loosen.

6. Use an impact driver and loosen the oil pump mounting bolts (A and B, **Figure 9**). Remove the bolts.

7. Remove the oil pump assembly (C, **Figure 9**) and O-ring from the crankcase. Hold the *open end* of the oil pump up so the rotors do not fall from the body.

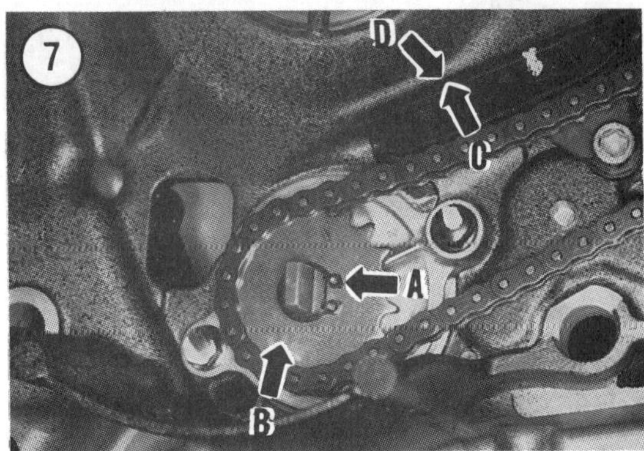

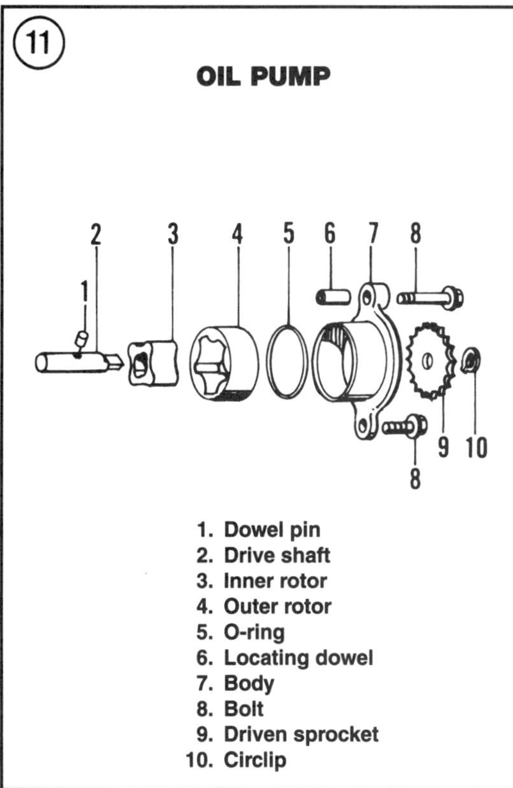

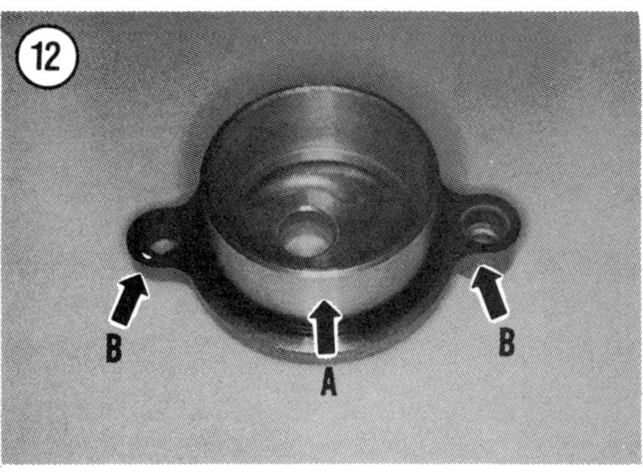

Do not lose the dowel located behind the forward mounting bolt (A, **Figure 9**).

8. Install by reversing the removal steps while noting the following:
   a. Be sure the dowel is in place in the pump housing. The dowel should sit inside the hole for the forward oil pump mounting bolt (A, **Figure 9**).
   b. Apply grease to the O-ring (**Figure 10**) on the oil pump body prior to installation.
   c. Apply Loctite 242 to the oil pump mounting bolts and torque the bolts to the specification in **Table 2**.
   d. Position the sprocket circlip with the sharp side edge facing away from the oil pump and install the circlip (A, **Figure 7**). Make sure it seats correctly in the shaft groove.
   e. Make sure the oil pump chain guide is in place and positioned correctly. When properly installed, the upper edge of the chain guide (C, **Figure 7**) will touch the flat surface on the crankcase (D, **Figure 7**). Torque the oil pump drive chain guide bolt to the specification in **Table 2**.

5

Disassembly/Inspection/Assembly

Refer to **Figure 11** for this procedure.

NOTE
Service specifications for the oil pump are not available. If excessive wear is noticed on any part, replace the pump.

1. Remove the driveshaft, dowel pin, inner rotor and outer rotor from the pump body.
2. Clean all parts in solvent and dry with compressed air.
3. Inspect the oil pump body (A, **Figure 12**) for cracks or bore damage. If worn or damaged, replace the oil pump.
4. Inspect the oil pump mounting bosses (B, **Figure 12**) for fractures or damage. If damaged, replace the oil pump.
5. Inspect the driveshaft for wear or damage. If worn or damaged, replace the oil pump.
6. Make sure the dowel pin fits tightly in the driveshaft. If loose, replace the oil pump.
7. Inspect the inner and outer rotors (**Figure 13**) for wear, abrasion or damage.

8. Lay the oil pump chain on a workbench and stretch a 20 pin segment as shown in **Figure 14**. Measure the 20-pin length at several places around the chain. Replace the chain if any measurement exceeds the service limit in **Table 1**.

10. Visually inspect the chain for damage or wear. Replace the chain, if necessary. If the chain is worn, also inspect the oil pump driven sprocket and the balancer shaft drive sprocket for wear or damage.

11. Coat all parts with clean engine oil.

12. Install the outer rotor into the oil pump body (**Figure 15**).

13. Position the inner rotor with the groove for the dowel pin facing up and install the inner rotor into the outer rotor (**Figure 16**).

14. Install the dowel pin (A, **Figure 17**) into the drive shaft.

15. Position the driveshaft with the flat tab going in first, and install the drive shaft (B, **Figure 17**) into the inner rotor. Make sure the dowel pin is properly seated in the inner rotor groove.

16. If removed, install the O-ring (**Figure 10**) onto the oil pump body.

PRIMARY DRIVE GEAR

Removal

1. Remove the clutch cover as described in Chapter Six.

2A. If the clutch assembly is still in place, perform the following:

   a. Stuff a shop cloth, penny or brass washer (A, **Figure 18**) between the clutch outer housing gear and the primary drive gear. This will prevent the gear from rotating while loosening the bolt.

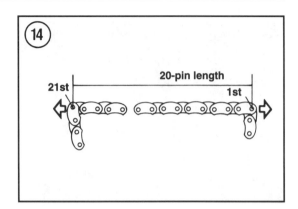

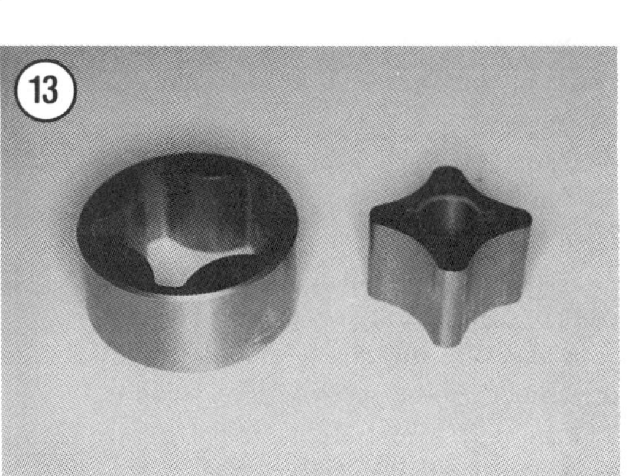

13

14

20-pin length
21st
1st

15

16

17

CAUTION

Any soft metal washer, copper, brass or aluminum, will work in the above step. However, do not use a steel washer. Steel will damage the gear teeth.

b. Loosen the primary drive gear bolt (B, **Figure 18**).

2B. If the clutch assembly is removed, perform the following:

a. If still in place, remove the piston from one of the connecting rods.

b. Insert a 1/2 in. drive socket extension or round drift through the small end of the connecting rod.

CAUTION

Use only a round extension or drift. Any other shape could cause damage to the piston pin hole.

c. Rotate the crankshaft until the extension or round drift in the connecting rod rests on the top surface of the crankcase.

d. Loosen the primary drive gear bolt (B, **Figure 18**).

e. Remove the socket extension or drift from the connecting rod.

3. Remove the primary gear flange bolt and the washer (A, **Figure 19**).

4. Slide the primary drive gear (B, **Figure 19**) off the end of the crankshaft.

5. Do not lose the Woodruff key (**Figure 20**) from the crankshaft. It is not necessary to remove the key unless it is loose.

6. Inspect all components as described in this chapter.

Installation

1. If removed, install the Woodruff key (**Figure 20**) in the slot in the crankshaft.

2. Align the keyway in the gear with the Woodruff key and install the primary drive gear (B, **Figure 19**).

3. Apply engine oil to the threads of the primary drive gear bolt and to the bolt seating surface on the primary gear. Install the bolt and washer (A, **Figure 19**).

4. Use the same tool arrangement (**Figure 21**) used in Step 2 to prevent the crankshaft from rotating while tightening the bolt.

5. Tighten the primary drive gear bolt to the torque specification listed in **Table 2**.
6. Install the crankcase right-hand side cover as described in this chapter.

Inspection

NOTE
*If the primary drive gear teeth are damaged, also inspect the gear teeth on the clutch outer housing, (**Figure 22**).*

1. Inspect the primary drive gear (**Figure 23**) for chipped or missing teeth, wear or damage. Replace the gear if necessary.
2. Check the keyway (**Figure 24**) for wear or damage and replace the gear if necessary.

BALANCER ASSEMBLY AND STARTER GEARS

The balancer system eliminates the vibration normally associated with a large displacement twin using a common crankpin. The engine and frame are designed to be compatible with this balancer system. If the balancer system is eliminated it will result in major fatigue and failure to engine and frame components. Do not eliminate this feature.

CAUTION
Any applicable manufacturer's warranty will be voided if the balancer system is modified, disconnected or removed.

Removal

Refer to the following illustrations for this procedure:

a. **Figure 25**—balancer gear assembly.
b. **Figure 26**—starter clutch gears.

1. Remove the alternator cover as described in Chapter Nine.

2A. If you have a flywheel holder:
   a. Hold the alternator rotor with the flywheel holder.
   b. Loosen the left-hand balancer bolt (A, **Figure 27**).

2B. If you do not have a flywheel holder:
   a. Remove the clutch cover as described in Chapter Six.
   b. Place a socket and wrench on the starter driven gear bolt (**Figure 28**) to hold the balancer shaft while you loosen the left-hand balancer bolt.
   c. Loosen the left-hand balancer bolt (A, **Figure 27**).

3. Remove the alternator rotor as described in Chapter Nine.

4. To remove the left-hand balancer, perform the following:

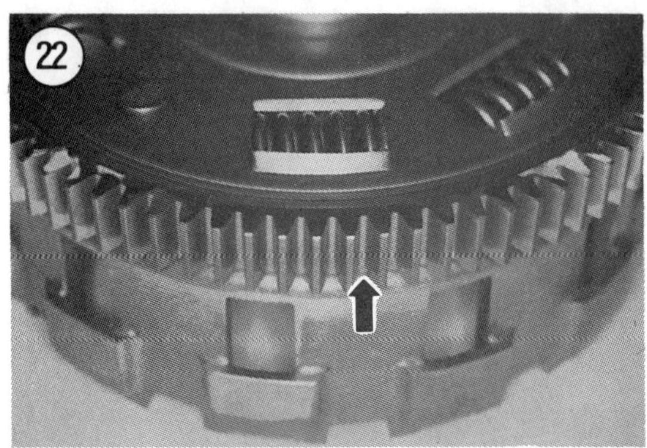

25

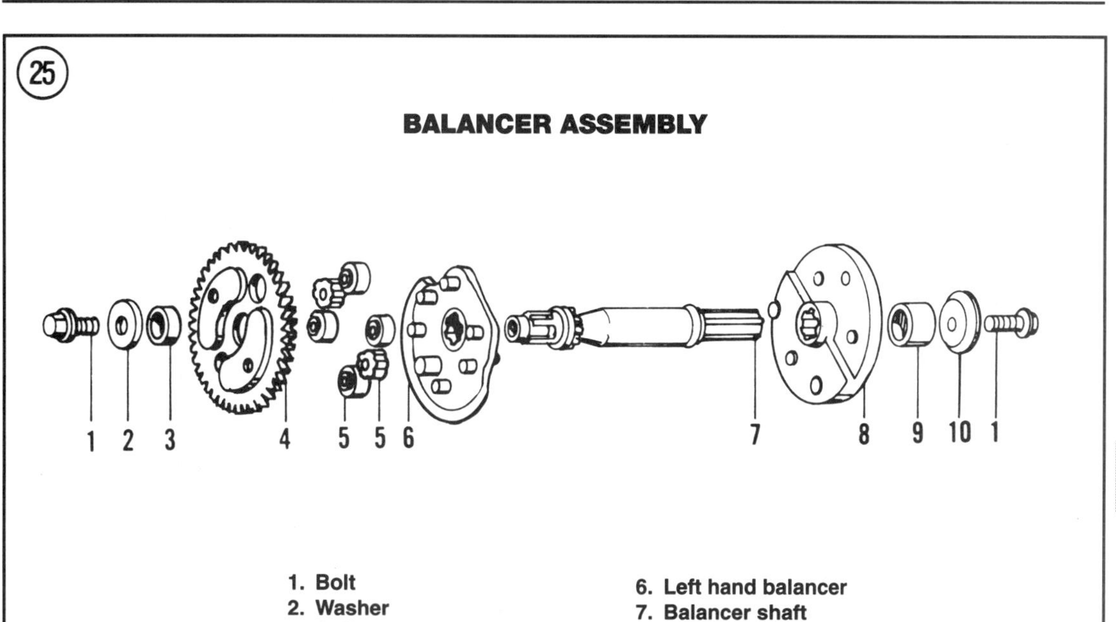

BALANCER ASSEMBLY

1. Bolt
2. Washer
3. Collar
4. Left-hand balancer gear
5. Rubber dampers
6. Left hand balancer
7. Balancer shaft
8. Right-hand balancer
9. Collar
10. Beveled washer

26

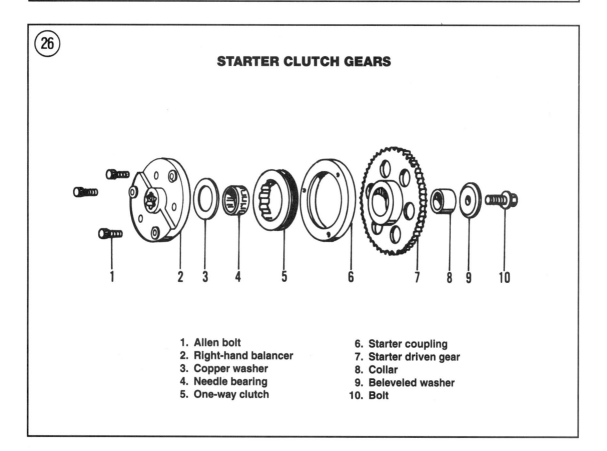

STARTER CLUTCH GEARS

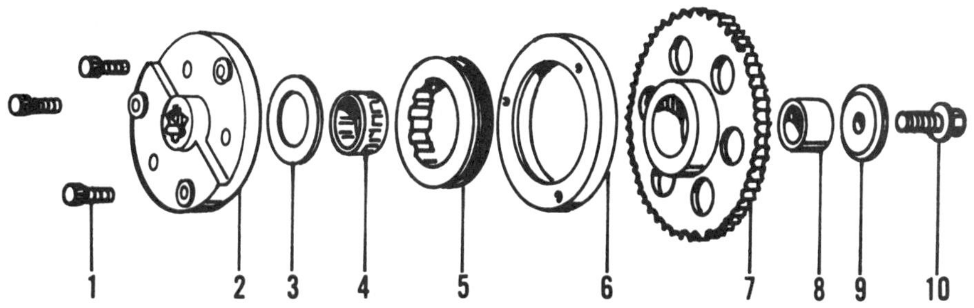

1. Allen bolt
2. Right-hand balancer
3. Copper washer
4. Needle bearing
5. One-way clutch
6. Starter coupling
7. Starter driven gear
8. Collar
9. Beleveled washer
10. Bolt

a. Remove the left-hand balancer bolt (A, **Figure 27**), washer (B, **Figure 27**) and collar (**Figure 29**).
b. The alignment mark on the balancer shaft can be difficult to see. Use a center punch to make your own alignment mark on the end of the balancer shaft prior to removing the balancer gear (A, **Figure 30**).
c. Remove the balancer gear (B, **Figure 30**) and left-hand balancer assembly from the balancer shaft.
d. If the balancer is hard to remove, use a two-jaw puller.
e. Clean any threadlocking compound from the threads of the balancer shaft.

5. To remove the right-hand balancer and starter gear, perform the following:

a. Remove the washer (A, **Figure 31**) from the starter idle gear.
b. Install the clutch holder tool onto the starter gear to prevent the gear from turning while loosening the bolt.
c. Loosen the starter gear bolt (B, **Figure 31**).

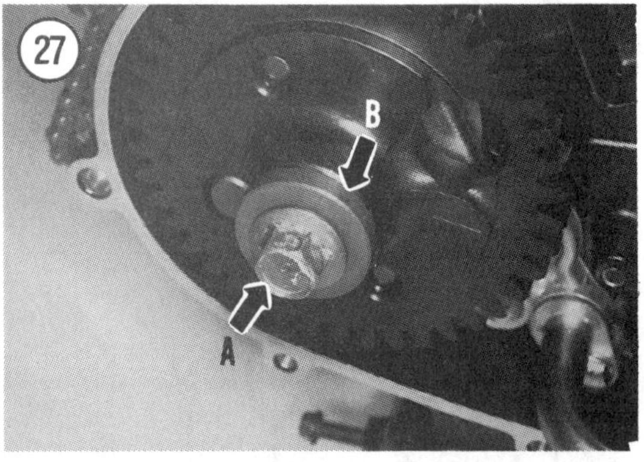

d. Remove the bolt and beveled washer (C, **Figure 31**).
e. Slide the starter driven gear (D, **Figure 31**) off the balancer shaft.
f. Remove the needle bearing (**Figure 32**) and collar (**Figure 33**).
g. Remove the copper washer (A, **Figure 34**).
h. Slide the right-hand balancer and starter clutch assembly (B, **Figure 34**) off the balancer shaft.
i. If the assembly is difficult to remove, use a two-jaw puller (**Figure 35**).

6. Remove the starter idle gear (A, **Figure 36**) from the crankcase.
7. Inspect all parts as described in this chapter.

Inspection

1. Separate the left-hand balancer (A, **Figure 37**) from the left-hand balancer gear (B, **Figure 37**).

CAUTION
*Two types of dampers are used on the right-hand balancer: four round dampers (A, **Figure 38**) and two gear-like dampers (B, **Figure 38**). When replac-*

*ing the dampers, be sure they are installed where shown in **Figure 38**.*

2. Inspect the six rubber dampers (**Figure 38**) for wear or deterioration. Replace as a set if any require replacement.
3. Inspect the six posts (**Figure 39**) on the left-hand balancer for wear or damage. Replace if necessary.
4. Inspect the left-hand balancer gear (**Figure 40**) for worn, chipped or missing teeth. Replace if necessary.
5. Inspect the inner splines in the right-hand balancer (**Figure 41**) and on the left-hand balancer (**Figure 42**) for wear or damage. Replace if necessary.
6. Inspect the outer splines on the balancer shaft for wear or damage. Replace if necessary.
7. Inspect the starter driven gear (A, **Figure 43**) for worn or damaged teeth. Replace the gear if necessary.
8. Inspect the starter idle gear (B, **Figure 43**) for wear or damage. Replace if necessary.
9. Inspect the starter driven gear outer surface (**Figure 44**) where it rides on the one-way clutch. If the surface is damaged, replace the gear.

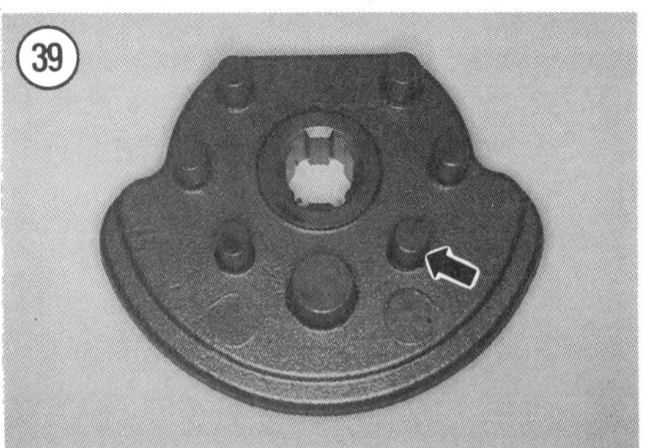

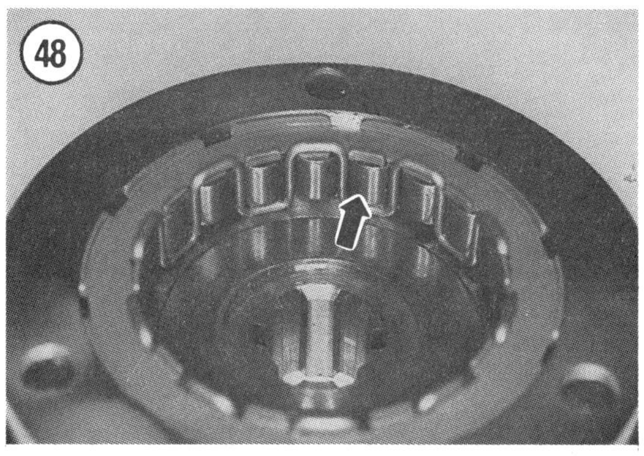

10. Inspect the starter driven gear inner surface (**Figure 45**) where it rides on the needle bearing. If the surface is damaged, replace the gear.

11. Inspect the needle bearing (**Figure 46**) for wear or damage. It must rotate freely.

12. Inspect the inner and outer surfaces of the collar for wear or damage. Insert the collar into the needle bearing (**Figure 47**) and rotate it. It should rotate freely. Replace the collar if necessary.

13. Inspect the rollers (**Figure 48**) of the one-way clutch for burrs, wear or damage. To remove the one-way clutch from the balancer, perform the following:

   a. Remove the Allen bolts (**Figure 49**) securing the one-way clutch (A, **Figure 50**) and coupling (B, **Figure 50**) to the right-hand balancer. Remove both parts.

   b. Install the one-way clutch (A, **Figure 50**) with the flanged side facing the right-hand balancer, then install the coupling (B, **Figure 50**).

   c. Apply Loctite 271 to the Allen bolt threads prior to installation. Install the bolts (**Figure 49**) and tighten to the torque specification listed in **Table 2**.

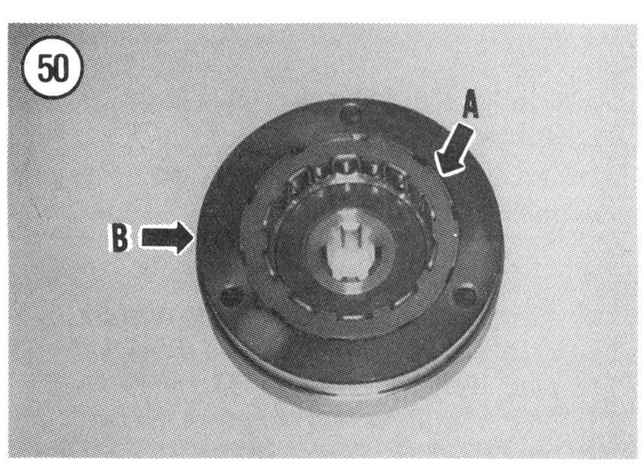

14. Assemble the left-hand balancer gear onto the left-hand balancer as follows:

a. Make sure all six rubber dampers (A, **Figure 51**) are in place.

CAUTION
The balancer and balancer gear must be assembled together correctly. If assembled incorrectly, the balance weight will be 180° out of alignment resulting in severe engine vibration that will lead to internal engine damage.

b. Position the balancer locating pin (B, **Figure 51**) so it will be inserted into the smaller diameter hole in the balancer gear (C, **Figure 51**).
c. Install the balancer onto the balancer gear and push them together.
d. Make sure the balancer locating pin is indexed correctly in the balancer gear *smaller diameter hole* (**Figure 52**). This alignment is necessary to ensure proper balancer operation.

Installation

Refer to the following illustrations for this procedure:

a. **Figure 25**—balancer assembly.
b. **Figure 26**—starter clutch gears.

CAUTION
Both balancer assemblies must be properly aligned and installed on the balancer shaft. If either balancer is installed incorrectly it will result in severe engine vibration leading to internal engine damage. Be sure to follow all alignment steps in this procedure to ensure proper installation of all components.

1. Install the starter idle gear (A, **Figure 36**) onto the crankcase.
2. To install the right-hand balancer and starter gear, perform the following:

CAUTION
*For the right-hand balancer to operate correctly, the index marks on the right-hand balancer (**Figure 53**) must be aligned with the index mark on the balancer shaft (B, **Figure 36**).*

a. Align the right-hand balancer index marks (**Figure 53**) with the balancer shaft index mark (B, **Figure 36**) and slide the right-balancer onto the shaft. Recheck the index marks to ensure proper alignment.

b. Install the copper washer (A, **Figure 34**) and center it.

c. Install the collar (**Figure 33**) and needle bearing (**Figure 32**). Make sure the collar fits in the center of the copper washer.

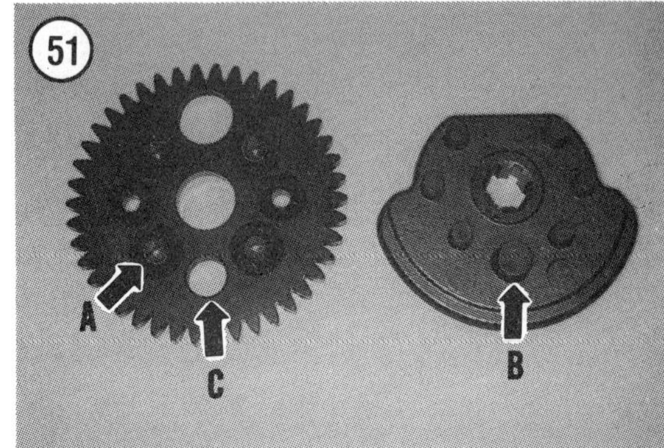

d. Slide the starter driven gear (D, **Figure 31**) onto the needle bearing on the balancer shaft. Rotate the gear clockwise as you simultaneously push it onto the shaft until you feel the gear bottom of the shaft.

e. Position the beveled washer with the beveled side going on first and install the washer (C, **Figure 31**).

f. Apply Loctite 242 to the threads of the starter driven gear bolt prior to installation.

g. Install the bolt (B, **Figure 31**).

h. Use the same tool setup used during removal to prevent the gear from turning while tightening the bolt.

i. Tighten the bolt to the torque specification listed in **Table 2**.

3. Install the washer (A, **Figure 31**) onto the starter idle gear.

4. To install the left-hand balancer, perform the following:

a. Align the index mark on the left-hand balancer (**Figure 54**) with the index mark on the balancer shaft (**Figure 55**) and slide the left-balancer onto the shaft. Recheck the index marks to ensure proper alignment (**Figure 30**).

b. Install the collar (**Figure 29**), and push it in until it bottoms.

c. Apply Loctite 242 to the threads of the left-hand balancer bolt prior to installation.

d. Install the bolt (A, **Figure 27**) along with the washer (B, **Figure 27**).

e. Use the same tool setup used during removal to prevent the gear from turning while tightening the bolt.

f. Tighten the bolt to the torque specification listed in **Table 2**.

5. Install the alternator rotor and alternator cover as described in Chapter Nine.

6. Install the clutch cover as described in Chapter Six.

54

55

CRANKCASE

Service to the lower end requires that the crankcase assembly be removed from the motorcycle frame and disassembled (split).

Disassembly

1. Remove the engine as described in this chapter.

2. Remove the following exterior assemblies from the crankcase assembly:

a. Cylinder head, cylinder block assemblies and pistons: Chapter Four.

b. Camshaft drive chains, guides and tensioners: (Chapter Four).

c. Starter motor: (Chapter Nine).

d. Oil filter: (Chapter Three).

e. Alternator: (Chapter Nine).

f. Balancer assembly: (this chapter).

g. Starter clutch assembly and starter idle gear: (this chapter).

h. External shift mechanism: (Chapter Seven).

i. Clutch: (Chapter Six).

j. Neutral switch: (Chapter Nine).

3. If still in place, remove the primary drive gear Woodruff key (**Figure 56**) from the crankshaft taper.

4. Remove the water pump impeller as described in Chapter Ten.

5. Shift the transmission into gear.

NOTE
Look for the countershaft collar and O-ring when you remove the transmission cover. They may come out with the cover.

6. On the left-side of the crankcase, remove the damper (A, **Figure 57**). Loosen the transmission cover bolts and remove the cover (B, **Figure 57**) and its gasket. Do not lose the two dowels (A, **Figure 58**) behind the cover.

7. Remove the collar (B, **Figure 58**) from the countershaft, then remove the O-ring (**Figure 59**).

8. Remove the bolts securing the oil filter plate (**Figure 60**) and remove the plate, the large and small O-rings and the gasket.

9. Turn the crankcase on its side with the right-hand side facing up.

10. On the right-hand side, loosen the four 6 mm crankcase bolts by 1/2 turns in a crisscross pattern, then remove the bolts. Make sure all four bolts are removed. Refer to **Figure 61** and **Figure 62**.

11. Turn the crankcase over so the left-hand side is facing up.

12. Loosen the crankcase bolts starting with the 6 mm bolts along the bottom and rear of the crankcase. Refer to **Figure 63** and **Figure 64**. Do not forget the two bolts (**Figure 65**) in the deep recesses at the rear. Loosen all bolts by 1/2 turn in a crisscross pattern, then remove the 6 mm bolts. Make sure to remove all eight 6 mm crankcase bolts.

13. Next, loosen the three 10 mm crankcase bolts (**Figure 66**) by 1/2 turn, then remove the 10 mm bolts. Make sure all three bolts are removed.

14. Turn the crankcase back over so the right-hand side is facing up.

CAUTION

If it is necessary to pry the crankcase apart, pry very carefully at the pry points located at the front and rear. Be careful that you do not mar or damage the gasket surfaces. If the gasket surface(s) is damaged, the crankcase will leak and require replacement. They cannot be repaired.

15. Carefully tap around the perimeter of the crankcase with a plastic mallet (do not use a metal hammer) to help separate the two case halves. Separate the case halves by pulling the right-hand crankcase up and off the left-hand case half.

16. After removing the right-hand crankcase half, the transmission and crankshaft assemblies should stay with the left-hand crankcase. Check the right-hand crankcase to make sure no transmission shims are stuck to the bearings. If found, reinstall them immediately in their original positions.

17. Remove the oil filter adapter bolt (**Figure 67**) and O-ring.

18. If loose, remove the two small dowel pins (A, **Figure 68**) from the left-hand crankcase half. If the

pins are secure in their receptacles, do not remove them.

19. Remove the transmission, shift forks and shift drum assemblies from the left-hand crankcase half as described in Chapter Seven.

20. Remove the oil pump and drive chain as described in this chapter.

21. Remove the crankshaft assembly as described in this chapter.

Inspection

The following procedure may require the use of some highly specialized and expensive measuring instruments. If such instruments are not readily available, have the measurements performed at a dealership or qualified machine shop.

1. Remove all old sealant residue from both crankcase half mating surfaces.

2. If necessary, use solvent to remove old gasket material from the crankcase mating surfaces. Soak the gasket material with solvent, then use a *dull* scraper to gently scrape off all gasket residue. Do not gouge the sealing surfaces as oil and air leaks will result.

3. On the inside of the left-hand crankcase half, remove the bolts (A, **Figure 69**) securing the internal oil pipe . Remove the oil pipe and the O-ring seals.

4. From the outside of the left-hand crankcase half:
   a. Remove the screws (A, **Figure 70**) securing the external oil pipe (B, **Figure 70**), and remove the oil pipe and O-ring seals.
   b. Remove the screws (C, **Figure 70**) securing the oil passage cover to the case half, and remove the cover (D, **Figure 70**)

5. From the inside of the right-hand crankcase half,
   a. Remove the bolts securing the internal oil pipe. Remove the oil pipe (A, **Figure 71**) and O-ring seals.
   b. Remove the oil pressure relief valve (B, **Figure 71**).
   c. Remove the circlip securing the water pump driveshaft (**Figure 72**) and remove the pump driveshaft by pulling it from the outside of the right-hand crankcase half.

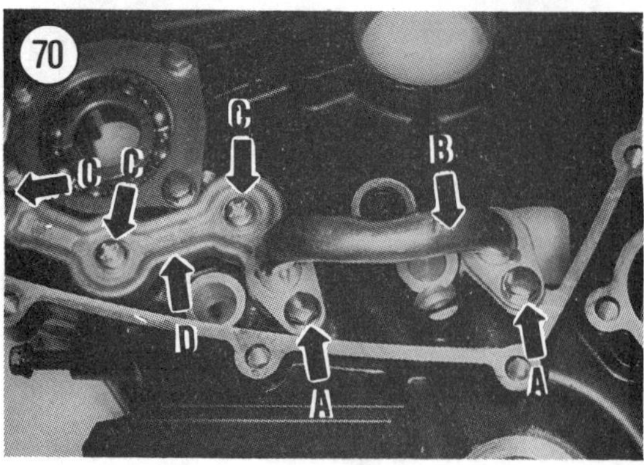

6. Thoroughly clean the inside and outside of both crankcase halves with cleaning solvent. Dry with compressed air. Make sure there is no solvent residue

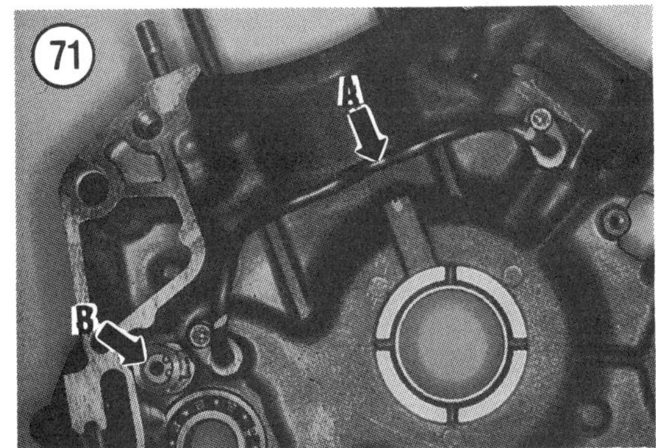

71

72

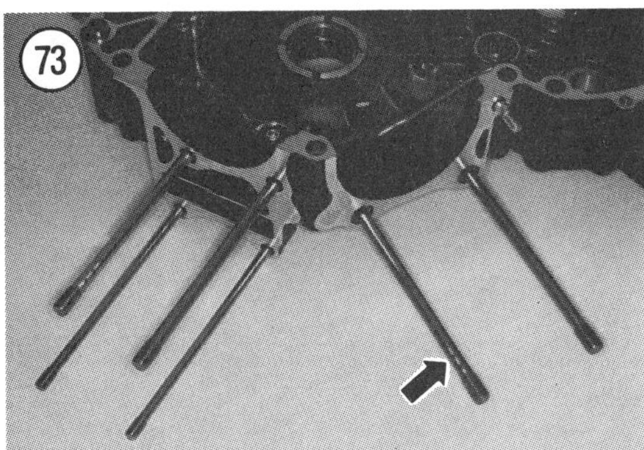

73

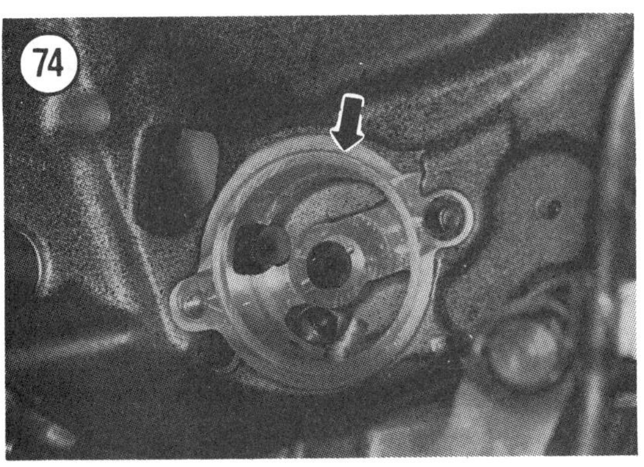

74

left in either half as it will contaminate new engine oil.

7. Make sure the crankcase studs (**Figure 73**) are tight in each half.

8. Check all studs and threaded holes for stripping, cross-threading or deposit buildup. Clean threaded holes using compressed air as dirt buildup in the bottom of a hole may prevent the bolt from being torqued properly. Replace damaged bolts and washers.

9. Inspect machined surfaces for burrs, cracks or other damage. Repair minor damage with a fine-cut file or oilstone.

10. Make sure that all oil passages throughout both crankcase halves are clean.

11. Make sure the oil passages in the oil pump housing (**Figure 74**) are clear with no sludge buildup.

12. Apply a light coat of engine oil to the bearing surfaces to prevent any rust formation.

13. Inspect the threads of the oil filter adapter bolt. Clean them off with a wire brush if necessary. If the threads are damaged, clean them up with an appropriate size metric thread die.

14. Inspect the crankcase bearings as described in this chapter.

15. Make sure the oil control holes are clear. Clean them out with a piece of wire and compressed air.

16. Be sure the oil pipes are clear. Clean them out with compressed air.

17. Inspect the oil pressure relief valve by performing the following:
   a. Use a small wooden dowel to push the valve's steel ball against the spring. The ball should move smoothly when you push it and when you release it.
   b. If you feel any rough spots, clean the valve with solvent, and blow it clear with compressed air.
   c. Replace the valve if cleaning does not solve the problem.

18. Inspect the oil seal (**Figure 75**) in the transmission cover. Replace the seal if it is worn or damaged.

19. Install all items removed during this inspection process. Pay attention to the following:
   a. Use new O-ring seals when installing the internal oil pipes (A, **Figure 69** and A, **Figure 71**) and the external oil pipe (B, **Figure 70**). Lubricate the O-rings with clean engine oil prior to installation. Apply Loctite 242 to the

5

threads of the oil pipe mounting bolts and torque the bolts to the specification in **Table 2**.

b. Use a new gasket when installing the oil passage cover (D, **Figure 70**). Apply Loctite 242 to the threads of the oil passage cover screws and torque the screws to the specification listed in **Table 2**.
c. Apply Loctite 242 to the threads of the oil pressure relief valve (B, **Figure 71**) and torque the valve to the specification listed in **Table 2**.
d. Install the water pump shaft (**Figure 72**) by pushing it through the bearing from the outside of the right-hand crankcase half.

Crankcase Bearings Inspection

1. After cleaning the crankcase halves in cleaning solvent and drying with compressed air, lubricate the bearings with engine oil.
2. With your fingers, rotate the transmission bearing inner races (B, **Figure 69**) and the balancer shaft bearing inner race (**Figure 76** and **Figure 77**) while checking for play or roughness. Replace any bearing that is noisy or does not spin smoothly.
3. Inspect the crankshaft main bearings (**Figure 78**) for wear (bluish tint) or damage. Make sure they are locked in place. Measure the bearing inside dimension as described in this chapter. Replace the bearings if damaged or worn.

Crankcase Bearing Replacement

Crankshaft main bearings

Remove and install the crankshaft main bearings using a hydraulic press and special tools. After the new bearings are installed, they must be honed to size.

To avoid damage to a costly set of crankcase halves, this procedure should be entrusted to a Kawasaki dealership or machine shop. Improper removal and installation of the bearings could result in costly crankcase damage.

All other bearings (except crankshaft main bearings)

1. On bearings equipped with retainers, perform the following:

NOTE

The bearing retainer screws are secured with threadlocking compound and may be difficult to remove. To avoid damage or rounding off of the screw head, use the recommended tool in this procedure.

a. Use an impact driver with the appropriate size bit to loosen the screws securing the bearing retainers.
b. Remove the screws and retainers.

75

76

77

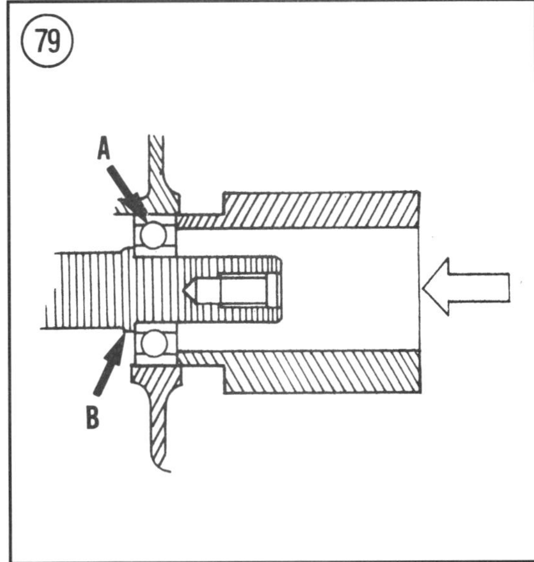

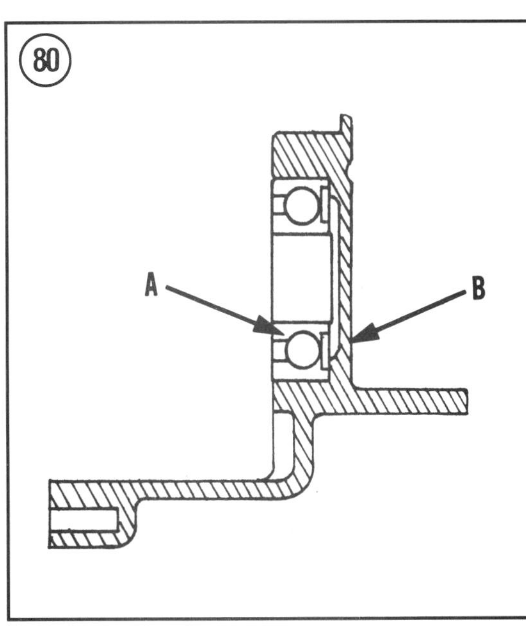

2. Heat the crankcase to approximately 205-257° (96-125° C) in an oven or on a hot plate. Do not attempt bearing removal by heating the crankcases with a torch. This type of localized heating may warp the cases.
3. Wear a pair of gloves for protection while moving the case from the oven and placing it on wooden blocks for support.
4. Drive the bearing out with a suitable size drift placed on the outside bearing race. A large socket also works well for bearing removal.
5. Install new crankcase bearings by reversing the removal steps, noting the following:
   a. Installation of the bearings is easier if the bearings are first placed in a freezer for approximately 30 minutes. Reheat the crankcase half and install the cold bearing by driving it squarely into position. If the bearing cocks in its bore, remove and reinstall the bearing. It may be necessary to refreeze the bearing and reheat the case half.
   b. Lubricate the bearing races with clean engine oil after installation.
   c. On bearings with retainers, install the retainer.

5

Apply Loctite 271 to the screw threads, and tighten the screw with an impact driver and appropriate bit.

Right-hand balancer bearing

1. Press the bearing (A, **Figure 79**) into the right crankcase until the bearing is even with the outer edge of the right-hand crankcase half.
2. Once the left-hand balancer is installed, press the bearing until it bottoms against the shoulder of the balancer shaft (B, **Figure 79**).

Countershaft bearing

Install the countershaft bearing (A, **Figure 80**) into the housing in the right-hand crankcase half with the sealed side against the crankcase (B, **Figure 80**). The marks should face the outboard side of the case half.

Left-hand crankcase needle bearings

In general, bearings and oil seals are installed with their manufacturer's marks facing out. These are an exception to this rule. Follow the procedure below when installing the left-hand crankcase needle bearings.

1. Install the needle bearing (A, **Figure 81**) into the housing in the left-hand crankcase so the manufacturer's marks face the *inside* of the crankcase.
2. Install the bearing so it is flush with the outer edge (B, **Figure 81**) of the crankcase half.

Water pump shaft bearing and seal

Refer to Chapter Ten when installing the water pump shaft bearing and seal.

Crankcase Assembly

1. Prior to installation, coat all rotating parts with assembly oil or engine oil.
2. Place the left-hand crankcase on wooden blocks.
3. Install the shift drum, shift forks and transmission assemblies as described in Chapter Seven.
4. Install the crankshaft as described in this chapter. Make sure the connecting rods (A, **Figure 82**) are positioned correctly within the connecting rod and piston openings (B, **Figure 82**) in the crankcase half.
5. If removed, install the two small dowel pins (A, **Figure 68**) into the left-hand crankcase half.
6. Apply oil to the bearing surfaces for the transmission shafts, crankshaft and balancer shaft.
7. Clean the crankcase mating surfaces of both halves with aerosol electrical contact cleaner. Wipe them dry with a lint-free cloth.
8. Make sure both crankcase half sealing surfaces are perfectly clean and dry.

NOTE

To seal the crankcase, use black RTV, ThreeBond 1207 or equivalent gasket sealer. If using an equivalent, avoid thick and hard-setting materials.

9. Apply a light coat of gasket sealer to the sealing surfaces of the left-hand half. Make the coating as thin as possible.
10. Install the oil filter adapter bolt (**Figure 67**).
11. Align the right-hand crankcase bearings with the left-hand assembly and join the halves together. Be sure the tab on the oil pump shaft (**Figure 83**) fits into the slot on the water pump shaft (**Figure 72**). Lightly tap the case halves together with a plastic mallet. Do not damage the cases by using a metal hammer.

CAUTION

The crankcase halves should fit together without force. If the crankcase halves do not fit together, do not attempt to pull them together with the crankcase bolts. Separate the crankcase halves and investigate the cause of the interference. If the transmission shafts were disassembled, make sure that a gear is not

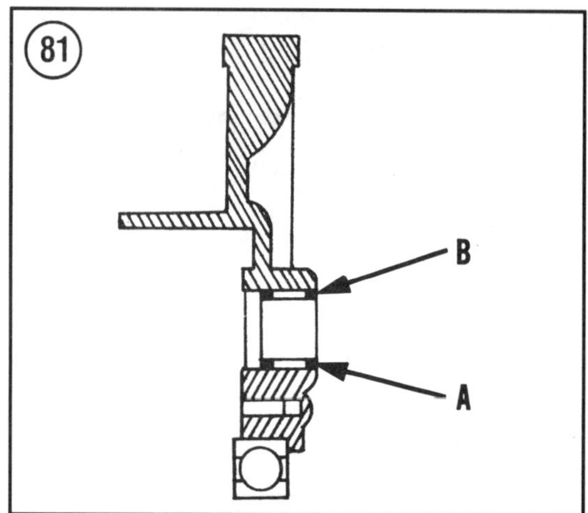

installed backward. Do not risk damage by trying to force the cases together.

12. Set the crankcase on its side so the right-hand side is facing up.

NOTE

Install all bolts in the crankcase half so that all bolt heads protrude up from the surface of the crankcase the same amount. If a bolt is installed in the wrong location, remove the bolt and insert it in the correct hole.

13. Install and tighten the four 6 mm crankcase bolts. Refer to **Figure 84** and **Figure 85**. Tighten the bolts securely in a crisscross pattern in two stages, to the specification in **Table 2**.
14. Turn the crankcase so its left-hand side is facing up.
15. Tighten the three 10 mm crankcase bolts securely in two stages. Tighten the bolts in the sequence shown in **Figure 86** to the specification in **Table 2**.
16. Tighten the 6 mm crankcase bolts; two (**Figure 87**) in the deep recesses at the rear of the crankcase and six (**Figure 88** and **Figure 89**) along the bottom of the crankcase. Tighten the bolts securely in a crisscross pattern in two stages. Torque the bolts to the specification in **Table 2**.
17. Install new O-ring seals (**Figure 90**) onto the oil filter adapter bolt and inlet hole.
18. After the crankcase halves are assembled and the bolts tightened, apply a light coat of the gasket sealant to the cylinder block sealing surface where the two crankcase halves join near the oil filter plate (**Figure 91**). Perform this step at both cylinder block sealing surface areas on the crankcase assembly. Use

the same sealant that was used to seal the crankcase halves in Step 9.

19. Install a new gasket (**Figure 92**) onto the backside of the oil filter plate. Install the plate (**Figure 93**) and bolts. Torque the bolts to the specification in **Table 2**.

20. On the left-hand side of the crankcase, install the O-ring onto the countershaft (**Figure 94**) and install the collar. (B, **Figure 95**).

21. Install a new gasket onto the crankcase half. Be sure the two locating dowels are in place (A **Figure 95**).

22. Apply grease to the lips of the O-ring in the transmission cover and install the cover onto the crankcase (B, **Figure 96**)

23. Install the transmission cover bolts and torque them to the specification in **Table 2**.

24. If removed, install the damper (A, **Figure 96**).

25. Install the following exterior assemblies onto the crankcase assembly:

a. Neutral switch: (Chapter Nine).
b. Starter motor: (Chapter Nine).
c. Clutch: (Chapter Six).
d. External shift mechanism: (Chapter Seven).
e. Oil filter: (Chapter Three).
f. Starter clutch assembly: (this chapter).
g. Balancer assembly: (this chapter).
h. Install the water pump impeller: (Chapter Ten).
i. Alternator: (Chapter Nine).
j. Camshaft drive chains, guides and tensioners: (Chapter Four).
k. Pistons, cylinder block and cylinder head assemblies: (Chapter Four).

26. Install the engine as described in this chapter.

90

91

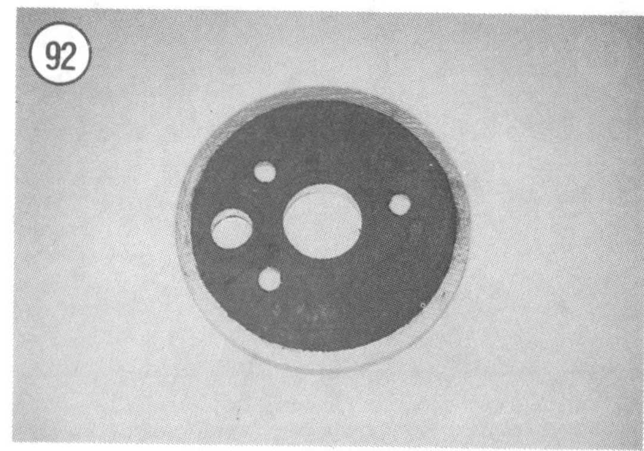
92

89

93

CRANKSHAFT AND CONNECTING RODS

Removal/Installation

1. Split the crankcase as described in this chapter.
2. Remove the crankshaft assembly (B, **Figure 97**) from the left-hand crankcase half.
3. Remove the connecting rod cap bolt nuts and separate the rods from the crankshaft.

NOTE
*The rear cylinder connecting rod (A, **Figure 98**) is located on the left-hand portion of the crankpin adjacent to the tapered end (B, **Figure 98**) of the crankshaft.*

4. Mark each rod and cap as a set. Also mark them with a F (front) and R (rear) to indicate which cylinder they were removed from.
5. If the inserts are going to be removed, mark each rod cap and bearing insert so it can be reinstalled in its original position.

CAUTION
If the old bearings are reused, they must be reinstalled in their exact positions.

CAUTION
If the connecting rods, bearing inserts or crankshaft are replaced, check the bearing clearance as described in this chapter.

6. If removed, install the bearing inserts (**Figure 99**) into each connecting rod and cap. Make sure they are locked in place correctly (**Figure 100**).
7. Lubricate the bearings and crankpins with molybdenum disulfide grease or engine oil.

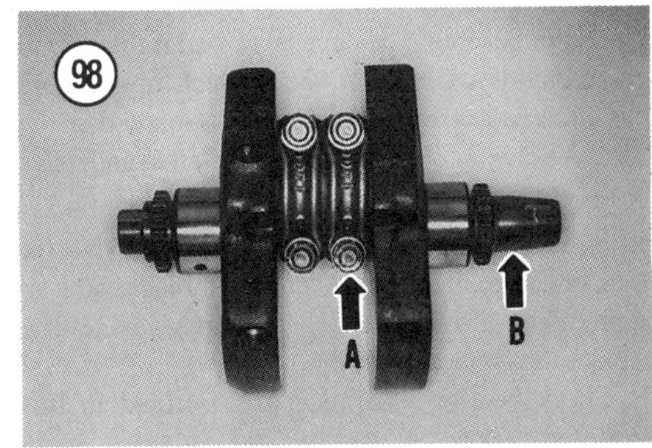

8. Position the connecting rod cap with the inner diameter code number (**Figure 101**) facing toward the *rear* of the engine.

9. The rear cylinder connecting rod (A, **Figure 98**) is located on the left-hand portion of the crankpin adjacent to the tapered end (B, **Figure 98**) of the crankshaft.

10. Install the caps and tighten the cap nuts (**Figure 102**) evenly, in two stages, to the torque specification listed in **Table 2**.

NOTE
When installing the crankshaft, make sure the connecting rods (A, ***Figure 82****) are positioned correctly within the connecting rod and piston openings (B,* ***Figure 82****) in the crankcase. Continue to check this alignment until the crankshaft is completely installed.*

11. Install the crankshaft with the tapered end in the left-hand crankcase half (**Figure 97**).

12. Assemble the crankcase as described in this chapter.

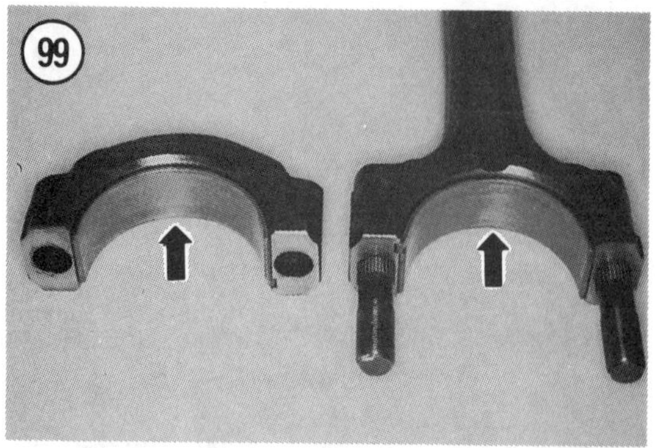

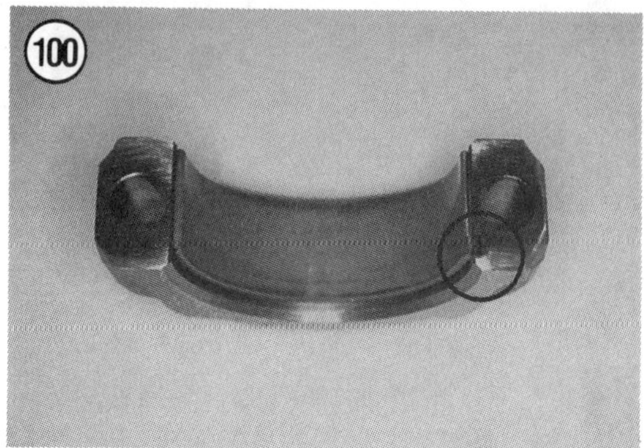

Connecting Rod Inspection

1. Check each rod and cap for obvious damage such as cracks and burrs.

2. Check the connecting rod small end for wear or scoring.

3. Insert the piston pin into the connecting rod small end (**Figure 103**). Rotate the pin to check for looseness or roughness.

4. Take the rods to a machine shop and have them checked for twisting and bending.

5. Examine the bearing inserts (**Figure 99**) for wear, scoring or burning. They can be reused if they are in good condition. Check the back of each insert before it is discarded to see if an undersize is marked on the back. A previous owner may have installed undersize bearings.

6. Inspect the connecting rod studs (**Figure 104**) for wear or damaged threads. Clean the threads using an appropriate size metric die. If damage is severe, replace the connecting rod.

7. Check bearing clearance as described in this chapter.

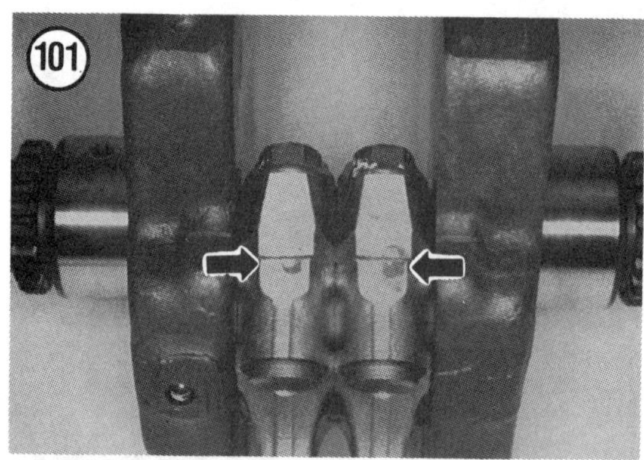

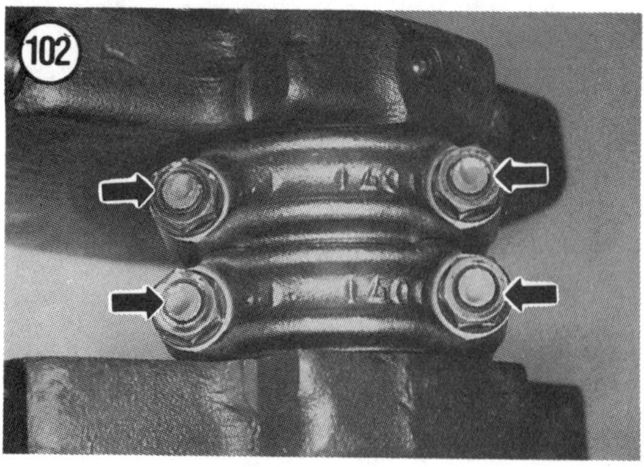

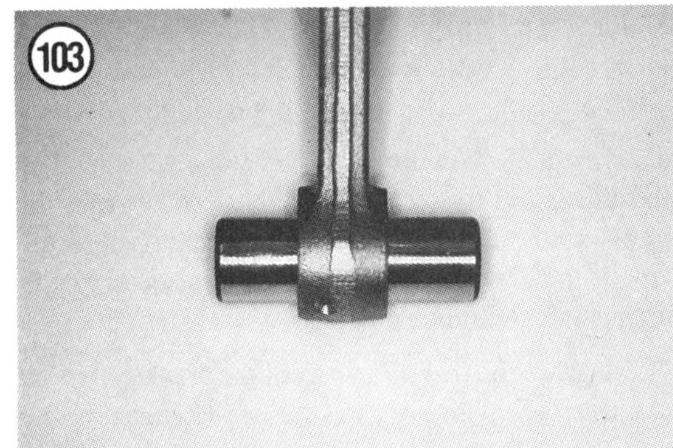

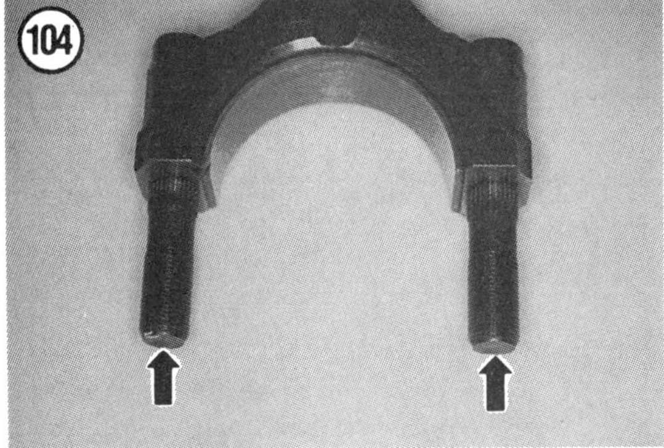

Connecting Rod Bearing Oil Clearance Measurement

CAUTION

If the old bearings will be reused, be sure that they are installed in their exact original locations.

1. Wipe the bearing inserts and crankpin clean. Install the bearing inserts into the rod and rod cap (**Figure 99**).
2. Place a piece of Plastigage on one crankpin parallel to the crankshaft.
3. Install the rod, rod cap and cap nuts. Tighten the nuts to the torque specification listed in **Table 2**.

CAUTION

Do not rotate crankshaft while the Plastigage is in place.

4. Remove the cap nuts and rod cap.
5. Use the Plastigage to check the crankpin taper by performing the following:
   a. Measure width of flattened Plastigage at each end.
   b. If the difference between these measurements is 0.025 mm (0.001 in.) or more, the crankpin is tapered. It may need to be ground or replaced. Measure the crankpin with a micrometer to get an exact journal diameter (**Figure 105**).
6. If the crankpin taper is within tolerance, use the same piece of Plastigage to check the bearing clearance. Compare the width of the flattened Plastigage to the bearing insert clearance listed in **Table 1**.
7. If the clearance is within specification, the existing bearing inserts are fine. No bearing insert replacement is necessary.
8. If the clearance is greater than specified, perform the following to select new bearing inserts.
   a. The connecting rods and caps either have a big end bore diameter mark (**Figure 101**) or are not marked at all.
   b. The crankshaft may have a crankpin diameter mark (**Figure 106**) at the counterbalancer or may be unmarked.
   c. Refer to **Table 3**, and select new bearings by cross-referencing the big end bore diameter marking with the crankpin diameter marking. Bearing inserts are identified by color. Install the indicated bearing.

5

9. After new bearings are installed, recheck the clearance with Plastigage. If the clearance is out of specification, either the connecting rod or the crankshaft is excessively worn.

Connecting Rod Side Clearance Measurement

1. With both connecting rods attached to the crankshaft, insert a flat feeler gauge between the counterweight and the connecting rod big end (**Figure 107**).
2. Compare the reading to the crankshaft side clearance specified in **Table 1**.
3. If the clearance is out of specification, replace the connecting rods and recheck the side clearance. If the clearance is still out of specification, replace the crankshaft assembly.

Crankshaft Inspection

1. Clean the crankshaft thoroughly with solvent. Clean the oil holes (**Figure 108**) with rifle cleaning brushes, then flush thoroughly and dry with compressed air. Lightly oil all journal surfaces immediately after cleaning to prevent rust.
2. Inspect the crankpin journals (A, **Figure 109**) and the main bearing journals (B, **Figure 109**) for scratches, ridges, scoring and nicks.
3. If the surfaces of all the bearing journals appear to be in acceptable condition, measure the diameter of the main bearing journals with a micrometer (**Figure 110**) and check for out-of-roundness and taper.
4. Inspect the camshaft chain sprocket (**Figure 111**) on the right-hand end and on the left-hand end (A, **Figure 112**) of the crankshaft. If either is worn or damaged, the crankshaft must be replaced.
5. Inspect the taper (B, **Figure 112**) where the alternator rotor is installed on the left-hand end. If it is worn or damaged, the crankshaft must be replaced.
6. Inspect the Woodruff key and slot on each end of the crankshaft for wear or damage. The key must fit tightly in the slot. If necessary, replace the Woodruff key. If the new key still does not fit in securely, the crankshaft should be replaced.
7. Measure the overall length of the crankshaft web (**Figure 113**) with a vernier caliper. Compare to the

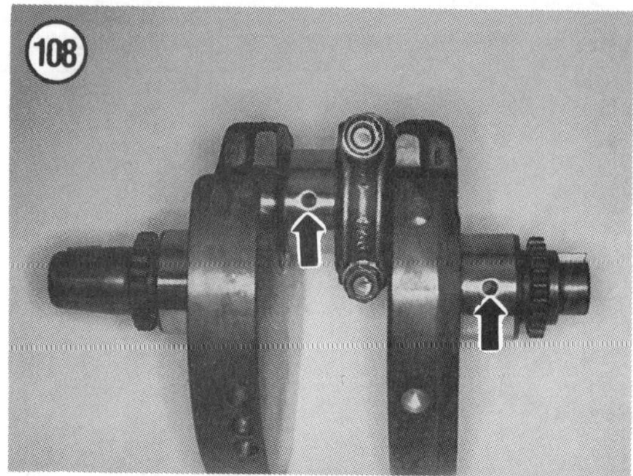

dimension listed in **Table 1**. If the web length is less than the service limit, replace the crankshaft.

Crankshaft Bearing and Oil Clearance Measurement

1. Wipe the bearing inserts in the crankcase and the main bearing journals clean.
2. Use a micrometer and measure the main journal diameter (**Figure 110**) at two places. If the journal diameter is less than the service limit listed in **Table 1**, replace the crankshaft.
3. Use a bore gauge and measure the main journal bore diameter (**Figure 114**) at two places (**Figure 115**). If the bore diameter exceeds the service limit in **Table 1**, replace both crankcase halves. The main bearings cannot be replaced on this model.

111

112

113

BREAK-IN

Following cylinder service (boring, honing, new rings or pistons) and major lower end work, the engine should be broken-in just as if it were new. The performance and service life of the engine depends greatly on a careful and sensible break-in. For the first 500 miles, use no more than one-third throttle and vary speed as much as possible within the one-third throttle limit. Avoid prolonged, steady running at one speed, no matter how moderate. Also avoid hard acceleration.

Following the 500-mile service, use increasingly more throttle but avoid full throttle until the motor-

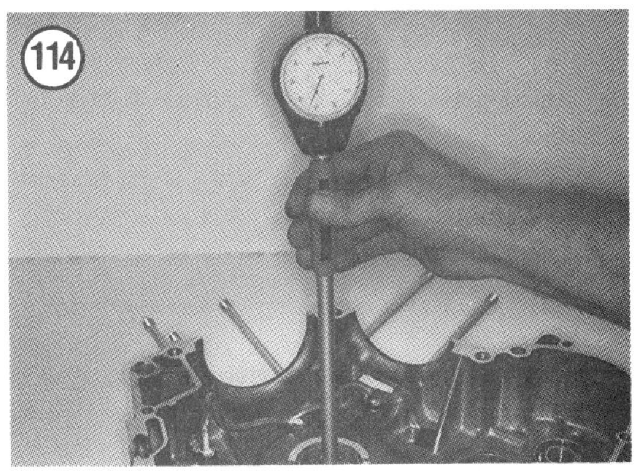
114

115

5

cycle has covered at least 1,000 miles. Then limit it to short bursts until 1500 miles have been logged.

During the break-in period, oil consumption may be higher than normal. It is therefore important to frequently check and correct the oil level. At no time, during break-in or later, should the oil level be allowed to drop below the bottom line on the inspection window. If the oil level is low, the oil will overheat causing insufficient lubrication and increased wear.

500-Mile Service

It is essential that the oil and filter be changed after the first 500 miles. In addition, it is a good idea to change the oil and filter at the completion of break-in (about 1,500 miles). This ensures that all of the particles produced during break-in are removed from the lubrication system. The small added expense is a smart investment that will pay off in increased engine life.

Table 1 ENGINE LOWER END SPECIFICATIONS

	Specification	Wear limit
Connecting rods		
Big end side clearance	0.16-0.46 mm (0.006-0.018 in.)	0.70 mm (0.027 in.)
Crankpin bearing clearance	0.026-0.054 mm (0.0010-0.0021 in.)	0.09 mm (0.0035 in.)
Big end bore diameter		
Marking: None	46.000-46.010mm (1.8110-1.8114 in.)	—
Marking: o	46.011-46.020 mm (1.8114-1.8118 in.)	—
Crankshaft		
Crankpin diameter		
Marking: none	42.984-42.992 mm (1.6923-1.6926 in.)	—
Marking: 1	42.993-43.000 mm (1.6926-1.6929 in.)	—
Main bearing journal diameter	42.984-43.000 mm (1.6923-1.6929 in.)	42.96 mm (1.6913 in.)
Runout	0.02 mm (0.00078 in.)	0.05 mm (0.0019 in.)
End play	0.05-0.055 mm (0.0019-0.0216 in.)	0.75 mm (0.0295 in.)
Web length	96.85-96.95 mm (3.8129-3.8169 in.)	96.6 mm (3.8031 in.)
Crankcase		
Main bearing bore diameter	43.025 -43.041 mm (1.6938- 1.6945 in.)	43.09 mm (1.6964 in.)
Oil pump		
Drive chain 20-link length	127.0-127.4 mm (5.0-5.02) in.)	128.9 mm (5.075 in.)

Table 2 LOWER END TIGHTENING TORQUES

Item	N•m	in.-lb.	ft.-lb.
Engine mounts			
Engine mounting nuts	44	—	32
Engine bracket mounting bolts	23	—	17
Downtube mounting bolts	44	—	32
Connecting rod cap nuts	46	—	34
Crankcase bolts			
6 mm	11	97	—
10 mm	39	—	29
Oil pump mounting bolts	11	97	—
Oil pump drive chain guide bolt	12	106	—
Oil filter	18	—	13
Oil filter plate mounting bolts	7.8	69	—
Oil screen plug	20	—	15
Oil pressure relief valve	15	—	11
Oil pressure switch	15	—	11
Oil pressure switch adapter	20	—	15
Oil pipe mounting bolts			
Inside crankcase	11	97	—
Outside crankcase	5.4	48	—
Oil passage cover screws	5.4	48	—
Primary gear bolt	155	—	114
Left-hand balancer bolt	69	—	51
Starter driven gear bolt	69	—	51
Starter one-way clutch Allen bolts	34	—	25
Transmission cover bolts	11	97	—

5

Table 3 CONNECTING ROD BEARING SELECTION

Connecting rod big end bore mark	Crankpin mark	Bearing insert size color	Bearing insert thickness	Part number
None	1	Brown	1.483-1.487 mm (0.0583-0.0585 in.)	13034-1059
None	None	Black	1.487-1.491 mm (0.0585-0.0587 in.)	13034-1058
o	1	Black	1.487-1.491 mm (0.0585-0.0587 in.)	13034-1058
o	None	Blue	1.491-1.495 mm (0.0587-0.0588 in.)	13034-1057

CHAPTER SIX

CLUTCH

This chapter provides complete service procedures for the clutch and clutch release mechanism.

The clutch is a wet multiplate type, which operates immersed in the engine oil. It is mounted on the right-hand end of the transmission main shaft. The inner clutch hub is splined to the main shaft and the outer housing can rotate freely on the main shaft. The outer housing is geared to the crankshaft. The clutch release mechanism is cable operated and requires routine adjustment as described in Chapter Three.

Specifications for the clutch are listed in **Table 1**. **Table 1** and **Table 2** are located at the end of this chapter.

CLUTCH CABLE

Removal

1. Remove the front exhaust pipe as described in Chapter Eight.
2. At the clutch release lever, move the dust cover (A, **Figure 1**) as necessary and completely loosen both clutch cable locknuts (B, **Figure 1**).
3. Move the clutch outer cable (C, **Figure 1**) forward to provide as much slack as possible.
4. At the handlebars, loosen the cable adjuster locknut (A, **Figure 2**) and turn the adjuster (B, **Figure 2**) all the way in to provide maximum slack in the cable.
5. Align the slots in the cable adjuster and the adjuster locknut. Disconnect the inner cable from the clutch lever and remove the clutch cable.
6. Release the inner cable from the clutch release lever (D, **Figure 1**), and remove the cable from the bracket (E, **Figure 1**) on the clutch cover.
7. Rotate the clutch release lever toward the front of the motorcycle and tape it in place so it will not fall from the clutch cover.

NOTE

If you do not intend to immediately install a new clutch cable, tie a length of string to the lower end of the old cable before removing it in the next step. Leave the string in place until you are ready to install the new cable. It will help you correctly route the new cable.

8. Slowly pull the clutch cable from the motorcycle. Note how the cable is routed along the frame so you can correctly route a new cable.

Installation

1. Correctly route the new cable along the frame.

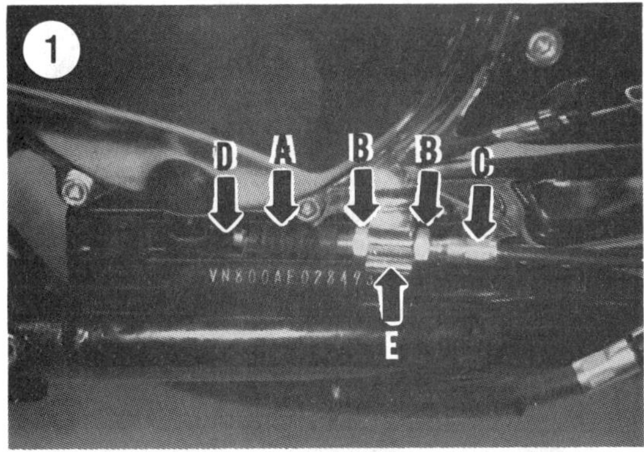

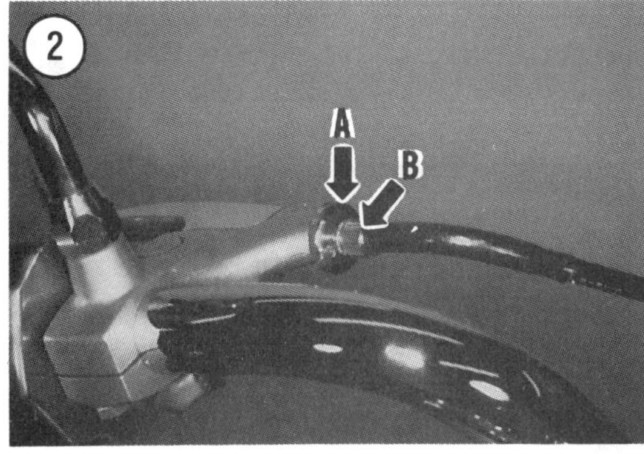

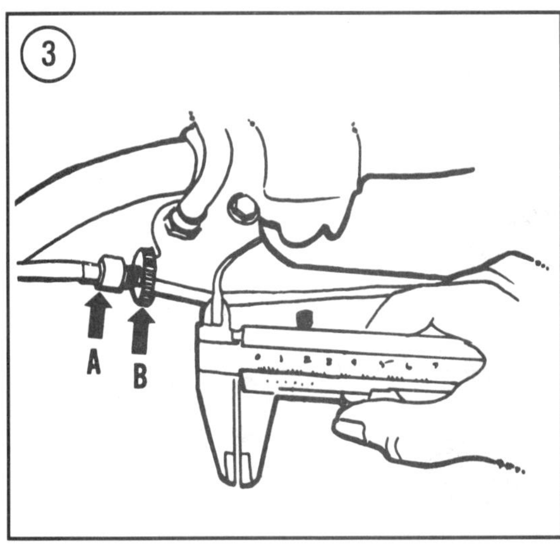

2. Fit the cable through the bracket on the clutch cover (E, **Figure 1**) and connect the inner cable to the clutch release lever (D, **Figure 1**).
3. At the handlebars, align the slots in the cable adjuster, the adjuster locknut and the cable lever. Fit the inner cable through the slot and connect it to the clutch lever.
4. Turn the clutch cable adjuster (A, **Figure 3**) until there's a 5-6 mm (3/16 to 1/4 in.) gap between the adjuster and the locknut (B, **Figure 3**).
5. Completely loosen the locknuts (B, **Figure 1**) at the clutch release lever.
6. Pull the clutch cable outer cable (C, **Figure 1**) until it is tight, then tighten both locknuts against the bracket (E, **Figure 1**).
7. Fit the dust cover (A, **Figure 1**) in place.
8. Loosen the locknut (A, **Figure 2**) at the clutch lever and turn the adjuster (B, **Figure 2**) until clutch lever free play is within the specification listed in **Table 1**.
9. Tighten the clutch lever locknut.
10. Install the front exhaust pipe as described in Chapter Eight.
11. Start the engine, and check the operation of the clutch. If further adjustment is required, refer to Chapter Three.

CLUTCH COVER

Removal

1. Place the bike on level ground, and support it with wooden blocks or a scissors jack.
2. Drain the engine oil and cooling system as described in Chapter Three.
3. Remove the front exhaust pipe as described in Chapter Eight.
4. Remove the radiator cover (A **Figure 4**) and remove the lower right-hand bolt securing the radiator to the frame downtube.
5. Disconnect the coolant hose from the fitting at the front of the crankcase cover (B, **Figure 4**).
6. Disconnect the clutch cable from the release arm as described in *Clutch Cable Removal* (in this chapter).

CAUTION

To avoid damaging the clutch release lever seal, rotate the clutch release lever toward the front of the motorcycle and tape it in place so it will not fall from the clutch cover.

7. Remove the rear brake pedal assembly as described in Chapter Thirteen.
8. Remove the frame downtube by performing the following.
   a. Remove the lower rear bolts (**Figure 5**) securing the frame downtube to the frame.
   b. Remove the upper front bolts (**Figure 6**) securing the frame downtube to the frame.
   c. Remove the two bolts securing the front engine bracket to the frame downtube (A, **Figure 7**), and then remove the frame downtube (B, **Figure 7**).
9. Remove the clutch cover bolts.

NOTE
If necessary, use the pry points to work the cover loose from the crankcase.

10. Rotate the clutch release arm rearward and remove the clutch cover and gasket. Work the coolant pipe (B, **Figure 8**) free from the fitting on the crankcase as you remove the cover. Do not lose the locating dowels in the crankcase cover.
11. Remove the coolant pipe from the fitting on the clutch cover and inspect the O-ring seals (**Figure 9**). Replace the O-rings if they are deteriorated or hard. Do not apply grease to the O-rings.
12. Install by reversing the removal steps while noting the following:
   a. Install the coolant pipe into the clutch cover. Apply soapy water to the coolant pipe O-rings, and push the pipe down into the clutch fitting until it bottoms.
   b. Be sure the washer (A, **Figure 10**) is in place on the starter idle gear.
   c. If removed, install the front locating dowel (B, **Figure 10**) and rear locating dowel (**Figure 11**) into the crankcase.
   d. Install a new clutch cover gasket.
   e. Install the clutch cover and insert the coolant pipe into the fitting in the crankcase. Apply soapy water to the pipe's O-ring and push the pipe into the fitting until it bottoms.
   f. Install the clutch cover bolts. Apply Loctite 242 to the threads of clutch cover mounting bolt (A, **Figure 8**). Torque all the clutch cover bolts to the specification listed in **Table 2**.
   g. Fill the engine with oil as described in Chapter Three.

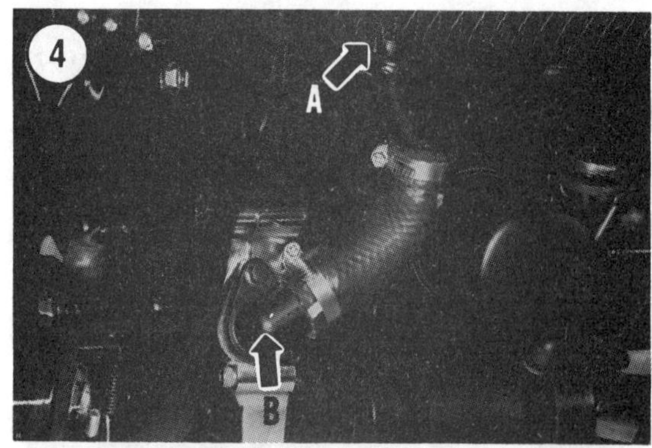

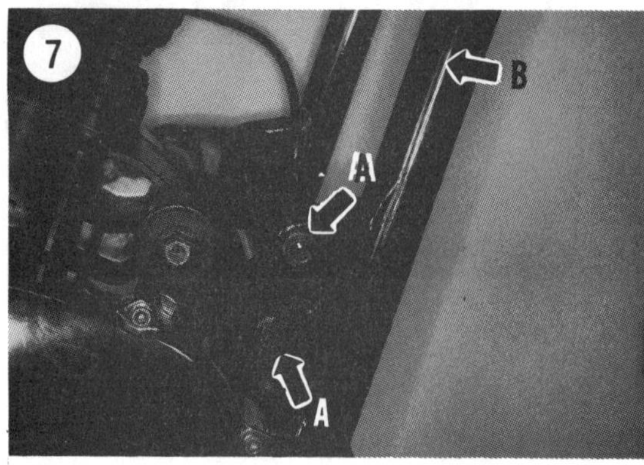

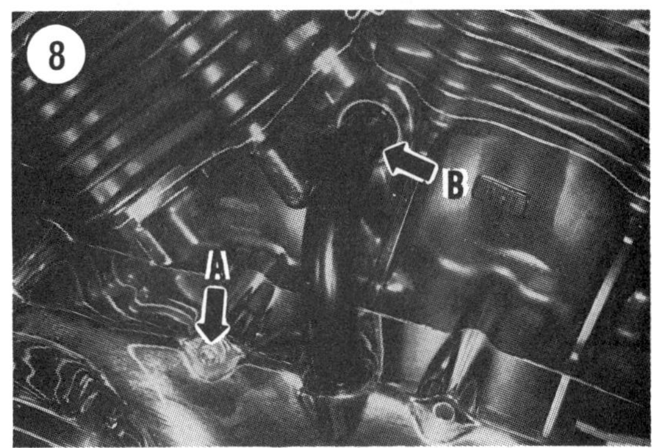

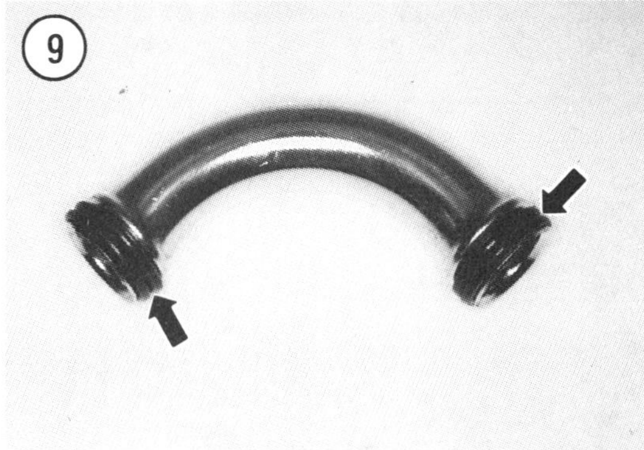

h. Refill the cooling system as described in Chapter Three.
i. Start the engine and check for leaks.

CLUTCH

Removal/Disassembly

The clutch assembly can be removed with the engine in the frame. This procedure is shown with the engine removed and partially disassembled for clarity.

Refer to **Figure 12** for this procedure.

1. Remove the clutch cover as described in this chapter.
2. Shift the transmission into gear.
3. Following a crisscross pattern, loosen the clutch bolts (**Figure 13**).
4. Remove the bolts.
5. Remove the clutch springs (**Figure 14**) and pressure plate (A, **Figure 15**). Do not lose the clutch push rod (B. **Figure 15**). It may come out with the pressure plate.
6. If still installed, remove the clutch push rod (A, **Figure 16**) and then remove the friction discs (B, **Figure 16**) and clutch plates.

CAUTION
Do not clamp the special tool too tight as it may damage the grooves in the clutch hub.

7A. Hold the clutch hub with a special tool such as the Grabbit and loosen clutch locknut (**Figure 17**).

7B. If you do not have a clutch holder, perform the following,

a. Stuff a shop cloth, penny or brass washer between the clutch outer housing gear and the primary drive gear. This will prevent the clutch from rotating while you loose the nut.

CAUTION:
Any soft metal washer (copper, brass or aluminum) will work to hold the clutch from turning. However, ***do not*** *use a steel washer. Steel will damage the gear teeth.*

8. Remove the clutch locknut (**Figure 18**) and washer (**Figure 19**).
9. Remove the special tool from the clutch hub.
10. Remove the clutch hub (**Figure 20**).

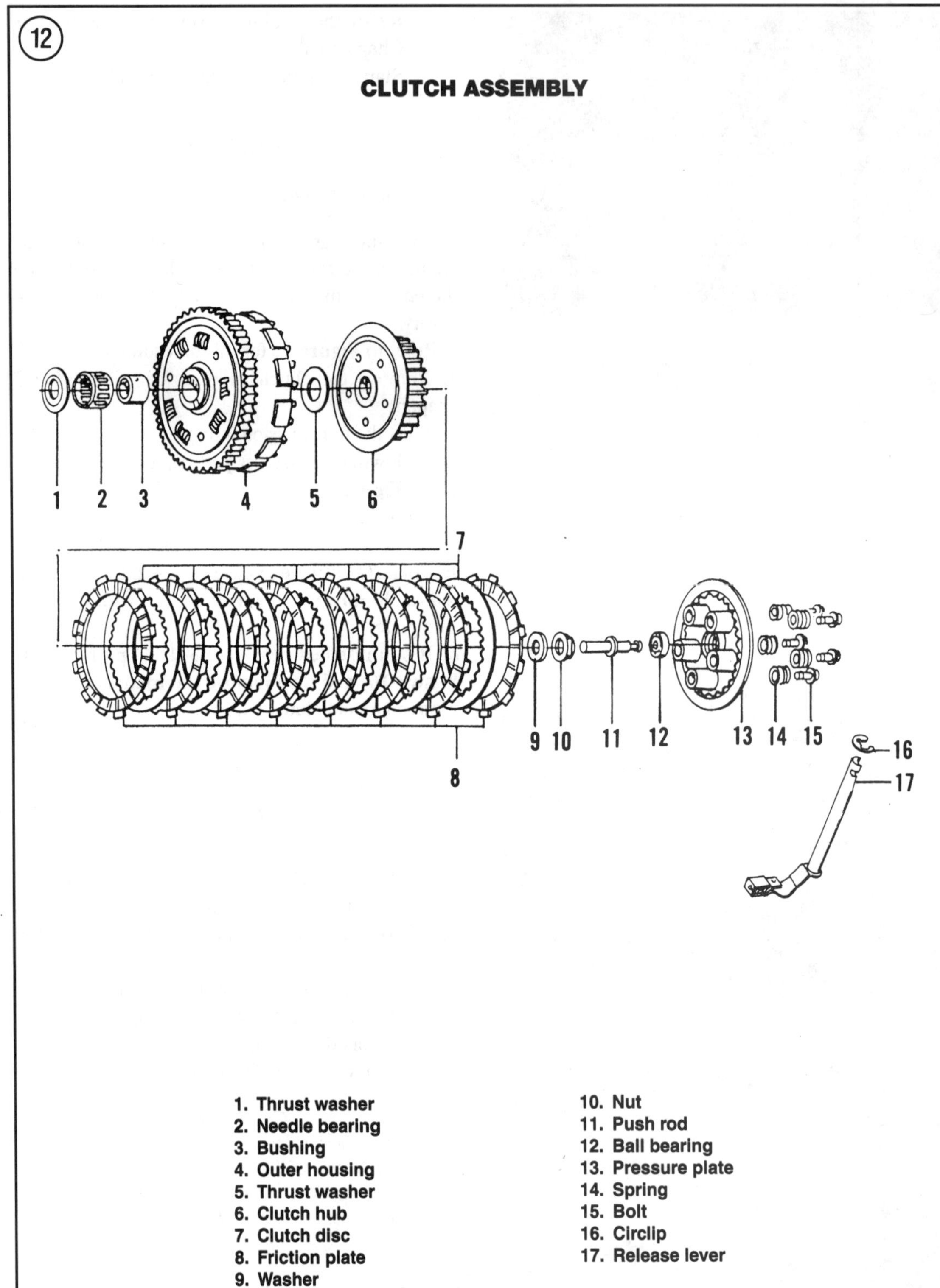

1. Thrust washer
2. Needle bearing
3. Bushing
4. Outer housing
5. Thrust washer
6. Clutch hub
7. Clutch disc
8. Friction plate
9. Washer
10. Nut
11. Push rod
12. Ball bearing
13. Pressure plate
14. Spring
15. Bolt
16. Circlip
17. Release lever

11. Remove the thrust washer (**Figure 21**).

CAUTION

The needle bearing and bushing may stay with the clutch outer housing when it is removed. Do not drop the bearing or bushing after the outer housing is removed.

12. Remove the clutch outer housing (**Figure 22**) from the transmission shaft.

6

13. If still in place, remove the needle bearing (**Figure 23**) from the transmission shaft.

14. Remove the bushing (A, **Figure 24**) and thrust spacer (B, **Figure 24**) from the transmission shaft.

Inspection

Refer to **Table 1** for clutch specifications.

1. Clean all clutch parts in a petroleum-based solvent such as kerosene and thoroughly dry with compressed air.

2. Measure the free length of each clutch spring as shown in **Figure 25**. Compare to the specification listed in **Table 1**.

3. Measure the thickness of each friction disc at several places around the disc as shown in **Figure 26**. Compare to the specifications listed in **Table 1**.

4. Check the friction discs (**Figure 27**) and clutch plates (**Figure 28**) for surface damage from heat or lack of oil. Replace any disc or plate that is damaged in any way.

5. Check the friction discs (**Figure 29**) and the clutch plates (**Figure 30**) for warp. Use a flat feeler

20

21

22

23

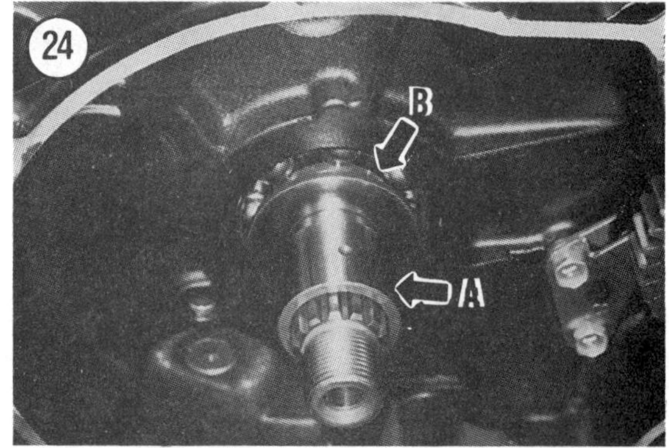

24

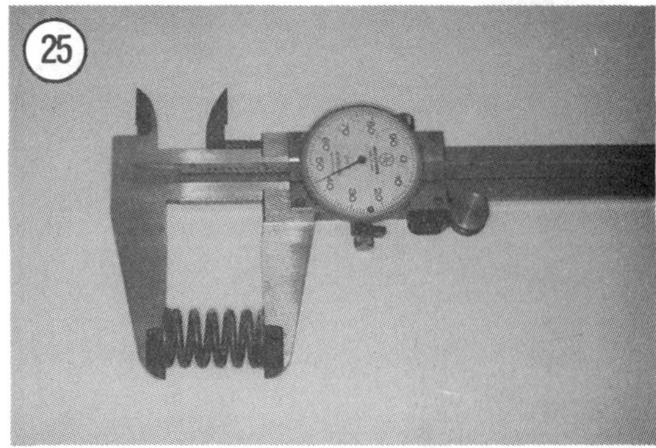
25

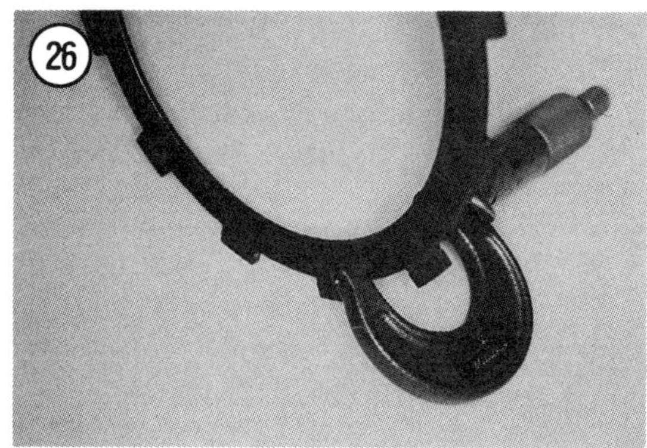

gauge on a surface plate such as a piece of plate glass. Compare to the specifications listed in **Table 1**.

NOTE
If any of the friction discs, clutch plates or clutch springs require replacement, replace all of them as a set to retain maximum clutch performance.

CAUTION
When installing new friction discs and clutch plates, apply engine oil to the surfaces of each plate to avoid clutch plate seizure.

6. Inspect the slots (**Figure 31**) and reinforcement ribs (**Figure 32**) in the clutch outer housing for cracks, nicks or galling. Pay particular attention to the area where they contact the friction disc tabs. If any damage is evident, the housing must be replaced.

7. Inspect the driven gear teeth (**Figure 33**) on the clutch outer housing for damage. Remove any small nicks with a file. If damage is severe, the clutch outer housing must be replaced.

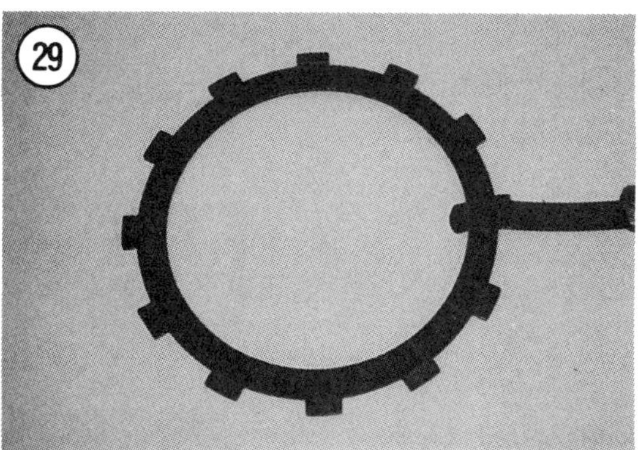

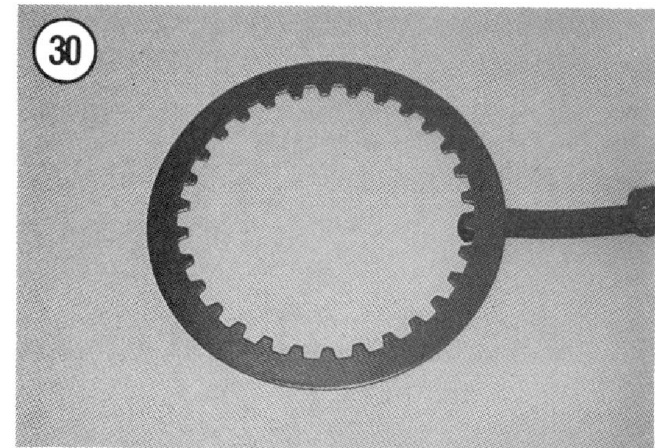

8. Inspect the damper springs (**Figure 34**). If they are sagged or broken, the housing must be replaced.

9. Inspect the outer grooves (**Figure 35**) and studs (**Figure 36**) in the clutch hub. If either is worn or galled, the clutch hub should be replaced.

10. Inspect the inner splines (**Figure 37**) in the clutch hub for damage. Remove any small nicks with a file. If damage is severe, the clutch hub must be replaced.

11. Inspect the spring receptacles (**Figure 38**) and inner grooves (A, **Figure 39**) in the clutch pressure plate for wear or damage. Replace the clutch pressure plate if necessary.

12. Check the inner surface (**Figure 40**) of the clutch outer housing, where it rides on the needle bearing. Replace the clutch outer housing if necessary.

13. Check the needle bearing (**Figure 41**). Make sure it rotates smoothly with no wear or damage. Replace if necessary.

14. Check the inner and outer surfaces of the bushing (**Figure 42**) for wear or damage. Replace if necessary.

34

35

32

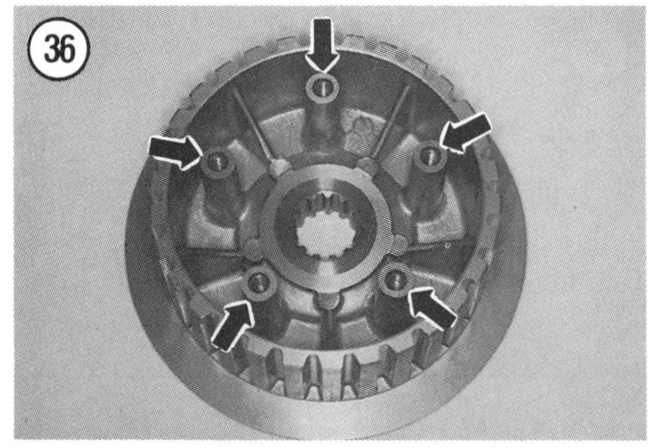
36

33

37

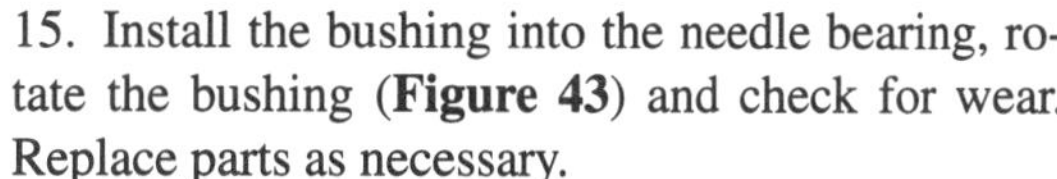

15. Install the bushing into the needle bearing, rotate the bushing (**Figure 43**) and check for wear. Replace parts as necessary.
16. Check the clutch push rod for wear or damage. Replace if necessary.
17. Check the clutch push rod bearing (B, **Figure 39**). Make sure it rotates smoothly with no wear or damage. Replace if necessary.

Assembly/Installation

Refer to **Figure 12** for this procedure.

1. Install the thrust spacer (B, **Figure 24**) onto the transmission shaft. Be sure the chamfered side of the thrust spacer (**Figure 44**) faces toward the engine.
2. Install the bushing (A, **Figure 24**) onto the transmission shaft.
3. Apply a good coat of clean engine oil to the needle bearing and install the needle bearing (**Figure 23**) onto the transmission shaft.
4. Install the clutch outer housing (**Figure 22**) onto the needle bearing on the transmission shaft.
5. Install the thrust washer (**Figure 21**) onto the transmission shaft.

6

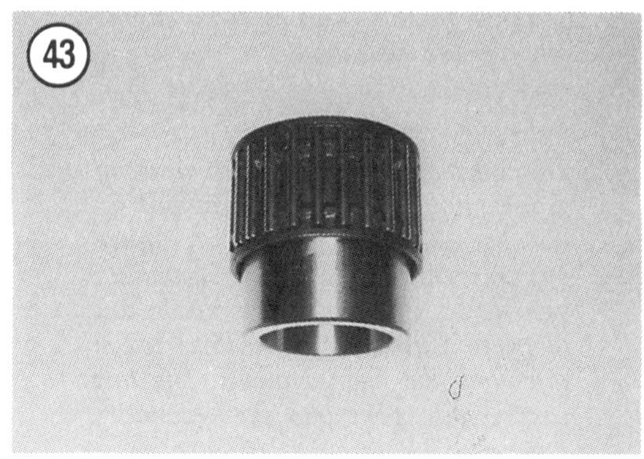

6. Install the clutch hub (**Figure 20**).

7. Install the washer (**Figure 19**) and a new clutch locknut (**Figure 18**). Apply oil to the threads of the locknut and to the surface of the nut that faces the washer.

CAUTION
Do not clamp the special tool on too tight as it may damage the grooves in the clutch hub.

8A. Attach a special tool such as the Grabbit to the clutch hub to keep it from turning and torque the clutch locknut to the specification listed in **Table 2**. See **Figure 45**.

CAUTION:
Any soft metal washer (copper, brass or aluminum) will work in the next step. However, ***do not*** *use a steel washer. Steel will damage the gear teeth.*

8B. If you do not have a clutch holding tool, stuff a shop cloth, penny or brass washer between the clutch outer housing gear and the primary drive gear. This will prevent the clutch from rotating while you loose the nut. Torque the clutch locknut to the specification listed in **Table 2**.

NOTE
On some models, the grooves cut into the friction discs radiate at an angle out from the center. On these models, position the friction discs so the groove runs toward the center in the direction of the clutch hub rotation (counterclockwise as viewed from the right-hand side).

NOTE
Soak the friction discs in clean engine oil prior to installation.

NOTE
The clutch outer housing has two sets of grooves that accept the tangs of the friction discs. The main grooves (A, ***Figure 46****) are reinforced while the secondary grooves (B,* ***Figure 46****) are not. Install all friction discs, except the last friction disc, into the main grooves. The last friction disc goes into the secondary grooves.*

9. First install a friction disc (A, **Figure 47**) onto the clutch hub with the friction disc tangs going into the *main grooves* (B, **Figure 47**).

10. Install a clutch plate (**Figure 48**) onto the clutch hub, then a friction disc.

11. Continue to install the clutch plates and friction discs, alternating them until all are installed except for the last friction disc. All of these friction disc tangs go into the main grooves.

44

45

46

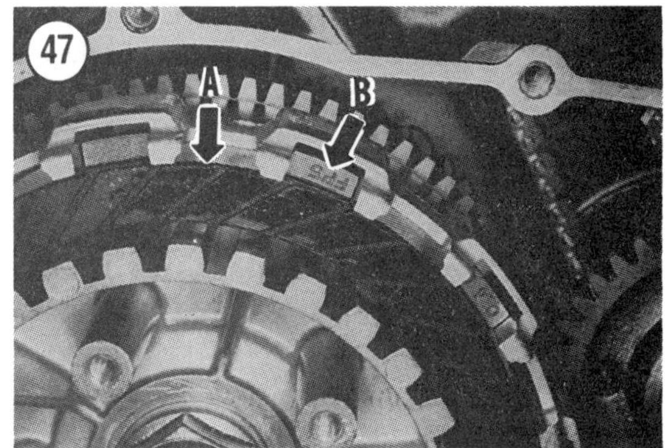

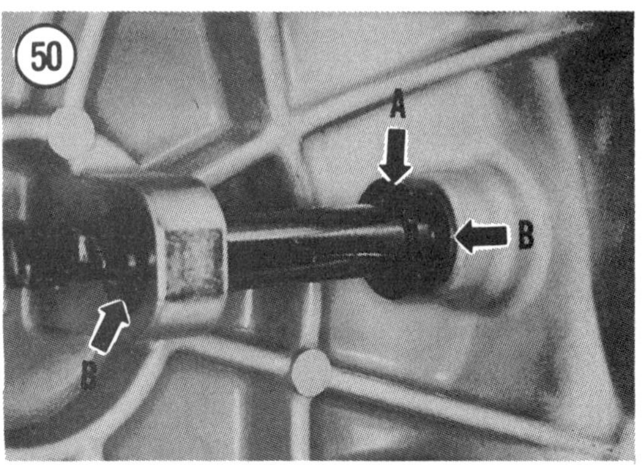

12. Install the *last* friction disc so its tangs go into the *secondary grooves* (**Figure 49**). This friction disc is the last disc or plate installed in the clutch housing.
13. Install the clutch push rod (A, **Figure 16**) into the clutch hub.
14. Install the clutch pressure plate (A, **Figure 15**).
15. Install the springs (**Figure 14**) and bolts.
16. Following a crisscross pattern, tighten the clutch bolts (**Figure 13**) to the torque specification listed in **Table 2**.
17. Reinstall the clutch cover as described in this chapter.

CLUTCH RELEASE ASSEMBLY

CAUTION

The clutch release mechanism is located in inside the clutch cover. Do not remove the release shaft from the clutch cover unless absolutely necessary. The seal can be damaged during removal and require replacement.

Removal

1. Remove the clutch cover as described in this chapter.
2. Remove the circlip (A, **Figure 50**) from the release shaft.
3. Carefully pull the release shaft from the clutch cover and remove it.
4. Inspect the seal and needle bearing in the clutch cover. Replace if necessary.

Installation

1. Apply a high-temperature grease to the lips of the seal in the clutch cover.
2. Lubricate the release shaft bearings (B, **Figure 50**) in the clutch cover with clean engine oil.

CAUTION

Take care not to disturb the seal spring when installing the release shaft.

3. Carefully insert the release shaft into place in the crankcase cover.
4. Install the circlip (A, **Figure 50**) onto the release shaft.

5. Reinstall the crankcase cover as described in this chapter.
6. Adjust the clutch as described in Chapter Three.
7. Start the engine and warm it to normal operating temperature. Then, stop the engine and check the oil level.

TABLE 1 CLUTCH SPECIFICATIONS

Item	Standard	Wear limit
Friction disc and clutch plate warp	2.9-3.1 (0.114-0.122 in.)	2.8 mm (0.110 in.)
Maximum friction disc and clutch plate warp	less than 0.2 mm	0.3 mm (0.0118 in.)
Clutch spring free length	34.2 mm (1.35 in.)	33.1 (1.30 in.)
Clutch lever free play	2-3 mm (0.079-0.118 in.)	—

TABLE 2 CLUTCH TIGHTENING TORQUES

Item	N•m	in.-lb	ft.-lb.
Clutch locknut	130	—	96
Clutch spring bolts	8.8	78	—
Clutch cover bolts	9.8	78	—

CHAPTER SEVEN

TRANSMISSION AND GEARSHIFT MECHANISMS

This chapter provides complete service procedures for the transmission shaft assemblies and the external and the internal shift mechanism.

Table 1 and **Table 2** are located at the end of this chapter.

SHIFT PEDAL/LEVER ASSEMBLY

NOTE
The shift pedal tie rod and shift lever are the only components that can be removed with the engine in the frame.

Removal/Installation

1. Place a mark on the end of the shift shaft (**Figure 1**) so the shift lever can be reinstalled in the same position on the shaft.
2. Loosen the pinch bolt on the shift lever (A, **Figure 2**).
3. Remove the two footpeg mounting bolts (B, **Figure 2**).
4. Pull the entire shift pedal/lever assembly straight out from the motorcycle until the splines of the shift lever disengage from those on the shift shaft.
5. Installation is the reverse of removal.
   a. Install the shift lever so it aligns with the mark you made on the shift shaft.
   b. When the shift pedal is properly installed, the shift pedal tie rod (A, **Figure 3**) will form a right angle with the shift lever (B, **Figure 3**). Also, the center of the foot pedal pad should be 4 mm (0.16 in.) above the center of the lower engine bracket mounting bolt (C, **Figure 3**). If necessary, adjust the shift pedal position as described in this chapter.

Adjustment

NOTE
The locknut at the knurled end of the tie rod has left-handed threads.

1. Loosen the front and rear locknuts (C, **Figure 2**) on the tie rod.
2. Turn the tie rod until the shift pedal is at the desired position.
3. Tighten each locknut securely.

EXTERNAL SHIFT MECHANISM

The gearshift ratchet mechanism is located on the left-hand side of the crankcase. The gearshift lever shaft is subject to a lot of abuse. Should it become bent, the shift shaft is very hard to straighten without subjecting the crankcase to abnormal stress where the shaft enters the crankcase. If the shaft is bent enough to prevent it from being withdrawn from the crankcase, there is little recourse but to cutoff the shaft very close to the crankcase. It is much less expensive to replace the shaft than the crankcase assembly.

To gain access to the external shift mechanism, it is necessary to remove the engine as described in Chapter Five.

Removal

Refer to **Figure 4** for this procedure.

1. Remove the engine as described in Chapter Five.
2. Remove the six bolts (**Figure 5**) securing the external shift mechanism cover to the crankcase. Remove the cover and its gasket.
3. Do not lose the locating dowels (**Figure 6**) in the crankcase.
4. Remove the washer (A, **Figure 7**) from the shift shaft and remove the shift shaft assembly (B, **Figure 7**) from the housing.
5. Remove the bolt (A, **Figure 8**) securing the gear position lever (B, **Figure 8**) to the housing and remove the lever along with its spring.
6. Remove the securing screw (A, **Figure 9**) and remove the shift drum cam (B, **Figure 9**). Be sure the washer behind the shift drum cam comes out with the cam. Also look for the indexing pin. It could come out with the cam or remain behind in the shift drum.

Inspection

1. Inspect the shift shaft assembly for damage.
   a. If the shaft (A, **Figure 10**) is bent or if its splines are damaged, replace the shaft.
   b. Inspect the return spring (B, **Figure 10**) and spring (C, **Figure 10**) on the shaft assembly. If either is broken or weak, it must be replaced.
   c. Inspect the shift pawl (D, **Figure 10**). Replace the pawl if it is damaged in any way.
2. Inspect the roller (**Figure 11**) on the gear position lever for wear or damage and replace if necessary.
3. Inspect the gear position lever spring. Replace the spring if any damage is noted.
4. Check the ramps on the shift drum cam (**Figure 12**) for wear or roughness. If any ramp has excessive wear or damage, replace the shift drum cam.
5. Be sure the stud (C, **Figure 8**) for the shift shaft return spring is tight in the crankcase half. If it is loose, remove and reinstall the stud. Apply Loctite 242 and torque the stud to the specification in **Table 2**.

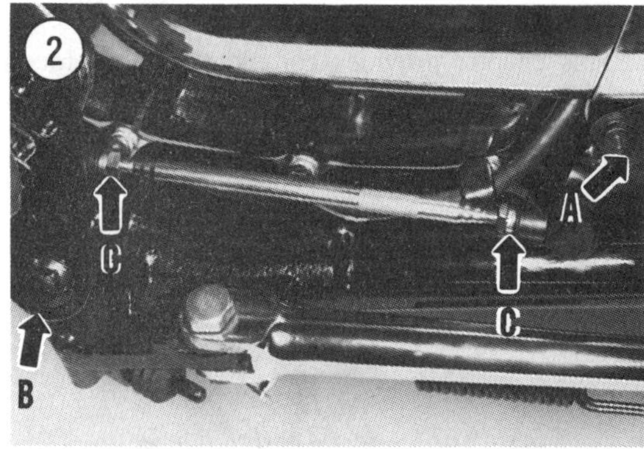

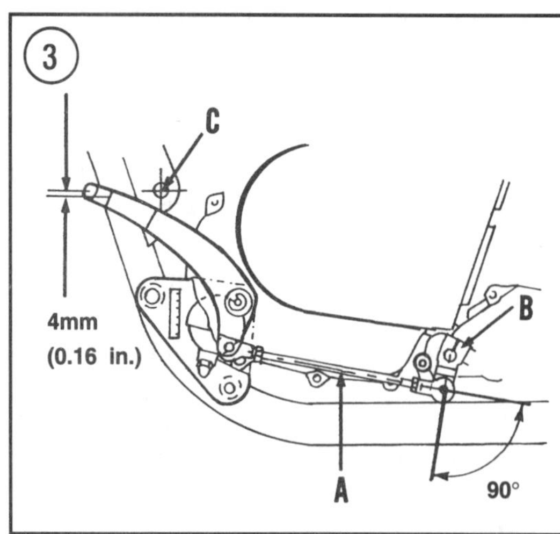

4

SHIFT PEDAL/EXTERNAL SHIFT MECHANISM

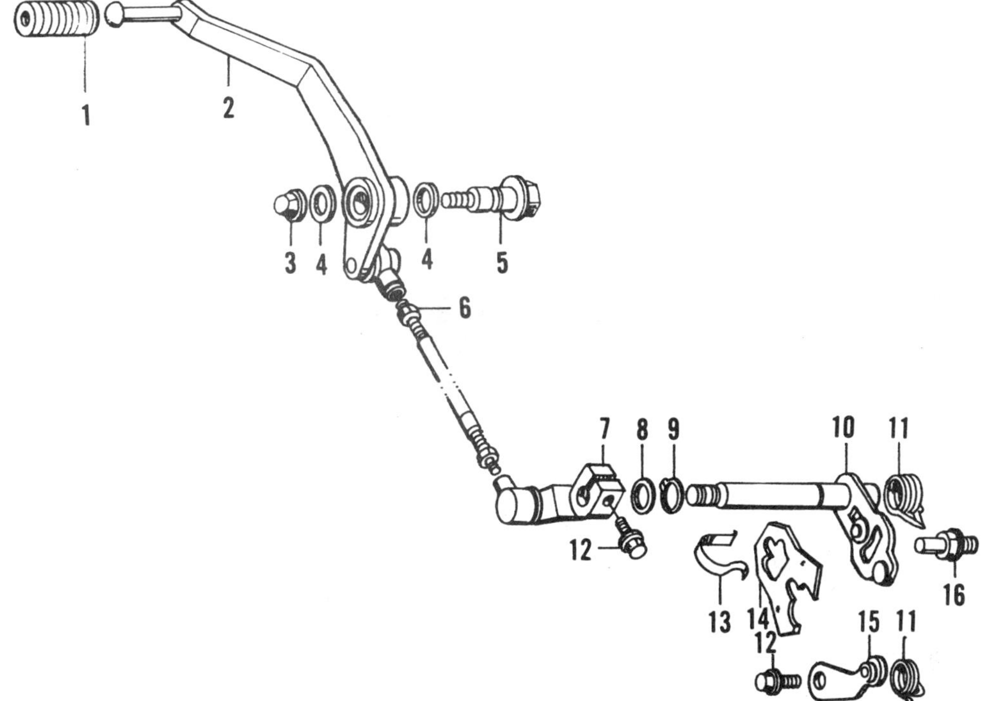

1. Rubber pad
2. Shift pedal lever
3. Cap nut
4. Seal
5. Shift pedal bolt
6. Tie rod
7. Shift lever
8. Washer
9. Circlip
10. Shift shaft
11. Return spring
12. Bolt
13. Spring
14. Shift pawl
15. Gear position lever
16. Return spring stud

Installation

1. If removed, install the indexing pin into the shift drum in the crankcase.
2. Install the shift drum cam and its washer onto the shift drum. Be sure the pin in the shift drum engages the indexing hole in the shift drum cam.
3. Apply Loctite 242 to the threads of the shift drum cam mounting screw (A, **Figure 9**) and install the screw. Tighten the screw securely.
4. Fit the gear position lever and its return spring into place in the left crankcase half. Be sure the inboard end of the return spring engages the hole in the crankcase (A, **Figure 13**) and that the outboard end engages the gear position lever (B, **Figure 13**). Partially install the gear position lever bolt.
5. Move the gear position lever **(Figure 8)** into place against the shift drum cam and torque the gear position lever bolt to the specification in **Table 2**.
6. Install the shift shaft into the crankcase half. Be sure shift shaft return spring engages the stud in the crankcase (A, **Figure 14**) and that the shift pawl (B, **Figure 14**) engages the shift drum cam.
7. If they were removed, install the circlip and washer (A, **Figure 7**) onto the shift lever shaft.

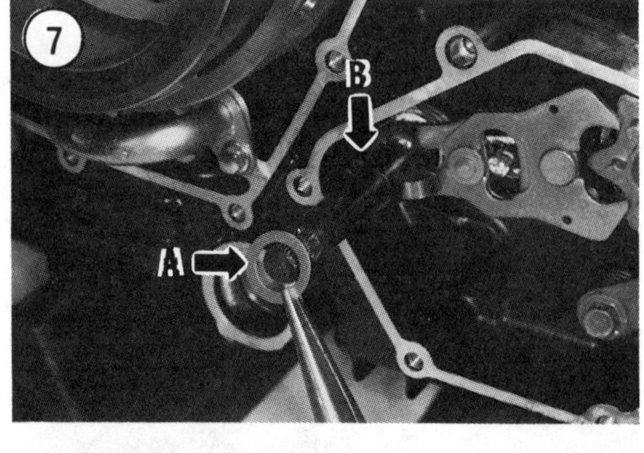

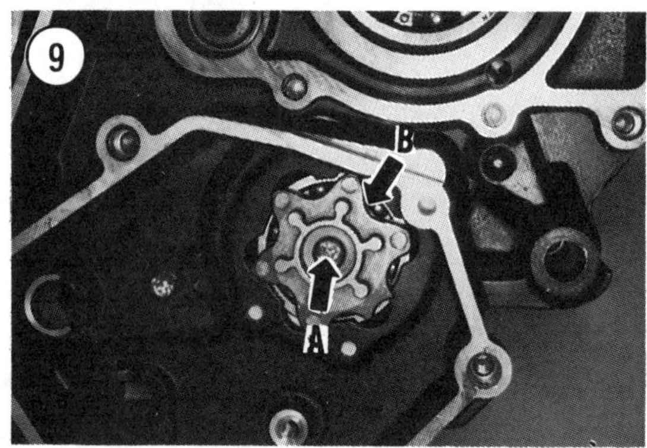

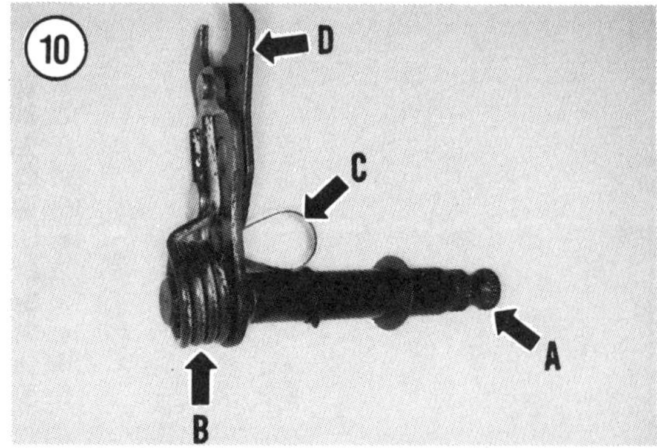

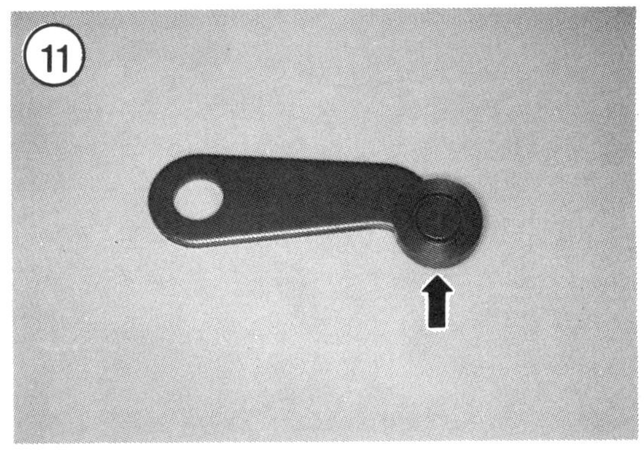
11

12

13

14

8. Install the dowels (A, **Figure 6**) into the crankcase half and install a new gasket.
9. Apply high-temperature grease to the seal lips (**Figure 15**) in the external shift mechanism cover and install the cover.
10. Install the cover bolts and torque them to the specification in **Table 2**.
11. Reinstall the engine as described in Chapter Five.

TRANSMISSION AND INTERNAL SHIFT MECHANISM

To gain access to the transmission and internal shift mechanism (shift drum and shift forks), it is necessary to remove the engine and disassemble the crankcase as described in Chapter Five.

The internal shift mechanism (except the shift drum) is removed along with the transmission shaft assemblies. The shift drum can be removed after the transmission shafts are removed.

Refer to **Table 1** at the end of the chapter for transmission and gearshift mechanism specifications.

Removal/Installation

1. Remove the engine as described in Chapter Five.
2. Disassemble the external shift mechanism as described in this chapter.
3. Disassemble the crankcase as described in Chapter Five.
4. Remove the crankshaft assembly (**Figure 16**).
5. Remove the shift fork shaft (**Figure 17**).
6. Move each shift fork so its guide pin disengages from the shift drum.

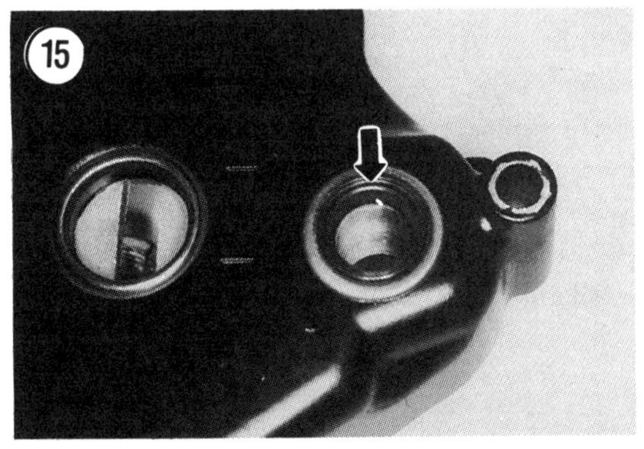
15

7. Remove the shift drum. Do not lose the indexing pin (**Figure 18**) from the end of shift drum.

NOTE

The right-hand and left-hand shift forks are identical, but each should be reinstalled in its original location during assembly. Mark each of them for identification as soon as they are removed from the crankcase.

8. Remove the shift forks (**Figure 19**)from the transmission assemblies.
9. Remove the mainshaft (A, **Figure 20**) and countershaft (B, **Figure 20**) as an assembly. Do not lose the two loose washers (**Figure 21**) from the left-hand end of the mainshaft assembly.
10. Inspect the transmission shaft assemblies as described in this chapter.
11. Inspect the internal shift components as described in this chapter.

NOTE

Coat all bearing surfaces with clean engine oil prior to installation.

CAUTION

*Hold the two washers (**Figure 22**) on the left-hand end of the mainshaft (A) during installation with your fingers. They must remain in place during installation of the transmission shaft assemblies.*

12. Install the mainshaft (A, **Figure 22**) and countershaft (B, **Figure 22**) as an assembly. Push both shaft assemblies all the way down until they bottom.

NOTE

Install the shift forks with their cast-in marks facing toward the left-hand crankcase half.

22

A

B

NOTE

*Position the left- and right-hand shift forks with the longer side of the boss (**Figure 23**) facing away from the left-hand crankcase half. Position the center shift fork as shown in **Figure 24**.*

13. Insert the left-hand shift fork (A, **Figure 25**) into the countershaft.

14. Insert the center shift fork (B, **Figure 25**) into the mainshaft.

15. Insert the right-hand shift fork (C, **Figure 25**) into the countershaft.

16. Position the shift forks so the guide pins will properly engage the shift drum.

17. Be sure the indexing pin is in place in the end of the shift drum (**Figure 18**) and install the shift drum into the left-hand crankcase half. Push it in until it bottoms in the bearing.

18. Rotate the shift drum to the neutral position.

19. Move each shift fork so its guide pin properly engages its groove in the shift drum. Make sure all three followers properly engage the shift drum (**Figure 19**).

20. Align the shift fork shaft holes and install the shift fork shaft (**Figure 17**). Push the shaft in until it bottoms.

21. After both transmission assemblies and the internal shift mechanism are installed, perform the following:

Shift both shafts into NEUTRAL. Hold the mainshaft and rotate the countershaft. The countershaft should rotate freely.

Rotate both shaft assemblies by hand. Make sure there is no binding. This is the time to find that something may be installed incorrectly—not after the crankcase is completely assembled.

22. Reassemble the crankcase as described in Chapter Five.

23. Reassemble the external shift mechanism as described in this chapter.

24. Reinstall the engine as described in Chapter Five.

Transmission Preliminary Inspection

After the transmission shaft assemblies are removed from the crankcase, clean and inspect the assemblies prior to disassembling them. Place an assembled shaft into a large can or plastic bucket and thoroughly clean all parts with a petroleum-based solvent, such as kerosene, and a stiff brush. Dry with compressed air or let it drip dry. Repeat this for the other shaft assembly.

NOTE
*Do not lose the two loose washers (**Figure 21**) from the end of the mainshaft. They are not held in place and may slide off the end of the shaft into the bucket.*

1. Visually inspect the transmission components for excessive wear. Any burrs, pitting or roughness on the teeth of a gear will cause wear on the mating gear. Minor roughness can be repaired with a file but do not attempt to remove deep scars.

NOTE
Defective gears must be replaced. Also consider replacing the mating gear on the other shaft even though it may not show as much wear or damage.

2. Carefully check the engagement dogs. If any are chipped, worn, rounded or missing, the affected gear must be replaced.

3. Inspect the transmission bearings (**Figure 26**) in both crankcase halves. Also check the starter drum bearing. Turn each bearing by hand, and check for roughness, noise and radial play. Any bearing that is in questionable condition should be replaced as described in Chapter Five.

4. If the transmission shafts are satisfactory and are not going to be disassembled, apply assembly oil or engine oil to all components and reinstall them in the crankcase as described in this chapter.

Transmission Service Notes

1. Use a divided container, such as a restaurant type egg carton to help maintain correct alignment and positioning of the parts. As you remove a part from the shaft, set it in the container in the same position from which it was removed. Refer to **Figure 27** for the mainshaft and **Figure 28** for the countershaft. This is an easy way to remember the correct relationship of all parts.

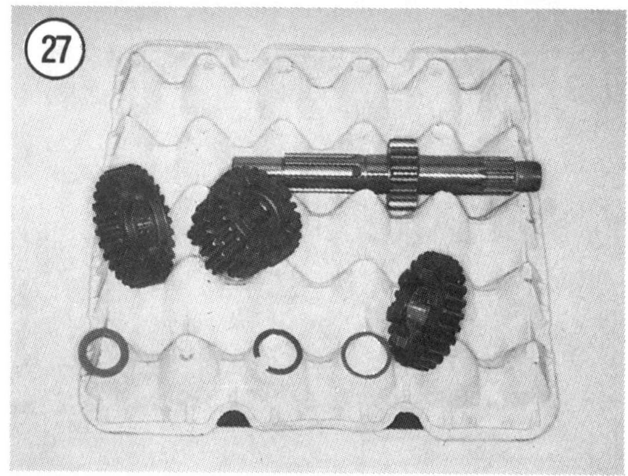

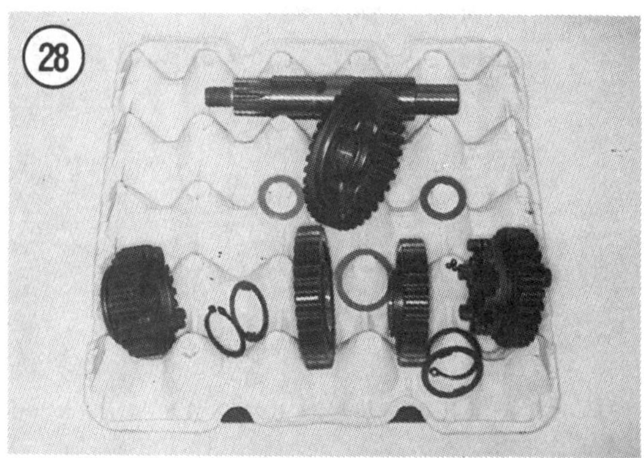

2. The circlips are a tight fit on the transmission shafts. Replacing all circlips during reassembly is recommended.

3. Circlips will turn and fold over making removal and installation difficult. To ease removal, open the circlips with a pair of circlip pliers while holding the back of the circlip with a pair of pliers. Repeat for installation.

Mainshaft Disassembly/Inspection

Refer to **Figure 29** for this procedure.

1. Place the assembled shaft into a large can or plastic bucket and thoroughly clean it with solvent and a stiff brush. Dry with compressed air or let it sit on rags to dry.
2. Slide both washers off the left-hand end of the shaft.
3. Slide off the fifth gear.
4. Slide off the second/third combination gear.
5. Remove the circlip, and slide off the washer.
6. Slide off the fourth gear.
7. Check each gear for excessive wear, burrs, pitting and chipped or missing teeth (A, **Figure 30**). Make

TRANSMISSION

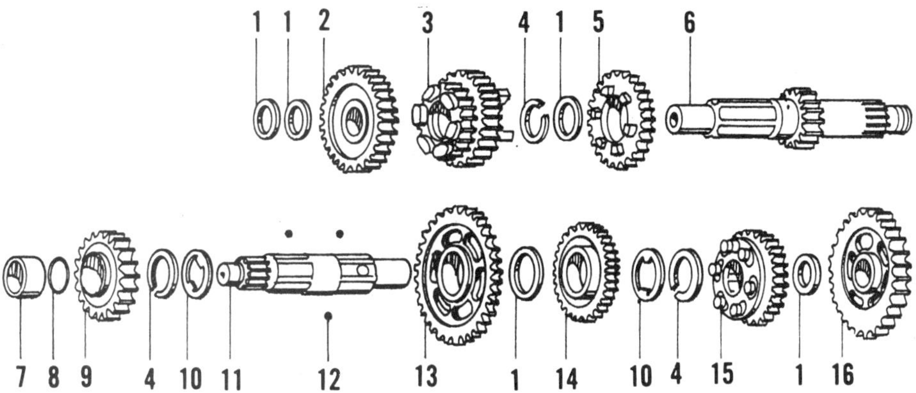

1. Washer
2. Mainshaft fifth gear
3. Mainshaft second/third combination gear
4. Circlip
5. Mainshaft fourth gear
6. Mainshaft/first gear
7. Collar
8. O-ring
9. Countershaft fifth gear
10. Splined washer
11. Countershaft
12. Steel balls (3)
13. Countershaft second gear
14. Countershaft third gear
15. Countershaft fourth gear
16. Countershaft first gear

sure the lugs (A, **Figure 31**) on the gears are in good condition.

8. Check the gear inner splines (B, **Figure 31**) for excessive wear or damage. Replace the gear if necessary.

9. Check the inner bearing surface (B, **Figure 30**) for excessive wear or damage. Replace the gear if necessary.

10. Inspect the splined washers for bending wear or damage. Replace if necessary.

11. Inspect the shift fork groove and any oil control holes. Make sure the oil holes are clear.

12. Inspect the shift fork-to-gear clearance as described under *Internal Gearshift Mechanism* in this chapter.

NOTE
The first gear (A, ***Figure 32****) is part of the mainshaft. If the gear is defective, the mainshaft must be replaced.*

13. Make sure that all gears and bushings slide smoothly on the mainshaft splines.

NOTE
It is recommended that all circlips be replaced every time the transmission is disassembled to ensure proper gear alignment. Do not expand a circlip more than necessary to slide it over the shaft.

14. Inspect the splines (B, **Figure 32**) and the circlip groove (C, **Figure 32**) of the mainshaft. If any are damaged, the shaft must be replaced.

15. Inspect the clutch hub splines (D, **Figure 32**) and clutch nut threads (E, **Figure 32**) of the mainshaft. If any splines are damaged, the shaft must be replaced. If the threads have burrs or have minor damage, clean them with a proper size metric thread

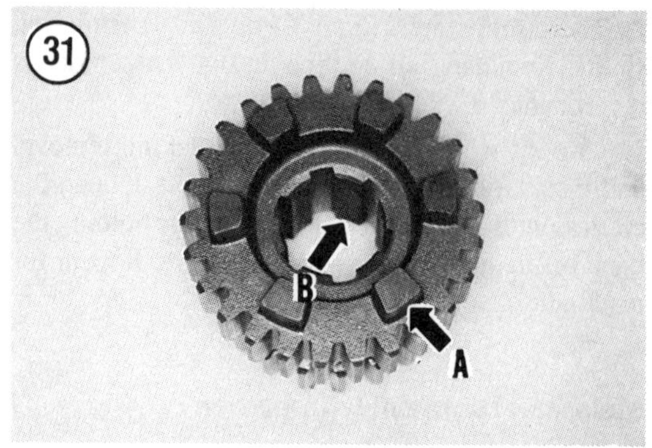

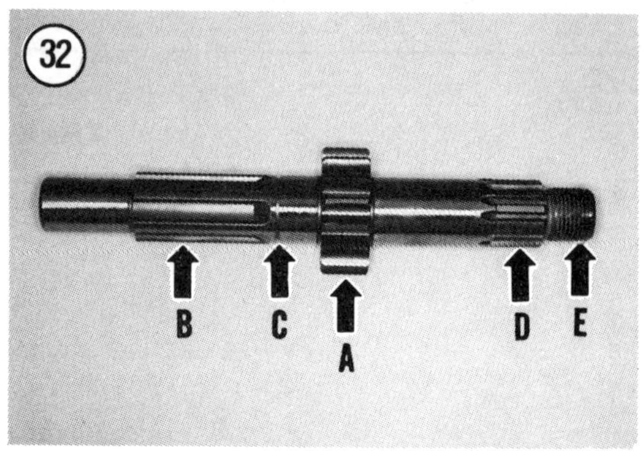

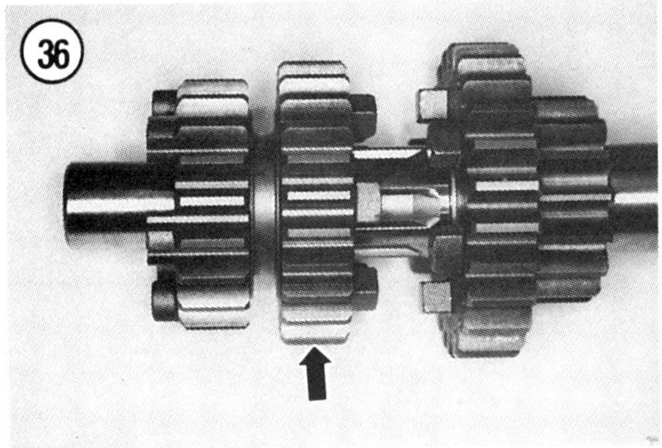

die. If thread damage is severe, the shaft must be replaced.

Mainshaft Assembly

1. Apply a light coat of clean engine oil to all sliding surfaces prior to installing any parts.
2. Position the fourth gear with its engagement dog side going on last and install the fourth gear (**Figure 33**).
3. Slide on the washer (A, **Figure 34**) and new circlip (B, **Figure 34**). Make sure the circlip is seated correctly in the mainshaft groove (**Figure 35**).
4. Position the second/third combination gear with the larger diameter gear (**Figure 36**) going on first and install the gear (**Figure 37**).
5. Position the fifth gear with its flush side going on last, and install the fifth gear (**Figure 38**).
6. Install both washers (**Figure 39**).
7. Refer to **Figure 40** for the correct placement of all gears. Make sure the circlip is correctly seated in the mainshaft groove.

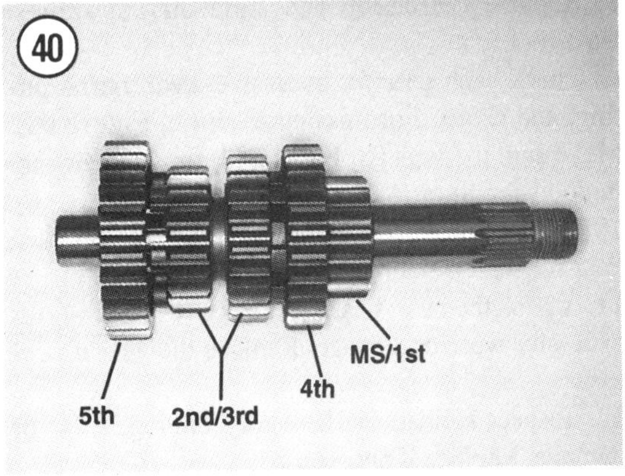

8. Make sure each gear properly engages the adjoining gear where applicable.

Countershaft Disassembly/Inspection

Refer to **Figure 29** for this procedure.

1. Place the assembled shaft into a large can or plastic bucket. Thoroughly clean the assembly with solvent and a stiff brush. Dry with compressed air or let it sit on rags to dry.
2. Slide off the first gear and washer.

NOTE

*The fourth gear is retained on the countershaft with three steel balls **(Figure 41)** that ride in the small receptacles in the raised splines of the shaft. These balls perform the function of a positive neutral detent mechanism.*

NOTE

Perform Step 3 over a small box or pan on the work bench to catch the small steel balls that fall out when the fourth gear is removed from the shaft.

3. Remove the fourth gear as follows:
   a. Hold the transmission shaft vertically with the fourth gear facing up.
   b. Hold onto the third gear with one hand. Quickly spin the fourth gear and shaft assembly while pulling up on the fourth gear.
   c. Remove the fourth gear and three small steel balls.
4. Remove the circlip, and slide off the splined washer.
5. Slide off the third gear and washer.
6. Slide off the second gear.
7. Slide the fifth gear from the other end of the shaft.
8. Remove the circlip and slide off the splined washer.
9. Check each gear for excessive wear, burrs, pitting, and chipped or missing teeth (A, **Figure 42**). Make sure the lugs (B, **Figure 42**) on the gears are in good condition.
10. Inspect the inner splines (**Figure 43**) on each gear for wear or damage. Replace if necessary.
11. Check the inner bearing surface (**Figure 44**) for excessive wear or damage. Replace the gear if necessary.
12. Inspect splined washers for bending, wear or damage. Replace if necessary.

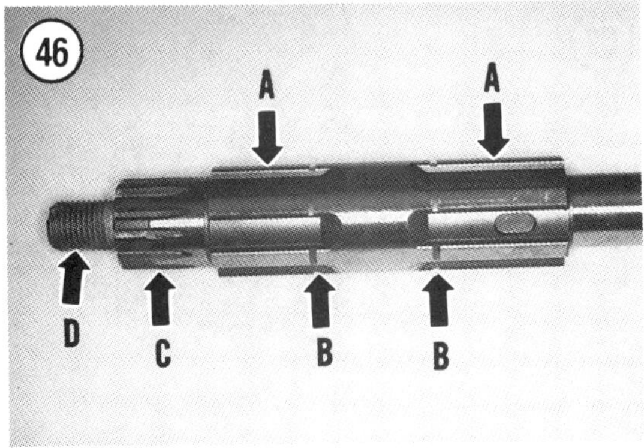

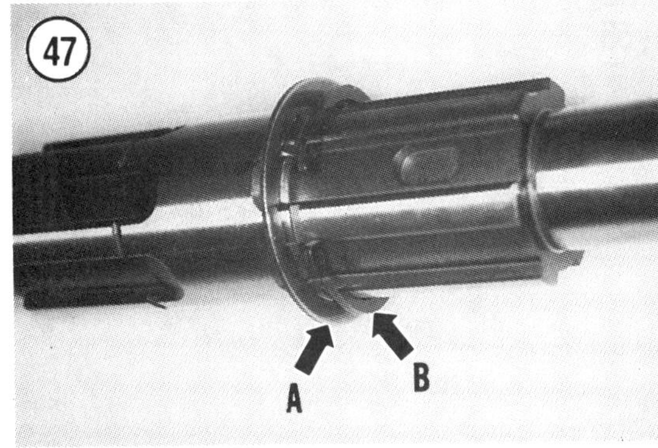

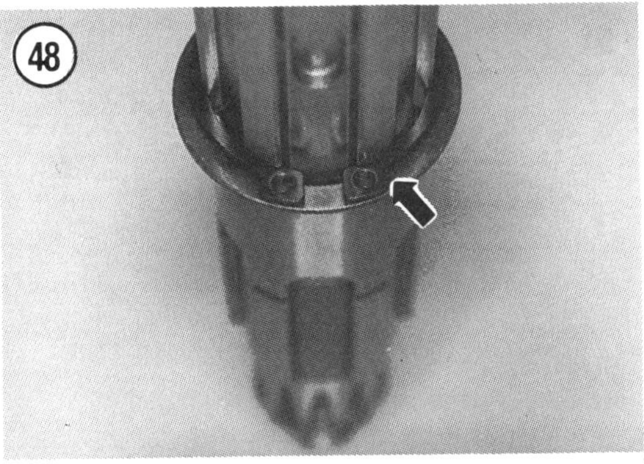

13. Inspect the shift fork groove (A, **Figure 45**) and any oil control holes (B, **Figure 45**). Make sure the oil holes are clear.
14. Inspect the shift fork-to-gear clearance as described under *Internal Gearshift Mechanism* in this chapter.

NOTE
Defective gears should be replaced. It is a good idea to replace the mating gear on the mainshaft as well.

15. Make sure that all gears slide smoothly on the countershaft splines.

NOTE
It is recommended that all circlips be replaced every time the transmission is disassembled to ensure proper gear alignment. Do not expand a circlip more than necessary to slide it over the shaft.

16. Inspect the splines (A, **Figure 46**) and circlip grooves (B, **Figure 46**) of the countershaft. If any are damaged, the shaft must be replaced.
17. Inspect the engine sprocket splines (C, **Figure 46**) and engine sprocket retaining nut threads (D, **Figure 46**) of the countershaft. If any of the splines are damaged, the shaft must be replaced. If the threads have burrs or minor damage, clean with a proper size metric thread die.

Countershaft Assembly

1. Apply a light coat of clean engine oil to all sliding surfaces prior to installing any parts.
2. Slide on the splined washer (A, **Figure 47**) and install a new circlip (B, **Figure 47**). Make sure the circlip (**Figure 48**) is correctly seated in the countershaft groove.

CAUTION
*Do **not** use grease to hold the three small steel balls in place within the receptacles in the fourth gear. If grease is used, the positive neutral detent mechanism will malfunction.*

3. Apply a light coat of clean engine oil to the three receptacles within the fourth gear.
4. Install the fourth gear as follows:
   a. Hold the fourth gear horizontally with the shift fork groove facing down.

b. Install the three steel balls (**Figure 49**) into the fourth gear (**Figure 50**).
c. Hold the transmission shaft vertically.
d. Align the fourth gear so the three small steel balls are aligned with the three receptacles in the raised splines on the shaft.
e. Slowly push the fourth gear onto the shaft until the steel balls fall into the receptacles in the shaft. Carefully move the fourth gear back and forth (**Figure 51**) on the shaft to make sure the steel balls are correctly seated.

5. Position the third gear with the long shoulder side going on last and slide the third gear (A, **Figure 52**) onto the countershaft.

6. Install the washer (B, **Figure 52**).

7. Position the second gear with its long shoulder side (**Figure 53**) going on last. Slide the second gear (**Figure 54**) onto the countershaft.

8. Slide on the splined washer (A, **Figure 55**) and install the circlip (B, **Figure 55**). Make sure the

circlip (**Figure 56**) is correctly seated in the countershaft groove.

9. Position the fifth gear with its shift fork groove going on last and install the fifth gear (**Figure 57**). Be sure the oil hole on the fifth gear is aligned with the oil hole in the shaft.

10. Install the washer (**Figure 58**) against the fourth gear at the other end of the shaft.

11. Position the first gear with its flush side going on last and slide the first gear (**Figure 59**) onto the countershaft.

12. Refer to **Figure 60** for correct placement of all gears. Make sure all circlips are correctly seated in the countershaft grooves.

13. After both transmission shafts are assembled, place the two assemblies against each other in the correct position (**Figure 61**). Make sure all gears properly engage. Make sure each is correctly assembled.

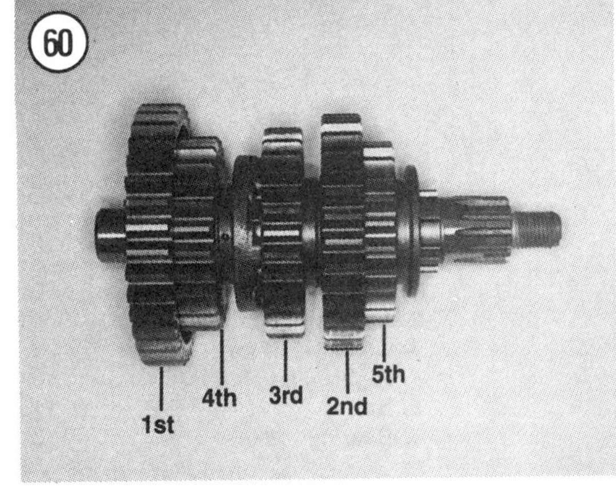

Internal Gearshift Mechanism Inspection

Refer to **Figure 62** for this procedure.

1. Roll the shift fork shaft on a flat surface such as a piece of plate glass and check for any bends. If the shaft is bent, it must be replaced.

2. Inspect each shift fork for wear or cracking. Check for any arc-shaped wear or burned marks on the fingers of the shift forks. This indicates that the fork fingers are excessively worn and the fork must be replaced

(62)

INTERNAL SHIFT MECHANISM

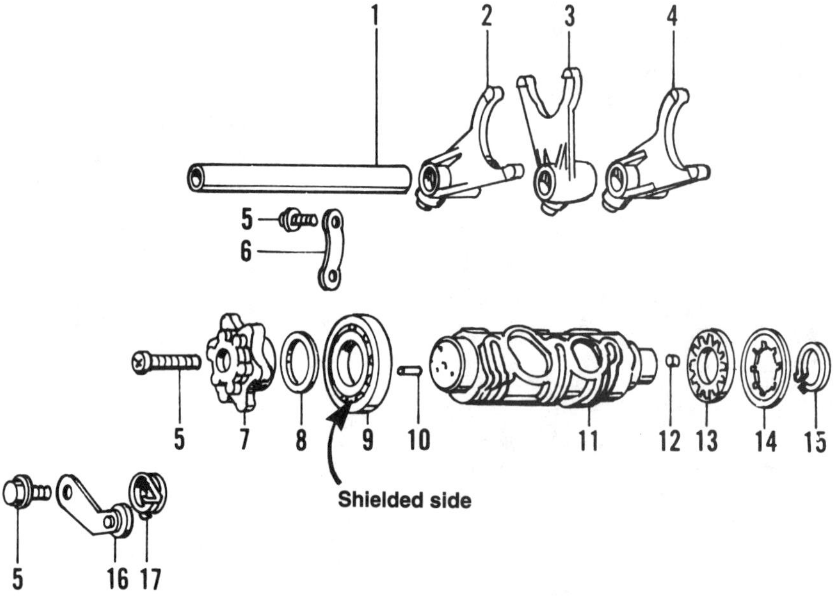

Shielded side

1. Shift fork shaft
2. Left-hand shift fork
3. Center shift fork
4. Right-hand shift fork
5. Bolt
6. Bearing retainer
7. Shift drum cam
8. Washer
9. Bearing
10. Pin
11. Shift drum
12. Roller
13. Shift drum holder
14. Spring
15. Circlip
16. Gear position lever
17. Spring

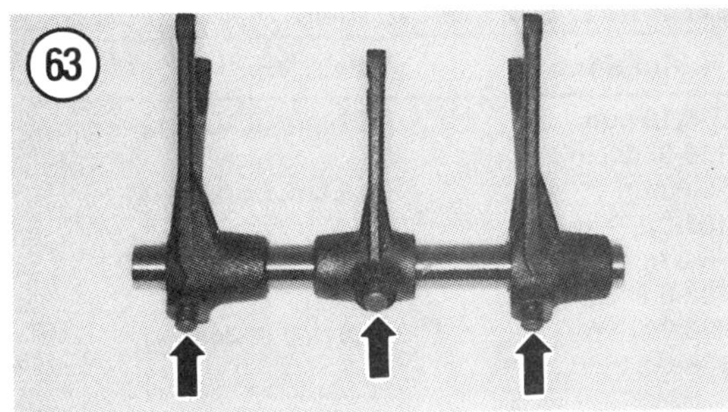

63

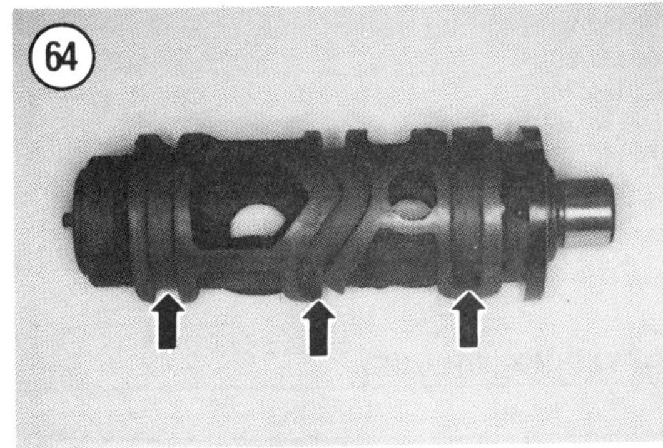

64

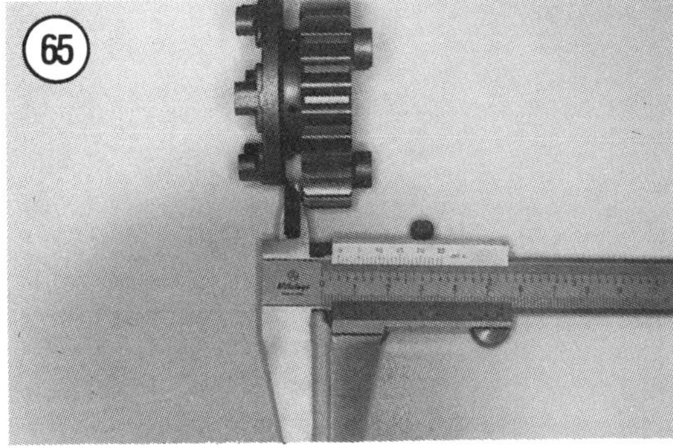

65

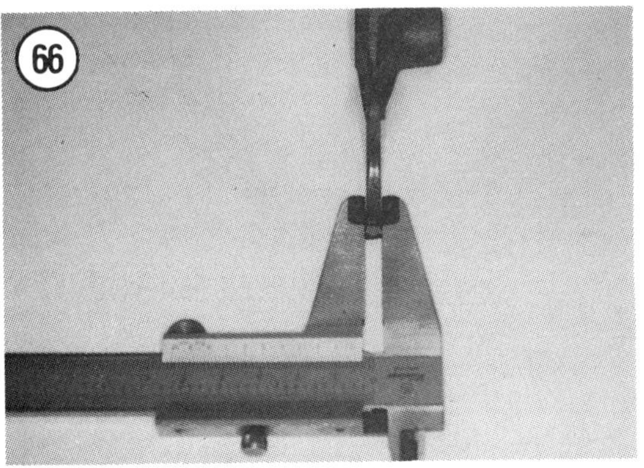

66

3. Check the bore of each shift fork and check the shift fork shaft for burrs, wear or pitting. Replace any worn parts.
4. Install each shift fork onto its shaft and make sure it moves freely on the shaft (**Figure 63**).
5. Check the guide pin (**Figure 63**) on each shift fork for wear or damage. Replace the shift fork(s) as necessary.
6. Check the grooves in the shift drum (**Figure 64**) for wear or roughness. If any of the groove profiles have excessive wear or damage, replace the shift drum.
7. Measure the width of the guide pin grooves in the shift drum. If any groove is worn beyond the service limit, replace the shift drum.

CAUTION

It is recommended that marginally worn shift forks be replaced. Worn forks can cause the transmission to slip out of gear, leading to more serious and expensive damage.

8. Measure the width of the shift fork groove in the gears with a vernier caliper as shown in **Figure 65**. Compare to the specifications listed in **Table 1**.
9. Measure the width of the shift fork fingers (**Figure 66**) with a micrometer or vernier caliper. Replace the shift fork(s) worn to the service limit listed in **Table 1**.
10. Measure the outer diameter of the shift fork guide pins (**Figure 67**) with a micrometer or vernier caliper. Replace the shift fork(s) if wear exceeds the service limit listed in **Table 1**.

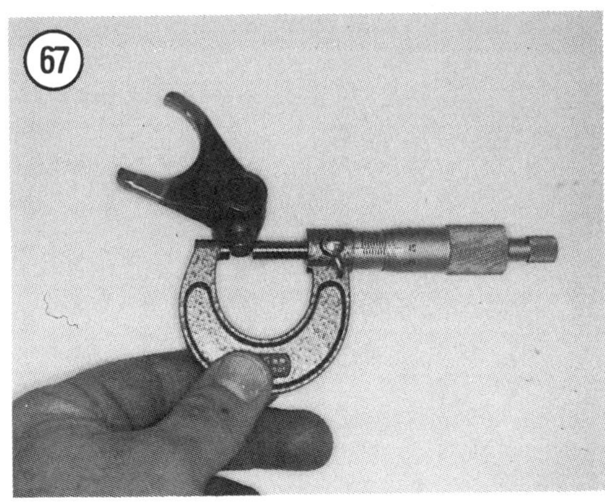

67

Table 1 TRANSMISSION AND GEARSHIFT SPECIFICATIONS

Item	Specifications	Wear limit
Shift fork groove (in gear)	5.05-5.15 mm (0.198-0.203 in.)	5.2 mm (0.205 in.)
Shift fork finger width	4.9-5.0 mm (0.193-0.197 in.)	4.8 mm (0.189 in.)
Shift fork guide pin diameter	5.9-6.0 mm (0.232-0.236 in.)	5.8 mm (0.228 in.)
Shift drum groove width	6.05-6.20 mm (0.238-0.244 in.)	6.3 mm (0.248 in.)
Transmission gear ratios		
1st gear	2.250 (36/16):1	
2nd gear	1.600 (32/20):1	
3rd gear	1.230 (32/26):1	
4th gear	1.000 (26/26):1	
5th gear	0.857 (24/28):1	
Primary reduction ratio	2.184 (83/38):1	
Final reduction ratio	2.875 (46/16):1	

Table 2 TRANSMISSION TIGHTENING TORQUES

Item	N•m	in.-lb.	ft.-lb.
Shift drum bearing retainer bolts	11	97	—
Transmission cover bolts	11	97	—
External shift mechanism cover bolts	11	97	—
Shift shaft return spring stud	29	—	21
Gear position lever bolt	11	97	—
Shift drum cam mounting screw			
Neutral switch	15	—	11
Shift pedal pivot bolt	29	—	21
Shift pedal pivot nut	29	—	21
Shift lever pinch bolt	12	106	—
Engine sprocket nut	125	—	92

CHAPTER EIGHT

FUEL, EMISSION CONTROL AND EXHAUST SYSTEMS

This chapter includes service procedures for all parts of the fuel system and exhaust system. Air filter service is covered in Chapter Three.

The fuel system consists of the fuel tank, shutoff valve, carburetor and air filter assembly. The exhaust system consists of two exhaust pipes and two mufflers. The emission controls consist of the evaporative emission control system on California models and the clean air system on both California and Swiss models.

Carburetor specifications are covered in **Table 1**, and fuel system torque specifications are in **Table 2**. Both tables located at the end of this chapter.

NOTE

Where differences occur relating to the United Kingdom (U.K.) models they are identified. If there is no (U.K.) designation relating to a procedure, photo or illustration, it is identical to the United States (U.S.) models.

WARNING

Gasoline is a known carcinogen as well as an extremely flammable liquid. It must be handled carefully. Wear latex gloves when working on any part of the fuel system. If gasoline gets on your skin, rinse it off immediately and thoroughly wash the area with soap and warm water.

CARBURETOR OPERATION

For proper operation, a gasoline engine must be supplied with air and fuel mixed in proper proportions by weight. An air/fuel mixture with too much fuel is said to be rich. A lean mixture is one that contains insufficient fuel. A properly adjusted carburetor supplies the correct air/fuel mixture to the engine under all operating conditions.

The carburetor consists of several major systems. A float and float valve mechanism maintains a constant fuel level in the float bowl. The pilot system supplies fuel at low speeds. The main fuel system supplies fuel at medium and high speeds. A starter (choke) system supplies the very rich mixture needed to start a cold engine.

CARBURETOR SERVICE

Perform major carburetor service (removal and cleaning) at the intervals indicated in Chapter Three or if poor engine performance, hesitation and little or no response to mixture adjustment is observed. Alterations in jet size, changes in jet needle position or other adjustments should be attempted only if you are experienced in this type of tuning work. A bad guess could result in costly engine damage or, at least, poor performance. If the bike does not perform correctly after you have serviced and adjusted the carburetor as described in this chapter (and if ignition condition and other factors affecting performance are correct), the bike should be checked at a dealership or a qualified performance tuning specialist.

CARBURETOR

NOTE
The carburetor has several air and vacuum hoses that must be removed during service. Label each hose and its fitting during removal so you can correctly reattach all lines during assembly.

Removal/Installation

1. Remove the seat as described in Chapter Fourteen.
2. Remove the fuel tank as described in this chapter.
3. Disconnect the battery negative lead as described in Chapter Three.
4. Remove the air filter housing as described in this chapter.
5. Loosen the jam nut and remove the choke cable from its mounting bracket on the left side of the motorcycle.
6. Remove the choke cable holder screws (**Figure 1**) from the top of the battery case.
7. Remove the bolts (A, **Figure 2**) securing the carburetor plate to the cylinder heads, and remove the carburetor plate (B, **Figure 2**).
8. Loosen the carburetor clamp screw (an Allen screw) securing the carburetor to the manifold boot (**Figure 3**).
9. Disconnect the vent hose (A, **Figure 4**) from its fitting on top of the carburetor and remove the vacuum line (B, **Figure 4**) from its fitting. Move the hoses out of the way.
10. Slowly move the carburetor assembly (C, **Figure 4**) partially up and away from the engine, then perform the following:
   a. Loosen the locknuts (A, **Figure 5**) at the mid-cable adjusters on both throttle cables. Turn the adjusters (B, **Figure 5**) all the way in to allow maximum slack in both cables.
   b. Disconnect the push and pull cables (A, **Figure 6**) from the throttle wheel. Label each cable and its location on the throttle wheel so you can correctly reattach the cables during assembly.
   c. Remove the idle adjust cable (B, **Figure 6**) from the throttle linkage.

NOTE
The string attached in the next step will be used to pull the fuel line back through the frame so it will be rerouted in exactly the same position during assembly.

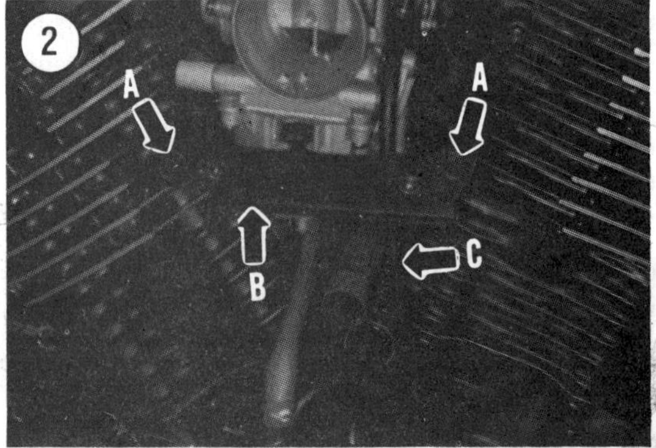

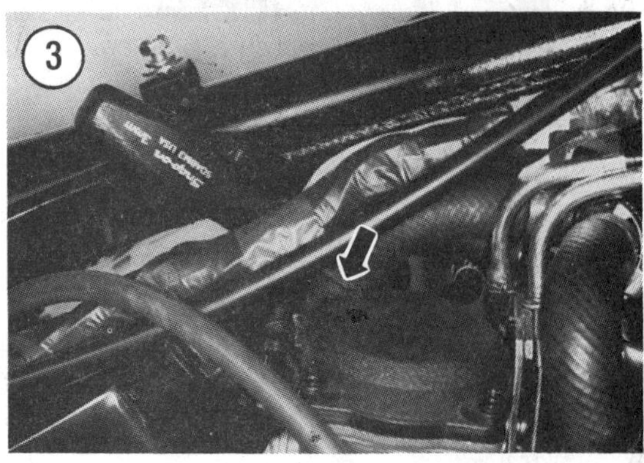

11. Tie a length of heavy string or cord to the petcock end of the fuel line. Wrap this end with masking or duct tape. Tie the other end of the string to the frame.

12. Carefully remove the carburetor assembly and the attached cables out of the frame. Remove the tape and untie the string from the fuel line. Take the assembly to a workbench for disassembly and cleaning.

13. Insert clean lint-free cloths into the intake manifold boot to prevent the entry of foreign matter.

14. Install by reversing these removal steps while noting the following:

a. Be sure the vacuum fitting boss on the carburetor slides under the spring clip on the manifold boot.
b. Make sure the screw on the manifold-boot clamping band is tight to avoid vacuum loss and possible valve damage due to a lean fuel mixture.
c. Be sure the starter plunger points upward.
d. Route the fuel line and choke cable in their original locations.
e. Route the idle adjust cable (C, **Figure 2**) behind the carburetor mounting plate (B, **Figure 2**).
f. Torque the carburetor mounting plate bolts to the specification in **Table 2**.
g. Adjust the throttle cable and the idle speed as described in Chapter Three.

CARBURETOR SERVICE

Disassembly

Refer to **Figure 7** for this procedure.

1. Remove the fuel line (A, **Figure 8**) from the carburetor.

2. Unscrew and remove the starter plunger assembly (B, **Figure 8**).

3. Remove the four screws (A, **Figure 9**) securing the top cover and remove the cover (B, **Figure 9**) from the carburetor.

4. Remove the vacuum piston/diaphragm assembly, including the spring and jet needle, from the carburetor (**Figure 10**).

5. Remove the spring, turn the vacuum piston/diaphragm assembly over and remove the jet needle (A, **Figure 11**) and spring seat (B, **Figure 11**).

6. Remove the screw securing the air cut valve cover and remove the cover (**Figure 12**).

7. Remove the spring (A, **Figure 13**) and the air cut valve diaphragm (B, **Figure 13**) from the carburetor. Do not lose the air cut valve O-ring (C, **Figure 13**).

8. Remove the screws securing the accelerator valve cover (A, **Figure 14**) to the bottom of the float bowl (B, **Figure 14**) and remove the cover.

9. Remove the accelerator valve spring (A, **Figure 15**) and the diaphragm (B, **Figure 15**). Do not lose the accelerator valve O-ring (C, **Figure 15**).

(7)

CARBURETOR ASSEMBLY

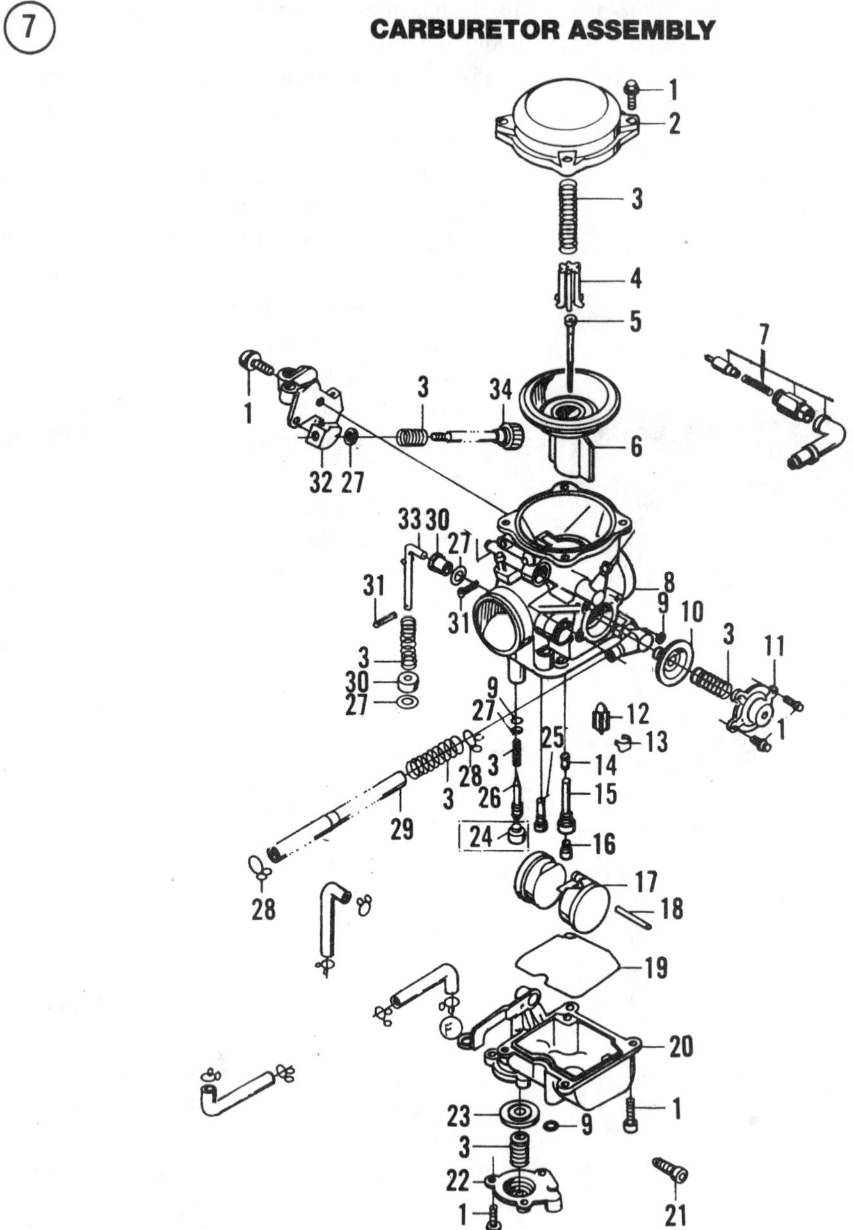

1. Screw
2. Top cover
3. Spring
4. Spring seat
5. Jet needle
6. Vacuum piston/ diaphragm assembly
7. Starter plunger
8. Carburetor body
9. O-ring
10. Air cut valve diaphragm
11. Air cut valve cover
12. Float valve needle
13. Clip
14. Needle jet
15. Needle jet holder
16. Main jet
17. Float
18. Float pin
19. O-ring gasket
20. Float bowl
21. Drain screw
22. Accelerator valve cover
23. Accelerator valve diaphragm
24. Plug (U.S., Canada and Switzerland models)
25. Pilot jet
26. Pilot air screw
27. Washer
28. Hose clamp
29. Hose
30. Collar
31. Cotter pin
32. Throttle lever
33. Rod
34. Idle adjust screw

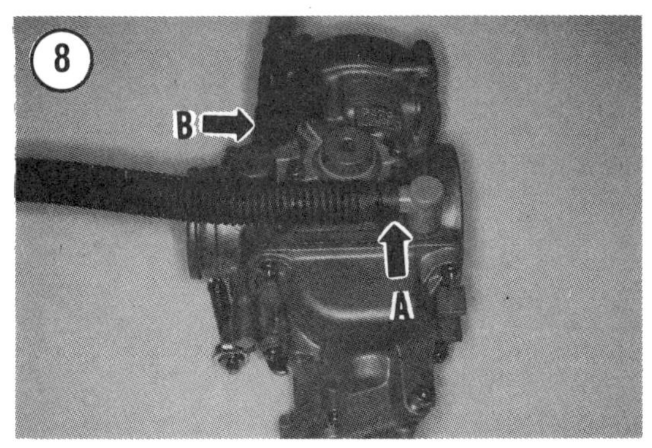
8
B
A

12
CVK
G200
AKFG
KEIHIN

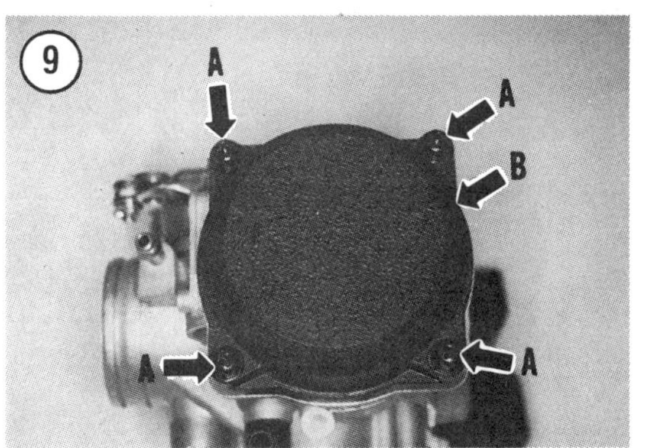
9
A
A
B
A
A

13
CVK
G200
AKFG
C
A
B

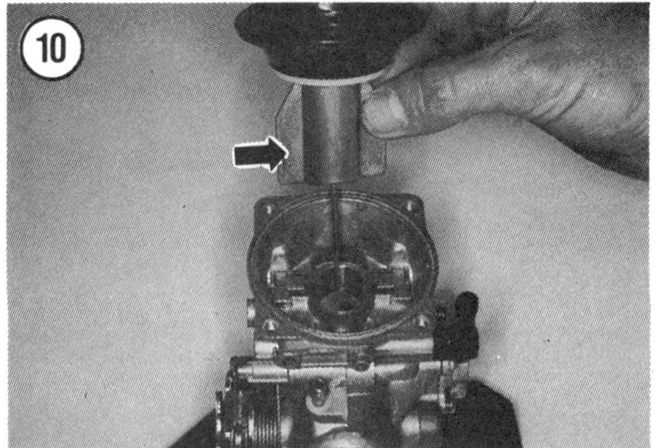
10

14
A
B

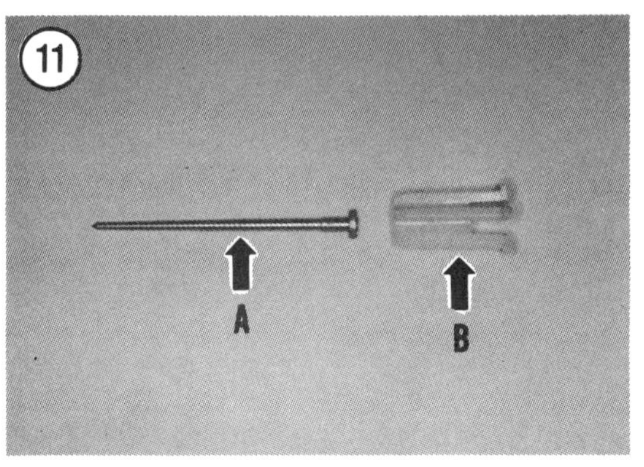
11
A
B

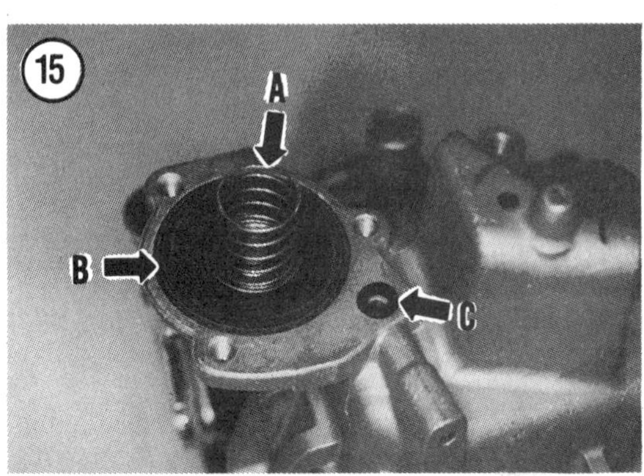
15
A
B
C

8

10. Remove the screws securing the float bowl to the carb body and remove the float bowl (B, **Figure 14**) and its O-ring seal.
11. Remove the float pin (**Figure 16**) from the float chamber mounting boss.
12. Lift the float and needle valve (B, **Figure 17**) from the float bowl.
13. Unscrew and remove the pilot jet (**Figure 18**).
14. Unscrew and remove the main jet (A, **Figure 19**) and then unscrew and remove the needle jet holder (B, **Figure19**).

NOTE
The pilot air screw is preset at the factory and should not be adjusted except during carburetor overhaul. If you must remove the pilot air screw, carefully perform the following steps so you can reinstall it in precisely the same factory-set position.

NOTE
U.S., Canadian and Swiss models have a plug to prevent tampering with the pilot air screw.

15. Unscrew and remove the pilot air screw by performing the following:
   a. On U.S., Canadian and Swiss models, drill a hole in the plug, and use an awl or other suitable tool to pry out the plug.
   b. Turn the pilot air screw (C, **Figure 19**) in, and record the number of turns it takes to lightly seat the pilot air screw. You will have to reset the pilot air screw to this same position during assembly.
   c. Unscrew and remove the pilot air screw and its spring.
16. If it's still in place, remove the O-ring gasket (**Figure 20**) from the float bowl.
17. Remove the drain screw (**Figure 21**) from the float bowl.

NOTE
*Further disassembly is neither necessary nor recommended. If throttle shaft (A, **Figure 22**) or valve (B, **Figure 22**) is damaged, take the carburetor body and/or float chamber to a dealer for replacement.*

18. Clean and inspect all parts as described in this chapter.

16

17

18

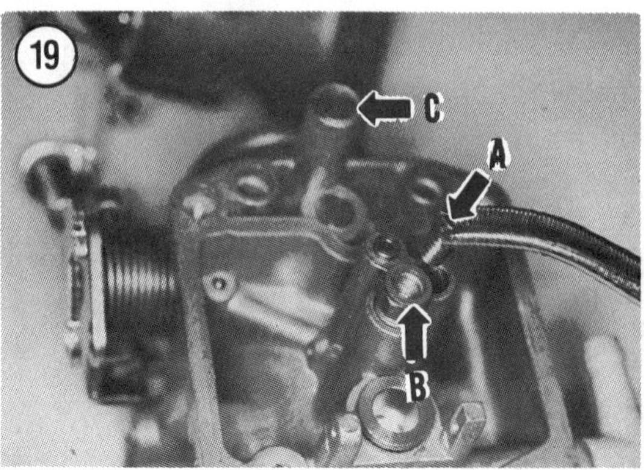

19

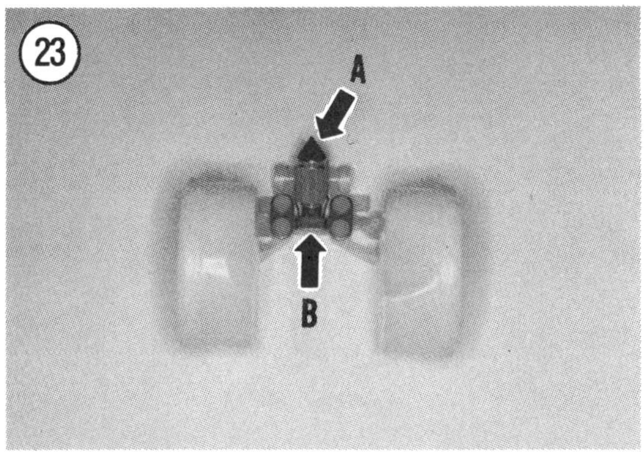

Assembly

1. Install the float and needle valve into the float chamber by performing the following:
   a. Make sure the needle valve (A, **Figure 23**) is still in place on the float arm (B, **Figure 23**).
   b. Install the float and needle valve (B **Figure 17**) into place in the float bowl.
   c. Install the pivot pin (A, **Figure 16**). Press down on the pivot pin only in the area of the mounting boss to avoid bending the pivot pin.
   d. After the pivot pin is installed, make sure the float pivots freely on the pin to ensure proper fuel flow.
2. Install the pilot air screw by performing the following:
   a. Screw in the pilot air screw (C, **Figure 19**) until it is lightly seated in the carburetor body.
   b. Back it out the same number of turns you recorded during removal.

CAUTION

Apply the bonding agent sparingly during the next step. Excessive bonding agent could permanently bond the pilot air screw to the carburetor body.

   c. On U. S., Canadian and Swiss models, apply a bonding agent to the circumference of a new plug and install the plug.
3. Install the needle jet holder (B, **Figure 19**) and tighten it securely.
4. Install the main jet (A, **Figure 19**) and tighten it securely.
5. Install the pilot jet (**Figure 18**), and tighten it securely.
6. Reinstall the drain screw (**Figure 21**) into the float bowl. Tighten it securely.
7. Install a new O-ring gasket (**Figure 20**) into the float bowl and reinstall the float bowl on the carburetor body. Make sure the O-ring seats completely against the carburetor body.
8. If removed, install the small O-ring (C, **Figure 15**) into the accelerator valve housing in the bottom of the float bowl.
9. Install the accelerator valve diaphragm (B, **Figure 15**), and install the spring (A, **Figure 15**) onto the diaphragm.
10. Install the accelerator valve cover (A, **Figure 14**), and secure it in place with the 3 screws.

11. If removed, install the small O-ring (C, **Figure 13**) into the air cut valve housing in the carburetor body.

12. Install the air cut valve diaphragm (B, **Figure 13**), and install the spring (A, **Figure 13**) onto the diaphragm.

13. Install the air cut valve cover (A, **Figure 12**) and secure it in place with the two screws.

14. Assemble the vacuum piston/diaphragm assembly by performing the following:

   a. Install the jet needle into the vacuum piston/diaphragm assembly. Make sure the jet needle is correctly positioned in the recess in the top of the vacuum piston/diaphragm assembly.
   b. Fit the spring onto the spring seat with its open end going in first. Refer to **Figure 24**.
   c. Align the ribs of the spring seat with the grooves in the raised boss in the vacuum piston/diaphragm assembly and install the spring and spring seat assembly. When correctly aligned, the spring seat will *not* block the hole in the base of the vacuum piston/diaphragm assembly. This hole must remain open for proper vacuum piston/diaphragm assembly operation.

15. Correctly position the vacuum piston/diaphragm assembly and install it into the carburetor body (**Figure 10**).

16. Set the top cover onto the spring so the spring fits into the receptacle in the top cover.

17. Install the top cover (B, **Figure 9**) and screws (A, **Figure 9**). Tighten the screws securely.

18. Screw the starter plunger assembly (B, **Figure 8**) into place and tighten it securely.

19. Connect the fuel line (A, **Figure 8**) to the carburetor.

20. Insert your finger into the carburetor venturi and slowly push the vacuum piston/diaphragm assembly up in the carburetor body. It should move up freely and the spring should push the assembly back down.

21. After the carburetor is assembled, adjust the idle speed as described in Chapter Three.

Cleaning and Inspection

1. Thoroughly clean and dry all parts. Kawasaki does not recommend the use of a caustic carburetor cleaning solvent. Instead, clean carburetor parts in a

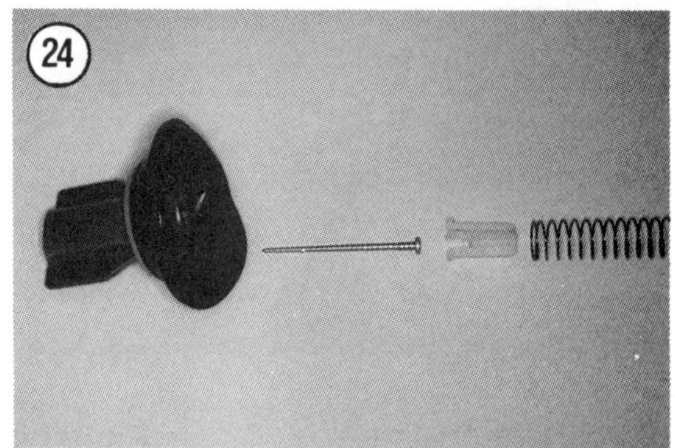
24

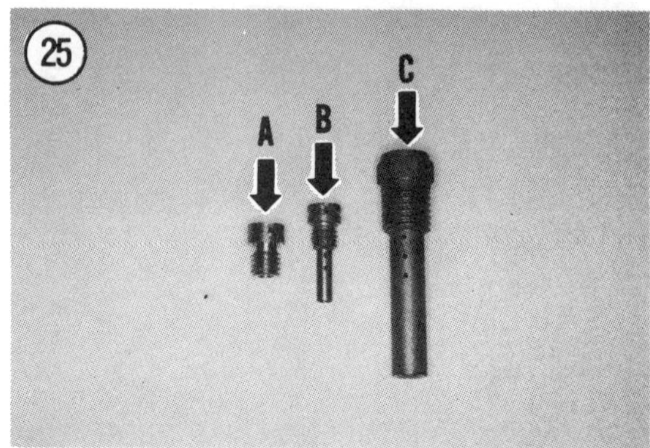

25

26

27

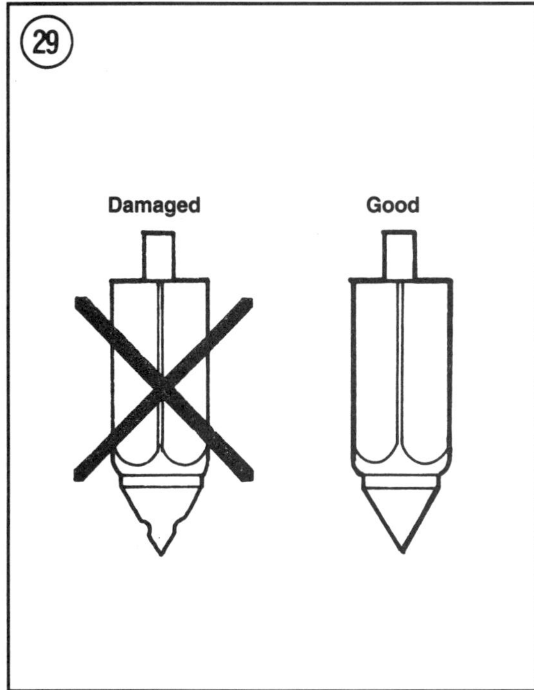

petroleum based solvent. Then rinse it in clean hot water.

2. Thoroughly dry the carburetor with compressed air before assembly. Be sure to blow out the jets and needle jet holder with compressed air.

3. Inspect the float chamber O-ring gasket (**Figure 20**) and all other O-rings. An O-ring tends to harden from prolonged use and, therefore, loses its ability to seal properly.

CAUTION

If compressed air is not available, allow the parts to air dry or use a clean lint-free cloth. Do not use a paper towel to dry carburetor parts. Small paper particles could plug openings in the carburetor body or jets.

CAUTION

Do not use a piece of wire to clean the jets. Minor gouges in a jet can alter flow rate and upset the air/fuel mixture.

4. Make sure the holes in the main jet (A, **Figure 25**), pilot jet (B, **Figure 25**) and needle jet holder (C, **Figure 25**) are clear. Clean them out if they are plugged in any way. Replace the holder and/or jets if you cannot unplug the holes.

5. Examine the jet needle, spring and spring seat (**Figure 24**) for wear or damage.

6. Make sure the diaphragm (**Figure 26**) is not torn or cracked. Replace any damaged or worn parts.

7. Inspect the piston valve (**Figure 27**) portion of the vacuum piston/diaphragm assembly for wear or damage. Replace the assembly if necessary.

8. Inspect the piston valve grooves (A, **Figure 28**) portion of the carburetor body for wear or damage. If damaged, replace the carburetor assembly.

9. Inspect the float (B, **Figure 23**) for deterioration or damage. If the float is suspected of leakage, place it in a container of non-caustic solution and push it down. If the float sinks or if bubbles appear (indicating a leak), replace the float assembly.

10. Inspect the end of the needle valve (**Figure 29**) and seat (A, **Figure 17**) for wear or damage; replace either or both parts if necessary.

11. Inspect the accelerator valve diaphragm, spring and cover (**Figure 30**) for damage. Make sure the opening in the cover is open.

12. Inspect the air cut valve diaphragm, spring and cover (**Figure 31**) for damage. Make sure the opening in the cover is open.

13. Make sure all openings in the carburetor body are clear. Refer to **Figure 32**, **Figure 33**, B, **Figure 28** and **Figure 34**.

14. Inspect the choke plunger (**Figure 35**) and spring for wear or damage. Replace if necessary.

15. Inspect the linkage for wear, looseness or damage; replace as necessary. Refer to **Figure 36**. Make sure the linkage moves smoothly.

16. Make sure all cotter pins are in place and that the ends are bent over completely.

CARBURETOR ADJUSTMENTS

Fuel Level Inspection

The fuel level must be checked with the carburetor assembly installed on the engine. This inspection *cannot* be performed with the carburetor removed.

1. Use a scissors jack or jack stands to securely support the bike on level ground. The bike must be in a true vertical position or the reading will be false.

2. Remove the fuel tank and air cleaner housing as described in this chapter.

3. Temporarily reattach the fuel tank and reconnect the fuel line (A, **Figure 37**) to the shutoff valve. Be sure the shutoff valve is turned to the ON or RES position.

4. Attach a piece of clear vinyl tubing to the drain outlet fitting (A, **Figure 38**) on the carburetor float bowl.

5. Connect the Kawasaki fuel level gauge (part No. 57001-1017) to the end of the vinyl tubing.

6. Hold the fuel level gauge in a vertical position next to the carburetor body. Position the gauge so its zero line (B, **Figure 38**) is several millimeters higher than the upper edge of the float bowl (C, **Figure 38**).

32

33

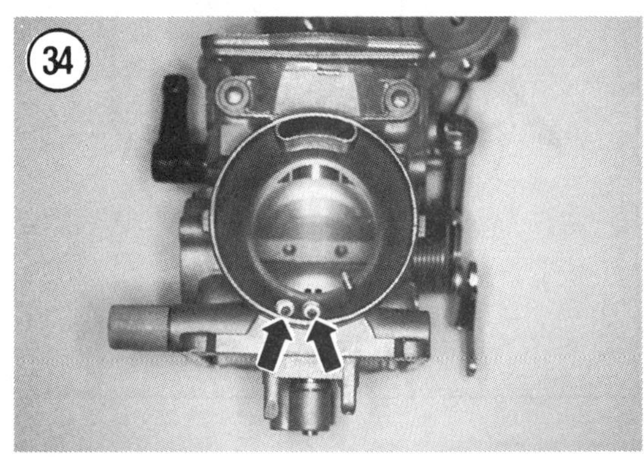

34

31

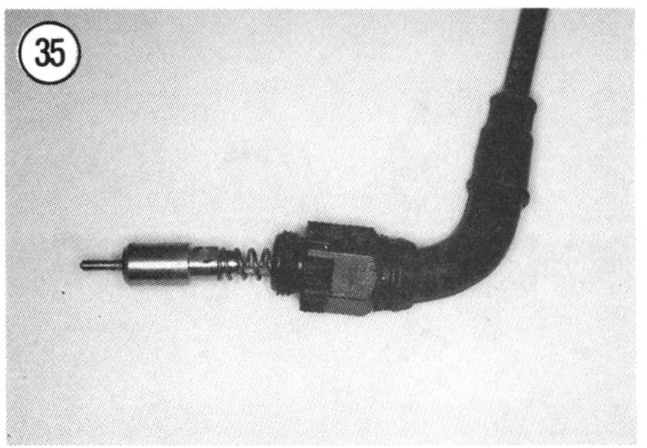

35

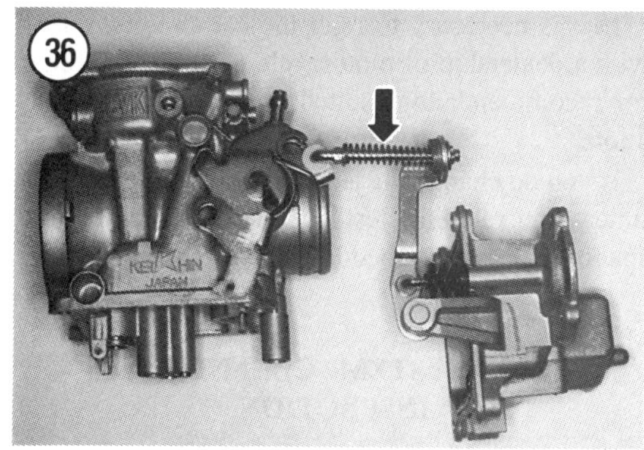

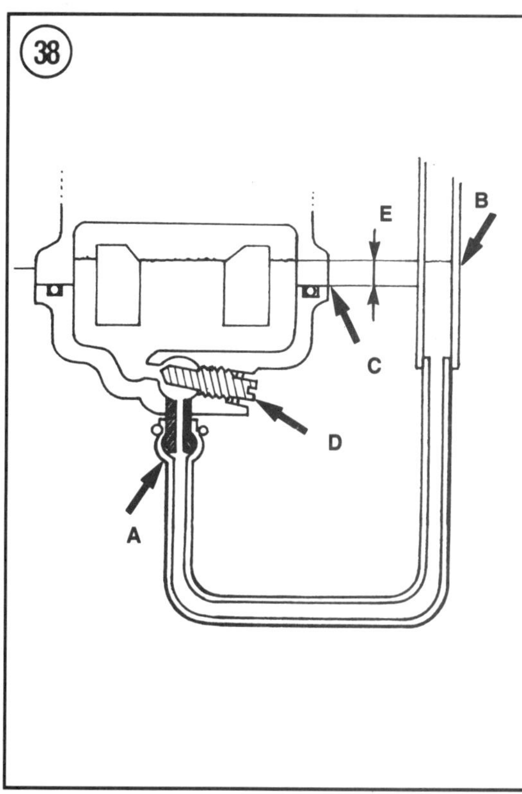

7. Turn the fuel shutoff valve to the PRI position (B, **Figure 37**).

8. Unscrew the carburetor drain screw (D, **Figure 38**) several turns to allow fuel to enter the fuel level gauge. Wait until the fuel level in the gauge settles.

NOTE

Do not lower the zero line on the fuel level gauge below the upper edge of the float bowl. If the fuel level gauge is lowered and then raised again, the fuel inside the fuel level gauge will be slightly higher than the actual fuel level, resulting in a false reading.

9. Keeping the gauge vertical, slowly lower the fuel level gauge until the zero line (B, **Figure 38**) is even with the upper edge of the float bowl (C, **Figure 38**). Read the fuel level in the gauge and record the reading.

10. Turn the fuel shutoff valve to the ON or RES position.

11. Tighten the carburetor drain screw. Drain the fuel in the gauge and hose into a container. Dispose of the fuel properly.

12. If necessary, adjust fuel level as described in this chapter.

13. Remove the fuel tank.

14. Reinstall the air cleaner housing and fuel tank as described in this chapter.

8

Fuel Level Adjustment

The carburetor assembly must be removed and partially disassembled for this adjustment.

1. Remove the carburetor assembly as described in this chapter.

2. Drain the fuel from the float bowl into a suitable container.

3. Remove the float bowl from the carburetor body.

4. Hold the float chamber almost vertically so the float contacts the spring-loaded rod (A, **Figure 39**) in the valve needle, but does not push it down.

5. Measure the distance between the top of the float and the surface of the float chamber (B, **Figure 39**).

6. If the float height is outside of the specification in **Table 1**, remove the float pin (**Figure 40**) from the mounting boss and remove the float.

7. Bend the float tang (**Figure 41**) *very slightly* until the float height is within specification. Increasing

the float height lowers the fuel level; decreasing the float height raises the fuel level.

8. Assemble the carburetor as described in this chapter.

9. Install the carburetor assembly as described in this chapter.

NOTE

If the float tang cannot be adjusted sufficiently to achieve the correct fuel level in the carburetor, either the float and/or the float valve may be faulty. Replace either of these parts as necessary.

10. Recheck the fuel level as described in this chapter to verify that the float tang was adjusted correctly.

Rejetting the Carburetors

Do not try to solve a poor running engine problem by rejetting the carburetor if all of the following conditions hold true:

a. The engine operated properly in the past with the standard jetting.
b. The engine is not modified.
c. The motorcycle is being operated in the same geographical region under the same general climatic conditions as in the past.
d. The motorcycle was and is being ridden at average highway speeds.

If these conditions all hold true, the chances are that the problem is due to a malfunction in the carburetor or in another component. Changing carburetor jet size probably will not solve the problem.

Rejetting the carburetor may be necessary if any of the following conditions hold true:

a. A non-standard type of air filter element is being used.
b. A non-standard exhaust system is installed on the motorcycle.
c. Any of the top end components in the engine (pistons, camshafts, valves, compression ratio have been modified.
d. The motorcycle is in use at considerably higher or lower altitudes or in a considerably hotter or colder climate than in the past.
e. The motorcycle is being operated at considerably higher speeds than before.
f. Someone has previously changed the carburetor jetting.
g. The motorcycle has never operated correctly.

If it is necessary to rejet the carburetors, check with a dealership or motorcycle performance tuner for recommendations suited to your specific situation.

If you do change the jets, do so only one size at a time. After rejetting, test ride the bike and read the spark plugs as described in Chapter Three.

FUEL SYSTEM CLEANLINESS INSPECTION

1. Use a scissors jack, wooden block, or jack stands to securely support the bike in an upright position on level ground.

2. Remove the fuel tank and air cleaner housing as described in this chapter.

3. Attach a piece of clear vinyl tubing to the drain outlet fitting (A, **Figure 38**) on the carburetor float bowl.

4. Place the loose ends in a *clean* transparent container.

5. Turn the fuel shutoff valve on the fuel tank to the PRI position (B, **Figure 37**).

6. Unscrew the bottom cover drain screw (D, **Figure 38**) several turns so fuel flows from the tube.

7. Tighten the carburetor drain screw and disconnect the tubing. Turn the shutoff valve back to the ON position.

8. Inspect the fuel for water, rust and other contaminates. If water is present in the fuel, it will be in a

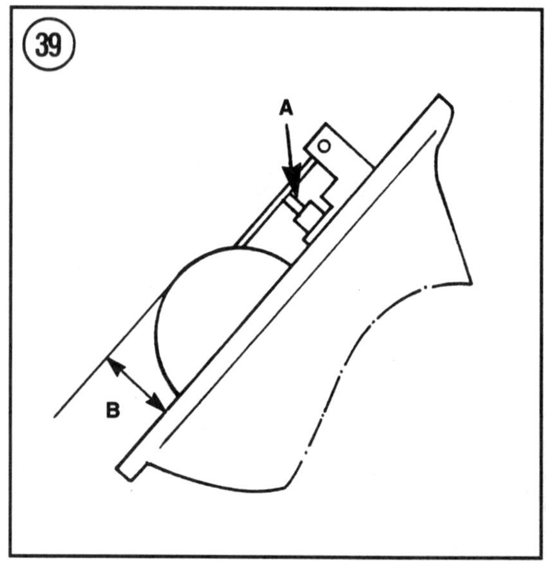

layer by itself below the fuel. Dispose of this fuel properly.

9. Water in the fuel usually is a result of water contaminated gasoline or from a leaking fuel filler cap that has allowed moisture to enter the fuel system.

10. Rust particles may have also come from contaminated gasoline or from an internally rusted fuel tank.

11. If water and/or rust are present in the fuel system, correct the problem as soon as possible.

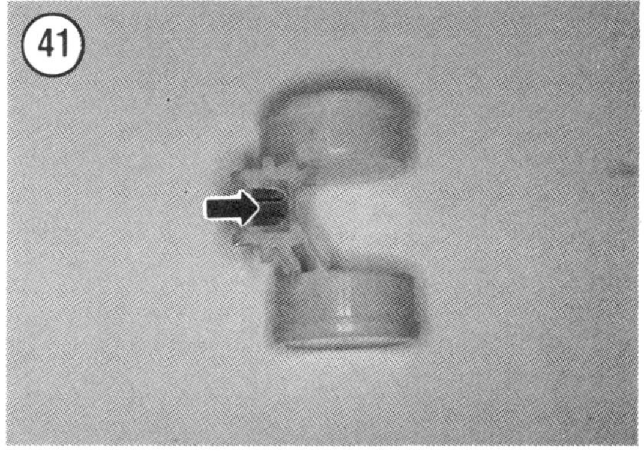

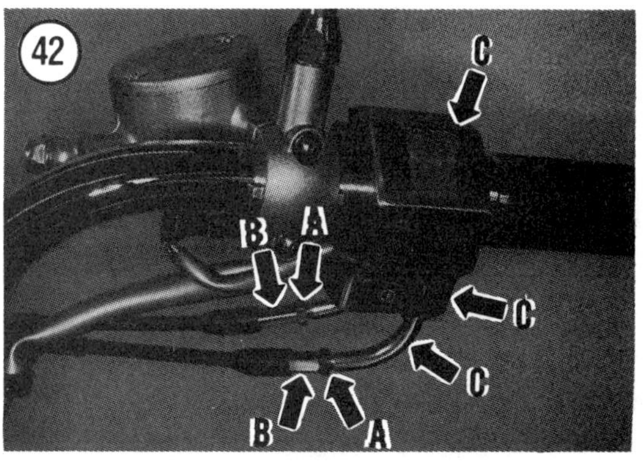

12. Remove and disassemble the carburetor. Clean all components to remove all contaminants. Make sure all jets are clear.

13. Remove the fuel shutoff valve from the fuel tank as described in this chapter and clean its integral fuel filter.

14. Remove the fuel tank as described in this chapter. Inspect the fuel tank for rust accumulation, and check the filler cap for any possible leaks. Have the fuel tank cleaned to remove any rust. Correct any possible fuel filler cap leaks.

THROTTLE CABLE REPLACEMENT

This procedure describes the replacement of both throttle cables from the throttle grip to the carburetor assembly.

NOTE
The throttle pull cable is shorter than the push cable. Also the pull cable has a guide at the carburetor end. Do not confuse one cable with the other during installation.

1. Remove the carburetor as described in this chapter.

2. At the throttle grip, loosen both throttle cable locknuts (A, **Figure 42**).

3. Remove the screws securing the right-hand switch assembly (C, **Figure 42**) together and separate the switch halves.

4. If necessary, turn the cable adjusters (B, **Figure 42**) to achieve the maximum amount of slack in both throttle cables. Disengage the throttle cables from the throttle grip. Mark the push and pull cable receptacles in the throttle grip so the new cables will be properly installed.

5. Remove the throttle cables from the upper half of the right-hand switch assembly.

NOTE
The piece of string attached in the next step will be used to pull the new throttle cables back through the frame so they will be routed in exactly the same position as the old ones were.

6. Tie a piece of heavy string or cord (approximately 3 ft. [1 m long]) to the carburetor end of both throttle cables. Wrap this end with masking or duct tape. Tie

the other end of the string to the frame in the adjacent area.

7. At the throttle grip end of the cable, carefully pull the cables (and attached string) out through the frame. Make sure the attached string follows the same path as the cable through the frame.

8. Remove the tape and untie the string from the old cables.

9. Lubricate the new cables as described in Chapter Three.

10. Tie the string to the carburetor end of both new throttle cables and wrap it with tape.

11. Carefully pull the string back through the frame routing the new cables along the same path as the old cables.

12. Remove the tape and untie the string from the cables and frame.

13. Attach both throttle cables to the throttle wheel. Be sure the push and pull cables are installed to the correct fitting on the throttle wheel.

14. Reinstall the carburetor as described in this chapter.

15. Temporarily tighten the locknuts (A, **Figure 43**) on the mid-cable adjusters.

16. Insert the throttle cables into the upper half of the right-hand switch assembly.

17. Connect each throttle cable to its receptacle in the throttle grip.

18. Fit the upper half of the switch assembly in place and install the screws securing the right-hand switch assembly (C, **Figure 42**) together.

19. Connect the battery negative lead as described in Chapter Three.

20. Install the fuel tank as described in this chapter.

21. Install the seat as described in Chapter Fourteen.

22. Adjust the throttle cables as described in Chapter Three.

23. Test ride the bike slowly at first, and make sure the throttle is operating correctly.

CHOKE CABLE REPLACEMENT

This procedure describes the replacement of the choke cable from the choke housing to the carburetor assembly.

1. Remove the seat as described in Chapter Fourteen.

2. Remove the fuel tank as described in this chapter.

3. Loosen the jam nut (A, **Figure 44**) securing the choke cable to its mounting bracket on the frame. Remove the cable from the bracket.

4. Remove the choke cable holder screws (**Figure 45**) from on top of the battery case.

5. Remove the carburetor as described in this chapter.

6. Remove the starter plunger (**Figure 46**) from the carburetor body and disconnect the choke cable from the starter plunger.

7. Connect the new cable to the starter plunger and reinstall the plunger.

8. Reinstall the carburetor.

9. Route the new cable though the frame.

10. Fit the choke cable into the cable holders beneath the frame.

11. Fit the choke cable into its mounting bracket and secure it in place by securely tightening the jam nut (A, **Figure 44**).

12. Tighten the choke cable holder screws (**Figure 45**) on top of the battery case.

13. Adjust the choke cable by turning the friction nut (B, **Figure 44**) until the choke operates properly. Apply the minimal amount of friction necessary to

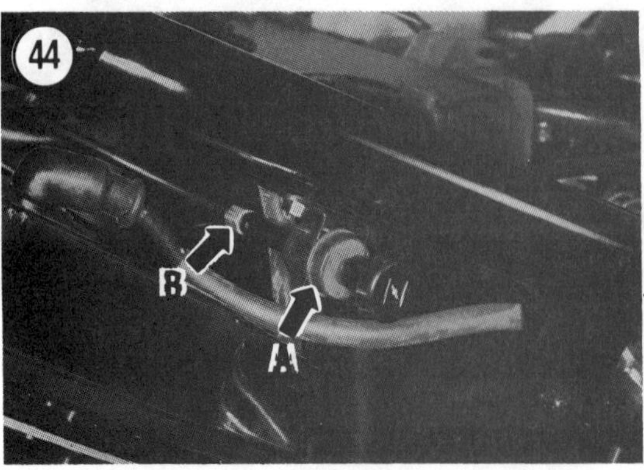

hold the choke open while also permitting smooth operation of the cable.

AIR FILTER

Air Filter Housing Removal/Installation

NOTE

Label each hose and its respective fitting on the air filter housing during the following procedure. This will help you correctly reattach all hoses during assembly.

Refer to **Figure 47** for this procedure.

1. Remove the seat as described in Chapter Fourteen.
2. Remove the fuel tank as described in this chapter.
3. Remove the bolts securing the surge tank to the frame (**Figure 48**) and remove the surge tank.

4. Remove the air filter cover bolt (A, **Figure 49**), the air filter cover (B, **Figure 49**), then remove the air filter element (**Figure 50**).
5. Remove the air filter housing bolts (A, **Figure 51**) and disconnect the housing (B, **Figure 51**) from the carburetor mounting plate.
6. Disconnect the engine breather hose (A, **Figure 52**) and the vacuum switch valve hose (B, **Figure 52**) from the back of the air filter housing.
7. On California models, remove the charcoal canister hose from the air filter housing.
8. Remove the breather hose (A, **Figure 53**) and remove the air filter housing drain line (B, **Figure 53**).
9. Remove the air filter housing.
10. Stuff a clean, lint-free cloth into the carburetor bore to keep out contaminants.
11. Blow the air filter element clean with compressed air as described in Chapter Three.
12. Inspect the air filter housing (**Figure 54**) for cracks and other damage. Pay particular attention to the hose fittings on the housing. Replace the housing if it is damaged.
13. Install by reversing the removal steps while noting the following:
    a. Be sure all hoses are connected to the correct fittings on the housing.
    b. Make sure the surge tank is seated correctly on the air filter housing duct.
    c. Refer to Chapter Three and clean the air filter element prior to installing it in the housing.

Surge Tank Removal/Installation

Refer to **Figure 47** for this procedure.

1. Remove the seat as described in Chapter Fourteen.
2. Remove the fuel tank as described in this chapter.
3. Remove the bolts securing the surge tank to the frame (**Figure 48**) and remove the surge tank.
4. Installation is the reverse of removal. Be sure the surge tank is seated correctly on the air filter housing duct.

FUEL TANK

Removal/Installation

Refer to **Figure 55** for this procedure.

1. Remove the seat as described in Chapter Fourteen.

2. Disconnect the battery negative lead as described in Chapter Three.

3. Remove the meter assembly from the tank as described in Chapter Nine.

4. Be sure the fuel shutoff valve is in the ON or RES position.

5. Disconnect the fuel line (A **Figure 56**) from the shutoff valve.

6. Disconnect the vacuum line (B, **Figure 56**) from the fitting on the fuel shutoff valve. Plug the end of the line to prevent the entry of foreign matter.

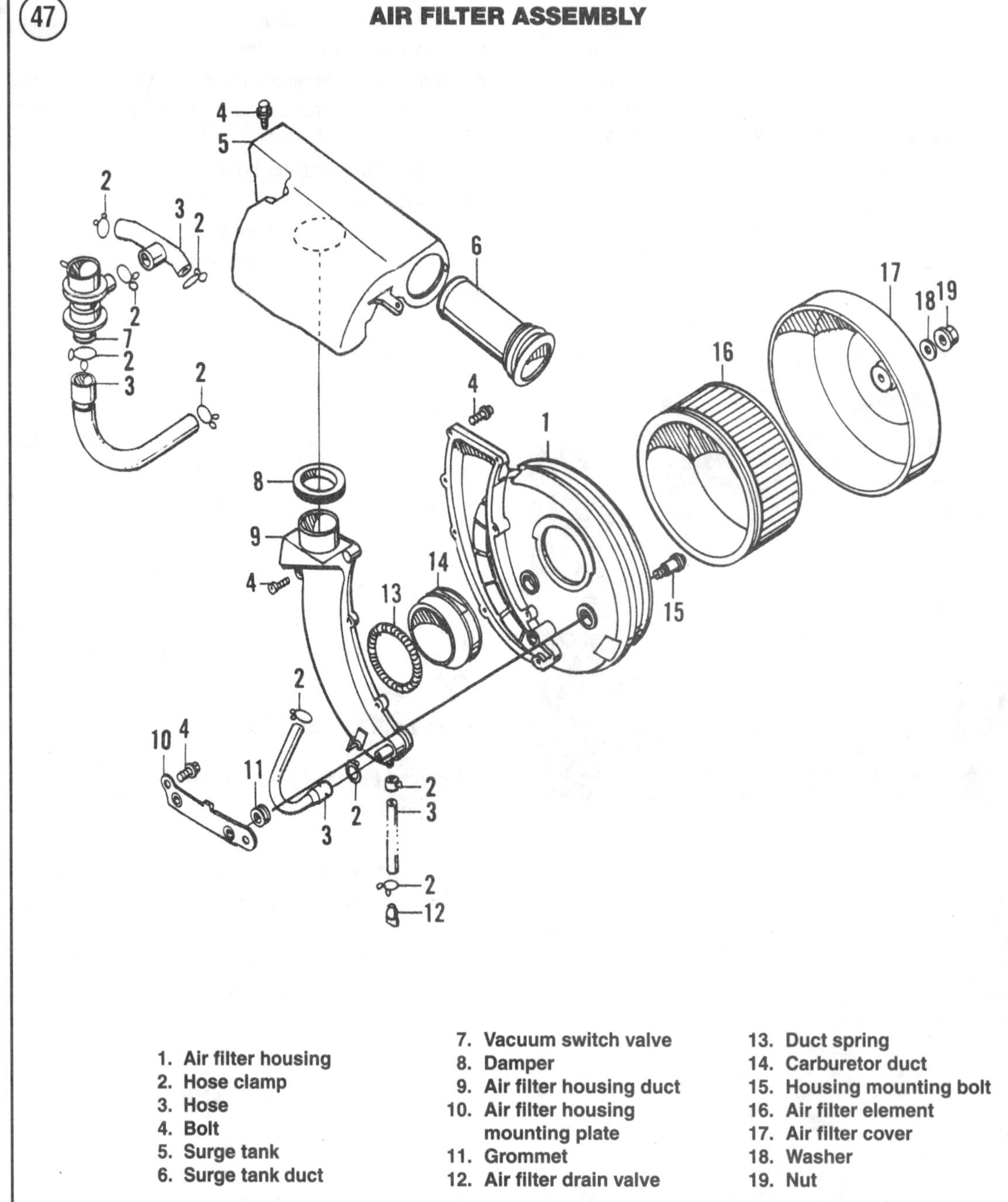

(47) **AIR FILTER ASSEMBLY**

1. Air filter housing
2. Hose clamp
3. Hose
4. Bolt
5. Surge tank
6. Surge tank duct
7. Vacuum switch valve
8. Damper
9. Air filter housing duct
10. Air filter housing mounting plate
11. Grommet
12. Air filter drain valve
13. Duct spring
14. Carburetor duct
15. Housing mounting bolt
16. Air filter element
17. Air filter cover
18. Washer
19. Nut

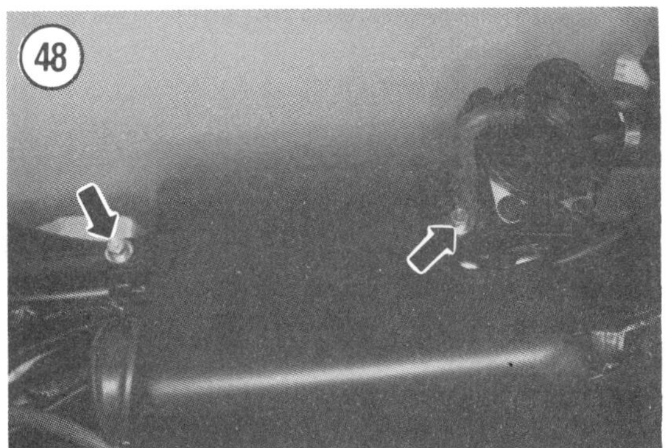

7. Remove the flange bolt securing the front of the fuel tank (**Figure 57**).

8. Remove the flange bolt (**Figure 58**) securing the rear of the fuel tank.

CAUTION
California models are equipped with an evaporative emission control system. If gasoline, water, or other contaminants enter the canister, it must be replaced. Plug the evaporative emissions control lines to prevent entry of contaminants.

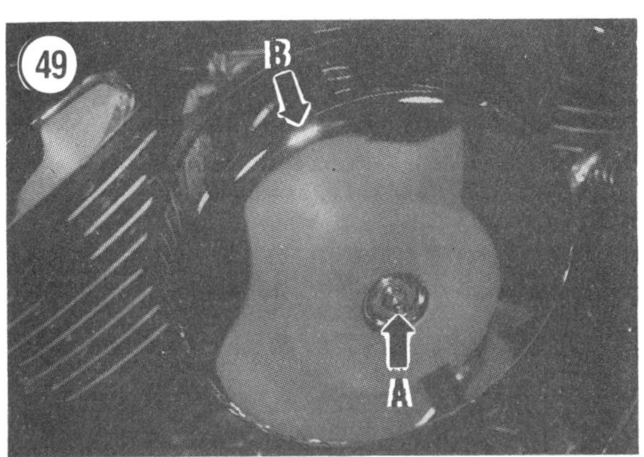

8

FUEL TANK

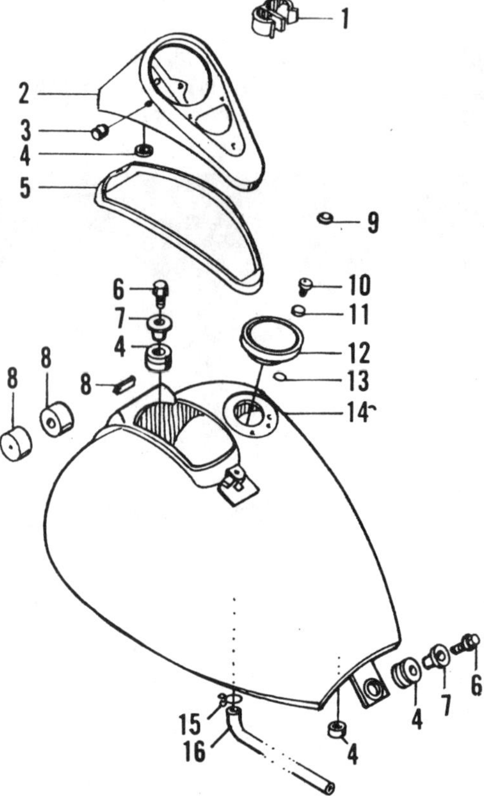

1. Clamp
   (except California models)
2. Meter assembly
3. Trip knob
4. Grommet
5. Meter damper
6. Bolt
7. Collar
8. Damper
9. Cap seal
   (California models only)
10. Screw
11. Washer
12. Fuel cap
13. O-ring
14. Fuel tank
15. Hose clamp
16. Hose

9. On California models, partially lift the tank at the rear and disconnect the evaporative emission system vent lines from the fuel tank. Plug each line.

10. Lift up the tank, pull it rearward and remove the fuel tank from the frame.

11. Inspect the fuel tank mounting tabs (A, **Figure 59**) for cracks or damage.

12. Open the fuel filler cap and inspect the cap gasket (A, **Figure 60**). Replace if it has started to deteriorate or harden.

13. Make sure the breather hole (B, **Figure 60**) is clear. If the hole is plugged, replace the filler cap.

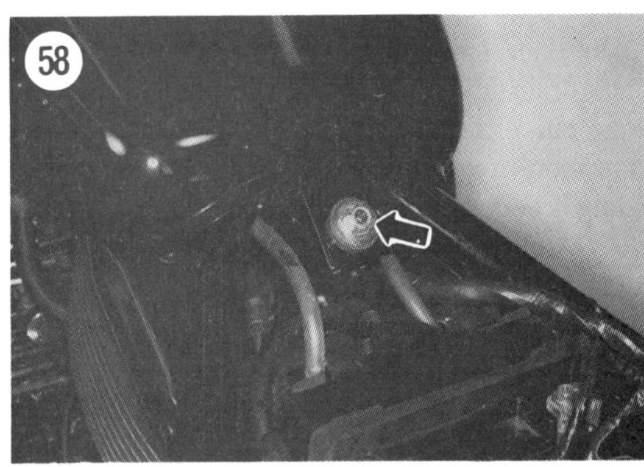

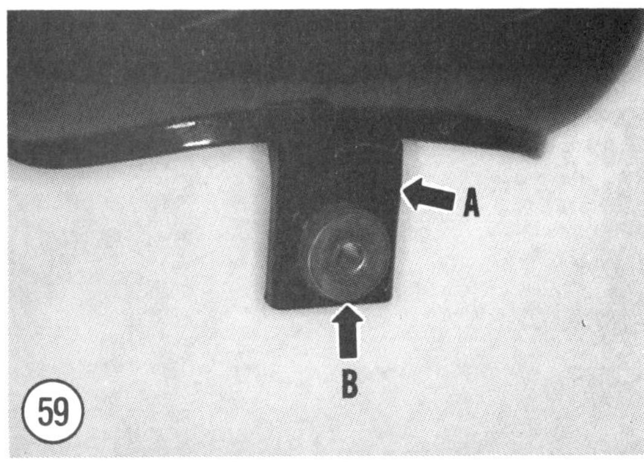

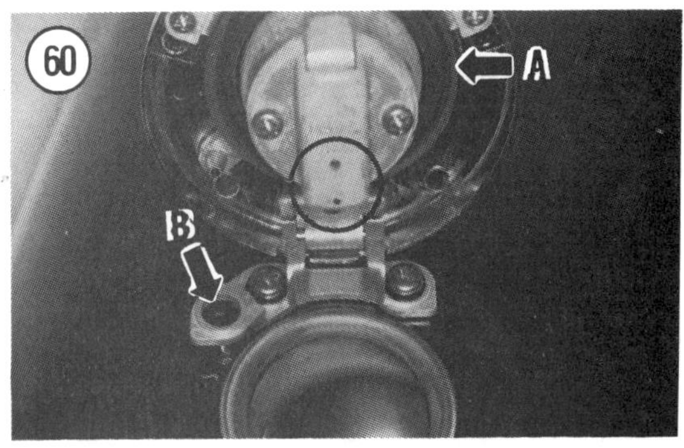

14. Install by reversing the removal steps while noting the following:

a. Make sure the rubber cushion and metal collar (B, **Figure 59**) are in place in each tank mount.
b. Be sure the two rubber dampers are in place on the frame.
c. Make sure the fuel line (A, **Figure 56**) and vacuum line (B, **Figure 56**) are secure on the shutoff valve.
d. Turn the fuel shutoff valve to the ON position. Start the engine and check for fuel leaks.

FUEL SHUTOFF VALVE AND FILTER

Removal/Installation

Refer to **Figure 61** for this procedure.

WARNING
Some fuel may spill in the following procedure. Work in a well-ventilated area at least 50 ft. (15m) from any sparks or flames, including gas appliance pilot lights. Do not allow anyone

8

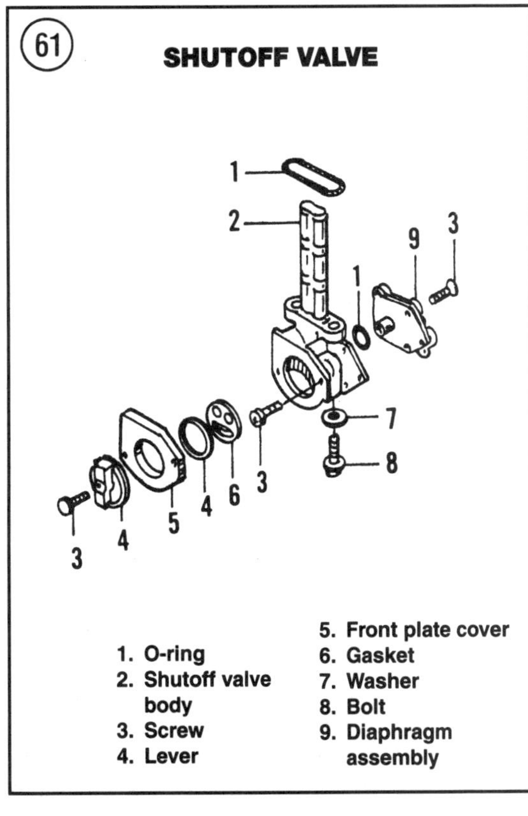

to smoke in the area. Keep a B/C rated fire extinguisher nearby.

1. Remove the fuel tank as described in this chapter.
2. Place a blanket or several towels on the workbench to protect the surface of the fuel tank.
3. Drain the fuel from the tank into a clean, sealable container.
4. Turn the fuel tank on its side with the fuel shutoff valve side facing up.
5. Remove the screws (A, **Figure 62**) and nylon washers securing the shutoff valve to the fuel tank and remove the valve (B, **Figure 62**).
6. After removing the valve, insert the corner of a lint-free cloth into the opening in the tank to prevent the entry of foreign matter or tape it closed.
7. Inspect the shutoff valve mounting O-ring; replace if necessary.
8. Clean the filter portion of the valve with a medium soft toothbrush and blow out with compressed air. If the filter is broken in any area or starting to deteriorate, replace the shutoff valve. The filter is an integral part of the shutoff valve and cannot be replaced separately.
9. If the shutoff valve leaks or allows fuel to flow when the valve is in the ON or RES position, inspect the gasket and O-rings by performing the following:
   a. Remove the lever and cover plate from the valve body.
   b. Remove the diaphragm assembly from the valve body.
   c. Inspect the gasket and O-rings for deterioration or damage and replace as necessary.
10. Install by reversing the removal steps while noting the following:
   a. Be sure to use nylon washers under the valve mounting bolts. Do not substitute metal washers, as they will not seal the bolts sufficiently and cause a fuel leak.
   b. Pour a small amount of gasoline into the tank after installing the valve and check for leaks. If a leak is present, solve the problem immediately—do not reinstall the fuel tank with a leaking valve.

CRANKCASE BREATHER SYSTEM (U.S. ONLY)

To comply with clean air standards, all models are equipped with a closed crankcase breather system. The system routes the engine combustion gases into the air filter housing. From here they are drawn into the intake tract and burned in the combustion chamber.

Inspection/Cleaning

Make sure the hose clamps at each end of both hoses are tight. Check the hose for deterioration and replace as necessary.

NOTE
California models are not equipped with a collector at the end of the air filter housing drain hose.

Disconnect the collector (**Figure 63**) from the end of the drain tube attached to the air filter housing and drain out all residue. Perform this cleaning procedure more frequently if a considerable amount of riding is done at full throttle or in the rain.

EVAPORATIVE EMISSION CONTROL SYSTEM (CALIFORNIA MODELS ONLY)

To comply with the California Air Resources Board (CARB) regulations, an evaporative emission control system is installed on all models sold in California.

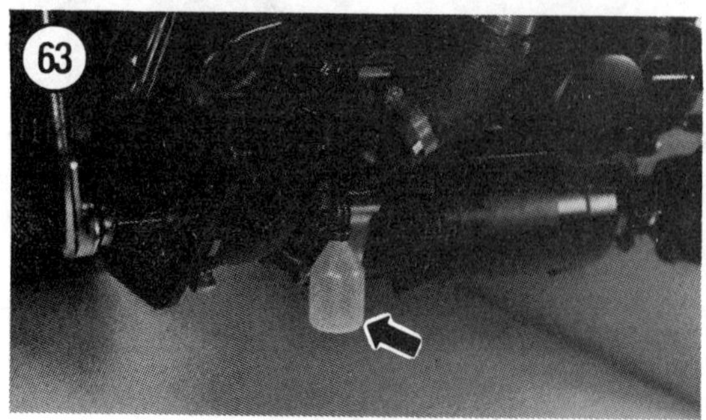

Fuel vapor from the fuel tank is routed into a charcoal canister where the vapor is stored when the engine is not running. When the engine is running, the vapor is drawn through a purge hose, into the air filter housing and into the carburetor to be burned. **Figure 64** shows the hose routing and components of the system.

Insert all hoses and fittings as indicated in **Table 1** of Chapter Three. Make sure all hose clamps are tight. Check all hoses for deterioration and replace as necessary.

Before removing the hoses from any part of this system, mark each hose and its fitting so you can easily determine where each hose goes during as-

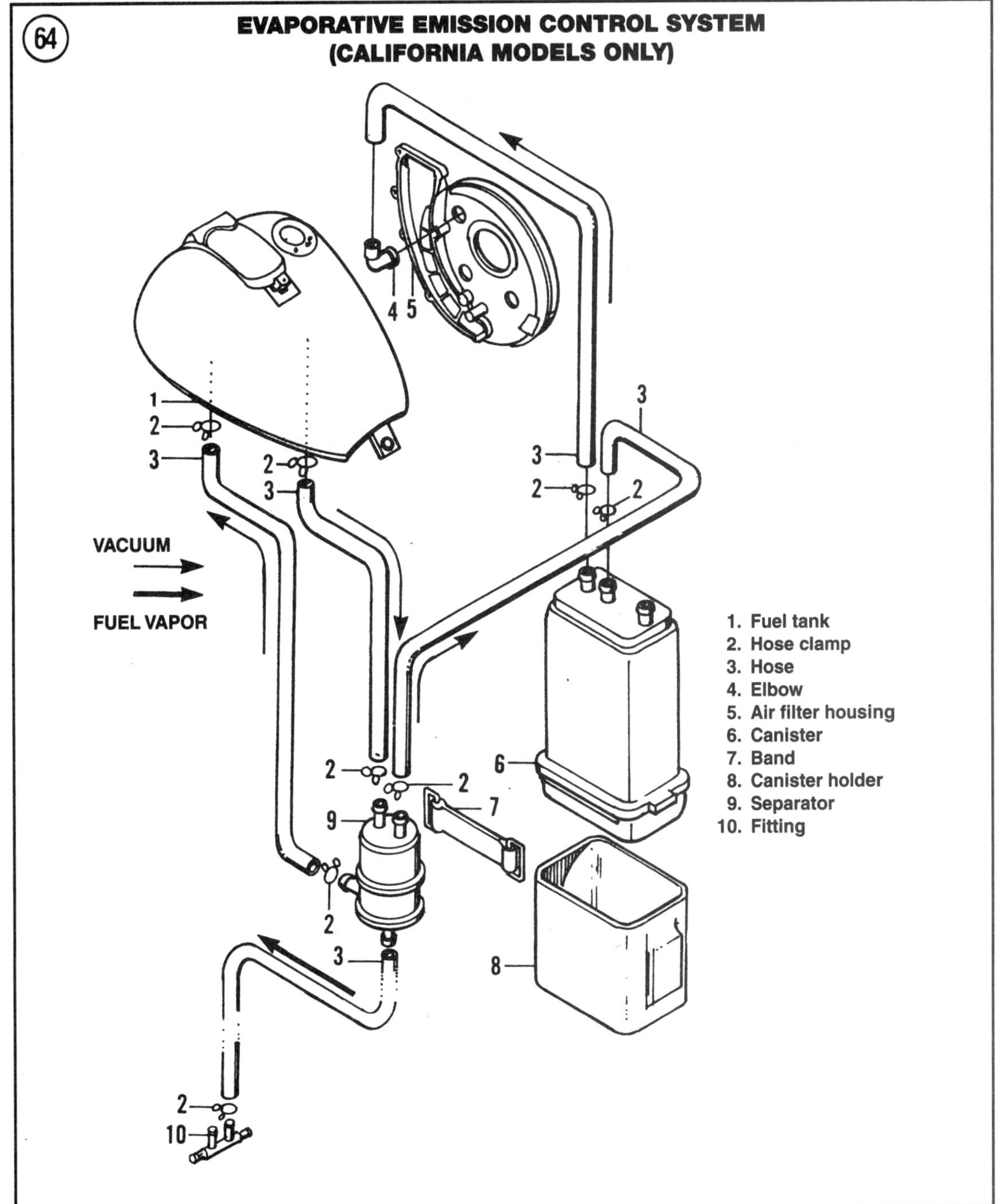

sembly. There are many vacuum hoses on these models. One can easily be installed incorrectly. Make the effort to ensure that all hoses are properly routed during assembly. The system will not operate correctly if any hose is installed on the wrong fitting.

Separator and Charcoal Canister Removal/Installation

1. Remove the rear exhaust pipe as described in this chapter.
2. Remove the right-hand side cover as described in Chapter Fourteen.
3. Remove the three screws (A, **Figure 65**) and remove the lower cover (B, **Figure 65**) from the storage box.

NOTE
Prior to removing the hoses from the separator and the charcoal canister, mark the hose and the fitting for assembly reference.

4. Unhook the rubber strap and remove the separator from the mounting bracket. Disconnect the hoses from the separator.
5. Carefully pull the charcoal canister and the rubber holder from the mounting bracket. Remove the canister from the bracket and disconnect the hoses from the canister.
6. If necessary, remove the screws securing the canister mounting bracket to the frame and remove the bracket.
7. Install by reversing the removal steps while noting the following:
   a. Be sure to install the hoses on their correct fittings on the charcoal canister and the separator.
   b. Make sure the hoses are not kinked, twisted or in contact with any sharp surfaces.

Inspection

1. Remove the separator and canister as described in this chapter.
2. Inspect the separator and the canister for cracks or damage.
3. If there is any type of exterior damage, replace the separator and/or canister.

VACUUM SWITCH VALVE

Removal/Installation

1. Remove the fuel tank as described in this chapter.
2. Disconnect the air filter housing line (A, **Figure 66**) from the inlet fitting on the vacuum switch valve.
3. Disconnect the vacuum line (B, **Figure 66**) from the fitting on the vacuum switch valve.
4. Disconnect the fresh air hose (C, **Figure 66**) from the fitting on each cylinder head cover and remove the vacuum switch valve (D, **Figure 66**).
5. Inspect all hoses for deterioration or damage; replace as necessary.
6. Inspect the vacuum valve switch as described in this chapter.
7. Install by reversing the removal steps while noting the following:
   a. Install all hoses onto their correct fittings without flattening or kinking them. They must be unobstructed to allow maximum flow.
   b. Make sure all hose clamps are on tight.

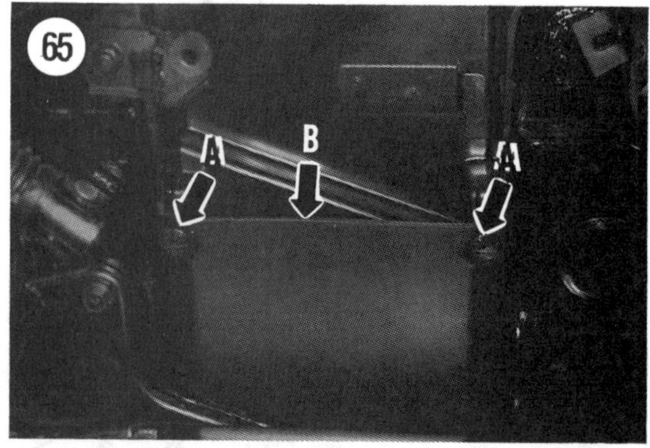

Inspection

When the throttle is open or during normal riding conditions, the vacuum switch valve should remain open and allow air to flow. During engine braking with the throttle closed, the valve should close and not allow air to flow through the valve.

1. Remove the vacuum switch valve as described in this chapter.

2. Attach a hand operated vacuum pump and gauge to the vacuum line fitting (B, **Figure 66**) in the valve.

3. Apply vacuum and check the operation of the valve as follows:

   a. At low vacuum, the valve should allow air to flow. Blow through the inlet fitting (A, **Figure 66**). You should feel air flowing from the outlet hose (C, **Figure 66**).

   b. Increase vacuum to 57-65 kPa (16.93-19.29) in. Hg. Blow through the inlet fitting. Air should not flow through the outlet hoses.

4. If the vacuum switch valve fails to operate as specified, replace the valve.

67

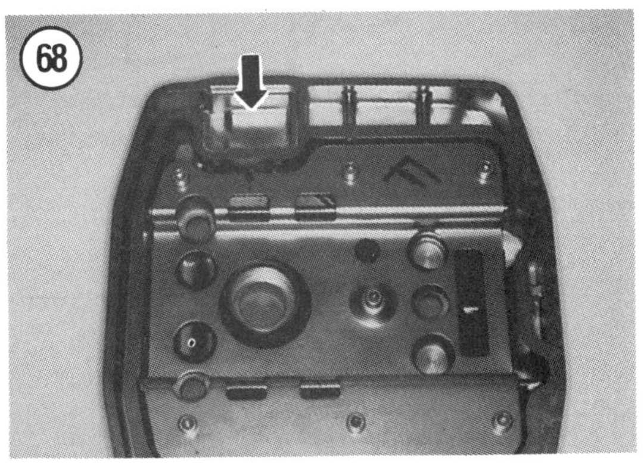

68

AIR SUCTION VALVE

Removal/ Installation

The air suction valve is a reed valve assembly that sits in cylinder head. The air suction valve allows fresh air to flow from the air filter housing into the exhaust port while blocking the flow of air out of the exhaust port and back to the filter housing.

1. Remove the cylinder head cover as described in Chapter Four.
2. Remove the air suction valve (**Figure 67**) from its housing in the cylinder head.
3.Inspect the air suction valve as described in this chapter.
4. Replacement parts are not available for the air suction valve assembly. If there is any question about the condition of the reed valve, replace it along with both gaskets.

NOTE
Make sure all parts of the reed valve are clean. Any contamination can cause a small amount of distortion in the reed plate. Any dirt that may be stuck between the reed valve and stopper will keep the reed valve from opening completely.

5. Make sure the air inlet opening in the cylinder head cover (**Figure 68**) is open.
6. Install the air suction valve (**Figure 67**) into its housing in the cylinder head. Be sure the valve stopper faces down into the cylinder head.
7. Reinstall the cylinder head cover as described in Chapter Four.
8. Repeat for the other air suction valve if necessary.

Inspection

1. Visually inspect the reed (**Figure 69**) for cracks, folds warps, heat damage or any other visible damage.
2. Check the reed contact area (B, **Figure 69**) of the valve holder. It should be free of grooves, scratches, heat damage or separation.

CAUTION
The air suction valve cannot be serviced. If any damage is noted, replace the valve as an assembly.

3. Replace the air suction valve if any damage is discovered.

4. Also check for carbon or other foreign material between the reed and the reed contact area. Wash the valve as necessary with solvent.

EXHAUST SYSTEM

The exhaust system is a vital performance component. Because of its design, it is a vulnerable piece of equipment. Check the exhaust system for deep dents and fractures. Repair them immediately or replace the damaged component. Check the exhaust system frame mounting flanges for cracks or fractures. Check the cylinder head mounting flanges for tightness.

Exhaust Pipe and Muffler Removal/Installation

Refer to **Figure 70** for this procedure.

1. Remove the two clamp bolts and remove the exhaust pipe cover. Note how the exhaust pipe cover engages the grommets on the exhaust pipe. The cover must be reinstalled in the same manner.

2. Loosen the clamp securing the front-to-rear muffler union. (A, **Figure 71**).

3A. On 1995 and 1996 VN800 models, remove the two bolts securing the exhaust pipe to the exhaust port.

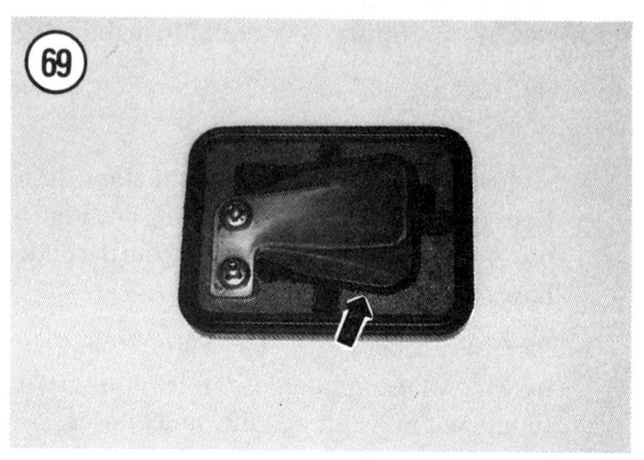

69

70

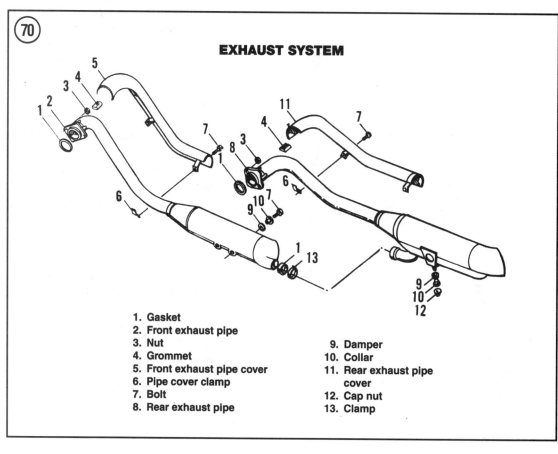

EXHAUST SYSTEM

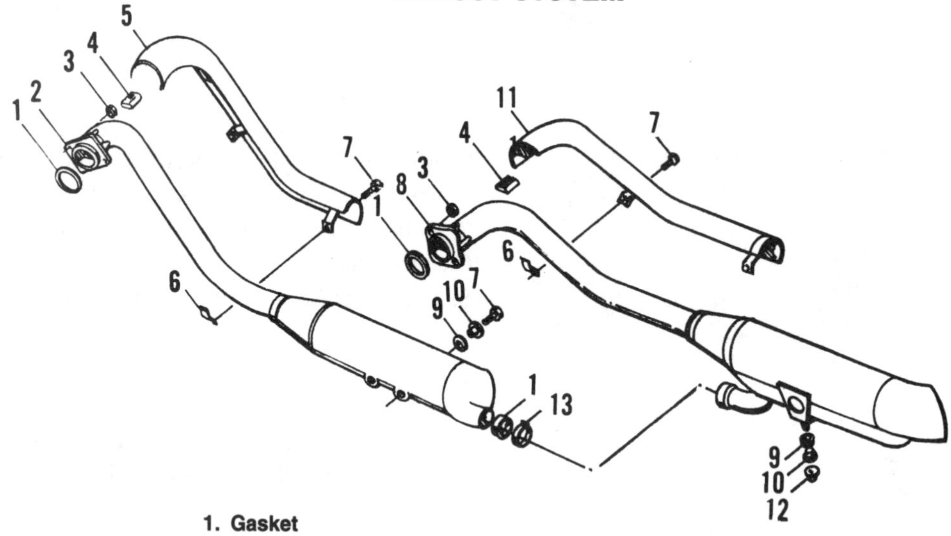

1. Gasket
2. Front exhaust pipe
3. Nut
4. Grommet
5. Front exhaust pipe cover
6. Pipe cover clamp
7. Bolt
8. Rear exhaust pipe
9. Damper
10. Collar
11. Rear exhaust pipe cover
12. Cap nut
13. Clamp

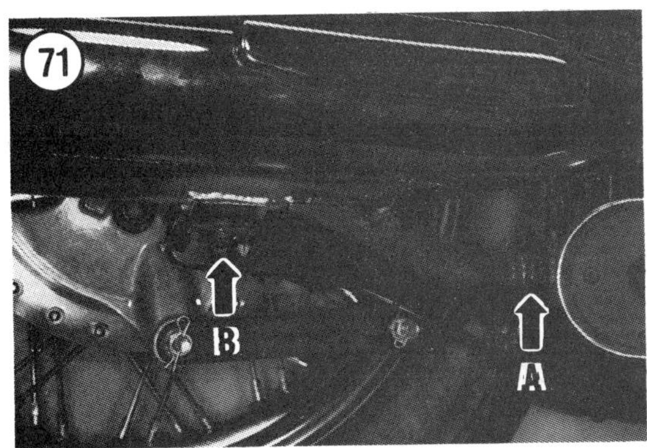

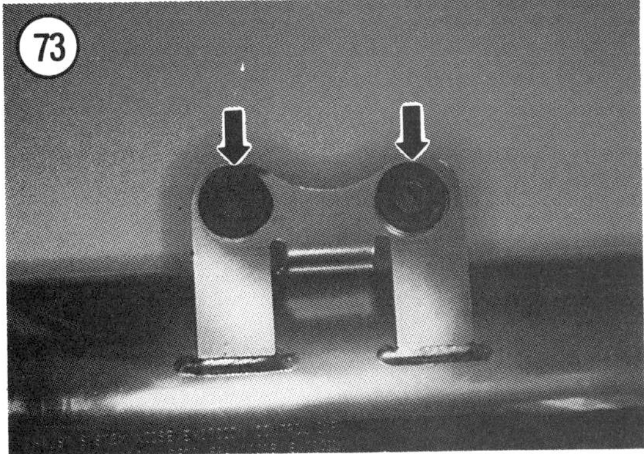

3B. On 1997 and 1998 VN800 and VN800 Classic models, remove the two nuts (**Figure 72**) securing the exhaust pipe to the exhaust port.

4A. When removing the front exhaust pipe, remove the two bolts securing the muffler bracket to the frame.

4B. When removing the rear exhaust pipe, remove the cap nut securing the muffler to the muffler stay (B, **Figure 71**).

5. Carefully remove the pipe from the cylinder head, disconnect the front-to-rear muffler union and remove the exhaust pipe.

6. Repeat the procedure to remove the other exhaust pipe if necessary.

7. Installation is the reverse of removal. Pay attention to the following:

   a. On the front exhaust pipe, be sure the damper and collar are installed on each fitting on the mounting bracket (**Figure 73**).
   b. On the rear exhaust pipe, be sure the damper and collar are installed on the mounting bracket on the frame (B, **Figure 71**)
   c. Install a new exhaust gasket on each exhaust pipe (**Figure 74**).
   d. Install a new gasket at the front-to-rear muffler union (A, **Figure 71**).

8. To minimize the chance of exhaust leakage, loosely assemble all mounting hardware, then tighten the hardware in the following order:

   a. First, tighten the exhaust pipe cylinder head nuts (**Figure 72**).
   b. Next, tighten the hardware securing the muffler mounts to the frame. See **Figure 73** (front) and **Figure 75** (rear).
   c. Finally, tighten the front muffler-to-rear muffler union clamp (A, **Figure 71**).

9. Start the engine and check for exhaust leakage.

8

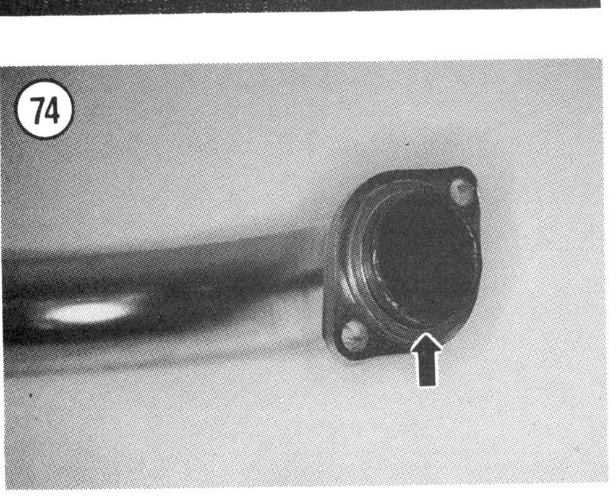

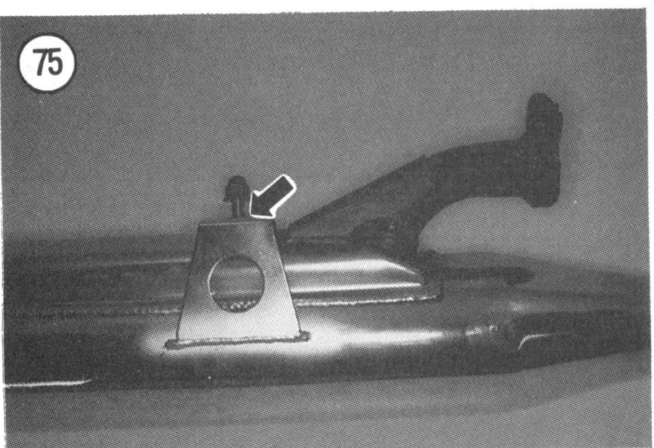

Table 1 CARBURETOR SPECIFICATIONS

Carburetor type	Keihin CVK36
Main jet number	135
Main air jet	100
Needle jet	6
Jet needle	N2PE
Needle clip position	Fixed
Pilot jet	48
Pilot air jet	70
Pilot air screw initial setting	1 3/4 turns out
Starter jet	70
Fuel level	2.0 1 mm (0.079 0.039 in.) above float chamber edge
Float height	16.5-2 mm 0.649- 0.079 in.)
Idle speed	
U.S. and Swiss models	1250-1350 rpm
Other models	950-1050 rpm

Table 2 FUEL SYSTEM TIGHTENING TORQUES

Item	N•m	in.-lb.
Air cleaner cover nut	11	97
Air cleaner housing bolts	11	97
Carburetor mounting plate bolts	11	97

CHAPTER NINE

ELECTRICAL SYSTEM

This chapter contains test and service procedures for electrical and ignition components. Information regarding the battery and spark plugs are covered in Chapter Three.

The electrical system includes the following systems:

a. Charging system.
b. Ignition system.
c. Starting system.
d. Lighting system.
e. Radiator fan system.
f. Turn signal system.
g. Switches.
h. Various electrical components.

Tables 1-4 are located at the end of this chapter.

NOTE
Where differences occur relating to the United Kingdom (U.K.) models they are identified. If there is no U.K. designation relating to a procedure, photo or illustration, it is identical to the United States (U.S.) models.

NOTE
Most motorcycle dealerships and parts suppliers will not accept a returned electrical part. Therefore, when testing electrical components, follow the test procedure as described. Also, be sure your test equipment is operating correctly and know how to operate it.

ELECTRICAL CONNECTORS

The Kawasaki Vulcan and Vulcan Classic are equipped with many electrical components, connectors and wires. Corrosion-causing moisture can enter these electrical connectors and cause poor electrical contact and component failure. Troubleshooting an electrical circuit with one or more corroded electrical connectors can be time-consuming and frustrating.

When attaching electrical connectors, pack them with a dielectric grease compound. Dielectric grease is especially formulated for sealing and waterproofing electrical connectors and will not interfere with the current flow through the electrical connectors. Use only this compound or an equivalent designed for this specific purpose. Do *not* use a substitute that may interfere with the current flow within the electrical connector. Do *not* use silicone sealant.

After cleaning both the male and female connectors, make sure they are thoroughly dry. Pack the interior of one of the connector halves with dielectric grease before joining the connector halves. On multipin connectors, pack the male side and on single-wire connectors, pack the female side. For best results, fill the entire inner area of the connector with the compound. On multipin connectors, also pack the backside of both the male and female side with dielectric grease to prevent moisture from entering the backside of the connector. After the connector is fully packed, wipe any excessive compound from the exterior.

Get into the practice of cleaning and sealing all electrical connectors every time they are unplugged. This may prevent a breakdown on the road and may also save you time when troubleshooting a circuit.

Always make sure all ground connections are free of corrosion and are tight.

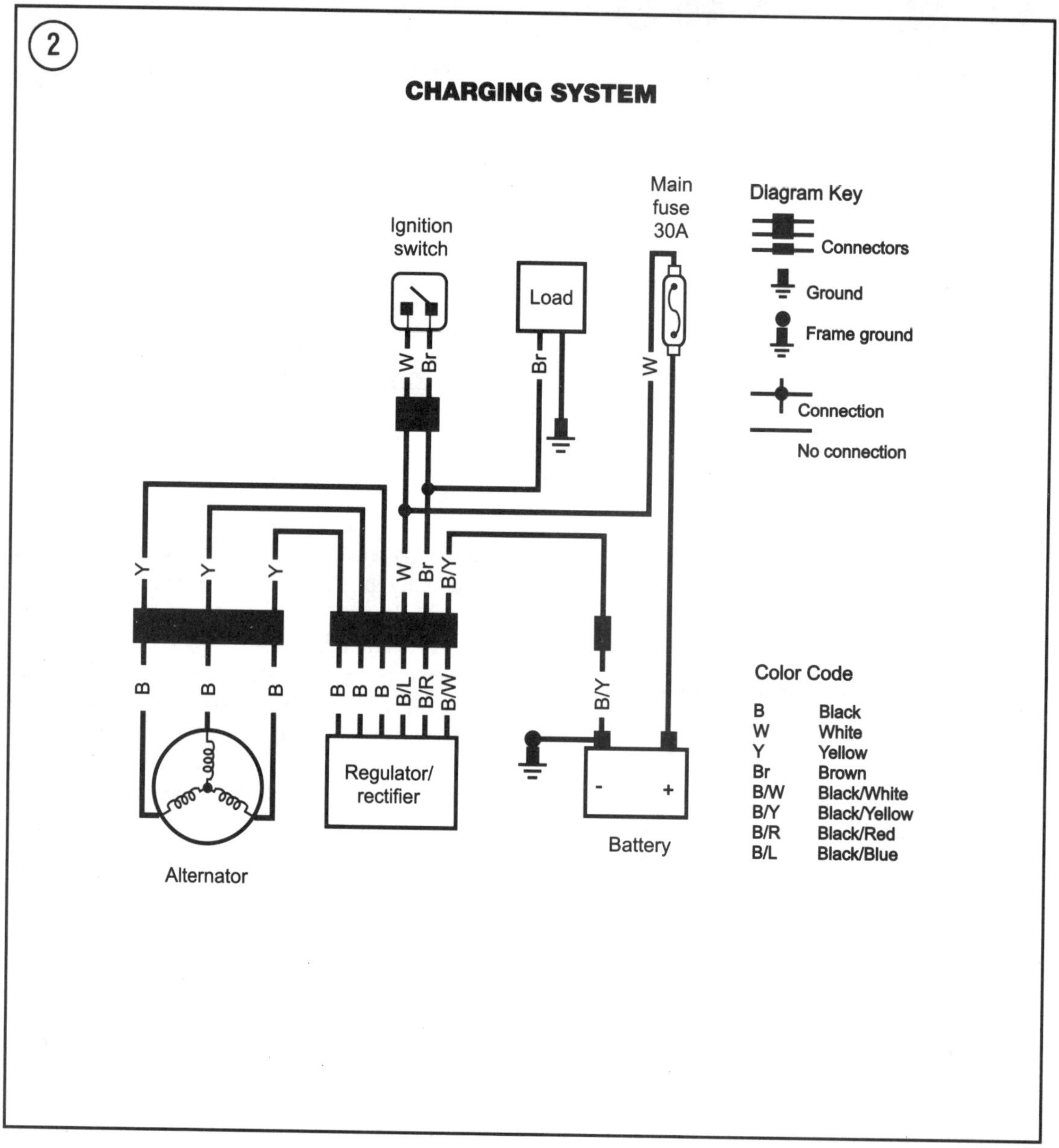

2

CHARGING SYSTEM

Ignition switch

Load

Main fuse 30A

Alternator

Regulator/ rectifier

Battery

Diagram Key

Connectors

Ground

Frame ground

Connection

No connection

Color Code

B	Black
W	White
Y	Yellow
Br	Brown
B/W	Black/White
B/Y	Black/Yellow
B/R	Black/Red
B/L	Black/Blue

BATTERY NEGATIVE TERMINAL

Some of the component replacement procedures and some of the test procedures in this chapter require disconnecting the battery negative (–) lead as a safety precaution.

1. Securely support the bike on level ground.
2. Remove the seat as described in Chapter Fourteen.
3. Remove the bolt and disconnect the battery negative (**Figure 1**) cable from the terminal.
4. Reach into the battery case and move the negative lead out of the way so it will not accidentally make contact with the battery negative terminal.

CAUTION
Make sure the system is not shorted before permanently attaching the negative (ground) lead to the battery.

5. Connect the battery negative lead to the battery negative terminal and tighten the bolt securely.
6. Install the seat as described in Chapter Fourteen.

CHARGING SYSTEM

The charging system consists of the battery, alternator and a solid-state voltage regulator/rectifier (**Figure 2**).

Alternating current generated by the alternator is rectified to direct current. The voltage regulator maintains constant voltage to the battery and electrical loads regardless of engine speed and load.

A malfunction in the charging system generally causes the battery to remain undercharged. To prevent damage to the alternator and the regulator/rectifier when testing and repairing the charging system, note the following precautions:

1. Always disconnect the negative battery cable, as described in this chapter, before removing a component from the charging system.
2. When charging the battery, remove the battery from the motorcycle and charge it as described in Chapter Three.
3. Inspect the physical condition of the battery. Look for bulges or cracks in the case and check for leaking electrolyte or corrosion buildup.
4. Check the wiring in the charging system for chafing, deterioration or other damage.
5. Check the wiring for corroded or loose connections. Clean, tighten or reconnect as required.

Battery Drain Test

Perform this test prior to performing the output test to determine if an excessive drain is discharging the battery.

1. Turn the ignition switch OFF.
2. Disconnect the battery negative (–) lead (**Figure 1**) from the battery.

CAUTION
Before connecting the ammeter to the circuit in Step 3, set the meter to its highest amperage scale. This will prevent a large current flow from damaging the meter or blowing the meter's fuse, if so equipped.

3. Connect an ammeter between the negative (–) lead and the negative (–) terminal of the battery (**Figure 3**).
4. The ammeter should read less than 1.2 mA.
5. Any indicated drain in the system will eventually discharge the battery, but more than 1.2 mA is considered excessive.
6. Some probable causes of excessive drain are a short circuit in the electrical system or a load (such as light or radio) that is turned ON.

NOTE
The radiator fan is connected to the battery regardless of the position of the

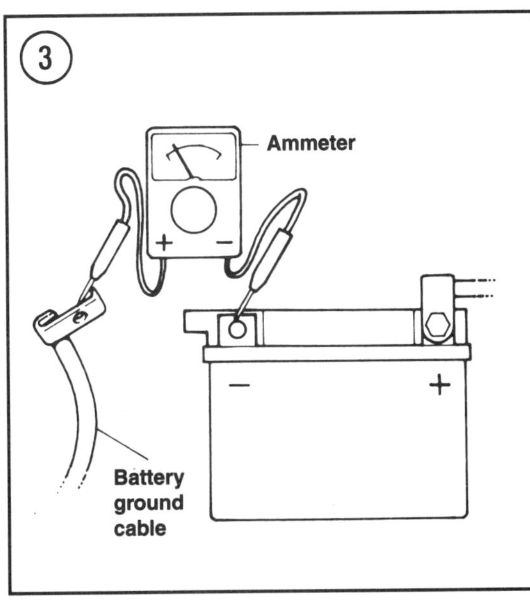

9

ignition switch. If the radiator fan runs continuously, check the radiator fan switch as described in this chapter.

7. Disconnect the ammeter and reconnect the battery negative lead.

Charging System Regulated Voltage Test

If a charging system problem is suspected, make sure the battery is fully charged and in good condition before going any further. Clean and test the battery as described in Chapter Three. Make sure all electrical connectors are tight and free of corrosion.

1. Start the engine and let it reach normal operating temperature. Shut off the engine and support the bike securely on level ground.
2. Remove the seat as described in Chapter Fourteen.
3. Start the engine and let it idle.
4. On models other than U.S., Canada and Australia, turn the headlight ON.
5. Connect a 0-20 DC voltmeter positive (+) test lead to the battery positive terminal and the voltmeter negative (–) test lead to the negative terminal (**Figure 4**).
6. Increase and then decrease engine speed and observe the voltmeter. The voltmeter should read close to battery voltage at idle, then as engine speed increases the voltage reading should rise to 14-15 volts.

7A. On U.S., Canada, and Australia models, disconnect the electrical connector (**Figure 5**) from the backside of the headlight bulb as described in this chapter.

7B. On models other than U.S., Canada and Australia, turn the headlight OFF.

8. Increase and then decrease engine speed and observe the voltmeter. The voltmeter should read battery voltage at idle, then as engine speed increases the voltage reading should rise but stay within 14-15 volts.
9. If the voltage readings are much higher than specified, the voltage regulator/rectifier is probably faulty. Test the voltage regulator/rectifier as described in this chapter.
10. If the voltage readings do not rise as engine speed increases, then the voltage regulator/rectifier is faulty or the alternator output is insufficient for the electrical load requirement. Test the voltage regulator/rectifier and the alternator as described in this chapter.
11. After the test is completed, perform the following:
    a. Shut OFF the engine.
    b. Disconnect the voltmeter.
    c. Install the seat.

Charging System Current Output Test

If a charging system malfunction is suspected, first make sure the battery is in acceptable condition. To obtain the best results, the battery should be slightly undercharged. Also make sure all electrical connectors are tight and free of corrosion.

1. Start the engine and warm it to normal operating temperature. Stop the engine.
2. Remove the seat as described in Chapter Fourteen.
3. Remove the junction box (A **Figure 6**) from under the frame member beneath the seat and re-

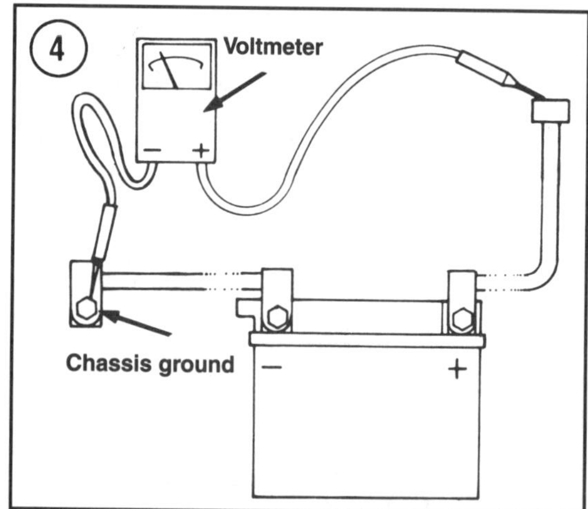

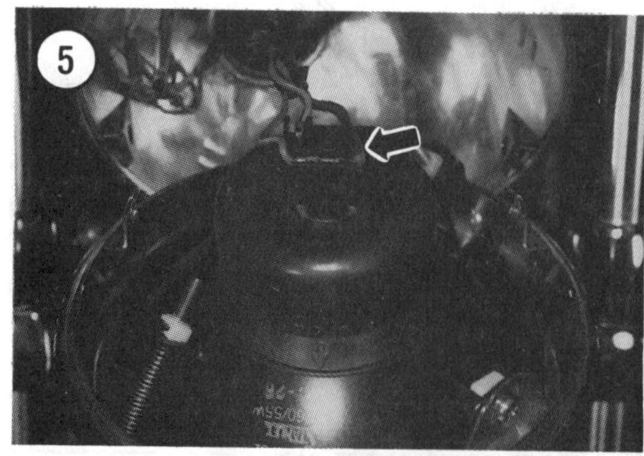

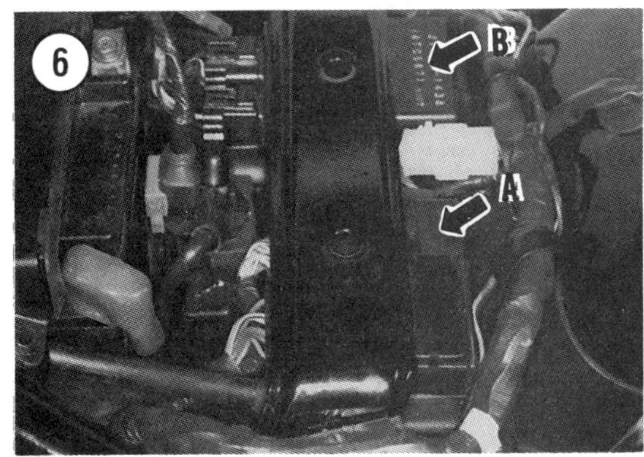

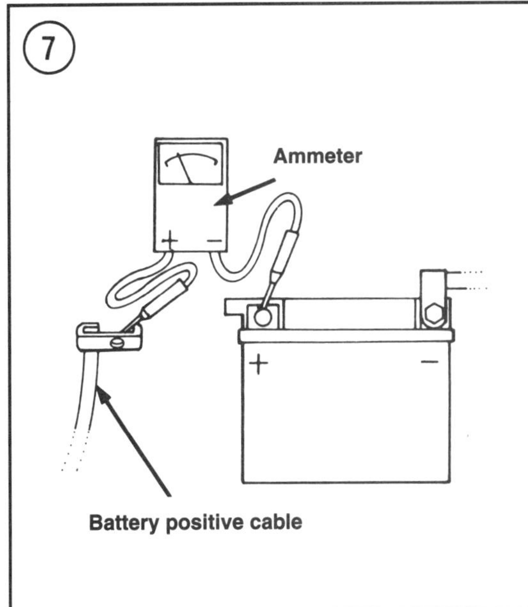

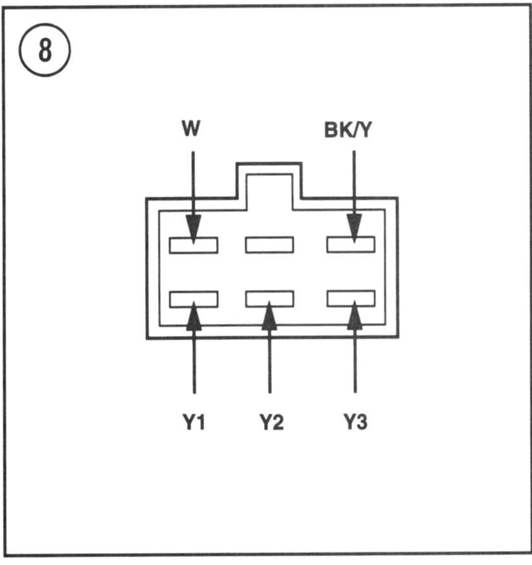

move the headlight and taillight fuses from the junction box. This is necessary to reduce the load on the charging system to only that required by the ignition system.

4. Start the engine, then connect an ammeter capable of reading 20 amperes DC (minimum to the battery as shown in **Figure 7**.
5. Run the engine at 1500 rpm while noting the ammeter. The ammeter should indicate positive amperage flow. As the battery returns to full charge, the current output should diminish.
6. If current output does not taper off as the battery reaches full charge, the voltage regulator is defective.

VOLTAGE REGULATOR/RECTIFIER

Inspection

If the charging system fails either the regulated voltage and/or current output test, check the voltage regulator/rectifier for an internal short or open.

1. Remove the left-hand side cover from the frame.
2. Disconnect the six-pin regulator/rectified connector from the voltage regulator/rectifier.
3. Perform the rectifier circuit check and the three regulator circuit checks described below.

9

NOTE

You'll need three 12-volt batteries and a 12-volt test lamp (3-6 W) to perform the three regulator circuit checks.

CAUTION

Do not use an ammeter to test the regulator. Excessive current could damage the regulator.

Rectifier circuit check

NOTE

Connect the ohmmeter test leads to the voltage regulator/rectifier electrical connector terminals.

1. Use an ohmmeter to check the resistance between the following pairs of terminals in the regulator rectifier connector (**Figure 8**):
   a. W—Y1.
   b. W—Y2.
   c. W—Y3.
   d. B/Y—Y1.

e. B/Y—Y2.
f. B/Y—Y3.

2. Check the resistance in both directions. The resistance should be relatively low in one direction, but it should be more than 10 times as much when you reverse the connections.

NOTE
The actual reading varies depending upon the ohmmeter setting. In general, the lower reading should be between zero and half the scale.

3. If the reading for any pair of terminals is low or high in both directions, replace the regulator/rectifier.

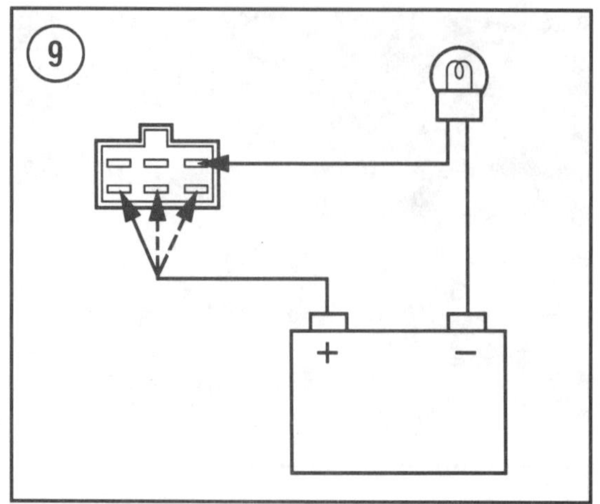

Regulator circuit check No.1

1. Connect the test lamp to the regulator/rectifier B/Y terminal and to the negative terminal of the battery as shown in **Figure 9**.
2. Connect the positive battery terminal to the Y1 terminal as shown in **Figure 9** and observe the test lamp.
3. Repeat this for terminals Y2 and Y3.
4. If the test lamp comes on during any check, replace the regulator/rectifier.

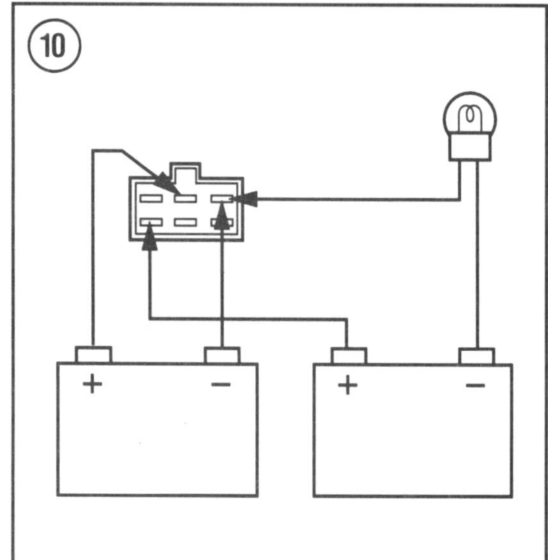

Regulator circuit check No. 2

1. Connect the test lamp to the regulator/rectifier B/Y terminal and to the negative terminal of the first battery as shown in **Figure 10**.
2. Apply 12 volts to the Br terminal by connecting the second battery to the regulator/rectifier B/Y and Br terminals as shows in **Figure 10**. Observe the test lamp.
3. Connect the positive terminal of the first battery to Y1 as shows in **Figure 10**, and observe the test lamp..
4. Check terminals Y2 and Y3 in the same manner.
5. If the test lamp comes on during any check, replace the regulator/rectifier.

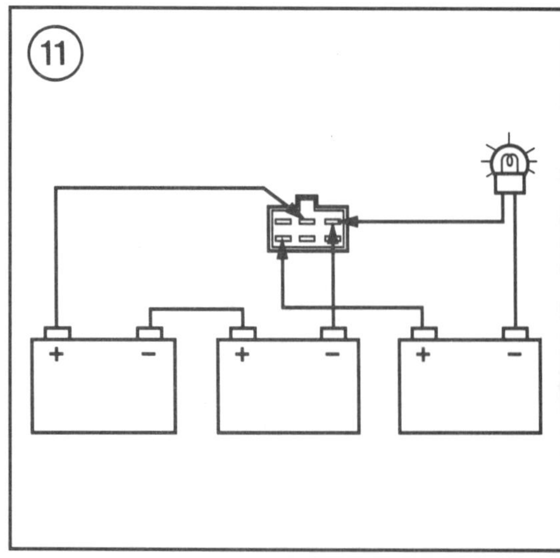

Regulator circuit check No. 3

1. Connect the test lamp to the regulator/rectifier BK/Y terminal and to the negative terminal of the first battery as shown in **Figure 11**.

2. Connect the positive terminal of the first battery to Y1 as shows in **Figure 11**.

> CAUTION
> *In the following step, do not apply 24 volts to the regulator/rectifier for more than a few seconds. The unit could be damaged.*

3. Briefly apply 24 volts to the regulator/rectifier by connecting a second and third battery to the Br and B/Y terminals as shown in **Figure 11**. Observe the test lamp. It should turn on when 24 volts are applied.
4. Repeat this test with the first battery connected to terminals Y2 and Y3.
5. If the test lamp does not turn on when 24 volts are applied during any check, replace the regulator/rectifier.

> NOTE
> *If the regulator/rectifier passes all four tests, it may still be defective. The only way to confirm its operation is to replace the regulator/rectifier with a known-good unit. Since electrical components usually cannot be returned, consider taking the bike to a dealership for this service.*

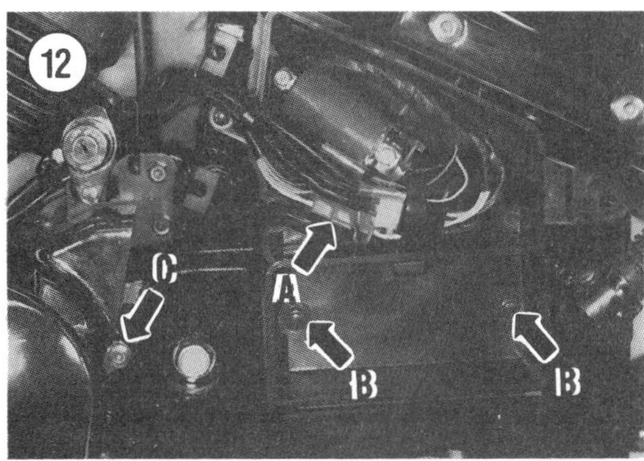

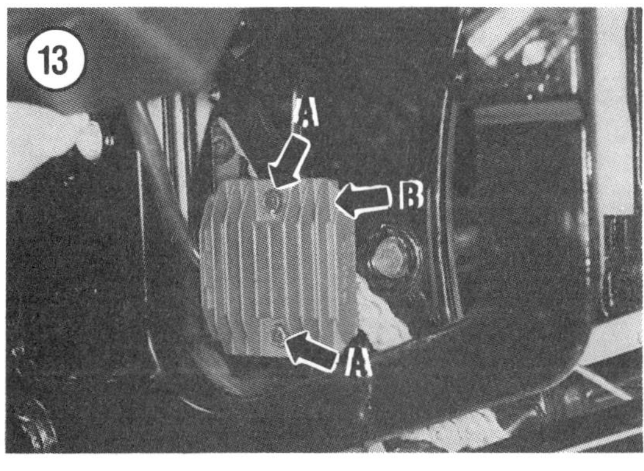

Removal/Installation

The voltage regulator/rectifier is mounted behind the toolbox on the left side of the frame.

1. Use a scissors jack or jack stands to securely support the bike on level ground.
2. Disconnect the battery negative (–) lead as described in this chapter.
3. Remove the left-hand side cover from the frame.
4. Disconnect the six-pin electrical connector (A, **Figure 12**) from the voltage regulator/rectifier.
5. Remove the tool kit and then pull the toolbox by removing the retaining bolts (B, **Figure 12**).
6. Remove the regulator/rectifier bolts (A, **Figure 13**) and remove the regulator/rectifier (B, **Figure 13**). Note how its connector wire is routed through the frame so you can route the wire correctly during installation.
7. Install by reversing these removal steps while noting the following:
   a. Tighten the mounting bolts securely.
   b. Make sure all electrical connections are tight and free of corrosion.
   c. Connect the battery negative (–) lead.

9

ALTERNATOR

The alternator is an electrical generator in which a magnetized field called a rotor revolves around a set of stationary coils called a stator assembly. As the rotor revolves, alternating current is induced in the stator coils. The current is then rectified to direct current and is used to operate the electrical systems on the motorcycle and to keep the battery charged. The rotor is permanently magnetized. Alternators generally suffer from one of three types of failures: a short, open or loss of rotor magnetism.

Alternator Cover Removal

1. Drain the engine oil as described in Chapter Three.
2. Remove the engine sprocket cover mounting bolt (A, **Figure 14**).
3. Pull the engine sprocket cover (B, **Figure 14**) rearward to disengage it from the alternator cover,

then remove engine sprocket cover from the motorcycle. Do not lose the trim that fits between the two covers (C, **Figure 14**).

4. Remove the left-hand side cover from the frame.

5. Remove the bolt securing the ignition switch. Remove the switch (A, **Figure 15**).

6. Disconnect the three-pin, alternator lead connector (B, **Figure 15**) and the two-pin, pickup coil connector (C, **Figure 15**).

7. Open the clamp (D, **Figure 15**) so the wires are free to move. Note how the wires are routed (A, **Figure 16**) through the frame. You will have to reroute them in the same locations during assembly.

8. Remove the shift pedal/lever assembly as described in Chapter Seven.

NOTE
The engine has been removed in the following illustration for clarity.

9. Remove the alternator cover mounting bolts. Note which bolt has a wire clamp behind it (A, **Figure 17**). You must reinstall the wire clamp in the same position.

NOTE
*Carefully pull the alternator wires from the frame as you remove the alternator cover (A, **Figure 16**). Note how they are routed so you can route them correctly during assembly. If necessary, tie a string to the alternator and pickup coil connectors before removing the cover. Once you have removed the cover, untie the string and leave it in place in the frame. Use the string to pull the wires back through the frame during assembly.*

10. Remove the alternator cover (B, **Figure 17**) and the gasket. Do not lose the dowels behind the cover.

Alternator Cover Installation

1. If removed, install the locating dowels (**Figure 18**) and then install a new gasket.

2. Install the alternator cover (B, **Figure 17**) and bolts.

3. Apply Loctite 242 to the threads of the alternator cover bolts and install the bolts. Be sure to install the electrical wire clamp (A, **Figure 17**) at its original location.

4. Tighten the bolts in a crisscross pattern in 2-3 stages. Torque the alternator cover bolts to the specification listed in **Table 1**.

5. Route the stator and pickup coil wires through the frame and reconnect them to their respective connectors above the tool box. Refer to **Figure 15**.

6. Be sure the wires are properly routed and secured in their clamps.

7. Fit the trim into place on the mating surface (B, **Figure 16**) of the alternator cover. Apply an adhesive to the trim if necessary.

8. Fit the engine sprocket cover in place (B, **Figure 14**). Be sure the groove in the engine sprocket cover fits over the trim in the alternator cover. Refer to C, **Figure 14**.

9. Install the engine sprocket cover mounting bolt (A, **Figure 14**) and tighten it securely.

10. Reconnect the ignition switch (A, **Figure 15**).

11. Reinstall the left-hand side cover.

12. Install the shift pedal/lever assembly as described in Chapter Seven.

13. Add engine oil to the level described in Chapter Three.

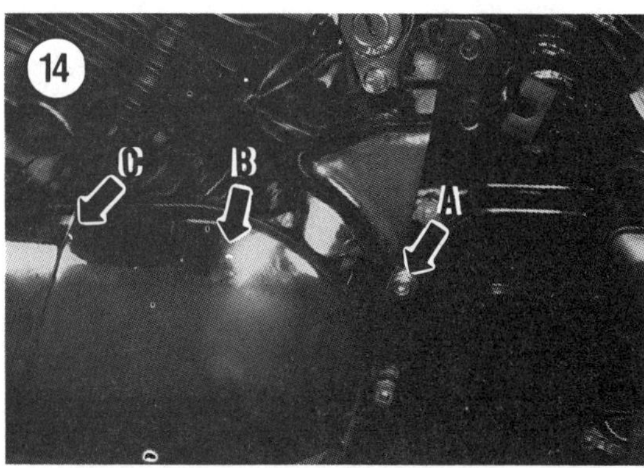

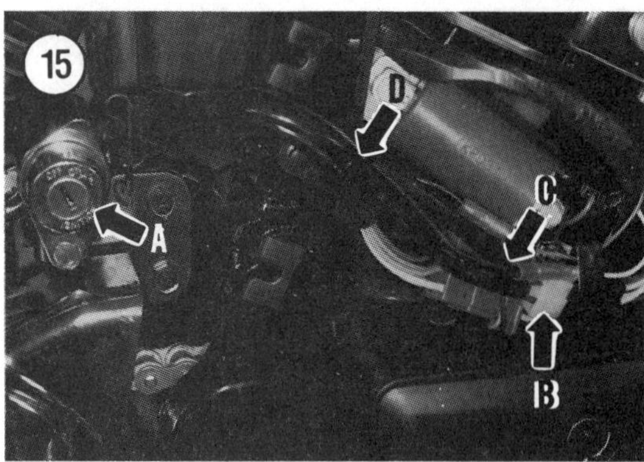

Rotor Testing

The rotor is permanently magnetized and cannot be tested except by replacing it with a known good one. The rotor can lose magnetism from old age or a sharp hit. If defective, the rotor must be replaced. It cannot be remagnetized.

Alternator Testing

1. Remove the left-hand side cover.

2. Start the engine and let it reach normal operating temperature. Shut off the engine.
3. Disconnect the 3-pin alternator connector (B, **Figure 15**) above the toolbox.
4. Perform the alternator output voltage and stator tests described below.

Alternator Output Voltage

1. Set the voltmeter to the 250 volt AC range.
2. Connect the voltmeter across two of the black terminals on the alternator side of the connector.
3. Start the engine and check the voltage at 4000 rpm.
4. Connect the voltmeter across another pair of black terminals and check the voltage at 4000 rpm.
5. Repeat this check for the remaining pair of black terminals in the connector. At this point, you should have checked the voltage across each pair of black terminals in the connector (taken a total of three readings).

6A. If the alternator output is within the specification in **Table 3**, the alternator is operating properly. The regulator/rectifier is most likely defective. Check the voltage regulator/rectifier as described in this chapter.

6B. If any of the three readings is less than the specified value in **Table 3**, the alternator is defective. Perform the stator test described below.

Stator Test

1. Stop the engine if it is still running.
2. Use an ohmmeter set at R × 1, and check resistance between each of the three black terminals on the alternator side of the connector. You should take a total of 3 measurements. Compare your measurements to the specified resistance as listed in **Table 3**.
3. If the resistance across any pair of black terminals is greater than specified, the stator must be replaced. If the resistance is less than specified, the stator must be replaced.
4. Use an ohmmeter set to the highest range setting, and check continuity between each black terminal on the alternator side of the connector and ground.
5. Replace the stator assembly if any black terminal has continuity to ground.

NOTE
Prior to replacing the stator assembly, check the stator wires and connector for an open circuit or poor connections.

6. If the stator assembly fails either of these tests, it must be replaced as described in this chapter.
7. If the stator checks good, but the alternator output voltage is less than specified, the rotor magnets are weakened. Replace the rotor as described in this chapter.
8. If the alternator is in acceptable condition, reconnect the alternator connector. Make sure all terminals are free of corrosion and that the connection is tight.
9. Install the frame left-hand side cover.

Stator Assembly/Removal

Refer to **Figure 19** for this procedure.

1. Remove the alternator cover as described in this chapter.
2. Remove the three bolts (A, **Figure 20**) securing the pickup coil lead clamp to the alternator cover and remove the pickup coil lead clamp (B, **Figure 20**). Note how the pickup coil leads are routed. You must route these wires in the same location during assembly.
3. Remove the two bolts (A **Figure 21**) securing the alternator lead clamp (B **Figure 21**) in place and remove the clamp.
4. Note how the pickup coil and stator leads are routed.

NOTE
The upper rubber grommet contains the pickup coil wires, the lower grommet contains the alternator stator wires.

5. Carefully pull both rubber grommets (C, **Figure 21**) and electrical wires loose from the cover.
6. Remove the stator coil bolts (C, **Figure 20**), and remove the stator (D, **Figure 20**) from the alternator cover.

Stator Assembly/ Installation

1. Fit the stator assembly into the alternator cover.
2. Apply adhesive to each grommet.
3. First install the grommet containing the stator electrical wires. Then install the rubber grommet containing the pickup coil electrical wires.

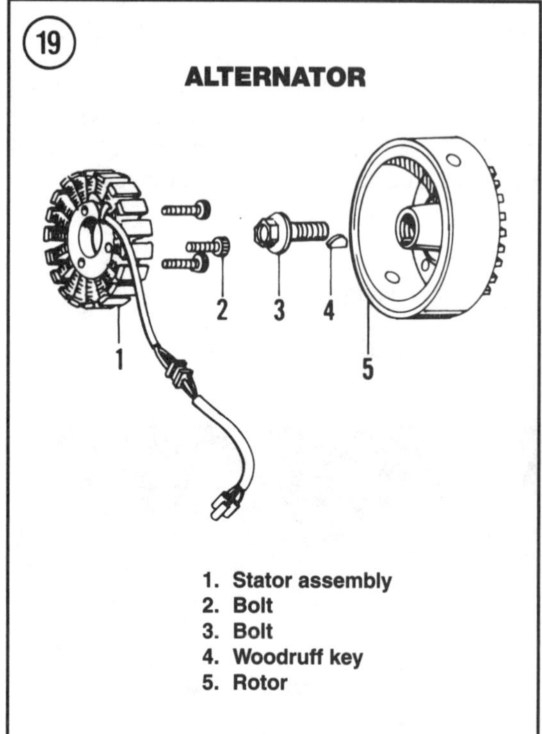

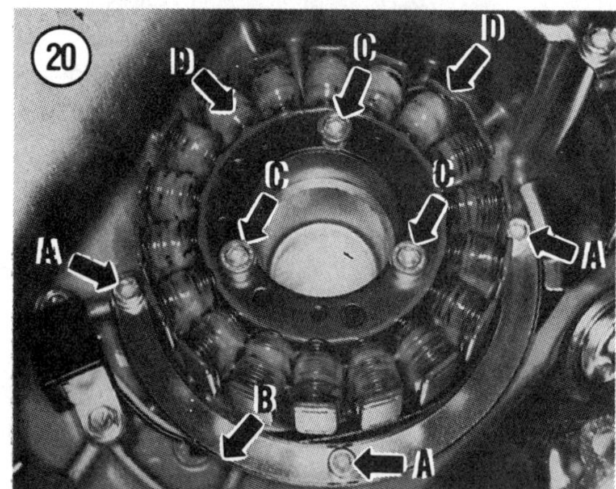

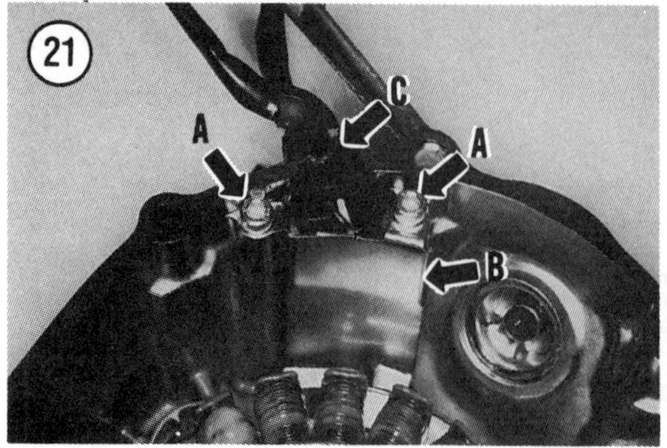

4. Make sure both rubber grommets (C, **Figure 21**) are installed correctly in the cover. Push them down until they seat tightly in the cover groove.
5. Apply Loctite 242 to the stator bolt threads prior to installation. Install the stator bolts (C, **Figure 20**) and tighten to the torque specification listed in **Table 1**.
6. Confirm that the wires are routed correctly and install the alternator lead clamp (B, **Figure 21**). Torque the alternator lead clamp bolts (A, **Figure 21**) to the specification in **Table 1**.
7. Install the pickup coil lead clamp (B, **Figure 20**). Torque the bolts (A, **Figure 20**) to the specification in **Table 1**.
8. Reinstall the alternator cover as described in this chapter.

Rotor Removal/Installation

Refer to **Figure 19** for this procedure.

NOTE
The engine is removed in the following procedure for clarity. The rotor can be removed with the engine installed in the frame.

1. Remove the alternator cover as described in this chapter.
2. Wipe oil off the rotor.
3A. Hold the rotor with a flywheel holder (A, **Figure 22**) and remove the rotor bolt.
3B. If you do not have a flywheel holder, place a penny or brass washer between the alternator rotor gear and the left-hand balancer gear where they mesh at the upper portion of the gears. This will prevent the alternator rotor from turning in the next step.

CAUTION:
Any soft metal washer (copper, brass or aluminum) will work in the above step. However, ***do not*** *use a steel washer. Steel will damage the gear teeth.*

4. Loosen, then remove the alternator rotor 17 mm bolt (B, **Figure 22**). If you used a washer to hold the flywheel, remove the washer.

CAUTION
Do not try to remove the rotor without a puller; any attempt to do so will ultimately lead to some form of damage to the engine and/or rotor. Many aftermarket pullers are available from motorcycle dealerships or mail order houses. A puller is relatively inexpensive and it makes an excellent addition to any mechanic's tool box. If you cannot buy or borrow one, have a dealership remove the rotor.

5. Install the Kawasaki rotor puller (part No. 57001-1216), or equivalent (**Figure 23**) onto the threads of the rotor. Screw it on until it stops against the end of the crankshaft.
6A. Hold the flywheel with the flywheel holder.
6B. If you do not have a flywheel holder, place a penny or brass washer between the alternator rotor gear and the left-hand balancer gear where they mesh at the lower portion of the gears. This will prevent the alternator rotor from turning in the next step.
7. Turn the rotor puller (**Figure 23**) with an open-end wrench. Turn the puller until the rotor disengages from the crankshaft taper. If you used a washer to hold the flywheel, remove the washer.

NOTE
If the rotor is difficult to remove, strike the end of the puller (not the rotor) a few times with a hammer. This will usually break it loose.

CAUTION
If normal rotor removal attempts fail, do not force the puller. This could strip the threads from the rotor causing expensive damage. Take the bike to a dealership and have the rotor removed.

8. Remove the rotor from the crankshaft and then unscrew the rotor puller from the rotor.
9. Inspect the inside of the rotor (**Figure 24**) for small bolts, washers or other metal particles that may have been picked up by the magnets. These small metal bits can cause severe damage to the alternator stator assembly.
10. Inspect the rotor keyway (**Figure 24**) for wear or damage. If damage is severe, replace the rotor.
11. Install by reversing the removal steps while noting the following:
   a. Use an aerosol electrical contact cleaner and clean all oil residue from the crankshaft taper where the rotor slides onto it and the matching tapered surface of the rotor. This is to ensure that the rotor fits tightly onto the crankshaft.
   b. If removed, install the Woodruff key in the crankshaft slot and center it.

CAUTION
The alignment between the alternator rotor and the left-hand balancer gear is necessary for proper synchronization of the balance shaft assembly with the engine. The balancer shaft system eliminates the vibration normally associated with large displacement V-twins.

CAUTION
Any applicable manufacturer's warranty will be voided if the balancer system is modified or eliminated.

   c. Align the keyway in the rotor with the Woodruff key on the crankshaft and partially install the rotor onto the crankshaft.

NOTE
*The alignment mark on the rotor is difficult to see in a photograph. A pointer is used in **Figure 25** to show its location.*

   d. Rotate the left balancer gear and align the index line mark on the rotor with the punch mark or index line on the left balancer gear. Refer to **Figure 25**.
   e. After alignment is correct, push the rotor onto the crankshaft until it stops. Make sure the index marks on the rotor and left-hand balancer gear are still aligned. If not; remove the rotor and realign the two parts.
   f. Apply oil to the threads and mating surface of the alternator rotor bolt.
   g. Hold the rotor and torque the alternator rotor bolt to the specification listed in **Table 1**.

TRANSISTORIZED IGNITION SYSTEM

The Kawasaki Vulcan is equipped with a solid-state system that uses no mechanical parts such as cams or breaker points and requires no routine maintenance. The ignition circuit diagram is shown in **Figure 26**.

The ignition signal generation consists of a single raised tab on the alternator rotor and a pickup coil, which is attached to the alternator inner cover next

to the alternator stator coil assembly. As the crankshaft turns the alternator rotor, the raised tab passes the pickup coil and sends a signal to the IC ignitor unit. This signal turns the IC ignitor unit transistor alternately ON and OFF. As the transistor turns ON and OFF, the current passing through the primary windings of the ignition coil also turns ON and OFF. This induces the secondary current in the ignition coil's secondary windings and produces the current necessary to fire the spark plug.

Transistorized Ignition System Precautions

1. Never connect the battery backward. If the battery polarity is wrong, damage will occur to the voltage regulator/rectifier, IC ignitor unit and alternator stator assembly.
2. Do not disconnect the battery when the engine is running. The resulting voltage surge will damage the voltage regulator/rectifier and possibly burn out light bulbs.

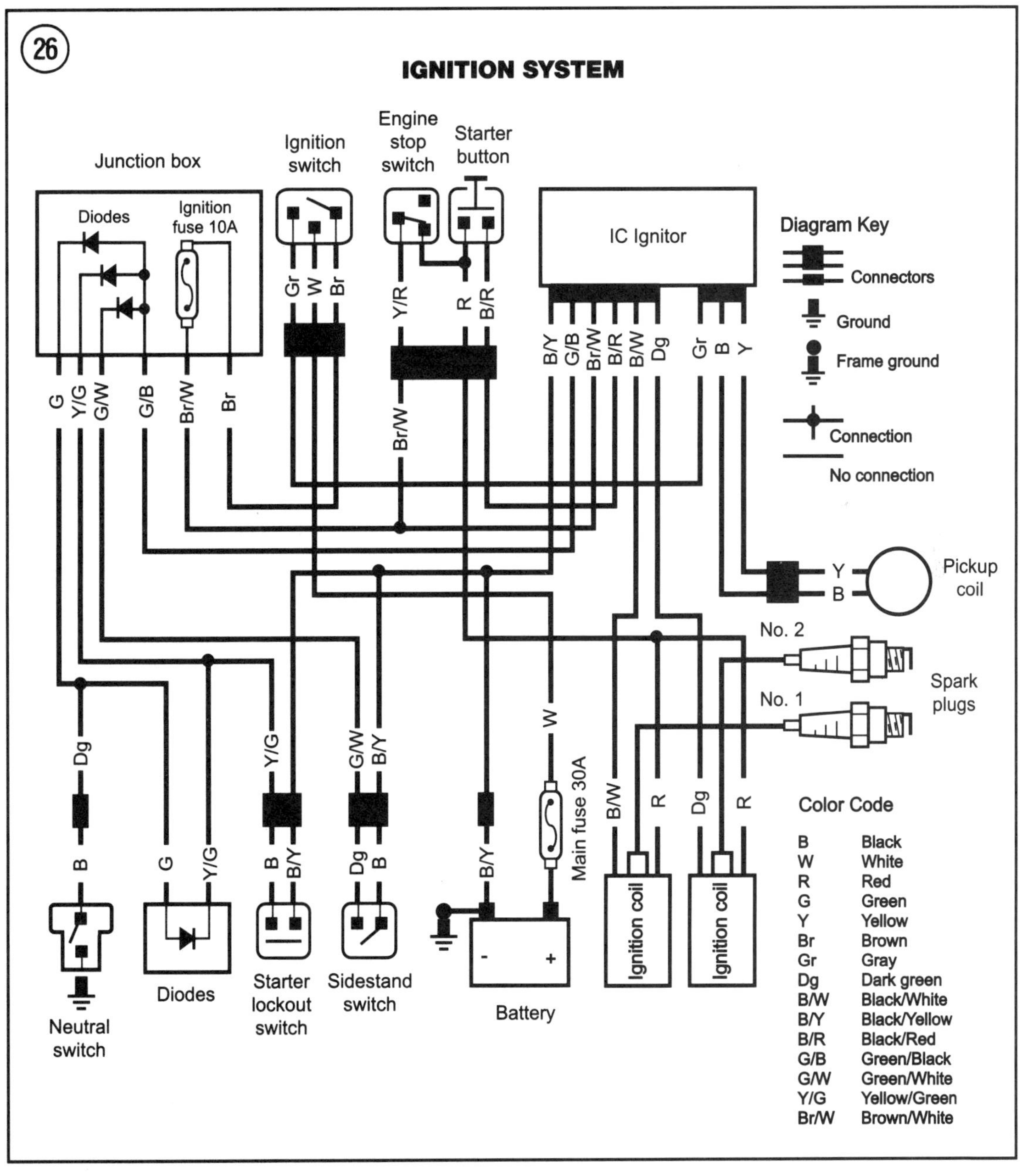

3. Never disconnect any electrical connection while the engine is running.
4. Keep all ignition system wiring and connectors clean and tight. Be sure that the wiring connectors are pushed together firmly to help keep out moisture. Also pack the connectors with dielectric grease as described at the beginning of this chapter.
5. Do not substitute another type of ignition coil.
6. Most components are mounted in a rubber vibration isolator. Always be sure that the isolator is in place when installing the units in the system.
7. Prior to inspecting or troubleshooting the ignition system, check the battery charge as described in Chapter Three. For best test results, the battery must be fully charged. A lower voltage reading will yield inaccurate test readings.
8. Cranking the engine with the spark plug wire(s) in an open circuit will destroy the IC igniter. Do not crank the engine unless the spark plug wires are firmly attached to the spark plugs or securely grounded to the engine.

Troubleshooting

A weak spark or no spark indicates problems with the transistorized ignition system. Refer to **Table 2**. Refer to **Table 3** for ignition component specifications.

Pickup Coil Testing

1. Remove the frame left-hand side cover.
2. Disconnect the pickup coil two-pin electrical connector (C, **Figure 15**).
3. Set an ohmmeter to the R × 100 scale and calibrate (zero) the meter.
4. Check the resistance across the two terminals on the pickup coil side of the connector.

Compare your reading to the specified resistance is listed in **Table 3**.

5. If the measured resistance is not as specified, the pickup coil assembly must be replaced as described in this chapter.
6. Set the ohmmeter to its highest scale and calibrate (zero) the meter.
7. Check for continuity between each of the terminals in the pickup coil side of the connector and chassis ground. Any continuity indicates a short and the pickup coil assembly must be replaced as described in this chapter.
8. If the pickup coils are in good condition, reconnect the electrical connector. Make sure the electrical connector is free of corrosion and is tight.
9. Install the left-hand side cover.

Pickup Coil Assembly Removal/Installation

1. Remove the alternator cover as described in this chapter.
2. Remove the three bolts (A, **Figure 20**) securing the pickup coil wire clamp to the alternator cover and remove the pickup coil lead clamp (B, **Figure 20**). Note how the pickup coil wires are routed. You must route the wire in the same location during assembly.
3. Remove the two bolts (A, **Figure 21**) securing the alternator lead clamp (B, **Figure 21**) and remove the clamp.

NOTE

The upper rubber grommet contains the pickup coil electrical wires, the lower grommet contains the alternator stator electrical wires.

4. Carefully remove the upper rubber grommet from the alternator cover (C, **Figure 21**). It contains the pickup coil wires. Leave the lower grommet in place. It contains the alternator stator electrical wires.
5. Remove the bolts (A, **Figure 27**) securing the pickup coil (B, **Figure 27**) to the alternator cover, and remove the pickup coil.
6. Install the new pickup coil. Torque the pickup coil bolts to the specification given in **Table 1**.

7. Correctly route the pickup coil wire around the stator assembly and reinstall its grommet into the alternator cover (C, **Figure 21**).

8. Install the alternator lead clamp (B **Figure 21**). Torque the alternator lead clamp bolts (A **Figure 21**) to the specification in **Table 1**.

9. Install the pickup coil lead clamp (B, **Figure 20**). Torque the bolts (A, **Figure 20**) to the specification in **Table 1**.

10. Reinstall the alternator cover as described in this chapter.

Ignition Coil

The ignition coil is a transformer that develops the high voltage required to jump the spark plug gap. Maintenance consists of keeping the electrical connections clean and tight and occasionally checking the tightness of the coil fasteners.

If the condition of the coil(s) is questionable, there are several checks that may be made.

Performance Test

NOTE
The spark plug must be grounded against a piece of bare metal on the engine or frame. If necessary, carefully scrape away some of the engine paint.

First, disconnect the high voltage (**Figure 28**) lead from the spark plug and remove the spark plug as described in Chapter Three. Connect a new or good spark plug to the high-voltage lead and place the spark plug's base on a good ground like the engine cylinder head. Position the spark plug so you can see the electrodes.

WARNING
If it is necessary to hold the high voltage lead, do so with a pair of insulated pliers. The high voltage generated by the signal generator could produce serious or fatal shocks.

Crank the engine with the starter. If a fat blue spark occurs, the coil is in good condition; if not, proceed as follows. Make sure that you are using a known-good spark plug for this test. If the spark plug used is defective, the test results will be incorrect.

Reinstall a known-good spark plug into the cylinder head and connect the high voltage lead.

9

Resistance Test

NOTE
To get accurate resistance measurements, the coil must be at 20°C (68° F).

NOTE
The following shows the procedure for testing the rear-cylinder ignition coil. The procedure is identical for the front cylinder ignition coil.

1. Remove the fuel tank as described in Chapter Eight.
2. Disconnect the battery negative lead as described in this chapter.
3. Remove the left-hand side cover from the frame.
4. Disconnect both primary leads (A, **Figure 29**) from the ignition coil.
5. Disconnect the high-voltage lead (B, **Figure 29**) from the spark plug.

NOTE
In Step 5 and Step 6, the resistance specification is not as important as the fact that there is continuity between the terminals. If the ignition coil windings are in good condition, the resistance will be close to those specified.

6. Set an ohmmeter to R×1, and calibrate (zero) the meter.
7. Measure the primary coil resistance between the primary wire terminals on the ignition coil as show in **Figure 30**. The specified resistance is listed in **Table 3**.
8. Set the ohmmeter to R×1000, and calibrate (zero) the meter.
9. Measure the secondary coil resistance as shown in **Figure 31**. The specified resistance is listed in **Table 3**.
10. If necessary, repeat Steps 5-9 for the other ignition coil.
11. If any coil resistance does not meet (or come close to) either of these specifications, the coil must be replaced. If the coil exhibits visible damage, it should be replaced as described in this chapter.
12. If the coil(s) is in good condition, reconnect all ignition coil wires to the ignition coil.
13. Install the fuel tank as described in Chapter Seven.
14. Install the frame left-hand side cover.

Ignition Coil Removal/Installation

NOTE
The following procedure shows the removal and installation of the rear cylinder ignition coil. The procedure is identical for the front cylinder ignition coil.

1. Remove the fuel tank as described in Chapter Eight.
2. Disconnect the battery negative lead as described in this chapter.
3. Remove the frame left-hand side cover.
4. Disconnect both primary leads (A, **Figure 29**) from the ignition coil.
5. Disconnect the high-tension lead (B, **Figure 29**) from the spark plug.
6. Remove the bolts (C, **Figure 29**) securing the ignition coil to the frame and remove the coil. Note how the high tension lead is routed so you can route the high-tension lead in the same position during assembly.
7. Install by reversing these removal steps. Make sure all electrical connections are free of corrosion and are tight.

IC Ignitor Unit

Complete testing of the IC ignitor unit requires a special Kawasaki Hand Tester (part No. 57001-1394) and should be tested at a Kawasaki dealership service department. This test procedure is provided if you are able to procure this piece of test equipment and choose to perform this test yourself. *Do not* perform the resistance tests with a meter other than the Kawasaki Hand Tester. Other testers may yield inaccurate results.

The dealership will either test the ignitor unit with the special tool or perform a remove and replace test to see if the ignitor unit is faulty. This type of R/R test is expensive for an individual to perform. Remember if you purchase a new IC ignitor unit and it does *not* solve your particular ignition system problem, you *cannot* return the ICignitor unit for a refund. Most motorcycle dealers will *not* accept returns on any electrical component since they could be damaged internally even though they look good externally.

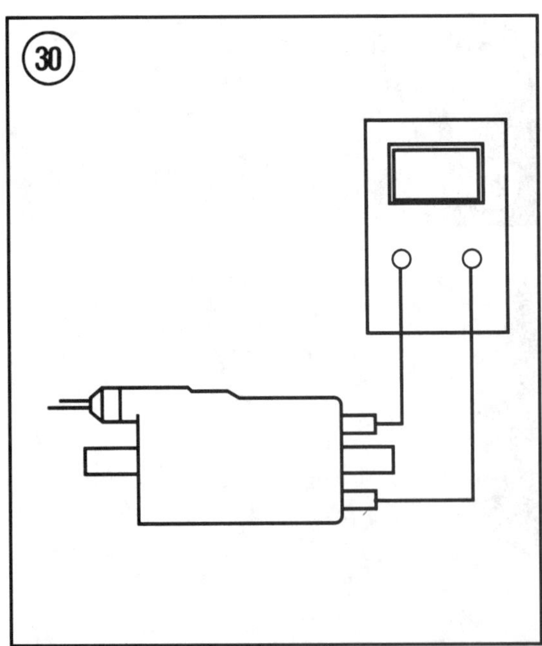

Make sure all connections between the various components are clean and tight. Be sure that the wiring connectors are pushed together firmly and packed with a dielectric compound to help keep out moisture.

Performance Test

1. Remove the fuel tank as described in Chapter Eight.
2. Remove the frame right-hand side cover.
3. Disconnect the high-tension lead (**Figure 28**) from one of the spark plugs. Remove the spark plug from the cylinder head as described in Chapter Three.

NOTE
The spark plug must ground against a piece of bare metal on the engine or frame. If necessary, carefully scrape away some of the paint to reach bare metal.

4. Connect a new or known-good spark plug to the high-tension lead and place the spark plug base on a good ground like the engine cylinder head cover. Position the spark plug so you can see the electrodes.

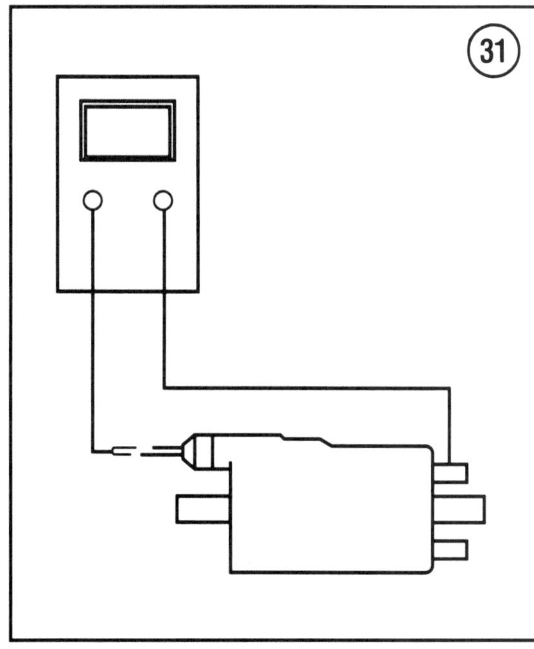

WARNING
If it is necessary to hold the high-tension lead, do so with an insulated pair of pliers. The high voltage generated by the ignitor unit could produce serious or fatal shocks.

5. Crank the engine with the starter and check for a spark. If there is a fat blue spark, the ignitor unit is working properly.
6. If a weak spark or no spark is obtained, and if the pickup coils and ignition coils are both good, test the IC ignitor or have it tested at a Kawasaki dealership.
7. Reinstall the spark plug and connect the high-tension lead onto the spark plug.
8. If all of the ignition components are good, then check the following:
   a. Check for an open or short in the wire harness between each component in the system.
   b. Again, make sure all connections between the various components are clean and tight. Be sure that the wiring connectors are pushed together firmly to help keep out moisture.

Resistance Test

NOTE
*You **must** use the Kawasaki Hand Tester (part No. 57001-1394) when performing this test. Another tester may yield inaccurate readings, leading to an incorrect diagnosis of the situation. Another tester could also damage the IC ignitor.*

1. Remove the seat as described in Chapter Fourteen.
2. Disconnect the battery negative lead as described in this chapter.
3. Disconnect the eight-pin and four-pin electrical connectors (**Figure 32**) from the IC ignitor.
4. Set the Kawasaki Hand Tester to R × 1000 scale.
5. Check the resistance between the indicated wire terminals in the IC ignitor side of the eight-pin and four-pin electrical connector.
6. Refer to **Figure 33** for terminal identification. Refer to **Figure 34** and **Figure 35** for test lead placement and specified resistance readings.
7. If the IC ignitor unit fails any portion of this test, the unit is faulty and must be replaced as described in this chapter.

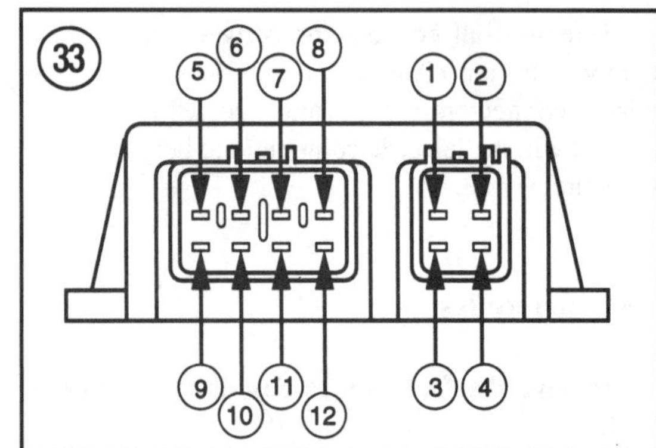

34

IC IGNITOR INTERNAL RESISTANCE (4 PIN)

(kΩ)

		Tester (+) Lead Connection			
	Terminal	1	2	3	4
(–)	1		∞	∞	∞
	2	∞		0-1	30-150
	3	∞	0-1		30-150
	4	∞	28-150	28-150	

Tester (–) Lead Connection

IC IGNITOR INTERNAL RESISTANCE (8 PIN)

(kΩ)

		Tester (+) Lead Connection							
	Terminal	5	6	7	8	9	10	11	12
(–)	5		∞	∞	∞	∞	∞	∞	∞
	6	35-400		∞	22-100	35-400	50-500	∞	18-80
	7	∞	∞		∞	∞	∞	∞	∞
	8	5-20	6-26	∞		5-20	4-16	∞	2.2-9.5
	9	∞	∞	∞	∞		∞	∞	∞
	10	∞	∞	∞	∞	∞		∞	∞
	11	∞	∞	∞	∞	∞	∞		∞
	12	1.8-7.5	2.4-10	∞	2-8	1.8-7.5	7-30	∞	

Tester (–) Lead Connection

8. If the IC ignitor checks good, reconnect the eight-pin and four-pin electrical connectors to the IC ignitor unit (**Figure 32**). Make sure the electrical connectors are free of corrosion and are tight.
9. Connect the battery negative lead as described in this chapter.
10. Install the seat as described in Chapter Fourteen.

Ignitor Unit Replacement

1. Remove the seat and fender as described in Chapter Fourteen.
2. Disconnect the battery negative lead as described in this chapter.
3. Disconnect the eight-pin and four-pin electrical connectors (**Figure 32**) from the IC ignitor.
4. Remove the flange bolts securing the ignitor unit.
5. Remove the ignitor unit (**Figure 36**) from beneath the frame member.
6. Install a new ignitor unit and tighten the bolts securely.
7. Connect the eight-pin and four-pin connectors. Make sure all electrical connections are tight and free of corrosion.
8. Reconnect the negative battery lead.
9. Reinstall the rear fender and seat as described in Chapter Fourteen

STARTER SYSTEM

The starter system includes an ignition switch, starter switch, clutch interlock switch, sidestand interlock switch, starter relay, battery and starter motor as shown in **Figure 37**. Each component of this system is covered separately in this chapter except for the battery, which is covered in Chapter Three.

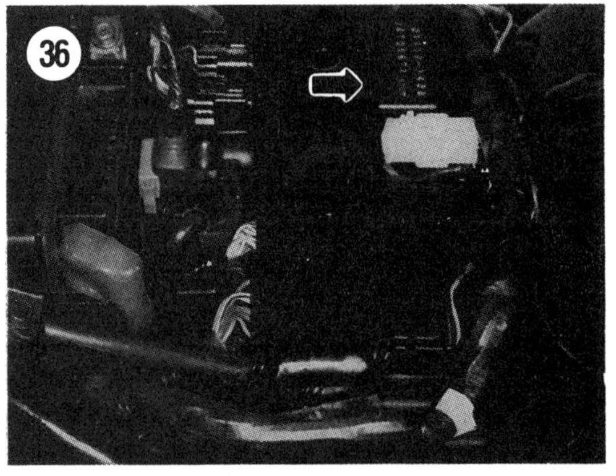

The starter clutch and gears are covered in Chapter Five.

ELECTRIC STARTER

Removal/Installation

1. Drain the engine oil as described in Chapter Three.
2. Disconnect the battery negative (–) lead as described in this chapter.
3. Slide back the rubber boot (A, **Figure 38**) on the starter cable connector.
4. Remove the nut and disconnect the starter cable from the starter motor (B, **Figure 38**).
5. Remove the two bolts securing the starter motor to the crankcase.

NOTE
*There is an interference fit between the starter motor mounting bosses and the crankcase. After the two mounting bolts are removed, the starter motor **cannot** be easily removed from the crankcase without force.*

CAUTION
Do not use a metal hammer to tap on the starter motor as the starter motor case may be damaged.

6. Use a soft-faced or plastic-faced mallet and gently tap on the case of the starter motor to dislodge it from the crankcase boss.
7. Pull the starter motor toward the left-hand side of the motorcycle to disengage it from the idle gears. Remove the starter motor (B, **Figure 38**) from the opening in the crankcase.
8. Inspect the starter motor as described in this chapter.
9. Install by reversing these removal steps while noting the following:
   a. Make sure the O-ring seal (A, **Figure 39**) is in place on the end of the starter. Apply a light coat of clean engine oil to the O-ring prior to installing the starter motor in the crankcase.
   b. Clean the mounting surface (C, **Figure 41**) on the starter motor and the mating surface on the crankcase. This is how the starter is grounded. These surfaces must be clean.
   c. If the starter motor gear will not properly engage the idle gear, slightly rotate the starter

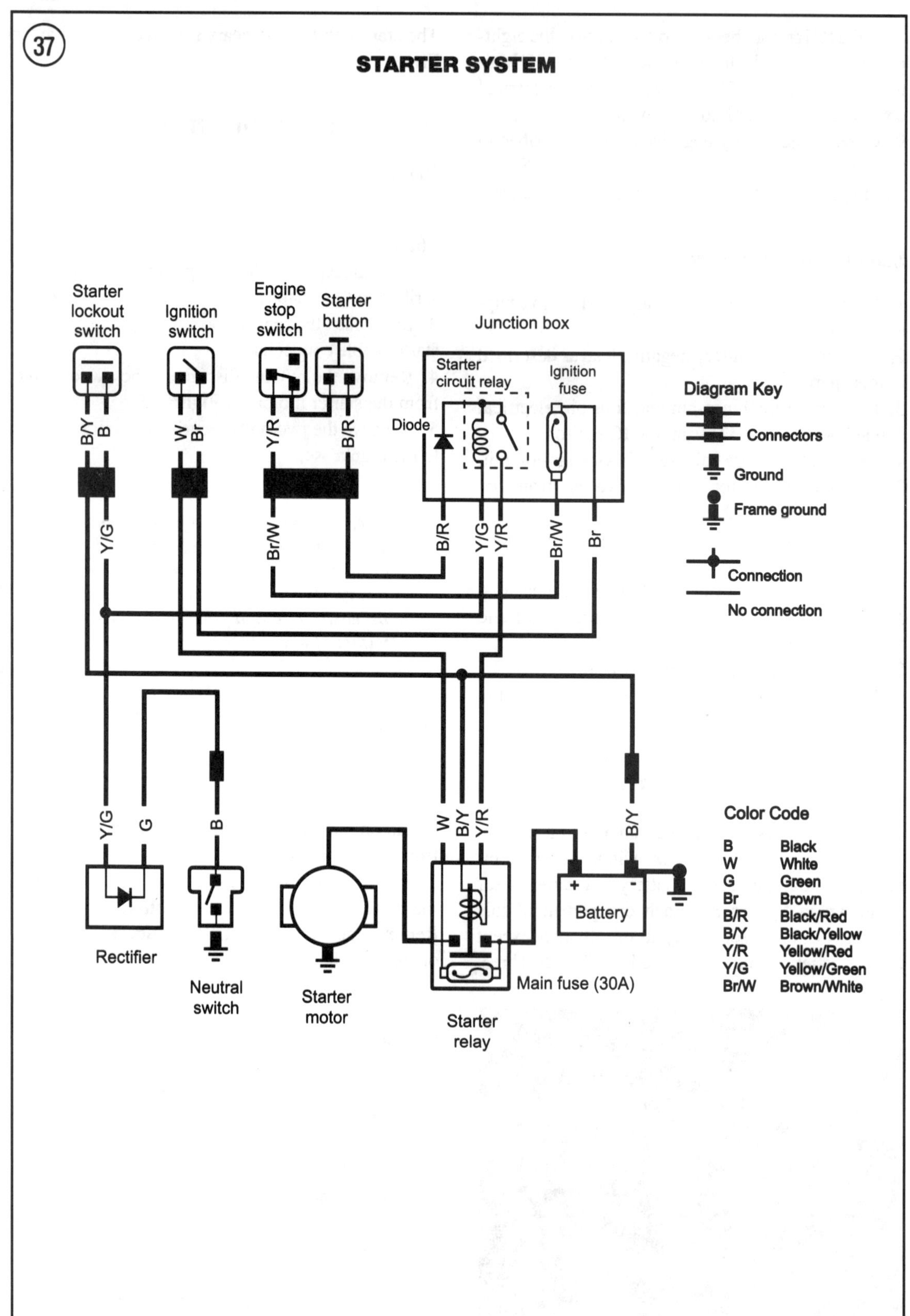
37
STARTER SYSTEM
Starter lockout switch
Ignition switch
Engine stop switch
Starter button
Junction box
Starter circuit relay
Ignition fuse
Diode
B/Y
B
W
Br
Y/R
B/R
Y/G
Br/W
B/R
Y/G
Y/R
Br/W
Br
Diagram Key
Connectors
Ground
Frame ground
Connection
No connection
Y/G
G
B
W
B/Y
Y/R
B/Y
Rectifier
Neutral switch
Starter motor
Starter relay
Main fuse (30A)
Battery
+
-
Color Code
B Black
W White
G Green
Br Brown
B/R Black/Red
B/Y Black/Yellow
Y/R Yellow/Red
Y/G Yellow/Green
Br/W Brown/White

motor gear and try again until alignment is correct.

d. Push the starter motor all the way into the crankcase until it bottoms against the crankcase surface. Torque the starter motor mounting bolts to the specification listed in **Table 1**.

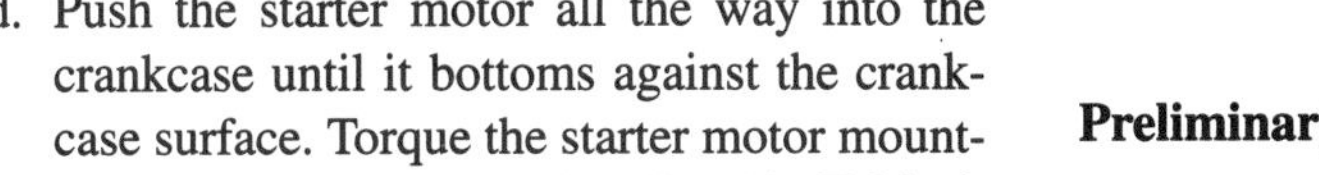

e. Reconnect the starter cable, and torque the cable nut to the specification listed in **Table 1**.

f. Refill the engine with oil as described in Chapter Three.

g. Start the engine and check for proper operation.

Preliminary Inspection

The overhaul of a starter motor is best left to a specialist. This procedure shows how to detect a defective starter.

Inspect the O-ring seal (A, **Figure 39**). O-ring seals tend to harden and lose their ability to seal

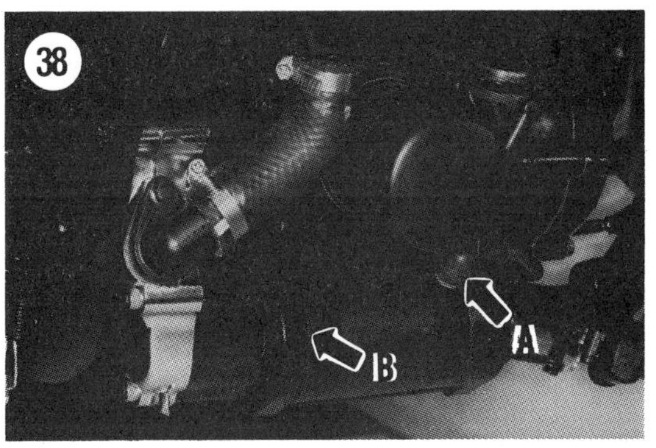

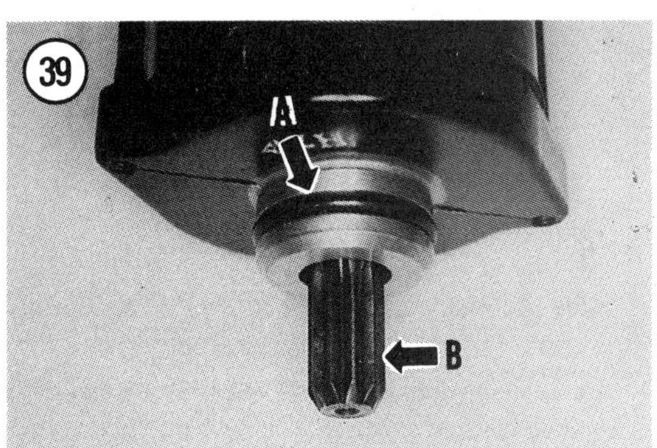

(40)

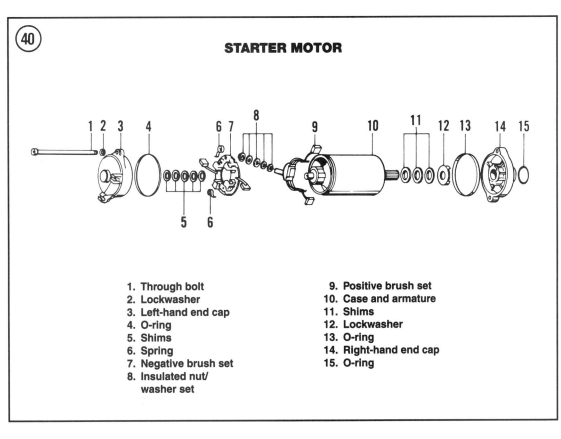

STARTER MOTOR

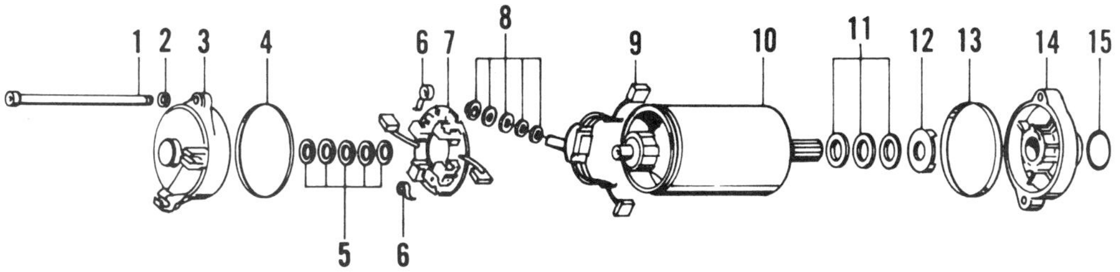

1. Through bolt
2. Lockwasher
3. Left-hand end cap
4. O-ring
5. Shims
6. Spring
7. Negative brush set
8. Insulated nut/ washer set
9. Positive brush set
10. Case and armature
11. Shims
12. Lockwasher
13. O-ring
14. Right-hand end cap
15. O-ring

9

properly after prolonged use and exposure to heat. Replace as necessary.

Inspect the gear (B, **Figure 39**) for chipped or missing teeth. If damaged, the starter assembly must be replaced.

Disassembly

Refer to **Figure 40** for this procedure.

1. Remove the case through-bolts and lockwashers (A, **Figure 41**).
2. Remove the right-hand end cap (**Figure 42**) from the case.

NOTE
*Record the number of shims (A, **Figure 43**) used on the shaft next to the right-hand end cap.*

3. Slide the lockwasher (A, **Figure 44**) and shims (B, **Figure 44**) from the armature shaft.
4. Remove the left-hand end cap (B, **Figure 41**) from the case.

NOTE
*Record the number of shims (**Figure 45**) used on the shaft next to the commutator and next to the left-hand end cap.*

5. Slide the shims (**Figure 46**) from the armature shaft.
6. Partially remove the negative (–) brush holder (A, **Figure 47**) from the case. Disengage the positive (+) brushes (B, **Figure 47**) from the negative brush holder, then remove the negative brush holder.
7. Withdraw the armature (**Figure 48**) from the case.

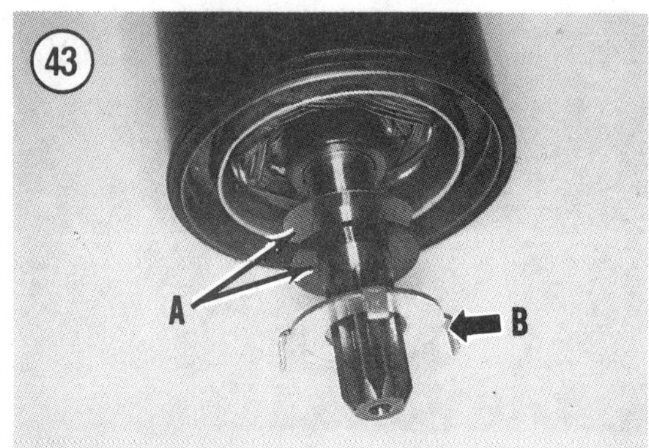

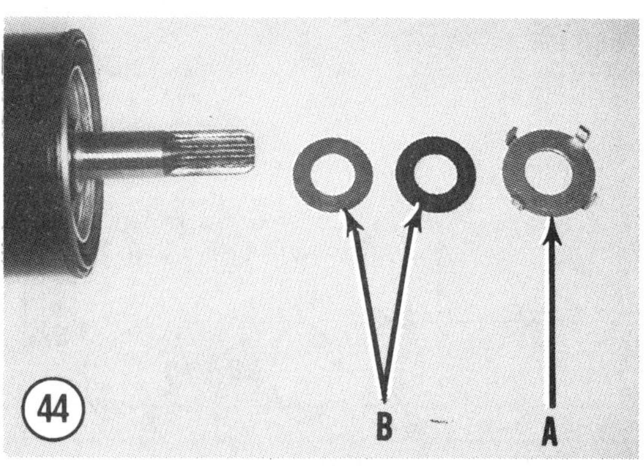

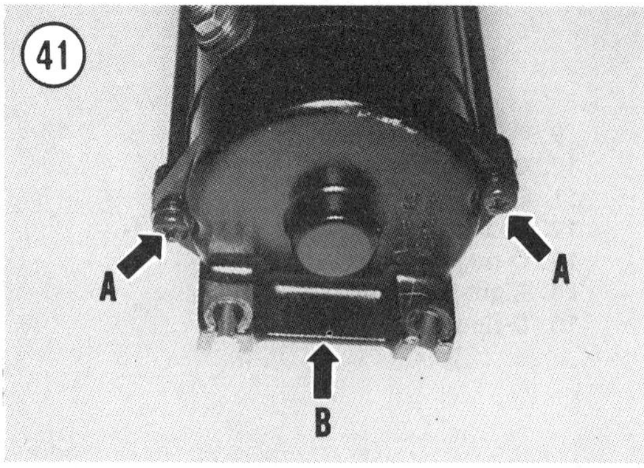

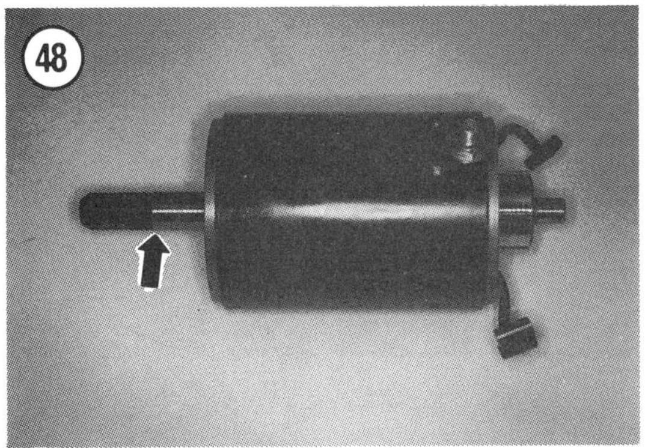

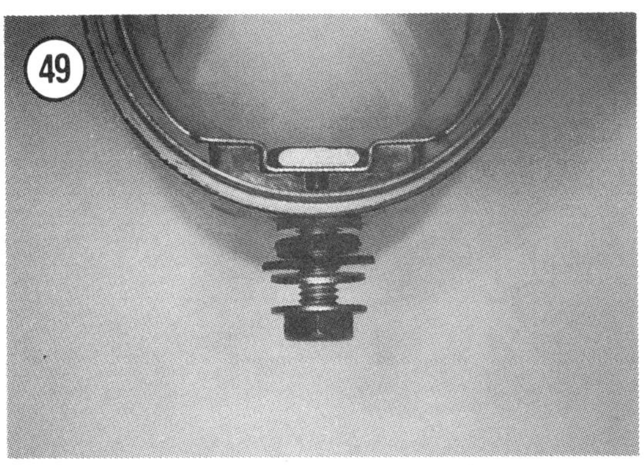

NOTE

*Before removing the nuts, washers and O-ring (**Figure 49**), record their description and order. They must be reinstalled in the same order to insulate the brushes from the case.*

8. If necessary, remove the nut, washers and O-ring (A, **Figure 50**) securing the brush positive (+) brush set and remove the set (B, **Figure 50**).

CAUTION

Do not immerse the wire windings in the case or the armature coil in solvent as the insulation may be damaged. Wipe the windings with a cloth lightly moistened with solvent and thoroughly dry.

9. Clean all grease, dirt and carbon from all components.
10. Inspect the starter motor components as described in this chapter.

Assembly

Refer to **Figure 40** for this procedure.

NOTE

In the next step, install all parts in the same order as noted during disassembly. This is essential to insulate the positive (+) brushes from the case.

1. If removed, install the positive (+) brush holder (B, **Figure 50**), O-ring, washers and nut (A, **Figure 50**). Tighten the nut securely.
2. Position the armature coil assembly so the armature end is installed into the case where the positive

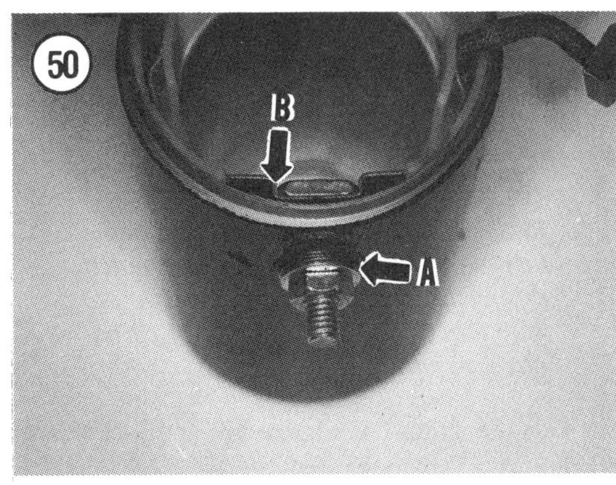

brush set is located. Insert the armature (**Figure 48**) into the end of the case.

3. If removed, install an O-ring seal (**Figure 51**) onto each end of the case. Apply a light coat of clean engine oil to the O-rings.

NOTE
*To ease the installation of the brush assemblies onto the commutator, carefully pull the brush spring off the backside of the brush and insert a small plastic or metal washer (**Figure 52**) between the brush and the spring. This will keep the spring pressure off the brush and the brushes will remain retracted in their holders.*

4. Partially install the negative brush holder (A, **Figure 47**) onto the armature. Carefully insert the positive brush electrical wires through the slots in the negative brush holder (A, **Figure 53**). Make sure they are correctly routed so they will not get pinched during final assembly.
5. Insert the positive brushes onto their holders and install the washer (B, **Figure 53**) as described in the previous Note.
6. Align the locating tab (C, **Figure 53**) on the negative (–) brush holder with the locating notch (D, **Figure 53**) in the left-case and push the holder assembly into place.

NOTE
*In the next step, install the exact same number of shims (**Figure 46**) as noted during disassembly. This is necessary to maintain the correct amount of armature end play.*

7. Slide the shims (**Figure 46**) onto the armature shaft.
8. Align the raised tab (A, **Figure 54**) on the negative brush holder with the locating notch (B, **Figure 54**) in the left-hand end cap and install the left-hand end cap (**Figure 55**).

NOTE
*In the next step, install the exact same number of shims (B, **Figure 44**) as noted during disassembly. This is necessary to maintain the correct amount of armature end play.*

9. Slide the shims (A, **Figure 43**) and lockwasher (B, **Figure 43**) onto the shaft.

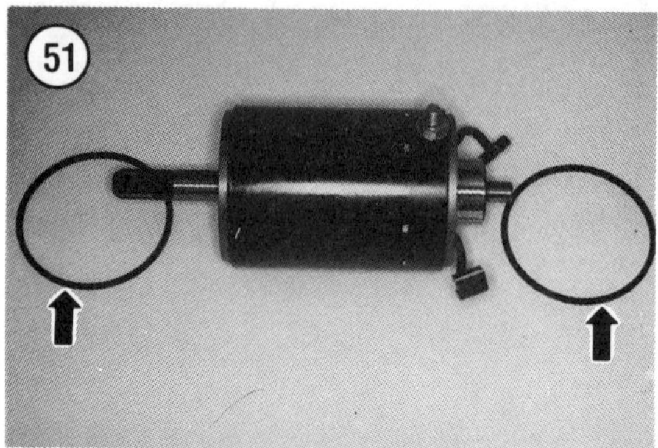
51

52

53

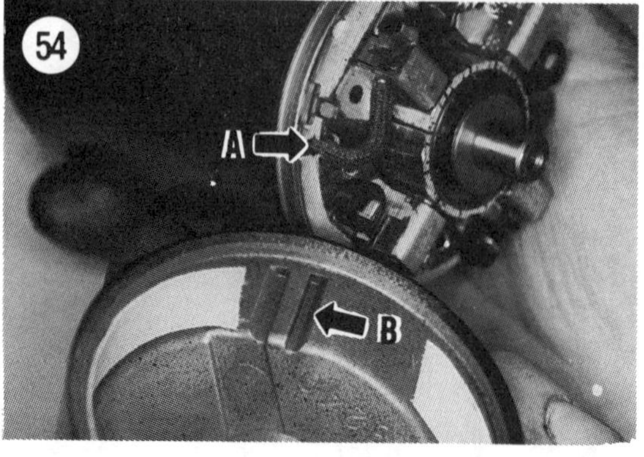

54

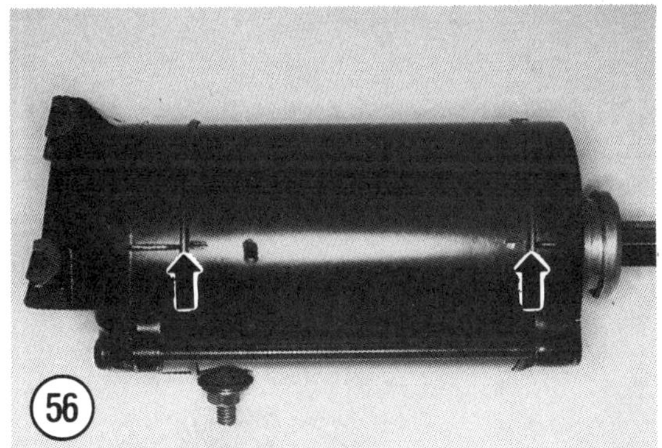

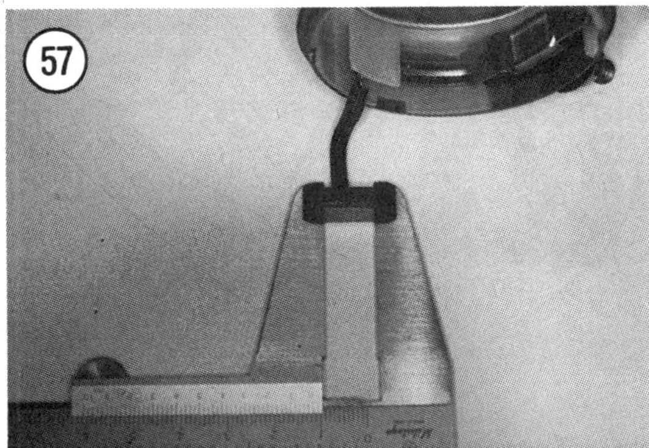

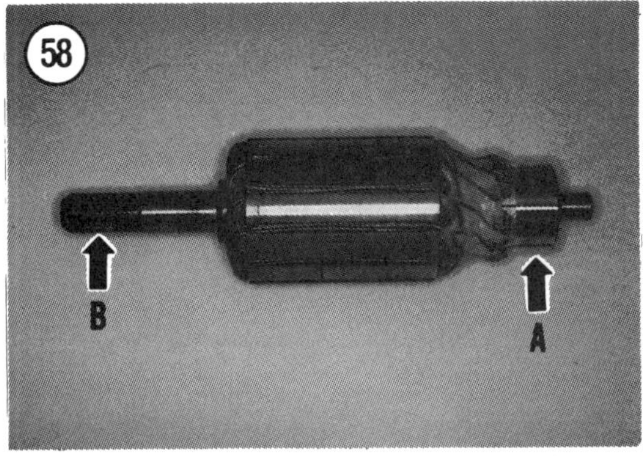

10. Install the right-hand end cap (**Figure 42**). Slightly rotate it back and forth to make sure the lockwasher is seated correctly in the right-hand end cap.

11. Align the match marks on the end caps with the marks on the case (**Figure 56**).

12. Apply a small amount of Loctite 242 to the case through-bolt threads prior to installation. Install the case through-bolts and lockwashers (A, **Figure 41**) and then torque the bolts to the specification in **Table 1**.

Inspection

1. Measure the length of each brush (**Figure 57**) with a vernier caliper. If the length for any one of the brushes is less than the service limit listed in **Table 3**, both brush sets must be replaced. A brush set cannot be replaced individually.

2. Inspect the commutator (A, **Figure 58**). The mica should be just below the surface of the copper bars. On a worn commutator, the mica and copper bars may be worn to the same level (**Figure 59**). If necessary, have the commutator serviced at a dealership or electrical repair shop.

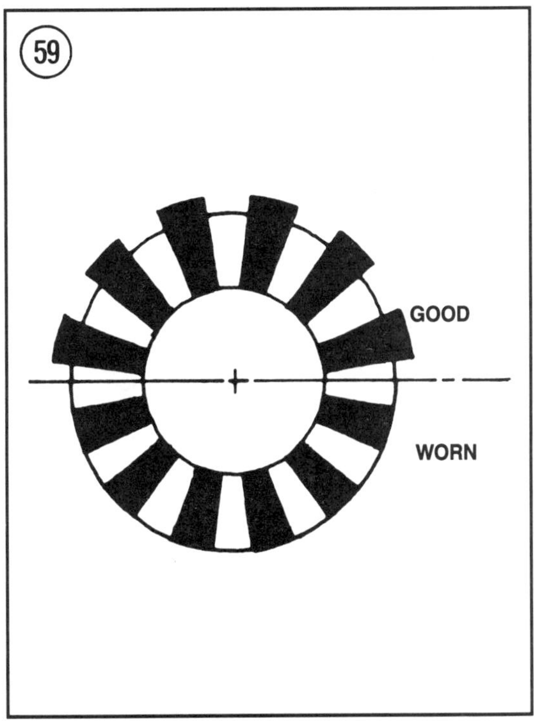

3. Inspect the commutator segments (**Figure 60**) for discoloration. If a pair of segments are discolored, grounded armature coils are indicated.
4. Use an ohmmeter and perform the following:
   a. Check for continuity between the commutator segments (**Figure 61**); there should be continuity between any two of the segments.
   b. Check for continuity between the commutator segments and the shaft (**Figure 62**); there should be *no* continuity.
   c. If the unit fails either of these tests, the starter assembly must be replaced. The armature cannot be replaced individually.
5. Use an ohmmeter and perform the following:
   a. Check for continuity between the starter cable terminal and the starter case; there should be no continuity.
   b. Check for continuity between the starter cable terminal and the brush wire terminal; there should be no continuity.
   c. If the unit fails either of these tests, the starter assembly must be replaced. The case/field coil assembly cannot be replaced individually.
6. Inspect the seal (A, **Figure 63**) and needle bearing (B, **Figure 63**) in the right-hand end cap for wear, damage or deterioration. Neither part is available as a replacement part. If either is damaged, replace the right-hand end cap.
7. Inspect the left-hand end cap for wear or damage and replace if necessary.
8. Inspect the left-hand end cap bushing (**Figure 64**) for wear or damage. The bushing is not available as a replacement part. If either is damaged, replace the left-hand end cap.
9. Inspect the case assembly for wear or damage. Make sure the field coils (**Figure 65**) are bonded

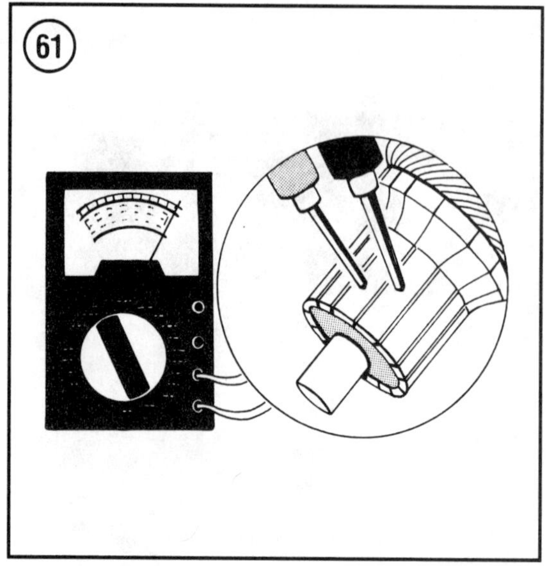

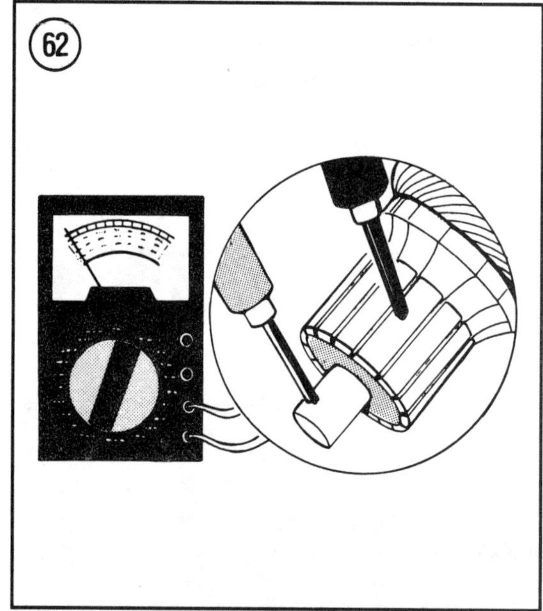

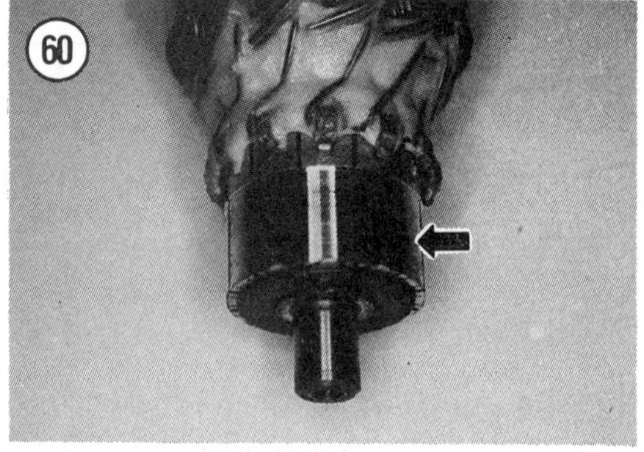

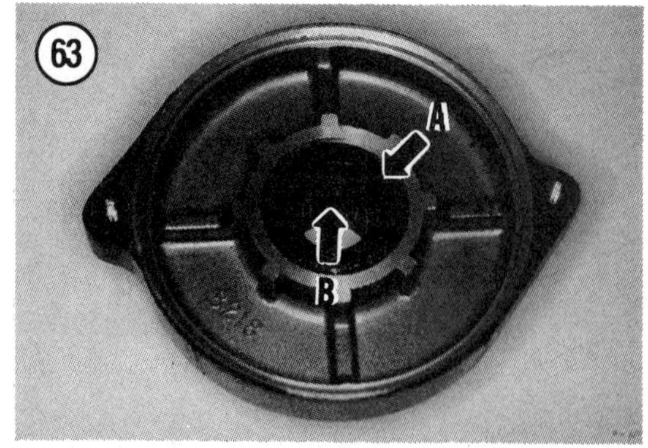

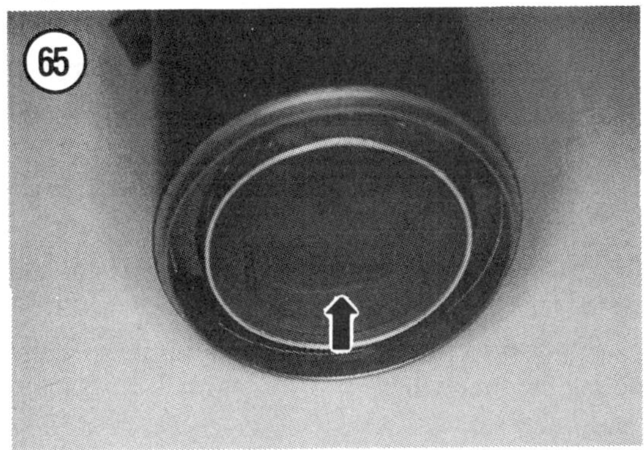

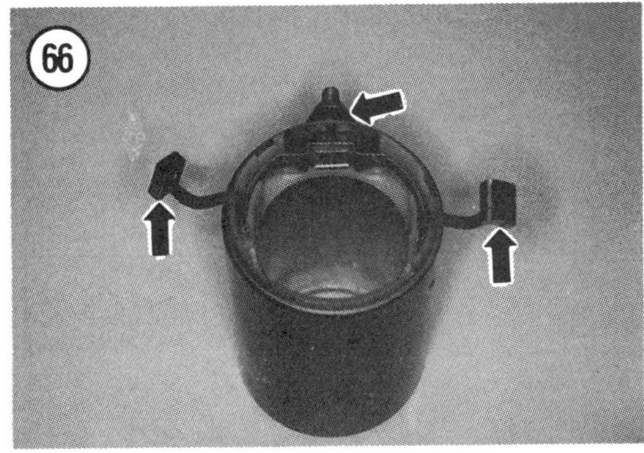

securely in place. If any field coils are loose or damaged, replace the case assembly.

10. Inspect the positive brush holder (**Figure 66**) assembly for wear or damage; replace any damaged parts.

11. Inspect the negative brush holder and brush springs (**Figure 67**) assembly for wear or damage. The springs are the only replacement parts available for this assembly.

12. Inspect the gear splines (B, **Figure 58**) on the armature coil assembly for wear or damage. If damaged, replace the starter motor assembly.

STARTER RELAY

Testing

1. Remove the seat as described in Chapter Fourteen.
2. Shift the transmission into neutral.

CAUTION

Because the battery positive (+) lead at the starter relay is connected directly to the battery, do not allow the end of the lead to touch any part of the bike during the following procedure. This would result in a direct short—even when the ignition switch is OFF.

3. Move the rubber boots back off the electrical connectors (A, **Figure 68**) on top of the starter relay.
4. Remove the nuts and washers and disconnect the starter motor lead and the battery positive cable from the starter relay terminals.
5. Position the switches in the following positions in order to run this test correctly:
   a. Ignition switch—ON.

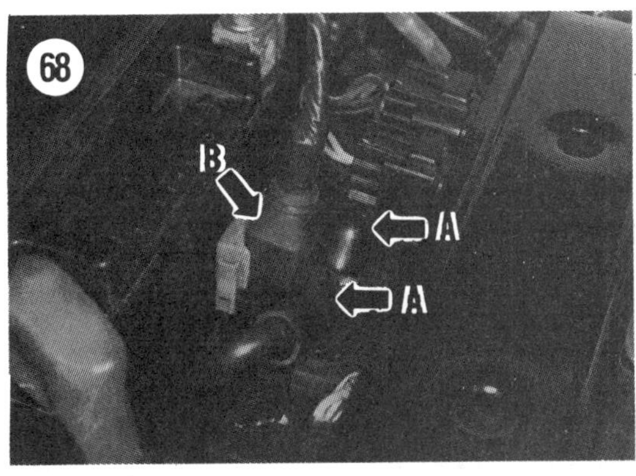

b. Engine stop switch—RUN.
c. Neutral switch—ON (transmission in neutral).
d. Starter button—ON.

6. Set the ohmmeter to R× 1 and calibrate (zero) the meter.

7. Connect the ohmmeter between the relay large terminals (the starter motor and battery terminals), press the start button and observe the following:

a. If the relay makes a single clicking sound and the meter reads zero resistance, the relay is good.
b. If the relay clicks, but the meter reads a value greater than zero, the relay is defective and must be replaced.
c. If the relay does not click, the relay is defective and must be replaced.

8. If the relay checks good, install all electrical wires to the relay and tighten the nuts securely. Make sure the electrical connectors are secured to the terminals and that the rubber boots are properly installed to keep out moisture.

9. If the relay is faulty, replace it as described in this chapter.

10. Install the seat and frame right-hand side cover.

Removal/Installation

1. Remove the seat as described in Chapter Fourteen.

2. Move the rubber boots back off the electrical connectors (A, **Figure 68**) on top of the starter relay.

3. Remove the nuts and washers and disconnect the starter motor lead and the battery positive (+) cable from the starter relay.

4. Disconnect the harness connector (B, **Figure 68**) containing 3 wires (1 yellow/red, 1 black/yellow and 1 white) from the relay.

5. Pull the rubber isolator from the mounting tab on the frame.

6. Withdraw the relay from the rubber isolator and install a new one.

7. Replace by reversing the removal steps while noting the following:

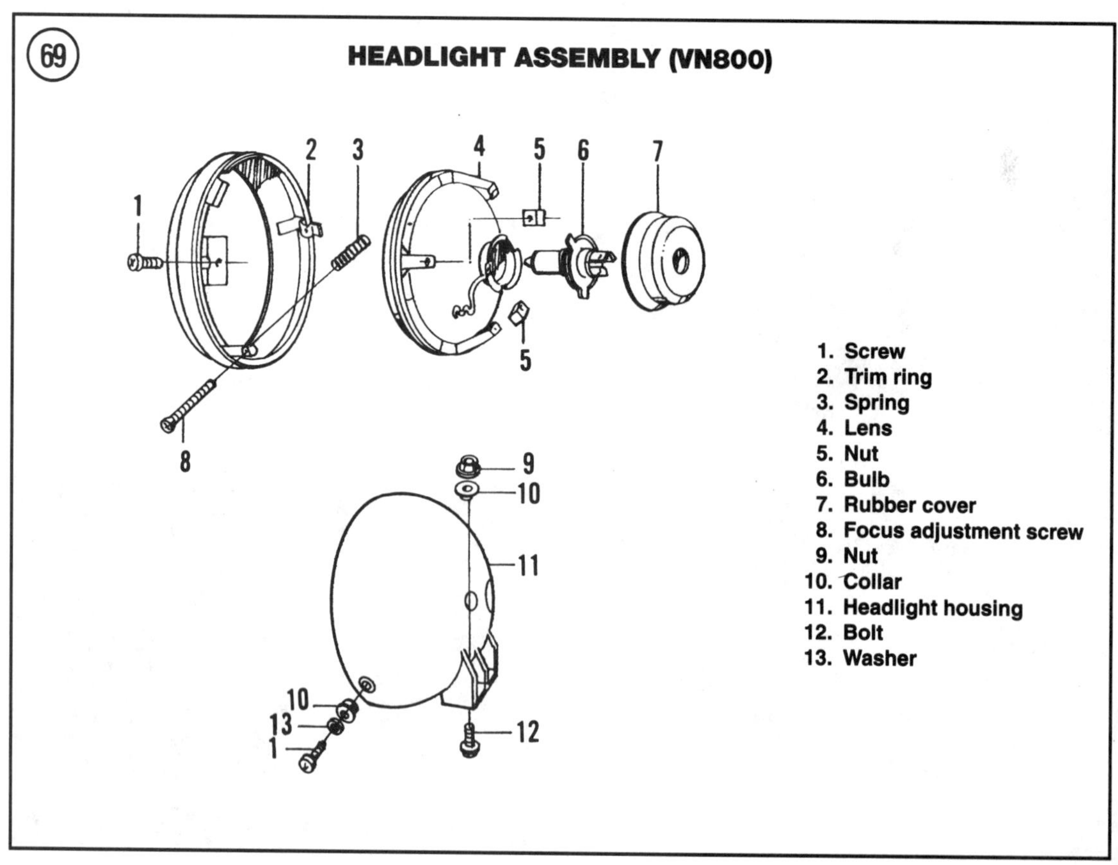

a. Install all electrical wires to the relay. Tighten the nuts securely.
b. Make sure the electrical connectors are on tight and that the rubber boots are properly installed (**Figure 68**) to keep out moisture.

LIGHTING SYSTEM

The lighting system consists of a headlight, taillight/brakelight, directional lights, indicator lights and meter illumination lights. **Table 4** lists replacement bulbs for these components. Always use the correct wattage bulb as indicated in this section. A larger wattage bulb will produce a dim light and a smaller wattage bulb will burn out prematurely.

U.S., Canadian, and Australian models have a headlight relay found in the junction box. On these models, the headlight does not come on when the ignition switch is first turned on. The light comes on and remains on after the starter button is released. Once on, the headlight will momentarily go out whenever the starter button is pressed.

Headlight Bulb and Lens Replacement

For this procedure, refer to **Figure 69** and **Figure 70** for headlight components. Also refer to **Figure 71** and **Figure 72** the headlight circuit diagrams.

1. Remove the mounting screw (A, **Figure 73**), lockwasher and collar (VN800 only) from each side of the headlight housing.

NOTE
The tabs at the top of the headlight housing are very fragile. Exercise great care to prevent breaking tabs.

2. Gently lift out the bottom of the headlight trim ring (B, **Figure 73**) to disengage it from the retaining tabs at the top of the headlight housing. Remove the trim ring and headlight lens unit assembly from the case.
3. Disconnect the electrical connector (A, **Figure 74**) from the backside of the lens unit.
4. Remove the rubber cover (B, **Figure 74**) from the back of the headlight lens unit.

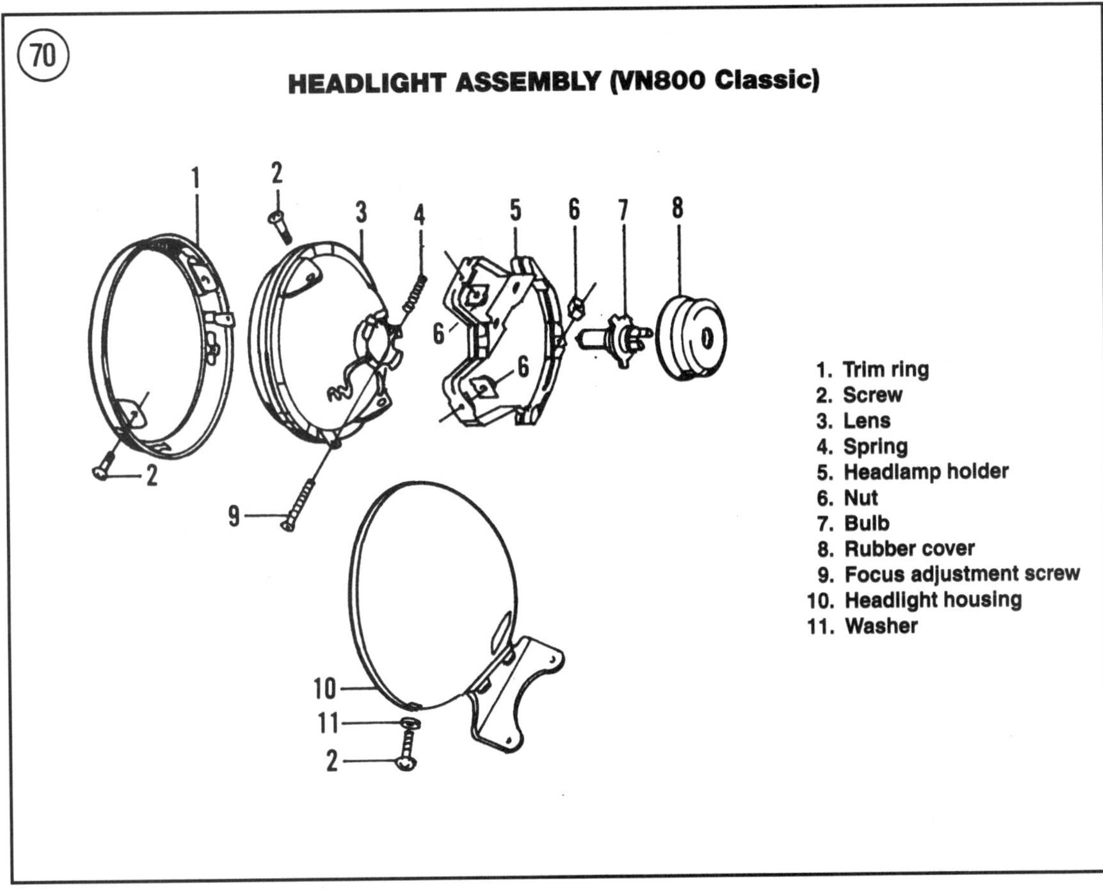

9

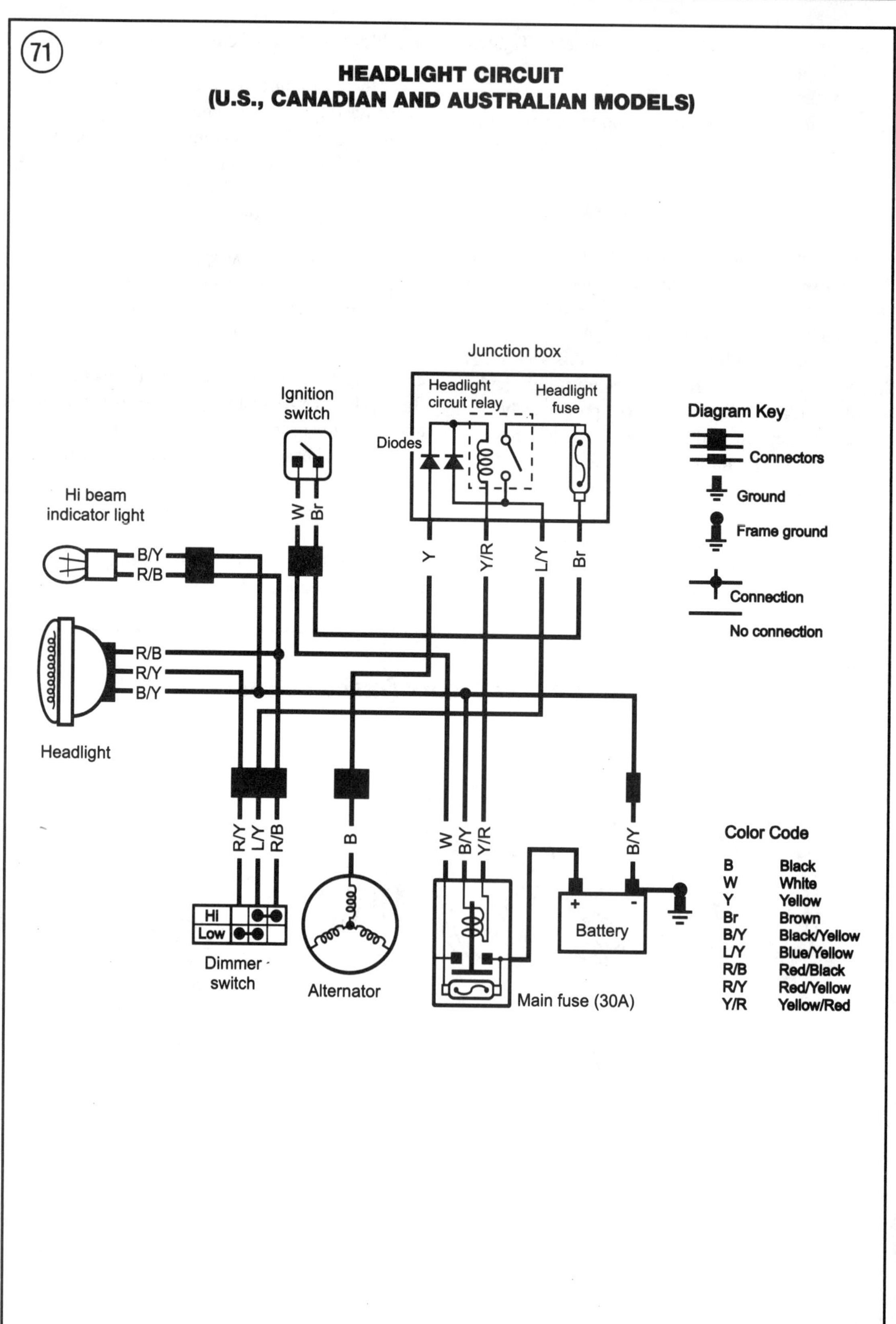
71
HEADLIGHT CIRCUIT
(U.S., CANADIAN AND AUSTRALIAN MODELS)
Junction box
Headlight circuit relay
Headlight fuse
Diodes
Ignition switch
W
Br
Hi beam indicator light
B/Y
R/B
Y
Y/R
L/Y
Br
Diagram Key
Connectors
Ground
Frame ground
Connection
No connection
R/B
R/Y
B/Y
Headlight
R/Y
L/Y
R/B
B
W
B/Y
Y/R
B/Y
Hi
Low
Dimmer switch
Alternator
Main fuse (30A)
Battery
Color Code
B Black
W White
Y Yellow
Br Brown
B/Y Black/Yellow
L/Y Blue/Yellow
R/B Red/Black
R/Y Red/Yellow
Y/R Yellow/Red

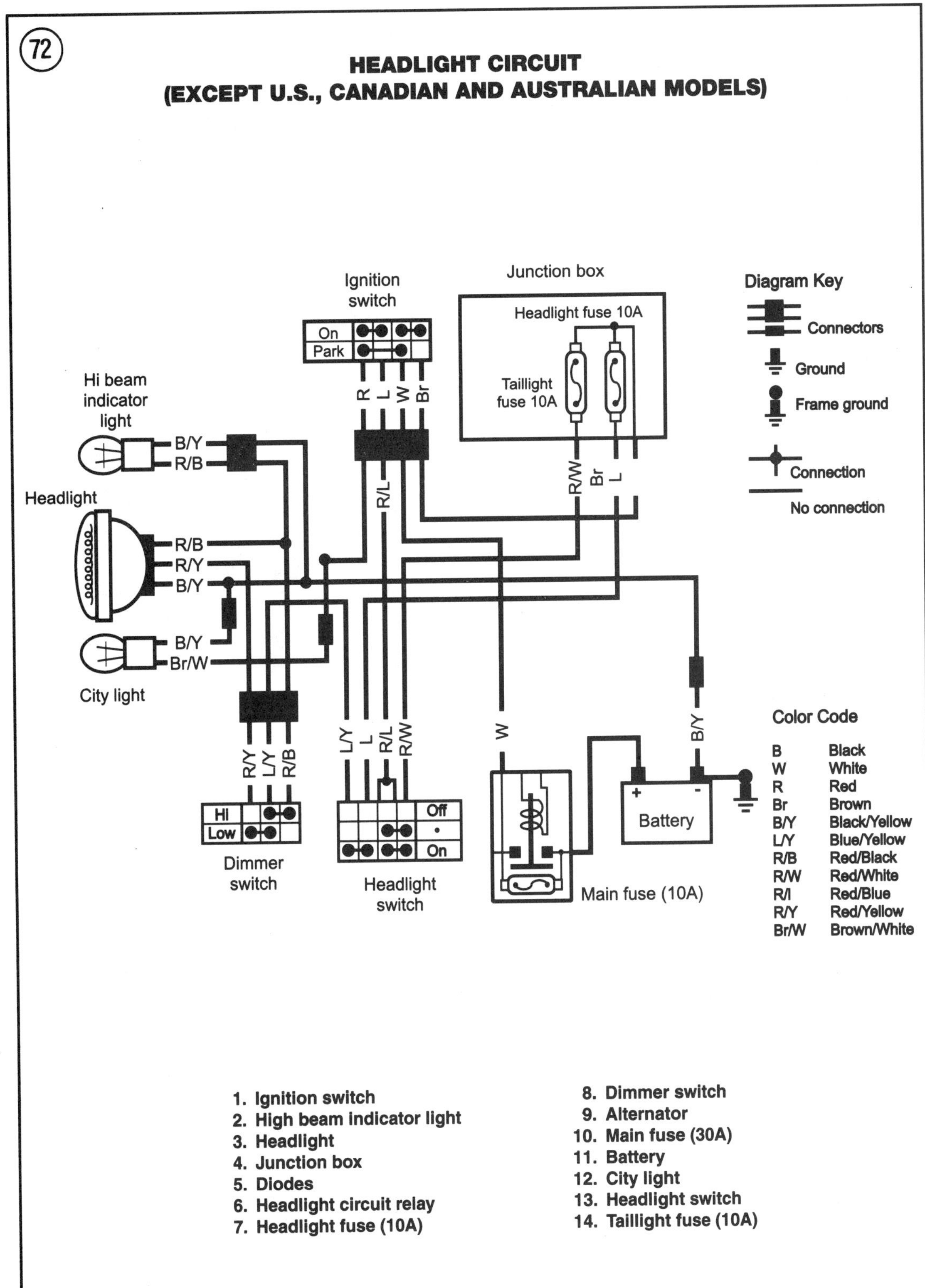

1. Ignition switch
2. High beam indicator light
3. Headlight
4. Junction box
5. Diodes
6. Headlight circuit relay
7. Headlight fuse (10A)
8. Dimmer switch
9. Alternator
10. Main fuse (30A)
11. Battery
12. City light
13. Headlight switch
14. Taillight fuse (10A)

CAUTION

Carefully read all instructions shipped with the replacement quartz bulb. Do not touch the bulb glass with your finger. Any contamination on the quartz halogen bulb will drastically reduce bulb life. Clean any traces of oil from the bulb with a cloth moistened in alcohol or lacquer thinner.

5. Unhook the retaining clip (A, **Figure 75**) and release the clip from the lens unit.

6. Remove the light bulb (B, **Figure 75**) and replace it (**Figure 76**).

7A. On VN800 models, remove the trim ring from the headlight lens unit by performing the following:

a. Remove the adjustment screws (A, **Figure 77**).

b. Remove the screws, washers and spacers (B, **Figure 77**) that secure the lens unit to the trim ring.

c. Remove the trim ring (C, **Figure 77**) from the lens unit.

7B. On VN800 Classic models, remove the trim ring from the headlight lens unit by performing the following:

a. Remove the adjustment screws.

b. Remove the screws, washers and spacers that secure the lens holder to the trim ring.

c. Remove the lens holder and trim ring from the lens unit.

8. Install by reversing these removal steps while noting the following.

a. Install the headlight lens unit so the TOP mark (**Figure 78**) on the front of the headlight lens faces up.

b. Install the rubber cover with the TOP mark (**Figure 79**) facing upward.

c. Make sure the electrical connector (A, **Figure 74**) is on tight and that the rubber cover is properly installed to keep out moisture.

d. On VN800 models, be sure to install the collar (**Figure 80**) on the mounting screw. Do not overtighten the screw as the plastic headlight housing mounting area may fracture.

e. Adjust the headlight as described in this chapter.

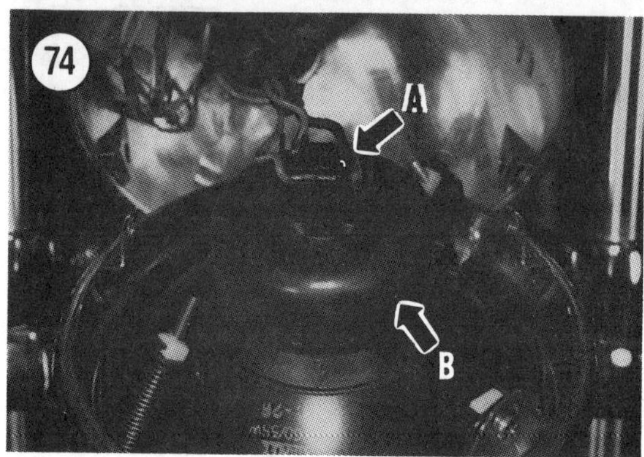

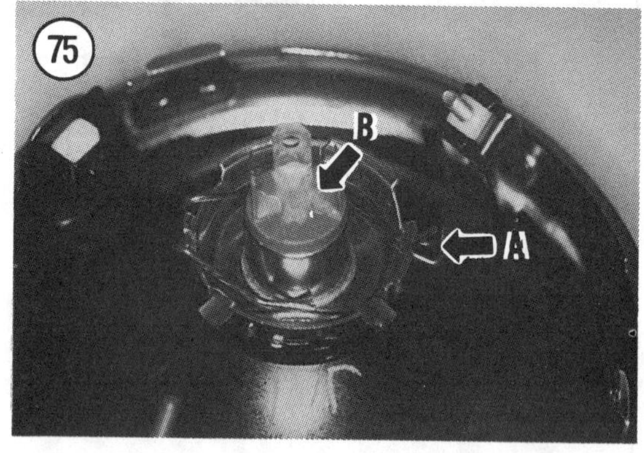

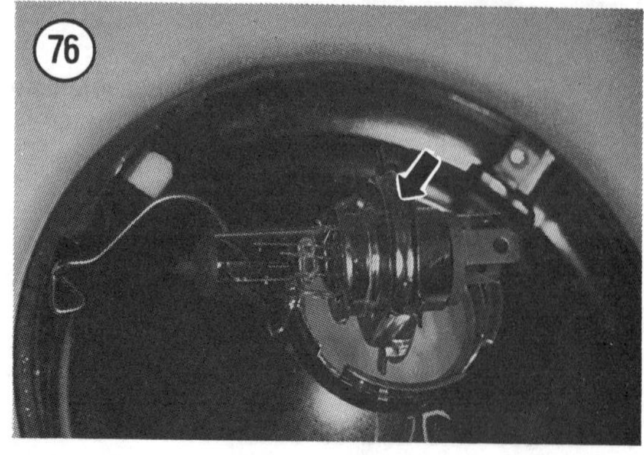

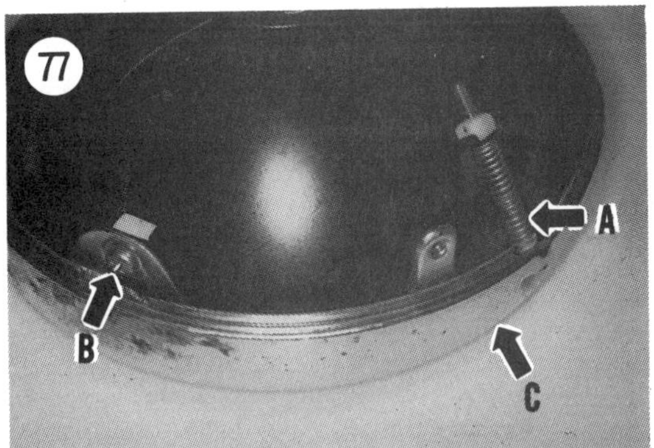

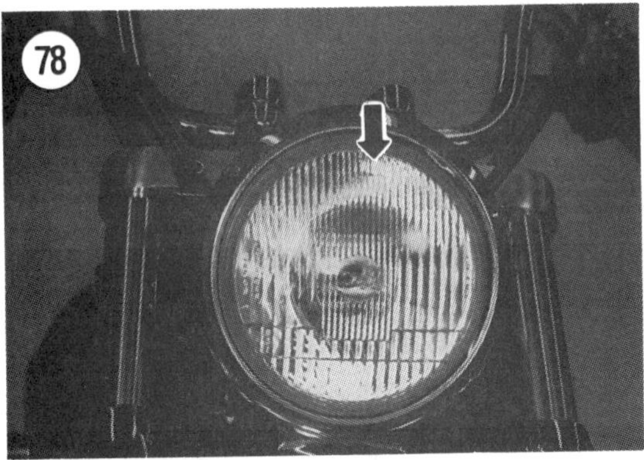

Front Position Light Bulb Replacement (U.K. Models)

1. Reach up under the headlight housing and remove the socket/bulb and electrical connector from the headlight housing.
2. Remove the bulb from the socket.
3. Replace the bulb and install the socket assembly.

Headlight Housing Removal/Installation

For this procedure, refer to **Figure 69** and **Figure 70** for headlight components. Also refer to **Figure 71** and **Figure 72** the headlight circuit diagrams.

1. Remove the headlight bulb and lens assembly from the headlight housing as described in this chapter.
2. Disconnect the electrical wire connectors (A, **Figure 81**) located inside the headlight housing.
3. Remove the bolts and nuts securing the headlight housing to the lower fork bridge.
4. Partially remove the housing and withdraw the wires from the opening in the back of the headlight housing. (B, **Figure 81**).
5. Remove the housing from the lower fork bridge.
6. Install by reversing the removal steps while noting the following:
   a. Make sure the collar and rubber damper are in place in the mounting hole on each side of the headlight housing.
   b. Do not overtighten the nuts as the plastic headlight housing mounting area may fracture.
   c. Adjust the headlight as described in this chapter.

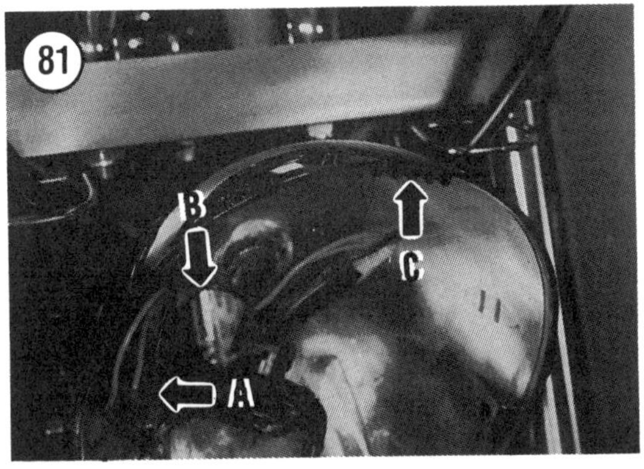

9

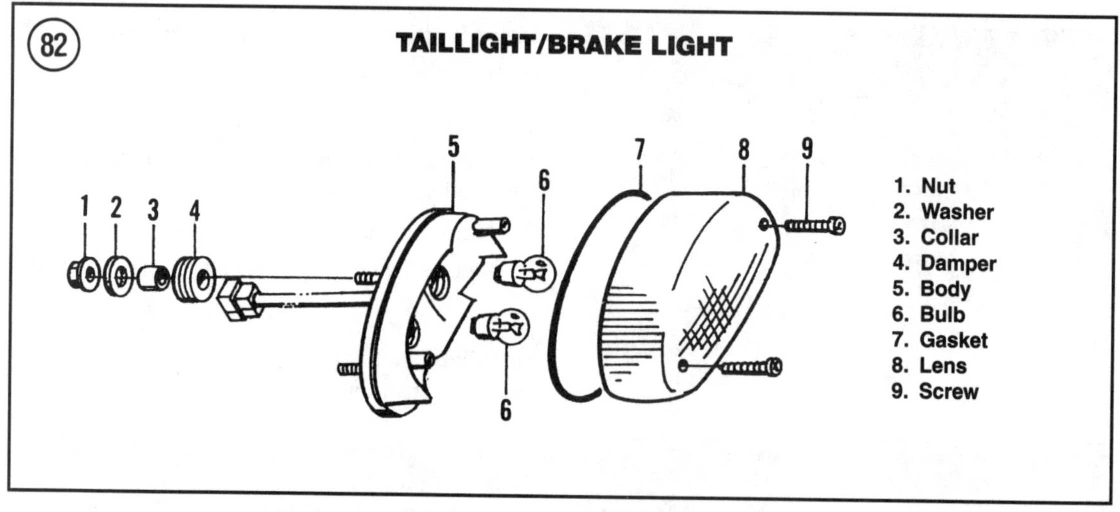
82
TAILLIGHT/BRAKE LIGHT
1
2
3
4
5
6
7
8
9
6
1. Nut
2. Washer
3. Collar
4. Damper
5. Body
6. Bulb
7. Gasket
8. Lens
9. Screw

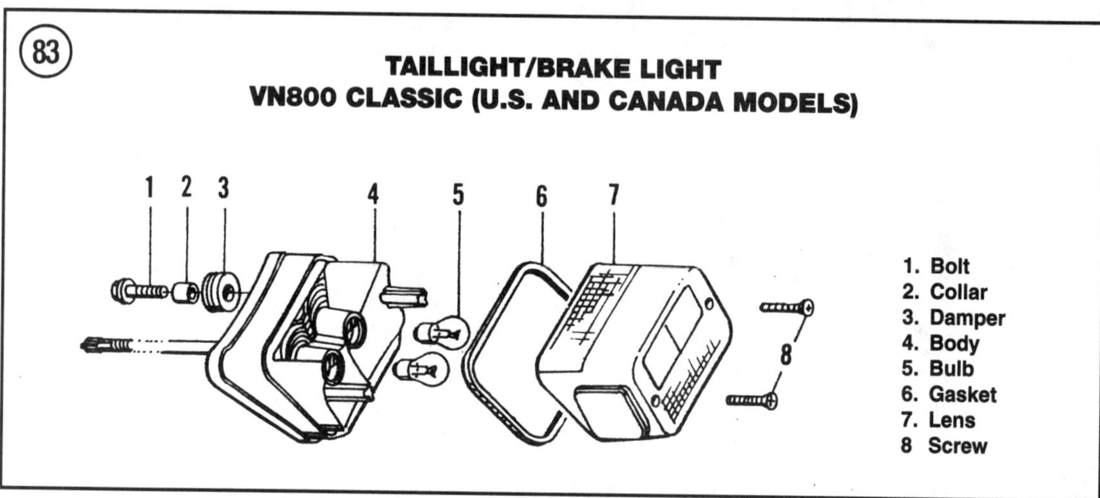
83
TAILLIGHT/BRAKE LIGHT
VN800 CLASSIC (U.S. AND CANADA MODELS)
1
2
3
4
5
6
7
8
1. Bolt
2. Collar
3. Damper
4. Body
5. Bulb
6. Gasket
7. Lens
8 Screw

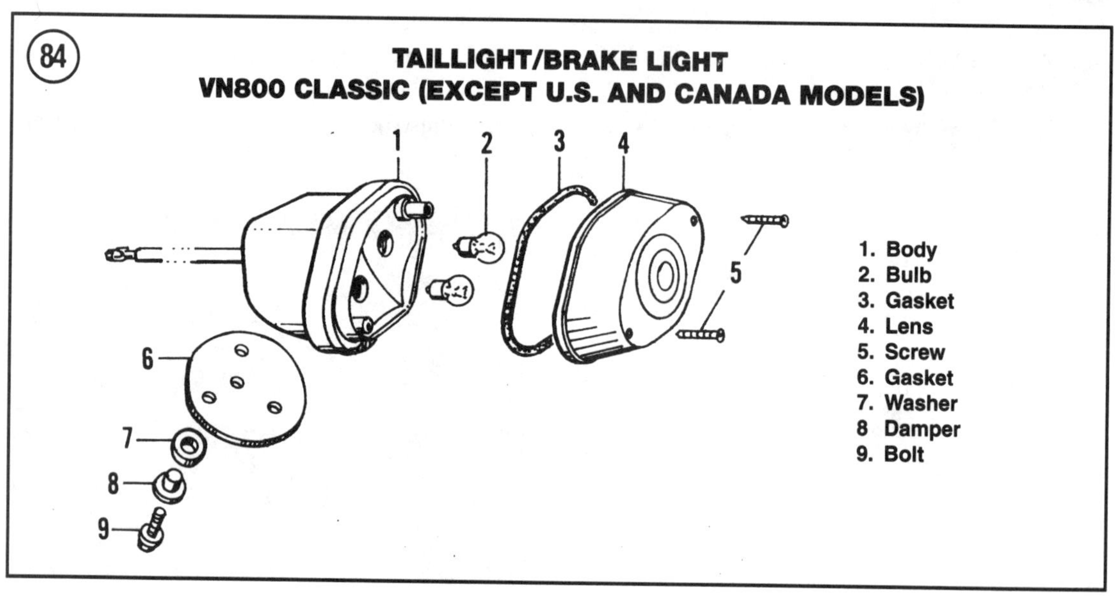
84
TAILLIGHT/BRAKE LIGHT
VN800 CLASSIC (EXCEPT U.S. AND CANADA MODELS)
1
2
3
4
5
6
7
8
9
1. Body
2. Bulb
3. Gasket
4. Lens
5. Screw
6. Gasket
7. Washer
8 Damper
9. Bolt

Headlight Adjustment

Adjust the headlight horizontally and vertically according to the Department of Motor Vehicle regulations in your area.

To adjust the headlight vertically, turn the lower adjustment screw on the left-hand side of the trim ring, until the aim is correct. Turning the screw clockwise moves the headlight beam down toward the road.

To adjust the headlight horizontally, turn the upper adjustment screw on the right-hand side of the trim ring (C, **Figure 73**). Turning the screw clockwise moves the headlight beam toward the left-hand side of the road.

Taillight/Brake Light Bulb Replacement

Refer to **Figure 82**, **Figure 83** and **Figure 84** for this procedure.

1. Remove the screws securing the lens and remove the lens and gasket.
2. Wash the inside and outside of the lens with a mild detergent and wipe it dry.

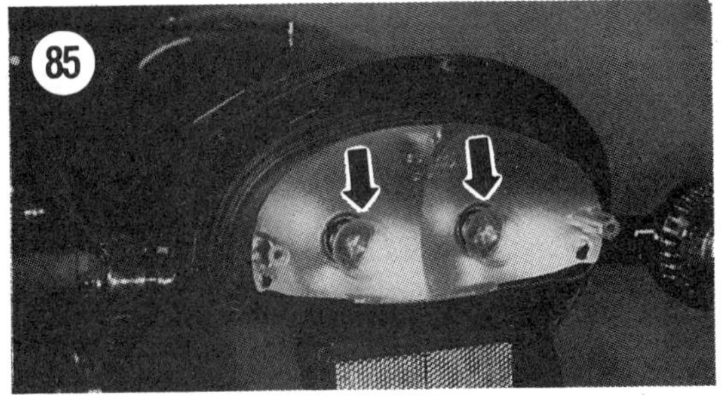

3. Inspect the lens gasket. Replace the gasket if it is damaged or deteriorated.
4. Remove a bulb (**Figure 85**) by pushing it in and turning it counterclockwise.
5. Carefully wipe off the reflector surface behind the bulb with a soft cloth.
6. Replace the bulb and install the lens and gasket; do not over-tighten the screws as the lens may crack.

Taillight/Brake Light Body Removal/Installation

Refer to **Figure 82**, **Figure 83** and **Figure 84** for this procedure.

1. Remove the taillight/brake light lens, gasket and bulbs from the body as described in this chapter.
2. Disconnect the electrical connector for the taillight/brake light assembly.
3. Remove the hardware securing the taillight/brake light body to the rear fender. Remove the body and gasket (where equipped).
4. Install by reversing these removal steps while noting the following:
   a. Replace the body gasket (where equipped) if it is starting to harden or deteriorate.
   b. Make sure the electrical connector is tight and free of corrosion.

License Plate Light Bulb Replacement (VN800 Classic, Except U.S. and Canadian models)

Refer to **Figure 86** for this procedure.

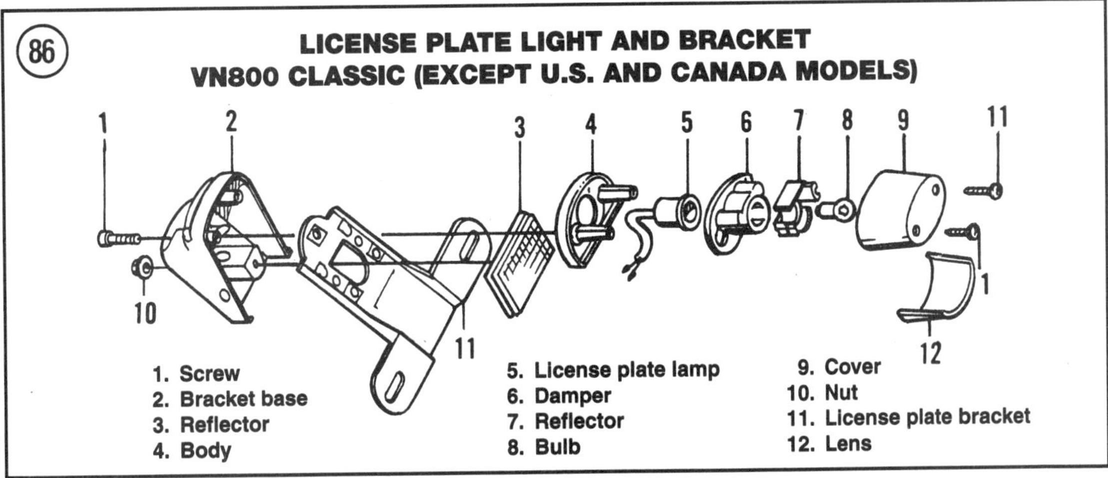

1. Remove the screws securing the bulb cover/lens assembly to the body, and remove the bulb cover/lens assembly.
2. Wash out the inside of the bulb cover/lens with a mild detergent and wipe dry.
3. Inspect the sealing surface of the damper and body. Replace the damper if it is damaged or deteriorated.
4. Remove the bulb by pushing it in and turning it counterclockwise.
5. Replace the bulb and install the bulb cover/lens assembly; do not over-tighten the screws as the bulb cover/lens may crack.

License Plate Light AssemblyRemoval/Installation (VN800 Classic, Except U.S. and Canadian models)

Refer to **Figure 86** for this procedure.

1. Remove the bulb cover/lens and bulb as described in this chapter.
2. Disconnect the two individual electrical wires for the license plate assembly.
3. Remove the screws securing the body to the body bracket and remove the body/lamp assembly.
4. Install by reversing these removal steps while noting the following:
   a. Replace the damper if it is starting to harden or deteriorate.
   b. Make sure the electrical connectors are tight and free of corrosion.

Turn Signal Light Bulb Replacement

For this procedure, refer to **Figure 87** for turn signal components and to **Figure 88** for the turn signal circuit diagram.

1. Remove the screws securing the lens, and remove the lens.

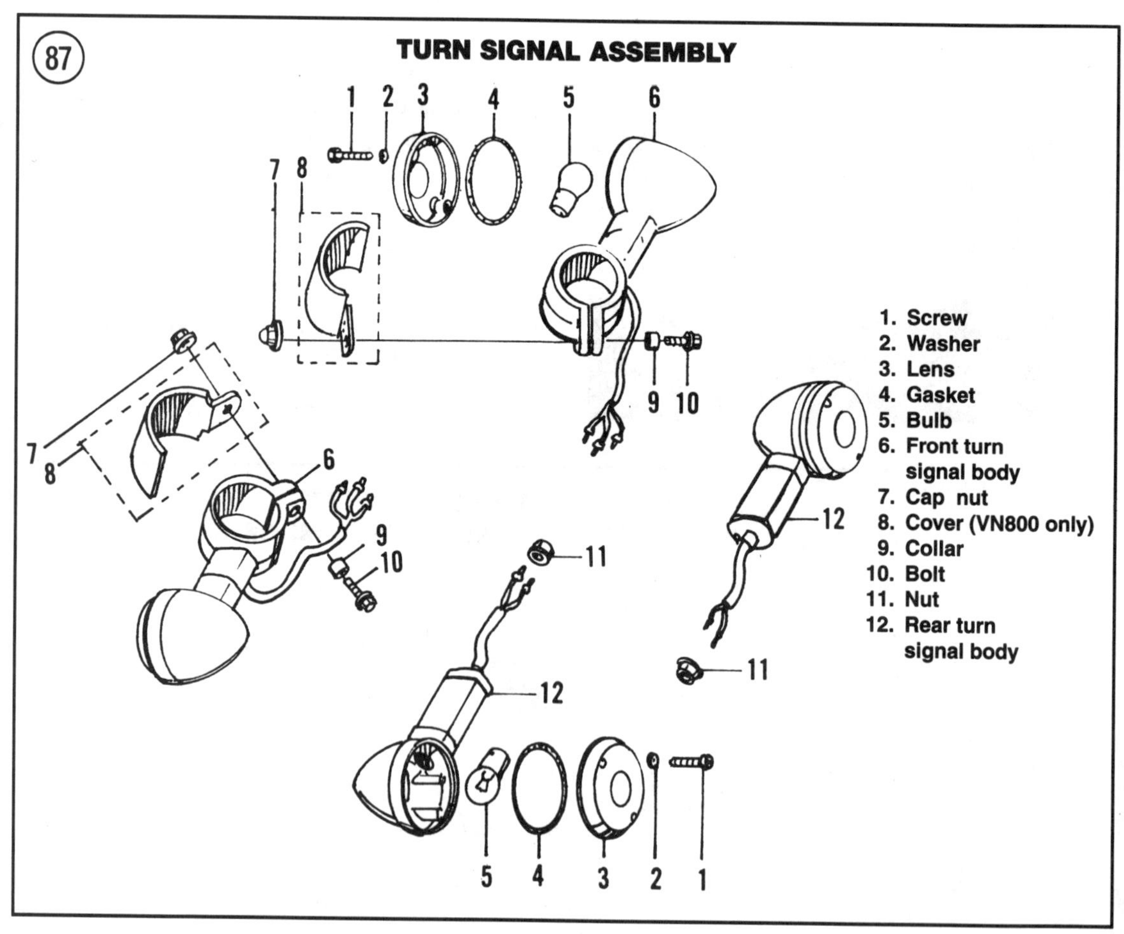

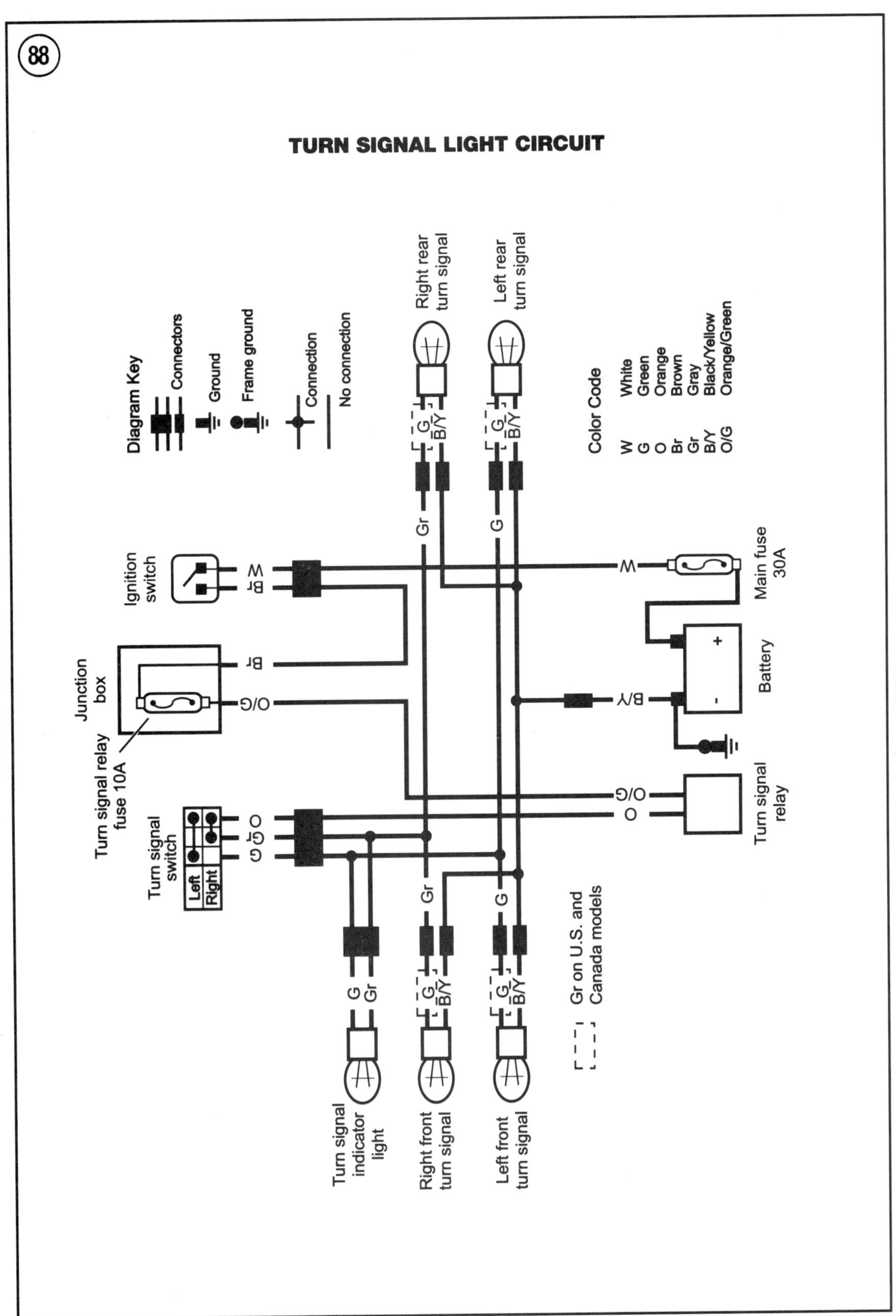
88
TURN SIGNAL LIGHT CIRCUIT
Diagram Key
Connectors
Ground
Frame ground
Connection
No connection
Right rear turn signal
Left rear turn signal
Color Code
W White
G Green
O Orange
Br Brown
Gr Gray
B/Y Black/Yellow
O/G Orange/Green
Ignition switch
Junction box
Turn signal relay fuse 10A
Turn signal switch
Left
Right
Main fuse 30A
Battery
Turn signal relay
Turn signal indicator light
Right front turn signal
Left front turn signal
Gr on U.S. and Canada models
W
Br
O/G
O
G
Gr
B/Y

2. To remove a bulb, push it in and turn it counterclockwise.
3. Wash the inside and outside of the lens with a mild detergent and wipe dry.
4. Carefully wipe off the reflector surface behind the bulb with a soft cloth.
5. Inspect the lens gasket. Replace the gasket if it is damaged or deteriorated.
6. Replace the bulb and install the lens and gasket. Be sure to install the small plastic washer (**Figure 89**) on the lens mounting screws. Do not over-tighten the screws as the lens may crack.

Turn Signal Light Assembly Removal/Installation

For this procedure, refer to **Figure 87** for turn signal components and to **Figure 88** for the turn signal circuit diagram.

1. Disconnect the two (or three) individual electrical connectors for the turn signal light assembly.
2. When removing a front turn signal assembly:
   a. Remove the cap nut from the assembly clamp bolt. Do not lose the clamp bolt collar.
   b. On VN800 models, remove the cover.
   c. Note how the wires are routed, and carefully remove the turn signal body from the fork down tube.
3. When removing a rear turn signal assembly:
   a. Remove the nut securing the turn signal body to the rear fender stay.
   b. Carefully pull the electrical wires out through the opening in the mounting surface and remove the turn signal body.
4. Install by reversing these removal steps. Make sure the electrical connectors are tight and free of corrosion.

Turn Signal Relay Removal/Inspection

1. Remove the seat as described in Chapter Fourteen
2. Remove the turn signal relay (**Figure 90**) from the electrical box.
3. Connect the relay, turn signals and a fully charged battery as shown in **Figure 91**, and observe the turn signals. Count the number of times the lights flash per minute.
4. Replace the relay if the lights do not operate as specified in **Figure 92**.

5. Install the relay by reversing the removal steps.

SWITCHES

Switches can be tested for continuity with an ohmmeter (see Chapter One) or a self-powered test

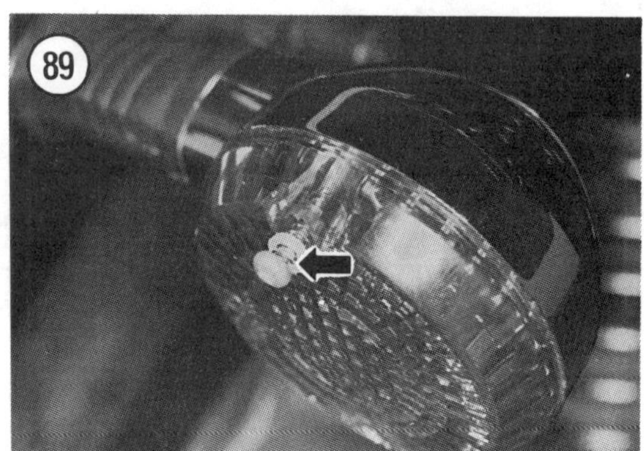

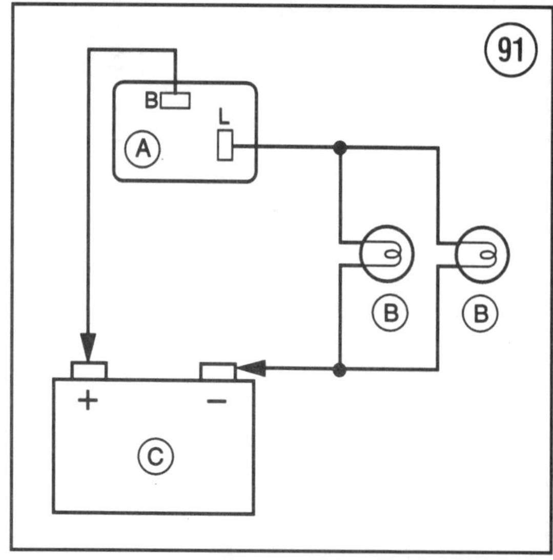

TURN SIGNAL RELAY

Load		Flashing times (c/m)*
The Number of Turn Signal Lights	Wattage (W)	
1	21 or 23	Light stays on
2	42 or 46	75-95

*Cycles(s) per minute

lamp at the switch connector plug by operating the switch in each of its operating positions. For example, **Figure 93** shows a continuity diagram for a typical ignition switch. It shows which terminals should show continuity when the ignition switch is in a given position.

When the ignition switch is in the PARK position, there should be continuity between the white and red terminals. This is indicated by the line on the continuity diagram. An ohmmeter connected between these two terminals should indicate little or no resistance and a test lamp should light. When the ignition switch is OFF, there should be no continuity (infinite resistance) between any of the terminals.

(93)

IGNITION SWITCH CONNECTIONS

	Ignition	Battery 1	Ignition	Tail 1	Tail 2
Color	Br	W	G/Y	Bl	R
OFF, LOCK					
ON	•	•	•	•	•
P (PARK)		•			•

R = Red
W = White
Br = Brown
Bl = Blue
G = Green
Y = Yellow

Testing

If the switch or button does not perform properly, replace it. Refer to the following figures when testing the switches:

a. Ignition switch—**Figure 93**.
b. Engine stop switch—**Figure 94**.
c. Sidestand switch—**Figure 95**.
d. Starter lockout switch (clutch)—**Figure 96**.
e. Starter button switch—**Figure 97**.
f. Headlight switch (U.K.)—**Figure 98**.
g. Front brake switch—**Figure 99**.
h. Rear brake switch—**Figure 100**.
i. Dimmer switch—**Figure 101**.
j. Turn signal switch—**Figure 102**.
k. Oil pressure switch—**Figure 103**.
l. Horn switch—**Figure 104**.

9

(94)

ENGINE STOP SWITCH CONNECTIONS

	R	Y/R
Off		
Run	•	•

R = Red
Y = Yellow
R = Red

(95)

SIDESTAND SWITCH CONNECTIONS

	Bk/Y	G/W
When sidestand is up	•	•
When sidestand is down		

Bk = Black
Y = Yellow
G = Green
W = White

96

STARTER LOCKOUT SWITCH

Color	Bk/Y	Bk
Clutch lever		
Released		
Pulled in	●	●

Bk = Black
Y = Yellow

97

STARTER BUTTON CONNECTIONS

	Bk/R	Bk/R
Free		
Push on	●	●

Bk = Black
R = Red

98

HEADLIGHT SWITCH CONNECTIONS (U.K.)

	R/W	R/Bl	Bl	Bl/Y
OFF				
■	●	●		
ON	●	●	●	●

R = Red
W = White
Bl = Blue
Y = Yellow

99

FRONT BRAKE SWITCH CONNECTIONS

	Bk	BK
When brake lever is pulled on	●	●

Bk = Black

100

REAR BRAKE SWITCH CONNECTIONS

	Br	Bl
When brake pedal is pushed down	●	●

Br = Brown
Bl = Blue

101

DIMMER SWITCH

Color	R/Y	Bl/Y	R/Bk
LO	●	●	
HIGH		●	●

R = Red
Y = Yellow
Bl = Blue
Bk = Black

102

TURN SIGNAL SWITCH

Color	G	O	G/Y
R		●	●
OFF/PUSH			
L	●	●	

Y = Yellow
O = Orange
G = Green

(103) OIL PRESSURE SWITCH CONNECTIONS

	SW Terminal	⏚
When engine is stopped	●———	———●
When engine is running		

HORN BUTTON CONNECTIONS

	Bk/W	Bk/Y
Free		
Push on	●———	———●

(104)

Bk = Black
W = White
Y = Yellow

NEUTRAL SWITCH CONNECTIONS

Color	G	⏚
When transmission is in neutral	●———	———●
When transmission is not in neutral		

(105)

G = Green

(106)

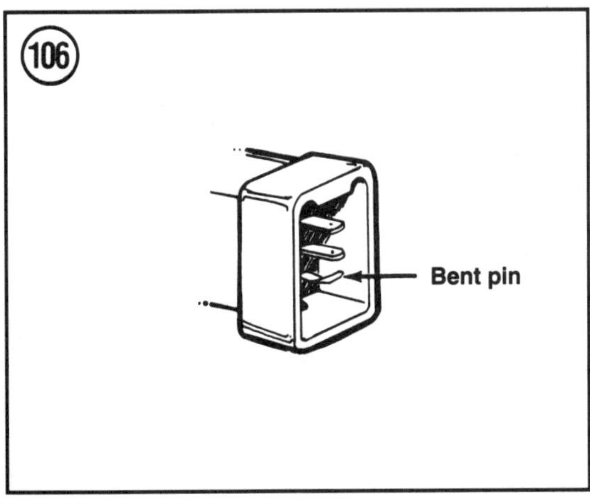

m. Neutral indicator switch—**Figure 105**.

When testing switches, note the following:

a. First check the fuses as described in this chapter.

b. Check the battery as described in Chapter Three; charge the battery to the correct state of charge.

c. Disconnect the negative (–) cable from the battery, as described in this chapter, if the switch connectors are not disconnected in the circuit.

CAUTION
Do not attempt to start the engine with the battery negative (–) cable disconnected or you will damage the wiring harness.

d. When separating two electrical connectors, depress the retaining clip and pull on the electrical connector housings and *not* the wires.

NOTE
Electrical connectors can be serviced by disconnecting them and cleaning the terminals with aerosol electrical contact cleaner. Pack multiple pin connectors with a dielectric compound (available at most automotive and motorcycle supply stores).

e. After locating a defective circuit, check the electrical connectors to make sure they are clean and properly connected. Make sure there are no bent metal pins on the male side of the connector (**Figure 106**). Check all wires going into an electrical connector housing to make sure each wire is properly positioned and that the wire end is not loose (**Figure 107**).

f. To attach the electrical connectors properly, push them together until they click and are locked in place (**Figure 108**).

g. When replacing handlebar switch assemblies, make sure the wiring is routed correctly so that it is not crimped when the handlebar is turned from side to side. Also secure the wiring to the handlebar with the plastic tie wraps.

Ignition Switch Removal/Installation

1. Disconnect the battery negative (–) lead as described in this chapter.
2. Remove the left-hand frame cover.
3. Remove the bolt securing the switch assembly to the left side of the motorcycle and remove the switch (**Figure 109**).
4. Disconnect the ignition switch six-pin electrical connector.
5. Connect the six-pin connector to the new switch. Make sure the electrical connectors are free of corrosion and are tight.
7. Install the new ignition switch and tighten the bolts securely.
8. Install the left-hand frame cover
9. Connect the battery negative (–) lead as described in this chapter.

Right-hand Combination Switch Removal/Installation

The right-hand combination switch assembly contains the engine start button, engine stop switch and on U.K. models the headlight switch. If any portion of the switch is faulty, the entire switch assembly must be replaced.

1. Remove the seat as described in Chapter Fourteen.
2. Disconnect the battery negative (–) lead as described in this chapter.
3. Remove the fuel tank as described in Chapter Eight.
4. Remove any tie wraps (A, **Figure 110**) securing the switch wiring harness to the handlebar.

NOTE
The location of the electrical connectors and the color of the wiring vary with the different years and country in which the bike was originally sold. Therefore the exact location of the connector(s) is not shown in this procedure.

5. Disconnect the electrical connector (B, **Figure 110**) from the front brake light switch. The brake light switch wires are part of the right-hand switch electrical wiring harness.
6. Follow the right-hand switch wiring harness on the handlebar to the frame area.
7. Locate and disconnect the electrical connector(s).
8. Remove the electrical wire harness from any clips on the frame and carefully pull the harness out from the frame.
9. Remove the screws securing the right-hand combination switch together and remove the switch assembly (C, **Figure 110**).
10. Install a new switch and tighten the screws securely. Do not over-tighten the screws or the plastic switch housing may crack.

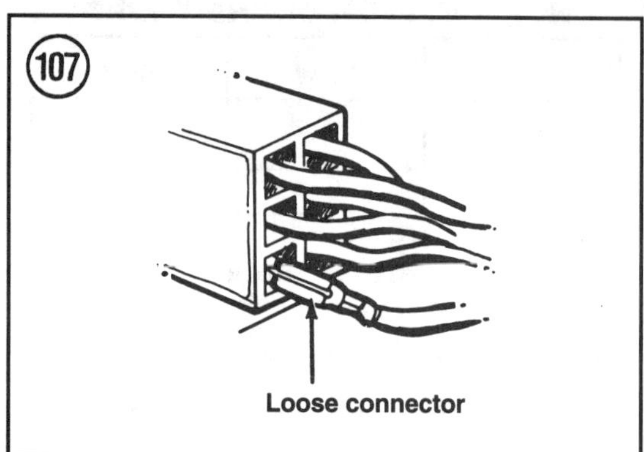

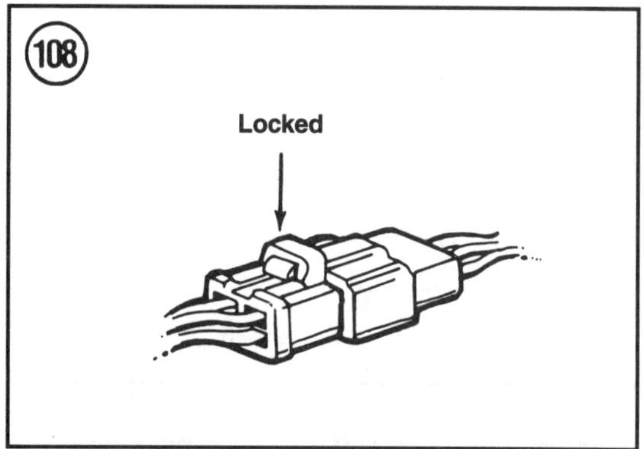

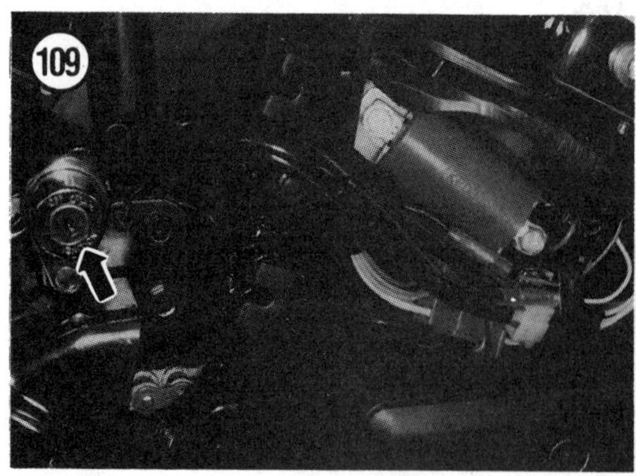

11. Reconnect the electrical connector(s)
12. Make sure the electrical connector(s) are free of corrosion and are tight. Install the tie wrap to hold the electrical wires to the front of the frame. The wires must be retained in this manner to allow room for the fuel tank.
13. Connect the battery negative (–) lead as described in this chapter.
14. Install the fuel tank as described in Chapter Eight.
15. Install the seat as described in Chapter Fourteen.

Left-hand Combination Switch and Starter Interlock Switch Removal/Installation

The left-hand combination switch assembly contains the headlight dimmer switch, turn signal switch and horn switch. If any portion of the switch is faulty, the entire switch assembly must be replaced.

1. Remove the seat as described in Chapter Fourteen.
2. Disconnect the battery negative (–) lead as described in this chapter.

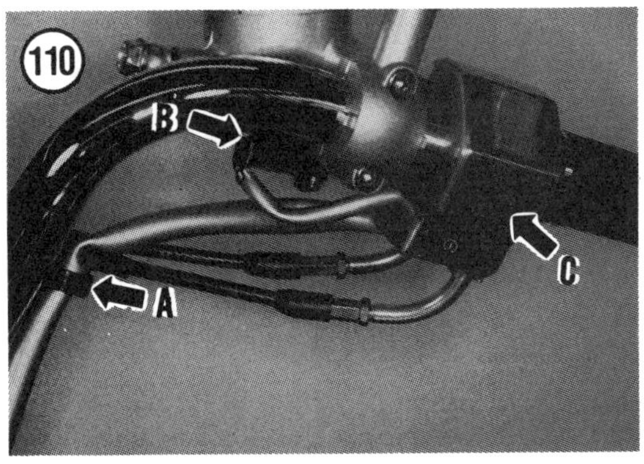

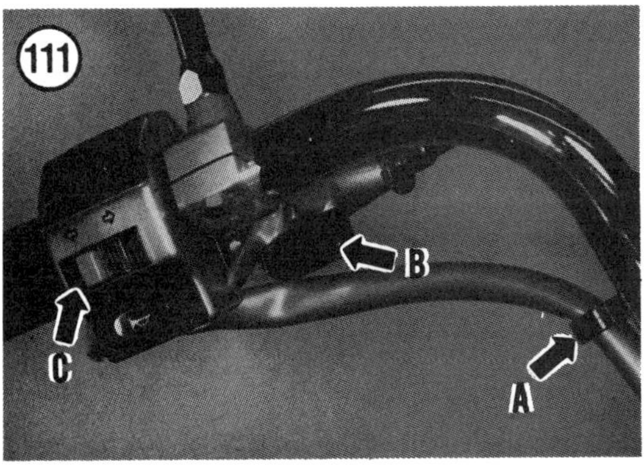

3. Remove the fuel tank as described in Chapter Eight.
4. Remove any tie wraps (A, **Figure 111**) securing the wiring harness to the handlebars.

NOTE

The location of the electrical connectors and the color of the wiring vary with the different years and country in which the bike was originally sold. Therefore, the exact location of the connector(s) is not shown in this procedure.

5. Disconnect the electrical connector (B, **Figure 111**) from the starter interlock switch. The starter interlock switch wires are part of the left-hand switch electrical wiring harness.
6. Follow the left-hand switch electrical wiring harness on the handlebar to the frame area.
7. Locate and disconnect the electrical connector(s).
8. Remove the electrical wire harness from any clips on the frame and carefully pull the harness away from the frame.
9. Remove the screws attaching halves of the left-hand combination switch together, then remove the switch assembly (C, **Figure 111**).
10. Install a new switch onto the handlebar and tighten the screws securely. Do not over-tighten the screws or the plastic switch housing may crack.
11. Attach the electrical connector(s).
12. Make sure the electrical connector(s) are free of corrosion and are tight. Install the tie wrap to hold the electrical wires to the frame.
13. Connect the battery negative (–) lead as described in this chapter.
14. Install the fuel tank as described in Chapter Eight.
15. Install the seat as described in Chapter Fourteen.

Starter Interlock Switch Removal/Installation

1. Disconnect the electrical connector from the starter interlock switch (clutch switch).
2. Remove the screw securing the switch to the clutch lever assembly and remove the switch.
3. Install the new switch and tighten the screws securely.
4. Make sure the electrical connectors are free of corrosion and are tight.

Front Brake Light Switch Removal/Installation

1. Disconnect the electrical connectors (B, **Figure 110**) from the front brake light switch.
2. Remove the screw securing the brake light switch to the master cylinder and remove the switch.
3. Install the new switch and tighten the screws securely.
4. Make sure the electrical connectors are free of corrosion and are tight.

Rear Brake Light Switch Removal/Installation

1. Remove the seat and frame right-hand side cover as described in Chapter Fourteen.

NOTE
The footpeg bracket is removed to better show the brake switch in this procedure. You do not have to remove the footpeg to remove the rear brake light switch.

2. Disconnect the return spring (A, **Figure 112**) from the switch located behind the right-hand footpeg bracket.
3. Locate and disconnect rear brake light switch connector.
4. Remove the switch (B, **Figure 112**) from its mount on the footpeg bracket.
5. Install by reversing these removal steps while noting the following:
   a. Make sure the electrical connectors are free of corrosion and are tight.
   b. Adjust the switch as described in this chapter.

Rear Brake Light Switch Adjustment

1. Turn the ignition switch to the ON position.
2. Depress the brake pedal. The brake light should come on just as the brake begins to actuate.
3. To make the brake light come on earlier, hold the brake light switch body (B, **Figure 112**) and turn the adjusting nut *clockwise* as viewed from the top. Turn the adjusting nut (C, **Figure 112**) *counterclockwise* to delay brake light illumination.

NOTE
Some riders prefer that brake light come on a little early. This way, they can tap the pedal without braking to warn drivers who are following too closely.

Neutral Switch Removal/Installation

The neutral switch (**Figure 113**) is located on the rear of the right-hand crankcase just behind the clutch cover.

1. Securely support the bike in an upright position on level ground.
2. Drain the engine oil as described in Chapter Three.
3. Disconnect the electrical connector from the neutral switch (**Figure 113**).
4. Remove the neutral switch and washer from the right-hand crankcase.
5. Apply a nonhardening gasket sealer to the neutral switch threads prior to installation.
6. Install the neutral switch and washer. Tighten the switch to the torque specification listed in **Table 1**.
7. Attach the electrical connector and make sure it is free of corrosion and is tight.

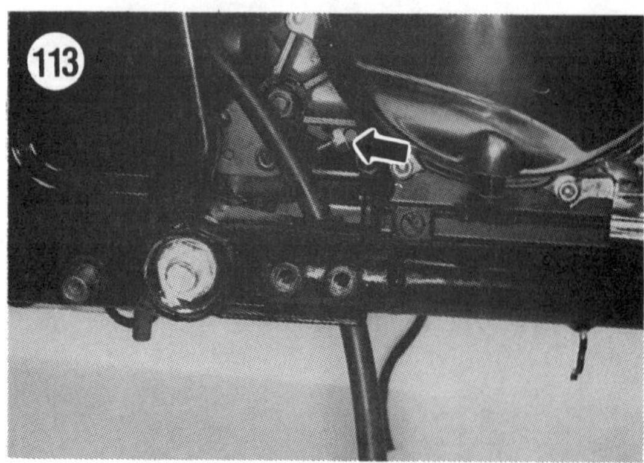

8. Refill the engine with oil as described in Chapter Three.

Sidestand Switch Removal/Installation

1. Use a scissors jack or jack stands to securely support the bike in an upright position on level ground.
2. Follow the sidestand switch electrical wiring harness (A, **Figure 114**) up the left-hand side of the frame.
3. Locate and disconnect the sidestand switch electrical connector.
4. Disconnect the electrical connector from the main wiring harness.
5. Unhook the tie wraps securing the wiring harness to the frame.

NOTE
The footpeg bracket is removed to better show the sidestand switch in this procedure. You do not have to remove the footpeg bracket to remove the sidestand switch.

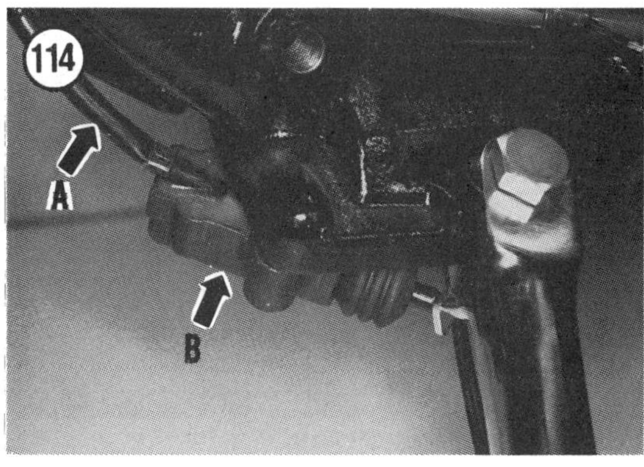

6. Remove the screws securing the switch (B, **Figure 114**) to the frame and remove the switch.
7. Install by reversing the removal steps while noting the following:
   a. Make sure the electrical connector is free of corrosion and is tight.
   b. Secure the electrical harness to the frame with tie wraps.

Oil Pressure Switch Removal/Installation

1. Drain the engine oil as described in Chapter Three.
2. Pull the cover (**Figure 115**) from the oil pressure switch.
3. Unscrew the electrical terminal from the end of the oil pressure switch and remove the wire from the switch.
4. Unscrew the oil pressure switch from the fitting in the crankcase.
5. Apply a light coat of RTV sealer to the threads of the new switch prior to installation.
6. Install the oil pressure switch into the fitting in the crankcase. Tighten the switch to the torque specification listed in **Table 1**.
7. Connect the oil pressure switch wire to the switch and tighten the screw securely.
8. Fit the cover in place over the oil pressure switch.
9. Refill the engine with oil as described in Chapter Three.

ELECTRICAL COMPONENTS

This section contains information on electrical components other than switches. Some of the test procedures in this section involve touching a meter lead to a terminal inside an electrical connector. Under these conditions make sure that the meter test lead has penetrated into the connector and is touching the bare metal wire *not* the insulation on the wire. If the test lead does not touch the bare metal wire, the readings will be false and may lead to the unnecessary purchase of an expensive electrical part that cannot be returned for a refund. Most dealers and parts houses will not accept any returns on electrical parts.

If you are having trouble with some of these components, performing some quick preliminary checks may save you a lot of time.

a. Disconnect each electrical connector and make sure there are no bent metal pins on the male side of the electrical connector (**Figure 106**). A bent pin will not connect to its mating receptacle in the female end of the connector causing an open circuit.
b. Check each female end of the connector. Make sure that the metal connector on the end of each wire is pushed in all the way into the plastic connector. If not, carefully push them in with a small screwdriver.
c. Check all electrical wires where they enter the metal terminals in both the male and female plastic connector (**Figure 107**).
d. Push the connectors together and make sure they are fully engaged and locked together (**Figure 108**).

Battery Case Removal/Installation

1. Remove the seat and rear fender as described in Chapter Fourteen.
2. Remove the fuel tank as described in Chapter Eight.
3. Remove the coolant reservoir hose (A, **Figure 116**) from the top of the thermostat housing.
4. Remove the surge tank (B, **Figure 116**).
5. Remove the battery as described in Chapter Three.
6. Disconnect the electrical connectors from the indicated components and remove the components:
   a. IC ignitor (A, **Figure 117**).
   b. Junction box (B, **Figure 117**).
   c. Starter relay and main fuse (C, **Figure 117**).
   d. Turn signal relay (D, **Figure 117**).
7. Remove the choke cable holder screws (E, **Figure 117**).
8. Remove the fuel tank drain hose (F, **Figure 117**) and the coolant hose (G, **Figure 117**) from the battery case. Note how each hose is routed through the frame so you can route them correctly during assembly .
9. On California models, remove the evaporative emission system hoses from the battery case.
10. Slide the battery case rearward and pull it out from under the frame crossmember.
11. If the battery case is corroded by electrolyte spillage, thoroughly clean it with a solution of baking soda and water. Rinse the case thoroughly, clean it with solvent, and dry it completely. Repaint any areas of bare metal.
12. Install by reversing the removal steps while noting the following:
   a. Make sure all electrical connectors are free of corrosion and are tight.
   b. Tighten the battery case mounting bolts securely.

Meter Assembly (Speedometer and Indicator Lights) Removal/Installation

Refer to **Figure 118** for this procedure.

1. Remove the screw securing the meter assembly to the tank.
2. Lift the rear of the meter assembly and disengage the assembly tongue (A, **Figure 119**) from the tank.
3. Unscrew the speedometer drive cable from the speedometer assembly (B, **Figure 119**) and disconnect the electrical connectors (C, **Figure 119**).
4. Installation is the reverse of removal.

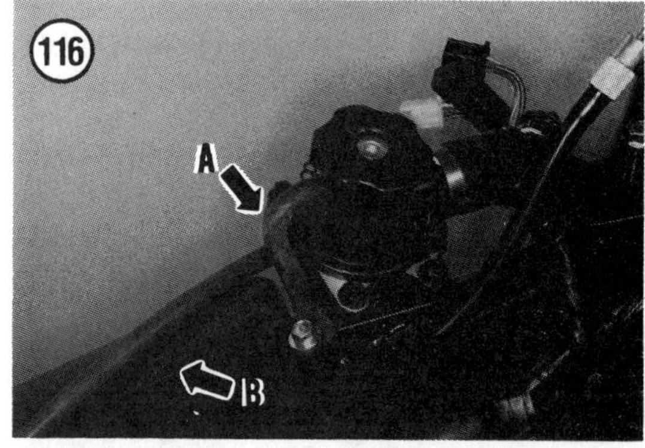

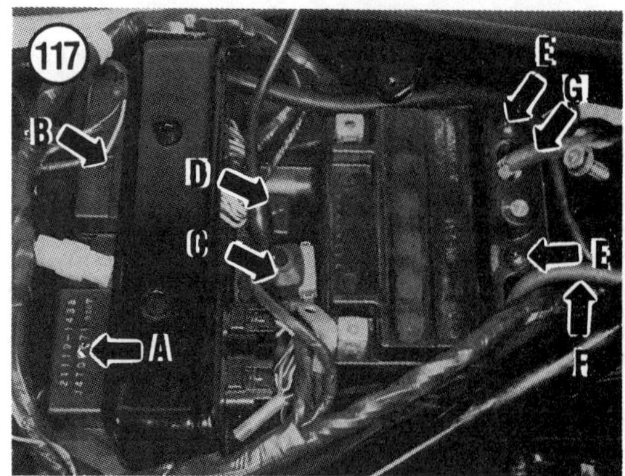

a. Be sure the electrical connections are tight and free of corrosion.

b. Be sure that the tongue in the meter assembly engages the slot in the tank.

Meter Assembly/Disassembly

NOTE
This procedure includes the steps for replacing bulbs in the speedometer and indicator lights. Perform only those steps necessary for removing the bulbs that require replacement.

1. Remove the meter assembly as described in this chapter.

2. Take the meter assembly to the bench and set it face down on a clean cloth or some other suitable material.

3. Remove the set screw from the side of the trip knob and remove the trip knob.

4. Remove the speedometer mounting screws and remove the speedometer from the meter assembly. Do not lose the washer and damper behind the speedometer screws.

5. Carefully pull the appropriate lamp holder assembly from the backside of the speedometer or from the indicator light housing.

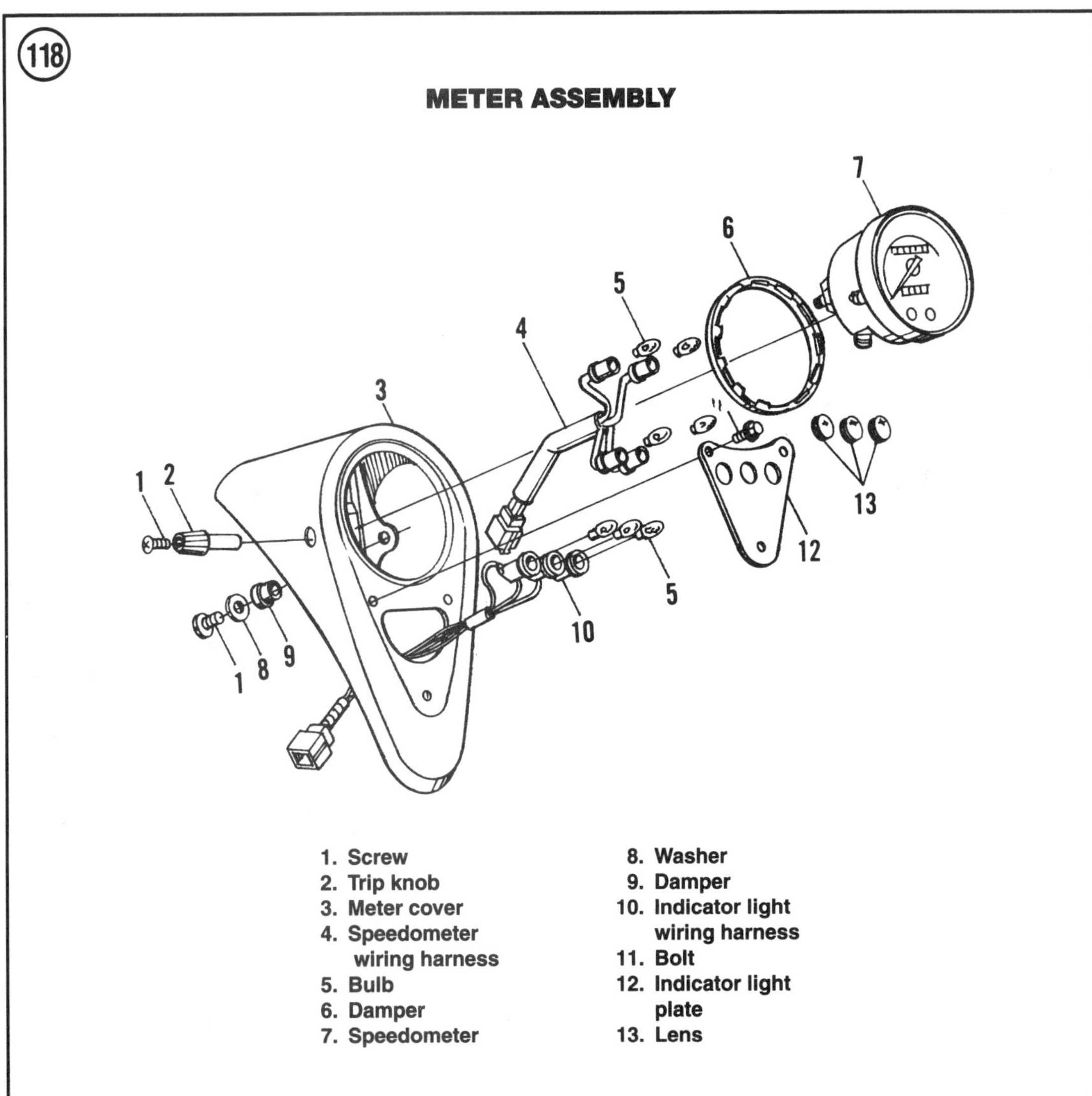

1. Screw
2. Trip knob
3. Meter cover
4. Speedometer wiring harness
5. Bulb
6. Damper
7. Speedometer
8. Washer
9. Damper
10. Indicator light wiring harness
11. Bolt
12. Indicator light plate
13. Lens

6. Pull the bulb straight out of the holder and replace the defective bulb.

NOTE
If a new bulb will not work, check the wire connections for loose or broken wires. Also check the bulb socket for corrosion. Replace as necessary.

7. Push the lamp holder assembly back into the speedometer or indicator light housing. Make sure it is completely seated to prevent the entry of water and moisture.
8. Reassemble the meter assembly by reversing the above procedure.

Radiator Fan Switch Removal/Testing/Installation

The radiator fan switch operates the radiator fan based on engine coolant temperature. When the coolant temperature is in the hot range, the radiator fan should operate. The radiator fan switch (A, **Figure 120**) is mounted to the upper right-hand side of the radiator .

Refer to **Figure 121** for the radiator fan circuit diagram.

NOTE
If the radiator fan is not operating correctly, check the radiator fan fuse before starting this test. Also clean any rust or corrosion from the electrical terminals on the radiator fan switch.

1. Disconnect the two electrical leads from the radiator fan switch (A, **Figure 120**).
2. Use a jumper wire to connect these two electrical leads together.
3. Turn the ignition switch ON. The radiator fan should start running.
   a. If the radiator fan does not run, either the fan or the electrical wiring to the fan is faulty.
   b. If the fan runs, the radiator fan switch may be defective. Test the switch as follows.
4. Partially drain the cooling system as described in Chapter Three. Drain just enough coolant to lower the coolant level in the radiator to below the radiator upper hose. This will reduce the loss of coolant when the sensor is removed.
5. Remove the fuel tank as described in Chapter Eight.
6. Unscrew the radiator fan switch from the radiator.

WARNING
Wear safety glasses or goggles and gloves during this test. Protect yourself accordingly as the coolant is heated to a high temperature.

7. Place the radiator fan switch into a small pan of distilled water and antifreeze. The radiator fan switch must be positioned so that all of its threads are submerged in the coolant.
8. Place a shop thermometer in the pan (use a thermometer that is rated higher than the test temperature).
9. Use an ohmmeter and check for continuity between the terminals on the switch as shown in **Figure 122**. At room temperature there should be no continuity (infinite resistance).
10. Do not let the switch or the thermometer touch the pan as it will give a false reading.
11. Heat the coolant slowly until the temperature reaches 93-103° C (199-217° F). Watch the ohmmeter needle while the coolant is heating. The needle should move from infinity to 0.5 ohm. Maintain this

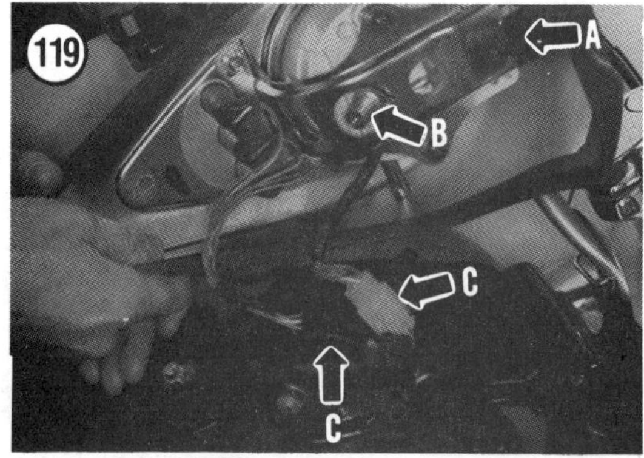

temperature for at least 3 minutes before taking the final reading. A sudden change in temperature will cause a different ohmmeter reading. After this 3 minute interval is complete, check the ohmmeter; there should be continuity (0.5 ohms).

12. Turn the heat off and keep the ohmmeter test leads attached. When the coolant temperature falls to 91-95° C (196-203° F), check the ohmmeter; there should be no continuity (infinite resistance).

13. If the radiator fan switch does not operate as described, the switch must be replaced.

14. Apply a light coat of RTV based sealant to the threads of the radiator fan switch and install the switch in the radiator.

15. Tighten the radiator fan switch to the torque specification listed in **Table 1**.

16. Refill the cooling system with coolant. Refer to Chapter Three.

17. Attach the electrical wires to the radiator fan switch. Make sure the connections are tight and free from oil and corrosion.

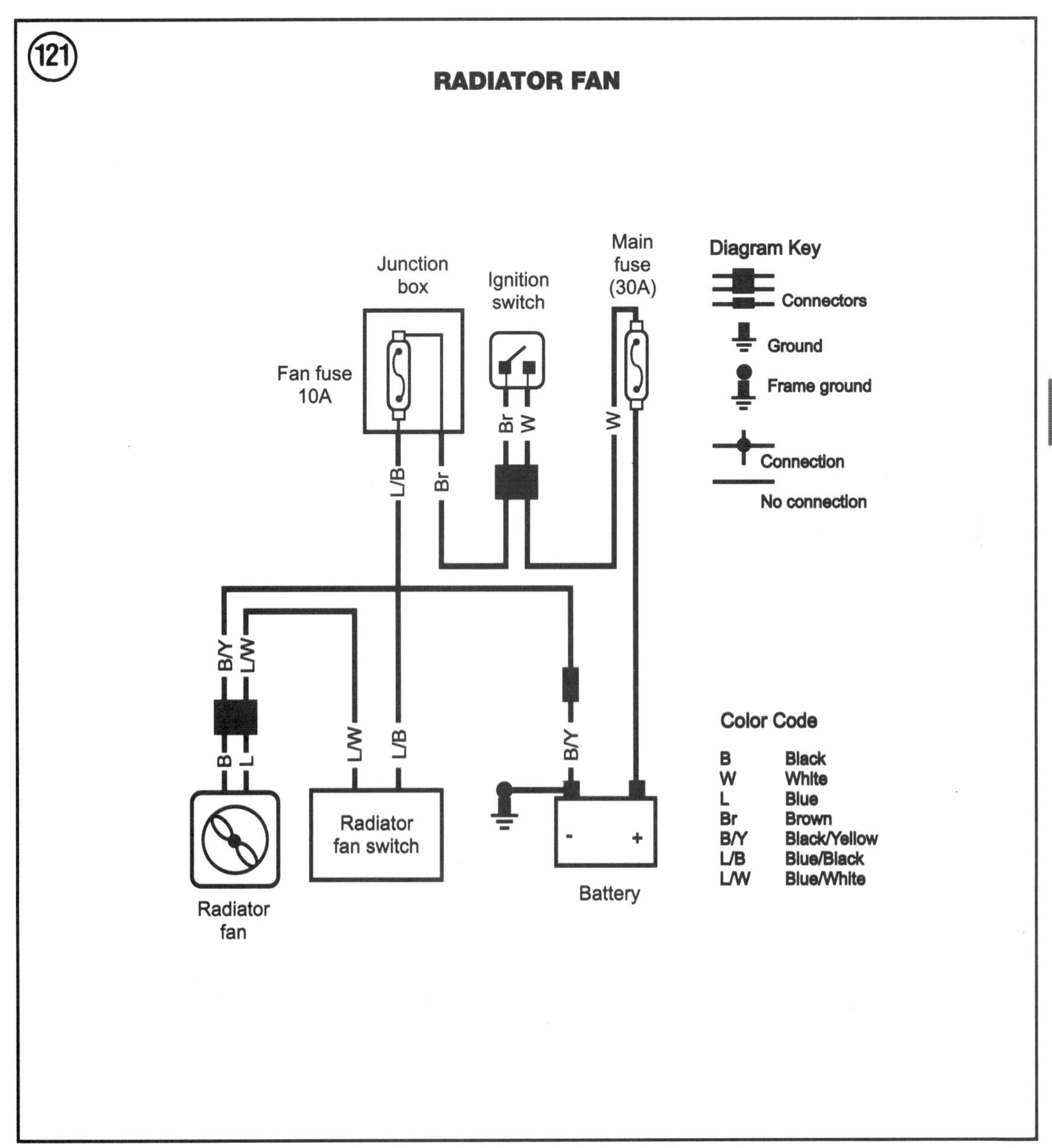

9

Coolant Temperature Sensor Removal/Testing/Installation

The coolant temperature sensor (B, **Figure 120**) controls the coolant temperature indicator light on the instrument cluster. This sensor is attached to the thermostat housing.

1. Remove the fuel tank as described in Chapter Eight.
2. Partially drain the cooling system as described in Chapter Three. Drain just enough coolant to lower the coolant level in the radiator to below the radiator upper hose. This will reduce the loss of coolant when the sensor is removed.
3. Disconnect the electrical connector from the end of the coolant temperature sensor.
4. Unscrew the coolant temperature sensor from the thermostat housing.

WARNING
Wear safety glasses or goggles and gloves during this test. Protect yourself accordingly as the coolant is heated to a very high temperature and can result in severe burns if not handled properly.

5. Place the coolant temperature sensor in a small pan of distilled water and antifreeze. Position the coolant temperature sensor so that all of its threads are submerged in the coolant.
6. Place a shop thermometer in the pan (use a thermometer that is rated higher than the test temperature).
7. Use an ohmmeter and check for continuity between the terminal on the switch and ground (side of switch) as shown in **Figure 123**. At room temperature there should be no continuity (infinite resistance).
8. Do not let the switch or the thermometer touch the pan as it will give a false reading.
9. Heat the coolant slowly until the temperature reaches 113-117° C (235-243° F). Watch the ohmmeter needle while the coolant is heating. The needle should move from infinity to 0.5 ohm. Maintain this temperature for at least 3 minutes before taking the final reading. A sudden change in temperature will cause a different ohmmeter reading. After this 3 minute interval is completed, check the ohmmeter; there should be continuity (0.5 ohm).
10. Turn the heat off and keep the ohmmeter test leads attached. When the coolant temperature falls below 108° C (226° F), check the ohmmeter. There should be no continuity (infinite resistance).
11. If the coolant temperature sensor fails to operate as described, the sensor must be replaced.
12. Let the sensor cool down and remove it from the small pan.
13. Apply a light coat of silicone based sealant to the threads of the coolant temperature sensor. Install the sensor in the radiator (B, **Figure 120**) and torque the sensor to the specification in **Table 1**.
14. Attach the electrical connector to the coolant temperature sensor. Make sure the connection is tight and free from oil and corrosion.
15. Refill the cooling system with coolant. Refer to Chapter Three.

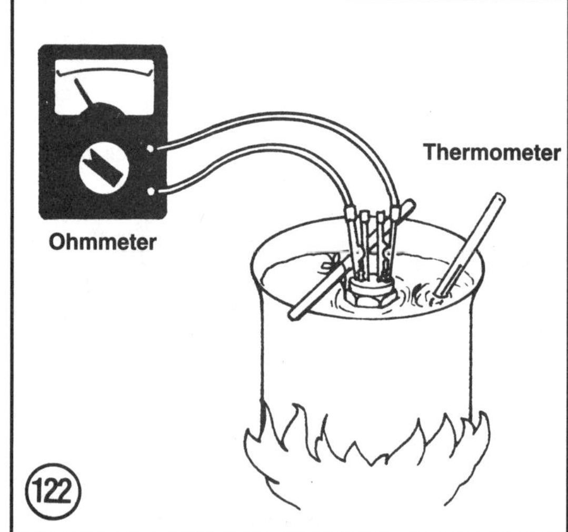

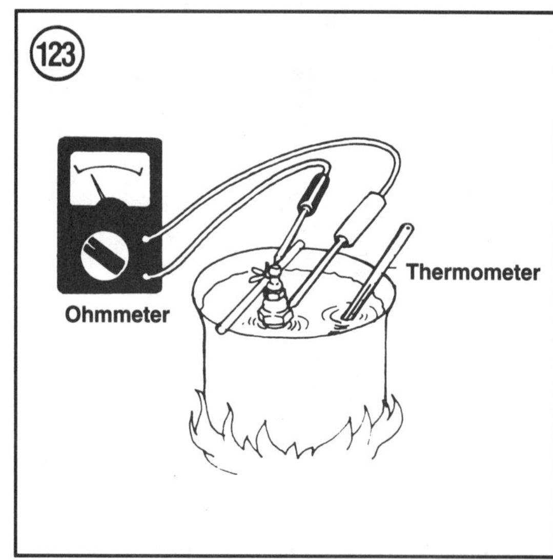

16. Install the fuel tank as described in Chapter Eight.

Radiator Fan Circuit Testing

1. Disconnect the two leads from the radiator fan switch (A, **Figure 120**).
2. Turn on the ignition switch.
3. Use a jumper to connect the two radiator fan leads.
4. If the fan operates, inspect the radiator fan switch.
5. If the fan does not operate, inspect the following:

a. Leads and connectors.
b. Main fuse.
c. Fan fuse.
d. Fan motor.

Radiator Fan Motor Inspection

1. Remove the fuel tank as described in Chapter Eight.
2. Disconnect the radiator fan two-pin electrical connector.
3. Using two jumper wires, apply battery power to the fan side of the connector.
4. If the fan does not rotate, replace the motor. Refer to Chapter Ten.

Horn Testing

1. Disconnect the horn wires from the harness.
2. Connect a 12-volt battery to the horn.
3. If the horn sounds, it is good; if it does not, replace the horn.

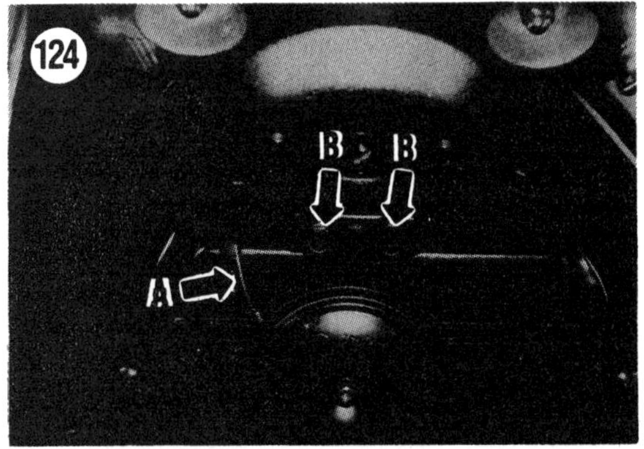

Horn Removal/Installation

1. Disconnect the electrical lead (A, **Figure 124**) from the two terminals on the horn.
2. Remove the horn mounting bolts (B, **Figure 124**) and remove the horn.
3. Install by reversing the removal steps. Make sure the electrical connectors are free of corrosion and are tight.

JUNCTION BOX

The junction box is located under seat. The junction box circuit diagram for U.S., Canadian and Australian models is shown in **Figure 125**. The circuit diagram for all other models is shown in **Figure 126**.

The junction box includes fuses, relays and diodes. The relays and diodes *cannot* be removed. Fuses are the only components that can be removed. If a fuse blows, determine the reason for the failure before replacing the fuse. Usually, the trouble is a short circuit in the wiring. This may be caused by worn-through insulation or a disconnected wire shorting to ground.

Removal/Installation

1. Remove the seat as described in Chapter Fourteen.
2. Slide the junction box (B, **Figure 117**) and its rubber damper out from under the frame crossmember.
3. Remove both multipin connectors from the junction box (B, **Figure 117**).
4. Reinstall the junction box and rubber damper under the frame crossmember.
5. If removed, reinstall both multipin electrical connectors. Be sure each of the connections are free of corrosion and are tight.
6. Reinstall the seat.

Fuse Replacement

CAUTION

Never substitute metal foil or wire for a fuse. Never use a higher amperage fuse than specified. An overload could result in a fire and complete loss of the bike.

CAUTION
When replacing a fuse, make sure the ignition switch is in the OFF position. This will lessen the chance of a short circuit.

1. Remove the junction box as described in this chapter.

2. Unhook the fuse panel cover and remove the cover.

3. Pull the fuse straight up with your fingers or needlenose pliers and inspect it. If the fuse is blown, there will be a break in the element (**Figure 127**).

4. The fuse location and description label is attached to the backside of the fuse panel cover. A spare fuse is stored in the junction box.

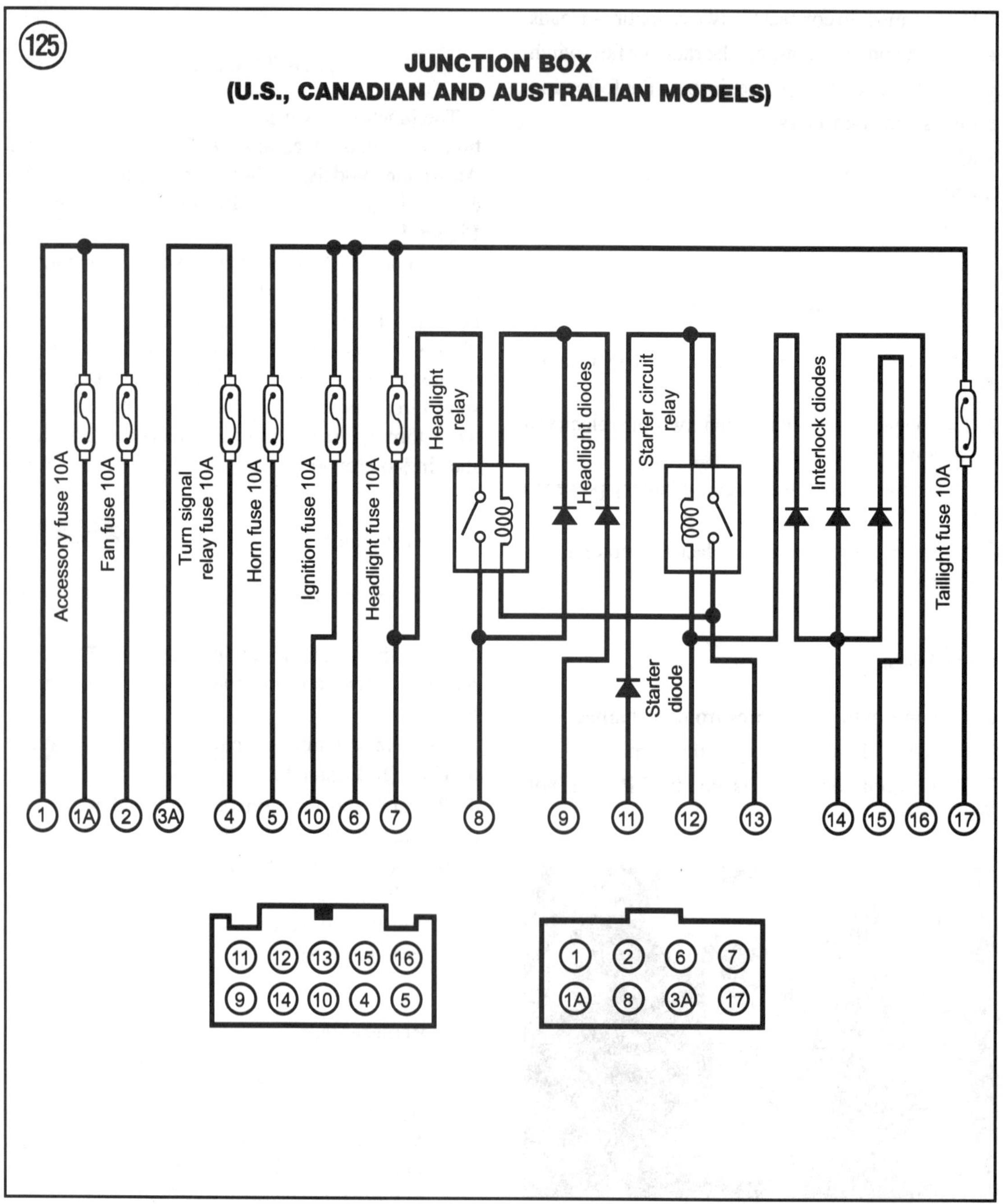

NOTE
The junction box includes a slot for storing a spare fuse. After using the spare, replace it as soon as possible to avoid being stranded.

5. Install the new fuse and push it all the way down until it seats completely. Install the cover onto the junction box. Push the lower end of the cover onto the box until it locks in place.

Fuse Circuit Inspection

1. Remove the junction box as described in this chapter.

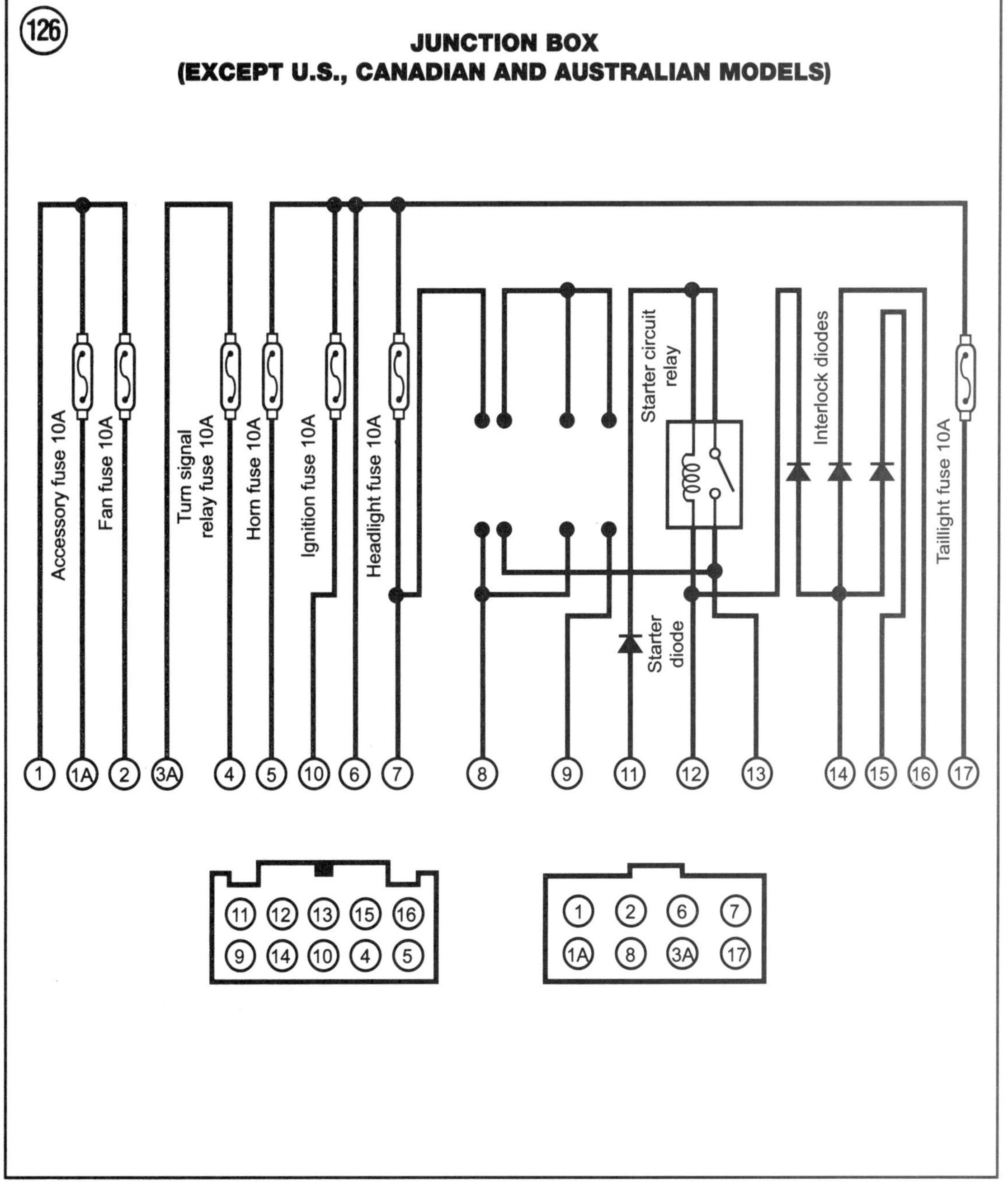

2. Remove both multi-pin connectors from the junction box.
3. Use an ohmmeter to check the resistance between the junction box terminals show in **Figure 128**.
4. If any test reading does not match the specified value, replace the junction box.

Starter Circuit Relay Inspection

1. Remove the junction box as described in this chapter.
2. Disconnect both multi-pin connectors from the junction box.
3. Use an ohmmeter to check the continuity at the following terminals on the junction box:
   a. Check the continuity between terminals 9 and 11. There should be no continuity across these terminals (infinite resistance).
   b. Check the continuity between terminals 12 and 13. There should be no continuity across these terminals (infinite resistance).
   c. Connect the ohmmeter's positive probe to terminal 13 and the negative probe to terminal 11. There should be no continuity across these terminals (infinite resistance).
   d. Connect the ohmmeter's positive probe to terminal 12 and the negative probe to terminal 11. There should be continuity across these terminals.
4. Use a battery and ohmmeter to check resistance by performing the following:
   a. Connect the positive terminal from the battery to terminal 11 on the junction box. Connect the negative terminal from the battery to terminal 12 on the junction box.
   b. Connect the ohmmeter's positive probe to terminal 13 on the junction box and the negative probe to terminal 11. There should be continuity across these terminals.
5. If any test does not yield the specified results, the starter circuit relay is defective. Replace the junction box.

Headlight Relay Inspection (U.S., Canadian and Australian models only)

1. Remove the junction box as described in this chapter.
2. Disconnect both multi-pin connectors from the junction box.

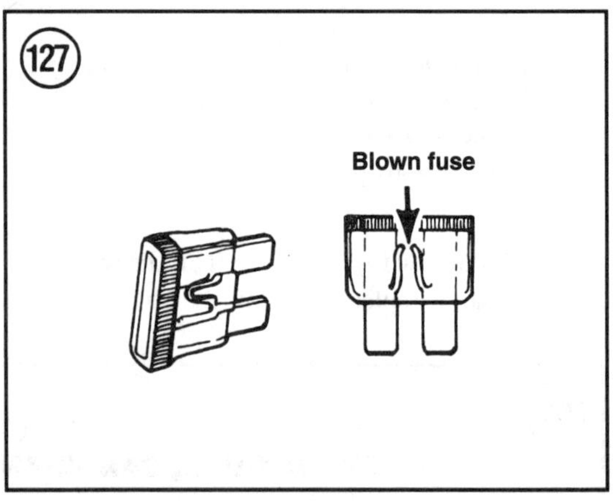

FUSE CIRCUIT INSPECTION

Tester Connection	Tester Reading (Ω)
1 to 1A	0
1A to 8	∞
1 to 2	0
2 to 8	∞
3A to 4	0
3A to 8	∞
6 to 5	0
6 to 2	∞
6 to 10	0
6 to 3A	∞
6 to 7	0
17 to 3A	∞
6 to 17	0

3. Use an ohmmeter to check the continuity at the following terminals on the junction box:
   a. Check the continuity between terminals 7 and 8. There should be no continuity across these terminals (infinite resistance).
   b. Check the continuity between terminals 7 and 13. There should be no continuity across these terminals (infinite resistance).
   c. Connect the ohmmeter's positive probe to terminal 13 and the negative probe to terminal 9. There should be continuity across these terminals.
4. Use a battery and ohmmeter to check continuity by performing the following:
   a. Connect the positive terminal from the battery to terminal 9 on the junction box. Connect the negative terminal from the battery to terminal 13 on the junction box.
   b. Check the resistance between terminals 7 and 8 on the junction box. The meter should read zero.
5. If any test does not yield the specified results, the starter circuit relay is defective. Replace the junction box.

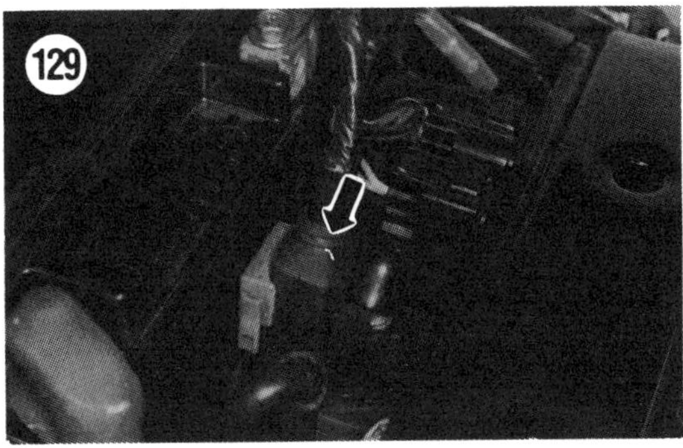

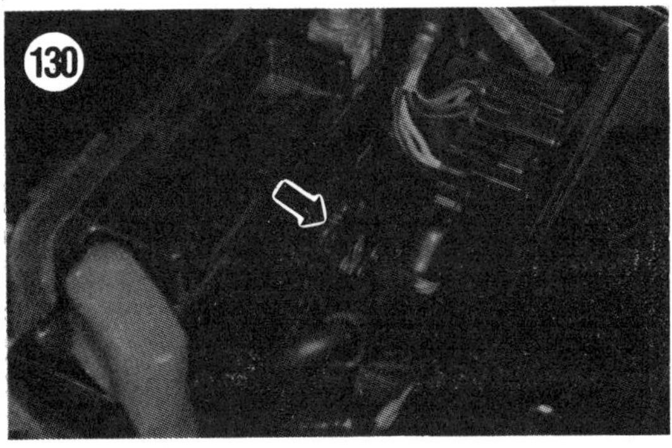

Diode Circuit Inspection

1. Remove the junction box as described in this chapter.
2. Disconnect both multi-pin connectors from the junction box.
3. Use an ohmmeter to check the resistance across each pair of terminals in both directions.
   a. Terminals 13 and 8 (U.S., Canadian and Australian models only).
   b. Terminals 13 and 9 (U.S., Canadian and Australian models only).
   c. Terminals 12 and 11.
   d. Terminals 12 and 14.
   e. Terminals 15 and 14.
   f. Terminals 16 and 14.
4. Check the resistance in both directions. The resistance should be relatively low in one direction, but it should be more than 10 times higher when you reverse the connections.

NOTE
The actual reading varies depending upon the ohmmeter setting. In general, the lower reading should be between zero and half the scale.

5. If a diode is low in both directions or high in both directions, replace the junction box.

MAIN FUSE

The 30-amp main fuse is located on top of the starter relay beneath the seat.

1. Remove the seat as described in Chapter Fourteen.
2. Remove the harness connector (**Figure 129**) from the starter relay.
3. Remove the fuse from its holder on the starter relay (**Figure 130**).
4. Inspect the fuse. Replace it if necessary.
5. Reinstall the harness connector. Be sure the connections are tight and free of corrosion.
6. Reinstall the seat.

WIRING DIAGRAMS

Wiring diagrams for all models are located at the end of this book.

Table 1 ELECTRICAL SYSTEM TIGHTENING TORQUES

Item	N•m	in.-lb.	ft.-lb.
Alternator cover bolts	12	106	—
Alternator lead clamp bolt	7.8	69	—
Alternator rotor bolt	155	—	114
Timing inspection cover screw	4.9	43	—
Stator coil bolts	13	115	—
Pickup coil bolts	2.9	26	—
Pickup coil lead clamp bolts	7.8	69	—
Starter motor mounting bolts	11	97	—
Starter motor through bolts	4.9	43	—
Starter motor terminal nut	11	97	—
Starter motor cable nuts	4.9	43	—
Side stand switch mounting bolts	3.9	35	—
Oil pressure switch	15	—	11
Neutral switch	15	—	11
Radiator fan switch	18	—	13
Coolant temperature switch	7.8	69	—
Spark plugs	18	—	13

Table 2 IGNITION TROUBLESHOOTING

Symptom	Probable cause
Weak spark	Poor connections in circuit (clean and retighten all connections) High voltage leak (replace defective wire) Defective ignition coil (replace coil)
No spark	Broken wire (replace wire) Defective ignition coil (replace coil) Defective signal generator (special ignitor unit) Faulty engine stop switch (replace switch)

Table 3 ELECTRICAL SYSTEM SPECIFICATIONS

Regulator/rectifier output voltage	14-15 VDC
Battery	Maintenance free
Capacity	12V/2 amp hour
Starter motor	
Brush length	12.0-12.5 mm (0.472-0.492 in.)
Brush length wear limit	5.5 mm (0.217 in.)
Commuator diameter	28 mm (1.102 in.)
Commutator diameter wear limit	27 mm (1.063 in.)
Alternator output voltage	50-80 VAC @ 4000 rpm
Stator coil resistance	0.3-0.5 ohm
Pickup coil resistance	380-570 ohms
Ignition coil resistance	
Primary coil	2.3-3.5 ohms
Secondary coil	12,000-18,000 ohms
Spark plug gap	0.7-0.8 mm (0.028-0.031 in.)
Radiator fan switch resistance	
With temp rising, 93-103° C (199-217° F)	less than 0.5 ohm
With temp falling, 91-95° C (196-203° F)	more than 1000 ohms
Coolant temperature sensor resistance	
With temp rising, 113-117° C (235-243° F)	less than 0.5 ohm
With temp falling 108° C (226° F) and lower	more than 1000 ohms

Table 4 REPLACEMENT BULBS

U.S. and Canadian Models **Item**	**Voltage/wattage**
Headlight (high/low beam)	12V 60/55W
Tail/brake light	12V 8/27W
Turn signals	
Front/running position light	12V 23/8W
Rear	12V 23W
Turn signal indicator light	12V 3.4W
Coolant temperature warning light	12V 1.7W
Oil pressure warning light	12V 1.7W
Speedometer lights	12V 1.7W
Neutral indicator light	12V 3W
High beam indicator light	12V 3W

Except U.S. and Canadian Models **Item**	**Voltage/wattage**
Headlight (high/low beam)	12V 60/55W
City light	12V 4W
Tail/brake light	12V 5/21W
Turn signals	
Front	12V 21W
Rear	12V 21W
Turn signal indicator light	12V 3.4W
Coolant temperature warning light	12V 1.7W
Oil pressure warning light	12V 1.7W
Speedometer lights	12V 1.7W
Neutral indicator light	12V 3W
High beam indicator light	12V 3W
License plate light	
VN800 Classic	12V 5W

CHAPTER TEN

COOLING SYSTEM

The pressurized cooling system consists of a radiator, radiator cap, thermostat, electric cooling fan and a coolant reservoir.

The coolant temperature indicator light on the meter assembly illuminates if coolant temperature becomes excessive. If this light turns on during operation, stop the engine and let the coolant and engine cool down. Then check the coolant level. It is important to keep the coolant level at the FULL mark on the coolant reservoir (A, **Figure 1**). Always add coolant to the reservoir, not the radiator.

CAUTION
Drain and flush the cooling system at least every two years. Refill it with a mixture of ethylene glycol antifreeze (formulated for aluminum engines) and purified water. Do not reuse old coolant as it deteriorates with use. ***Never*** *operate the cooling system with only purified water (even in climates where antifreeze protection is not required). This is important because the engine is all aluminum. It will not rust, but it will oxidize internally. When changing the coolant, follow the procedure described in Chapter Three.*

WARNING
Antifreeze (coolant) is a toxic waste material. Drain it into a suitable container and dispose of it according to local toxic waste regulations. Do not store coolant where it is accessible to children or pets.

This chapter describes the repair and replacement of the cooling system components. **Table 1** at the end of this chapter lists the cooling system specifications. **Table 2** lists torque specifications. For routine maintenance of the system, refer to Chapter Three.

WARNING
*Do not remove the radiator cap (**Figure 2**) when the engine is hot. The coolant is very hot and is under pressure. Severe scalding could result if the coolant comes in contact with your skin.*

WARNING
Whenever the engine is warm or hot, the fan may operate even with the main (ignition) switch turned OFF. Never work around the fan or touch the fan until the engine and coolant are completely cool.

The cooling system must be cooled prior to removing any component of the system.

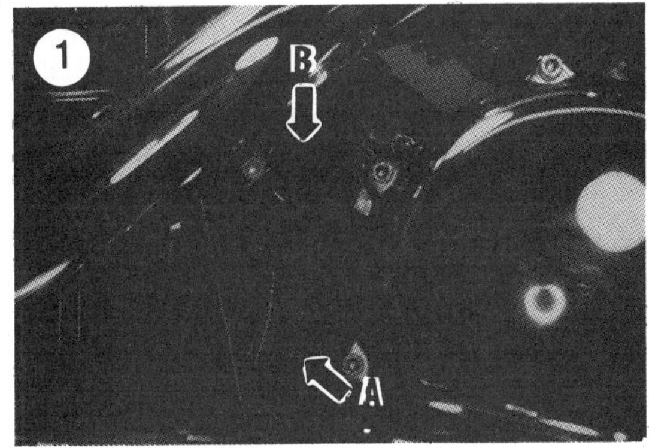

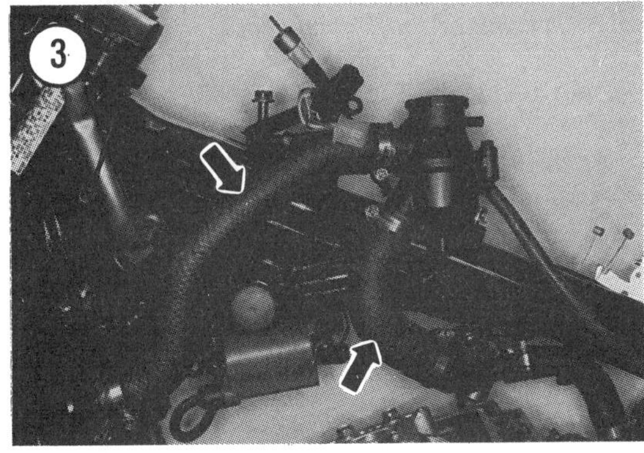

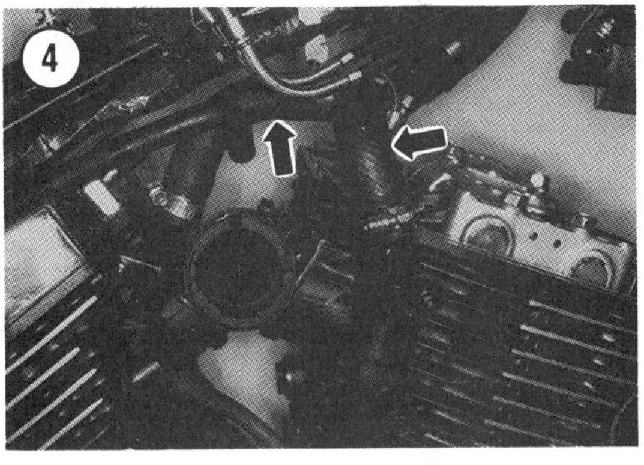

HOSES AND HOSE CLAMPS

Hoses deteriorate with age and should be replaced periodically or if they are cracked or leaking. To be safe, replace the hoses (**Figure 3** and **Figure 4**) every 2 years. The spray of hot coolant from a cracked hose can injure the rider and passenger. Loss of coolant can also cause the engine to overheat.

Whenever any component of the cooling system is removed, inspect the hoses and determine if replacement is necessary.

The small diameter coolant hoses are very stiff and are sometimes difficult to install onto the fittings of the various cooling system parts. Prior to installing the hoses, soak the ends in hot water to make them pliable, and they will slide on much easier. *Do not* apply any type of lubricant to the inner surfaces of the hoses.

Always use the screw adjusting type hose clamps. This type of clamp has superior holding ability, and it is easily released with a screwdriver.

1. Be sure the cooling system is cool before replacing the hoses.
2. Be sure to replace the hoses with Kawasaki replacement hoses. They are formed to a specific shape and of the correct length and inner diameter to fit correctly onto all components.
3. Drain the cooling system as described in Chapter Three.
4. Loosen the hose clamp and slide the clamp back off of the fitting.

CAUTION

When trying to remove a stubborn hose from the fittings, especially the fragile aluminum radiator inlet and outlet fittings, do not twist too hard. The fittings may be damaged, which could lead to expensive radiator repair.

5. Twist the hose to release it from the fitting. If the hose has been on for some time, it will probably be difficult to break loose. If so, carefully cut the hose parallel to the fitting with a knife. Carefully pry the hose from the fitting with a broad-tipped screwdriver.
6. Examine the fitting for cracks or other damage. Repair or replace the fitting as necessary. If the fitting is good, use sandpaper and clean any hose residue from the fitting. Wipe clean with a cloth.
7. Inspect the hose clamps and replace if necessary. The hose clamps are as important as the hoses. If

they do not hold the hose tightly in place, there will be a coolant leak. For best results, always use the screw type hose clamps.

8. With the hose installed correctly on the fitting, position the hose clamp back away from the end of the hose by about ½ in (12.7 mm). Make sure the hose clamp is still positioned over the fitting and tighten the clamps securely but not so tight that it damages the hose.
9. Install all removed components.
10. Refill the cooling system with coolant. Refer to Chapter Three.
11. Start the engine and check for leaks.

COOLING SYSTEM INSPECTION

1. Run the engine until it reaches operating temperature. A pressure surge should be felt when the outlet hose is squeezed while the engine is running.
2. If thick steam is observed at the muffler(s), a head gasket might be damaged. If enough coolant leaks into a cylinder, the cylinder could hydrolock and prevent the engine from being cranked. If so, coolant may also be present in the engine oil. If the engine oil is foamy or milky, there is coolant in the oil. If so, correct the problem before returning the bike to service.

CAUTION
After the cooling system is repaired, drain and thoroughly flush the engine oil system to eliminate all coolant residue. Refill with fresh engine oil; refer to Chapter Three.

3. Check the radiator for plugged or damaged fins. If more than 15 percent of the radiator fin area is damaged, repair or replace the radiator.
4. Check all coolant hoses for cracks or damage. Replace all questionable parts. Make sure all hose clamps are secure but not so tight that they cut the hoses.
5. Pressure test the cooling system as described in Chapter Three.

COOLANT RESERVOIR

Removal/Installation

1. Remove the seat as described in Chapter Fourteen.
2. Remove the fuel tank as described in Chapter Eight.
3. Remove the rear wheel and the shock absorber as described in Chapter Twelve, then remove the mud guard.
4. Remove the bolts (A, **Figure 5**) securing the coolant reservoir (B, **Figure 5**).
5. Remove the hose (C, **Figure 5**) from the reservoir and remove the coolant reservoir.
6. Remove filler cap and drain the coolant from the reservoir. Dispose of the coolant properly.
7. If necessary, clean the inside of the reservoir with a detergent and thoroughly rinse it with clean water. Remove all detergent residue from the reservoir.
8. Install by reversing the removal steps. Be sure to properly route the coolant hose through the clamps on the reservoir without kinking the hose.

RADIATOR AND RADIATOR FAN

WARNING
Whenever the engine is warm or hot, the fan may start even if the main (ignition) switch turned OFF. Never work around the fan or touch it until the engine and coolant are completely cool.

Removal/Installation

Refer to **Figure 6** for this procedure.

1. Remove the seat as described in Chapter Fourteen.
2. Remove the fuel tank as described in Chapter Eight.
3. Drain the cooling system as described in Chapter Three.

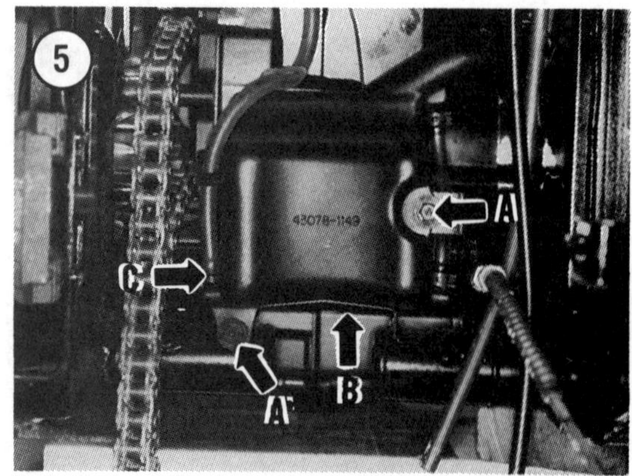

(6) **COOLING SYSTEM**

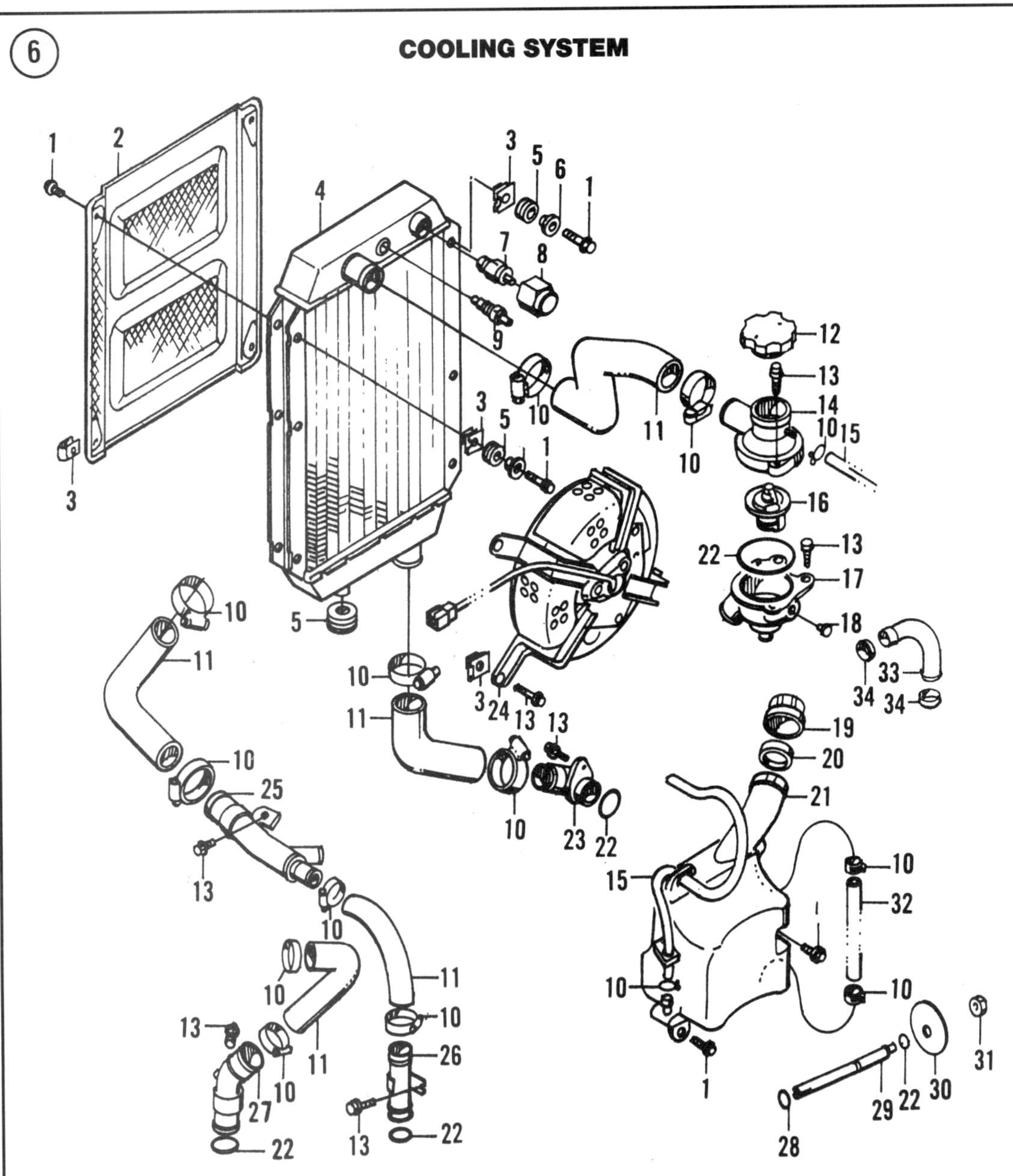

1. Screw
2. Radiator screen
3. Nut
4. Radiator
5. Damper
6. Collar
7. Fan switch
8. Fan switch cover
9. Coolant temerature sensor
10. Hose clamp
11. Coolant hose
12. Radiator cap
13. Bolt
14. Thermostat housing cover
15. Overflow hose
16. Thermostat
17. Thermostat housing
18. Oil line plug
19. Reservoir cap
20. Gasket
21. Reservoir
22. O-ring
23. Coolant pipe (crankcase inlet)
24. Fan assembly
25. Connector pipe
26. Coolant pipe (rear cylinder head)
27. Coolant pipe (front cylinder head
28. Circlip
29. Impeller shaft
30. Impeller
31. Nut
32. Sight gauge
33. Coolant pipe (crankcase outlet)
34. Seal

4. Disconnect the battery negative lead as described in Chapter Nine.

5. Disconnect the two leads (A, **Figure 7**) from the horn, remove the two horn mounting bolts (B, **Figure 7**) and remove the horn.

6. Loosen the hose clamp securing the lower radiator hose (**Figure 8**) to the fitting on the radiator.

7. Disconnect the radiator fan two-pin electrical connector (**Figure 9**). Carefully pull the electrical cable out through the frame and steering stem area.

8. Disconnect the electrical connectors from the radiator fan switch (A, **Figure 10**) and from the coolant temperature sensor (B, **Figure 10**).

9. Loosen the clamp securing the upper radiator hose to the fitting on the radiator.

10. Remove the bolts and collars (C, **Figure 10**) securing the radiator to the frame.

11. Pull the radiator slightly forward and disengage the upper radiator hose from the radiator fitting.

12. Pull the radiator up to disengage the lower radiator hose (**Figure 8**) from the radiator fitting.

13. Carefully remove the radiator from the frame.

14. Inspect the radiator as described in this chapter.

15. Install by reversing the removal steps while noting the following:

   a. Replace all radiator hoses if they are starting to deteriorate or are damaged in any way.
   b. Make sure the connectors for the radiator fan, radiator fan switch and coolant temperature switch are free of corrosion and are tight.
   c. Refill the cooling system with coolant as described in Chapter Three.

Radiator Inspection

1. Remove the radiator fan assembly as described in this chapter. This allows access to the back portion of the radiator for inspection.

2. Remove the protective screen (**Figure 11**) from the front of the radiator.

3. If compressed air is available, use short spurts of air directed from the *backside* of the radiator core and blow out dirt and insects.

4. Flush the exterior of the radiator with a garden hose on low pressure. Spray both the front and the back to remove all road dirt and bugs. Carefully use a whisk broom or stiff paint brush to remove any stubborn dirt from the cooling fins.

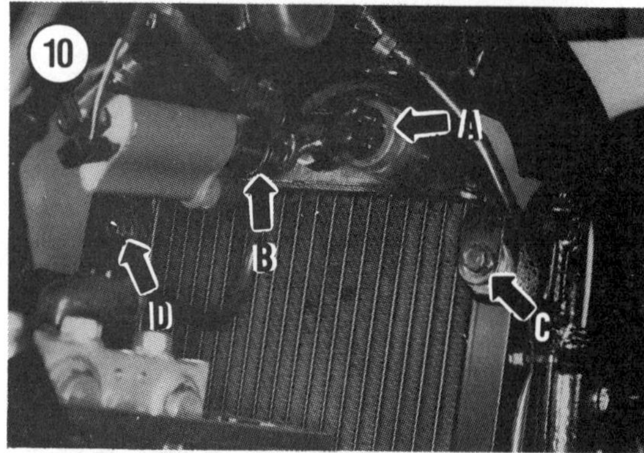

CAUTION
Do not press too hard or the cooling fins and tubes may be damaged causing a leak.

5. Carefully straighten any bent cooling fins using a broad tipped screwdriver or putty knife.

6. Check for cracks or leakage (usually a moss-green colored residue) at the inlet hose fitting (A, **Figure 12**), outlet hose fitting (B, **Figure 12**) and the seams of both end tanks (C, **Figure 12**).

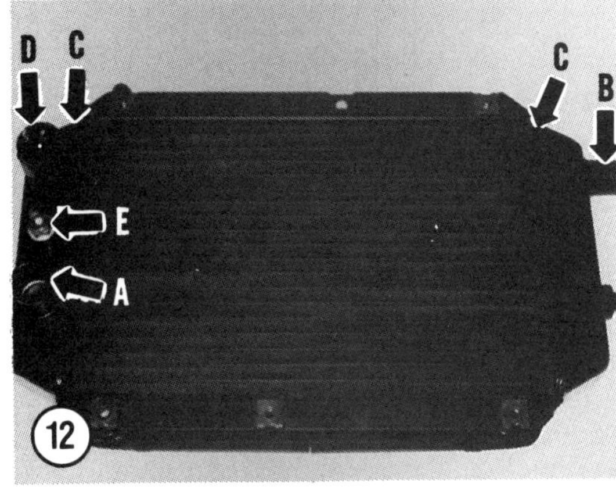

7. To prevent oxidation to the radiator, touch up any area where the black paint is worn off. Use good quality spray paint and apply several light coats of paint. Do not apply heavy coats. A heavy layer of paint will cut down on the cooling efficiency of the radiator.

8. Inspect the rubber dampers at the radiator mounts on the frame. Replace either damper if it is damaged or starting to deteriorate.

9. Check the radiator fan switch (D, **Figure 12**) and coolant temperature switch (E, **Figure 12**) for leakage. Be sure each switch is tight.

RADIATOR FAN

Removal/Installation

Replacement parts for the fan assembly are not available. If the fan motor is defective the entire fan assembly must be replaced.

Refer to **Figure 6** for this procedure.

1. Remove the radiator as described in this chapter.
2. Remove the bolts (A, **Figure 13**) securing the fan and carefully detach the fan assembly from the radiator.
3. Test the cooling fan as described in Chapter Nine.
4. Install by reversing the removal steps. Be sure to attach the ground wire (B, **Figure 13**).

THERMOSTAT

Removal/Installation

The thermostat is located beneath the meter assembly on the main frame member.

Refer to **Figure 6** for this procedure.

1. Drain the coolant from the system as described in Chapter Three.
2. Remove the seat as described in Chapter Fourteen.
3. Remove the fuel tank as described in Chapter Eight.
4. Remove the coolant reservoir hose (A, **Figure 14**) from the thermostat housing cover.
5. Loosen the clamp (B, **Figure 14**) on the radiator hose.

6. Remove the two bolts (C, **Figure 14**) securing the thermostat housing cover (D, **Figure 14**) to the housing.
7. Remove the thermostat housing cover and remove the thermostat from the thermostat housing.
8. If necessary, test the thermostat as described in this chapter.
9. Install by reversing the removal steps while noting the following:
   a. Inspect the O-ring seal on the housing cover. If is damaged, deteriorated or starting to harden, replace it with a new O-ring seal.
   b. Install a new O-ring seal in the thermostat housing cover. Apply a light coat of cold multipurpose grease to hold the O-ring in place during installation.
   c. Refill the cooling system with coolant as described in Chapter Three.

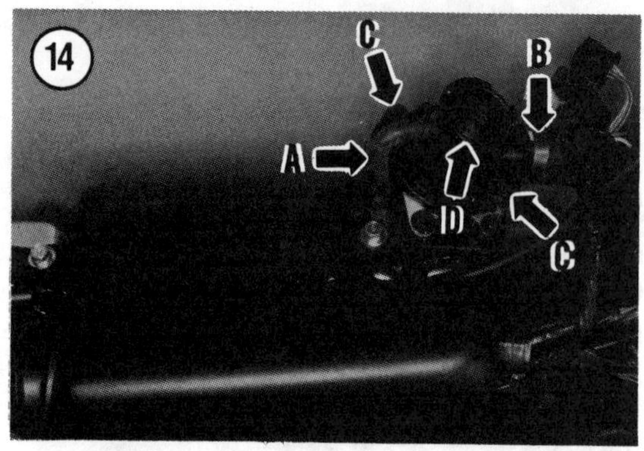

Testing

Test the thermostat to ensure proper operation. Replace the thermostat if it remains open at normal room temperature or stays closed after the specified temperature is reached during the test procedure.

Suspend the thermostat in a pan of water (**Figure 15**). Place a thermometer in the pan of water (use a cooking or candy thermometer that is rated higher than the test temperature). Gradually heat the water and continue to gently stir it until the water temperature reaches the opening temperature in **Table 1**. At this temperature the thermostat valve should open.

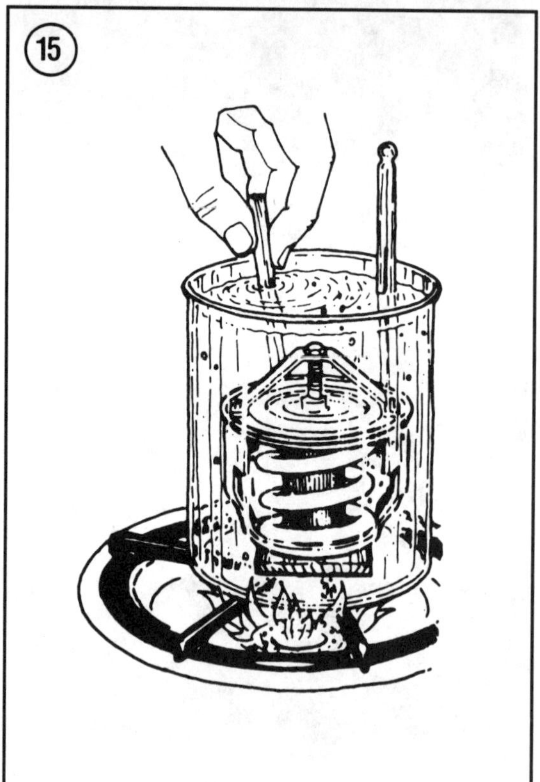

NOTE

Valve operation is sometimes sluggish. It usually takes 3-5 minutes for the valve to operate properly and to open completely. If the valve fails to open, the thermostat must be replaced (it cannot be serviced). Be sure to replace the thermostat with one of the same temperature rating.

WATER PUMP

The water pump is not a separate unit that can be removed as an assembly. It is an integral part of the right-hand crankcase half. The only parts that can be serviced are the impeller, the impeller drive shaft and the mechanical seal.

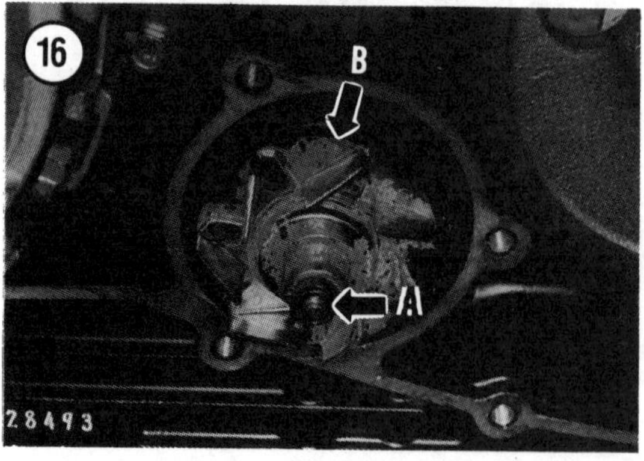

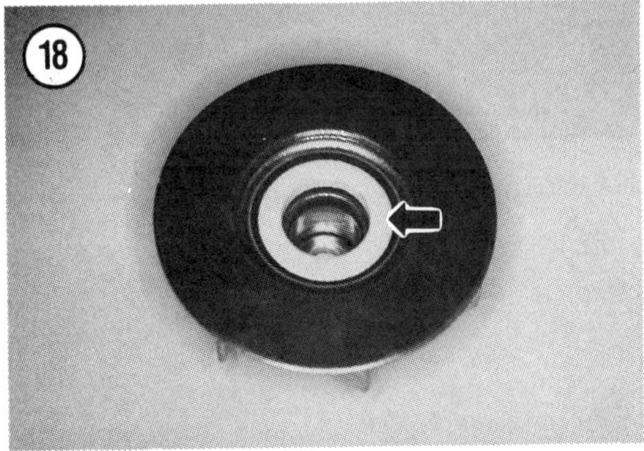

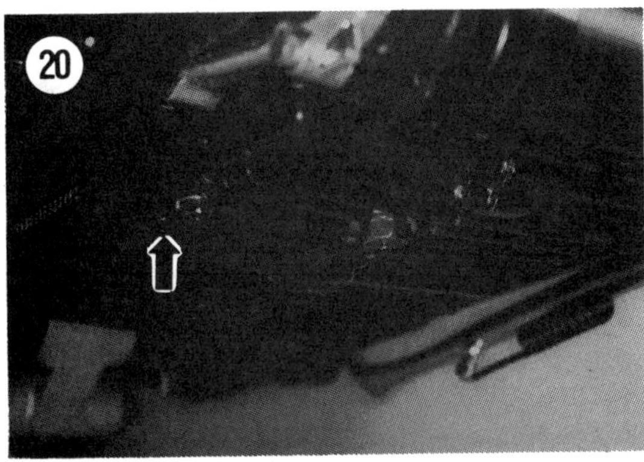

Impeller Removal/Inspection/Installation

1. Drain the engine oil as described in Chapter Three.
2. Drain the cooling system as described in Chapter Three.
3. Remove the clutch cover as described in Chapter Six.
4. Turn the impeller shaft and check the bearing for excessive noise or roughness. If the bearing operation is rough, replace the bearings as described in Chapter Five.
5. Remove the impeller nut (A, **Figure 16**) and remove the impeller (B, **Figure 16**).
6. Check the impeller blades (**Figure 17**) for corrosion or damage. Replace the impeller if it is corroded or if the impeller blades are cracked or broken.
7. Press a new rubber seal and new seal seat into the back of the impeller until they bottom (**Figure 18**).
8. Lubricate the mating surfaces of the impeller sealing seat and the mechanical seal with fresh coolant.
9. Apply grease to a new O-ring (**Figure 19**) and install it onto the impeller shaft.
10. Install the impeller and torque the nut to the specification in **Table 2**.
11. Refill the engine with oil and the cooling system with coolant as described in Chapter Three.

Water Pump Inspection

1. Inspect the drainage outlet (**Figure 20**) beneath the impeller on the right side of the crankcase.
2. If you notice evidence of leakage, coolant is leaking past the mechanical seal and out through the drainage outlet. Replace the mechanical seal and the impeller.

Mechanical Seal Removal/Installation

1. Drain the engine oil as described in Chapter Three.
2. Drain the cooling system as described in Chapter Three.
3. Remove the clutch cover as described in Chapter Six.
4. Remove the impeller as described in this chapter.
5. Use a suitable tool to pry the mechanical seal flange from the crankcase (**Figure 21**).

CAUTION
Do not damage the inner surface of the crankcase bore or the water pump shaft while removing the mechanical seal.

6. Use needlenose pliers and carefully pull the mechanical seal from the crankcase. Discard the old seal.

NOTE
The body of the mechanical seal is coated with an adhesive. Do not apply any liquid gasket sealer to the mechanical seal or to the seal housing in the crankcase.

7. Fit the new mechanical seal (A, **Figure 22**) over the water pump shaft and into place in the crankcase.

CAUTION
Take care not to damage the water pump shaft or the mechanical seal during the next step.

8. Use a suitably sized socket and extension (B, **Figure 22**) to press the mechanical seal into the crankcase until it bottoms.
9. Install the impeller as described in this chapter.
10. Install the clutch cover as described in Chapter Six.
11. Refill the engine with oil and the cooling system with coolant as described in Chapter Three.

Water Pump Shaft Removal/Installation

1. Split the crankcase as described in Chapter Five.
2. Remove the mechanical seal as described in this chapter.
3. Remove the circlip (A, **Figure 23**) from the water pump shaft (B, **Figure 23**).
4. Remove the shaft by pulling it from the outside of the crankcase half.
5. Install the water pump shaft by pushing it into the crankcase from the outside.
6. Install a new mechanical seal as described in this chapter.
7. Reassemble the crankcase as described in Chapter Five.

Water Pump Shaft Bearings and Seals

In general, bearings and seals are installed with their manufacturer's marks facing out. The water

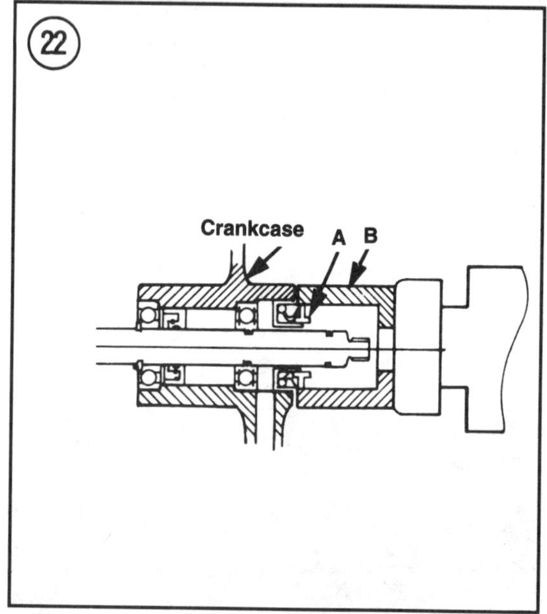

pump shaft bearings and seals, however, are an exception to this rule. Follow the procedure below when replacing them.

1. Use the appropriate size bearing driver or socket to press the seal into the housing on the internal side of the right-hand crankcase half. Install this seal with it's manufacturer's marks facing the outboard side of the crankcase half.
2. Use the appropriate size bearing driver or socket to press the unsealed ball bearing into the housing on the inboard side of the crankcase half.
3. Use the appropriate size bearing driver or socket to press the sealed ball bearing into the housing on the outboard side of the right-hand crankcase half.
4. Install the water pump shaft and mechanical seal as described in this chapter.

Table 1 COOLING SYSTEM SPECIFICATIONS

Total system coolant capacity	2.4 liters (2.5 U.S. qt. [2.1 Imp. qt.])
Radiator cap relief pressure	93-123 kPa (14-18 psi)
Thermostat	
Opening temperature	80-84° C (176-183° F)
Minimum valve lift	8 mm (0.015 in.) @ 95° C (203 ° F)

Table 2 COOLING SYSTEM TIGHTENING TORQUES

Item	N•m	in.-lb.
Impeller nut	11	97
Coolant pipe mounting bolt	11	97
Coolant drain bolt	11	97

CHAPTER ELEVEN

FRONT SUSPENSION AND STEERING

This chapter describes the repair and maintenance for the front wheel, front forks and steering components.

Front suspension torque specifications are covered in **Table 1**. **Tables 1-4** are at the end of this chapter.

NOTE
Where differences occur relating to United Kingdom (U.K.) models they are identified. If there is no (U.K.) designation relating to a procedure, photo or illustration, it is identical to the United States (U.S.) models.

FRONT WHEEL

Removal

CAUTION
Care must be taken when removing, handling and installing a wheel with a disc brake rotor. The rotor is relatively thin in order to dissipate heat and to minimize unsprung weight. The rotor is designed to withstand tremendous rotational loads, but it can be damaged when subjected to side impact loads. If the rotor is knocked out of true by a side impact, a pulsation will be felt in the front brake lever during braking. The rotor is too thin to be trued and must be replaced if damaged. Protect the rotor when transporting a wheel to a dealership or tire specialist for tire service. Do ***not*** *place a wheel in a car trunk or pickup bed without protecting the rotor from side impact.*

1. Loosen the front axle nut (**Figure 1**)
2. Use a scissors jack or jack stands to securely support the bike with the front wheel off the ground.
3. Loosen the front axle pinch bolt (A, **Figure 2**).
4. Remove the front axle nut (**Figure 1**) from the left-hand side.
5. Withdraw the front axle from the right-hand side.
6. Pull the wheel down and forward to remove it from the front fork and the brake caliper.

NOTE
Insert a piece of vinyl tubing or wood into the caliper in place of the brake disc. With the tubing/wood in place, the piston (pistons on VN800 Classic models) will not be forced out of the cylinder(s) if the brake lever is inadvertently squeezed. If this does happen, the caliper may have to be disassembled to reseat the piston(s) and the system will have to be bled.

CAUTION
Do not set the wheel down on the disc surface as it may get scratched or warped.

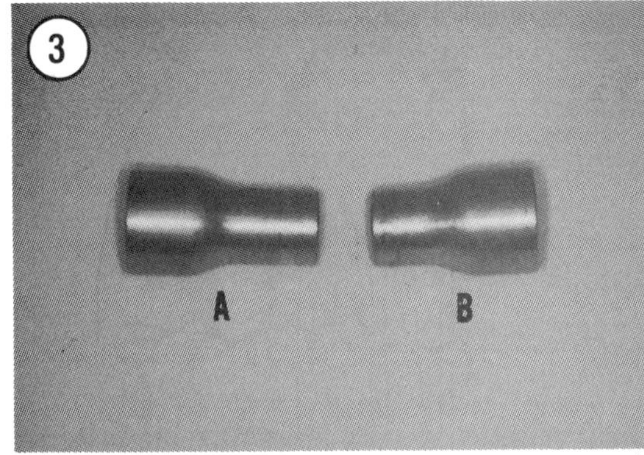

NOTE

***Figure 3** shows the cone-shaped spacers from a VN800. The spacers on a VN800 Classic are cylindrical. The installation and removal procedure, however, apply to both models.*

7. Remove the right-hand spacer (A, **Figure 3**) and the left-hand spacer (B, **Figure 3**) from the hub.
8. Inspect the wheel as described in this chapter.

Installation

1. Make sure the axle bearing surfaces of the fork sliders and axle are free from burrs and nicks.
2. Apply grease to the axle on each side of the hub.

NOTE:

The two front hub spacers are not interchangeable. The longer spacer goes on the right-hand side of the hub; the shorter spacer on the left.

3. Install both spacers onto the hub. The longer spacer (A, **Figure 3**) goes into the right-hand side of the hub; the shorter spacer (B, **Figure 3**) goes into the left-hand side.
4. Position the wheel in place. Insert the brake disc into the caliper being careful not to damage the brake pads.
5. Apply a light coat of grease to the front axle. Insert the front axle through the right-hand fork leg and through the wheel hub.
6. Make sure the axle passes through the spacers on the right-hand (B, **Figure 2**) and left-hand (A, **Figure 4**) side of the hub.
7. Install front axle nut, but do not tighten it.
8. Place a long drift into the hole in the right-hand end of the front axle to prevent it from turning. Tighten the front axle nut (B, **Figure 4**) to the torque specification listed in **Table 1**. Remove the drift from the front axle.
9. Remove the jack or jack stands from under the crankcase. Leave the bike on the sidestand.
10. With the front brake applied, push down hard on the handlebars and pump the forks several times to seat the front axle.
11. Tighten the front axle pinch bolt (A, **Figure 2**) to the torque specification listed in **Table 1**.
12. After the wheel is completely installed, rotate it several times to make sure that it rotates freely. Apply the front brake as many times as necessary to

make sure the brake pads seat against the brake disc correctly.

Inspection

1. Remove any corrosion on the front axle with a piece of fine emery cloth. Clean it with solvent, then wipe the axle clean with a lint-free cloth.
2. Check axle runout. Place the axle on V-blocks and place the tip of a dial indicator in the middle of the axle (**Figure 5**). Rotate the axle and check runout. If the runout exceeds the specification listed in **Table 4**, replace the axle. Do not attempt to straighten it.
3. Check rim runout as follows:
   a. Remove the tire from the rim as described in this chapter. Reinstall the wheel (without the tire) as described in this chapter.
   b. Measure the radial (up and down) runout of the wheel rim with a dial indicator as shown in **Figure 6**. If runout exceeds the specification listed in **Table 4**, check the wheel bearings.
   c. Measure the axial (side to side) runout of the wheel rim with a dial indicator as shown in **Figure 7**. If runout exceeds the specification listed in **Table 4**, check the wheel bearings.
   d. Check the wheel bearings as described in this chapter. If necessary, replace the front wheel bearings.
   e. If the wheel bearings are in good condition, check for loose or bent spokes. Some runout can be removed by adjusting the spokes as described in this chapter. If adjusting the spokes does not bring axial runout within specification, the rim is badly bent and must be replaced.

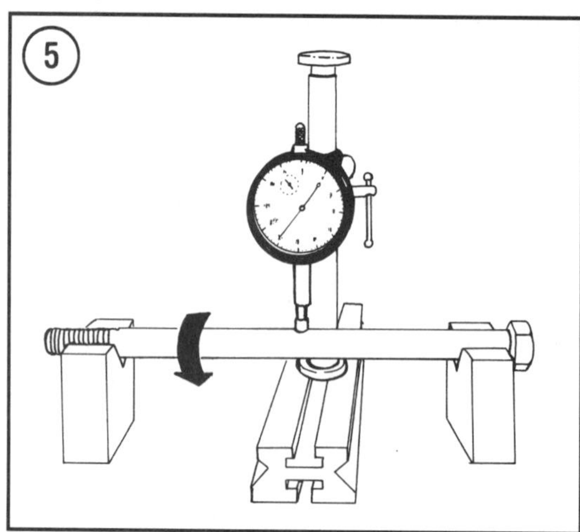

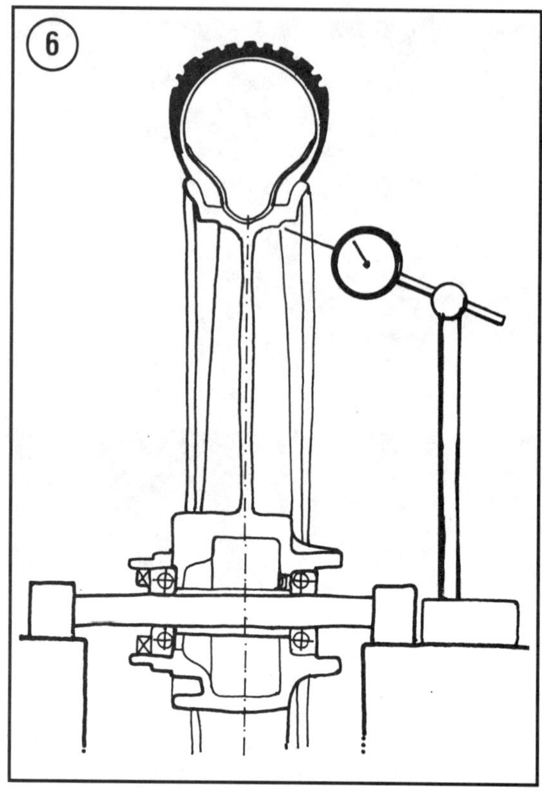

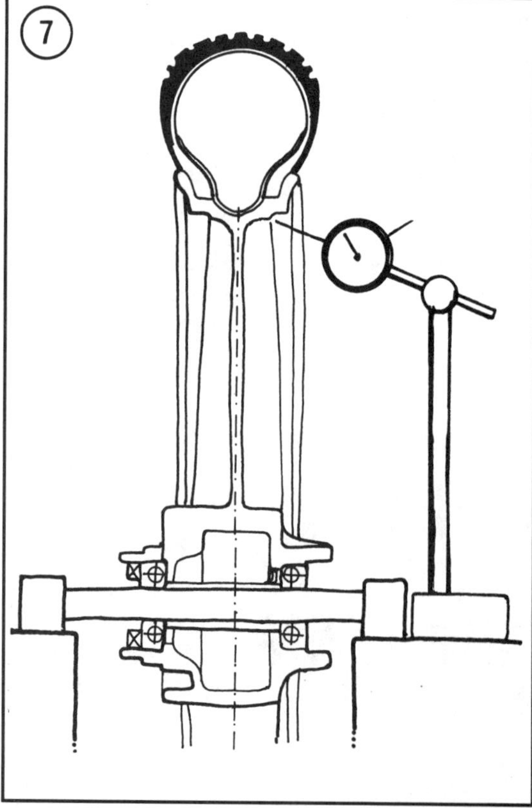

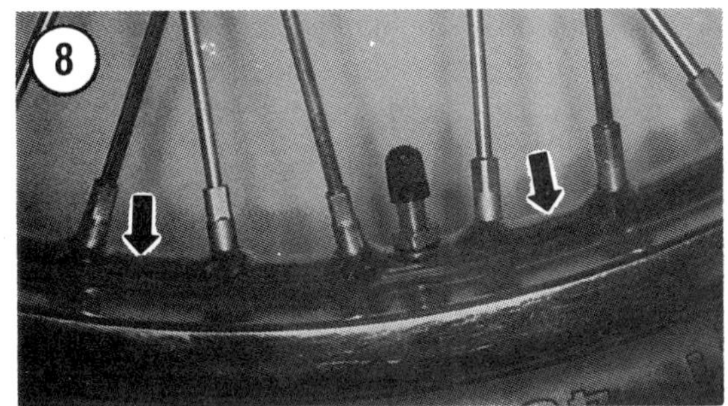

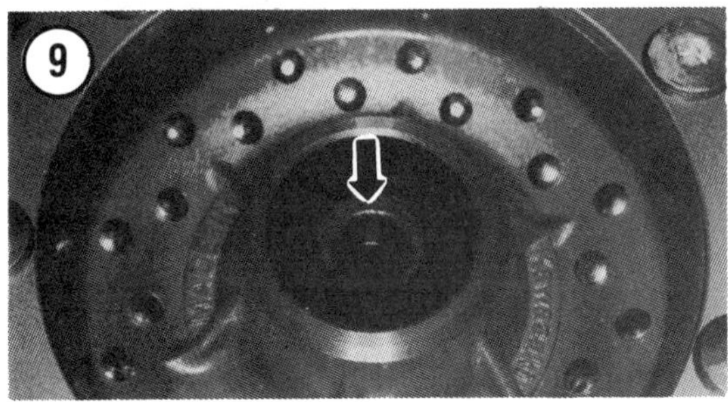

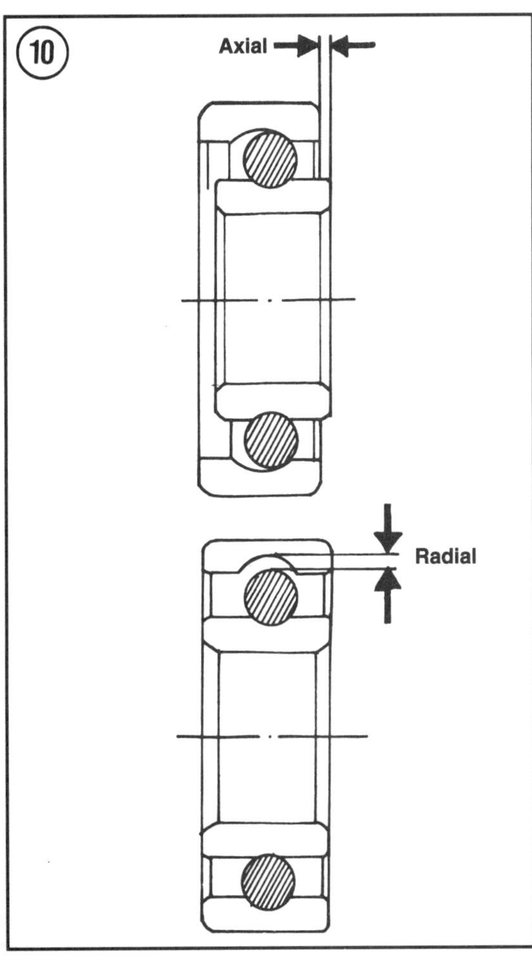

4. Inspect the wheel rim (**Figure 8**) for dents, bending or cracks. Check the rim and rim sealing surface for scratches deeper than 0.5 mm (0.01 in.). If any of these conditions are present, the wheel is unsafe for use and should be replaced.

FRONT HUB

Bearing Inspection

Inspect each wheel bearing prior to removing it from the wheel hub.

CAUTION
Do not remove the wheel bearings for inspection because they will be damaged during the removal process. Remove wheel bearings only if they must be replaced.

CAUTION
Do not set the wheel down on the disc surface as it may get scratched or warped.

1. Remove the front wheel as described in this chapter.
2. Turn the inner race of each bearing by hand. Make sure the bearings turn smoothly.
3. Inspect the play of the inner race (**Figure 9**) of each wheel bearing. Check for excessive axial play and radial play (**Figure 10**). Replace the bearing if it has an excessive amount of free play.

NOTE
When replacing the bearing, always replace them as a complete set. When purchasing new bearings, take your old bearings along to ensure a perfect matchup.

NOTE
Fully sealed bearings are available from many bearing specialty shops. Fully sealed bearings provide better protection from dirt and moisture than unsealed bearings.

Disassembly

Refer to **Figure 11** for this procedure.

1. Remove the front wheel as described in this chapter.

CAUTION
Do not set the wheel down on the disc surface as it may get scratched or warped.

2. Remove the right-hand spacer from the hub.

3. If necessary, remove the bolts (**Figure 12**) securing the brake disc to the hub and remove the disc.

4. Before proceeding further, inspect the wheel bearings as described in this chapter. If they must be replaced, proceed as follows:

5. On the left-hand side of the hub, perform the following:
   a. Remove the axle seal (**Figure 13**).
   b. Remove the circlip securing the bearing.

6. Remove the axle seal from the right side of the hub.

(11)

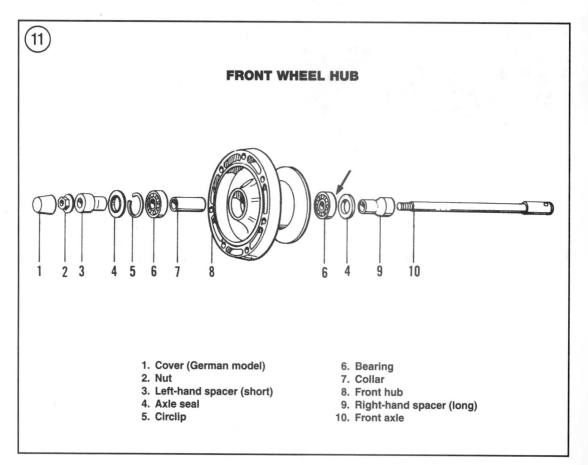

FRONT WHEEL HUB

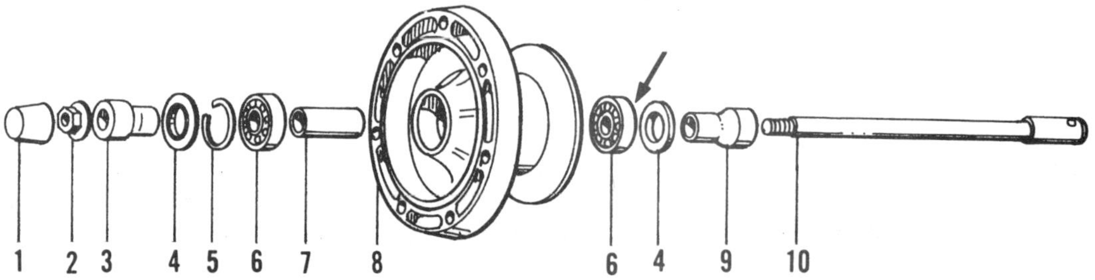

1 2 3 4 5 6 7 8 6 4 9 10

1. Cover (German model)
2. Nut
3. Left-hand spacer (short)
4. Axle seal
5. Circlip
6. Bearing
7. Collar
8. Front hub
9. Right-hand spacer (long)
10. Front axle

7. To remove the right- and left-hand bearings and distance collar, insert a soft aluminum or brass drift into one side of the hub (**Figure 14**).

8. Push the distance collar to one side and place the drift on the inner race of the lower bearing.

9. Tap the bearing out of the hub with a hammer, working around the perimeter of the inner race.

10. Repeat for the bearing on the other side.

11. Clean the inside and the outside of the hub with solvent. Dry with compressed air.

Assembly

1. On unsealed bearings, pack the bearings with a high temperature bearing grease. Work the grease in between the balls thoroughly; turn the bearing by hand a couple of times to make sure the grease is distributed evenly inside the bearing.

2. Blow any dirt or foreign matter from the hub prior to installing the bearings.

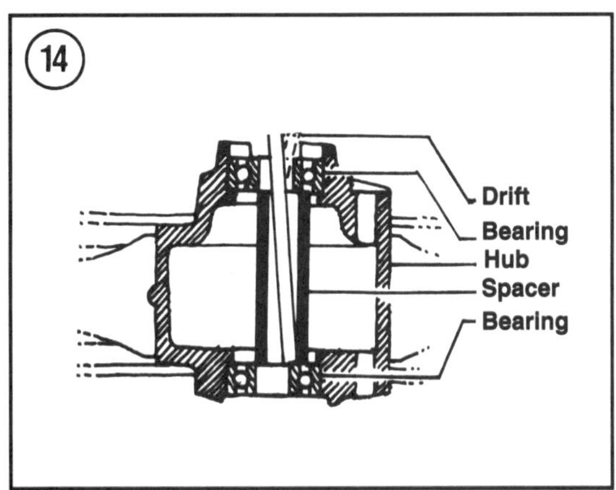

CAUTION

Install the unsealed bearings with the single sealed side or the manufacturer's marks facing outward. Tap the bearings squarely into place, and tap on the outer race only. Do not tap on the inner race or the bearing might be damaged. Be sure that the bearings are completely seated.

3. Set the left-hand bearing in place in the hub.

4. Select a socket (**Figure 15**) or bearing driver that matches the outer race diameter and set it on the bearing. Tap the left-hand bearing squarely into place until it bottoms in the hub. Take care to tap on the outer race only. Do not tap on the inner race or the bearing might be damaged. Be sure that the bearing is completely seated in the hub.

5. Turn the wheel over (right-hand side up) on the workbench and install the distance collar.

6. Drive in the right-hand bearing squarely into place until it bottoms in the hub.

7. Turn the wheel over, and install a new circlip into the left-hand side of the hub. Be sure the circlip is securely seated in the groove in hub.

8. Install a new axle seal into each side of the hub.
   a. Pack the seal with a high temperature grease.
   b. Tap the grease seal squarely into place. Use a socket (**Figure 15**) or bearing driver that matches the seal's outer diameter and tap the seal into place in the hub. Be sure the seal is flush with the outer surface of the hub.

9. If the brake disc was removed, perform the following:
   a. Apply Loctite 271 to the brake disc bolts prior to installation.
   b. Install the brake disc (**Figure 12**) and bolts. Torque the bolts to the specifications listed in **Table 1**.

10. Install the front wheel as described in this chapter.

WHEELS

Wheel Balance

An unbalanced wheel is unsafe. Depending upon the degree of imbalance and the speed of the motorcycle, the rider may experience anything from a mild vibration to a violent shimmy that may result in loss of control.

Kawasaki offers balance weights of 10, 20 and 30 grams each. These weights fit onto the spokes (**Figure 16**), and are crimped into place with ordinary pliers.

Before you attempt to balance the wheel, make sure that the wheel bearings are in good condition and properly lubricated. The wheel must rotate freely. Also check that the tire balance mark (yellow paint mark on the tire) is aligned with the valve stem (**Figure 17**). If not, break the tire loose from the rim and align it correctly prior to balancing the wheel.

NOTE
When balancing the wheels, do so with the brake disc attached. The disc rotates with the wheel and affects the balance.

1. Remove the wheel as described in this chapter.
2. Mount the wheel on a fixture such as the one shown in **Figure 18** so it can rotate freely.
3. Give the wheel a spin and let it coast to a stop. Mark the tire at the lowest point (6 o'clock).
4. Spin the wheel several more times. If the wheel keeps coming to rest at the same point, it is out of balance.
5. Loosely attach a balance weight onto a spoke at the upper or light side (12 o'clock) of the wheel.
6. Rotate the wheel 1/4 turn (3 o'clock). Release the wheel and observe the following:
   a. If the wheel does not rotate (if it stays at the 3 o'clock position), the correct balance weight is installed. The wheel is balanced.
   b. If the wheel rotates and the weighted portion goes up, replace the weight with the next heavier size.
   c. If the wheel rotates and the weighted portion goes down, replace the weight with the next lighter size.
   d. Repeat this step until the wheel remains at rest after being rotated 1/4 turn. Rotate the wheel another 1/4 turn, and another 1/4 turn, and another turn to see if the wheel is correctly balanced.
7. Firmly crimp the balance weight in place with a pair of pliers (**Figure 19**).

CAUTION
Do not attach more than 60 grams of balance weight to the wheel. If the balance weight required exceeds this amount, take the wheel to a Kawasaki dealership for inspection and balancing.

Spoke Adjustment

Spokes loosen with use and should be checked periodically. If all spokes appear to be loose, first tighten all the spokes on one side of the hub, then tighten all the spokes on the other side. One half to one turn should be sufficient. Do not overtighten the

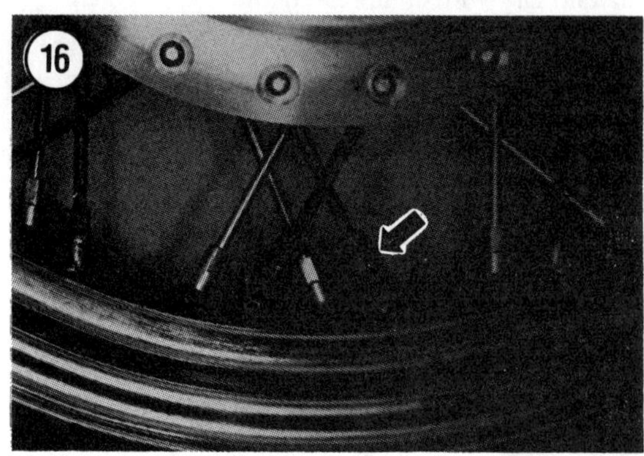

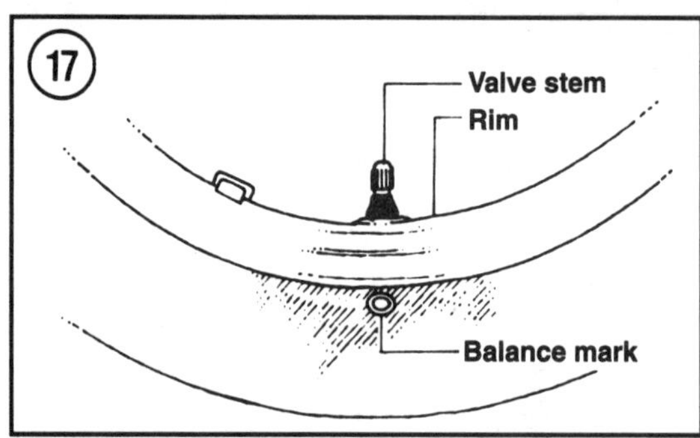

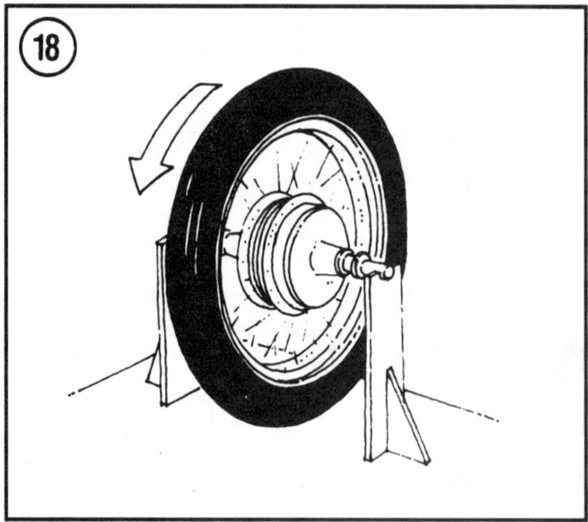

spokes. After tightening all the spokes, check rim runout to be sure you have not pulled the rim out of shape.

To check rim runout, mount a dial indicator onto the front fork so the gauge bears against one side of the rim. If you do not have a dial indicator, improvise a device like the one shown in **Figure 20**. Adjust the position of the bolt so it just clears the rim. Rotate the wheel and note whether the clearance increases or decreases. Mark the tire with chalk or crayon at areas that produce significantly larger or smaller clearances. Clearance must not change by more than the rim runout limit shown in **Table 4**.

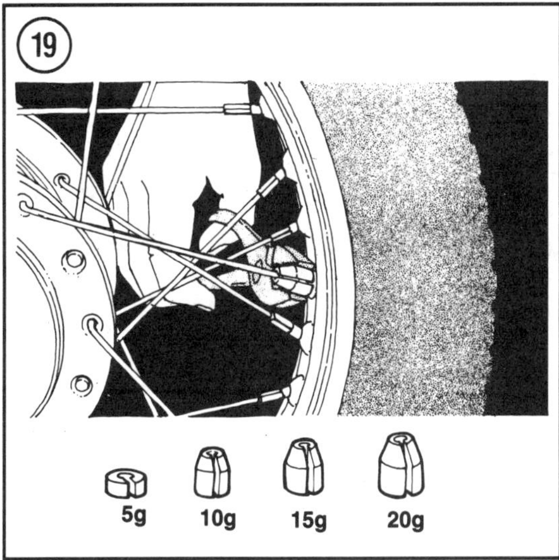

To pull the rim out, tighten the spokes that terminate on the same side of the hub and loosen the spokes that terminate on the opposite side of the hub (**Figure 21**). In most cases, only a slight amount of adjustment is necessary to true a rim. After adjustment is complete, rotate the wheel and make sure another area has not been pulled out of true. Continue adjustment and checking until runout does not exceed the specification in **Table 4**.

Wheel Alignment

The swing arm has alignment scales on each side for checking wheel alignment. The wheels should be properly aligned when the notches on the left-hand and right-hand chain adjusters point to the same mark on their respective alignment scales. (**Figure 22**).

Wheel alignment can also be checked by performing the following procedure. Refer to **Figure 23** for this procedure.

1. Measure the tires at their widest point.

2. Subtract the smaller dimension from the larger dimension.

3. Make an alignment tool out of wood, approximately 7 ft. (2m) long, with an offset equal to one-half the dimension obtained in Step 2. Refer to D, **Figure 23**.

11

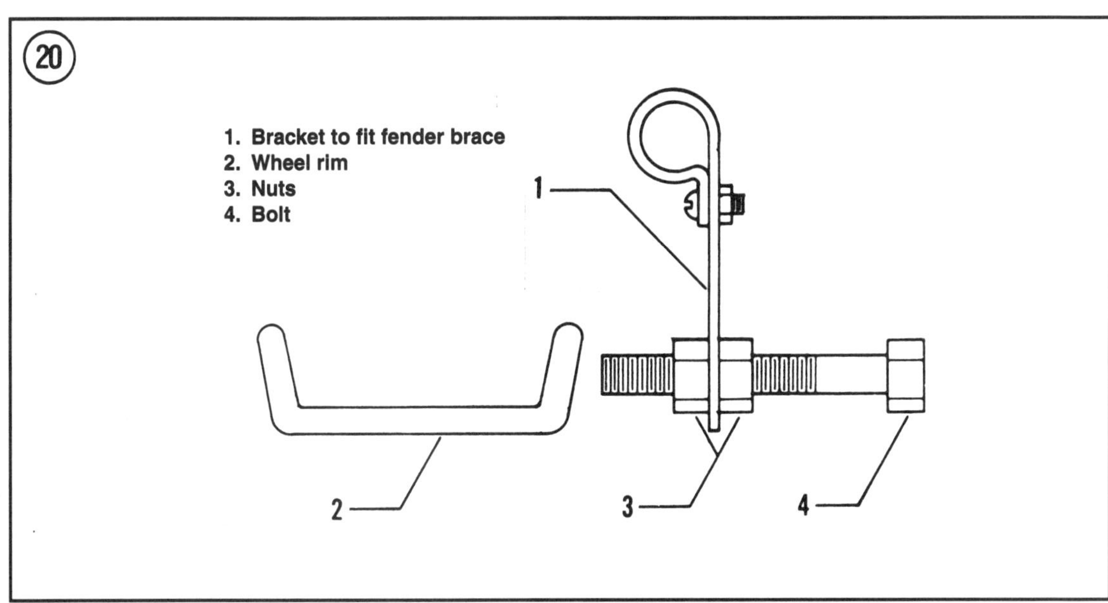

4. If the wheels appear as shown in either A or C in **Figure 23**, the rear wheel must be shifted to correct the alignment.
5. Use the drive chain adjuster to align the wheels as described Chapter Three.

TIRES

Tire Safety

After installing new tires on the bike, break them in correctly. Remember that a new tire has relatively poor adhesion to the road surface until it is broken in properly. Do not subject a new tire to any high-speed riding for at least the first 60 miles (100 km).

TIRE CHANGING

The wheels can easily be damaged during tire removal. Special care must be taken to avoid scratching and gouging the outer rim surface. Insert scraps of leather between the tire iron and the rim to protect the rim from damage. The stock wire wheels are designed for use with tube type tires.

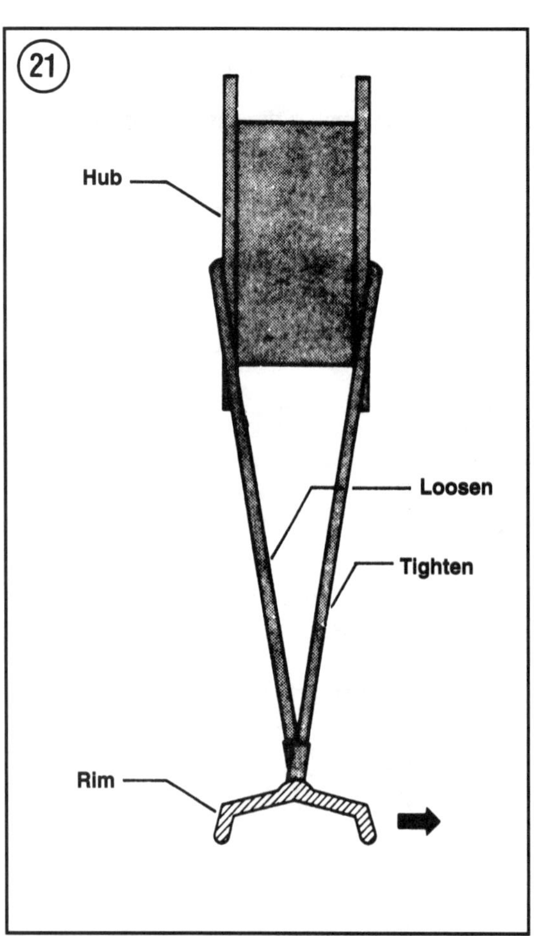

Removal

1. If you are going to reinstall the existing tire, mark the valve stem location on the tire (**Figure 17**) so the tire can be installed in the same position for easier balancing.

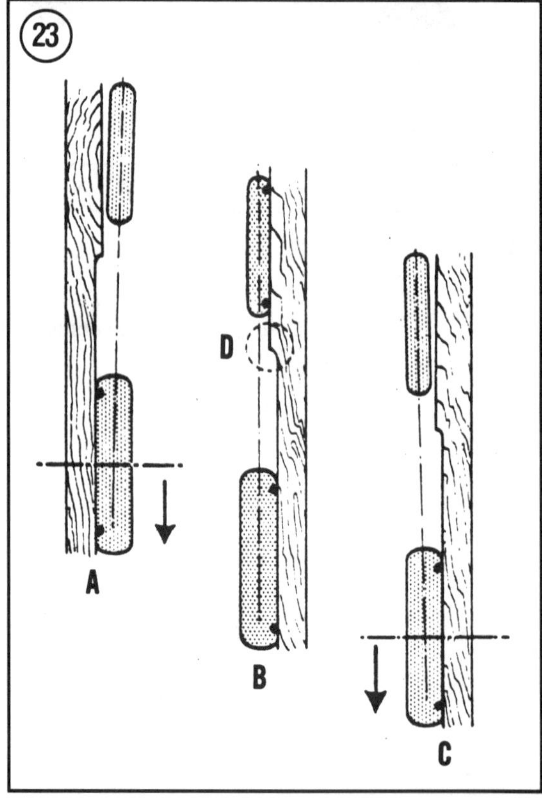

2. Remove the valve stem core to deflate the tire.
3. Press the entire bead on both sides of the tire into the center of the rim. Make sure the tire is broken loose around the entire perimeter of the wheel.
4. Lubricate the beads with soapy water.

CAUTION
Use rim protectors or insert scraps of leather between the tire irons and the rim to protect the rim from damage.

5. Insert the tire iron under the bead next to the valve (**Figure 24**). Force the bead on the opposite side of the tire into the center of the rim and pry the bead over the rim with the tire iron.
6. Insert a second tire iron next to the first to hold the bead over the rim. Then work around the tire with the first tire iron, prying the bead over the rim. Be careful not to pinch the inner tube with the tire irons.
7. Stand the tire on its end or turn it over. Insert the tire iron between the second bead and the side of the rim that the first bead was pried over (**Figure 25**). Force the bead on the opposite side from the tire iron into the center of the rim. Pry the second bead off the rim, working around as with the first. Remove the tire from the rim.
8. Inspect the rim as described in this chapter.

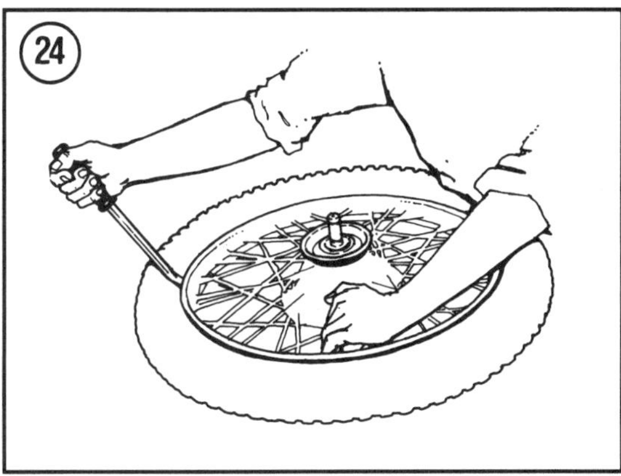

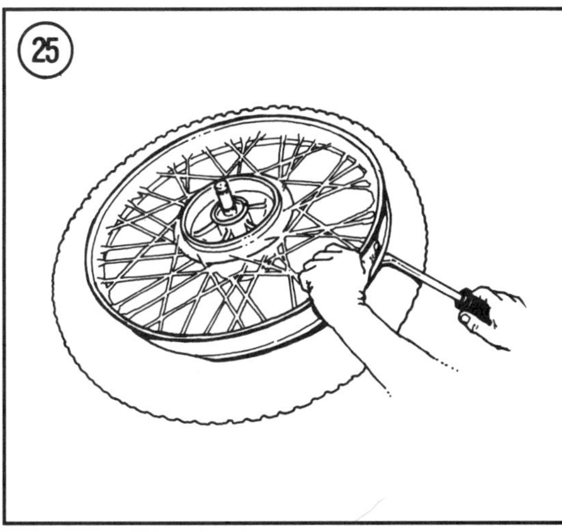

Tire and Rim Inspection

1. Wipe off the inner surfaces of the wheel rim. Clean off any rubber residue or oxidation.
2. If any one of the following is observed, replace the tire.
   a. Cracks or splits in the tire.
   b. Swelling or high spots in the tire.
   c. Damage to the inside of the tire.
   d. Flat spots in the tread from skidding or other abnormal wear patterns.
   e. For original equipment tires, if the tread depth is less than the wear limit in **Table 2**. The wear limit on aftermarket tires may vary.
3. Inspect the valve stem hole in the rim. Remove any dirt or corrosion from the hole and wipe it dry with a clean cloth.

Installation

1. A new tire may have balancing rubbers inside. These are not patches. Do not remove or disturb them.
2. Check the spoke ends. They should not protrude through the nipples into the center of the rim. If they do, they will puncture the inner tube. File off any protruding spoke ends.
3. Make sure the rubber rim tape is in place with the rough side toward the rim.
4. Be sure you have the correct tire, either front or rear, for the rim and that the direction arrow on the tire (**Figure 26**) faces the direction of wheel rotation.
5. Install the valve stem core into the valve stem in the tube and place the inner tube into the tire. Be sure the valve stem is aligned with the valve stem mark (**Figure 17**) you made during Step 1 of *Removal.* If you are installing a new tire, align the valve stem with the yellow paint mark (indicating a lighter point on the tire) on the new tire.
6. Inflate the tube just enough to round it out. Too much air will make installation difficult; too little air will increase the chances of pinching the tube with tire irons.

7. Lubricate both beads of the tire with soapy water. Pull the tube partly out of the tire at the valve. Squeeze the beads together to hold the tube and insert the valve into the hole in the rim (**Figure 27**). The lower bead should go into the center of the rim with the upper bead outside the rim.

8. Place the lower bead of the tire into the center of the rim on each side of the valve stem. Work around the tire in both directions (**Figure 28**). Use a tire iron for the last few inches of bead (**Figure 29**).

9. Press the upper bead into the rim opposite the valve stem. Pry the bead into the rim on both sides of the initial point with a tire iron, working around the rim to the valve (**Figure 30**).

10. Wiggle the valve stem to be sure the tube is not trapped under the tire bead. Set the valve squarely in the rim hole before screwing on the valve stem nut.

11. Check the bead on both sides of the tire for an even fit around the rim.

12. Bounce the wheel several times, rotating it each time. This will force the tire beads against the rim flanges. After the tire beads are in contact with the rim evenly, inflate the tire to seat the beads.

WARNING

In the next step, inflate the tire to approximately 10-15% over the recommended inflation pressure. Do not exceed this pressure as the tire could burst, causing severe injury. Never stand directly over a tire while inflating it.

13. Inflate the tire to 10-15% more that the recommended inflation pressure to initially seat the beads on the rim flanges. Once the beads are seated correctly, deflate the tire to the recommend pressure. If the beads will not seat, deflate the tire and lubricate the rim and beads again with soapy water.

14. Install the valve stem cap (B, **Figure 8**). Always install the cap onto the valve stem. It prevents small pebbles and dirt from collecting in the valve stem; this could allow air leakage or result in incorrect tire pressure readings.

15. Balance the wheel as described in this chapter.

TIRE REPAIRS

Patching an inner tube on the road is very difficult. A can of pressurized tire sealant may inflate the tire

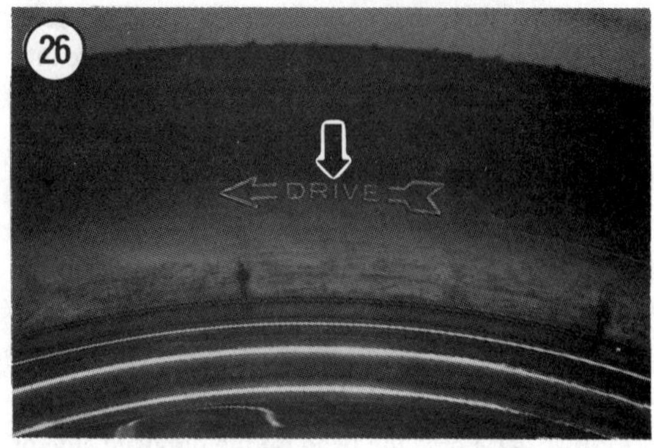

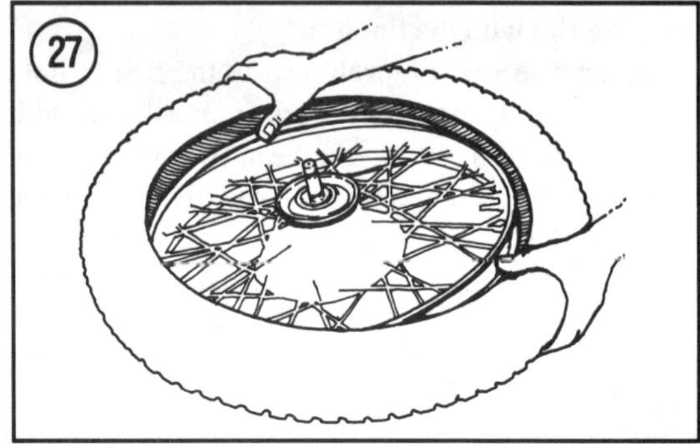

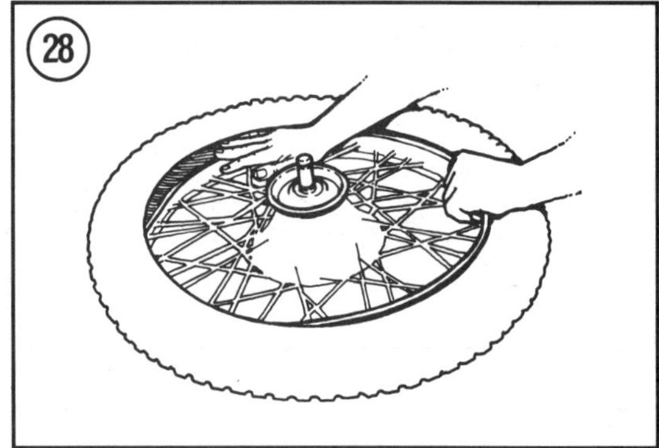

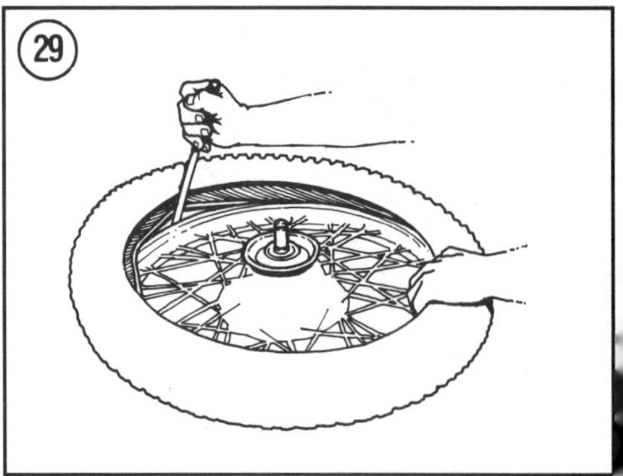

and seal the hole, although this is only a temporary fix.

Another solution is to carry a spare inner tube.

Do not run with a patched inner tube for any length of time. The patch may rub off resulting in another flat. Install a new inner tube as soon as possible.

HANDLEBAR

Handlebar Assembly Removal/Installation

NOTE

If it is not necessary to remove the components from each end of the handlebar for service, perform the following steps. If component removal is necessary, disassemble the handlebar as described in this chapter.

Refer to **Figure 31** when performing this procedure.

1. Remove the fuel tank as described in Chapter Eight.
2. Disconnect the brake light switch electrical connector (**Figure 32**) from the brake lever.
3. Disconnect the starter lockout switch electrical connector (**Figure 33**) from the clutch lever.

CAUTION

Cover the surrounding area with a heavy cloth or plastic tarp to protect it from accidental spilling of clutch and brake fluid. Wash any spilled fluid from any painted or plated surface immediately, as it will destroy the finish. Use soapy water and rinse thoroughly.

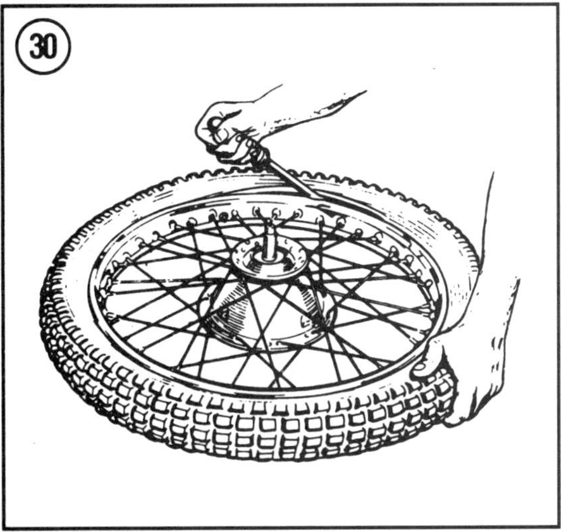

4. Remove the trim caps from the handlebar holder Allen bolts.

5A. For 1997 and 1998 VN800 models and for VN800 Classics models:
   a. Remove the Allen bolts (**Figure 34**) securing the handlebar upper holders.
   b. Remove the upper handlebar holders and remove the handlebar assembly.

5B. For 1995 and 1996 VN800 models:
   a. Remove the Allen bolt from the handlebar holder (**Figure 31**).
   b. Slide the collars out from the handlebar holders.
   c. Carefully open the handlebar holders and remove the handlebar assembly.

6. Move the handlebar assembly back and rest it on the frame.
7. Secure the handlebar assembly so the brake master cylinder reservoir remains in an upright position. This will minimize the loss of hydraulic fluid and keep air from entering the brake system. It is not necessary to remove the hydraulic line.
8. Install by reversing these removal steps while noting the following:
   a. Tighten the handlebar holder Allen bolts to the torque specification listed in **Table 1**.
   b. On 1995 and 1996 VN800 models, be sure the punch mark on the handlebar aligns with the gap in the handlebar holder (**Figure 35**).
   c. On 1997 and 1998 VN800 models and VN800 Classics models, tighten the front Allen bolts first and then tighten the rear Allen bolts. There should be no gap at the front and an even gap at the rear between the handlebar upper and lower holders (**Figure 36**). Be sure that the punch mark on the handlebar assembly aligns with the gap between the upper and lower holders.
   d. Check the throttle operation. If necessary, adjust the throttle as described in Chapter Three.

WARNING

After installation is complete, make sure the brake lever does not contact the throttle grip assembly when it is pulled on fully. If it does, the brake fluid may be low in the reservoir; refill if necessary. Refer to Chapter Thirteen.

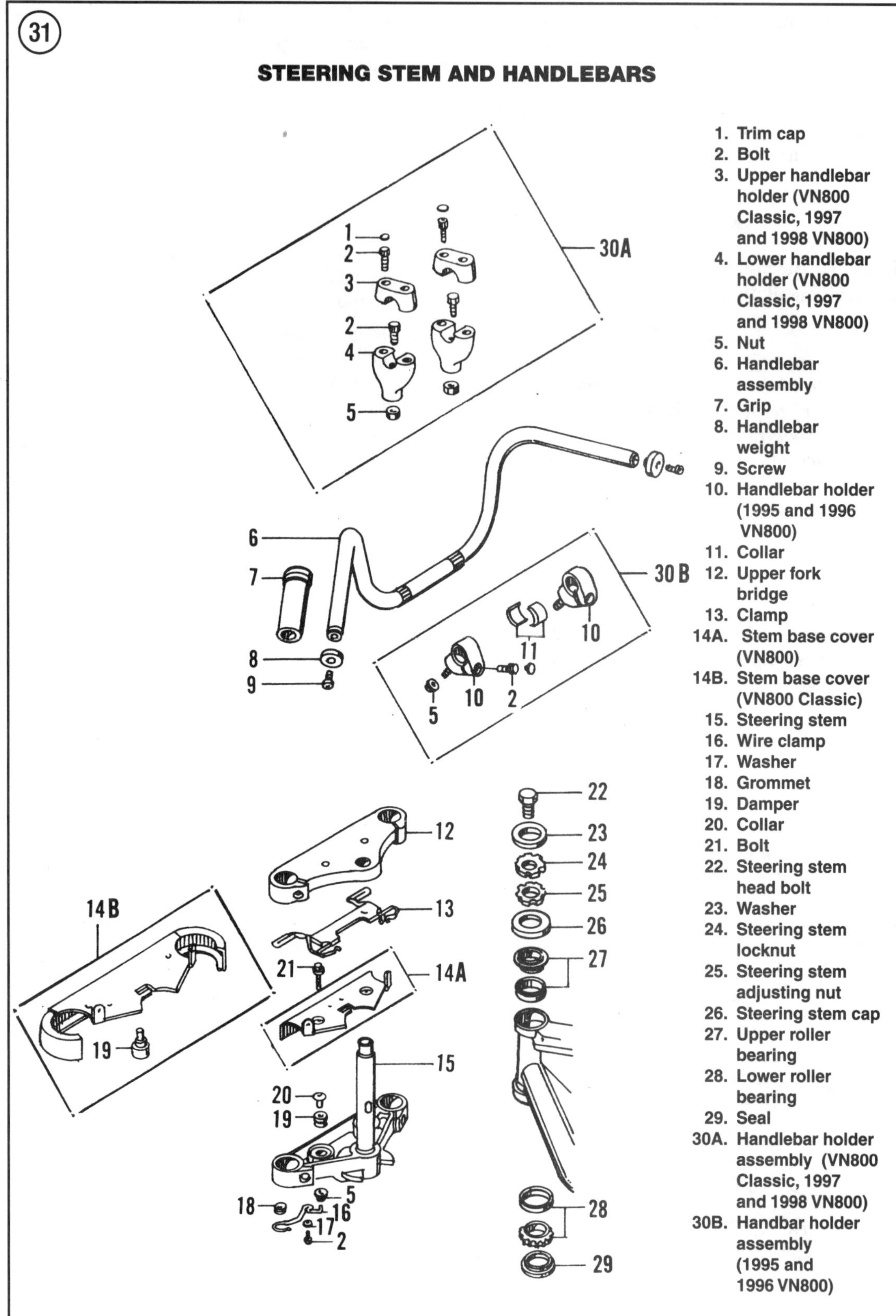
31
STEERING STEM AND HANDLEBARS
1. Trim cap
2. Bolt
3. Upper handlebar holder (VN800 Classic, 1997 and 1998 VN800)
4. Lower handlebar holder (VN800 Classic, 1997 and 1998 VN800)
5. Nut
6. Handlebar assembly
7. Grip
8. Handlebar weight
9. Screw
10. Handlebar holder (1995 and 1996 VN800)
11. Collar
12. Upper fork bridge
13. Clamp
14A. Stem base cover (VN800)
14B. Stem base cover (VN800 Classic)
15. Steering stem
16. Wire clamp
17. Washer
18. Grommet
19. Damper
20. Collar
21. Bolt
22. Steering stem head bolt
23. Washer
24. Steering stem locknut
25. Steering stem adjusting nut
26. Steering stem cap
27. Upper roller bearing
28. Lower roller bearing
29. Seal
30A. Handlebar holder assembly (VN800 Classic, 1997 and 1998 VN800)
30B. Handbar holder assembly (1995 and 1996 VN800)

Handlebar and Component Removal/Installation

NOTE
*If it is necessary to remove the components from the handlebar for service, perform the following procedure. If component removal is not necessary, refer to **Handlebar Removal/Installation** in this chapter.*

Right-hand side of handlebar

1. Remove the fuel tank as described in Chapter Eight.

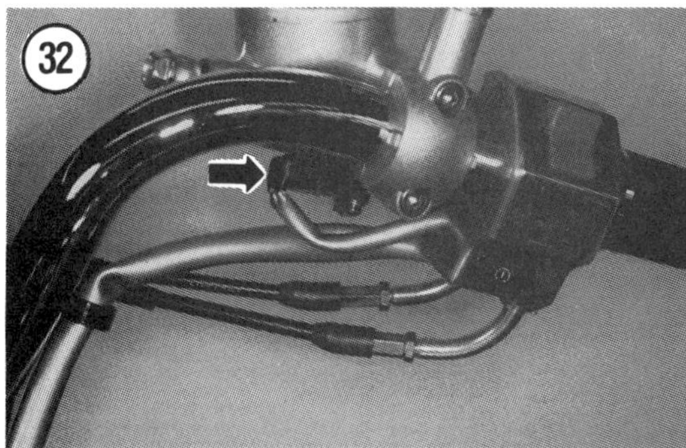

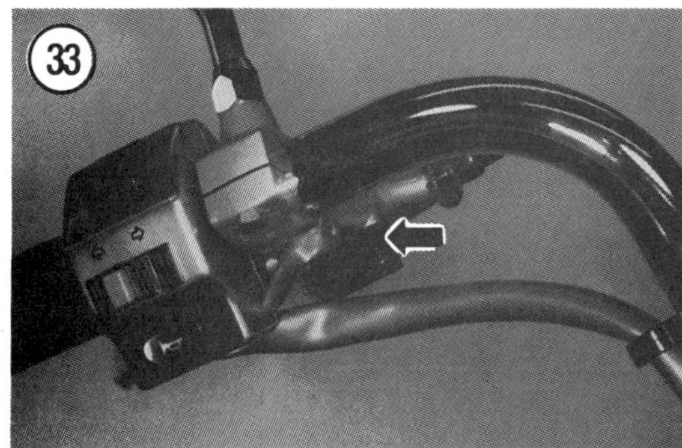

2. Disconnect the brake light switch electrical connector (**Figure 32**) from the brake switch.
3. Unscrew and remove the rear view mirror (A, **Figure 37**) from the master cylinder.
4. Remove the screws securing the right-hand handlebar switch assembly (B, **Figure 37**) together.
5. Partially remove the upper half and disconnect the throttle cables from the throttle assembly. Carefully lay the throttle cable over the fender or back over the frame. Be careful that the cable does not get crimped or damaged.
6. Remove the lower half of the right-hand switch assembly from the handlebar and lay it over the fender or back over the frame.
7. Remove the throttle grip screw from the end of the handlebar and remove the handlebar weight.
8. Remove the throttle grip assembly (C, **Figure 37**).

CAUTION
Cover the surrounding area with a heavy cloth or plastic tarp to protect it

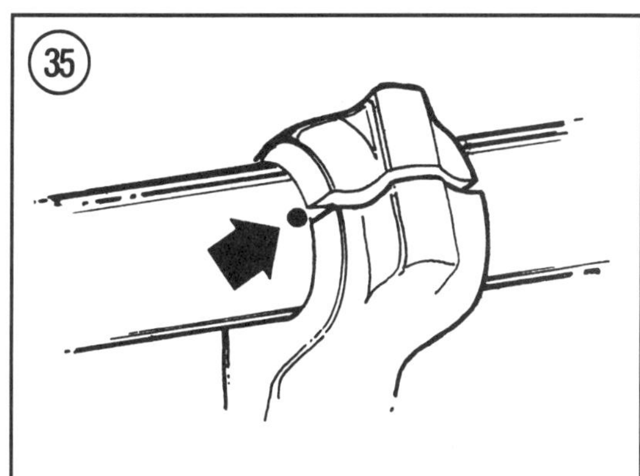

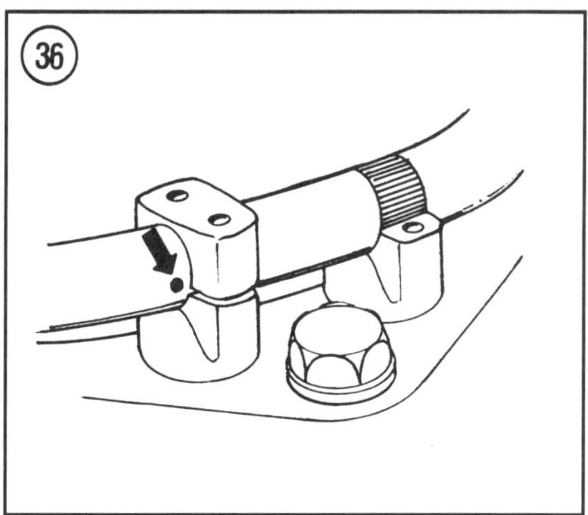

11

from accidental spilling of brake fluid. Wash any spilled fluid off painted or plated surfaces immediately as it will destroy the finish. Use soapy water and rinse thoroughly.

9. Remove the clamp bolts and clamp securing the front brake master cylinder (D, **Figure 37**) to the handlebar.
10. Remove the front brake master cylinder from the handlebar. Tie the master cylinder to the frame and keep the reservoir in an upright position. This will the minimize loss of brake fluid and keep air from entering the brake system. It is not necessary to remove the hydraulic brake line.
11. Remove the components from the left-hand side of the handlebar as described in this chapter.

12A. For 1997 and 1998 VN800 models and VN800 Classic models, remove the handlebars by performing the following:

 a. Remove the trim caps and remove the Allen bolts (**Figure 34**) securing the handlebar upper holders.
 b. Remove the upper holders and the handlebar assembly.
 c. Move the handlebar assembly back and rest it on the frame.

12B. For 1995 and 1996 VN800 models, remove the handlebars by performing the following:

 a. Remove the trim caps, and then remove the Allen bolts from the handlebar holders (**Figure 31**).
 b. Slide the collars out from the handlebar holders.
 c. Carefully open the handlebar holders and remove the handlebar assembly.
 d. Move the handlebar assembly back and rest it on the frame.

13. Install by reversing these removal steps while noting the following:

 a. Tighten the handlebar holder Allen bolts to the torque specification listed in **Table 1**.
 b. On 1997 and 1998 VN800 models and VN800 Classic models, tighten the front Allen bolts first, then tighten the rear Allen bolts. There should be no gap at the front and an even gap at the rear between the handlebar upper and lower holders (**Figure 36**). Be sure that the punch mark on the handlebar assembly aligns with the gap between the upper and lower holders.
 c. On 1995 and 1996 VN800 models, be sure the punch mark on the handlebar assembly aligns with the gap in the handlebar holder.
 d. When installing the master cylinder, be sure the line formed by the mating surfaces of the two halves of the master cylinder aligns with the punch mark on the handlebar.
 e. Apply a light coat of multipurpose grease to the throttle grip area on the handlebar prior to installing the throttle grip assembly.
 f. When installing the handlebar weight, apply Loctite 242 to the threads of the throttle grip screw.
 g. Tighten the upper clamp bolt on the front brake master cylinder first, then the lower clamp bolt. Tighten the clamp bolts securely.
 h. Check the throttle operation. If necessary, adjust the throttle operation as described in Chapter Three.

WARNING

After installation is complete, make sure the brake lever does not contact the throttle grip assembly when it is pulled on fully. If it does, the brake fluid may be low in the reservoir. Refill if necessary. Refer to ***Front Disc Brakes*** *in Chapter Thirteen.*

Left-hand side of handlebar

1. Remove the fuel tank as described in Chapter Eight.
2. Disconnect the starter lockout switch electrical connector (**Figure 33**) from the clutch lever.

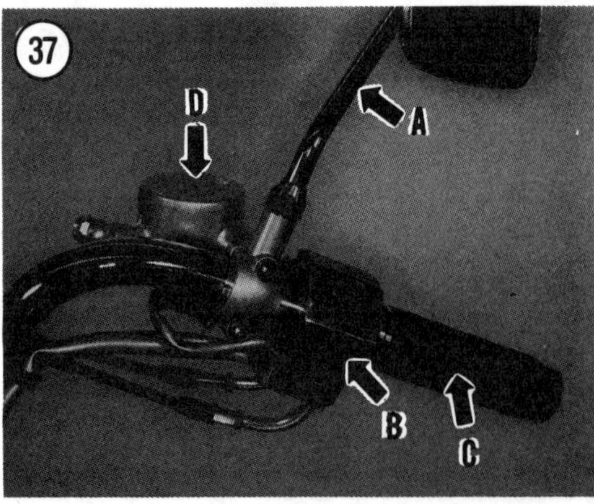

races) as a set if either bearing is faulty. Refer to the procedure in this chapter.

4. Check the roller bearing outer races for pitting, galling and corrosion. If any of these conditions exist, replace both races (including bearings) as a set. Follow the procedure described in this chapter.

5. Check the steering stem for cracks, damage or wear. If damaged in any way, replace the steering stem.

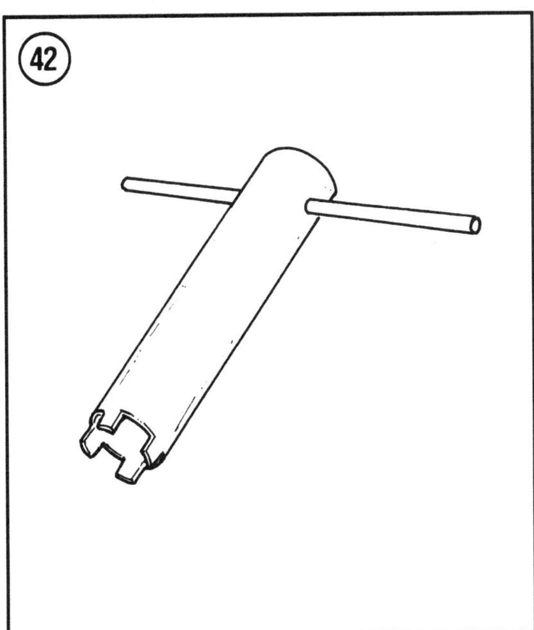

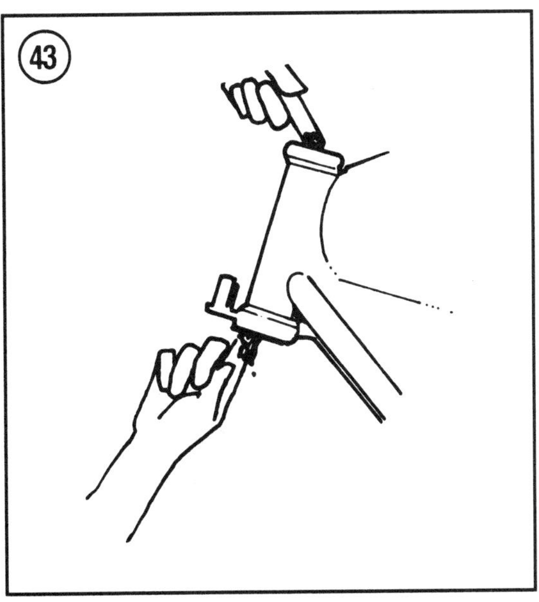

Steering Stem Assembly

Refer to **Figure 31** for this procedure.

1. Make sure the roller bearing outer races are properly seated in the steering head.
2. Apply an even, complete coat of wheel bearing grease to the steering head outer races (**Figure 43**) and to both bearings.
3. Install the upper roller bearing into the steering head.
4. Install the steering stem into the head tube and hold it firmly in place.
5. Install the steering stem cap.
6. Install the steering stem adjusting nut so the stepped side faces down into the steering head. Finger tighten the adjust nut.

NOTE
The following step is best performed using the Kawasaki stem nut wrench, part No. 57001-1100.

7. Seat the steering stem bearings as follows:
   a. Tighten the bearing adjusting nut to 39 N•m (29 ft.-lb.) using a stem nut wrench (**Figure 44**) or equivalent. If using a stem nut wrench with the dimensions shown in **Figure 44**, apply a 22.2 kg (49 lb.) force to the end of the stem nut wrench to obtain the specified torque.

   NOTE
   If the special tool (stem nut wrench) is not used, it will be necessary to tighten the steering stem adjust nut by feel.

   b. When the steering stem adjust nut is tightened properly, the steering stem should turn smoothly with no play.
   c. Loosen the steering stem adjust nut a fraction of a turn until it turns lightly.
   d. Turn the adjust nut lightly *clockwise*, as viewed from the top, until it just becomes hard to turn. Do not overtighten or the steering will be too tight.
   e. Turn the steering stem by hand to make sure it turns freely and does not bind. Repeat if necessary.
8. Install the steering stem locknut. Lock the steering stem adjust nut in its present location by tightening the locknut securely.
9. Fit the front fork into place in the lower fork bridge.

10. On VN800 Classic models, secure the lower fork covers to the lower fork bridge.

11. Install the stem base cover onto the lower fork bridge. Be sure the damper and collar are in place and tighten the cap nut securely.

12. Fit the turn signals onto each fork leg, however; do not tighten the clamp bolts at this time.

13. On VN800 Classic models, install the upper fork cover onto each fork leg.

14. Install the handlebar/upper fork bridge assembly. Be sure the top of the forks are flush with the top surface of the upper fork bridge (**Figure 45**).

15. Torque the upper fork bridge clamp bolts and lower fork bridge clamp bolts to the specification listed in **Table 1**.

16. Install the steering stem head bolt and washer, then tighten to the torque specification listed in **Table 1**.

17. Tighten the turn signal clamp bolts securely.

18. Install the brake caliper as described in Chapter Thirteen.

19. Install the front wheel as described in this chapter.

20. Install the headlight housing as described in Chapter Nine.

21. Reconnect the starter lockout switch connector to the clutch lever and reconnect the brake light switch connector to the brake lever.

22. Reinstall the fuel tank as described in Chapter Eight.

STEERING HEAD BEARING RACES

The headset and steering stem bearing races are pressed into the headset portion of the frame. The races are easily bent so they should not be removed unless they require replacement.

Headset Bearing Race Removal/Installation

1. Remove the steering stem as described in this chapter.

2A. A special Kawasaki tool (stem bearing remover part No. 57001-1107) can be used to remove the headset bearing race as follows:

a. Install the outer race remover (A, **Figure 46**) into one of the outer races.
b. Insert an aluminum rod or a drift (B, **Figure 46**) against the top of the outer race remover.
c. Tap on the end of the rod or drift with a hammer and drive the outer race from the

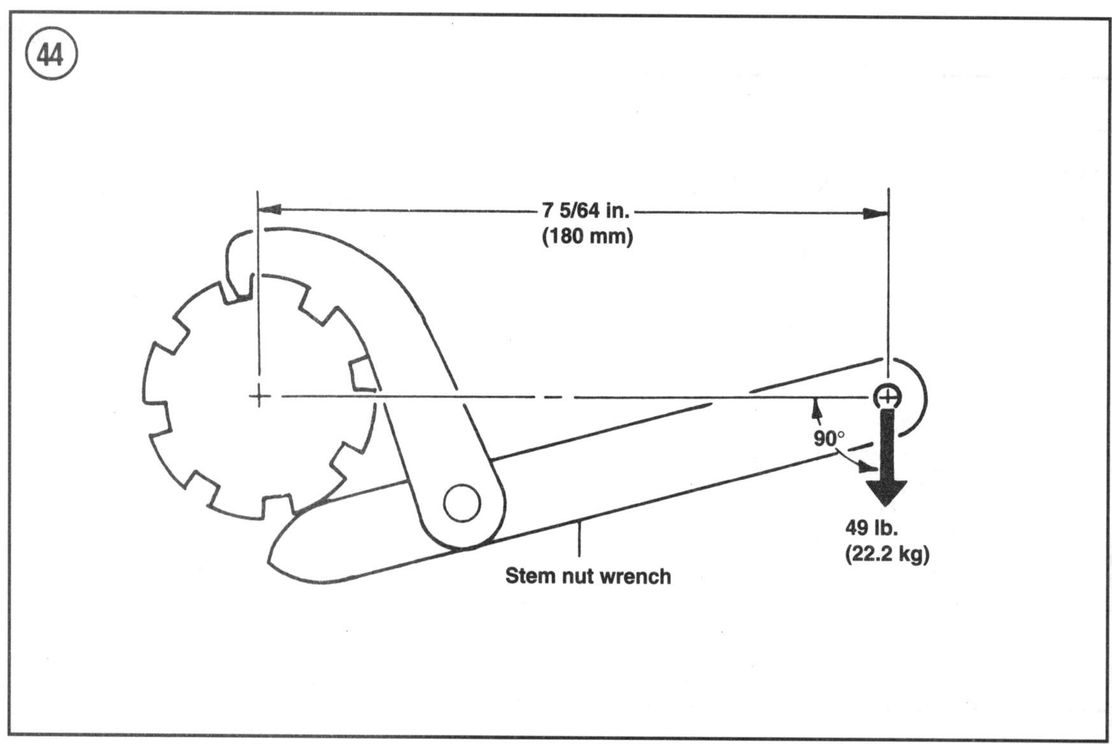

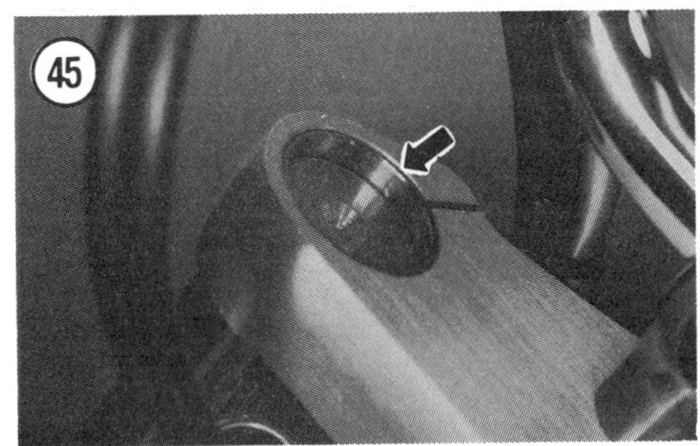

45

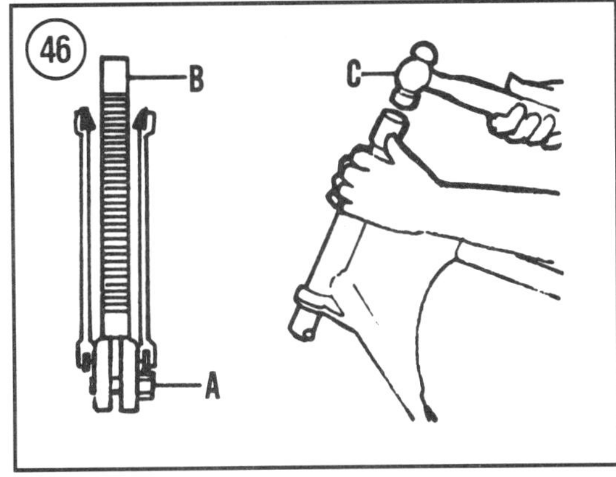

46

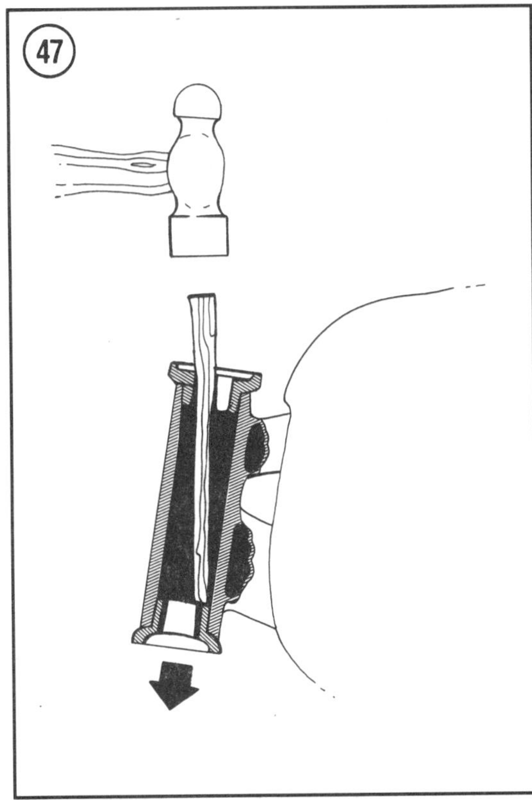

47

steering head. Remove the special tool from the outer race.

d. Repeat for the bearing outer race at the other end of the headset.

2B. If the special tools are not used, perform the following:

a. Insert a hardwood stick or soft punch into the head tube and carefully tap the outer race out (**Figure 47**).
b. Work around the outer race so that neither the race nor the head tube is damaged.
c. Repeat for the bearing outer race on the other end of the steering head.

3. Thoroughly clean the bearing receptacles in the steering head with solvent and thoroughly dry with compressed air.

4. Inspect the bearing bore for damage or burrs. Carefully remove any burrs prior to installing new bearing races.

5. Apply a light coat of multi-purpose grease to the steering head bearing bores and to the outer surface of the new bearing races.

6A. A special Kawasaki tool setup (driver press shaft part No. 57001-1075, driver 57001-1106 and driver 57001-1076) can be used to install the bearing outer race as follows:

a. Position both outer races into the steering head and start them into position lightly with a soft-faced mallet. Just tap them in enough to hold them in place until the special tools can be installed.
b. Install the bearing drivers into both of the outer races.
c. Tighten the nut (**Figure 48**) on the bearing driver press shaft and pull the outer races into place in the headset. Tighten the nut until both bearing outer races are completely seated in the headset and are flush with the steering head surface.
d. Remove the special tool.

6B. If the special tools are not used, perform the following:

a. Position one of the outer races into the steering head and lightly start it into position using a soft-faced mallet. Just tap it in enough to hold it in place.
b. Tap the outer race in slowly with a block of wood, a suitable size socket or piece of pipe (**Figure 49**). Make sure that the race is squarely seated in the headset race bore before

tapping it into place. Tap the race in until it is flush with the steering head surface.

c. Repeat for the other outer race.

Steering Stem Lower Bearing Removal/Installation

1. Install the steering stem adjust nut and locknut onto the steering stem to protect the threads during this procedure.
2. Clamp the steering stem shaft in a vise with soft jaws.
3. Carefully drive the bearing and seal up from the base of the steering stem with a chisel and hammer (**Figure 50**) working around in a circle so that the bearing will not bind on the stem.
4. Remove the steering stem from the vise.
5. Remove the steering stem locknut and adjust nut.
6. Remove the bearing and seal from the steering stem shaft and discard both parts.
7. Clean all old grease from the steering stem bearing area.
8. Inspect the bearing location of the steering stem for damage or burrs. Carefully remove any burrs before installing new bearing races.
9. Apply a light coat of multipurpose grease to the steering stem and to the inner surface of the new bearing.
10. Install the seal and the lower bearing on the steering stem. Slide the bearing down onto the top of the shoulder at the base of the steering stem.
11. Align the bearing with the machined surface of the steering stem and slide an appropriate size pipe or driver down against the *inner* bearing race (**Figure 51**).

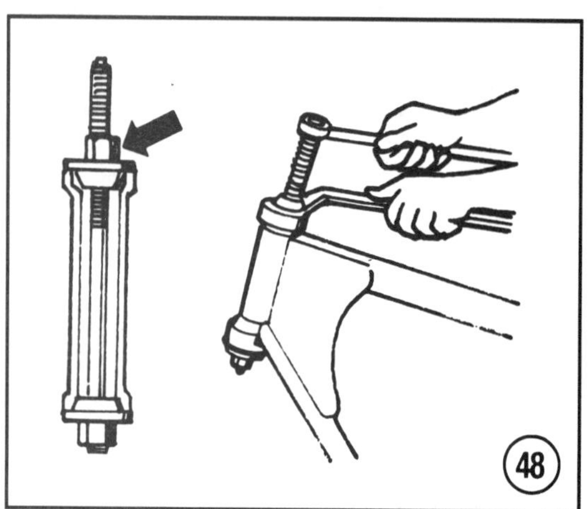

48

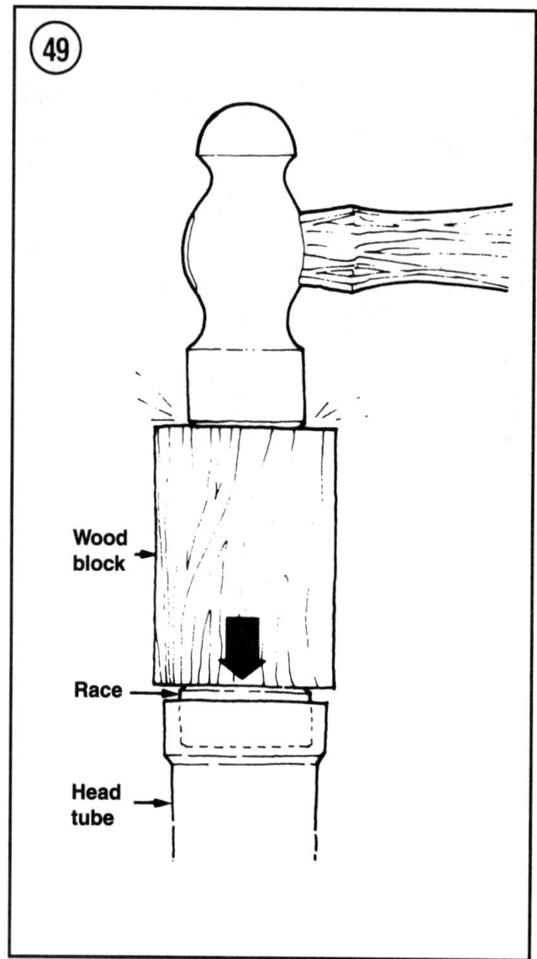

49

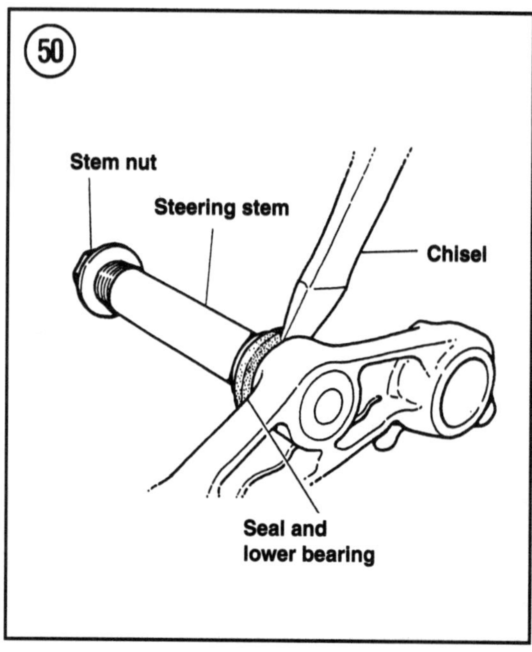

50

(51)

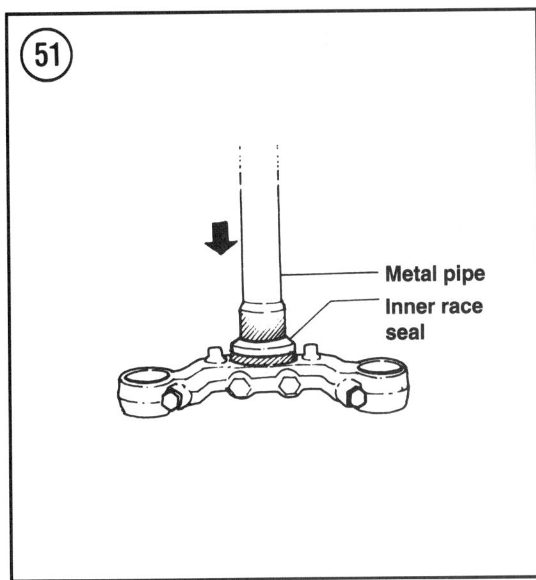

12. Use a hammer and carefully tap the lower bearing into place. Tap it into place until it bottoms.
13. Remove the pipe.
14. Make sure it is seated squarely and is all the way down.

FRONT FORK

Front Fork Service

To simplify fork service and to prevent mixing parts, service the legs individually.

Changing Fork Oil

Refer to **Figure 52** during the disassembly and assembly procedure.

(52)

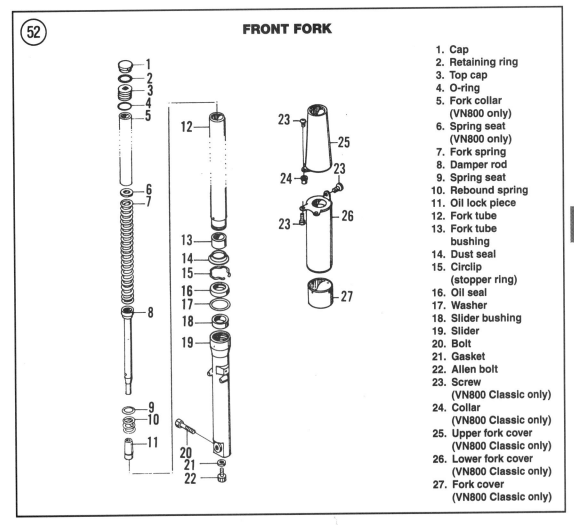

FRONT FORK

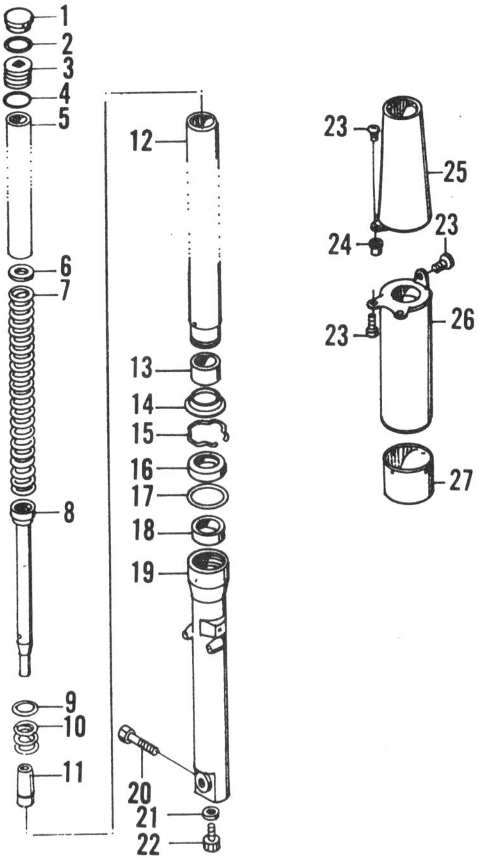

1. Cap
2. Retaining ring
3. Top cap
4. O-ring
5. Fork collar (VN800 only)
6. Spring seat (VN800 only)
7. Fork spring
8. Damper rod
9. Spring seat
10. Rebound spring
11. Oil lock piece
12. Fork tube
13. Fork tube bushing
14. Dust seal
15. Circlip (stopper ring)
16. Oil seal
17. Washer
18. Slider bushing
19. Slider
20. Bolt
21. Gasket
22. Allen bolt
23. Screw (VN800 Classic only)
24. Collar (VN800 Classic only)
25. Upper fork cover (VN800 Classic only)
26. Lower fork cover (VN800 Classic only)
27. Fork cover (VN800 Classic only)

1. Remove the front fork leg as described in Removal/Installation in this chapter.
2. Secure the fork leg in a vise with soft jaws.
3. Use a Phillips screwdriver to depress the top cap while removing the retaining ring (**Figure 53**). Discard the old retaining ring. A new one must be installed every time the ring is removed.
4. Remove the top cap and O-ring.

5A. On VN800 models, remove the collar, spring seat, and fork spring.

5B. On VN800 Classic models, remove the fork spring.

6. Turn the fork assembly upside down and pour the fork oil into a suitable container. Pump the fork several times by hand to expel most of the remaining oil. Dispose of the fork oil properly.
7. Hold the fork in an upright position, and secure it in a vise.

NOTE
Kawasaki recommends accurately measuring the fork oil level to ensure a more accurate filling.

NOTE
To measure the correct amount of fluid, use a plastic baby bottle or a mixing container. These containers have measurements in milliliters (ml) on the side.

8. Add the recommended amount of fork oil to the fork assembly. Refer to **Table 3** for the recommended viscosity and quantity.
9. Compress the fork assembly completely, hold it in this position and measure the fork oil level.
10. Use an accurate ruler or oil level gauge (**Figure 54**) to attain the correct oil level listed in **Table 3**.

NOTE
*An oil level measuring device can be made as shown in **Figure 55**. Secure the hose clamp on the tool so that the distance between the clamp's lower edge and the small diameter hole equals the specified oil level listed in **Table 3**. Position the tool so the hose clamp rests on the top edge of the fork tube and draw out the excess oil. Draw oil out until the level reaches the small diameter hole. A precise oil level can be achieved with this simple device.*

11. Allow the oil to settle completely and recheck the oil level measurement. Adjust the oil level if necessary.
12. Extend the fork slider.

13A. On VN800 models, install the fork spring, spring seat and collar. Install the spring so the end with the smaller diameter coils faces down.

13B. On VN800 Classic models, install the fork spring. Install the spring so the end with the smaller diameter coils faces down.

14. Install the O-ring and the top cap.

WARNING
Be sure the retaining ring is properly seated in the fork tube groove. If the ring works loose while riding, the fork as-

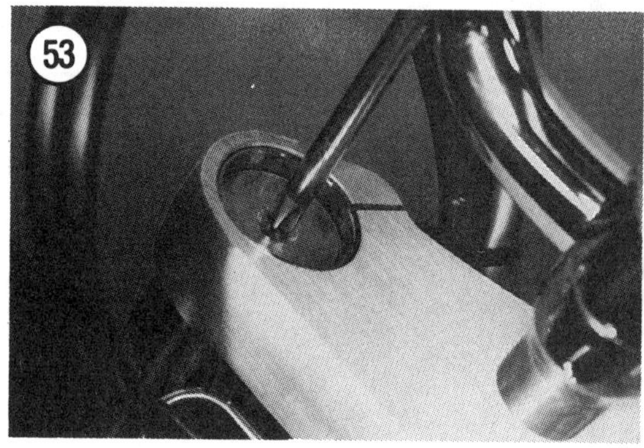

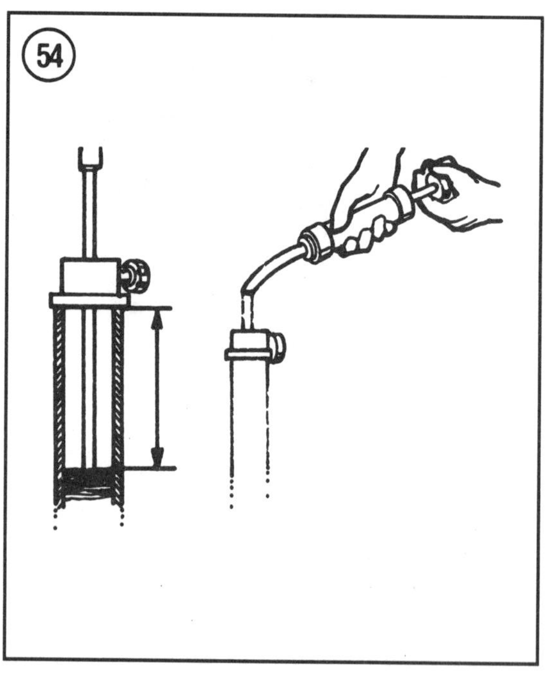

sembly will compress and could result in an accident.

15. Use a Philips screwdriver to depress the top cap and spring. Install a *new* retaining ring (**Figure 53**) and make sure the retaining ring is seated correctly in the fork tube groove.
16. Reinstall the fork tube as described in this chapter.
17. Repeat the procedure for the other fork leg.

Removal/Installation

1. Use a scissors jack or jack stand to support the bike on a level surface.

NOTE
Insert a piece of vinyl tubing or wood into the caliper in place of the brake disc. Then, the piston (pistons on VN800 Classic models) will not be forced out of the cylinder(s) if the brake lever is inadvertently squeezed. If this does happen, the caliper must be disassembled to reseat the piston(s) and the system will have to be bled.

2. Remove the brake caliper as follows:
   a. Loosen, then remove the bolts (A, **Figure 56**) securing the brake caliper assembly to the front fork.
   b. Remove the caliper assembly (B, **Figure 56**) from the brake disc.
3. Remove the brake hose clamp (C, **Figure 56**) from the left fork slider.
4. Remove the front wheel as described in this chapter.
5. Remove the bolts (**Figure 57**) securing the front fender brace to the fork slider and remove the fender.
6. Remove the cap (**Figure 58**) from the top of the fork tube.

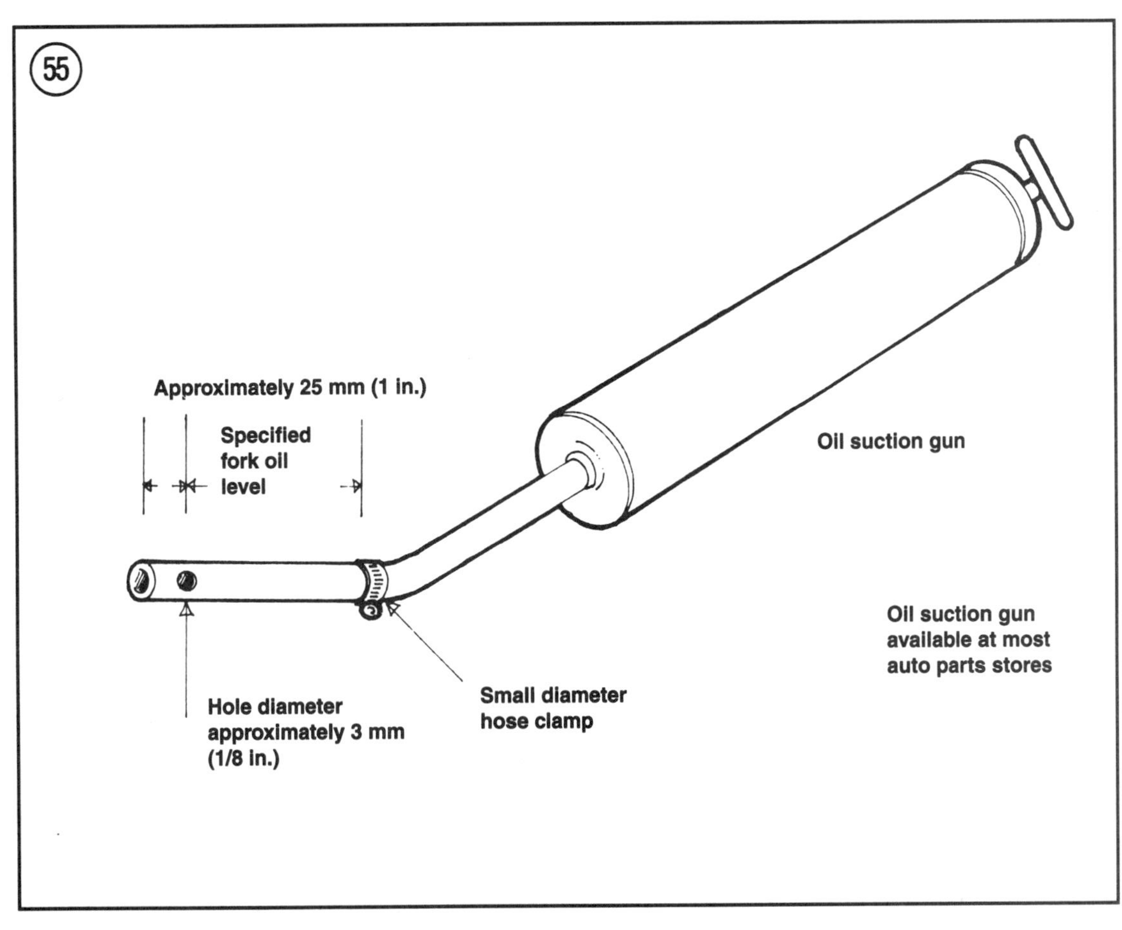

11

NOTE
The Allen bolt at the base of the slider is secured with threadlocking compound. It is often very difficult to remove because the damper rod will turn inside the slider. It sometimes can be removed with an air impact driver. If you are unable to remove it, take the fork tubes to a dealership and have the bolts removed.

7. If the fork assembly must be disassembled, use an Allen wrench to loosen the Allen bolt at the base of the slider. If the bolt is loosened too much, fork oil may start to drain from the slider.

NOTE
The fuel tank is removed in the following steps for clarity. You do not need to remove the tank in order to remove the front forks.

8. Loosen the clamp bolt on the turn signal assembly (A, **Figure 59**).
9. Loosen the upper fork bridge clamp bolt (B, **Figure 59**) and lower fork bridge clamp bolt (C, **Figure 59**).

NOTE
On VN800 Classic models, the fork tube can be removed with the fork covers installed on the upper and lower fork bridges.

10. Twist the fork assembly slightly and withdraw it from the upper and lower fork bridges.
11. Install by reversing these removal steps while noting the following:
    a. Install the fork assembly through the lower fork bridge, through the turn signal clamp and into the upper fork bridge. Be sure the top of the fork assembly is flush with the top surface of the upper fork bridge (**Figure 45**).
    b. Install the front axle into both fork sliders to ensure correct alignment between both fork legs.
    c. Tighten the upper and lower fork bridge bolts to the torque specifications listed in **Table 1**.
    d. Remove the front axle from both fork sliders.

Disassembly

Refer to **Figure 52** during the disassembly and assembly procedures.

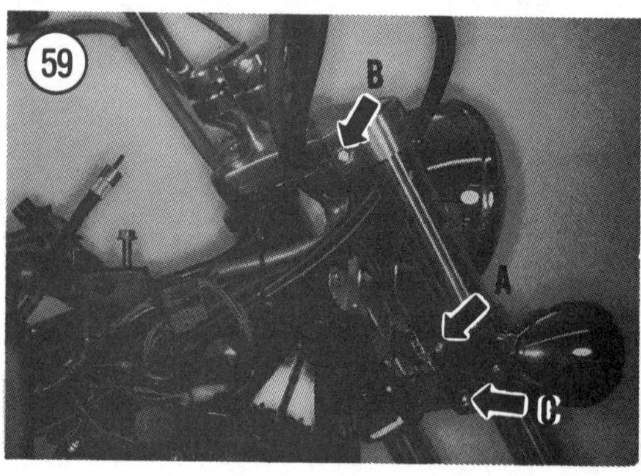

1. Secure the fork assembly in a vise with soft jaws.
2. Use a Phillips screwdriver to depress the top cap in the fork (**Figure 53**) while removing the retaining ring. Discard the old retaining ring as a new one must be installed every time the ring is removed.
3. Remove the top cap and O-ring.
4. On VN800 models, remove the collar and spring seat.
5. Carefully withdraw the fork spring from the fork tube.
6. Turn the fork assembly upside down and drain the fork oil into a suitable container. Pump the fork several times by hand to expel most of the remaining oil. Dispose of the fork oil properly.
7. Remove the Allen bolt and gasket from the bottom of the slider. If the Allen bolt was not loosened during the removal procedure, use the Kawasaki special tools and perform the following:
   a. Install the adapter (part No. 57001-1057) onto the extension bar and handle (part No. 57001-183).
   b. Insert this tool into the fork tube and index it into the hex receptacle in the top of the damper rod to hold the damper rod in place.
   c. Using an Allen wrench, loosen then remove the Allen bolt and washer from the base of the slider.
8. Remove the dust seal from the slider.
9. Remove the stopper ring from the top of the slider.

NOTE
On this type of fork, force is needed to remove the fork tube from the slider.

10. Secure the fork assembly in a vise with soft jaws.
11. There is an interference fit between the bushing in the fork slider and the bushing on the fork tube. To remove the fork tube from the slider, pull hard on the fork tube using quick in-and-out strokes (**Figure 60**). Doing so will withdraw the bushing, washer and seal from the slider. Discard the seal and slider bushing.

NOTE
It may be necessary to slightly heat the area on the slider around the seal prior to removal. Use a rag soaked in hot

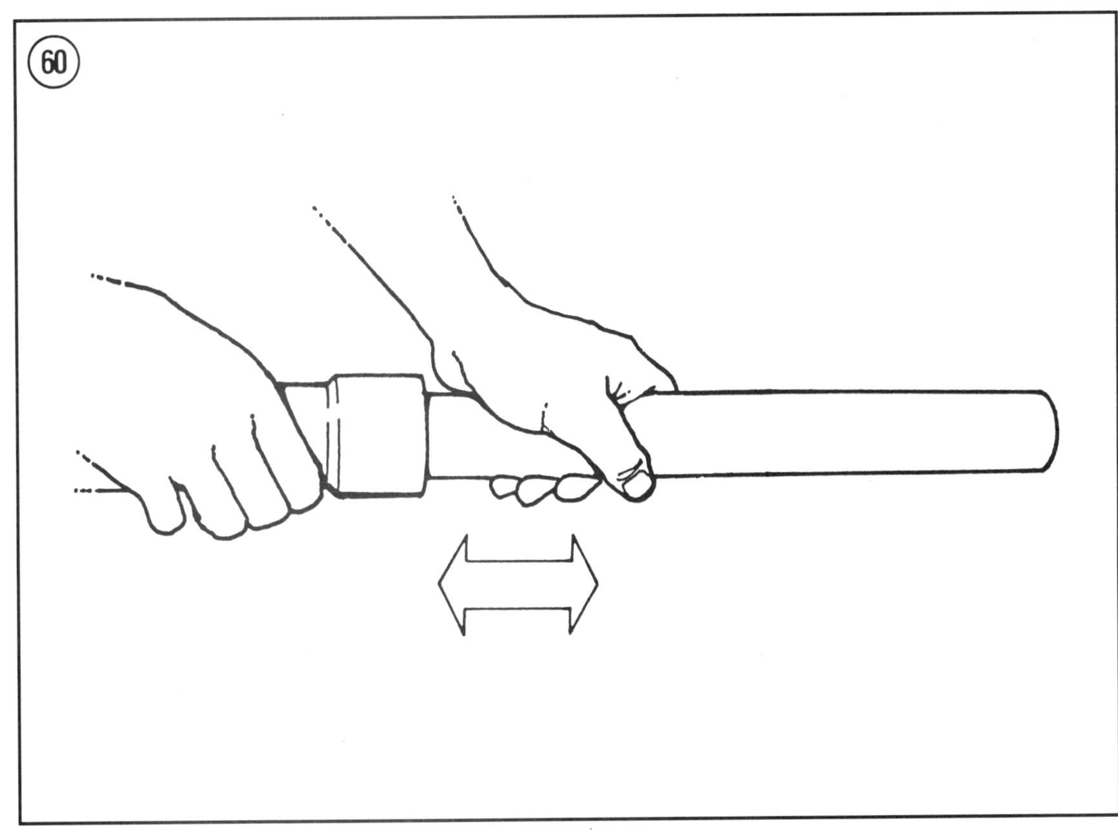

11

water; do not apply flame directly to the fork slider.

12. Withdraw the fork tube from the slider. Remove and discard the fork tube bushing. It must be replaced.
13. Remove the oil lock piece (**Figure 61**) from the damper rod.
14. Remove the damper rod and rebound spring (**Figure 62**) from the slider.
15. Inspect the components as described in this chapter.

Inspection

1. Thoroughly clean all parts in solvent and dry them with compressed air. Check the fork tube for wear or scratches.
2. Check the damper rod for straightness. **Figure 63** shows one method. Replace the damper rod if the runout exceeds the specification in **Table 3**.
3. Make sure the oil holes (**Figure 64**) in the damper rod are clear.
4. Inspect the damper rod (**Figure 65**) and its piston ring (**Figure 66**) for wear or damage. Replace as necessary.
5. Check the fork tube for straightness. If bent or scratched, it must be replaced.
6. Check the slider for dents or exterior damage that may cause the upper fork tube to bind during riding. Replace if necessary.
7. On the left-hand slider, inspect the brake caliper mounting bosses and the front axle boss for cracks or damage. On the right-hand slider, inspect the axle boss (A, **Figure 67**) and pinch bolt area (B, **Figure 67**). If damage is found, replace the slider.

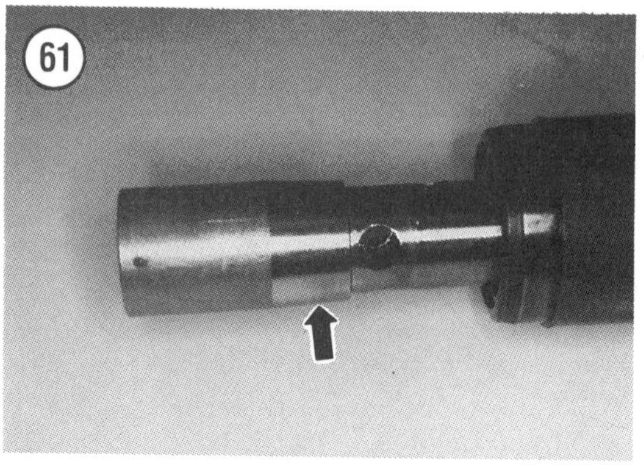
61

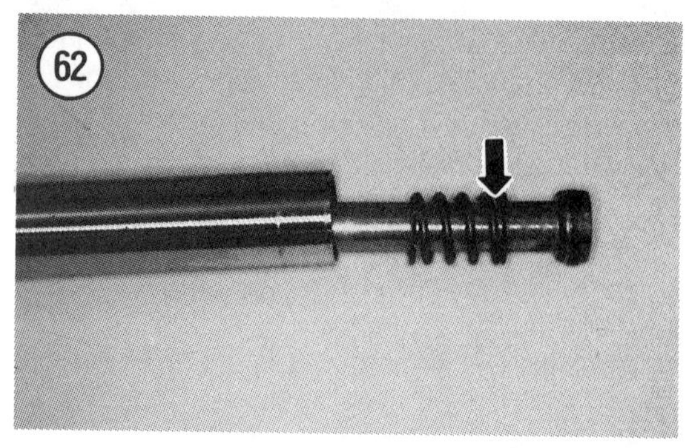
62

63

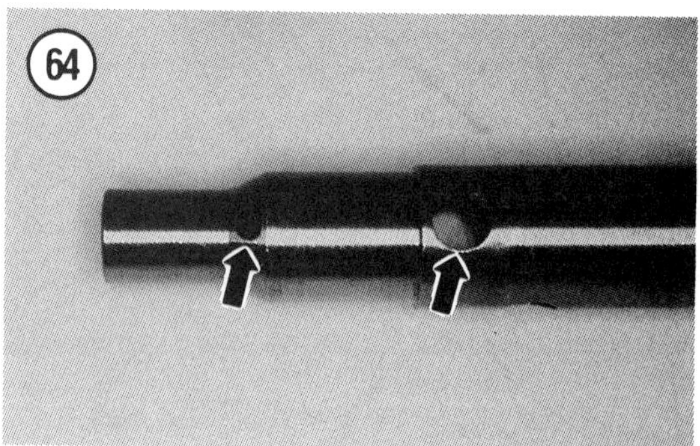
64

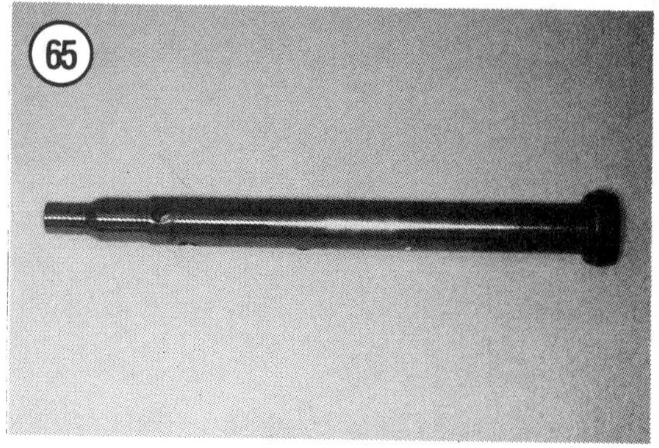
65

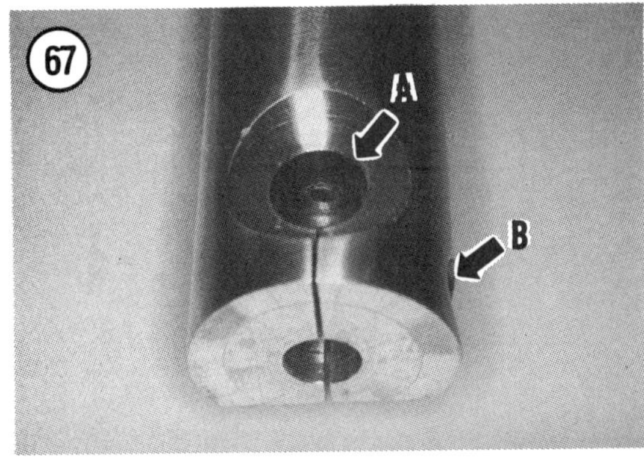

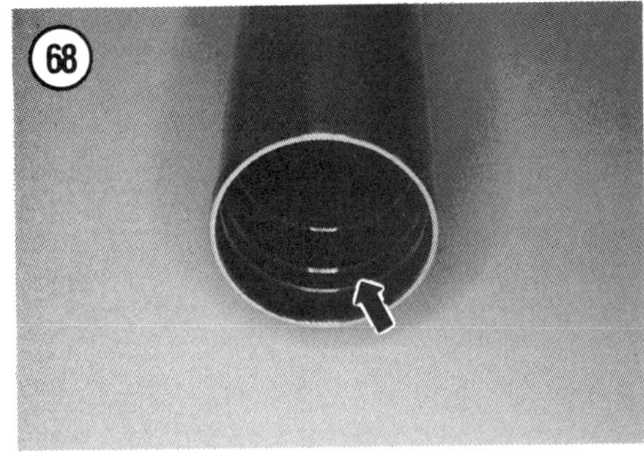

8. Inspect the fork cap retaining ring groove (**Figure 68**) in the fork tube for wear or damage. The groove should not be rounded off at the upper portion since that would allow the retaining ring to slip out when riding. If necessary, replace the fork tube.

9. Inspect the fork top cap for wear or damage. Check the O-ring seal for hardness or deterioration.

10. Inspect the seal seating area (**Figure 69**) in the slider for damage or burrs. Clean up if necessary.

11. Inspect the gasket on the Allen bolt (**Figure 70**) and replace if damaged.

12. Inspect the fork spring for wear or damage and replace if necessary. Measure the spring free length (**Figure 71**). Replace the spring if it is outside the specification in **Table 3**.

Assembly

Refer to **Figure 52** when performing this procedure.

1. Coat the sliding portions of all parts with fresh SAE 10W fork oil prior to installation.

2. Install the new bushing (**Figure 72**) onto the fork tube.

3. Install the spring seat and rebound spring onto the damper rod (**Figure 73**) and insert this assembly into the fork tube (**Figure 62**). Push the damper rod in until it exits the bottom of the fork tube (**Figure 74**).

4A. On VN800 models temporarily install the fork spring (A, **Figure 75**), the spring seat (B, **Figure 75**) and collar (C, **Figure 75**) to hold the damper rod in place. Push the collar in until it bottoms (**Figure 76**).

4B. On VN800 Classic models, temporarily install the fork spring (**Figure 77**) to hold the damper rod in place. Push the spring in until it bottoms.

5. Apply a strip of duct tape (**Figure 78**) over the end of the fork tube to temporarily hold the fork spring in place.

6. Position the oil lock piece with its tapered end (A, **Figure 61**) going on first, and install it onto the damper rod. Push it on until it stops.

7. Install the damper rod/fork tube assembly into the slider (**Figure 79**).

8. Make sure the gasket (**Figure 70**) is on the Allen bolt.

9. Apply Loctite 242 to the threads of the Allen bolt prior to installation. Install it into the bottom of the fork slider and screw it into the base of the damper rod. Tighten to the torque specification listed in **Table 1**.

10. Remove the strip of duct tape from the top of the fork tube.

11A. On VN800 models, remove the collar, spring seat, and fork spring. They will be installed after fork oil is added.

11B. On VN800 Classic models, remove the fork spring. It will be installed after fork oil is added.

12. Slide a new fork slider bushing (A, **Figure 80**) and washer (B, **Figure 80**) down the fork tube until they rest on top of the fork slider.

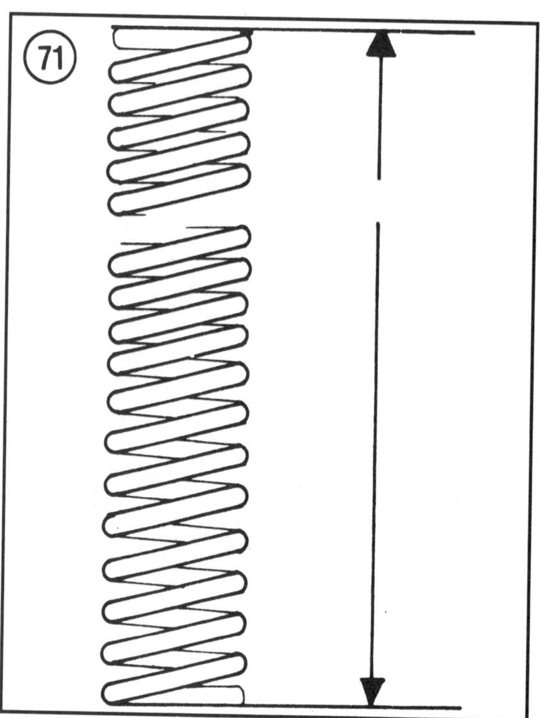

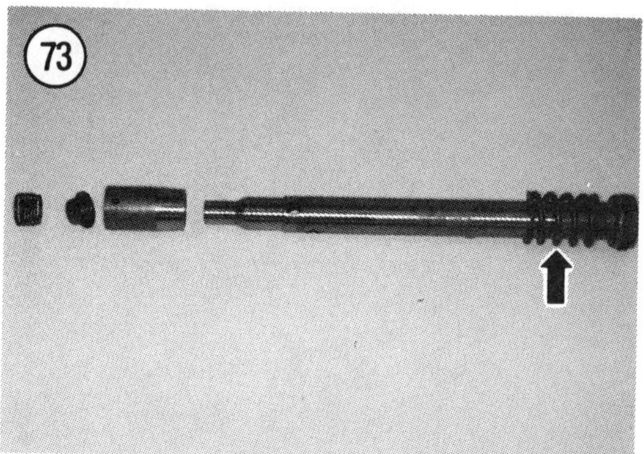

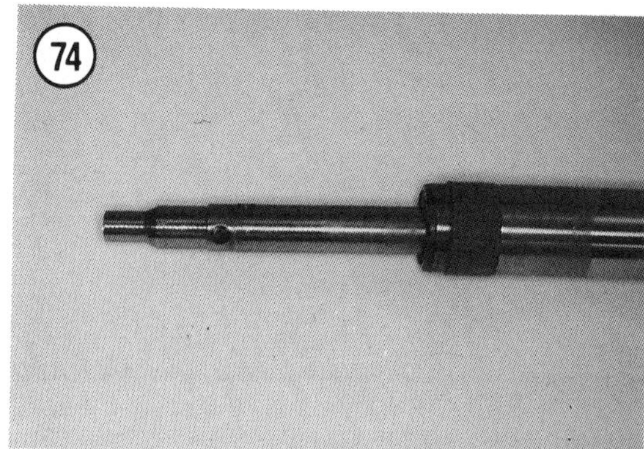

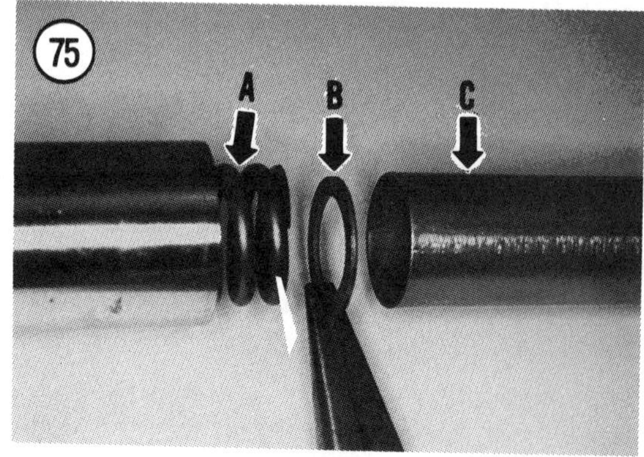

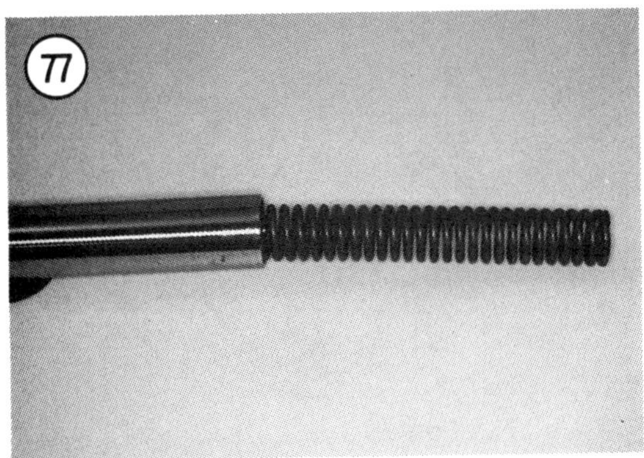

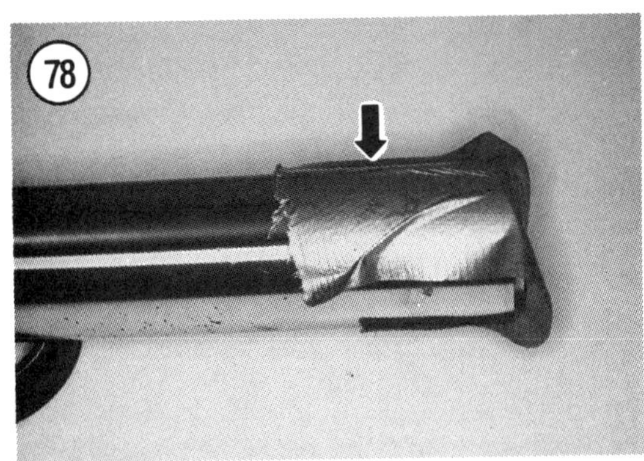

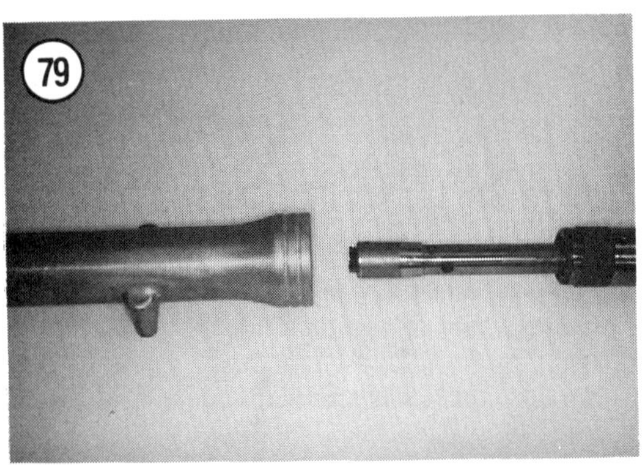

NOTE
The following special tool is very expensive. If you work on a lot of different bikes, this special tool is a must for your tool box. It is adjustable and will work on almost all Japanese fork assemblies (including Japanese Showa forks installed on some late model Harley-Davidson motorcycles).

13. Install the special tool (A, **Figure 81**) down onto the washer (B, **Figure 81**) and slider bushing (C, **Figure 81**).
14. Drive the slider bushing into the slider with the special tool. Drive the bushing in until it bottoms in the slider.
15. Remove the special tool.

CAUTION
Do not use a reclosable type of plastic bag as the closure portion of the bag is thick and can damage the seal when it passes over it. If using this type of bag, cut off the closure portion, then use the modified bag.

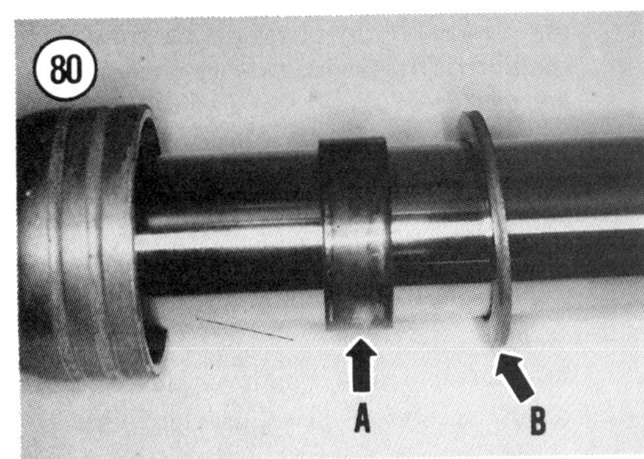

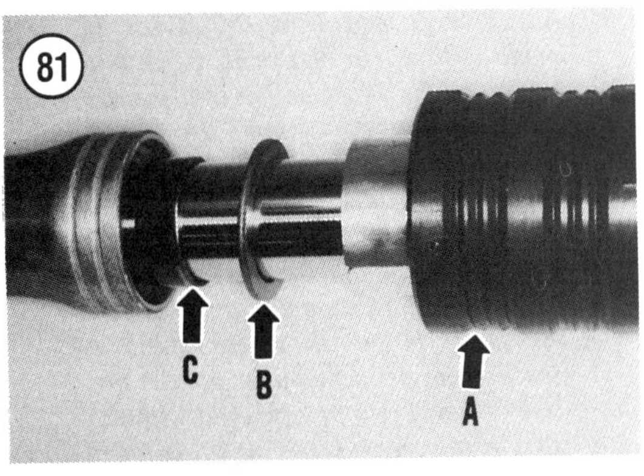

16. Place a small plastic bag (**Figure 82**) over the top of the fork tube to protect the seal during installation over the sharp top surface opening of the fork tube.

17. Coat a new seal with fresh SAE 10W fork oil.

18. Position the seal with its open groove facing upward (**Figure 83**). Slide the seal (**Figure 84**) over the plastic bag and down the fork tube.

19. Remove the plastic bag.

20. Use the same special tool setup used in Step 14 to drive in the seal (A, **Figure 85**).

21. Drive the seal into the slider with the special tool (B, **Figure 85**) until the groove in the slider can be seen above the top surface of the seal.

22. Remove the special tool.

23. Slide the stopper ring down the fork tube until it is at the fork slider.

24. Install the stopper ring into the fork slider. Make sure it is completely seated in the groove in the slider (**Figure 86**).

25. Install the dust seal (**Figure 87**) into the slider. Press it in until it is completely seated.

NOTE
To measure the correct amount of fluid, use a plastic baby bottle or a mixing container. These containers have measurements in milliliters (ml) on the side.

26. Add the recommended amount of fork oil to the fork assembly. Refer to **Table 3** for the recommended viscosity and quantity.

27. Compress the fork assembly completely, hold it in this position, and measure the fork oil level.

28. Use an accurate ruler or oil level gauge (**Figure 54**) to attain the correct oil level listed in **Table 3**.

NOTE
*An oil level measuring device can be made as shown in **Figure 55**. Secure the hose clamp on the tool so that the distance between the clamp's lower edge and the small diameter hole equals the specified oil level listed in **Table 3**. Slightly overfill the fork leg. Position the tool so the hose clamp rests on the top edge of the fork tube and draw out the excess oil. Draw oil out until the level reaches the small diameter hole. A precise oil level can be achieved with this simple device.*

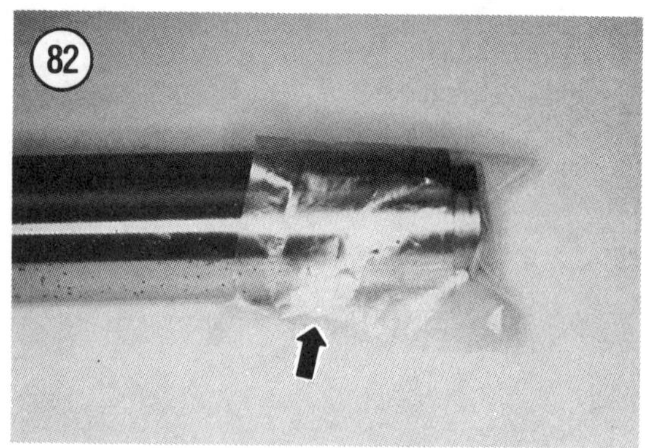

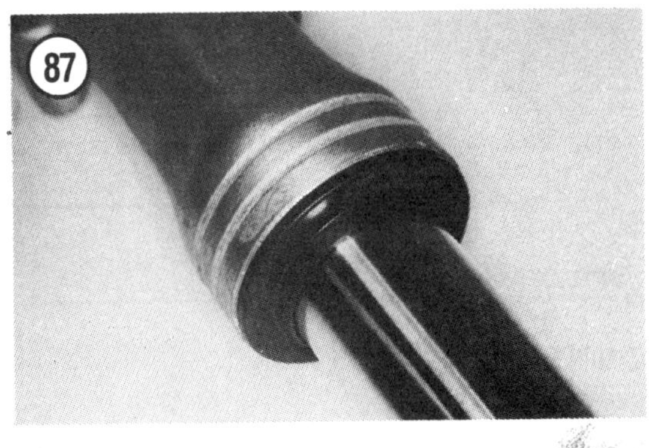

29. Allow the oil to settle completely and recheck the oil level measurement. Adjust the oil level if necessary.
30. Extend the fork slider.
31A. On VN800 models, install the fork spring, spring seat, and collar. Install the spring so the end with the smaller diameter coils faces down.
31B. On VN800 Classic models, install the fork spring. Install the spring so the end with the smaller diameter coils faces down.
32. Install the O-ring and the top cap.

WARNING
Be sure the retaining ring is properly seated in the fork tube groove. If the ring works loose while riding, the fork assembly will compress and could result in an accident.

33. Use a Philips screwdriver to depress the top cap and spring. Install a *new* retaining ring (**Figure 53**) and make sure the retaining ring is seated correctly in the fork tube groove.
34. Reinstall the fork tube as described in this chapter.

Table 1 FRONT SUSPENSION and STEERING TIGHTENING TORQUES

Item	N•m	in.-lb.	ft.-lb.
Front axle nut			
VN800	110	—	81
VN800 Classic	88	—	65
Front axle clamp bolt	34	—	25
Spoke nipples	3.9	35	—
Upper fork bridge clamp bolts	20	—	15
Lower fork bridge clamp bolts	34	—	25
Fork bottom Allen bolts	20	—	15
Handlebar holder Allen bolts	59	—	44
Handlebar holder mounting nuts	34	—	25
Steering stem head bolt	44	—	32
Steering stem nut	4.9	43	—
Brake disc mounting bolts	23	—	17
Master cylinder clamp bolts	11	97	—

Table 2 TIRE SPECIFICATIONS

Tire Size	Front	Rear
VN800	80/90-21 48H tube	140/90-16 71H tube
VN800 Classic	130/90-16 67H tube	140/90-16 71H tube

(continued)

Table 2 TIRE SPECIFICATIONS (continued)

Tread Depth	Standard	Wear limit
Front	4.3 mm (0.17 in.)	1 mm (0.04 in.)
Rear		
Up to 130 km/h (80 m/h)	7.7 mm (0.30 in.)	2 mm (0.8 in)
Over 130 km/h (80 m/h)	7.7 mm (0.30 in.)	3 mm (0.12 in.)

Tire Inflation Pressure (Cold)	Front		Rear	
Load	psi	kPa	psi	kPa
Up to 215 lbs (97.5 kg)				
VN800	28	200	32	200
VN800 Classic	28	200	28	200
215 to 397 lbs (97 to 180 kg)	28	200	32	225

*Tire inflation pressure for original equipment tires. Aftermarket tires may require different inflation pressure; refer to aftermarket manufacturer's specifications.

Table 3 FRONT FORK SPECIFICATIONS

Fork oil	
Viscosity	SAE 10W fork oil
Capacity per leg	
Oil change only	
VN800	290 ml (9.80 U.S. oz. [10.21 Imp. oz.])
VN800 Classic	265 ml (8.96 oz. [9.33 Imp. oz.])
After disassembly	
VN800	336-344 ml (11.36-11.63 U.S. oz. [11.83-12.11 Imp. oz.])
VN800 Classic	306-314 ml (10.35-10.62 U.S. oz. [10.77-11.05 Imp. oz.])
Oil level each leg (measured from top of fully compressed fork tube, without spring)	
VN800	290-294 mm (11.42-11.65 in.)
VN800 Classic	284-288 mm (11.18-11.34 in.)
Fork spring	
Free length	
VN800	469.6 mm (18.49 in.)
Minimum length	460 mm (18.11 in.)
VN800 Classic	547.2 mm (51.54 in.)
Minimum length	540 mm (21.25 in.)
Maximum damper rod runout	0.2 mm (0.008 in.)

Table 4 FRONT SUSPENSION SPECIFICATIONS

Item	Standard	Wear limit
Front axle runout	Less than 0.05 mm (0.002 in.)	0.2 mm (0.0078 in.)
Front wheel rim runout		
Radial	1.0 mm (0.039 in.)	2.0 mm (0.078 in.)
Axial	0.8 mm (0.031 in.)	2.0 mm (0.078 in.)

CHAPTER TWELVE

REAR SUSPENSION

The Kawasaki Uni-Track link-type suspension consists of a single shock absorber, a shock lever assembly and a swing arm. The pivot joints on all components must be disassembled, inspected and lubricated frequently to provide proper operation of the suspension as well as maximum service life.

The shock absorber, which has pivots at each end, is mounted between the swing arm and the shock lever assembly.

The link-type suspension allows the rear wheel to move easily over small bumps for a comfortable ride, and it provides progressively more compression damping as the rear wheel moves closer to the limit of suspension travel.

This chapter includes repair and replacement procedures for the rear wheel and rear suspension components. Refer to Chapter Eleven tire changing and wheel balancing.

Refer to **Table 1** for rear suspension torque specifications. **Table 1** and **Table 2** are located at the end of this chapter.

REAR WHEEL

Removal

1. Remove the rear exhaust pipe as described in Chapter Eight.
2. Back out the speedometer set screw (A, **Figure 1**) and remove the speedometer cable (B, **Figure 1**) from its housing in the rear hub.
3. Remove and discard the cotter pin from the rear axle nut (C, **Figure 1**). Never reuse a cotter pin. The ends could break off and the cotter pin may fall out.
4. Hold the left-hand end of the axle with a wrench while you loosen the rear axle nut (C, **Figure 1**). Do not remove the nut at this time.
5. Remove the safety clip, then remove the nut (D, **Figure 1**) securing the torque link arm to the rear brake panel. Remove the bolt from the brake panel and swing the torque link arm down and out of the way.
6. Completely unscrew the rear brake adjusting nut (A, **Figure 2**).
7. Depress the brake pedal and remove the brake rod (B, **Figure 2**) from the pivot joint in the brake arm. Remove the pivot joint from the brake lever. Install the pivot joint and adjusting nut onto the brake rod to avoid misplacing them.
8. Remove the two chain guard mounting bolts (A, **Figure 3**), and remove the chain guard (B, **Figure 3**).
8. Securely support the bike on level ground with the rear wheel off the ground. If necessary, place a small jack, with a piece of wood, under the crankcase for protection.

9. Remove the rear axle nut (C, **Figure 1**).
10. Withdraw the axle (C, **Figure 3**) from the motorcycle. Do not lose the collar between the swing arm and the coupler on the left-hand side of the hub.
11. Move the wheel forward, disengage the drive chain from the rear sprocket and remove the wheel.
12. Inspect the wheel as described in this chapter.

Installation

1. Apply a light coat of grease to the axle, bearings and collar.
2. If removed, install the collar into the coupling on the left-hand side of the hub.
3. Position the rear wheel in the frame and install the drive chain onto the sprocket.
4. Install the rear axle (C, **Figure 3**) from the left-hand side. Be sure the axle passes through the collar (**Figure 4**) between the swing arm and coupling.
5. Install the axle nut (C, **Figure 1**). Fingertighten the nut at this time.
6. Rotate the rear wheel and apply the rear brake several times. This will center the brake panel within the brake drum, resulting in a solid feel to the rear brake.
7. To install the brake torque link, perform the following:
   a. Swing the torque link up and into position on the brake panel.
   b. Install the torque link bolt and nut. Torque the nut to the specification listed in **Table 1**.
   c. Install the safety clip into the hole in the bolt (D, **Figure 1**).
8. Place a wrench on the axle (C, **Figure 3**) to keep it from turning.
9. Tighten the rear axle nut to the torque specification listed in **Table 1**.

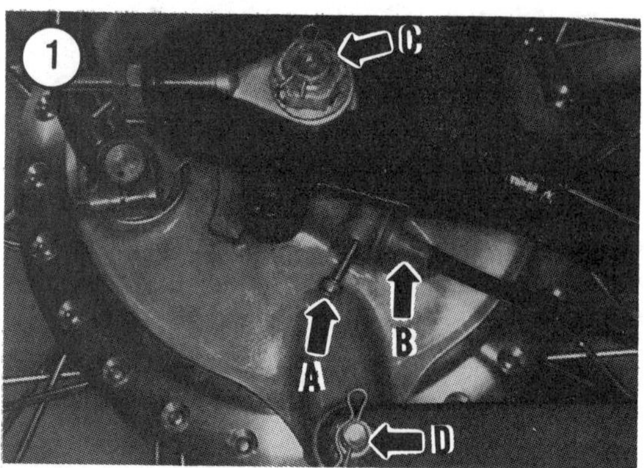

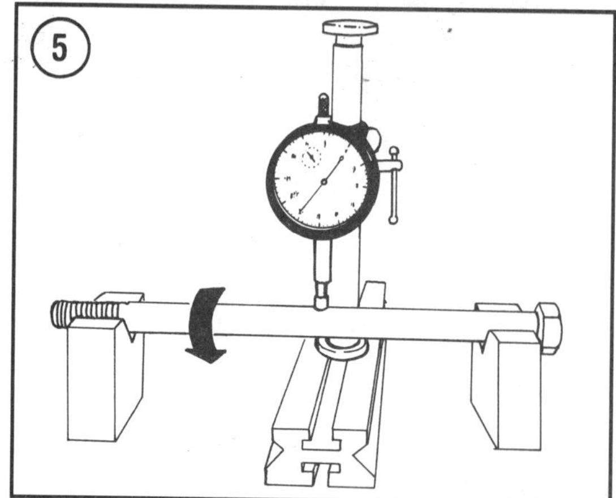

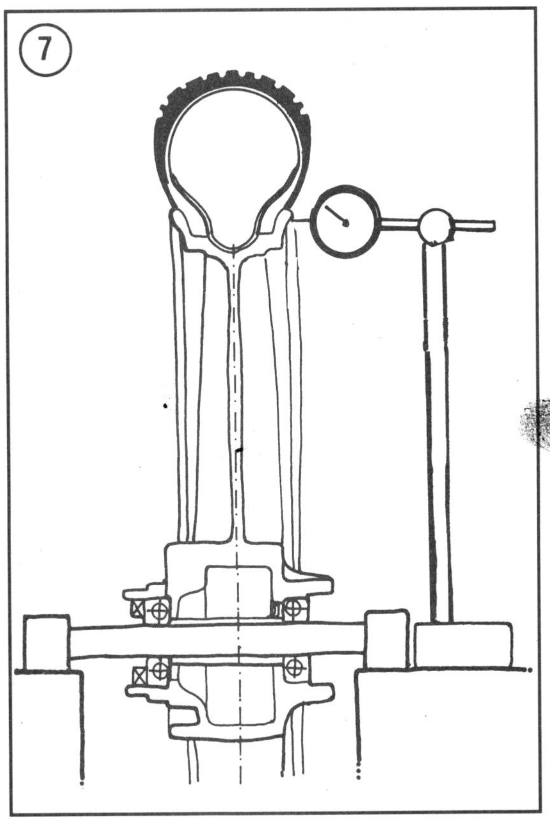

10. Install a new cotter pin and bend the ends over completely.
11. Remove the rear brake adjusting nut and pivot joint from the brake rod.
12. Install the pivot joint into the brake lever.
13. Depress the brake pedal and insert the brake rod through the pivot joint in the brake arm. Install the adjust nut onto the brake rod and turn the nut in until the brake can be operated by depressing the brake pedal.
14. Install the speedometer cable (B, **Figure 1**) into the housing on the brake panel and tighten the set screw (A, **Figure 1**).
15. Reinstall the chain guard (B, **Figure 3**) and adjust the chain tension as described in Chapter Three.
16. After the wheel is installed, rotate it and apply the brake several times. Be sure the wheel rotates freely and that the brake works properly.
17. Adjust the rear brake free play as described in Chapter Three.

Inspection

1. Remove any corrosion on the rear axle using a piece of fine emery cloth. Clean the axle with solvent, then wipe it clean with a lint-free cloth.
2. Check axle runout. Place the axle on V-blocks and place the tip of a dial indicator in the middle of the axle (**Figure 5**). Rotate the axle and check runout. If the runout exceeds the specification listed in **Table 2**, replace the axle. Do not attempt to straighten it.
3. Check rim runout as follows:
   a. Remove the tire from the rim as described in Chapter Eleven.
   b. Measure the radial (up and down) runout of the wheel rim with a dial indicator as shown in **Figure 6**. If runout exceeds the specification listed in **Table 2**, check the wheel bearings.
   c. Measure the axial (side to side) runout of the wheel rim with a dial indicator as shown in **Figure 7**. If runout exceeds the specification listed in **Table 2**, check the wheel bearings.
   d. Check the wheel bearings as described in this chapter. If necessary, replace the rear wheel bearings.
   e. If the wheel bearings are in good condition, check for loose or bent spokes. Some runout

can be removed by adjusting the spokes (Chapter Eleven). If adjusting the spokes does not bring axial runout within specification, the rim is badly bent and must be replaced.

5. Inspect the wheel rim (**Figure 8**) for dents, bending or cracks. Check the rim and rim sealing surface for scratches deeper than 0.5 mm (0.01 in.). If any of these conditions are present, the wheel is unsafe for use and should be replaced.

REAR HUB

Inspection

NOTE
The rear wheel is equipped with three bearings. Two fully sealed bearings are installed in the wheel hub. A conventional, unsealed bearing is installed in the rear wheel coupling.

CAUTION
Do not remove any of the bearings for inspection. These bearing will be damaged during removal. Remove the wheel bearings only if you intend to replace them.

1. Turn each bearing inner race by hand. The bearing should turn smoothly without excessive noise or play. Questionable bearings must be replaced.
2. Replace the bearings if necessary; always replace the bearings as a complete set. When buying the bearings, be sure to take your old bearings along to ensure a perfect matchup.
3. Inspect the seal on each of the sealed bearings in the hub. If either seal is damaged, replace the bearings as a set.
4. Inspect the raised ribs (A, **Figure 9**) in the hub. Look for wear or fractures. If damage is noted or if any of the ribs are missing, replace the rear hub.
5. Inspect each rubber damper (A, **Figure 13**) for wear or deterioration. Replace if necessary.
6. Inspect the rear wheel coupling as described in this chapter.

Disassembly

Refer to **Figure 10** for this procedure.

1. Remove the rear wheel as described in this chapter.
2. Pull the brake panel (**Figure 11**) straight up and remove it from the hub.
3. Pull the rear wheel coupling (**Figure 12**) straight up and remove it from the hub. Do not lose the sleeve. It could come out with the coupling or it could remain in the hub.
4. Remove the rubber dampers (A, **Figure 13**) from the rear hub.
5. Before proceeding further, inspect the wheel bearings (B, **Figure 13**) as described in this chapter. If they must be replaced, proceed as follows.

6A. If you do not have the special tools, remove the bearings and distance collar by performing the following:

a. On the right-hand side of the hub, remove the circlip from the hub and remove the speedometer receiver (**Figure 14**).
b. On the left-hand side of the hub, remove the sleeve if it is still in place in the hub. Remove the circlip (B, **Figure 9**) from the hub.
c. Insert a soft aluminum or brass drift into one side of the hub (**Figure 15**).

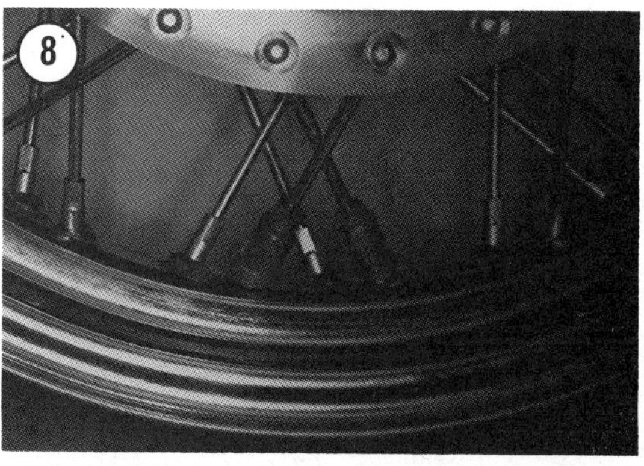

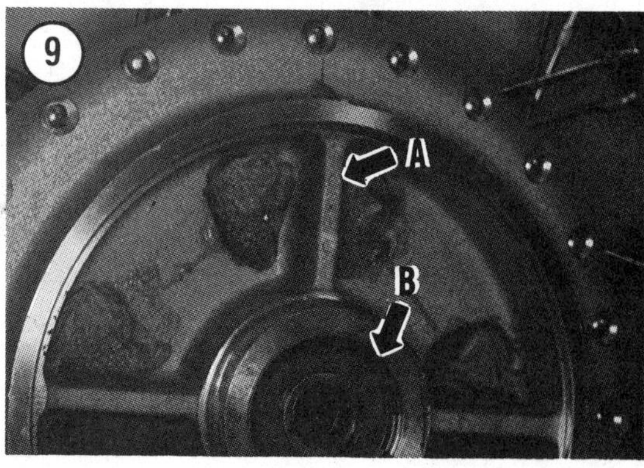

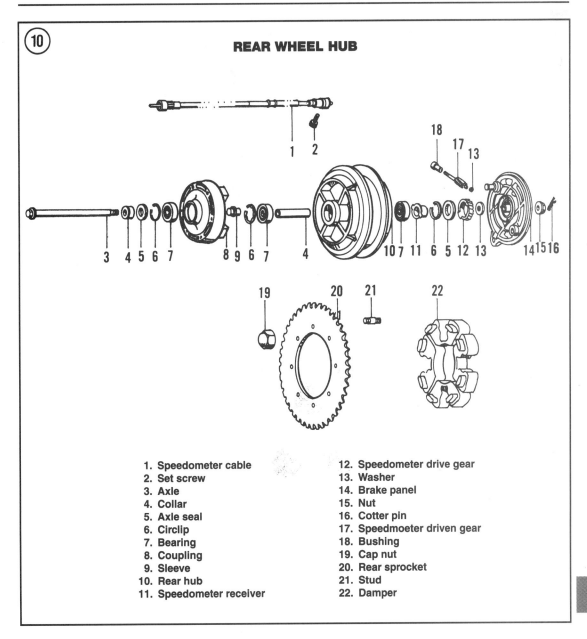

(10)

REAR WHEEL HUB

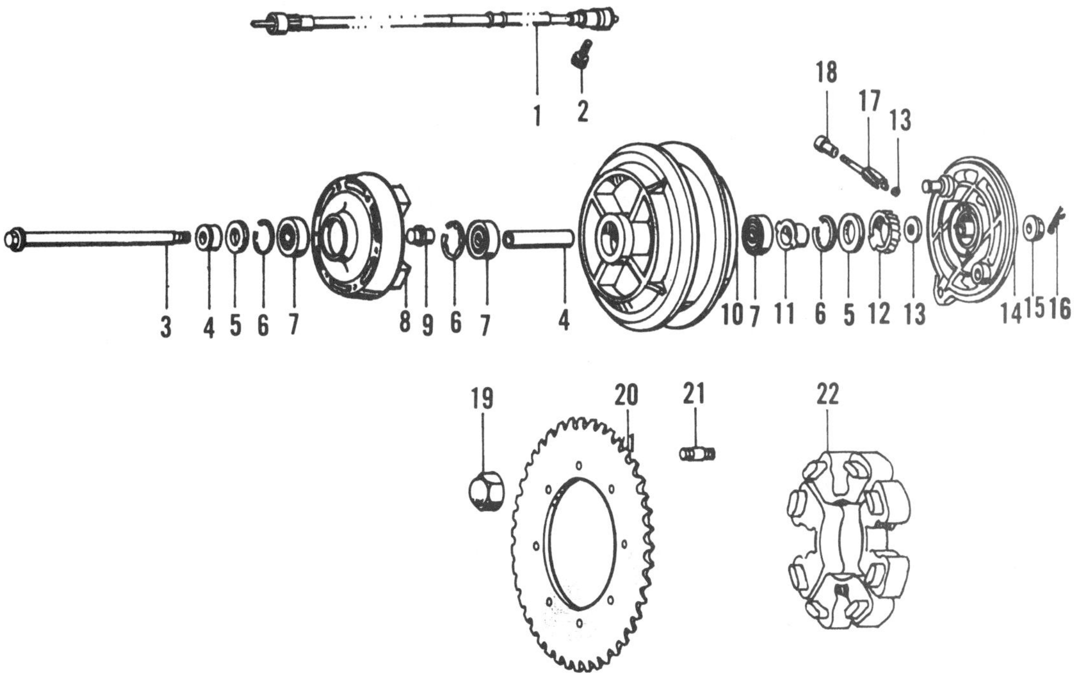

1. Speedometer cable
2. Set screw
3. Axle
4. Collar
5. Axle seal
6. Circlip
7. Bearing
8. Coupling
9. Sleeve
10. Rear hub
11. Speedometer receiver
12. Speedometer drive gear
13. Washer
14. Brake panel
15. Nut
16. Cotter pin
17. Speedmoeter driven gear
18. Bushing
19. Cap nut
20. Rear sprocket
21. Stud
22. Damper

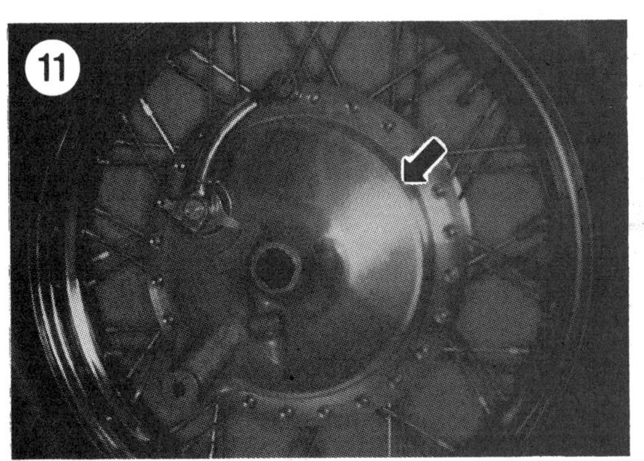

d. Push the distance collar over to one side and place the drift on the inner race of the lower bearing.
e. Tap the bearing out of the hub with a hammer, working around the perimeter of the inner race. Remove the distance collar.
f. Turn the wheel over and repeat this procedure for the remaining bearing.

6B. If you have the Kawasaki bearing remover shaft 57001-1265 and bearing remover head 57001-1267, remove the bearings and distance collar by performing the following:

a. On the right-hand side of the hub, remove the circlip from the hub and remove the speedometer receiver (**Figure 14**).
b. On the left-hand side of the hub, remove the sleeve if it is still in place in the hub. Remove the circlip (B, **Figure 9**) from the hub.
c. Insert the remover head into one of the bearings. Refer to **Figure 16**.
d. Turn the wheel over and insert the remover wedge into the back of the remover head.
e. Tap the end of the wedge with a hammer and drive the bearing from the hub. Remove the bearing and the distance collar.
f. Repeat this procedure for the remaining bearing.

7. Clean the inside and the outside of the hub with solvent. Dry with compressed air.

Assembly

The rear hub bearings are fully-sealed bearings. They are packed with grease and sealed at time of manufacture. This type of bearing cannot be packed with new grease.

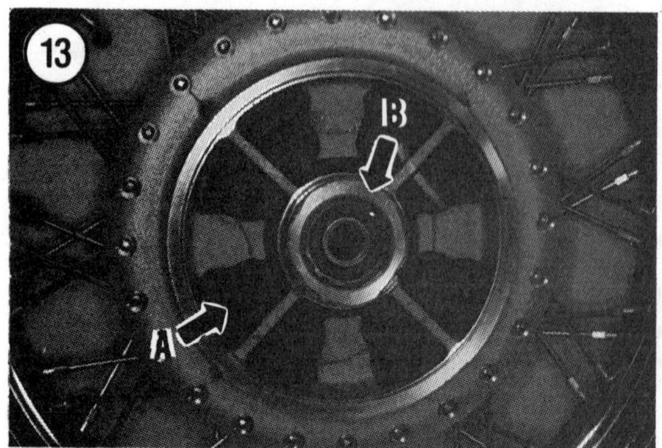

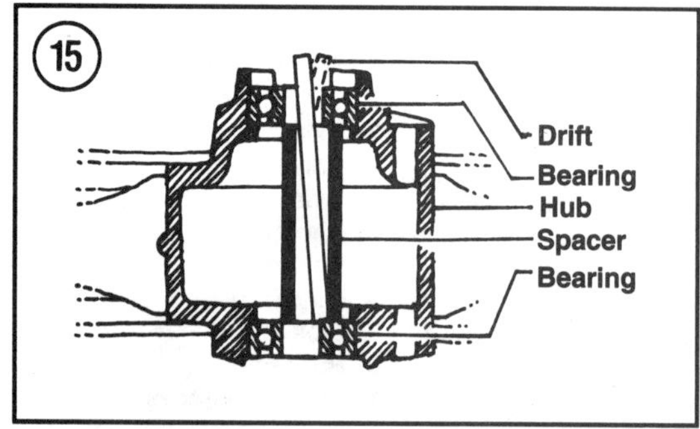

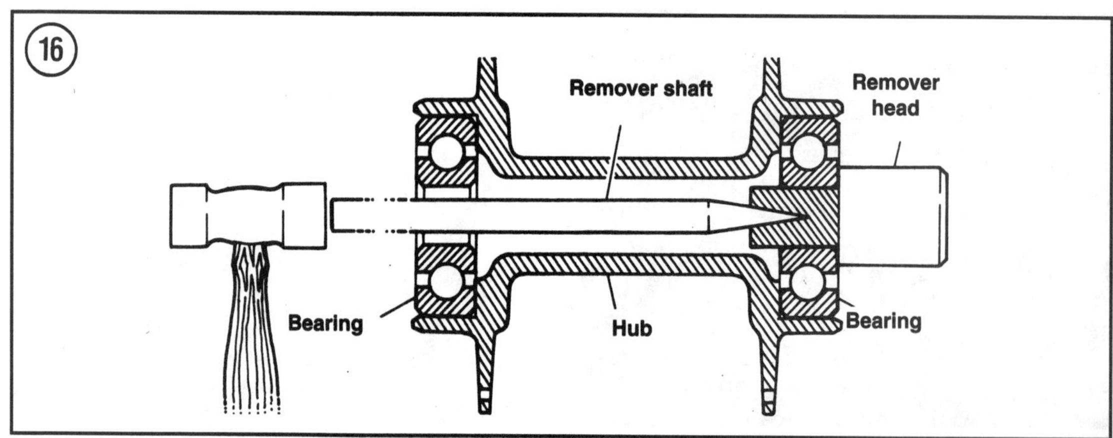

1. Blow any dirt or foreign matter out of the hub prior to installing the bearings.

CAUTION
Position the bearings with their marked side facing outward.

2. Install the right-hand bearing by performing the following:

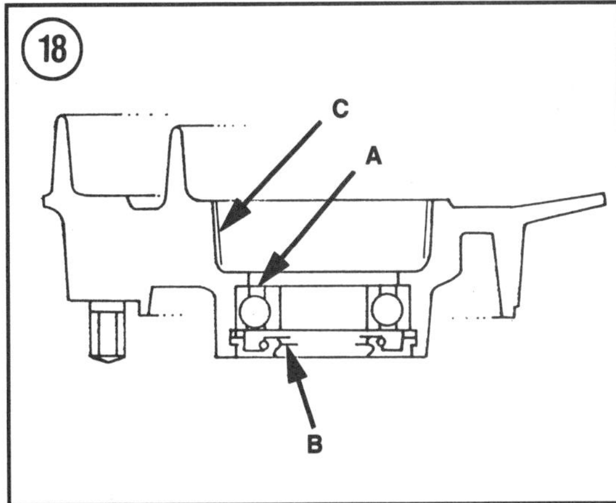

a. Set the right-hand bearing squarely into place in the hub.
b. Select a bearing driver that matches the outer race diameter and set it in place on the bearing.
c. Install the bearing by tapping it squarely into place. Be sure to tap only on the bearing's outer race. Do not tap on the inner race or the bearing might be damaged. Be sure the bearing is completely seated in the hub (**Figure 17**).

3. Install the speedometer receiver (**Figure 14**) and install a new circlip. Position the circlip with its sharp side facing out and install the circlip. Make sure the circlip is correctly seated in the hub groove.
4. Turn the wheel over (left-hand side up) on the workbench. Apply a light coat of grease to the distance collar and install it into the hub.
5. Drive in the left-hand bearing into the hub until the circlip groove is exposed.
6. Position a new circlip with its sharp side facing out and install the circlip in the hub (B, **Figure 9**). Be sure the circlip is completely seated in the hub groove.
7. Make sure that each bearing is installed squarely in the hub. Manually turn each bearing inner race. The bearing must turn smoothly. If it does not, it was damaged during installation. Remove and replace the bearing.
8. Install the rubber dampers (A, **Figure 13**) into the hub. Make sure they are properly seated between the ribs.
9. Install the sleeve into the left-hand side of the hub.
10. Apply grease to the bearings (A **Figure 18**), seal (B **Figure 18**) and inner surface of the coupling (C **Figure 18**). Fit the rear wheel coupling into place on the left-hand side of the rear hub. Push it straight down until it is completely seated in the rear hub.
11. Install the brake panel assembly (**Figure 11**) onto the right-hand side of the hub. Be sure the tangs on the speedometer drive gear (A, **Figure 19**) in the brake panel engage the cutout in the speedometer receiver (B, **Figure 19**).
12. Install the rear wheel as described in this chapter.

Speedometer Gear Inspection and Lubrication

Refer to **Figure 10** for this procedure

1. Remove the rear wheel as described in this chapter.
2. Remove the brake panel from the hub.
3. Inspect the seal in the brake panel for leaks.
4. Inspect the tangs of the speedometer drive gear (A, **Figure 19**) in the brake panel for wear or damage.
5. If necessary, remove the seal (C, **Figure 19**) with a hook.
6. Remove and inspect the speedometer drive gear. If the teeth on the speedometer drive gear are worn or damaged, replace the speedometer drive gear and the speedometer driven gear.
   a. Remove the bushing from the cable inlet (**Figure 20**) on the gear housing and remove the speedometer driven gear.
   c. Clean all old grease from the gear housing and gears.
   d. Apply a coat of high-temperature grease, and install the speedometer driven gear into the cable inlet.
   e. Apply a good coat of high-temperature grease and install the speedometer drive gear (A, **Figure 19**) into the housing. Be sure the speedometer drive gear properly engages the speedometer driven gear.
   f. Install the bushing into the cable inlet.
   g. Install a new seal (C, **Figure 19**).
7. Inspect the speedometer receiver (B, **Figure 19**) in the rear hub for wear or damage. If necessary, replace the speedometer receiver as follows:
   a. Remove the circlip from the rear hub and remove the speedometer receiver (B, **Figure 19**) from the hub.
   b. Install a new speedometer receiver into the hub.
   c. Position a new circlip with its sharp side facing out and install the circlip. Make sure the circlip is correctly seated in the hub groove.

REAR WHEEL COUPLING AND REAR SPROCKET

CAUTION
Do not remove the coupling bearing for inspection. The bearing will be damaged during removal. Remove the rear wheel coupling bearing only if it must be replaced.

NOTE
Fully sealed bearings are available from many bearing specialty shops. Fully sealed bearings provide better protection from dirt and moisture contamination than unsealed bearings.

Disassembly

Refer to **Figure 10** for this procedure.

1. If it is still in place, remove the sleeve from the right-hand side of the coupling (A, **Figure 21**).
2. Before proceeding further, use your finger to inspect the coupling bearing as described in this chapter. If it must be replaced, remove it by performing the following:
   a. If it is still in place, remove the collar (**Figure 22**) from the left-hand side of the coupling.
   b. Use a screwdriver or other suitable tool to pry the seal (A, **Figure 23**) from the coupling. Place a rag under the screwdriver to protect the coupling.
   c. Remove the circlip from the coupling.
   d. Turn the coupling over so the right-hand side faces up.

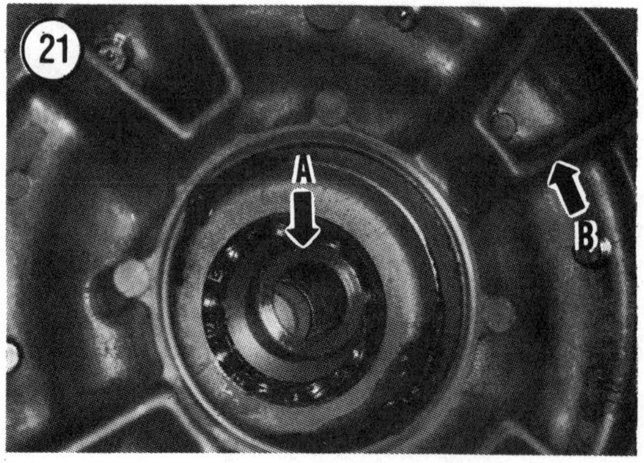

e. Use an appropriate sized bearing driver to drive the bearing from the coupling.

3. If the rear sprocket must be replaced, remove the rear sprocket nuts (B, **Figure 23**) and remove the rear sprocket from the coupling.

4. Clean the inside and the outside of the rear wheel coupling with solvent. Dry with compressed air.

Assembly

1. Install the sprocket onto the coupling. Be sure the side with the number of teeth stamped on its surface faces outward (C, **Figure 23**).

2. Install the rear sprocket nuts and torque them to the specification in **Table 1**.

3. If necessary, install a new bearing by performing the following:
   a. Carefully pack the new bearing with a good-quality, high-temperature grease.
   b. Set the bearing into place in the coupling. Be sure the sealed side of the bearing faces out.
   c. Select a bearing driver or socket that matches the outer race diameter and set it in place on the bearing.

   d. Install the bearing by tapping it squarely into place. Be sure to tap only on the bearing's outer race. Do not tap on the inner race or the bearing might be damaged. Be sure that the bearing is completely seated in the coupling.
   e. Position a new circlip with the sharp side facing out and install the circlip. Be sure the circlip is completely seated in the groove in the coupling.
   f. Manually inspect the operation of the bearing. If it does not move smoothly, the bearing was damaged during installation. Remove and replace the bearing.
   g. Apply a light coat of grease to a new seal and to the seal housing in the coupling.
   h. Set the seal in place with its manufacturer's marks facing out.
   i. Select a bearing driver or socket that matches the outer diameter of the seal.
   j. Tap the seal (A, **Figure 23**) squarely into place until it is flush with the surface of the coupling. Be sure to tap on the outer diameter of the seal only.

4. Apply a light coat of grease to the collar and install it into the coupling (**Figure 22**).

5. Turn the coupling over. Apply a light coat of grease to the sleeve (A, **Figure 21**) and install it in the coupling.

Inspection

1. Inspect the raised bosses (B, **Figure 21**) on the coupling for cracks or damage. 12

2. Inspect the entire coupling for cracks or warping.

3. Replace the rear wheel coupling if any of these areas are damaged.

4. Visually inspect the teeth on the rear sprocket. If the teeth are worn (**Figure 24**), replace the sprocket.

CAUTION

If the rear sprocket must be replaced, also replace the engine sprocket and the drive chain. Never install a new drive chain over worn sprockets. Also never install a worn drive chain over new sprockets.

DRIVE CHAIN

Removal/Installation

WARNING
The original drive chain is a continuous closed-loop chain without a master link. To prevent chain failure, do not cut and reinstall this type of chain.

NOTE
If an aftermarket drive chain is installed, it may be equipped with a master link. If so, follow the chain manufacturer's removal and installation instructions.

1. Remove the rear wheel as described in this chapter.
2. Remove the swing arm as described in this chapter.
3. Remove the engine sprocket cover as described in Chapter Five.
4. Disengage the chain from the engine sprocket (**Figure 25**), and remove the chain.
5. Install the chain by reversing these steps.
6. Adjust the chain tension as described in Chapter Three.

TIRE CHANGING AND TIRE REPAIR

Refer to Chapter Eleven.

SHOCK ABSORBER

Removal/Installation

NOTE
This procedure is shown with the rear wheel removed for clarity. It is not necessary to remove the wheel for this procedure.

1. Use a scissors jack or jack stands to support the bike securely with the rear wheel off the ground. If you do not have a bike stand, place a wooden block under the engine or frame.
2. Remove the exhaust pipes as described in Chapter Eight.
3. Remove the storage box and tool kit container as described in Chapter Fourteen.
4. Remove the nut and bolt (A, **Figure 26**) securing the lower end of the shock absorber to the rocker arm.
5. Remove the nut and bolt (B, **Figure 26**) securing the lower end of the tie rod to the rocker arm.
6. Move the tie rod out of the way.
7. Remove the nut and bolt (**Figure 27**) securing the upper end of the shock absorber to the mounting tab on the frame.

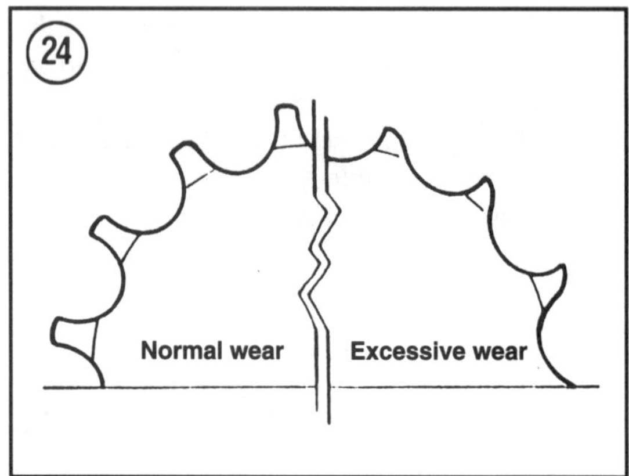

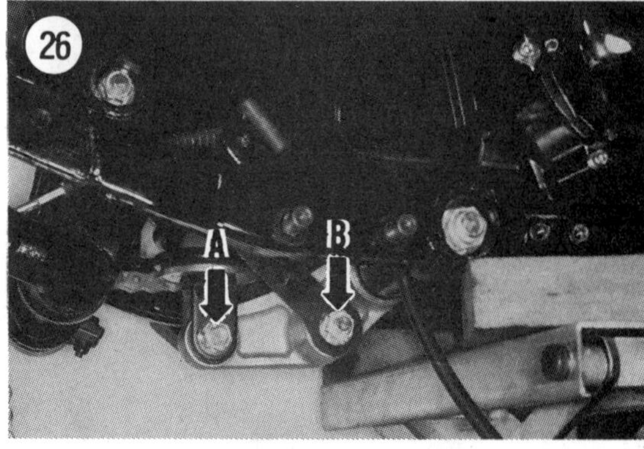

8. Lower and remove the shock absorber from the frame.

9. Inspect the shock absorber as described in this chapter.

10. Clean the mounting bolts and nuts in solvent, and thoroughly dry them.

11. Apply plenty of waterproof grease to the rocker arm needle bearings.

12. Apply a light coat of waterproof grease to the shock absorber upper and lower mounting surfaces.

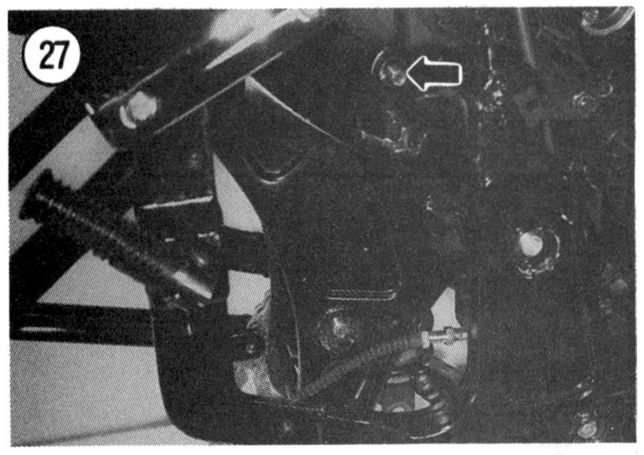

13. Position the shock absorber with the caution label facing rearward.

14. Move the shock absorber up and into the frame so the upper shock mount aligns with the mounting tab on the frame. Install the upper shock bolt from the left-hand side, and fingertighten the nut (**Figure 27**).

15. Move the rocker arm into position in the lower shock mount. Install the lower shock mounting bolt from the left-hand side, and fingertighten the nut (A, **Figure 26**).

16. Move the tie rod so its lower mount aligns with the middle mount in the rocker arm. Install the tie rod bolt from the left-hand side, and fingertighten the nut (B, **Figure 26**).

17. Torque all three mounting nuts to the specification listed in **Table 1**.

18. Remove the supports from under the bike, and push down on the rear to make sure the linkage is operating correctly.

19. Install the tool kit container and storage box as described in Chapter Fourteen.

20. Install the exhaust pipes as described in Chapter Eight.

Shock Absorber Inspection

The upper bushing is the only part of the shock absorber that can be replaced. If any other part of the shock absorber is faulty, replace the shock absorber.

1. Inspect the shock absorber for oil leakage (A, **Figure 28**).

2. Check the spring (B, **Figure 28**) for cracks or other damage.

3. Inspect the upper (A, **Figure 29**) and lower (C, **Figure 28**) shock mounts for wear or damage. Replace the upper bushing (A, **Figure 29**) if necessary.

4. If any part other than the upper bushing is worn or damaged, replace the shock absorber.

Shock Absorber Preload Adjustment.

The shock absorber has a seven-position preload adjuster. The factory sets the spring preload to the first position (B, **Figure 29**), which is the weakest setting. Turning the adjuster to a higher setting increases the spring preload; lowering the setting decreases the preload.

To adjust the preload, remove the shock absorber and use a steering stem wrench to turn the adjuster to the desired setting.

SWING ARM AND SHOCK LINKAGE

Refer to **Figure 30** and **Figure 31**. The swing arm is supported by two caged needle bearings on each side of the swing arm pivot. The lower end of the shock absorber is connected to the swing arm via the tie rod/rocker arm linkage. Service the swing arm bearings frequently to provide maximum bearing service life and to maintain proper suspension operation.

Swing Arm Bearing Preliminary Inspection.

The condition of the swing arm bearings can greatly affect handling performance. In time, the needle bearings will wear and require replacement.

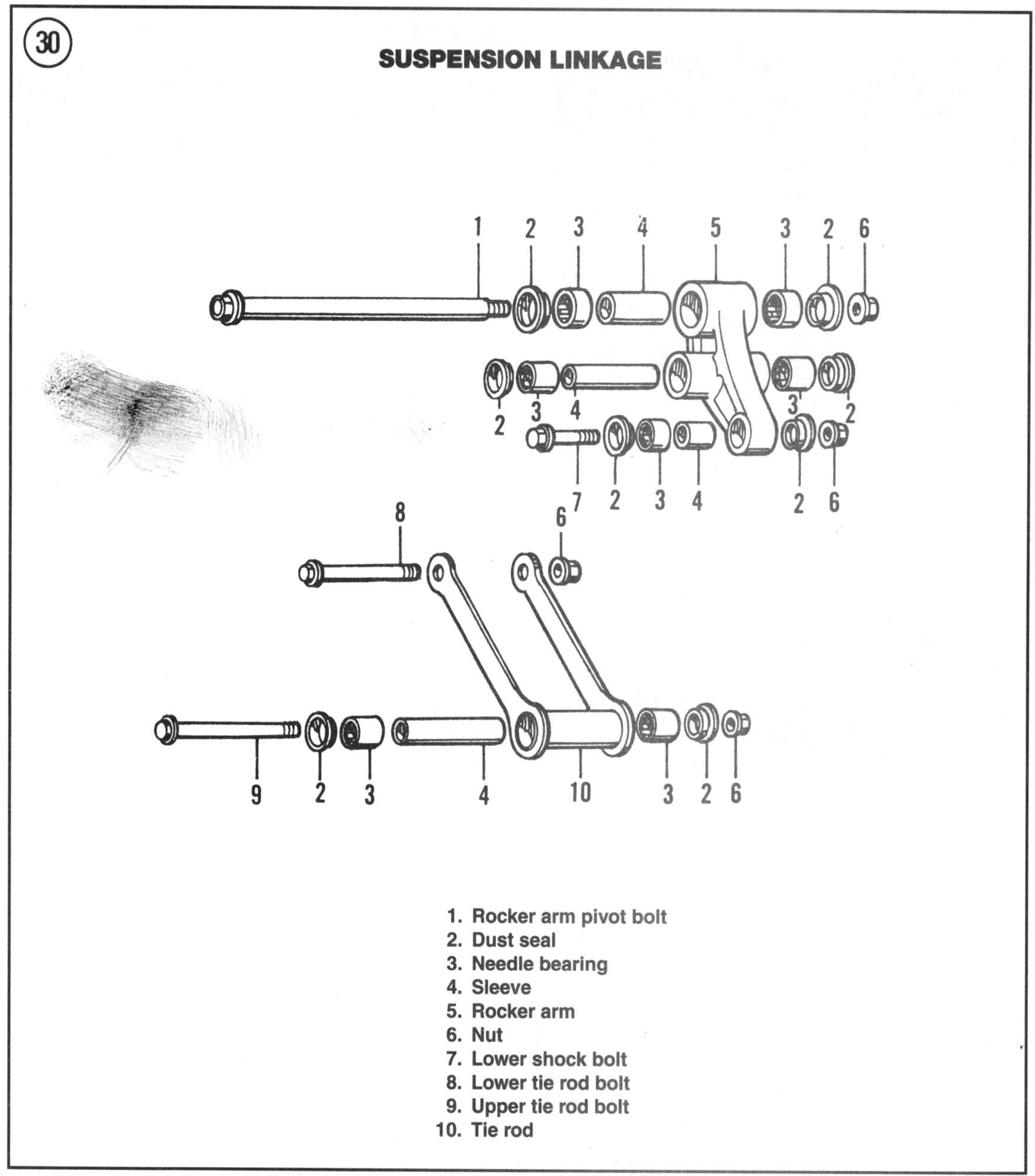

If worn parts are not replaced, they can produce erratic and dangerous handling. Common symptoms are wheel hop, pulling to one side during acceleration and pulling to the other side during braking.

1. Remove the exhaust pipes as described in Chapter Eight.
2. Remove the rear wheel as described in this chapter.
3. Remove the nut and bolt (A, **Figure 32**) securing the lower tie rod to the rocker arm.
4. Loosen and then tighten the swing arm pivot shaft nut (A, **Figure 33**). Torque the nut to the specification in **Table 1**.
5. The swing arm is now free to move under its own weight.

NOTE
Have an assistant steady the bike when performing Step 6.

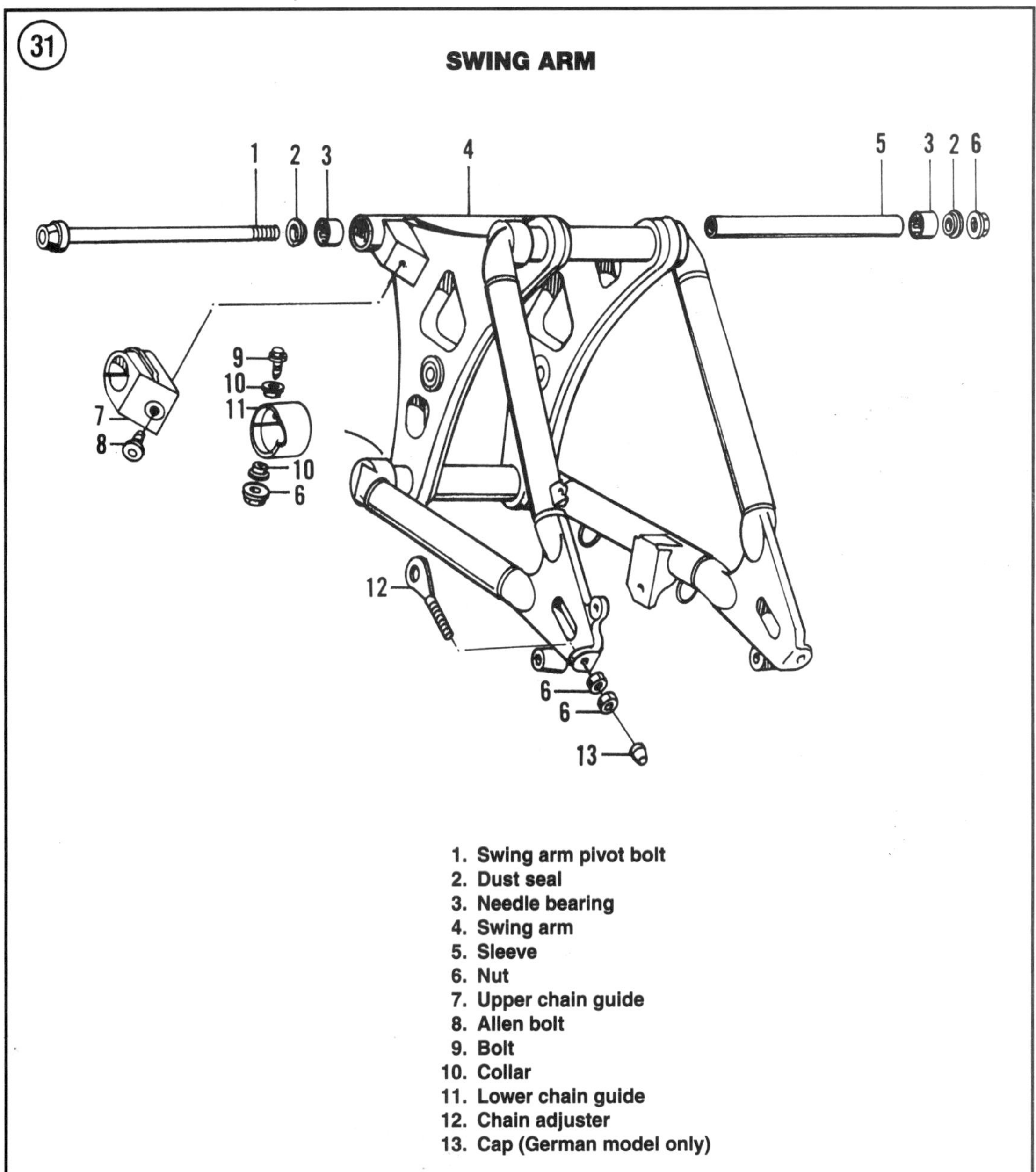

1. Swing arm pivot bolt
2. Dust seal
3. Needle bearing
4. Swing arm
5. Sleeve
6. Nut
7. Upper chain guide
8. Allen bolt
9. Bolt
10. Collar
11. Lower chain guide
12. Chain adjuster
13. Cap (German model only)

6. Grasp both ends of the swing arm and attempt to move it from side to side in a horizontal arc. If more than a slight amount of movement is felt, the bearings are worn and must be replaced.
7. Grasp both ends of the swing arm, and move it up and down. The swing arm should move freely or without any abnormal bearing noise. If there is binding or if the bearings are noisy, the bearings are worn and must be replaced.
8. Move the swing arm into position, and reattach the tie rod to the rocker arm. Insert the tie rod pivot bolt from the left-hand side, and torque the tie rod nut to the specification in **Table 1**.
9. Recheck the torque on the nut for the swing arm pivot bolt. If necessary, retighten the nut to the specification in **Table 1**.
10. Install the wheel as described in this chapter.
11. Install the exhaust pipes as described in Chapter Eight.

Swing Arm Removal/Installation

Refer to **Figure 30** for the suspension linkage and **Figure 31** for the swing arm.

1. Remove the exhaust pipes as described in Chapter Eight.
2. Remove the rear wheel as described in this chapter.
3. Remove the four mud guard bolts (A, **Figure 34**), and remove the mud guard (B, **Figure 34**).
4. Remove the shock absorber as described in this chapter.
5. Remove the upper tie rod nut (B, **Figure 32**), and carefully drive the pivot bolt from the swing arm.
6. Remove the tie rod. Do not lose the dust seals on each side of the tie rod. If you do not intend to service the tie rod bearings, place a strip of duct tape over the seals so the parts will not be lost.
7. Remove the swing arm pivot nut (A, **Figure 33**).
8. Carefully drive the pivot bolt from the frame and swing arm, and remove the bolt.
9. Carefully pull the swing arm rearward, and lower it to the ground.
10. Be sure the rear brake rod and the drive chain are clear of the swing arm, and remove the swing arm from the frame.
11. Inspect the swing arm and lubricate the bearings as described in this chapter.
12. Install by reversing the removal steps while noting the following:

a. Lubricate the swing-arm and tie rod bearings with waterproof grease.
b. Lubricate the pivot bolts and sleeves with waterproof grease prior to installation.

NOTE
Install the pivot bolts from the left-hand side; install the nuts on the right-hand side. To ensure maximum performance and service from the rear suspension, the bolts must be installed from the left-

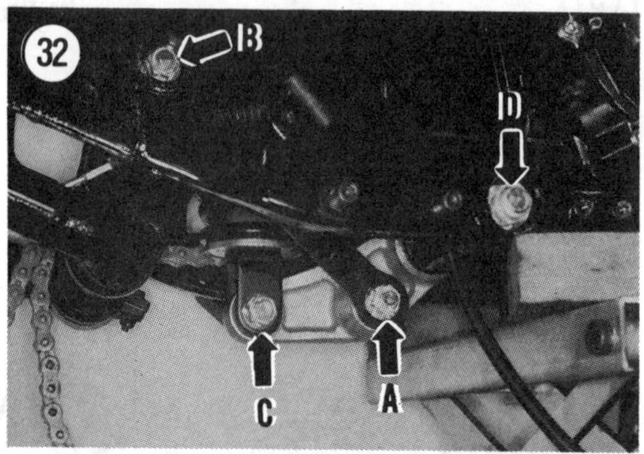

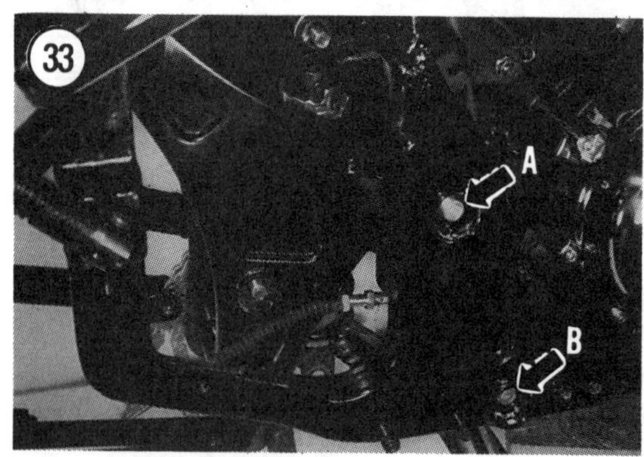

hand side as shown in **Figure 30** *and* **Figure 31**.

c. Install the sleeves, pivot bolts, and nuts as shown in **Figure 30** and **Figure 31**.
d. Be sure the dust seals are in place at all pivot points.
e. Tighten all rear suspension components to the torque specifications listed in **Table 1**.
f. Adjust the drive chain and rear brake as described in Chapter Three.

Rocker Arm Removal/Installation

NOTE
This procedure is shown with the rear wheel removed for clarity. It is not necessary to remove the wheel for this procedure.

Refer to **Figure 30** for this procedure.

1. Use a scissors jack or jack stands to support the bike securely with the rear wheel off the ground. If you do not have a bike stand, place a wooden block under the engine or frame.
2. Remove the exhaust pipes as described in Chapter Eight.
3. Loosen, but do not remove, the swing arm pivot nut (A, **Figure 33**).
4. Remove the nut and bolt (C, **Figure 32**) securing the lower end of the shock absorber to the rocker arm.
5. Remove the nut and bolt (A, **Figure 32**) securing the lower end of the tie rod to the rocker arm.
6. Move the tie rod out of the way.
7. Loosen the rocker arm pivot nut (D, **Figure 32**). Carefully drive the pivot bolt from the frame, and remove the rocker arm.
8. Inspect the rocker arm, and lubricate the bearings as described in this chapter.
9. Install by reversing the removal steps while noting the following:
   a. Lubricate the rocker arm bearings with waterproof grease.
   b. Lubricate the pivot bolts and sleeves with waterproof grease prior to installation.

NOTE
Install the pivot bolts from the left-hand side and the nuts on the right-hand side. To ensure maximum performance and service from the rear suspension, the bolts must be installed from the left-hand side as shown in **Figure 30**.

   c. Install the sleeves, pivot bolts, and nuts as shown in **Figure 30** and **Figure 31**.
   d. Be sure the dust seals are in place at all pivot bosses.
   e. Tighten all rear suspension components, including the swing arm pivot nut, to the torque specifications listed in **Table 1**.

Swing Arm Disassembly/Inspection/Assembly

Refer to **Figure 31** for this procedure.

Store the left- and right-hand bearing assemblies in separate containers so they will be installed in their original locations.

1. Carefully pry the left-hand dust seal (A, **Figure 35**) from the swing arm pivot boss.
2. Remove the sleeve (**Figure 36**) from the pivot boss.

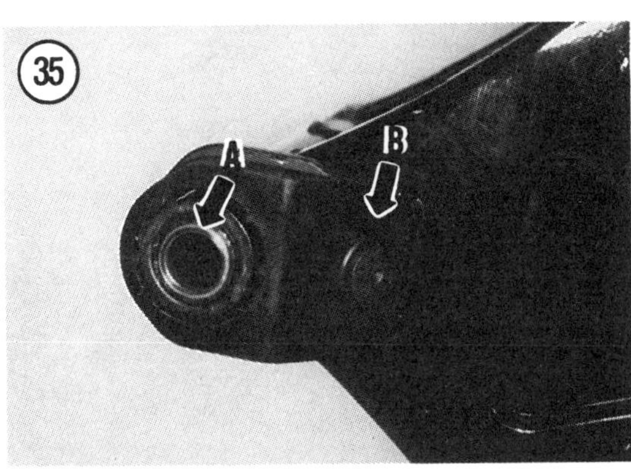

3. Carefully pry the right-hand dust seal from the pivot boss.
4. Clean the dust seals and sleeve in solvent, and thoroughly dry them.
5. Inspect the needle bearings in the pivot area as follows:
   a. Use a clean lint-free cloth to wipe excess grease from the needle bearings (**Figure 37**).
   b. Turn each bearing with your fingers. The bearing should turn smoothly without excessive play. Check the rollers for evidence of wear, pitting or rust.
   c. Reinstall the pivot sleeve (**Figure 36**), and slowly rotate the sleeve in the bearings. It must turn freely without noise, tight spots or excessive looseness.
6. Replace any worn or damaged needle bearing as described in this chapter.
7. Inspect the dust seals. Replace any seal that is torn or damaged.
8. Check the welded areas of the swing arm for cracks or fractures. See A, **Figure 38** and A, **Figure 39**.
9. Remove each drive chain adjuster assembly (B, **Figure 39**). Inspect the chain drive adjusters and inspect the adjuster boss on the swing arm (C. **Figure 39**) for cracks of other signs of damage.
10. Inspect the upper chain guard (B, **Figure 35**) and the lower chain guard (B, **Figure 38**) on the swing arm. Replace either if excessively worn or damaged.
11. Check the swing arm pivot bolt by rolling it along a surface plate or piece of plate glass. If you notice any warpage, replace the bolt.
12. Apply waterproof bearing grease to the needle bearings, pivot sleeve and dust seals.
13. Install the sleeve (**Figure 36**) into the left-hand side of the swing arm pivot boss. Push the sleeve in until it is centered within the pivot boss.
14. Install the left-hand dust seal (A, **Figure 35**) into the pivot boss.
15. Turn the swing arm over and set the right-hand dust seal in place on the pivot boss.
16. Use a driver that matches the outer diameter of the seal, and tap the seal until it is flush with the outer surface of the pivot boss.
17. Install the swing arm as described in this chapter.

Tie Rod Disassembly/Inspection/Assembly

1. Carefully pry the left-hand dust seal (A, **Figure 40**) from the tie-rod pivot boss.
2. Remove the sleeve (B, **Figure 40**) from the tie-rod pivot boss.
3. Carefully pry the right-hand dust seal from the pivot.
4. Clean the dust seals and sleeve in solvent, and thoroughly dry them.

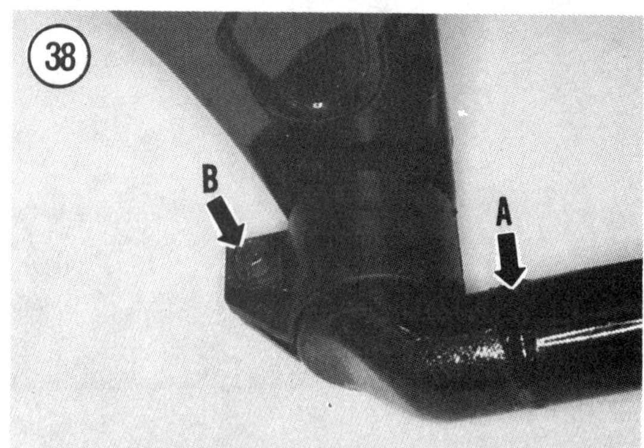

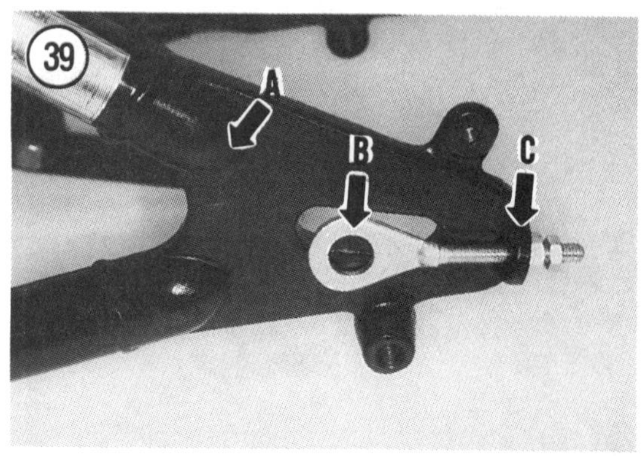

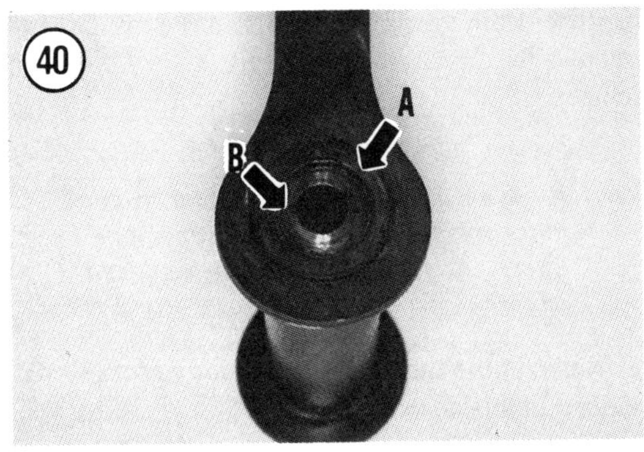

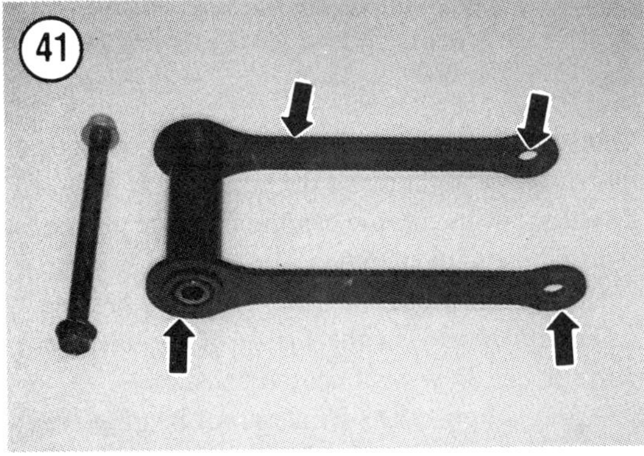

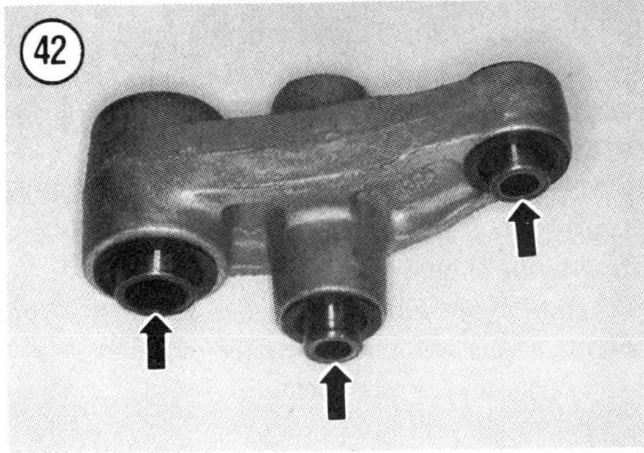

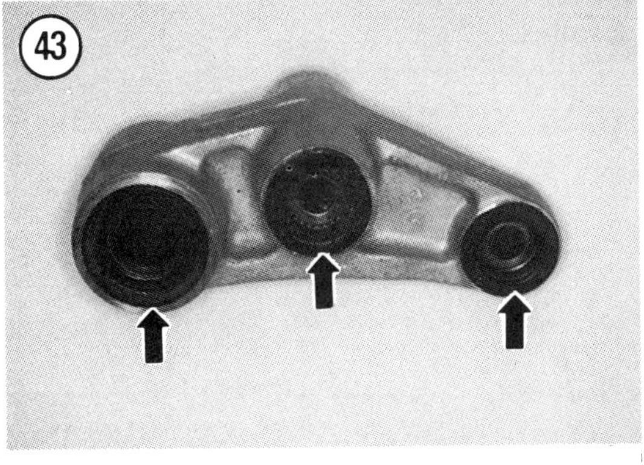

5. Inspect the needle bearings in the pivot boss as follows:
   a. Use a clean lint-free cloth to wipe excess grease from the needle bearings.
   b. Turn each bearing with your fingers. The bearing should turn smoothly without excessive play. Check the rollers for evidence of wear, pitting or rust.
   c. Reinstall the pivot sleeve, and slowly rotate the sleeve in the bearings. It must turn freely without noise, tight spots or excessive looseness.
6. Replace any worn or damaged needle bearing as described in *Needle Bearing Replacement* in this chapter.
7. Inspect the dust seals. Replace any that is torn or damaged.
8. Inspect the tie-rod to rocker-arm mount (**Figure 41**) in the tie rod.
9. Inspect the tie rod for cracks or damage. Replace the tie rod as necessary.
10. Apply waterproof grease to the needle bearings, pivot sleeve and dust seals.
11. Install the sleeve (B, **Figure 40**) into the left-hand side of the tie-rod pivot boss. Push the sleeve in until it is centered within the pivot boss.
12. Install the left-hand dust seal (A, **Figure 40**) into the pivot boss.
13. Turn the swing arm over and set the right-hand dust seal in place on the pivot boss.
14. Use a driver that matches the outer diameter of the seal, and tap the seal until it is flush with the outer surface of the pivot boss.
15. Install the tie rod as described in this chapter.

Rocker Arm Disassembly/Inspection/Assembly

NOTE

Three different length pivot sleeves are used in the rocker arm. Each sleeve must be reinstalled in the correct pivot boss. Note the location of each sleeve in the rocker arm so it can be reinstalled in its original location.

1. Remove the three pivot sleeves from the pivot bosses in the rocker arm (**Figure 42**).
2. Carefully pry the dust seals (**Figure 43**) from each pivot boss. Note the location of each dust seal. They must be reinstalled in their original locations.

3. Clean the dust seals and sleeves in solvent, and thoroughly dry them.
4. Inspect each needle bearing in the rocker arm as follows:
   a. Use a clean lint-free cloth to wipe excess grease from the needle bearings.
   b. Turn each bearing with your fingers. The bearing should turn smoothly without excessive play. Check the rollers for evidence of wear, pitting or rust.
   c. Reinstall the pivot sleeve, and slowly rotate the sleeve in the bearings. It must turn freely without noise, tight spots or excessive looseness.
5. Replace any worn or damaged needle bearing as described in *Needle Bearing Replacement* in this chapter.
6. Inspect the dust seals. Replace any that is torn or damaged.
7. Inspect the tie rod for cracks or other signs of damage. Replace the tie rod as necessary.
8. Apply waterproof bearing grease to the needle bearings, pivot sleeve and dust seals.
9. Install all six dust seals into their respective position in the rocker arm. (**Figure 43**). Be sure each dust seal is installed in its original position.

NOTE
Each pivot sleeve is a different length and must be reinstalled in the correct pivot boss in the rocker arm.

10. Install each pivot sleeve (**Figure 42**) into its respective pivot boss in the rocker arm.
11. Install the rocker arm as described in this chapter.

Needle Bearing Replacement

A Kawasaki tool (seal and bearing remover, part No. 57001-1058) is required to remove needle bearings from the swing arm and rocker arm. Do not remove the needle bearings unless they must be replaced.

NOTE
If the needle bearings are replaced, replace the pivot sleeve at the same time. These parts should always be replaced as a set.

1. Remove the dust seals and pivot sleeves as described in this chapter.

NOTE
This special tool grabs the inner surface of the bearing and withdraws it from the pivot boss.

2. Insert the bearing puller through the needle bearing, and expand it behind the bearing.
3. Withdraw the needle bearing from the pivot boss by using the slide hammer.
4. Repeat this process for the remaining bearing.
5. Thoroughly clean the inside of the pivot boss with solvent. Dry it with compressed air.
6. Apply a light coat of waterproof bearing grease to the exterior of the new bearing and to the inner surface of the pivot boss.
7. Locate and square the new bearing in the pivot.
8. Select a driver that matches the diameter of the bearing outer race. Set the driver on the bearing and tap the bearing into place.
9. Make sure the bearing is properly seated within the pivot boss. Turn each bearing with your fingers. The bearing should turn smoothly.
10. Thoroughly lubricate the needles of the new bearing with a waterproof bearing grease.
11. Repeat for the other bearing.
12. Prior to installing the new pivot sleeves, coat the inner surface of the bearing with waterproof bearing grease. Install the pivot sleeves and dust seals as described in this chapter.

Table 1 REAR SUSPENSION TIGHTENING TORQUES

Item	N•m	ft.-lb.
Rear axle nut	98	72
Rear sprocket nuts	74	54
Shock absorber mounting nuts	59	43
Tie rod nuts	59	43
Swing arm pivot shaft nut	98	72
Rocker arm pivot shaft nut	98	72
Torque link nuts	34	25

Table 2 REAR SUSPENSION SPECIFICATIONS

Item	Standard	Wear limit
Rear axle runout	Less than 0.05 mm (0.002 in.)	0.2 mm (0.0078 in.)
Rear wheel rim runout		
Radial	1.0 mm (0.039 in.)	2.0 mm (0.078in.)
Axial	0.8 mm (0.031 in.)	2.0 mm (0.078 in.)

CHAPTER THIRTEEN

BRAKES

The brake system on all models consists of a single disc brake on the front wheel and a drum brake on the rear. VN800 models use a single-piston front brake caliper and VN800 Classic models use a dual-piston caliper. This chapter describes repair and replacement procedures for all brake components.

Table 1 contains brake system torque specifications and **Table 2** contains brake system service specifications. **Table 1** and **Table 2** are located at the end of this chapter.

FRONT DISC BRAKES

The front disc brake is actuated by hydraulic fluid and is controlled by a hand lever that is attached to the front master cylinder. As the brake pads wear, the brake fluid level drops in the reservoir and automatically adjusts for wear.

When working on hydraulic brake systems, it is necessary that the work area and all tools be absolutely clean. Any tiny particles of foreign matter and grit in the caliper assembly or the master cylinder can damage the components. Also, sharp tools must not be used inside the caliper or on the piston. If there is any doubt about your ability to correctly and safely carry out major service on the brake components, take the job to a Kawasaki dealership or brake specialist.

Consider the following when servicing the disc brake system.

1. Disc brake components rarely require disassembly, so do not disassemble them unless necessary.

WARNING

Do not use silicone-based (DOT 5) brake fluid. It can damage brake components and lead to brake system failure.

2. Use only DOT 4 brake fluid from a sealed container.
3. Do not allow disc brake fluid to contact any plastic, painted or plated surfaces. Brake fluid will damage these surfaces.
4. Always keep the master cylinder reservoir and spare cans of brake fluid closed to prevent dust or moisture from entering. If moisture enters the brake fluid, it could result in brake fluid contamination and brake failure.

5. Use only DOT 4 disc brake fluid or isopropyl alcohol to wash parts. Never clean any internal brake components with solvent or any other petroleum based cleaners.

6. Whenever *any* component has been removed from the brake system, the system is considered opened and must be bled to remove air. Also, if the brake feels spongy, this usually means that air is present in the system. For safe brake operation, bleed the brake system in this chapter.

CAUTION
Do not use petroleum-based solvents of any kind on the brake system internal components. Petroleum-based solvents will cause the seals to swell and distort. When cleaning brake components (except brake pads) use new DOT 4 brake fluid or isopropyl alcohol.

WARNING
When working on the brake system, do ***not*** *inhale brake dust. It may contain asbestos, which can cause lung injury and cancer. Wear a facemask that meets OSHA requirements for trapping asbestos particles. Always wash your hands and forearms thoroughly after working on the brake system.*

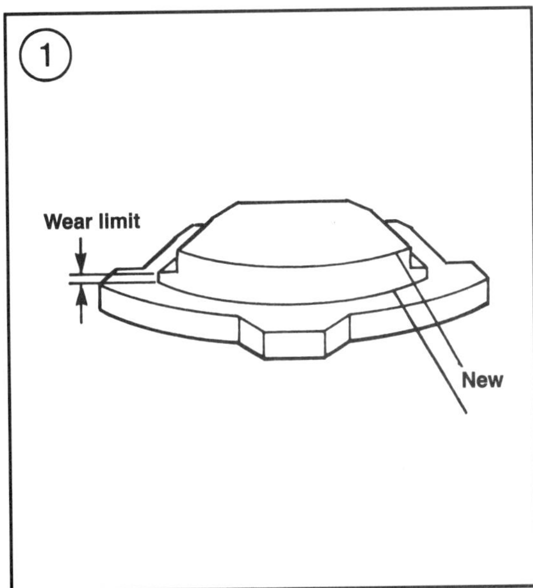

FRONT BRAKE PAD REPLACEMENT

There is no recommended mileage interval for changing the friction pads in the disc brakes. Pad wear depends greatly on riding habits and conditions. The pads should be checked for wear every six months and replaced when the wear indicator (**Figure 1**) reaches the edge of the brake disc. To maintain an even brake pressure on the disc always replace both pads at the same time.

Disconnecting the hydraulic brake hose from the brake caliper is not necessary for brake pad replacement. Disconnect the hose only if the caliper assembly must be removed and serviced.

CAUTION
Check the pads more frequently as the wear line approaches the disc. On some pads the wear line is very close to the metal backing plate. If pad wear happens to be uneven, the backing plate may contact the disc and cause damage.

Front Brake Pad Replacement

The following procedures show the removal and installation of the front brake pads on VN800 models. The procedures are similar for VN800 Classic models except for minor differences, which are noted.

Refer to **Figure 2** for VN800 models and **Figure 3** for VN800 Classic models.

1. Use a scissors jack or jack stands to securely support the bike on level ground.
2. Remove the caliper mounting bolts (A, **Figure 4**) and remove the caliper (B, **Figure 4**) from the disc.
3. On VN800 Classic models, remove the clip and withdraw the pad pin from the caliper.
4. Remove both brake pads from the caliper assembly.
5. Check the brake pad lining (**Figure 5**) for oil contamination or fraying. Check the pad plates for cracks or other damage. Measure the thickness of the brake pad lining with a vernier caliper (**Figure 6**). Replace the pads as a set if the lining is worn to the wear limit listed in **Table 2**.

WARNING
In order to maintain effective braking, the brake pads must be replaced as a set. When servicing front brakes, always replace both brake pads.

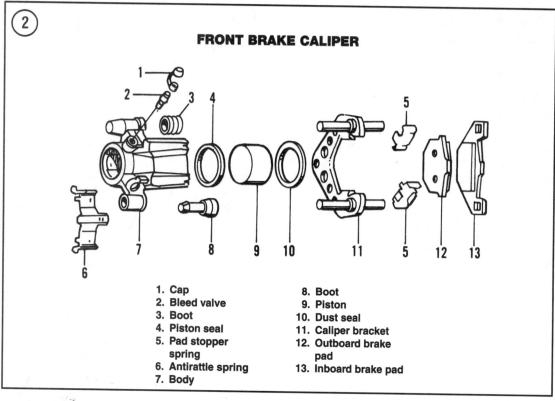

2

FRONT BRAKE CALIPER

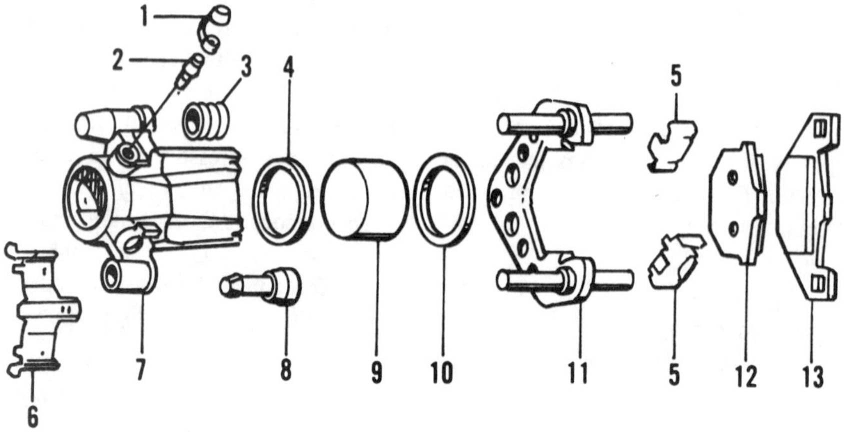

1. Cap
2. Bleed valve
3. Boot
4. Piston seal
5. Pad stopper spring
6. Antirattle spring
7. Body
8. Boot
9. Piston
10. Dust seal
11. Caliper bracket
12. Outboard brake pad
13. Inboard brake pad

3

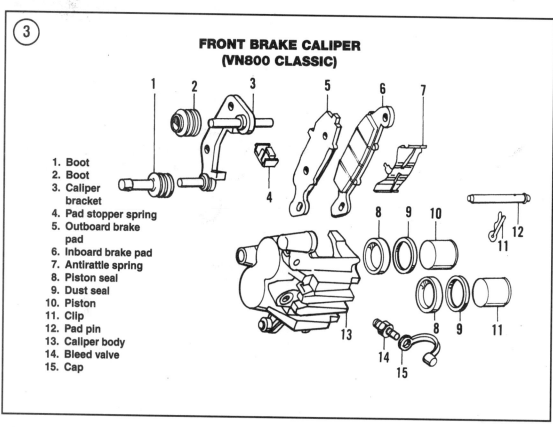

FRONT BRAKE CALIPER (VN800 CLASSIC)

1. Boot
2. Boot
3. Caliper bracket
4. Pad stopper spring
5. Outboard brake pad
6. Inboard brake pad
7. Antirattle spring
8. Piston seal
9. Dust seal
10. Piston
11. Clip
12. Pad pin
13. Caliper body
14. Bleed valve
15. Cap

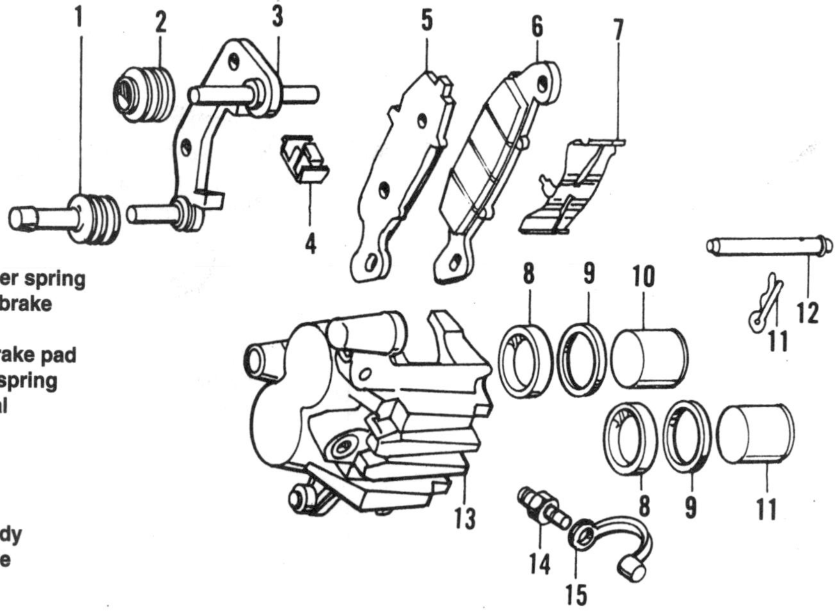

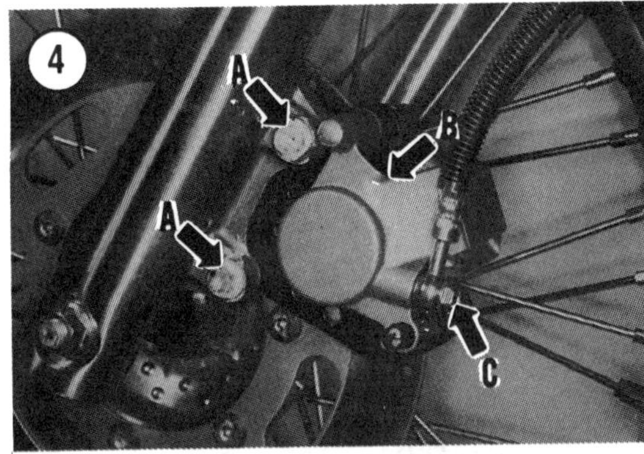

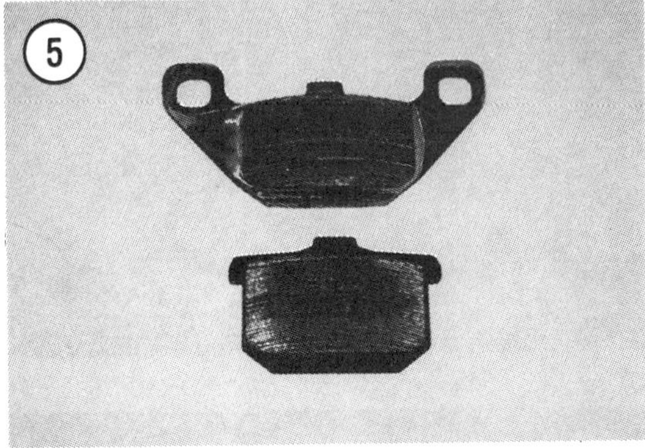

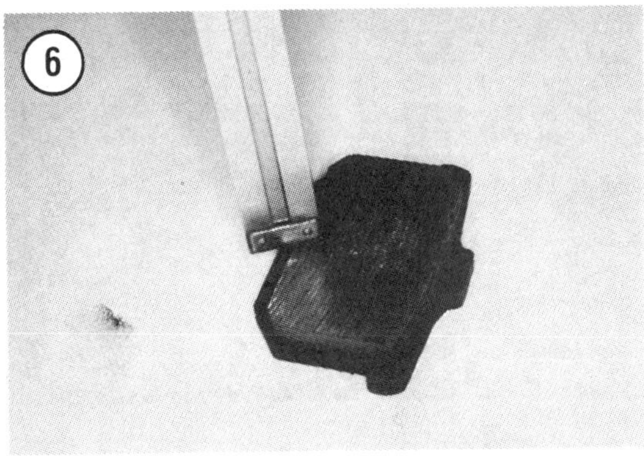

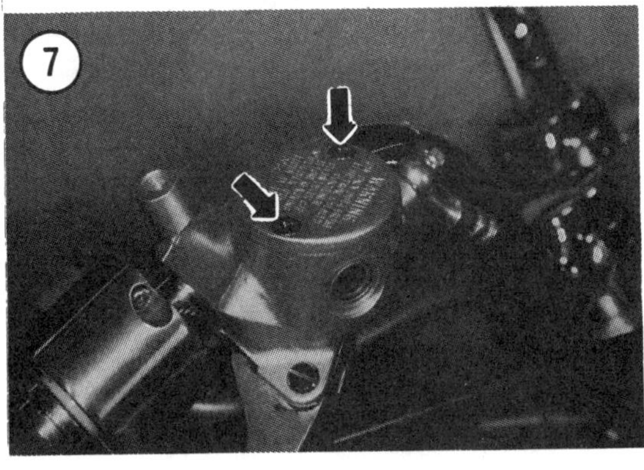

6. Clean the pad recess and the end of the piston(s) with a soft brush. Do not use solvent, a wire brush or any hard tool that would damage the cylinders or pistons.

7. Carefully remove any rust or corrosion from the disc.

8. When new pads are installed in the caliper, the master cylinder brake fluid level will rise as the caliper piston is repositioned. Perform the following:

a. Clean all dirt and foreign matter from the top of the master cylinder.
b. Remove the screws (**Figure 7**) securing the master cylinder cover. Remove the cover and the diaphragm (**Figure 8**) from the master cylinder.
c. *On VN800 models,* slowly push the caliper piston (A, **Figure 9**) into the caliper. *On VN800 Classic models,* slowly push both caliper pistons into the caliper.

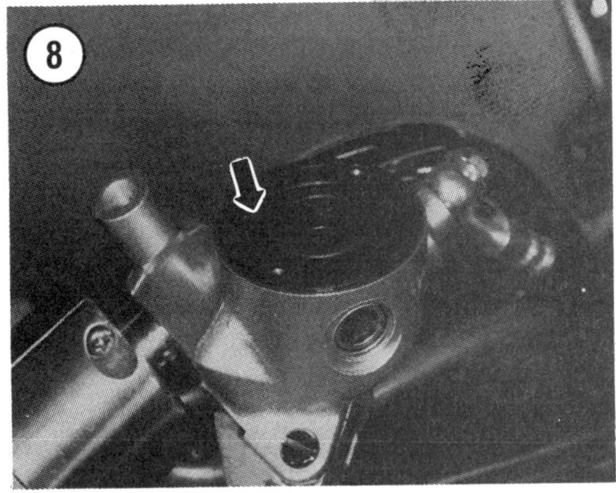

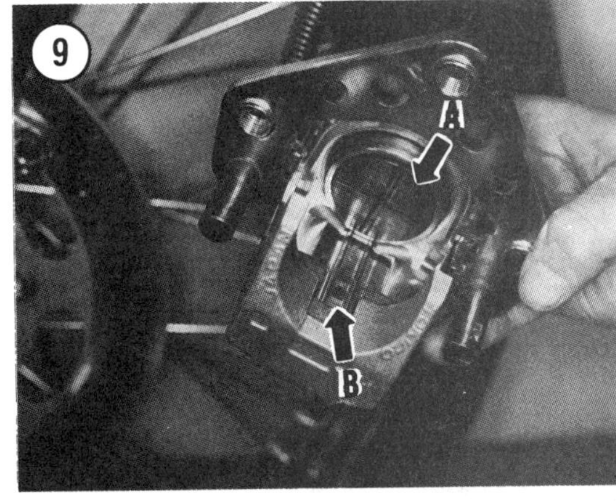

d. As you press the piston(s), constantly check the reservoir to make sure brake fluid does not overflow. Remove excess brake fluid, if necessary, before it overflows.

e. The piston(s) should move freely. If it does not, the caliper should be removed and serviced as described in this chapter.

9. Push in the caliper piston(s) until it bottoms in the cylinder(s) to allow room for the new pads.

10. Make sure the antirattle spring (B, **Figure 9**) is still in place in the caliper.

11. Install the outboard pad (A, **Figure 10**) into the caliper. Push it all the way down until it stops.

12. Push the posts on the caliper bracket (B, **Figure 10**) against the piston portion of the caliper to allow room for installation of the inboard pad.

12A. On VN800 models, install the inboard pad by performing the following:

a. Fit one hole of the inboard pad over the post on the caliper bracket (**Figure 11**).

b. Rotate the pad into the caliper until the pad rests on the other bracket post. (**Figure 12**).

c. Press the caliper bracket toward the piston portion of the caliper until the brake pad falls into place in the caliper.

d. Release the caliper bracket (A, **Figure 13**). Make sure the bracket posts (B, **Figure 13**) engage both holes on the inboard pad.

13B. On VN800 Classic models, install the inboard pad by performing the following:

a. Fit the hole in the pad over the bracket post, and rotate the pad until it is seated in the caliper.

b. Install the pad pin into the caliper. Be sure the pin passes through both pads, and that it is completely seated in the caliper.

c. Install the clip in the pad pin.

14. Hold the brake pads in position and install the caliper onto the brake disc, being careful not to damage the leading edge of the new pads on the disc.

15. Install the caliper mounting bolts (A, **Figure 4**), and torque them to the specification listed in **Table 1**.

16. Spin the front wheel and activate the front brake lever as many times as it takes to refill the cylinders in the caliper and correctly locate the brake pads.

WARNING

Use brake fluid clearly marked DOT 4 from a sealed container. Other types may cause brake failure. Always use the same brand name, because some brands are not compatible. Do not use silicone based (DOT 5) brake fluid. It can cause brake component damage leading to brake system failure.

17. Refill the master cylinder reservoir, if necessary. Be sure the fluid level in the viewing port is above

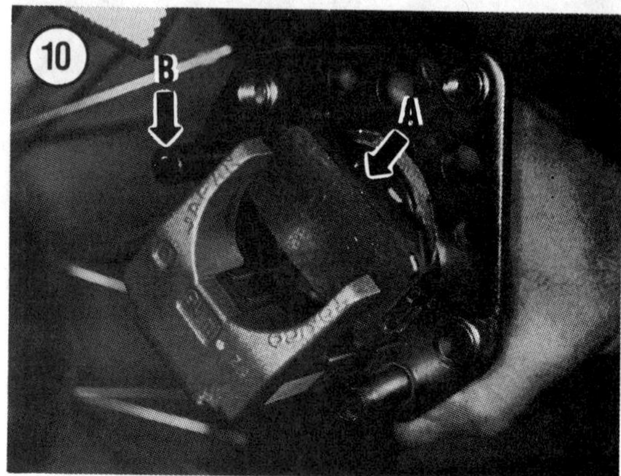

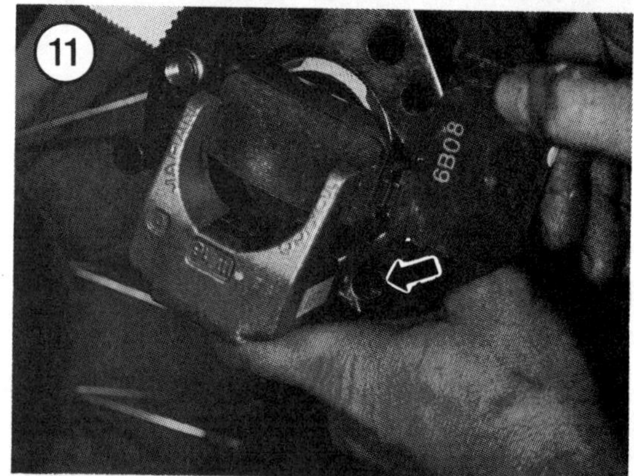

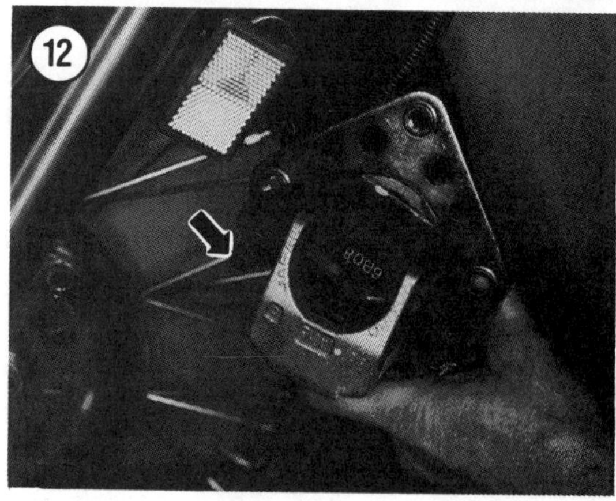

the lower line on the master cylinder (**Figure 14**). Install the diaphragm (A, **Figure 8**) and cover. Tighten the screws securely (**Figure 7**).

WARNING
Do not ride the motorcycle until you are sure the brakes are operating correctly with full hydraulic advantage. If necessary, bleed the brake as described in this chapter.

18. Bed the pads in gradually for the first 10 days of riding by using only light pressure as much as possible. Immediate hard application will glaze the new friction pads and greatly reduce the effectiveness of the brake.

FRONT BRAKE CALIPER

The following shows the procedures for removing, inspecting, rebuilding and installing the front brake caliper on VN800 models. The procedure is similar for VN800 Classic models except for minor differences, which are noted.

Removal

Refer to **Figure 2** for VN800 models and **Figure 3** for VN800 Classic models.

It is not necessary to remove the front wheel in order to remove the caliper assembly.

CAUTION
Do not spill brake fluid on the front fork or front wheel. Wash off any spilled brake fluid immediately, as it will destroy the finish. Use soapy water and rinse completely.

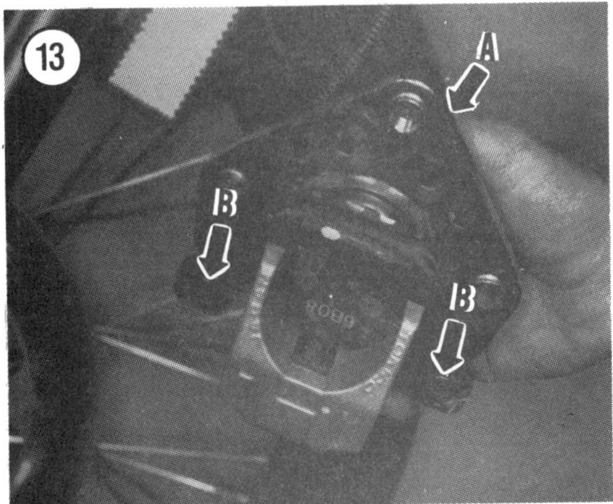

1. Use a scissors jack or jack stands to securely support the bike on level ground.
2. Clean all dirt and foreign matter from the top of the master cylinder.
3. Loosen the screws (**Figure 7**) securing the master cylinder cover. Slightly loosen the cover and the diaphragm. This will allow air to enter the reservoir so the brake fluid will drain more quickly in the next step.

NOTE
By performing Step 4, compressed air may not be necessary for piston removal during caliper disassembly.

4. If the caliper assembly is going to be disassembled for service, perform the following:
   a. Loosen and then remove the bolts (A, **Figure 4**) securing the brake caliper assembly to the front fork.
   b. Remove the caliper, and remove the brake pads as described in this chapter.
   c. Slowly apply the brake lever to push the piston (pistons on VN800 Classic models) part way out of the caliper assembly for ease of removal during caliper service.
5. Place a small drain under the caliper to catch the expelled brake fluid.
6. Loosen the union bolt (C, **Figure 4**) securing the brake hose to the caliper assembly.
7. Remove the union bolt, brake hose and sealing washers from the brake hose adapter nut, then let the brake fluid drain from the brake hose into the container. Dispose of this brake fluid—never reuse brake fluid.
8. If Step 4 was not performed, loosen and then remove the bolts (A, **Figure 4**) securing the brake caliper assembly to the front fork.
9. Remove the caliper assembly from the brake disc.
10. Place the loose end of the brake hose in a reclosable plastic bag to prevent brake fluid from dribbling out.

Installation

1. If removed, install the brake pads into the caliper as described in this chapter.

2. Carefully install the caliper assembly onto the disc being careful not to damage the leading edge of the brake pads.
3. Install the bolts (A, **Figure 4**) securing the brake caliper assembly to the front fork. Torque the bolts to the specification listed in **Table 1**.
4. Install the brake hose, with a *new* sealing washer on each side of the fitting, onto the caliper.
5. Install the union bolt through the sealing washers and fitting. Correctly position the brake hose onto the caliper, and tighten the union bolt (C, **Figure 4**) to the torque specification listed in **Table 1**.
6. Remove the master cylinder top cover and diaphragm.

WARNING
Use brake fluid clearly marked DOT 4 from a sealed container. Other types may cause brake failure. Always use the same brand name, because some brands are not compatible. Do not use silicone-based (DOT 5) brake fluid as it can cause brake component damage leading to brake system failure.

7. Refill the master cylinder reservoir, if necessary. Be sure the fluid level in the viewing port is above the lower line on the master cylinder (**Figure 14**). Install the diaphragm (**Figure 8**) and cover. Do not tighten the screws (**Figure 7**) and this time.
8. Bleed the brakes as described in this chapter.

WARNING
Do not ride the motorcycle until you are sure that the brakes are operating properly.

Front Caliper Rebuilding

NOTE
The following shows the procedure for rebuilding the single-piston front caliper used on VN800 models. VN800 Classic models, however, use a dual-piston caliper. When rebuilding the caliper for a VN800 Classic, perform the indicated services on both pistons and both cylinders in the caliper.

Refer to **Figure 2** for VN800 models and **Figure 3** for VN800 Classic models.
1. Remove the caliper and brake pads as described in this chapter.

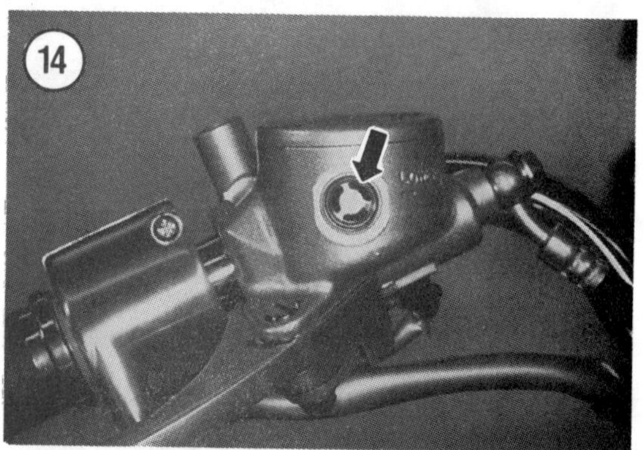
14

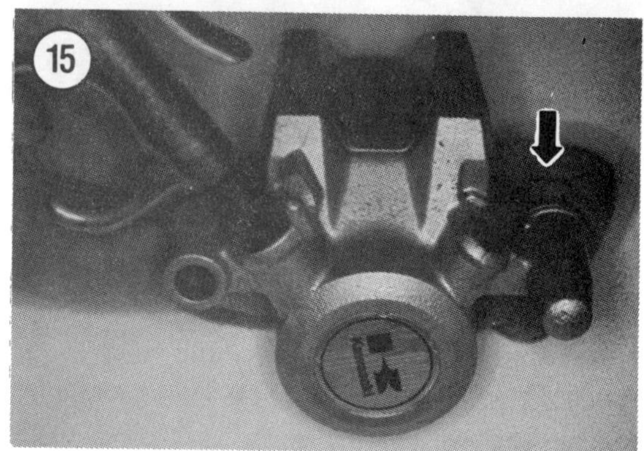
15

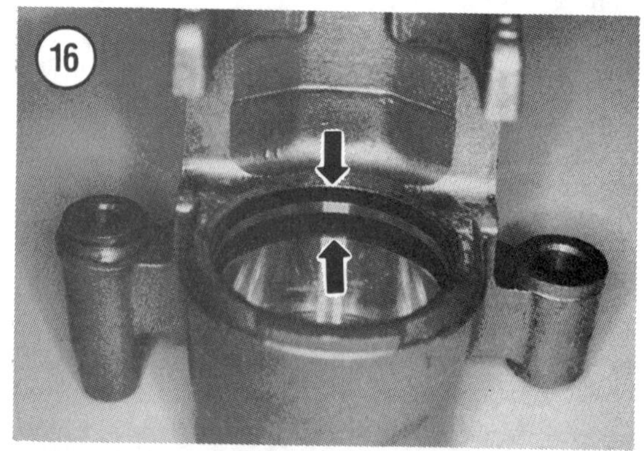
16

17

2. Remove the caliper bracket from the caliper body.

NOTE
If the piston(s) was partially forced out of the caliper body during removal, Steps 3-5 may not be necessary. If the piston or caliper bore is corroded or very dirty, compressed air may be necessary to remove the piston completely.

18

19

20

3. Place a shop cloth (**Figure 15**) or piece of soft wood over the end of the piston(s).
4. Perform this step close to a workbench top. Hold the caliper body with the piston(s) facing away from you.

WARNING
In the next step, the piston(s) may shoot out of the caliper body like a bullet. Keep your fingers out of the way. Wear shop gloves and apply air pressure gradually. Do not use high pressure air or place the air hose nozzle directly against the hydraulic line fitting inlet in the caliper body. Hold the air nozzle away from the inlet allowing some of the air to escape.

5. Apply the air pressure in short spurts to the hydraulic fluid passageway or brake hose inlet (**Figure 15**) and force the piston(s) out.

CAUTION
In the following step, do not use a sharp tool to remove the dust and piston seals from the caliper cylinder(s). Do not damage the cylinder surface.

6. Use a piece of plastic or wood and carefully push the piston and dust seals (**Figure 16**) out of their grooves.
7. Inspect the caliper as described in this chapter.

NOTE
Never reuse the old dust seals or piston seals. Very minor damage or deterioration can make the seals useless.

8. Coat the new dust seal and piston seal with fresh DOT 4 brake fluid.
9. Carefully install the new piston seal (**Figure 17**), then the dust seal (**Figure 18**) into their grooves in the caliper cylinder(s). Make sure the seals are properly seated in their respective grooves (**Figure 16**).
10. Coat the piston(s), seals and caliper cylinder(s) with fresh DOT 4 brake fluid. This will make piston installation easier.
11. Position the piston(s) with its machined side (**Figure 19**) going in first and install the piston(s) into the caliper cylinder(s) (**Figure 20**). Push the piston in until it bottoms.

12. Make sure the rubber boots (A, **Figure 21**) are installed on the caliper bracket.

13. Apply a thin coat of silicone grease to the caliper bracket posts (B, **Figure 21**).

14. Install the caliper bracket (A, **Figure 22**) onto the caliper body (B, **Figure 22**). Push the bracket into the caliper until it bottoms.

15. If removed, install the antirattle spring (**Figure 23**) into the caliper.

16. Install the brake pads and caliper as described in this chapter.

Front Caliper Inspection

NOTE
The following shows the procedure for inspecting the single-piston front caliper used VN800 models. VN800 Classic models, however, use a dual-piston caliper. When inspecting the caliper for a VN800 Classic, inspect both pistons and both cylinders in the caliper.

23

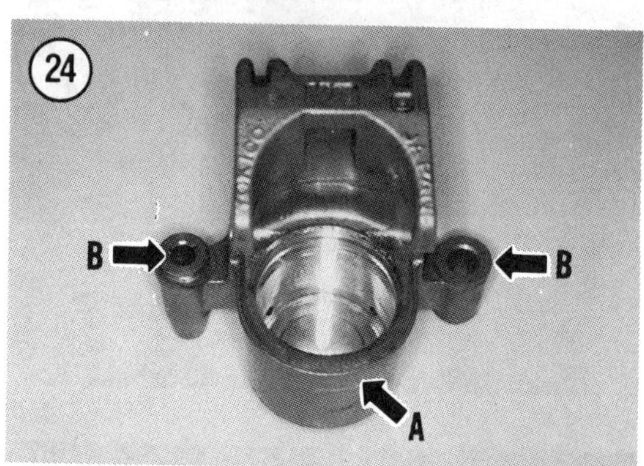

24

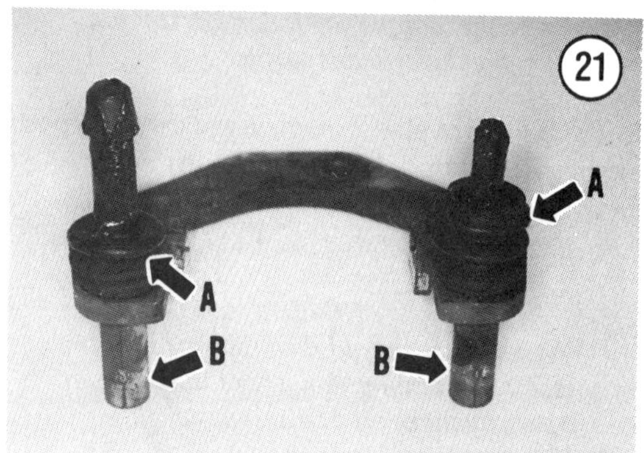

21

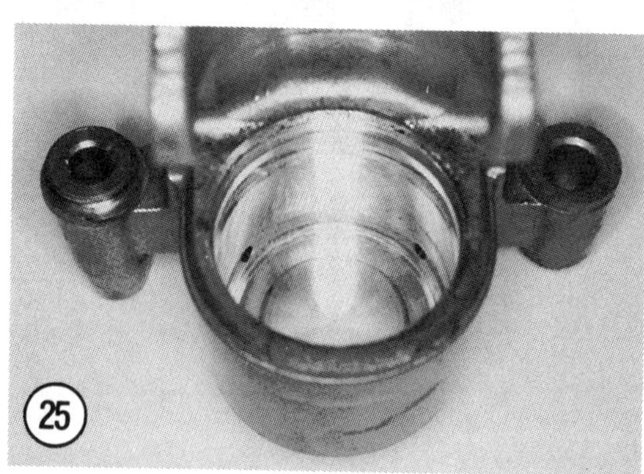
25

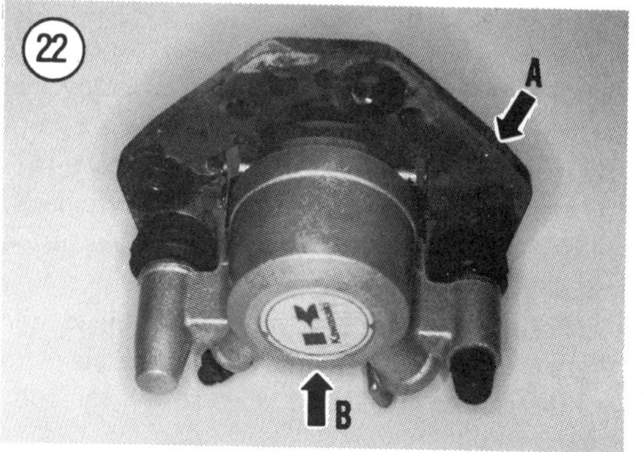

22

26

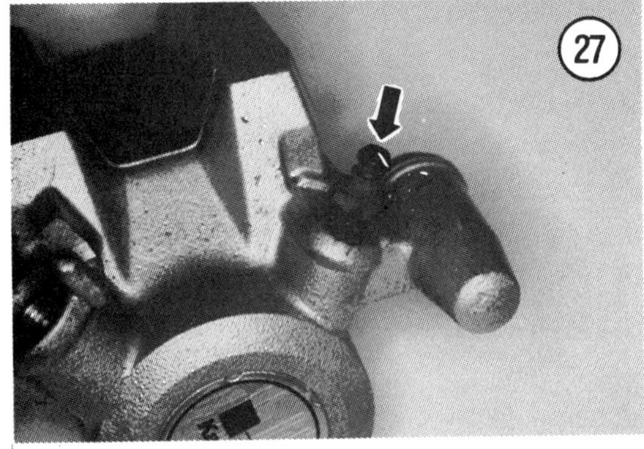

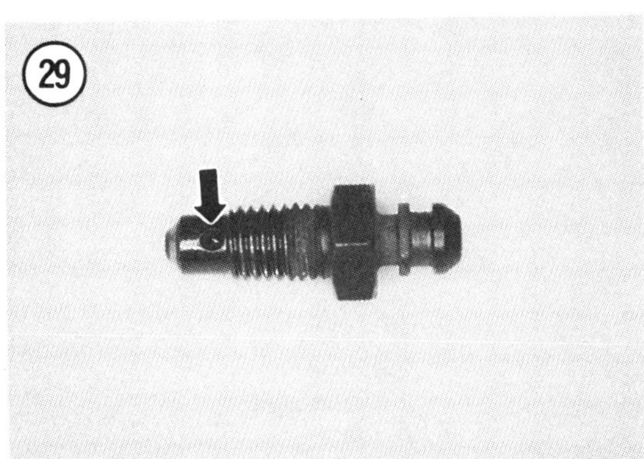

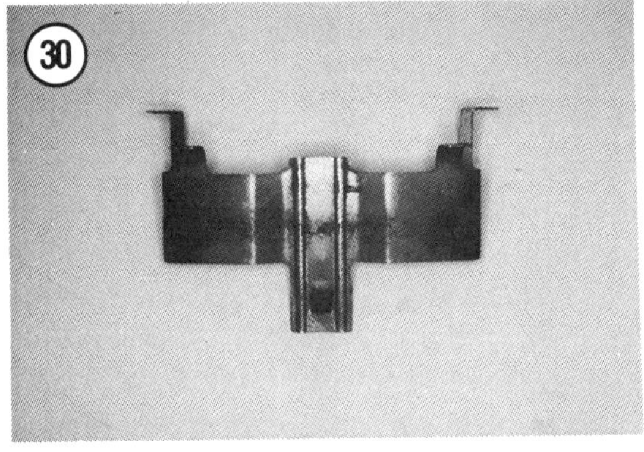

1. Inspect the piston and dust seal grooves in the caliper body for damage. If damaged or corroded, replace the caliper assembly.
2. Inspect the caliper body (A, **Figure 24**) for cracks or damage. Check mounting bolt holes (B, **Figure 24**). If worn or damaged, replace the caliper assembly.
3. Inspect the hydraulic fluid passageway (A, **Figure 25**) in the base of the piston bore. It must be clean and open. Apply compressed air to the opening and make sure it is clear. Clean out the passageway with fresh brake fluid if necessary.
4. Inspect the cylinder wall (B, **Figure 25**) and the piston(s) (**Figure 26**) for scratches, scoring or other damage. If either is rusty or corroded, replace either the piston or the caliper assembly.
5. Remove the bleed valve (**Figure 27**).
6. Inspect the threaded holes in the body for the bleed valve (A, **Figure 28**) and for the hydraulic line (B, **Figure 28**) for wear or damage. Clean out with an appropriate size metric tap and flush with solvent.
7. Inspect the bleed valve. The hole (**Figure 29**) must be clean and open. Apply compressed air to the opening and make sure it is clear. Clean out the hole with fresh brake fluid if necessary.

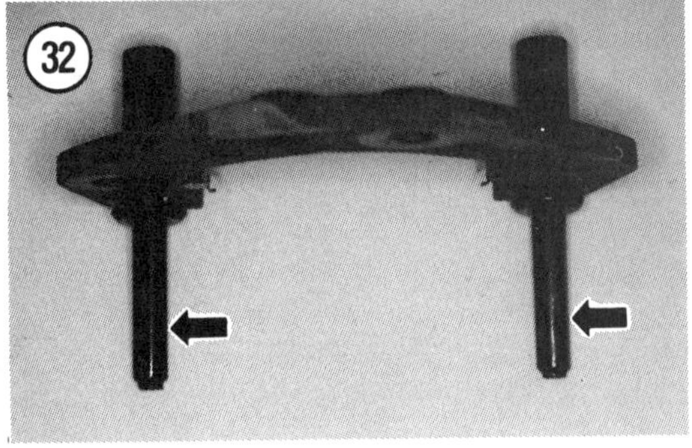

8. Inspect the antirattle spring (**Figure 30**) for wear or damage. Replace it if necessary.
9. If serviceable, clean the caliper body and piston(s) with fresh hydraulic brake fluid or isopropyl alcohol. Rinse them with fresh hydraulic brake fluid.
10. Inspect the caliper bracket (**Figure 31**) for fractures or damage. Replace it if necessary.
11. Inspect the caliper bracket posts (**Figure 32**) for burrs, wear or damage. Clean off any burrs or replace the bracket if necessary.

NOTE
Only one pad stopper spring is used in VN800 Classic models; two are used in VN800 models.

12. Make sure the pad stopper springs (**Figure 33**) are in good condition and stay in place on the caliper bracket. If they are loose, replace the springs.
13. Inspect the rubber boots (**Figure 34**) for wear, deterioration or tears. Replace both boots if either is damaged.

FRONT MASTER CYLINDER

Removal/Installation

CAUTION
Cover the surrounding areas with a heavy cloth or plastic tarp to protect them from accidental brake fluid spills. Wash brake fluid from any painted or plated surfaces or plastic parts immediately, as it will destroy the finish. Use soapy water and rinse completely.

Refer to **Figure 35** for this procedure
1. Unscrew the rear view mirror (A, **Figure 36**) from the master cylinder.

33

34

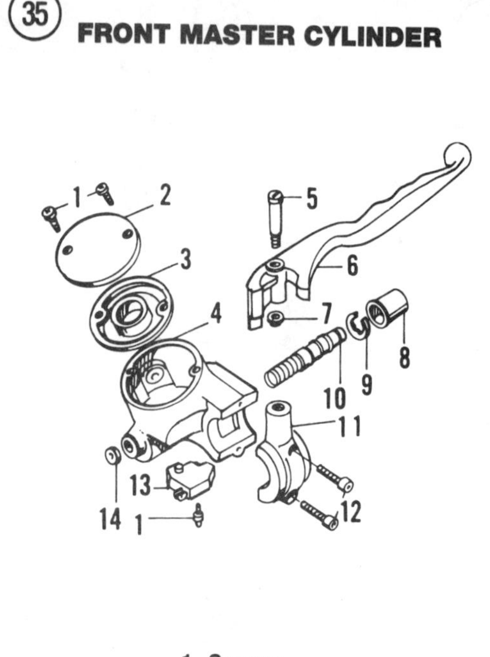

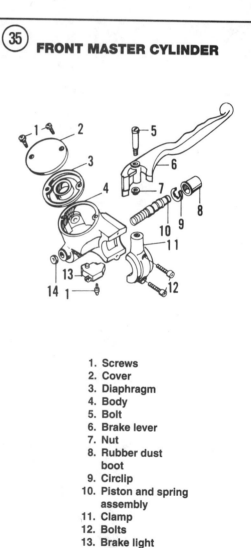

35
FRONT MASTER CYLINDER

1. Screws
2. Cover
3. Diaphragm
4. Body
5. Bolt
6. Brake lever
7. Nut
8. Rubber dust boot
9. Circlip
10. Piston and spring assembly
11. Clamp
12. Bolts
13. Brake light switch
14. Sealing washer

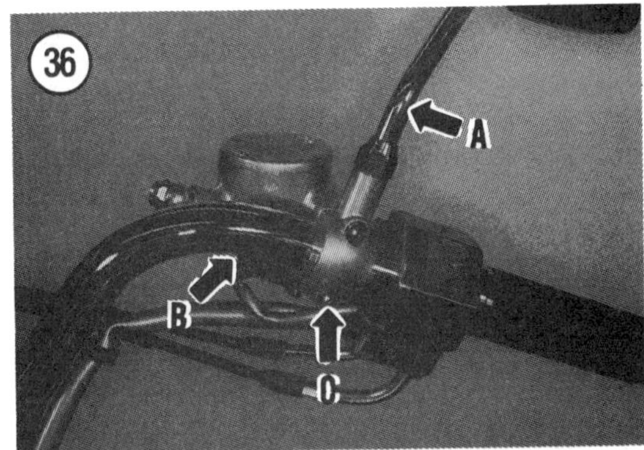

2. Disconnect the brake light switch electrical connector (B, **Figure 36**) from the brake switch.
3. Clean the top of the master cylinder of all dirt and foreign matter.
4. Remove the screws (**Figure 37**) securing the cover. Remove the cover and the diaphragm (A, **Figure 38**).

WARNING

*If a cooking baster is used for this purpose, do **not** reuse it for cooking purposes due to brake fluid residue within it.*

5. If you have a shop syringe or a cooking baster, draw all of the brake fluid out of the master cylinder reservoir.
6. Place a shop cloth under the union bolt to catch any spilled brake fluid that leaks out.
7. Unscrew the union bolt (B, **Figure 38**) securing the brake hose to the master cylinder. Do not lose the sealing washer from each side of the hose fitting.
8. Tie the loose end of the hose to the handlebar. Cover the loose end of the hose with a plastic bag to keep out moisture and foreign matter.
9. Remove the clamping bolts (C, **Figure 36**) that secure the master cylinder to the handlebar, remove the master cylinder.
10. Install by reversing these removal steps while noting the following:
   a. Position the clamp with its small projection facing toward the throttle grip.
   b. Apply grease to the end of each master cylinder clamp bolt.
   c. Install the master cylinder, clamp and bolts. Tighten the bolts to the torque specification listed in **Table 1**. Tighten the upper bolt first and then the lower bolt. There should be a gap at the bottom of the clamp after the bolts are torqued.
   d. Place a *new* sealing washer on each side of the brake hose fitting (**Figure 39**) and install the union bolt.
   e. Tighten the union bolt to the torque specification listed in **Table 1**.
   f. Bleed the system as described in this chapter.

Disassembly

Refer to **Figure 35** for this procedure:

1. Remove the master cylinder as described in this chapter.
2. If still in place, remove the cover (**Figure 40**) and diaphragm (**Figure 41**) from the master cylinder.
3. Remove the nut and pivot bolt (A, **Figure 42**), and remove the hand lever (B, **Figure 42**) from the master cylinder.
4. Remove the rubber dust boot (**Figure 43**) from the piston housing in the master cylinder.
5. Use circlip pliers to remove the internal circlip (**Figure 44**) from the piston housing.
6. Remove the piston assembly and the spring (**Figure 45**) from the piston housing.
7. If necessary, remove the screw securing the brake light switch to the master cylinder and remove the switch assembly (**Figure 46**).

Inspection

1. Clean all parts in fresh hydraulic brake fluid, isopropyl alcohol or ethyl alcohol.
2. Inspect the cylinder bore (**Figure 47**) surface for wear and damage. If less than perfect, replace the

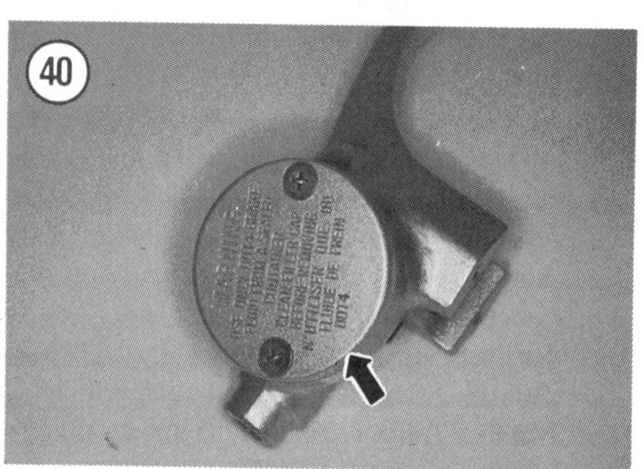

40

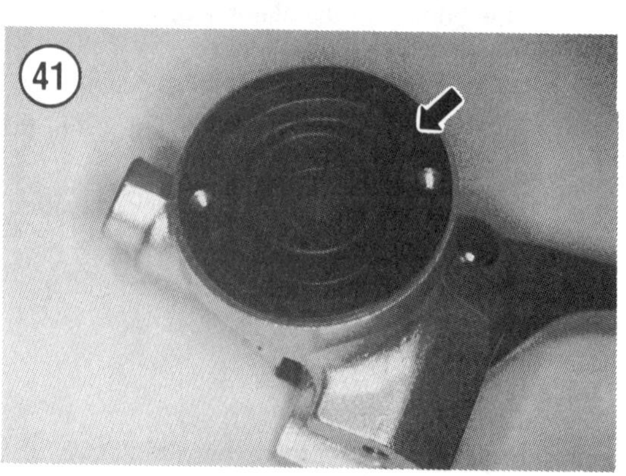

41

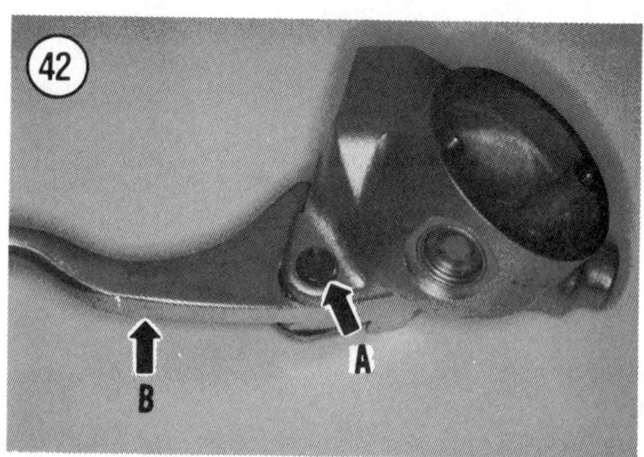

42

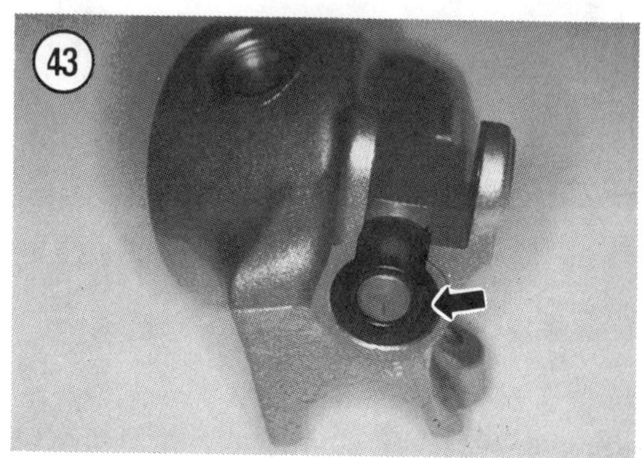

43

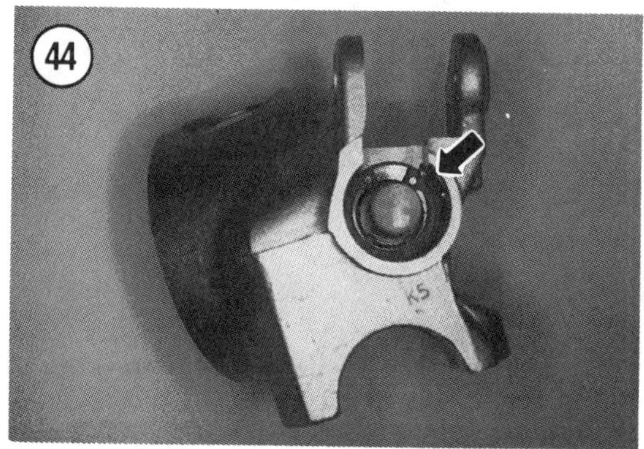

44

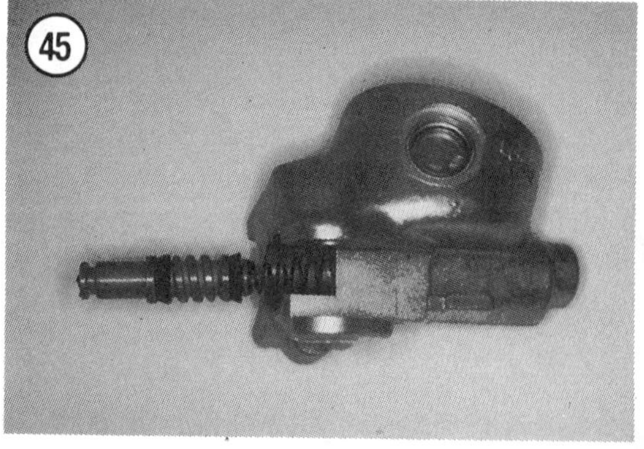

45

46

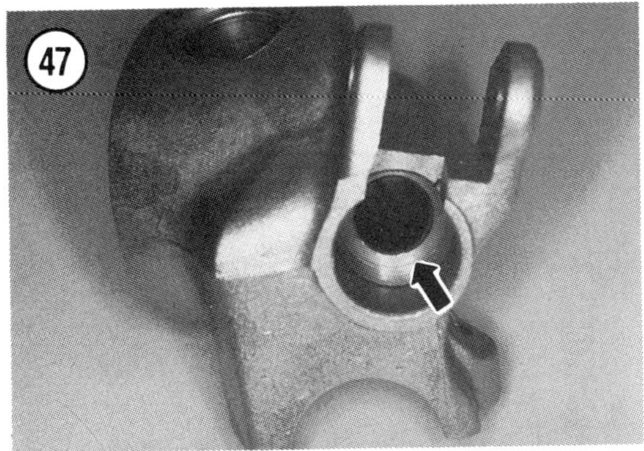

47

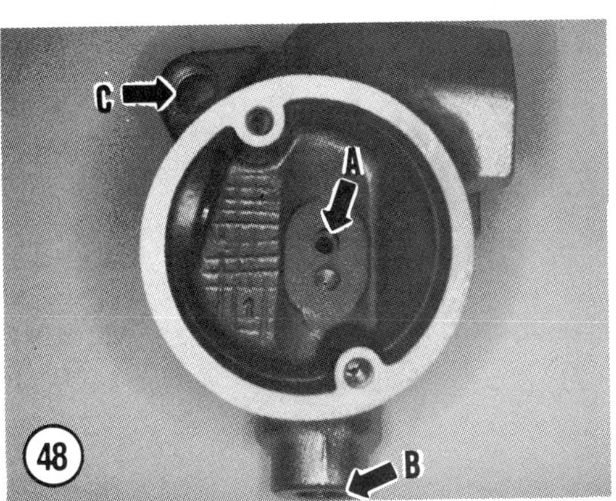

48

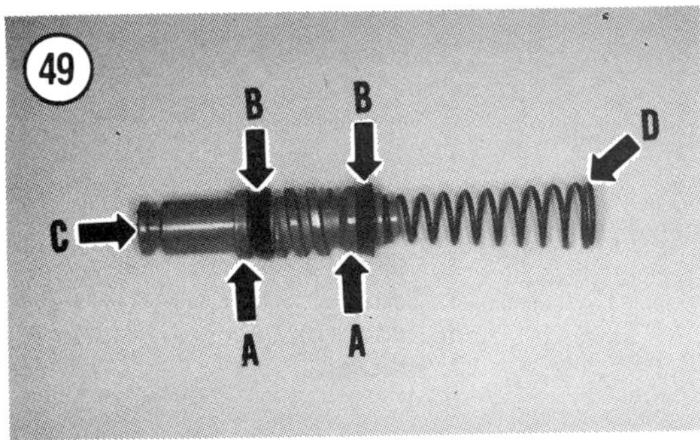

49

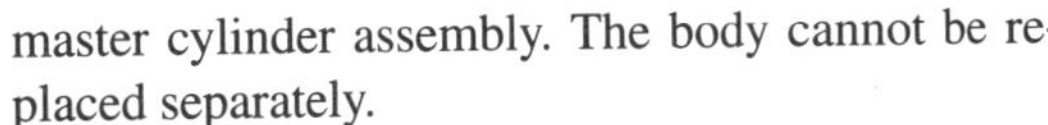
master cylinder assembly. The body cannot be replaced separately.

3. Make sure the ports (A, **Figure 48**) in the bottom of the master cylinder body are clear.
4. Inspect the threads for the union bolt (B, **Figure 48**) in the body. If worn or damaged, repair with a suitable size metric thread tap or replace the master cylinder assembly.
5. Check the hand lever pivot lugs (C, **Figure 48**) on the master cylinder body for cracks or elongation. If damaged, replace the master cylinder assembly.
6. Inspect the hand lever pivot area for fluid leakage. If any leakage is noted, replace the piston assembly.
7. Inspect the piston contact surfaces (A, **Figure 49**) for wear and damage. If less than perfect, replace the piston assembly.
8. Inspect the piston cups (B, **Figure 49**) for wear or damage. Cups are not available separately. If either is worn, replace the piston assembly.
9. Check the end of the piston (C, **Figure 49**) for wear caused by the hand lever. If worn, replace the piston assembly.
10. Check the piston spring (D, **Figure 49**) for wear or damage. If damaged, replace the piston assembly.

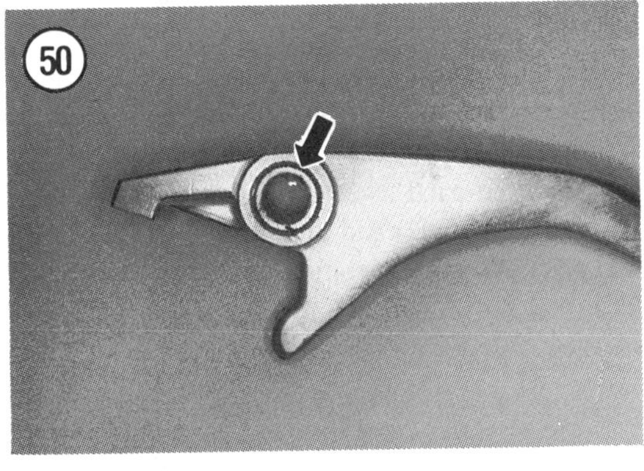

50

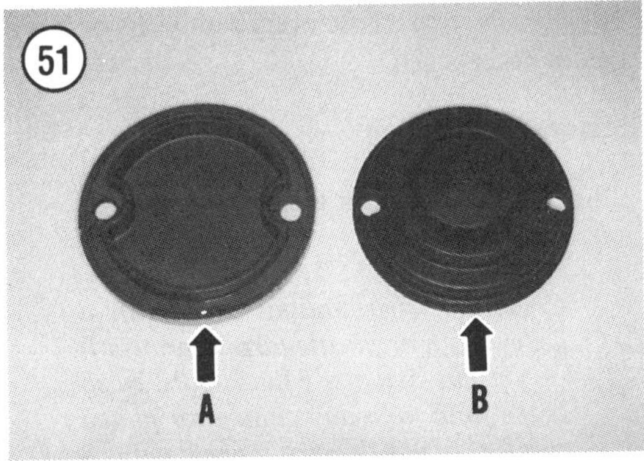

51

11. Inspect the pivot hole (**Figure 50**) in the hand lever. If worn or elongated, the lever must be replaced.
12. Inspect the cover (A, **Figure 51**) and the diaphragm (B, **Figure 51**) for wear or deterioration, replace if necessary.

Assembly

1. Soak the piston assembly and new cups in fresh brake fluid. Coat the inside of the cylinder bore with fresh brake fluid.

CAUTION
When installing the piston assembly, do not allow the cups to turn inside out. This will damage the cups and result in fluid leakage within the cylinder bore.

2. Be sure the tapered end of the spring faces toward the primary cup, and install the piston assembly into the housing in the master cylinder. (**Figure 45**).
3. Using circlip pliers, install the circlip into the body (**Figure 44**). Make sure it seats correctly in the groove in the body.
4. Install the rubber dust boot (**Figure 43**) over the end of the piston. Make sure the boot is seated correctly.
5. If removed, install the brake light switch (**Figure 46**) and screw to the master cylinder. Torque the screw to the specification listed in **Table 1**.
6. Install the hand lever (B, **Figure 42**), the pivot bolt (A, **Figure 42**) and nut. Torque the pivot bolt and pivot nut to the specifications listed in **Table 1**.
7. Install the master cylinder as described in this chapter.

FRONT BRAKE HOSE REPLACEMENT

Replace the brake hose every four years or if it is cracked or damaged.

Removal/Installation

Refer to **Figure 52** for this procedure.

CAUTION
Cover the surrounding area with a heavy cloth or plastic tarp to protect it from accidental brake fluid spills. Wash brake fluid from any painted or plated surfaces or plastic parts immediately, as

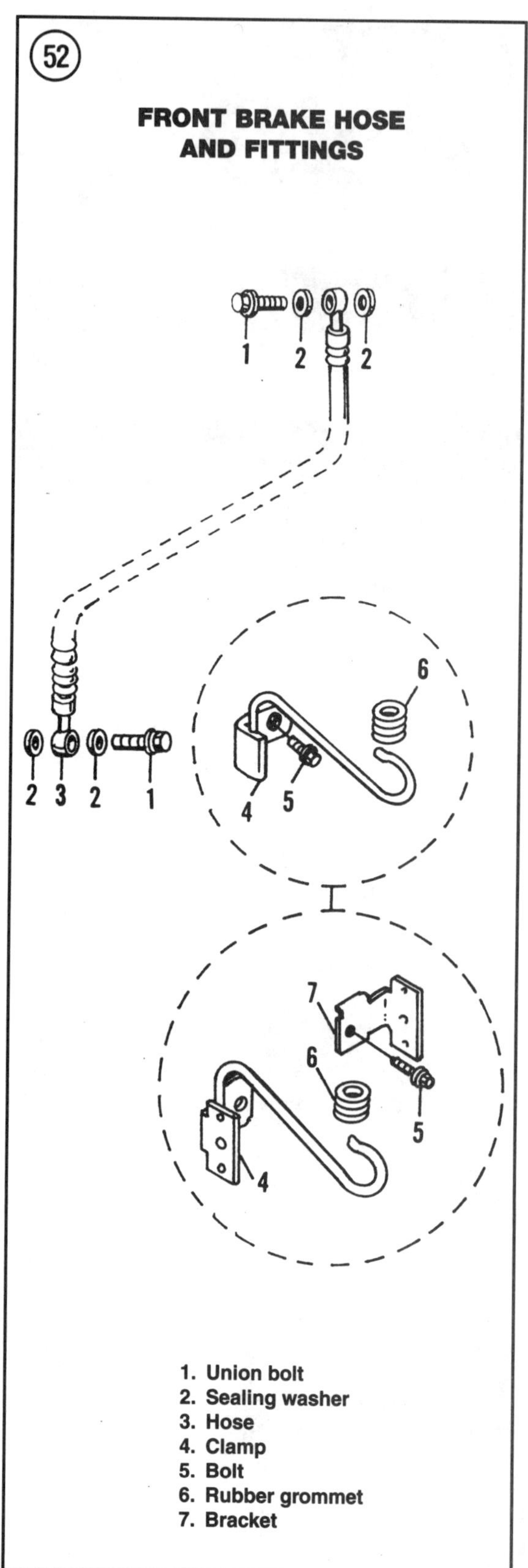

1. Union bolt
2. Sealing washer
3. Hose
4. Clamp
5. Bolt
6. Rubber grommet
7. Bracket

it will destroy the finish. Use soapy water and rinse completely.

1. Remove the caps from the bleed valve (A, **Figure 53**) on the front caliper.
2. Attach a piece of hose to the bleed screw and place the loose end in a container.
3. Open both bleed screw and operate the brake lever to pump the brake fluid from the master cylinder, the brake hose and the caliper assembly. Operate the lever until the system is clear of brake fluid.
4. Clean all dirt and foreign matter from the top of the master cylinder.
5. Remove the screws securing the master cylinder cover (**Figure 37**). Remove the cover and the diaphragm (A, **Figure 38**).

WARNING
*If a cooking baster is used for this purpose, do **not** reuse it for cooking purposes due to brake fluid residue within it.*

6. If you have a shop syringe or a cooking baster, draw any residual brake fluid from the master cylinder reservoir.
7. Unscrew the union bolt (B, **Figure 38**) securing the brake hose to the master cylinder. Do not lose the sealing washer on each side of the hose fitting.
8. Remove the union bolt and sealing washers (B, **Figure 53**) securing the lower hose to the brake calipers.
9. Remove the brake hose and allow residual brake fluid to drain into the container used in Step 2. Dispose of this brake fluid—never reuse brake fluid.
10. Unhook the brake hose from the clamps on the front fender and lower fork bridge. Remove the hose. Note how the hose is routed along the handlebars and through the fork bridge so you can route the new hose in the same location.
11. Install the new hose, sealing washers and union bolts in the reverse order of removal while noting the following:
    a. Be sure to install new sealing washers (**Figure 39**) in their correct positions on each side of the brake hose fittings.
    b. Tighten the union bolts to the torque specifications listed in **Table 1**.
    c. Bleed the brake system as described in this chapter.

FRONT BRAKE DISC

Removal/Installation

1. Remove the front wheel as described in Chapter Eleven.

NOTE
Place a piece of wood or vinyl tube in the caliper in place of the disc. Then if the brake lever is inadvertently squeezed, the piston(s) will not be forced out of the cylinder(s). If this does happen, the caliper must be disassembled to reseat the piston(s), and the system will have to be bled.

CAUTION
Always set the wheel down with the disc surface facing up. Do not set the wheel down on the disc surface, as it may get scratched or warped. If necessary, set the wheel on two blocks of wood.

2. Remove the bolts (**Figure 54**) securing the brake disc to the hub and remove the disc.

3. Install by reversing these removal steps while noting the following:
   a. Install the disc so the side with the wear limit stamping (**Figure 55**) faces up.
   b. Apply Loctite 242 to the disc mounting bolts prior to installation.
   c. Tighten the disc mounting bolts to the torque specifications listed in **Table 1**.

Inspection

It is not necessary to remove the disc from the wheel to inspect it. Small marks on the disc are not important, but radial scratches deep enough to snag a fingernail are. These can reduce braking effectiveness and increase brake pad wear. If these grooves are found, the disc should be replaced.

NOTE
*If the minimum thickness specification in **Table 2** differs from the minimum thickness stamped into the disc (A, **Figure 55**), reference the specification stamped into the disc.*

1. Measure the thickness of the disc at several locations around the disc with a micrometer (**Figure 56**). The disc must be replaced if the thickness in any area is less than the wear limit listed in **Table 2**.
2. Check disc runout by performing the following:
   a. Make sure the disc bolts are tight prior to running this check.
   b. Use a scissors jack or jack stands to securely support the bike with the front wheel off the ground.
   c. Check the disc runout with a dial indicator as shown in **Figure 57**. Rotate the wheel slowly, and watch the dial indicator. If the runout exceeds the specification listed in **Table 2**, the disc must be replaced.
3. Clean the disc (**Figure 55**) of any rust or corrosion and wipe clean with lacquer thinner. Never use an oil-based solvent that may leave an oil residue on the disc.

BLEEDING THE SYSTEM

Bleeding the system is not necessary unless the brakes feel spongy, there has been a leak in the system, a component has been replaced or the brake fluid has been replaced.

Bleeding the Master Cylinder

If *only* the master cylinder was removed for service, bleed the master cylinder by perform the following:

1. Fill the master cylinder reservoir with fresh brake fluid.

2. Pump the brake lever to expel air from the system.

3. Install the diaphragm (A, **Figure 38**) and master cylinder cover. Tighten the cover screws (**Figure 37**) securely.

4. Loosen the clamp bolts, and rotate the master cylinder so brake hose fitting is below the master cylinder as shown in **Figure 58**.

5. If necessary, add fluid to correct the fluid level in the reservoir.

55

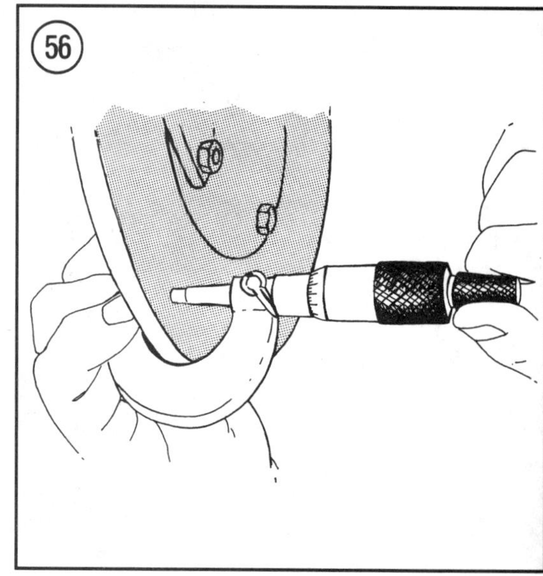
56

Bleeding the Entire System

1. Remove the dust cap from the bleed valve (A, **Figure 53**) on the caliper assembly.
2. Connect a piece of clear tubing to the bleed valve.
3. Place the other end of the tube into a clean container.
4. Fill the container with enough fresh brake fluid to keep the end of the tube submerged.

CAUTION
Cover the wheel with a heavy cloth or plastic tarp to protect it from the accidental spilling of brake fluid. Wash any brake fluid from any plastic, painted or plated surface immediately, as it will destroy the finish. Use soapy water and rinse completely.

5. Clean all dirt and foreign matter from the top cover of the master cylinder.

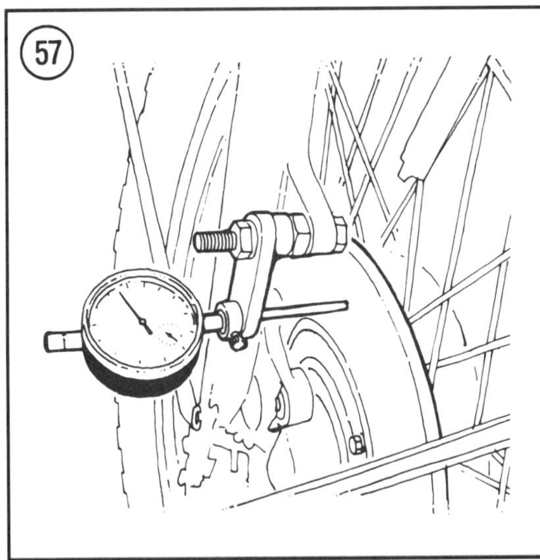

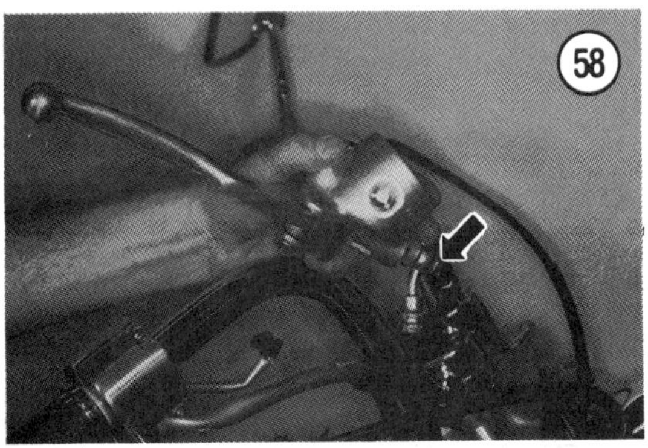

6. Remove the screws securing the cover (**Figure 37**). Remove the cover and the diaphragm (A, **Figure 38**).
7. Fill the reservoir almost to the top lip. Loosely fit the diaphragm and cover onto the master cylinder. Leave them in place during this procedure to prevent the entry of dirt.

WARNING
Use brake fluid from a sealed container marked DOT 4 only (specified for disc brakes). Other types may cause brake failure. Do not intermix different brands or types because some may not be compatible. Do not use a silicone based (DOT 5) brake fluid as it can cause brake component damage leading to brake system failure.

NOTE
During this procedure, it is very important to check the fluid level in the brake master cylinder reservoir often. If the reservoir runs dry, you will introduce more air into the system, which will require starting over.

8. Apply the brake lever and open the bleed valve by performing the following:
   a. Slowly pump the brake lever until it feels hard.
   b. Pull the brake lever and hold it in the applied position.
   c. Open the bleed valve on the caliper about one-half turn, and fully depress the brake lever. Watch the fluid emerging from the tube.
   d. When the brake lever is fully depressed, hold the lever against the throttle grip and tighten the bleed valve.
   e. Release the brake lever.
9. Repeat this procedure until the fluid emerging from the hose is completely free of air.
10. As brake fluid moves through the system, the fluid level will drop in the reservoir. Add brake fluid to the reservoir as necessary to maintain the level above the low-level limit so air will not be drawn into the system.

NOTE
Check the fluid level in the master cylinder frequently during this procedure. Be sure the reservoir does not run dry during the bleeding operation or more air will enter the system. If this occurs,

the entire bleeding process must be repeated.

11. Once all air is bled from the system, hold the brake lever in and tighten the bleed valve. Torque the valve to the specification listed in **Table 1**.

12. Remove the bleed tube, and install the bleed valve dust cap.

13. If necessary, add fluid to correct the fluid level in the reservoir.

14. Install the diaphragm (A, **Figure 38**) and the cover onto the front master cylinder. Tighten the screws (**Figure 37**) securely.

15. Test the feel of the brake lever. It should be firm and should offer the same resistance each time it is operated. If it feels spongy, it is likely that there is still air in the system. When all air is bled from the system and the fluid level is correct in the reservoir, check for leaks and tighten all fittings and connections.

NOTE

If you are having trouble getting all the air out of the system, bleed the system with the reverse flow method as described in this chapter.

WARNING

Before riding the bike, make certain that the brakes are operating correctly. Spin the front wheel and apply the lever several times. The wheel must come to a complete stop each time.

16. Test ride the bike slowly at first to make sure that the brakes are operating properly.

Reverse Flow Bleeding

This bleeding procedure can be used if you are having a difficult time freeing the system of all air.

With this procedure, the brake fluid is forced backward through the system. Brake fluid enters the caliper, flows through the brake hose and emerges in the master cylinder reservoir. If the system is already filled with brake fluid, the existing fluid is flushed out of the top of the master cylinder. Siphon fluid from the reservoir, then hold a shop cloth under the master cylinder reservoir to catch any additional fluid that will be forced out.

A special reverse flow tool called the EZE Bleeder is available or a homemade tool can be fabricated for this procedure.

To make this tool, perform the following:

NOTE

The brake fluid container must be plastic—not metal. Use vinyl tubing with the correct inner diameter to ensure a tight fit on the caliper bleed valve.

a. Purchase a 12 oz. (345 ml) *plastic* bottle of DOT 4 brake fluid.
b. Remove the cap, drill an appropriate size hole in the cap, and adapt a vinyl hose fitting onto the cap.
c. Attach a section of vinyl hose to the hose fitting on the cap, and secure it with a hose clamp. This joint must be a tight fit. You will squeeze the plastic brake fluid bottle and force the brake fluid out past this fitting and through the hose.
d. Remove the moisture seal from the brake fluid bottle, and screw the cap and hose assembly onto the bottle.

1. Clean all dirt and foreign matter from the top cover of the master cylinder.

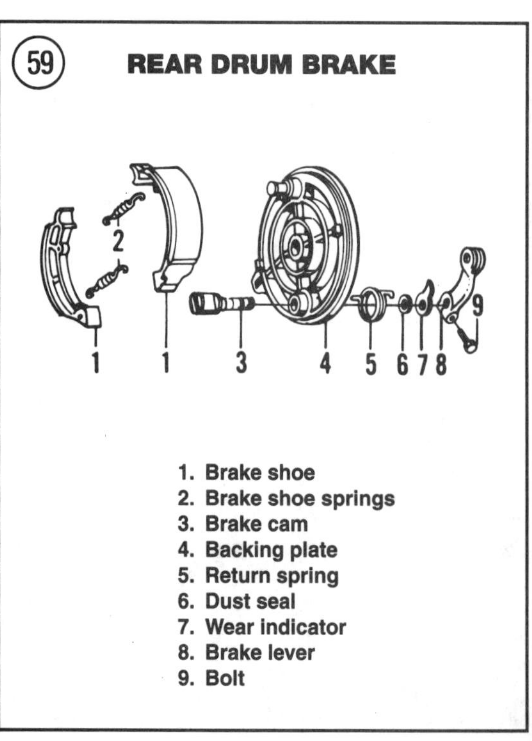

2. Remove the screws securing the cover (**Figure 37**). Remove the cover and the diaphragm (A, **Figure 38**).

3. Remove the dust cap from the bleed valve (A, **Figure 53**) on the caliper assembly.

4. Attach the vinyl hose from the tool onto the bleed valve. Make sure the hose is tight on the bleed valve.

5. Open the bleed valve, and squeeze the plastic bottle forcing this brake fluid into the system.

NOTE

If necessary, siphon brake fluid from the reservoir to avoid overflow of fluid.

6. Observe the brake fluid entering the master cylinder reservoir. Continue to apply pressure from the tool, or bottle, until the fluid entering the reservoir is free of air.

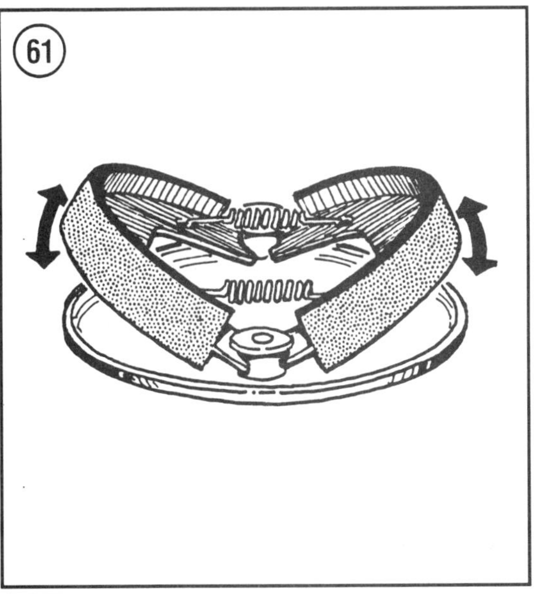

7. Close the bleed valve, and disconnect the bleeder or hose from the caliper bleed valve.

8. Torque the bleed valve to the specification listed in **Table 1**, and install the dust cap onto the caliper bleed valve.

9. At this time the system should be free of air. Apply the brake lever and check for proper brake operation. If the system still feels spongy, perform the typical bleeding procedure described at the beginning of this section.

10. Install the diaphragm (**Figure 38**) and the cover on the front master cylinder. Tighten the screws (**Figure 37**) securely.

REAR DRUM BRAKE

Pushing down on the brake foot pedal pulls the cable/rod assembly which moves the brake arm that in turn rotates the camshaft. The rotating camshaft forces the brake shoes out into contact with the brake drum.

Pedal free play must be maintained to minimize brake drag and premature brake wear and to maximize braking effectiveness. Refer to Chapter Three for the complete drum brake adjustment procedure.

Disassembly

Refer to **Figure 59** for this procedure.

WARNING

*When working on the brake system, do **not** inhale brake dust. It may contain asbestos, which can cause lung injury and cancer. Wear a face mask that meets OSHA requirements for trapping asbestos particles. Always wash your hands and forearms thoroughly after completing the work.*

1. Remove the rear wheel as described in Chapter Twelve.

2. Pull the brake assembly (**Figure 60**) straight up and out of the brake drum.

3. Carefully pull up on both brake shoes in a V-formation (**Figure 61**) and remove the brake shoes and return springs as an assembly.

4. Disconnect the return springs from the brake shoes.

NOTE
*Before removing the brake lever, mark the end of the cam (A, **Figure 62**) in relation to the split on the brake lever. This reference will be used during installation.*

5. If necessary, remove the pinch bolt (B, **Figure 62**) securing the brake lever to the shaft and remove the brake lever, wear indicator and return spring. Withdraw the camshaft from the backing plate and remove the dust seal from the backing plate.

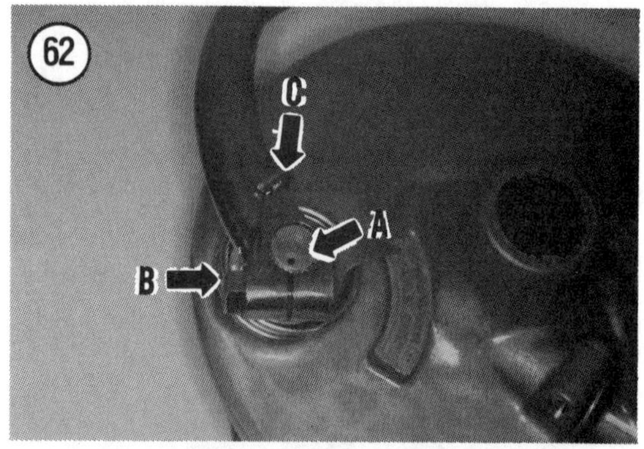

Inspection

1. Thoroughly clean and dry all parts except the brake linings.
2. Check the contact surface of the drum for scoring (**Figure 63**). If there are grooves deep enough to snag your fingernail, the drum should be resurfaced.
3. Measure the inside diameter of the brake drum (**Figure 64**). If the measurement is greater than the service limit listed in **Table 2**, the drum must be replaced.
4. If the drum can be machined and still stay within the maximum diameter, the linings will have to be replaced, and the new ones arced to conform to the new drum contour.
5. Measure the brake lining thickness with a vernier caliper (**Figure 65**). They should be replaced if the lining portion is worn to the service limit. Refer to specifications listed in **Table 2**.
6. Inspect the linings (**Figure 66**) for imbedded foreign material. Dirt can be removed with a stiff wire brush. Check for traces of oil or grease. If the linings are contaminated, they must be replaced.
7. Inspect the brake shoe assemblies (**Figure 67**) for wear, cracks or other damage. Replace the shoes as a set if necessary.
8. Inspect the cam lobe and pivot pins (A, **Figure 68**) for wear or corrosion. Minor roughness can be removed with fine emery cloth.
9. Inspect the backing plate (B, **Figure 68**) for wear, cracks or other damage. Replace if necessary.
10. Inspect the rear axle bushing (C, **Figure 68**) in the backing plate for wear, scoring or other damage. Replace the backing plate if necessary.
11. Inspect the brake shoe return springs (**Figure 69**) for wear. If they are stretched, they will not fully retract the brake shoes. Replace as necessary.

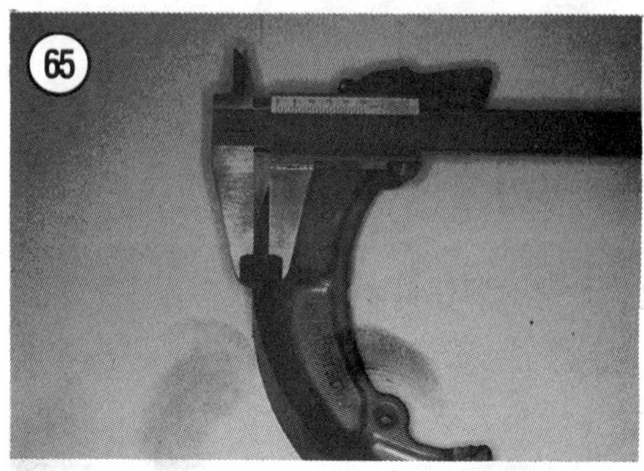

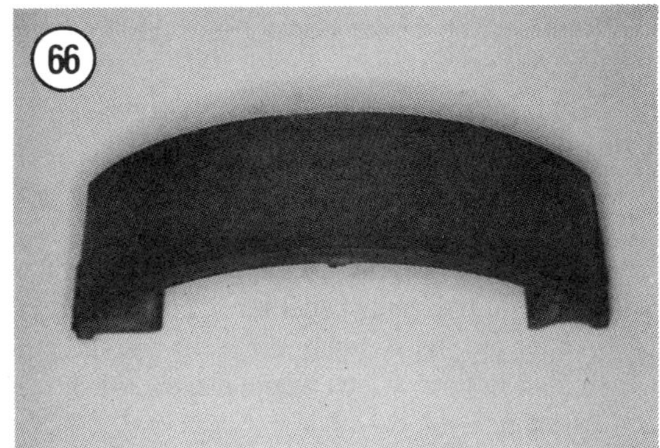

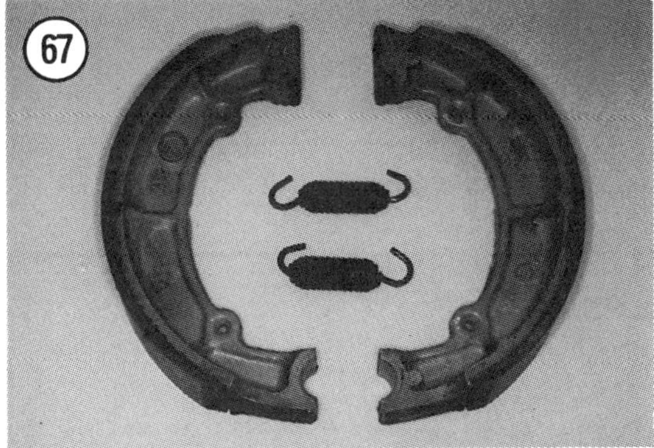

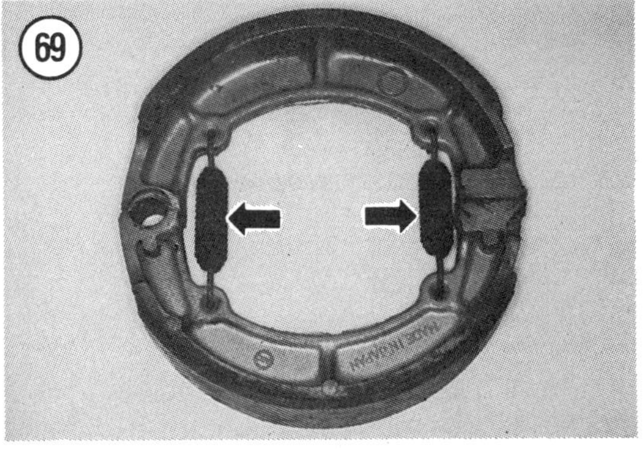

12. Measure the outside diameter of the cam and the inside diameter of the cam hole in the brake panel. Replace any part that is worn to the wear limit.

Assembly

1. If removed, grease the cam with a light coat of molybdenum disulfide grease. Install the cam into the backing plate from the backside with its triangular mark facing toward the center of the brake panel.
2. Install a new dust seal and wear indicator onto the camshaft from the outside of the backing plate.
3. Install the spring and the camshaft.
4. Align the brake lever split with the mark made on the end of the cam (A, **Figure 62**) and install the brake lever.
5. Index the spring onto the brake lever (C, **Figure 62**).
6. Install and securely tighten the brake lever pinch bolt (B, **Figure 62**).
7. Grease the cam and pivot post (A, **Figure 68**) with a light coat of molybdenum disulfide grease; avoid getting any grease on the brake backing plate where the brake linings may come in contact with it.
8. Assemble the return springs onto the brake shoes.
9. Hold the brake shoes in a V formation (**Figure 61**) with the return springs attached and snap them into place on the brake backing plate. Make sure they are firmly seated on it.
10. Install the brake panel assembly into the brake drum.
11. Install the rear wheel as described in Chapter Twelve.
12. Adjust the rear brake as described in Chapter Three.

REAR BRAKE PEDAL

Removal/Installation

Refer to **Figure 70** for this procedure.

1. Use a scissors jack or jack stands to support the bike on level ground.
2. Remove and discard the cotter pin (A, **Figure 71**) from the cleavis pin.
3. Pull the cleavis pin (B, **Figure 71**), and disconnect the brake cable from the brake pedal lever.
4. Remove the brake cable (C, **Figure 71**) from its bracket on the footpeg bracket.

5. Remove the two footpeg mounting bolts (A, **Figure 72**) and lower the footpeg (B, **Figure 72**) from the frame.

6. Loosen the locknut (A, **Figure 73**) on the pedal height adjust bolt and completely back off the adjust bolt (B, **Figure 73**).

7. Disconnect the brake pedal spring (C, **Figure 73**) and the brake switch spring (D, **Figure 73**) from the brake pedal lever.

8. Remove the brake switch (E, **Figure 73**) from its mount on the footpeg bracket.

9. Note the indexing marks (F, **Figure 73**) on the brake pedal lever and on the brake pedal pivot shaft. You must align these marks during assembly. If either mark is faint or difficult to see, use a punch or other suitable tool to enhance the marks.

10. Loosen the brake pedal lever clamp bolt, and remove the brake pedal lever from the pedal shaft.

11. Remove the brake pedal from the footpeg bracket.

12. Install by reversing these removal steps while noting the following:

   a. Apply a light coat of waterproof grease to all pivot areas prior to installation.
   b. Use a new cotter pin when securing the brake cable to the brake pedal lever. Never reuse a cotter pin. Its end may break off and the pin could fall out, which would disable the brake system.
   c. Align the indexing mark on the brake pedal lever with the mark on the brake pedal pivot shaft.
   d. Torque the brake pedal lever clamp bolt to the specification listed in **Table 1**.
   e. Securely tighten the bolts securing the footpeg bracket to the frame.

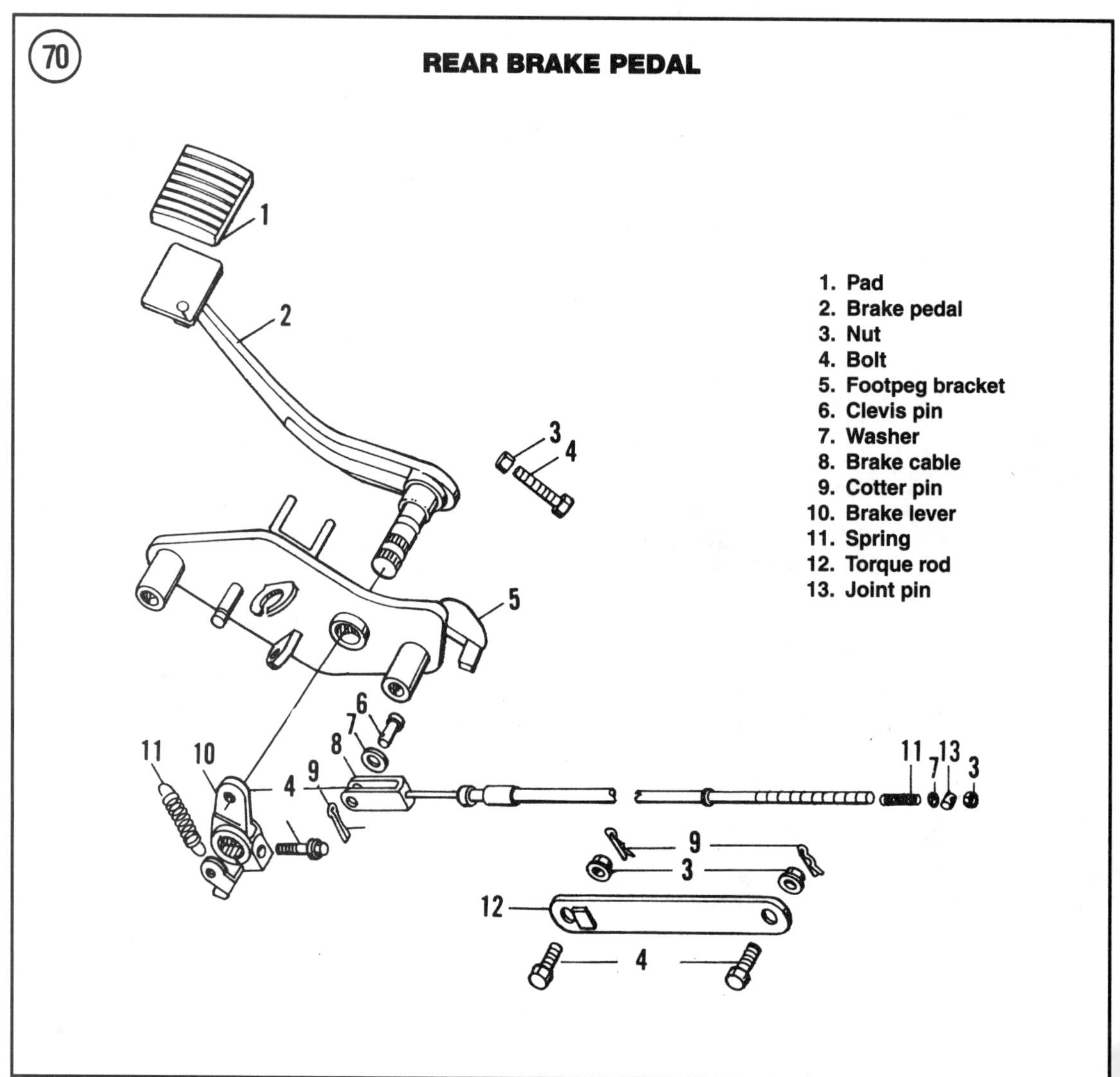

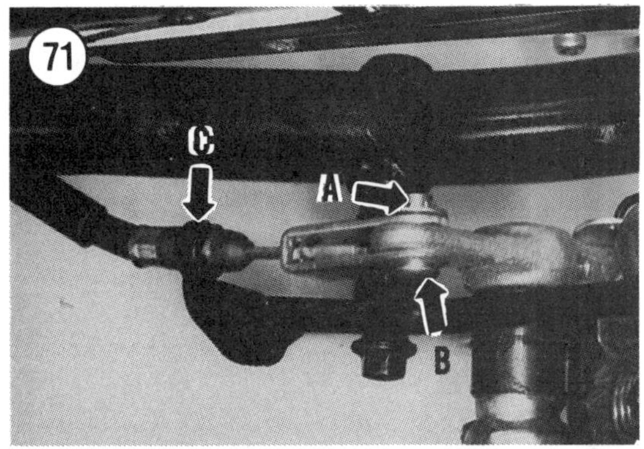

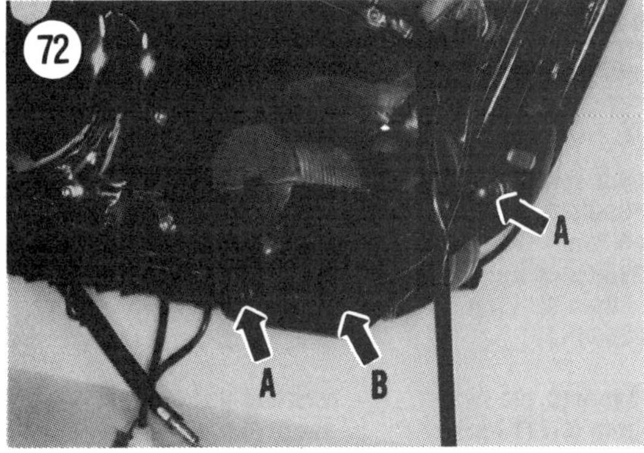

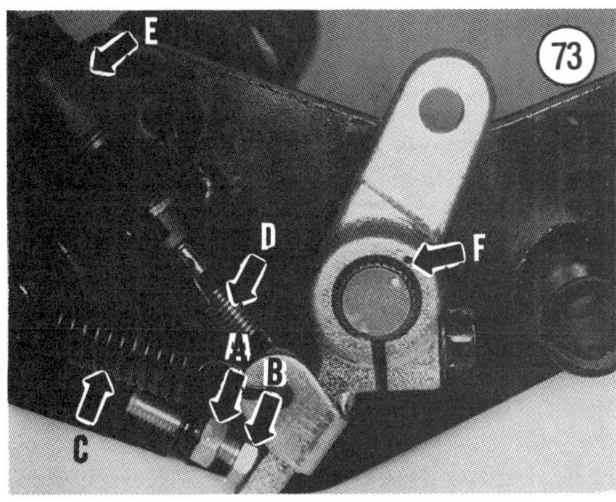

f. Adjust the rear brake as described in Chapter Three.

REAR BRAKE CABLE/ROD ASSEMBLY

Removal/Installation

1. Use a scissors jack or jack stands to support the bike on level ground.
2. Completely unscrew the rear brake-adjusting nut (A, **Figure 74**) from the brake rod.
3. Depress the brake pedal and remove the brake rod (B, **Figure 74**) from the pivot joint in the brake lever. Remove the pivot joint from the brake lever. Set the pivot joint and the adjusting nut aside to avoid misplacing them.
4. At the brake pedal, remove and discard the cotter pin (A, **Figure 71**) from the cleavis pin that secures the brake cable to the brake-pedal lever.
5. Pull the cleavis pin (B, **Figure 71**), and disconnect the brake cable from the brake pedal lever.
6. Remove the brake cable from its bracket (C, **Figure 71**) on the footpeg bracket.
7. Remove the storage box as described in Chapter Fourteen.
8. Loosen the cable/rod locknut from the mounting bracket on the frame (**Figure 75**).
9. Carefully withdraw the cable/rod assembly from behind the coolant reservoir. Do not lose the cable/rod locknut as you remove the assembly.
10. Install by reversing the removal steps while noting the following:
   a. Feed the new cable/rod through the locknut during installation.
   b. Always install new cotter pins—never reuse a cotter pin as the ends may break off and the cotter pin could fall out.
   c. Adjust the rear brake as described in Chapter Three.

Table 1 BRAKE SYSTEM TIGHTENING TORQUES

Item	N•m	in.-lb.	ft.-lb.
Rear brake			
Brake pedal lever clamp bolt	23	—	17
Front brake			
Brake hose union bolt	25	—	18
Brake lever pivot bolt	1.0	9	—
Brake lever pivot nut	5.9	52	—
Master cylinder clamp bolts	11	97	—
Brake switch screw	1.2	11	—
Brake caliper mounting bolts	34	—	25
Brake disc mounting bolts	23	—	17
Bleed screw	7.8	69	—

Table 2 BRAKE SYSTEM SPECIFICATIONS

Item	Specification	Wear limit
Front brake		
Disc thickness		
VN800	4.8-5.2 mm (0.189-0.205 in.)	4.5 mm (0.177 in.)
VN800 Classic	5.8-6.2 mm (0.228-0.244 in.)	5.5 mm (0.217 in.)
Disc runout	less than 0.15 mm (0.0059 in.)	0.3 mm (0.012 in.)
Brake pad lining thickness		
VN800	4.85 mm (0.191 in.)	1 mm (0.039 in.)
VN800 Classic	4.5 mm (0.177 in.)	1 mm (0.039 in.)
Rear brake		
Drum inner diameter	180.00-180.16 mm (7.086-7.093 in.)	180.75 mm (7.116 in.)
Shoe lining thickness	4.9-5.5 mm (0.193-0.217 in.)	2.6 mm (0.102 in.)
Pedal position	Approx 65mm (2.6 in.) above footpeg	—
Pedal free play	20-30 mm (0.79-1.18 in.)	—
Cam diameter	16.957-16.984 mm (0.668-0.669 in.)	16.88 (0.665 in.)
Camshaft hole diameter	17.0-17.010 mm (0.669-0.670 in.)	17.5 mm (0.689 in.)

CHAPTER FOURTEEN

FRAME

This chapter contains removal and installation procedures for all body panels and frame components. Frame component torque specifications are listed in **Table 1**, which is at the end of this chapter.

SEAT

Removal/Installation

1. Remove the bolt (**Figure 1**) securing the seat to the frame.
2. Move the seat to disengage the front tongue and rear hooks from the frame. Remove the seat.
3. To install the seat, insert the seat's front tongue under the retaining bracket (**Figure 2**) on the frame.

1

4. Push the seat forward. Make sure the front tongue is located correctly under the bracket, and that the rear hooks engage the holder on the fender (**Figure 3**).
5. Install the mounting bolt (**Figure 1**), and tighten it securely.

WARNING
After the seat is installed, pull up on it firmly to make sure it is securely locked in place. If the seat is not correctly locked in place, it may slide to one side while you are riding the bike. This could lead to a loss of control and a possible accident.

FRAME SIDE COVERS

Removal/Installation

The following shows the removal and installation of the left-hand side cover. The procedure is similar for the right-hand side cover except for minor differences, which are noted.

1A. On the left-hand side cover, remove the screw (**Figure 4**) securing the frame side cover to the frame rail.

14

1B. On the right-hand side cover, insert the key into the side cover lock, and release the lock by turning the key counterclockwise.

2. Carefully pull the rear of the side cover out from the frame, and slide the cover forward to disengage it from the front mounting brackets.

3. To install the side cover, make sure the rubber cushions are in place on the mounting brackets on the frame.

4. Set the side cover in place and push it rearward so the projections on the underside of the side cover (**Figure 5**) engage the rubber cushions on the frame. Make sure the side cover is securely in place.

5A. On the left-hand side cover, install the screw, and tighten it securely.

5B. On the right-hand side cover, lock the cover in place by turning the key clockwise.

STORAGE BOX

Removal/Installation

1. Remove the rear exhaust pipe as described in Chapter Eight.

2. Remove the right-hand side cover as described in this chapter.

3. Remove the three cover mounting screws (A, **Figure 6**), and remove the lower cover (B, **Figure 6**) from the storage box.

4. On California models, remove the separator and canister from the storage box by performing the following:

NOTE

Prior to removing the hoses from the separator and the charcoal canister, mark the hoses and the fittings with a piece of masking tape.

a. Unhook the rubber strap and remove the separator from the mounting bracket. Remove the separator from the bracket and disconnect the hoses from separator.
b. Carefully pull the charcoal canister and the rubber holder from the mounting bracket. Remove the canister from the bracket and disconnect the hoses from the canister.
c. If necessary, remove the screws securing the canister mounting bracket to the frame and remove the bracket.

5. Remove the storage-box mounting bolts (A, **Figure 7**) and the bracket (B, **Figure 7**). Remove the storage box (C, **Figure 7**) from the frame.

6. Install the storage box by reversing these removal steps.

7. On California models, note the following during assembly:

a. Be sure to install the hoses to their correct fittings on the charcoal canister and the separator.
b. Make sure the hoses are not kinked, twisted or in contact with any sharp surfaces.

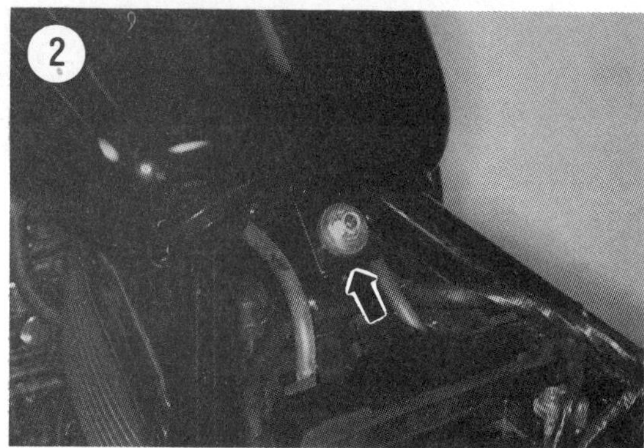

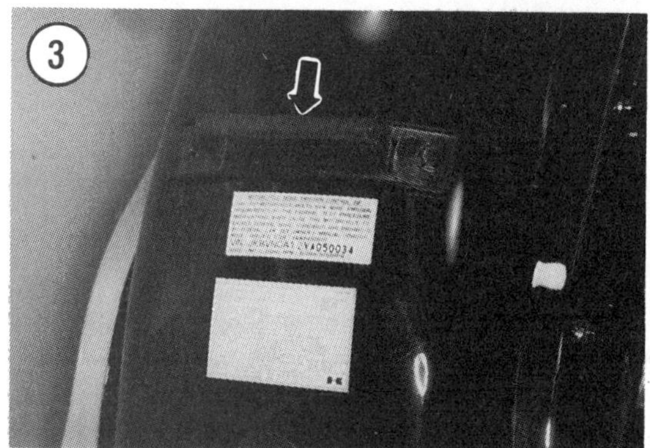

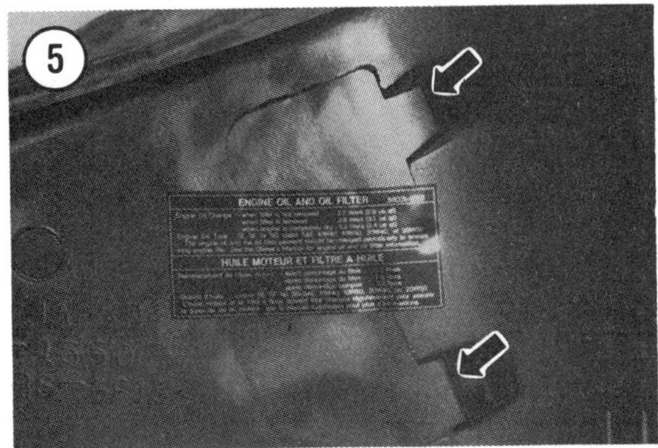

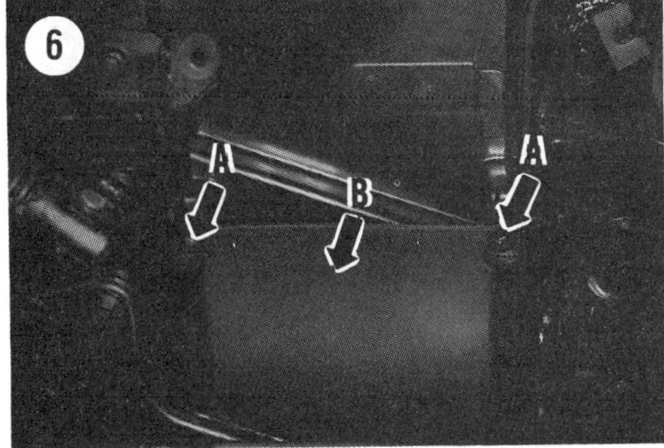

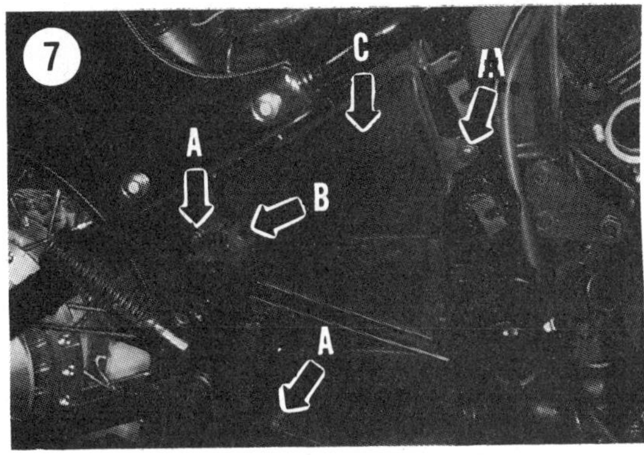

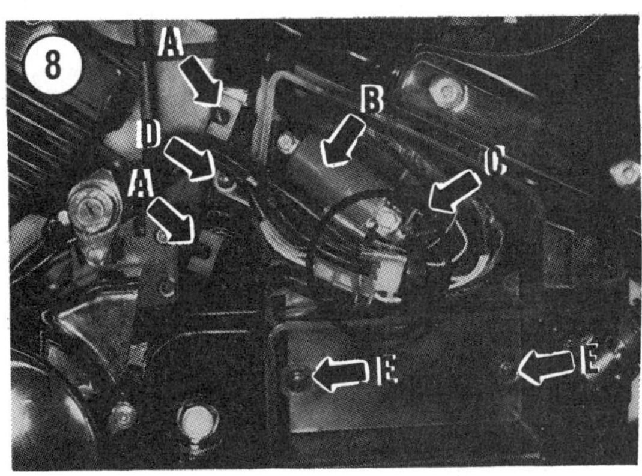

TOOL BOX

Removal/Installation

1. Remove the left-hand side cover as described in this chapter.
2. Remove the ignition coil (B, **Figure 8**) as described in Chapter Nine.

NOTE
If necessary, mark each wire before performing the following procedure so each wire can be easily reconnected to its mate during assembly.

3. Release the electrical wires from the wire clamp, and disconnect the electrical connectors (C, **Figure 8**).

NOTE
Note how the wires are routed so you can easily reroute them during assembly.

4. Remove the external mounting bolt (D, **Figure 8**).
5. Open the toolbox cover, and remove the two internal mounting bolts (E, **Figure 8**).
6. Lift the toolbox from the frame and carefully remove the electrical wires from the box.
7. Install the toolbox by reversing the removal steps.
   a. Be sure the electrical wires are correctly routed through the toolbox.
   b. Take care to reconnect each connector to its mate.

FOOTPEGS

Front Footpeg Removal/Installation

The following shows the removal and installation of the right-hand footpeg. The procedure is identical for the left-hand footpeg. 14

NOTE
Each front footpeg is attached to its respective footpeg bracket. Refer to the procedure described in Chapter Thirteen for removing the right-hand footpeg bracket. Refer to Chapter Six for removing the left-hand footpeg bracket.

1. Remove the E-clip (A, **Figure 9**) from the end of the pivot pin in the foot peg.
2. Withdraw the pivot pin (A, **Figure 9**) and remove the footpeg (B, **Figure 9**) and spring (C, **Figure 9**) from the bracket.
3. Install by reversing these removal steps while noting the following:
   a. Apply a light coat of multipurpose grease to the pivot pin prior to installation.
   b. Make sure the spring is positioned correctly to hold the footpeg in the *down* position.
   c. Make sure the E-clip is positioned correctly on the pivot pin.

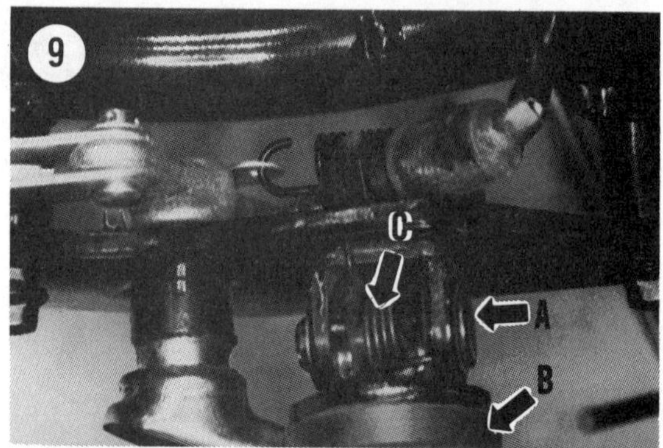

Rear Footpeg Removal/Installation

The following shows the removal and installation of the left-hand footpeg. The procedure is identical for the right-hand footpeg.

1. Remove the E-clip (A, **Figure 10**) from the end of the pivot pin.
2. Withdraw the pivot pin (B, **Figure 10**), and remove the footpeg (C, **Figure 10**) from the bracket.
3. Install by reversing these removal steps while noting the following:
   a. Apply a light coat of multipurpose grease to the pivot pin prior to installation.
   b. Make sure the E-clip is positioned correctly in the pivot shaft.
   d. Tighten the mounting bolts securely.

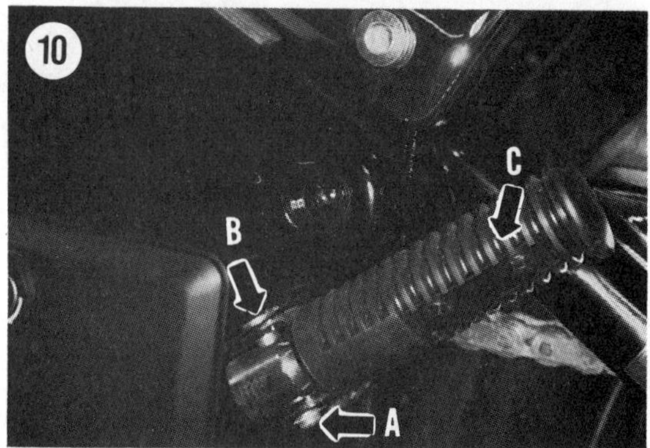

SIDESTAND

Removal/Installation

1. Use a scissors jack or jack stands to support the bike securely on level ground.
2. Place the sidestand in the up position.
3. Use locking pliers to disconnect the return spring (A, **Figure 11**) from the pin (B, **Figure 11**) on the sidestand.
4. Remove the nut from the pivot bolt securing the sidestand to the frame-mounting boss.
5. Withdraw the bolt (A, **Figure 12**) and remove the sidestand (B, **Figure 12**) from the frame.
6. Install by reversing the removal steps while noting the following:

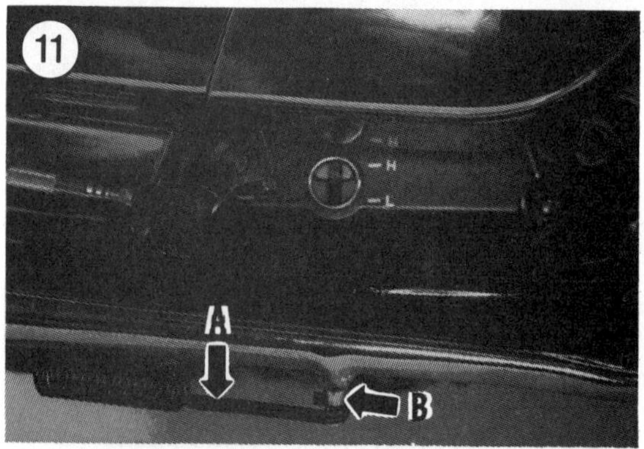

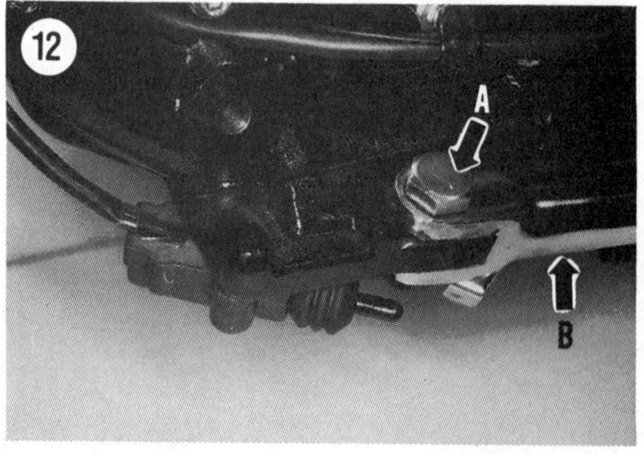

a. Apply a light coat of multipurpose grease to the pivot point on the frame, sidestand and pivot bolt prior to installation.
b. Install the pivot bolt and nut. Torque the pivot bolt to the specification listed in **Table 1**.

FRONT FENDER

Removal/Installation

1. Remove the front wheel as described under in Chapter Eleven.

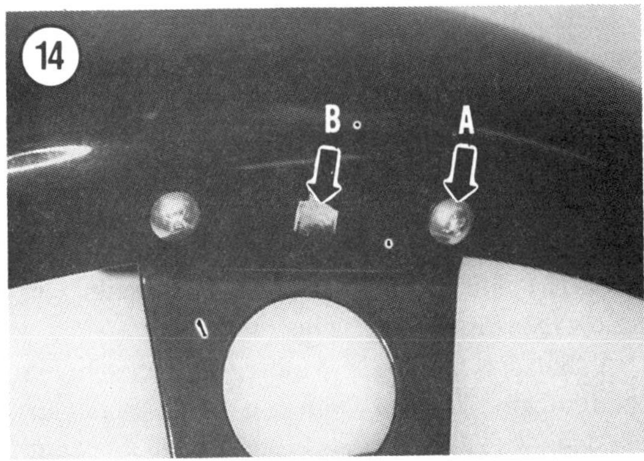

NOTE
Prior to removal, mark the front underside of the fender with a piece of tape with an F mark on it. This identification is necessary for installation.

2. Remove the four flange bolts (A, **Figure 13**) securing the front fender brace (B, **Figure 13**) to the mounts on the fork sliders, and remove the front fender/brace assembly.
3. If necessary, remove the four fender mounting screws (A, **Figure 14**), and remove the fender from the fender brace. Do not lose the collar behind each mounting screw.
4. Install by reversing the removal steps while noting the following:
   a. The front fender is not symmetrical and must be installed with the correct orientation.
   b. Position the front fender so the end with the forward mark you made during removal faces forward.
   c. When installing a new fender, be sure the arrow (B, **Figure 14**) on the fender points forward.
   d. Tighten the flange bolts securely. Do not overtighten as the plastic fender may fracture in the mounting hole area.

REAR FENDER

Removal/Installation

1. Remove the seat as described in this chapter.

NOTE
Mark the wires before disconnecting them in the next step. Correctly reconnecting these wires can be difficult if they are not labeled.

2A. On VN800 models and on U.S. and Canadian VN800 Classic models, disconnect the following electrical connectors.
   a. The taillight/brake light three-pin connector (A, **Figure 15**)
   b. The four individual connectors (B, **Figure 15**) for the turn signals.

2B. Except U.S. and Canadian VN800 Classic models—Disconnect the following electrical connectors:
   a. The three individual taillight/brake light.

b. The four individual connectors for the turn signals.

c. The two individual license-plate light connectors.

3. Remove the two screws securing the battery box to the fender.

4. Remove the two rear frame mounting bolts (**Figure 16**) from each side of the motorcycle.

5. Carefully pull the fender rearward, and remove the fender assembly from the frame. The rear frame members, taillight/brake light assembly and the license plate light assembly (except U.S. and Canadian VN800 Classic models) will come off with the rear fender.

6. Install by reversing the removal steps while noting the following:

a. Torque the rear frame mounting bolts (**Figure 16**) to the specification listed in **Table 1**.

b. Make sure the electrical connectors are free of corrosion and are tight.

FRAME

The frame does not require routine maintenance. However, it should be inspected immediately after any accident or spill.

Component Removal/Installation

Refer to **Figure 17** for this procedure.

1. Remove the seat and frame side covers.

2. Remove the fuel tank as described in Chapter Eight.

3. Remove the engine as described in Chapter Five.

4. Remove the headlight housing as described in Chapter Nine.

5. Remove the front wheel, steering stem and front fork as described in Chapter Eleven.

6. Remove the rear wheel, shock absorbers and swing arm as described in Chapter Twelve.

7. Remove the front and rear fenders as described in this chapter.

8. Remove the radiator as described in Chapter Ten.

9. Remove the battery as described in Chapter Three and the battery case as described in Chapter Nine.

10. Remove the wiring harness.

11. Remove the steering head races from the steering head tube as described in Chapter Eleven.

12. Inspect the frame for bends, cracks or other damage, especially around welded joints and areas that are rusted.

13. Assemble by reversing the removal steps.

Stripping and Painting

Remove all components from the frame. Thoroughly strip off all old paint. The best way is to have it sandblasted down to bare metal. If this is not possible, you can use a liquid paint remover, steel wool and a fine, hard wire brush.

CAUTION

The fenders and frame side covers are molded plastic, and the color is an integral part of the component. If you wish to change the color of these parts, consult an automotive paint supplier for the proper procedure. Do not use any type of paint remover on these components as it will damage the surface.

When the frame is down to bare metal, have it inspected for hairline and internal cracks. Magnaflux is the most common and complete process.

Make sure that the paint primer you use is compatible with the type of paint you are going to use for the finish color. Spray on one or two coats of primer as smoothly as possible. Let it dry thoroughly and use a fine grade of wet sandpaper (400-600 grit) to remove any flaws. Carefully wipe the surface clean and then spray a couple of coats of the final color. Use either lacquer or enamel base paint, and follow the manufacturer's instructions.

A shop specializing in painting will probably do the best job. However, you can do a surprisingly good job with a good grade of spray paint. Spending

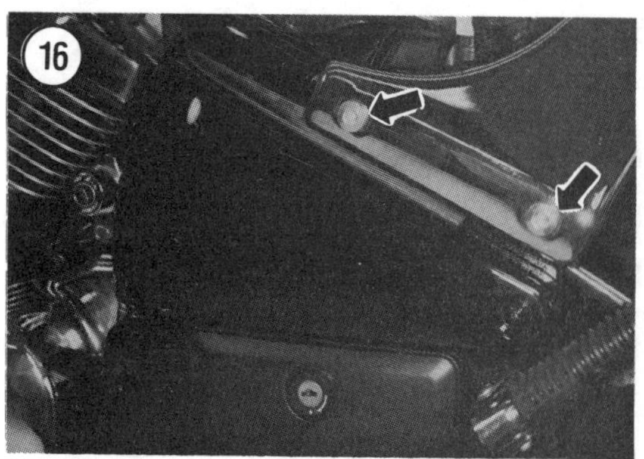

a few extra dollars to get a good grade of paint will make a difference in final looks and paint durability. It is a good idea to shake the can and make sure the ball inside the can is loose when you purchase the can of paint. Shake the can as long as is stated on the can. Then immerse the can *upright* in a pot or bucket of warm water (not over 120° F [49° C]).

WARNING
Higher temperature could cause the can to burst. Do ***not*** *place the can in direct contact with any flame or heat source.*

Leave the can in water for several minutes. When the paint is thoroughly warm, shake the can again and spray the frame. Be sure to get into all the crevices where there may be rust problems. Several light mist coats are better than one heavy coat. Spray painting is best done in temperatures of 70-80° F (21-27° C); any temperature above or below this will cause problems.

After the final coat has dried completely, at least 48 hours, any over spray or orange peel may be removed with a *light* application of Dupont rubbing compound (red color) and finished with Dupont polishing compound (white color). Be careful not to rub too hard or you will go through the finish.

Finish off with a couple coats of good wax prior to reassembling all the components.

It is a good idea to keep the frame touched up with fresh paint if any minor rust spots or scratches appear.

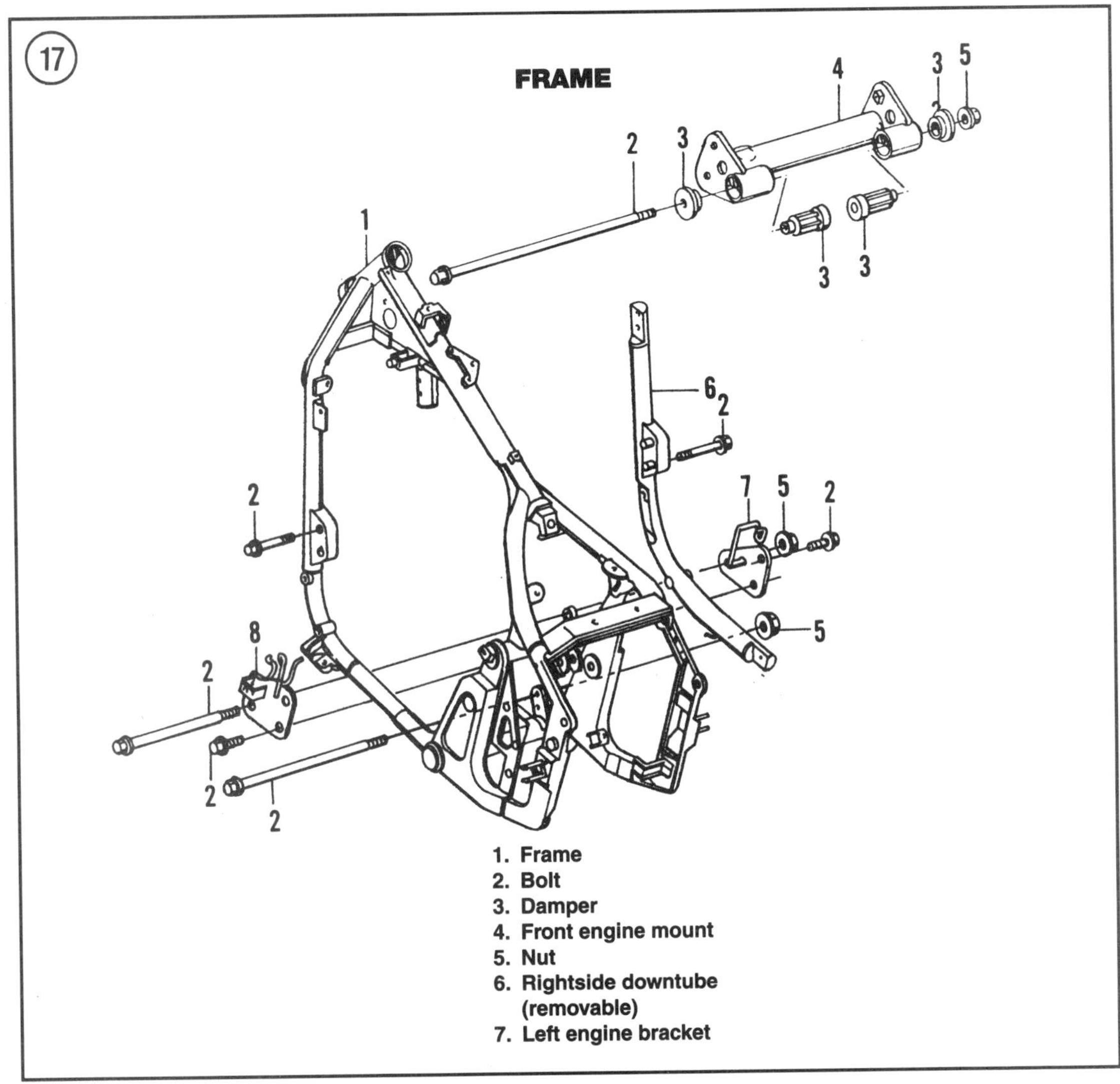

1. Frame
2. Bolt
3. Damper
4. Front engine mount
5. Nut
6. Rightside downtube (removable)
7. Left engine bracket

Table 1 FRAME COMPONENT TIGHTENING TORQUES

Item	N•m	ft.-lb.
Sidestand pivot bolt	44	32
Rear frame mounting bolts	44	32

INDEX

E

F

G

H

I

J

L

M

N

O

P

R

S

T

V

W

VN800 (U.S. AND CANADA)

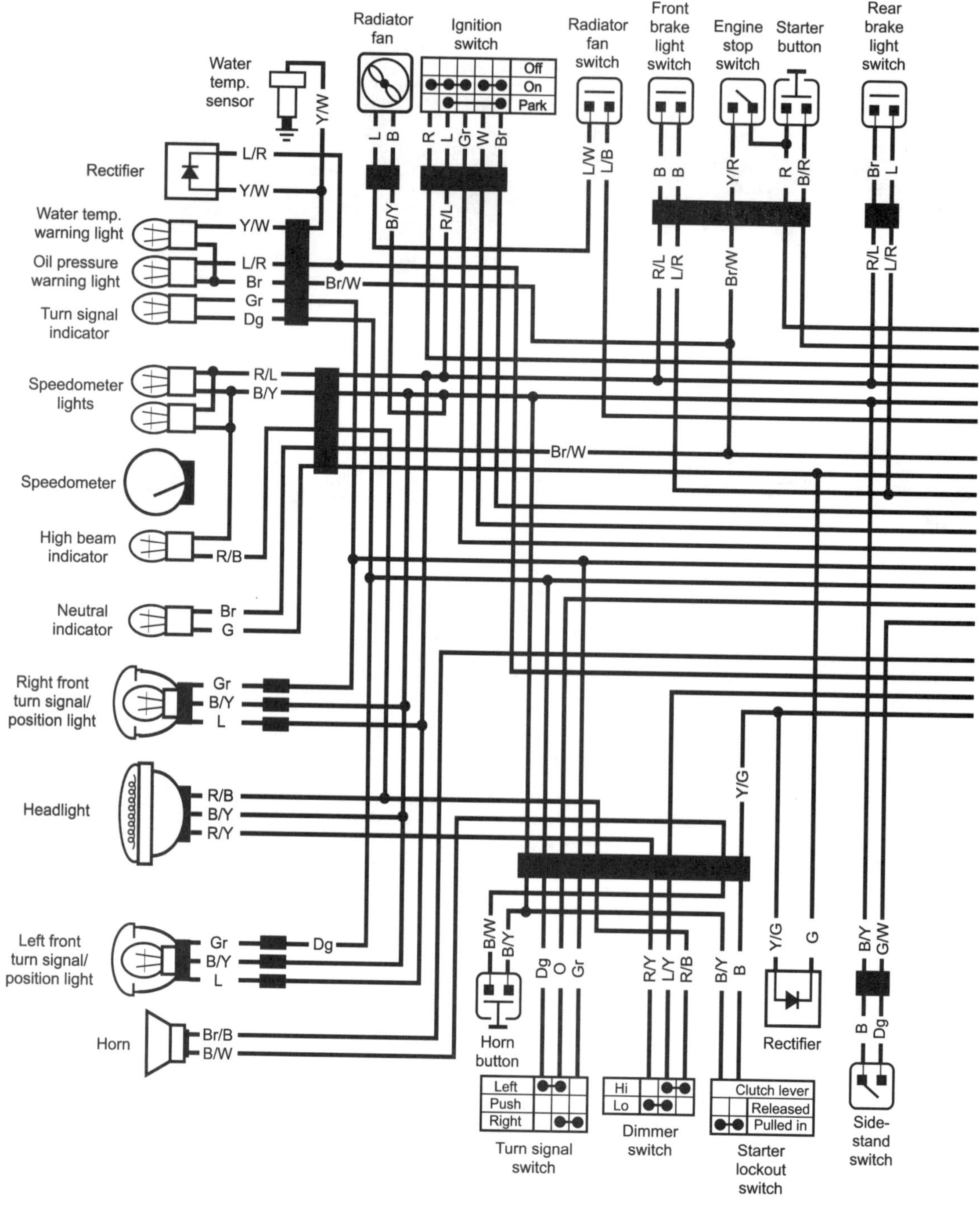

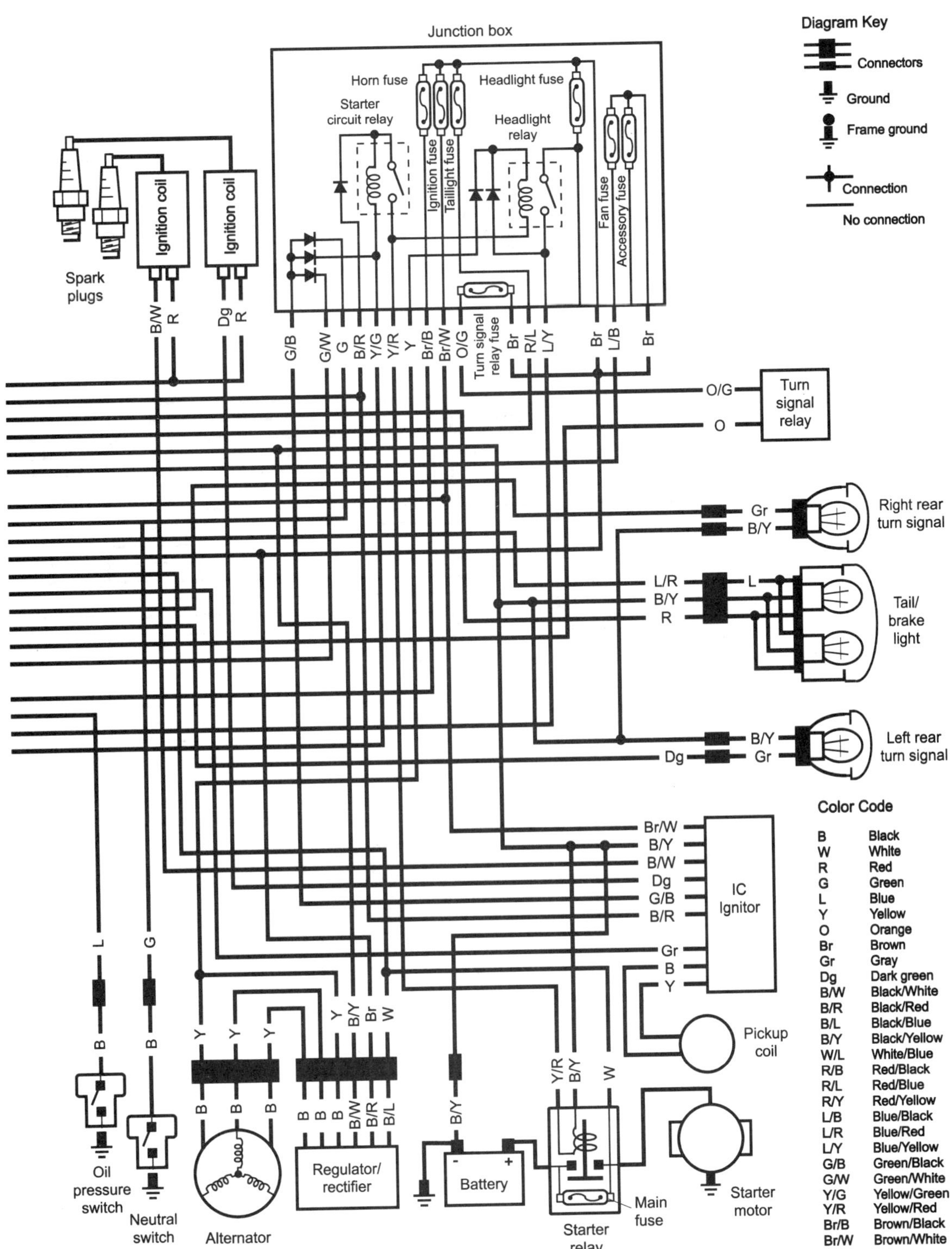

Junction box
Horn fuse
Starter circuit relay
Headlight fuse
Headlight relay
Ignition fuse
Taillight fuse
Fan fuse
Accessory fuse
Turn signal relay fuse
Ignition coil
Ignition coil
Spark plugs
Turn signal relay
Right rear turn signal
Tail/ brake light
Left rear turn signal
IC Ignitor
Pickup coil
Oil pressure switch
Neutral switch
Alternator
Regulator/ rectifier
Battery
Starter relay
Main fuse
Starter motor
Diagram Key
Connectors
Ground
Frame ground
Connection
No connection
Color Code
B Black
W White
R Red
G Green
L Blue
Y Yellow
O Orange
Br Brown
Gr Gray
Dg Dark green
B/W Black/White
B/R Black/Red
B/L Black/Blue
B/Y Black/Yellow
W/L White/Blue
R/B Red/Black
R/L Red/Blue
R/Y Red/Yellow
L/B Blue/Black
L/R Blue/Red
L/Y Blue/Yellow
G/B Green/Black
G/W Green/White
Y/G Yellow/Green
Y/R Yellow/Red
Br/B Brown/Black
Br/W Brown/White

16

VN800 (AUSTRALIA)

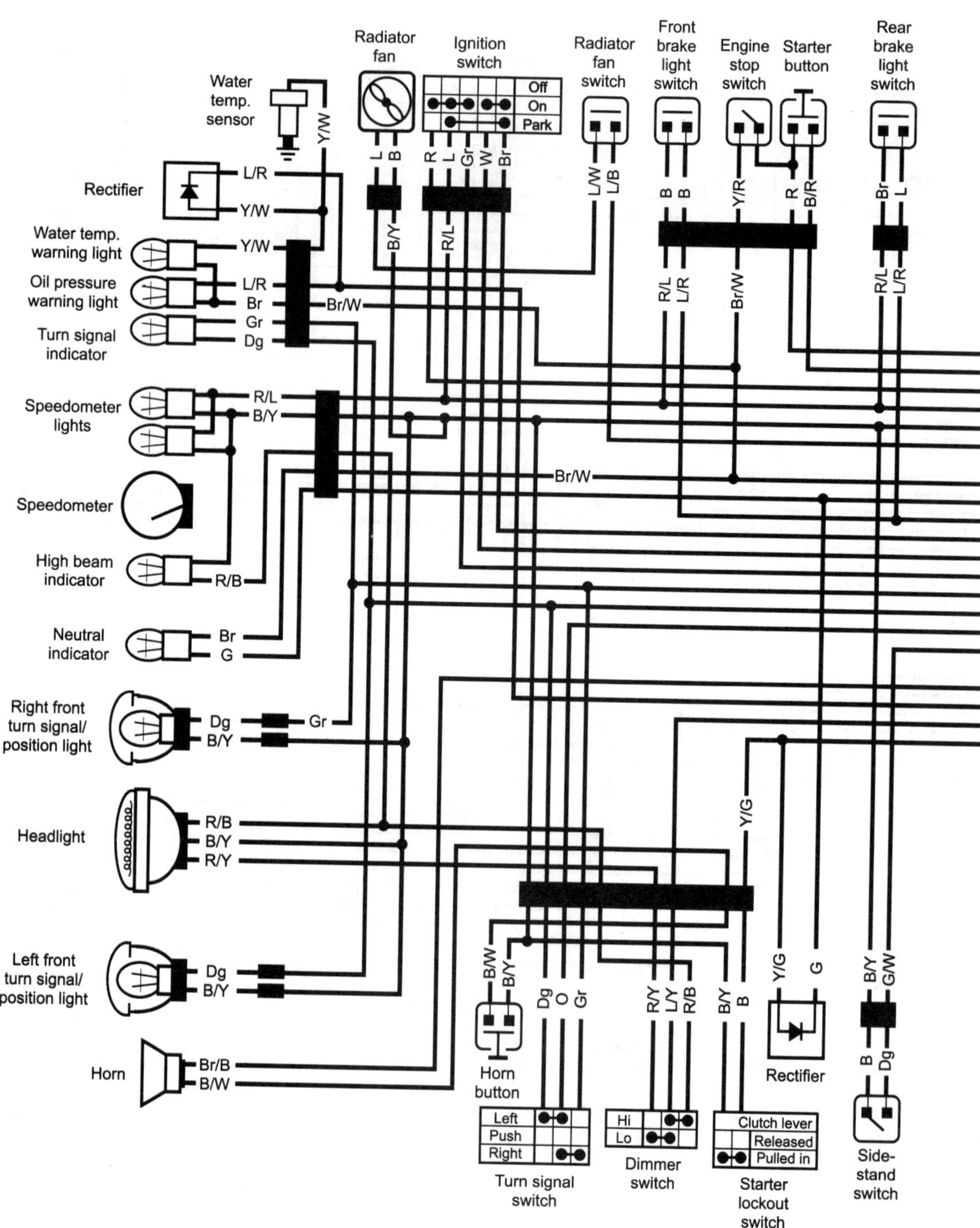

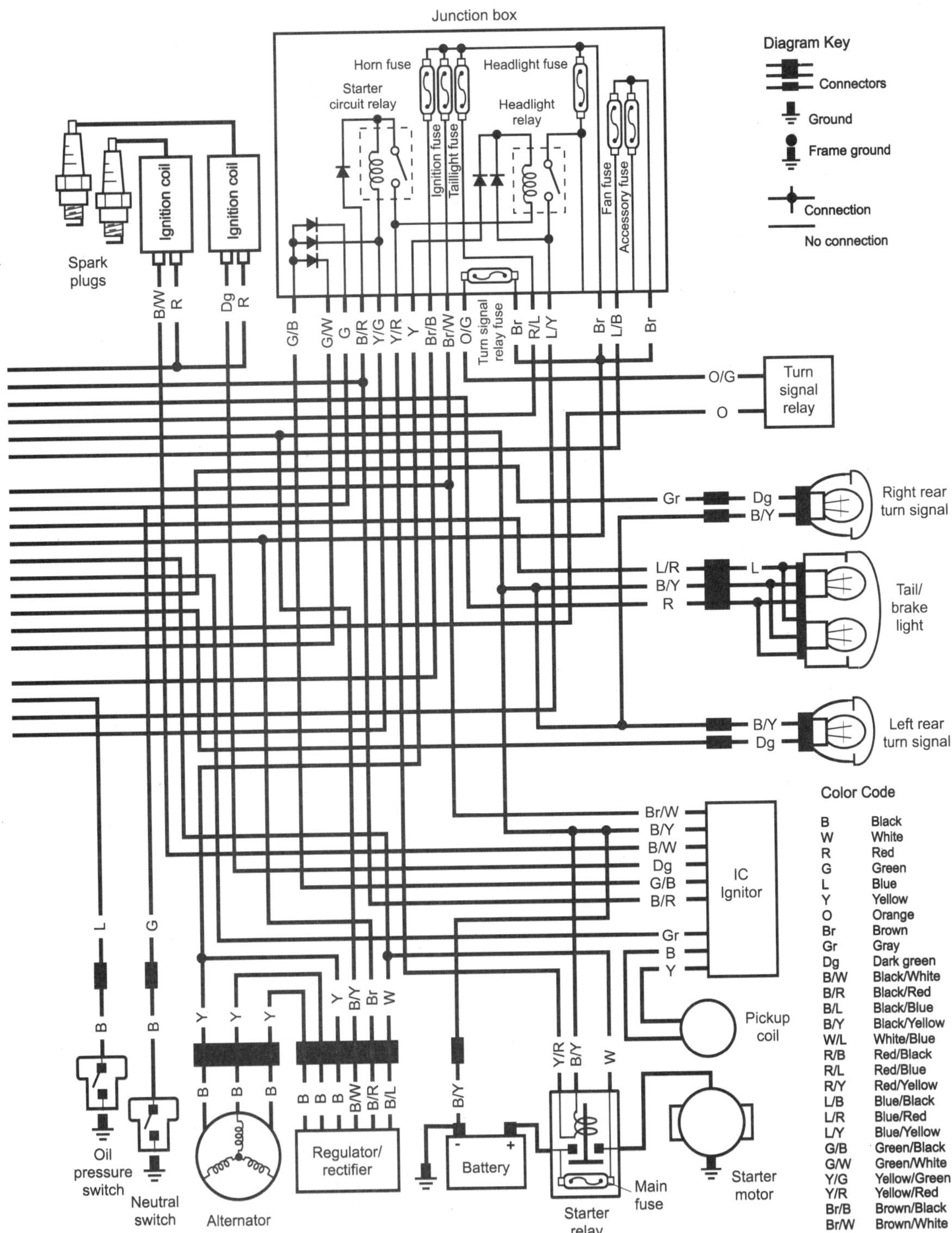
Junction box
Horn fuse
Starter circuit relay
Headlight fuse
Headlight relay
Ignition fuse
Taillight fuse
Fan fuse
Accessory fuse
Turn signal relay fuse
Spark plugs
Ignition coil
Ignition coil
B/W
R
Dg
R
G/B
G/W
G
B/R
Y/G
Y/R
Y
Br/B
Br/W
O/G
Br
R/L
L/Y
Br
L/B
Br
O/G
O
Turn signal relay
Gr
Dg
B/Y
Right rear turn signal
L/R
B/Y
R
L
Tail/ brake light
B/Y
Dg
Left rear turn signal
Br/W
B/Y
B/W
Dg
G/B
B/R
Gr
B
Y
IC Ignitor
Pickup coil
L
G
B
B
Y
Y
Y
Y
B/Y
Br
W
B
B
B
B
B
B
B/W
B/R
B/L
B/Y
Y/R
B/Y
W
Oil pressure switch
Neutral switch
Alternator
Regulator/ rectifier
Battery
Starter relay
Main fuse
Starter motor
Diagram Key
Connectors
Ground
Frame ground
Connection
No connection
Color Code
B Black
W White
R Red
G Green
L Blue
Y Yellow
O Orange
Br Brown
Gr Gray
Dg Dark green
B/W Black/White
B/R Black/Red
B/L Black/Blue
B/Y Black/Yellow
W/L White/Blue
R/B Red/Black
R/L Red/Blue
R/Y Red/Yellow
L/B Blue/Black
L/R Blue/Red
L/Y Blue/Yellow
G/B Green/Black
G/W Green/White
Y/G Yellow/Green
Y/R Yellow/Red
Br/B Brown/Black
Br/W Brown/White

VN800
(EXCEPT U.S., CANADA AND AUSTRALIA)

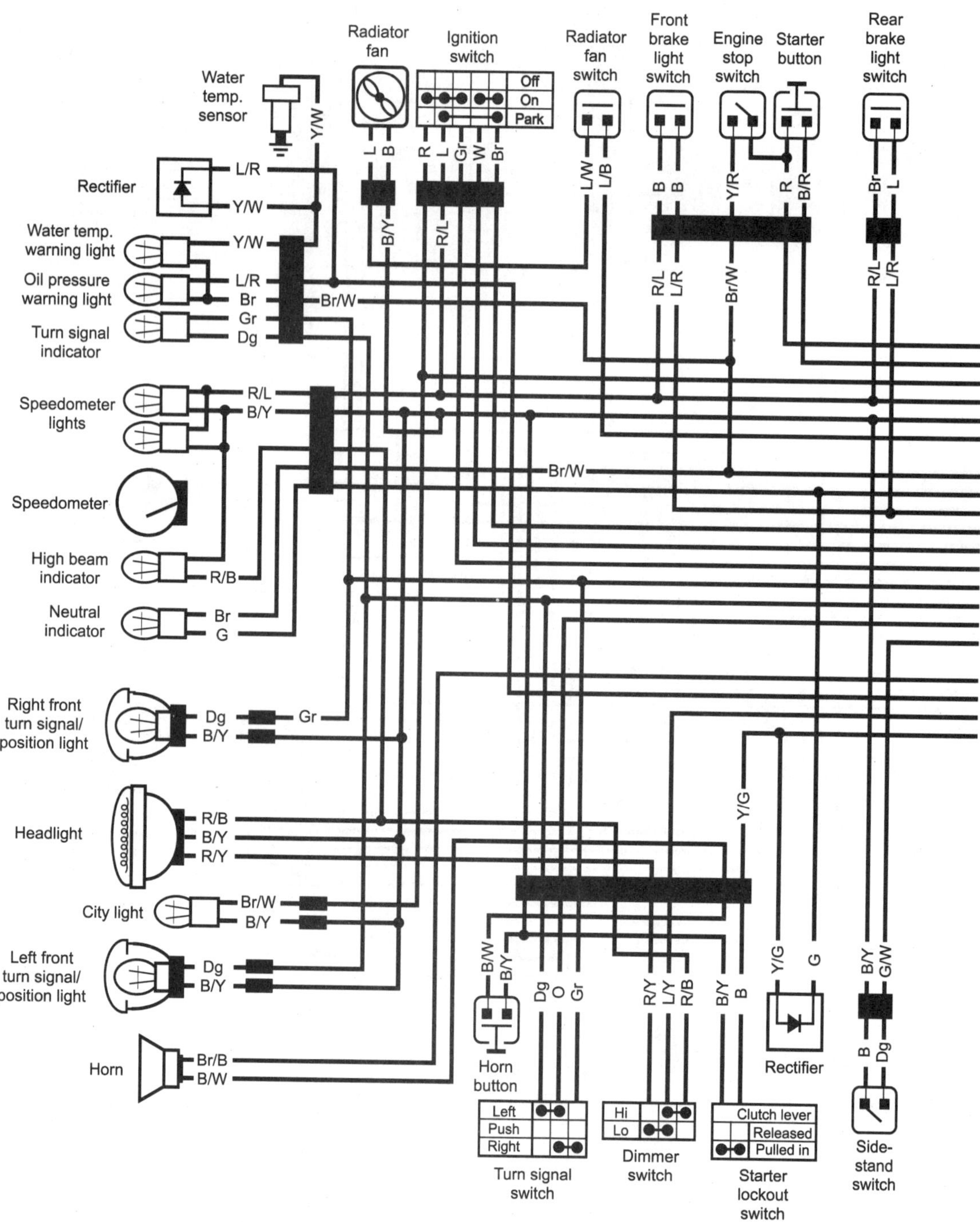

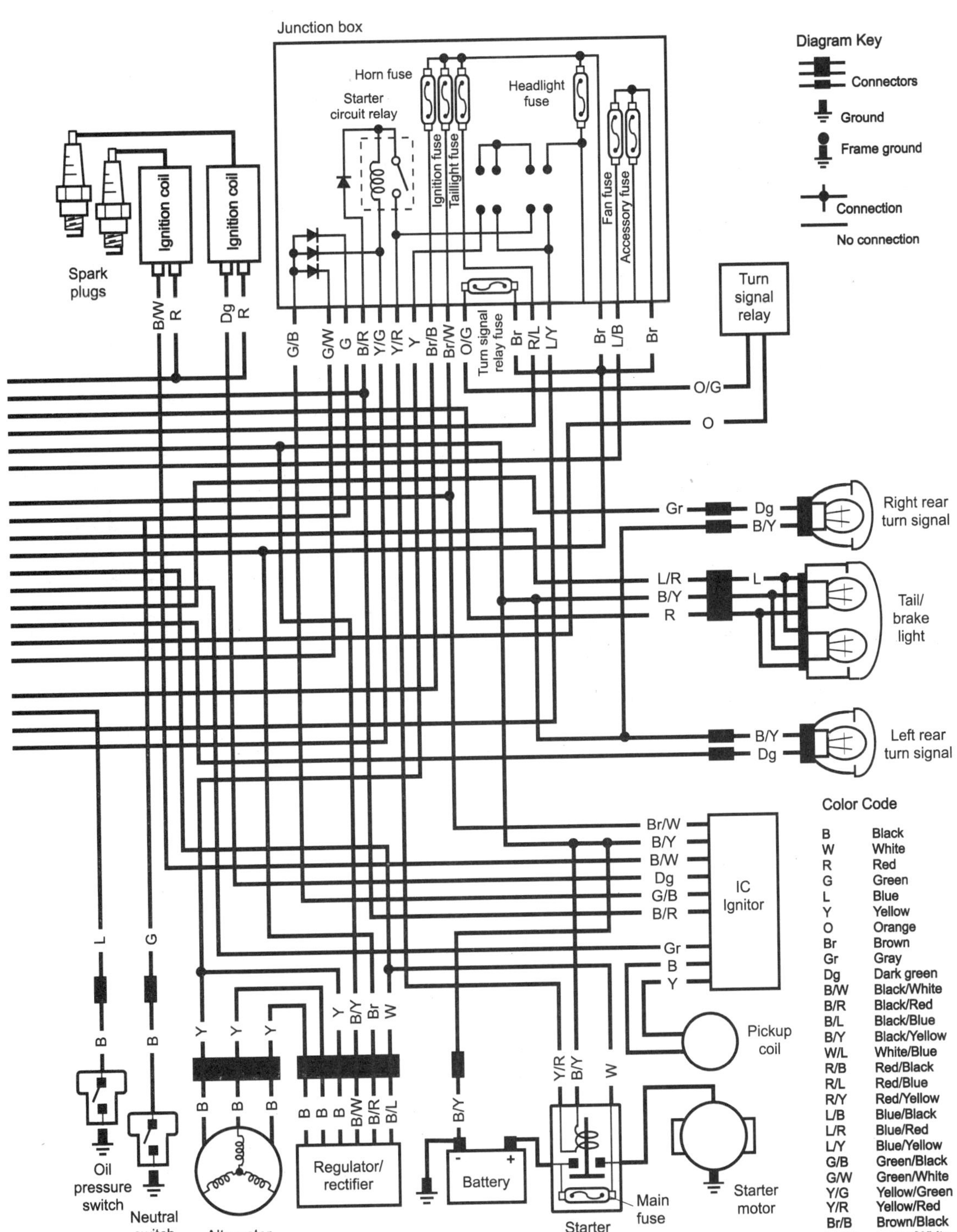
Junction box
Horn fuse
Starter circuit relay
Ignition fuse
Taillight fuse
Headlight fuse
Fan fuse
Accessory fuse
Turn signal relay fuse
Spark plugs
Ignition coil
Ignition coil
Turn signal relay
Diagram Key
Connectors
Ground
Frame ground
Connection
No connection
Right rear turn signal
Tail/ brake light
Left rear turn signal
IC Ignitor
Pickup coil
Oil pressure switch
Neutral switch
Alternator
Regulator/ rectifier
Battery
Starter relay
Main fuse
Starter motor
Color Code
B Black
W White
R Red
G Green
L Blue
Y Yellow
O Orange
Br Brown
Gr Gray
Dg Dark green
B/W Black/White
B/R Black/Red
B/L Black/Blue
B/Y Black/Yellow
W/L White/Blue
R/B Red/Black
R/L Red/Blue
R/Y Red/Yellow
L/B Blue/Black
L/R Blue/Red
L/Y Blue/Yellow
G/B Green/Black
G/W Green/White
Y/G Yellow/Green
Y/R Yellow/Red
Br/B Brown/Black
Br/W Brown/White

VN800 CLASSIC (U.S. AND CANADA)

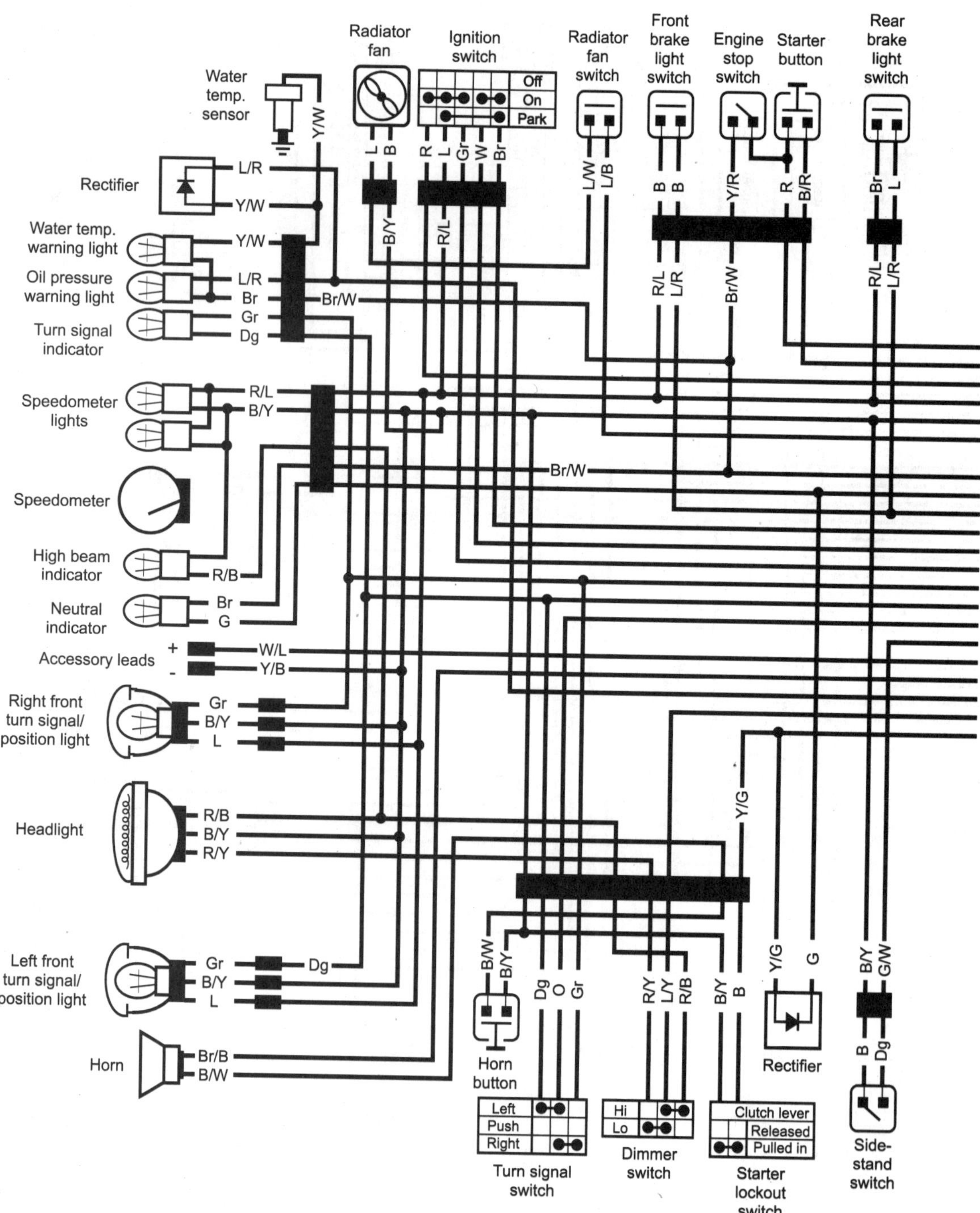

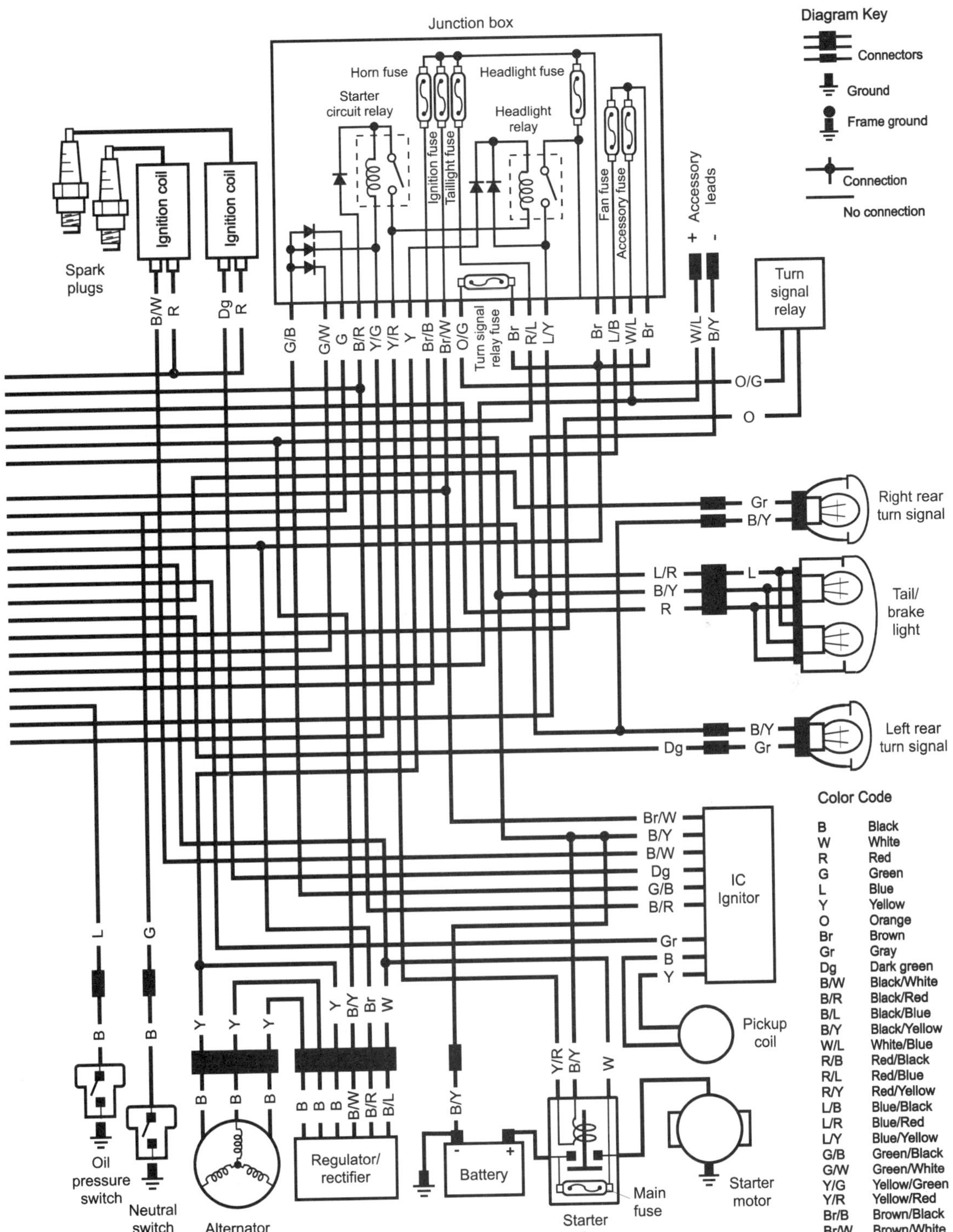
Junction box
Horn fuse
Starter circuit relay
Headlight fuse
Headlight relay
Ignition fuse
Taillight fuse
Fan fuse
Accessory fuse
Accessory leads
Turn signal relay fuse
Ignition coil
Ignition coil
Spark plugs
Turn signal relay
Right rear turn signal
Tail/ brake light
Left rear turn signal
IC Ignitor
Pickup coil
Oil pressure switch
Neutral switch
Alternator
Regulator/ rectifier
Battery
Starter relay
Main fuse
Starter motor
Diagram Key
Connectors
Ground
Frame ground
Connection
No connection
Color Code
B Black
W White
R Red
G Green
L Blue
Y Yellow
O Orange
Br Brown
Gr Gray
Dg Dark green
B/W Black/White
B/R Black/Red
B/L Black/Blue
B/Y Black/Yellow
W/L White/Blue
R/B Red/Black
R/L Red/Blue
R/Y Red/Yellow
L/B Blue/Black
L/R Blue/Red
L/Y Blue/Yellow
G/B Green/Black
G/W Green/White
Y/G Yellow/Green
Y/R Yellow/Red
Br/B Brown/Black
Br/W Brown/White

16

VN800 CLASSIC (AUSTRALIA)

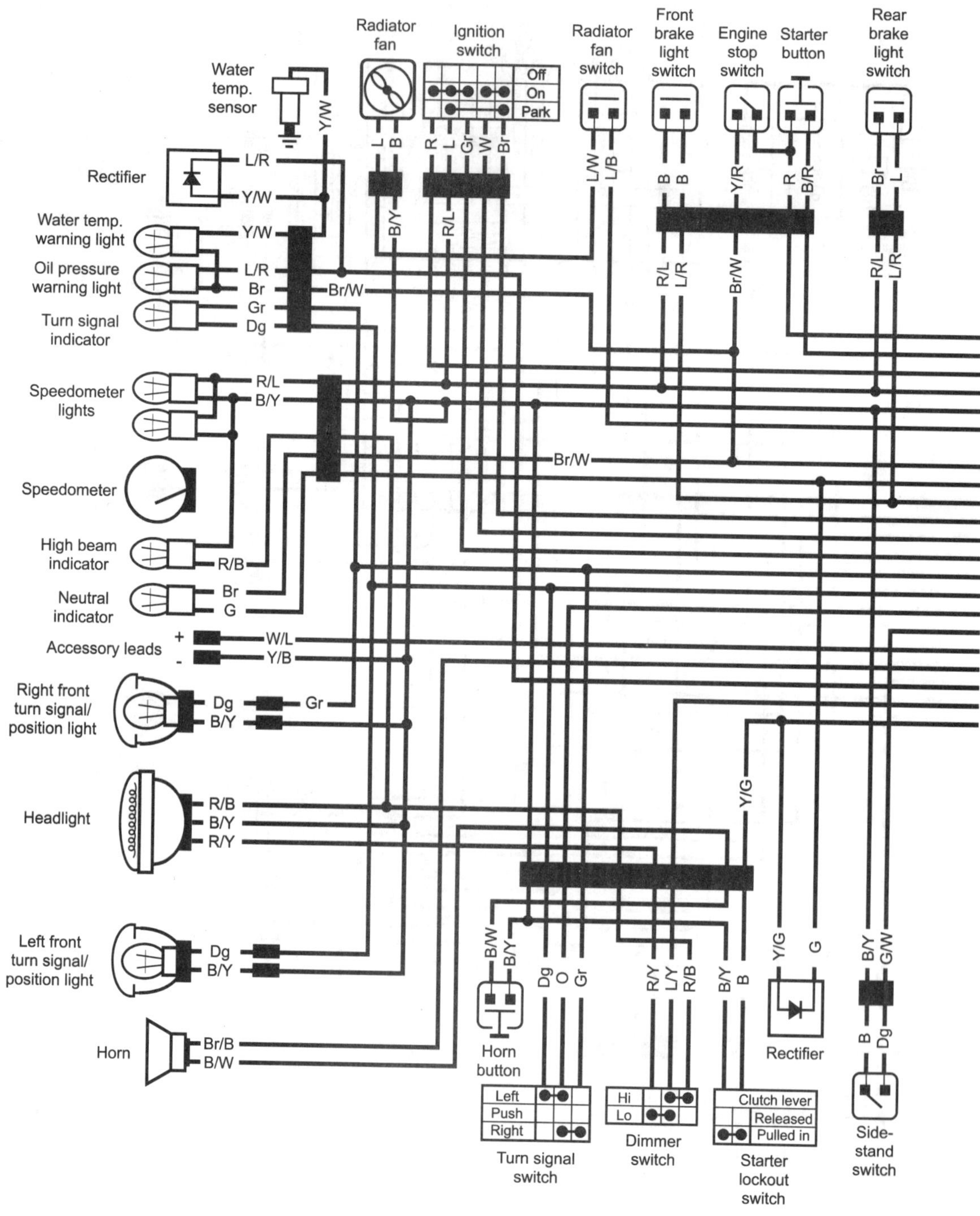

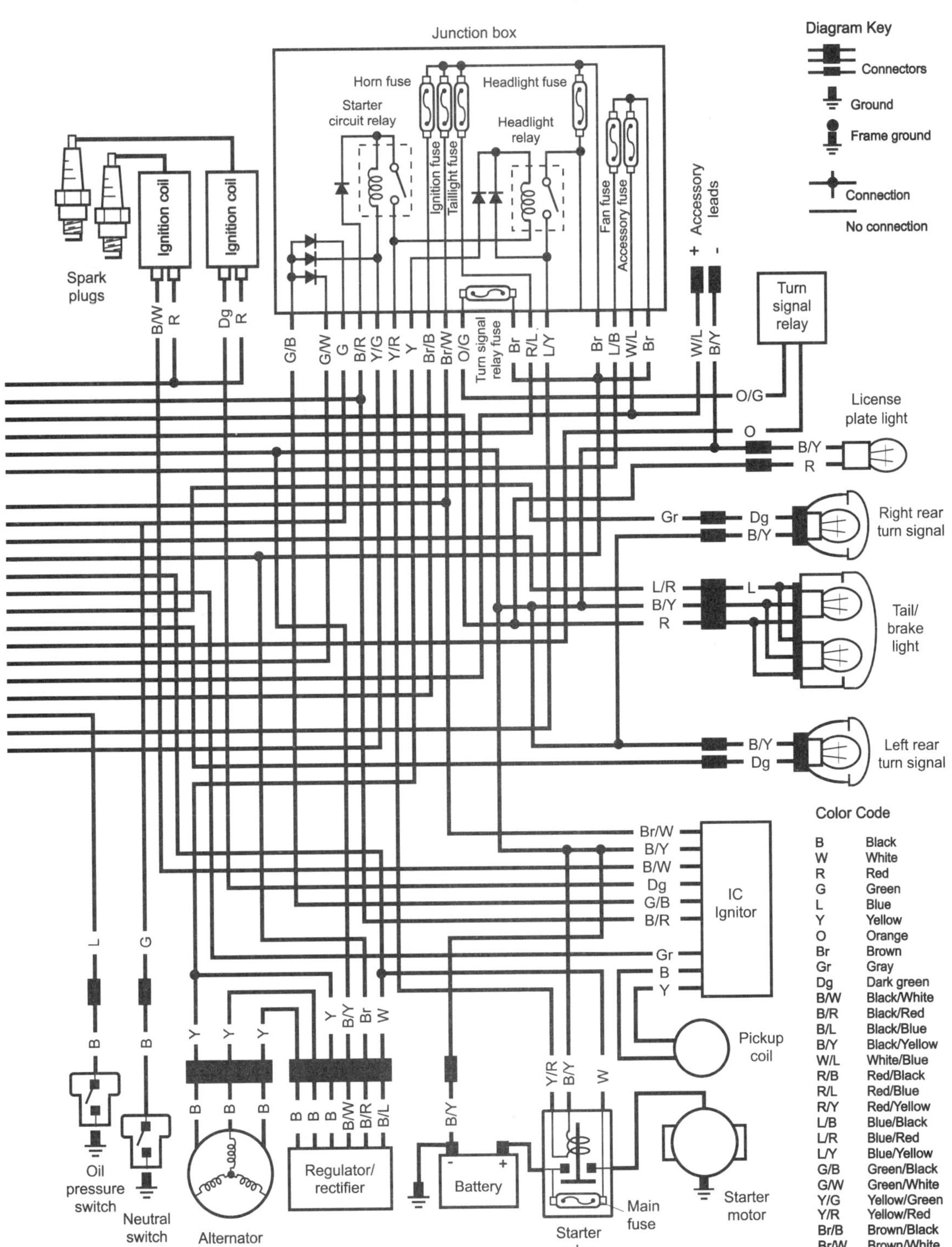

Junction box
Horn fuse
Starter circuit relay
Headlight fuse
Headlight relay
Ignition fuse
Taillight fuse
Fan fuse
Accessory fuse
Accessory leads
Turn signal relay fuse
Ignition coil
Ignition coil
Spark plugs
Turn signal relay
License plate light
Right rear turn signal
Tail/ brake light
Left rear turn signal
IC Ignitor
Pickup coil
Oil pressure switch
Neutral switch
Alternator
Regulator/ rectifier
Battery
Starter relay
Main fuse
Starter motor
Diagram Key
Connectors
Ground
Frame ground
Connection
No connection
Color Code
B Black
W White
R Red
G Green
L Blue
Y Yellow
O Orange
Br Brown
Gr Gray
Dg Dark green
B/W Black/White
B/R Black/Red
B/L Black/Blue
B/Y Black/Yellow
W/L White/Blue
R/B Red/Black
R/L Red/Blue
R/Y Red/Yellow
L/B Blue/Black
L/R Blue/Red
L/Y Blue/Yellow
G/B Green/Black
G/W Green/White
Y/G Yellow/Green
Y/R Yellow/Red
Br/B Brown/Black
Br/W Brown/White

VN800 CLASSIC (EXCEPT U.S., CANADA AND AUSTRALIA)

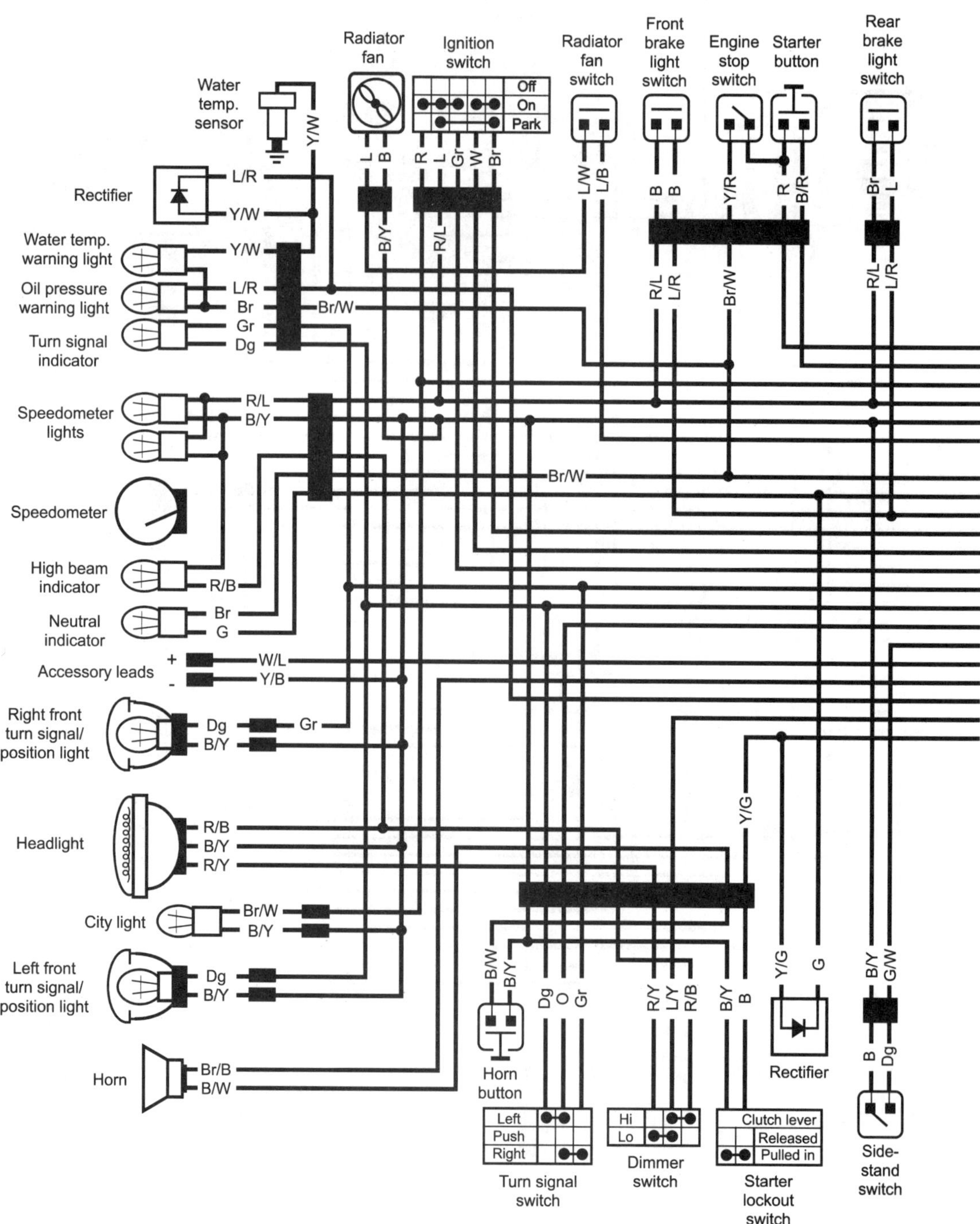

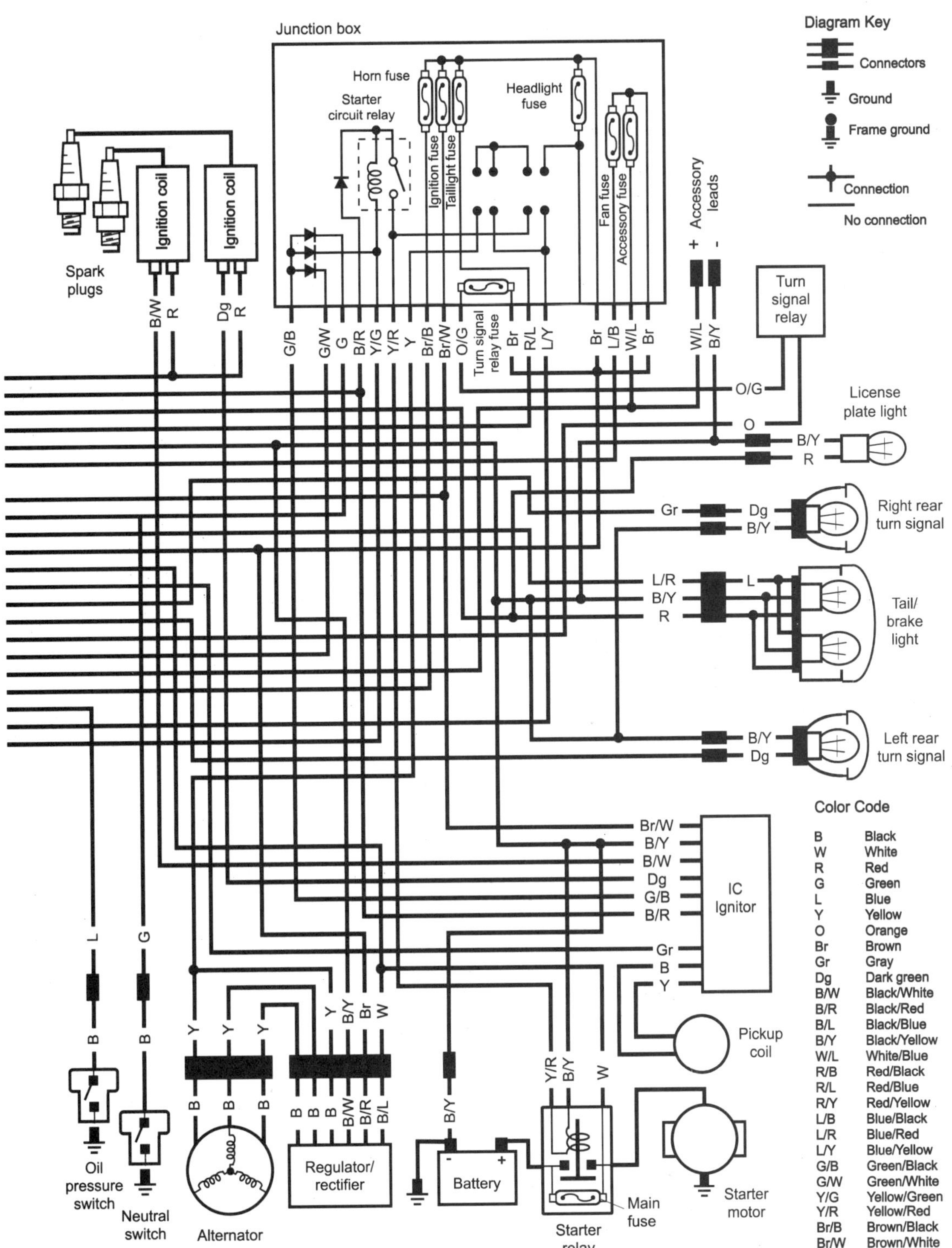

Color Code

B	Black
W	White
R	Red
G	Green
L	Blue
Y	Yellow
O	Orange
Br	Brown
Gr	Gray
Dg	Dark green
B/W	Black/White
B/R	Black/Red
B/L	Black/Blue
B/Y	Black/Yellow
W/L	White/Blue
R/B	Red/Black
R/L	Red/Blue
R/Y	Red/Yellow
L/B	Blue/Black
L/R	Blue/Red
L/Y	Blue/Yellow
G/B	Green/Black
G/W	Green/White
Y/G	Yellow/Green
Y/R	Yellow/Red
Br/B	Brown/Black
Br/W	Brown/White

NOTES

NOTES

NOTES

NOTES

MAINTENANCE LOG

Service Performed	Mileage Reading				
Oil change (example)	2,836	5,782	8,601		